DATE DUE

Traumatic Stress

From Theory to Practice

The Plenum Series on Stress and Coping

Series Editor:
Donald Meichenbaum, *University of Waterloo, Waterloo, Ontario, Canada*

Editorial Board: Bruce P. Dohrenwend, *Columbia University* • Marianne Frankenhauser, *University of Stockholm* • Norman Garmezy, *University of Minnesota* • Mardi J. Horowitz, *University of California Medical School, San Francisco* • Richard S. Lazarus, *University of California, Berkeley* • Michael Rutter, *University of London* • Dennis C. Turk, *University of Pittsburgh* • John P. Wilson, *Cleveland State University* • Camille Wortman, *University of Michigan*

Current Volumes in the Series:

BEYOND TRAUMA
Cultural and Societal Dynamics
Edited by Rolf J. Kleber, Charles R. Figley, and Berthold P. R. Gersons

COMBAT STRESS REACTION
The Enduring Toll of War
Zahava Solomon

COMMUTING STRESS
Causes, Effects, and Methods of Coping
Meni Koslowsky, Avraham N. Kluger, and Mordechai Reich

COPING WITH WAR–INDUCED STRESS
The Gulf War and the Israeli Response
Zahava Solomon

INTERNATIONAL HANDBOOK OF TRAUMATIC STRESS SYNDROMES
Edited by John P. Wilson and Beverley Raphael

PSYCHOTRAUMATOLOGY
Key Papers and Core Concepts in Post-Traumatic Stress
Edited by George S. Everly, Jr. and Jeffrey M. Lating

STRESS AND MENTAL HEALTH
Contemporary Issues and Prospects for the Future
Edited by William R. Avison and Ian H. Gotlib

TRAUMATIC STRESS
From Theory to Practice
Edited by John R. Freedy and Stevan E. Hobfoll

THE UNNOTICED MAJORITY IN PSYCHIATRIC INPATIENT CARE
Charles A. Kiesler and Celeste G. Simpkins

A Continuation Order Plan is available for this series. A continuation order will bring delivery of each new volume immediately upon publication. Volumes are billed only upon actual shipment. For further information please contact the publisher.

Traumatic Stress

From Theory to Practice

Edited by

John R. Freedy

Medical University of South Carolina
Charleston, South Carolina

and

Stevan E. Hobfoll

Kent State University
Kent, Ohio

PLENUM PRESS • NEW YORK AND LONDON

Library of Congress Cataloging-in-Publication Data

On file

ISBN 0-306-45020-8

©1995 Plenum Press, New York
A Division of Plenum Publishing Corporation
233 Spring Street, New York, N.Y. 10013

10 9 8 7 6 5 4 3 2 1

Printed in the United States of America

To my wife, Melba, and to my parents, Robert and Lucy Freedy

—JRF

To my aunt and uncle, Phyllis and Howard Mallin, and to Dr. Marvin and Marsha Cooper, for their loving support at many crossroads

—SEH

Contributors

Beverley K. Beach, Department of Psychology, West Virginia University, Morgantown, West Virginia 26506

Connie L. Best, National Crime Victims Research and Treatment Center, Department of Psychiatry and Behavioral Sciences, Medical University of South Carolina, Charleston, South Carolina 29425

Jonathan R. T. Davidson, Department of Psychiatry and Behavioral Sciences, Duke University Medical Center, Durham, North Carolina 27710

John C. Donkervoet, Family Services Center, Department of Psychiatry and Behavioral Sciences, Medical University of South Carolina, Charleston, South Carolina 29425

Carla A. Dunahoo, Applied Psychology Center, Department of Psychology, Kent State University, Kent, Ohio 44242

Sherry A. Falsetti, National Crime Victims Research and Treatment Center, Department of Psychiatry and Behavioral Sciences, Medical University of South Carolina, Charleston, South Carolina 29425

John P. Forsyth, Department of Psychology, West Virginia University, Morgantown, West Virginia 26506

John R. Freedy, National Crime Victims Research and Treatment Center, Department of Psychiatry and Behavioral Sciences, Medical University of South Carolina, Charleston, South Carolina 29425

Bonnie L. Green, Department of Psychiatry, Georgetown University School of Medicine, Washington, DC 20007

Rochelle F. Hanson, Center for Sexual Assault/Abuse Recovery and Education (CARE), Student Health Care Center, University of Florida, Gainesville, Florida 32611

Stevan E. Hobfoll, Applied Psychology Center, Department of Psychology, Kent State University, Kent, Ohio 44242

Marianne Kastrup, Rehabilitation and Research Centre for Torture Victims, Borgergade 13, DK-1300 Copenhagen K, Denmark

Terence M. Keane, Boston VA Medical Center, Boston, Massachusetts 02130

Dean G. Kilpatrick, National Crime Victims Research and Treatment Center, Department of Psychiatry and Behavioral Sciences, Medical University of South Carolina, Charleston, South Carolina 29425

Harold Kudler, Psychiatry Service, Durham VA Medical Center, and Department of Psychiatry and Behavioral Sciences, Duke University Medical Center, Durham, North Carolina 27705

Brett T. Litz, Boston VA Medical Center, Boston, Massachusetts 02130

Alexander C. McFarlane, Department of Psychiatry, University of Adelaide, P.O. Box 17, Eastwood, 5063 South Australia

Jeannine Monnier, Applied Psychology Center, Department of Psychology, Kent State University, Kent, Ohio 44242

Fran H. Norris, Department of Psychology, Georgia State University, Atlanta, Georgia 30303

Lynn M. E. Northrop, Department of Psychology, West Virginia University, Morgantown, West Virginia 26506

Heidi S. Resnick, National Crime Victims Research and Treatment Center, Department of Psychiatry and Behavioral Sciences, Medical University of South Carolina, Charleston, South Carolina 29425

David P. Ribbe, National Center for Posttraumatic Stress Disorder, VA Medical Center and Regional Office Center, White River Junction, Vermont 05009

Cheryl A. Rode, Department of Psychology, West Virginia University, Morgantown, West Virginia 26506

Joseph R. Scotti, Department of Psychology, West Virginia University, Morgantown, West Virginia 26506

Arieh Y. Shalev, Department of Psychiatry, Center for Traumatic Stress, Hadassah University Hospital, Jerusalem 91120, Israel

Susan D. Solomon, Violence and Traumatic Stress Research Branch, National Institute of Mental Health, Rockville, Maryland 20857

Zahava Solomon, Bob Shapell School of Social Work, Tel Aviv University, Ramat Aviv 69 978, Israel

Martie P. Thompson, Department of Psychology, Georgia State University, Atlanta, Georgia 30303

Peter Vesti, Rehabilitation and Research Centre for Torture Victims, Borgergade 13, DK-1300 Copenhagen K, Denmark

Frank W. Weathers, Boston VA Medical Center, Boston, Massachusetts 02130

Preface

This volume was conceived with very pragmatic purposes in mind. The editors wanted to produce a volume of direct relevance to mental health practice. Even a passing interest in daily news events confirms that violent crime, disasters, serious accidents, war, and other forms of traumatic events occur frequently and with great impact upon individuals, families, and communities. On a more scientific note, extant research studies have confirmed several crucial facts regarding the nature of traumatic events. These facts include: (1) that traumatic events occur frequently, impacting large numbers of people; (2) that exposure to traumatic events substantially increases the risk of several serious mental health problems; and (3) that it is possible to limit the impact of traumatic events through the application of prevention, assessment, and treatment strategies. This volume translates extant scientific knowledge concerning traumatic events and mental health into state-of-the-art prevention, assessment, and treatment activities for mental health professionals among whom intervention is their daily bread.

In developing this project, the editors agreed on the idea that critical gaps existed in the training of mental health professionals regarding the topic of traumatic stress. We concluded that many advanced training programs do not recognize either the high frequency of traumatic events or the potential devastating impact of such events for subsequent adjustment processes. By extension, we reasoned that few mental health professionals were fully informed regarding state-of-the-art prevention, assessment, and treatment approaches. The editors evaluated the accuracy of their assessment of the field, by consulting with a number of recognized experts in the field of traumatic stress. These leading experts agreed with our assessment of the field and have written chapters as a result. Therefore, this volume is intended to further inform mental health practitioners regarding: (1) the high prevalence of traumatic events; (2) the types of psychosocial problems associated with traumatic events; and (3) prevention, assessment, and treatment (psychosocial and biological) strategies available to alleviate trauma-engendered suffering.

As a practical matter, we have designed the book to be a clinical handbook for mental health professionals. We conceptualized this professional field in the broadest terms possible. In particular, the following practitioners may find the information in this volume of considerable utility: psychologists, psychiatrists, social workers, psychiatric nurses, or mental health counselors from related fields. Given the practical focus of the volume, it can be of use both to licensed practitioners as well as students in these various mental health fields. Indeed, the editors endorse the position that professional education should extend from the first day of professional school and throughout the entire clinical practice of the professional. The current volume should, therefore, be viewed as meeting the educational needs of both seasoned veterans as well as novice mental health professionals.

The 15 chapters in this volume have been organized into three sections in order to facilitate an understanding of the material. At the beginning of each of the three sections, the editors have written an introduction that provides detailed information concerning the nature of each of the chapters within the particular section. Here, the editors provide a broad description of the three sections of the volume. Part I contains four chapters that provide a broad overview of the entire field of traumatic stress. Topics covered include defining traumatic events, the prevalence of traumatic events, typical mental health problems, theoretical models concerning the traumatic events–adjustment linkage, a discussion of general treatment principles, a discussion of prevention strategies, and a consideration of biological strategies for limiting adverse mental health outcomes.

Part II contains five chapters that focus on five different types of traumatic events. The specific events include war-related trauma, violent crime, natural and technological disasters, accidental injury, and torture. The editors chose these topics because they represent common traumatic events that adversely impact many people on an ongoing basis. The five chapters in Part II provide basic knowledge concerning each of these types of traumatic events. Ideas addressed include defining the nature and prevalence of the specific traumatic event, describing factors that may increase the risk of negative adjustment, considering factors that may promote positive adjustment, describing a range of psychological and social outcomes, and examining the course of adjustment across time. Upon completing each chapter in Part II, the reader will possess a broad base of knowledge providing an appreciation of the scope and potential impact of traumatic events upon many people.

Part III contains five chapters that focus on state-of-the-art clinical practice. These five chapters are intended as companion chapters to each of the basic knowledge chapters from Part II of this volume. Thus, Part III contains separate chapters on these traumatic events: war-related trauma, violent crime, natural and technological disasters, accidental injury, and torture. Ideas addressed within the various chapters include models of assessment and treatment, specific assessment strategies, treatment procedures, and case examples. Upon considering the chapters from Part III, the reader will have learned how to apply the basic knowledge gained in reading Part II of this volume. In the interest of integration, Part III ends with a chapter that summarizes the content of the previous 14 chapters.

Many people deserve recognition regarding the conceptualization and production of this volume. Foremost, the editors wish to thank the authors of the chapters. These contributors provide a true all-star line-up concerning the topic of traumatic stress. Among the various chapter authors are well-known experts concerning research and clinical issues pertaining to the topic of traumatic stress. We are indebted to them for their time and expertise. The editors are also indebted to Don Meichenbaum for his excellent guidance and encouragement as the series editor for Plenum Press. In addition, Eliot Werner and the staff at Plenum Press provided excellent technical assistance that is highly appreciated. Also, support staff at both the Medical University of South Carolina and Kent State University have been both helpful and tolerant of the various demands made by the editors throughout the period of book production.

The editors want to pay a special tribute to the victims of traumatic events. This includes both direct victims and their family members. In total, this number includes many members of modern society. Our hope in developing this book has been to translate scientific theory and knowledge into information and techniques that can be applied by mental health professionals. This goal is reflected in our title, *Traumatic Stress: From Theory to Practice.* It is our intent that the application of the knowledge and techniques within this book will ultimately prevent and relieve unnecessary suffering by potential or actual victims of traumatic events. We hope that we have achieved this goal. For humanitarian reasons, it is essential that unnecessary suffering by fellow human beings be minimized.

JOHN R. FREEDY
STEVAN E. HOBFOLL

Contents

PART II. DEFINING THE NATURE OF TRAUMATIC EVENTS

PART III. ASSESSMENT AND TREATMENT ISSUES

Chapter 10. Helping Victims of Military Trauma 241

Zahava Solomon and Arieh Y. Shalev

Chapter 11. Helping the Victims of Violent Crime 263

Sherry A. Falsetti and Heidi S. Resnick

Chapter 12. Helping the Victims of Disasters 287

Alexander C. McFarlane

I

Overview of the Traumatic Stress Field

This section provides a broad overview of the field of traumatic stress. The issues discussed are intended to be core issues or ideas that have substantial relevance across different types of traumatic events. Thus, the ideas presented in this section will be substantially elaborated during later sections of this volume. In all, four chapters are included in this section. A brief overview of the focus of each chapter is offered here.

Chapter 1, written by John R. Freedy and John C. Donkervoet, is titled *Traumatic Stress: An Overview of the Field.* As this title suggests, the chapter addresses a broad range of issues relevant to the field of traumatic stress. The chapter begins with an overview section and is followed by a section concerning traumatic event prevalence. In a third section, mental health implications are considered, including: diagnostic models, posttraumatic stress disorder (PTSD), the relationship between event quality (e.g., injury, threat to life) and mental health, the time course of adjustment, and mental health comorbidity. The fourth section presents psychological, biological, and integrative models (psychological, social, and biological) concerning the etiology of posttrauma mental health problems. The fifth section outlines the core components that characterize successful mental health treatment for trauma victims (e.g., prevention-focused, trauma-focused components, skill building). Finally, a summary of major ideas is offered. Subsequent chapters throughout the volume serve to elaborate the more general facts and principles laid down in this lead chapter.

Chapter 2, written by Stevan E. Hobfoll, Carla A. Dunahoo, and Jeannine Monnier, is titled *Conservation of Resources and Traumatic Stress.* The main thrust of this chapter is to apply a general theory of stress (conservation of resources theory) to the specific case of traumatic events. A major contribution of the chapter is to introduce a creative theoretical framework to the area of traumatic stress. In this sense, the chapter is a substantial elaboration on the etiological models highlighted by Freedy and Donkervoet in Chapter 1. Hobfoll and colleagues remind the reader that traumatic events are dynamic processes that unfold across time and not static, time-bound entities. They then go on to argue that the experience of internal (e.g., self-efficacy) or external (e.g., home, employment) resource loss is responsible for many of the negative effects that follow traumatic events. Through the presentation of principles and examples, the authors crystallize their point of view. The inclusion of a measurement scale helps to make their ideas concrete. The authors intend their message to apply to a broad range of traumatic events and suggest the relevance of their ideas to the types of events discussed in Parts II and III of this volume.

Chapter 3, written by Fran H. Norris and Martie P. Thompson, is titled *Applying Community Psychology to the Prevention of Trauma and Traumatic Life Events*. This chapter is well reasoned and presents ideas that are taken from the tradition of the community psychology movement. Although the idea of preventing trauma-related mental health problems by preventing traumatic events from occurring may sound obvious, it is an idea that has not been sufficiently utilized by the mental health field. Toward this end, Norris and Thompson provide an excellent literature review and propose a comprehensive model concerning the implementation of prevention approaches ranging from political action through crisis counseling. It is most useful that the authors illustrate their various ideas with programs that have been tested in field work within various settings. These practical illustrations should stimulate readers into seeing (and hopefully pursuing) useful preventive strategies in their home communities.

Chapter 4, written by Harold Kudler and Jonathan R. T. Davidson, is titled *General Principles of Biological Intervention Following Trauma*. One of the major strengths of the chapter is the fact that it intelligently discusses the biology of posttrauma adjustment in a clinically relevant manner. The reader is informed about the thinking process of two expert psychiatrists as they try to clinically assess and determine the appropriate role for medication in the treatment of trauma victims. A range of medications are discussed, including antidepressants, anxiolytics, sleep aids, mood stabilizers, and antipsychotic medication. The authors are well reasoned in their approach and illustrate how to assess the effects of treatment and to modify biological approaches to treatment based upon the course of mental health symptoms across time. It is particularly important that these authors emphasize collaboration between and among treatment professionals, patients, and family members. It is also useful that Kudler and Davidson suggest that psychological, social, and biological treatment approaches must be integrated based upon mutual cooperation, respect, and communication between members of treatment teams from different professional disciplines.

1

Traumatic Stress

An Overview of the Field

JOHN R. FREEDY and JOHN C. DONKERVOET

CHAPTER OVERVIEW

A simple and powerful idea underlies this chapter as well as the volume as a whole. In essence it stipulates that good clinical practice must be guided by state-of-the-art knowledge concerning the topic of interest. Relevant sources of information may include: (1) psychosocial theory and associated empirical research; (2) prior clinical experience; (3) and personal life experiences. The remainder of the chapter provides an overview of available knowledge concerning the nature of traumatic stress. The material represents a synthesis of the aforementioned sources of information.

Of course, it is not the case that all sources of information provide equally valid or accurate information regarding the topic of traumatic stress. Professionals need to be selective regarding the amount of weight that is granted to any source of information. For example, replicated empirical findings should be weighed more heavily than a "clinical hunch" no matter how creative, or seemingly compelling, the latter source of information. Nevertheless, the current authors are suggesting that clinical work be guided by a reasonable (and well reasoned) openness to diverse sources of information.

The potential for synergy between theory, research, clinical work, and

JOHN R. FREEDY · National Crime Victims Research and Treatment Center, Department of Psychiatry and Behavioral Sciences, Medical University of South Carolina, Charleston, South Carolina 29425 • **JOHN C. DONKERVOET** • Family Services Center, Department of Psychiatry and Behavioral Sciences, Medical University of South Carolina, Charleston, South Carolina 29425.

Traumatic Stress: From Theory to Practice, edited by John R. Freedy and Stevan E. Hobfoll. Plenum Press, New York, 1995.

personal experience can be illustrated with an example. The first author (J.F.) was a resident of Charleston, South Carolina when Hurricane Hugo devastated this area in September, 1989. No amount of theory, research, or clinical work prepared him to understand what it was like to prepare for, survive, and work to recover from this hurricane. This personal experience provided a unique opportunity to develop an appreciation of the nature of traumatic events, suffering, and resiliency.

Despite the opportunity for personal growth following Hurricane Hugo, the first author believed it was important to test the accuracy of his impressions. He did not want to fall prey to using a personal experience to confirm preconceived ideas about traumatic stress. His learning process involved engagement in the following activities (in order of occurrence): (1) tending to basic needs for himself and his family (e.g., food, water, shelter); (2) offering to help neighbors, friends, and work colleagues to secure basic goods and services; (3) observing and discussing the psychological impact of the hurricane with professional colleagues, family, friends, and neighbors; (4) conducting clinical work with an increasing appreciation of the potential impact of environmental factors upon adjustment; and, (5) conducting research concerning the connection between natural disasters and psychosocial adjustment. His current level of knowledge represents a synthesis of his personal and professional experiences.

Like the first author, mental health professionals who wish to enhance expertise concerning the mental health impact of traumatic events will need to engage in a learning process on a sustained basis. As a step in this learning process, this chapter provides a broad overview of the traumatic event–adjustment linkage. These five areas are addressed: prevalence of traumatic events, mental health implications, conceptual models, intervention issues, and a chapter summary. The consideration of event prevalence includes a review of the growth of research on traumatic stress and a review of epidemiologic studies documenting the frequency of traumatic events. Under mental health implications, these issues are considered: conceptualizing adjustment, the symptoms of posttraumatic stress disorder (PTSD), PTSD prevalence as a function of exposure to different types of traumatic events, the typical time course of PTSD, and mental health disorders that may co-occur with PTSD (comorbidity). The consideration of conceptual models includes consideration of psychological, biological, and integrative models concerning the etiology and maintenance of mental health symptoms. Concerning intervention, general issues that characterize successful mental health intervention are suggested. Finally, a summary of the chapter is offered.

PREVALENCE OF TRAUMATIC EVENTS

Research Trends

The current century has witnessed steady growth in the number of publications concerning the mental health impact of traumatic events. A variety of military and civilian sources of trauma have been studied. The mental health impact of battle participation has been documented following a number of conflicts (Archibald, Long, Miller, & Tuddenham, 1962; Jordan et al., 1991; Laufer, Gallops, & Frey-Wouters, 1984; Solomon, Mikulincer, & Hobfoll, 1986). Additional work has considered the impact of war conditions upon civilians (e.g., concentration camp survivors, relatives of combatants, civilians living in war-torn regions) (Chodoff, 1963; Etinger, 1961; Hobfoll & London, 1986; Hobfoll, Lomranz, Eyal, Bridges, & Tzemach, 1989; Lomranz, Hobfoll, Johnson, Eyal, & Tzemach, 1994; Lewis, 1942; Solomon, 1988; Wolf & Ripley, 1947). Violent crime (e.g., sexual assault, physical assault) has also become a major area of inquiry (Kilpatrick et al., 1985; Kilpatrick & Resnick, 1993). Additional areas of inquiry include: natural disasters (Freedy, Kilpatrick, & Resnick, 1993; Gibbs, 1989; Rubonis & Bickman, 1991), disasters caused by technological failures (Baum, 1987; Butcher & Hatcher, 1988; Jacobs, Quevillon, & Strichetz, 1990; Green et al., 1990; Williams, Solomon, & Bartone, 1988), accidental injury (Kuch, Swinson, & Kirby, 1985; also see Chapter 8, this volume), refugee status (Burkle, 1983; Eisenbruch, 1991; Kinzie, 1989; Kinzie, Sach, Angell, Clark, & Ben, 1989), and torture (see Chapter 14, this volume) among others.

A recent review of research focused on traumatic events noted that 1596 references appeared in the 20 years between 1970 and 1990 (Blake, Albano, & Keane, 1992)! This review noted a gradual, but steady, upward trend in the number of articles published on the subject. Their findings indicate that theoretical and empirical work regarding traumatic stress stemming from either war or violent crime (e.g., sexual abuse or rape) were most common. However, numerous references were also located on the mental health impact of a number of other events such as: child abuse/incest, natural and technical (i.e., human caused) disasters, being held captive (e.g., as a prisoner of war), along with more general or theoretical articles.

Epidemiology

Several recent studies document the frequent occurrence of traumatic events across the life span. Breslau, Davis, Andreski, and Peterson (1991) interviewed a random sample of 1007 adults belonging to a health maintenance organization in Detroit, Michigan. Via structured interview, respondents were asked about the occurrence of any traumatic event; they were also given prompts in the form of several examples of different traumas. Surprisingly, it was discovered that more than one-third (39.1% of the sample) had experienced at least one traumatic event during their life span. The following types of events were reported: sudden injury/serious accident, physical assault, observing the death or serious injury of another person, news of sudden death or serious injury to a relative or friend, rape, natural disasters, and several other traumatic events.

Norris (1992) reported on the prevalence of traumatic events among a sample of 1000 adults living in four cities in the southeastern United States. A structured interview was used to inquire about experiencing traumatic events both during the previous year and over the life span. The majority of respondents (69.0%) had experienced at least one of the following events in their life span: robbery, physical assault, sexual assault, tragic death (family or close friend from accident, homicide, or suicide), motor vehicle crash involving injury, combat, fire, other disasters, and other hazards. In addition, 21.0% of respondents reported experiencing at least one of these events during the past 12 months!

Resnick and her colleagues conducted a crucial study concerning the prevalence of traumatic events (Resnick, Kilpatrick, Dansky, Saunders, & Best, 1993). A major strength of this study lies in the fact that responses were obtained from a national probability sample of 4009 American adult (age 18 or older) women. The respondents were specifically questioned regarding exposure to the following events: rape, molestations or attempted sexual assault, physical assault, homicide of a close friend or relative, and noncrime traumatic events (including natural disasters, serious accidents, serious injuries, life-threatening situations, events involving perceived life threat or threat of serious injury, and any other "extraordinarily stressful" event). Of this sample (68.9%) had experienced one or more of the events during their lifetime; moreover a substantial number (35.6%) reported experiencing at least one of the four traumatic "criminal" events during their lifetime.

Kilpatrick and colleagues reported on the lifetime prevalence of criminal victimization among a community-based sample of 391 adult females living in Charleston, South Carolina (Kilpatrick, Saunders, Veronen, Best, & Von, 1987). More than 75.0% of the sample had been victims of a crime. Lifetime prevalence rates were as follows for specific crime experiences: 23.3% completed rape, 13.1% attempted rape, 18.4% completed molestation, 4.6% attempted molestation, 3.9% other sexual assault, 9.7% aggravated assault, 5.6% robbery, and 45.3% burglary. Interview questions were worded descriptively to encourage respondents to report crime experiences with a higher degree of accuracy.

An additional study determined the lifetime prevalence of traumatic events among a mixed sample of treatment-seeking and non-treatment-seeking adults (Kilpatrick, Edmunds, & Seymour, 1992). This study was conducted as a field trial to determine PTSD symptom criteria for the fourth edition of the *Diagnostic and Statistical Manual of Mental Disorders* (DSM-IV) (APA, 1994). The total sample consisted of 528 adults (age 15 or older), 400 of whom were currently seeking treatment at outpatient clinics specializing in traumatic stress, and 128 of whom were selected from the community (non-treatment-seeking). Subjects were asked about the occurrence of the following events: completed rape, other sexual assault, serious physical assault, other violent crime, homicide death of family members or close friends, serious accidents, natural or man-made disasters, and military combat.

The results from the sample of this field trial were remarkable in the reported rates of traumatic event prevalence. The vast majority of the sample (86.4%) had experienced at least one traumatic event during their lifetime! Moreover, nearly two-thirds of the sample (64.3%) reported experiencing more than one traumatic event over the course of their lives. Most had experienced their first traumatic event (74.5%) prior to the age of 18 years. The early onset of traumatic events is particularly remarkable. Reducing early exposure to traumatic events may be one way to substantially reduce the risk of later mental health difficulties.

Based upon extant research, it is clear that traumatic events are neither rare nor unusual. Although prevalence rates do vary from study to study, the rates are uniformly high. Moreover, it is likely that a substantial portion of observed variation in prevalence rates results from methodological factors. For example, Resnick et al. (1993) have suggested that questions that seek descriptions of behavior (e.g., "Have you ever had a serious accident at work or elsewhere?") often lead to higher, and presumably more accurate, reporting rates. Also, as illustrated by the DSM-IV PTSD field trial, treatment-seeking samples are more likely than non-treatment-seeking samples to report prior exposure to traumatic events. Even when taking into account the methodology that may influence the reporting of traumatic events, it is apparent that prevalence rates remain astonishingly high. Clearly, the areas of both traumatic events and associated sequelae are well worth the consideration of mental health professionals.

MENTAL HEALTH IMPLICATIONS

Conceptualizing Adjustment

Mental health adjustment may be conceptualized according to different models. In fact, considerable professional debate has surrounded the development of systems to classify the nature of human behavior, ranging from normal or functional behavior to abnormal or dysfunctional behavior. At present, the classification of psychopathology typically represents a combination of underlying classification schemes. One particularly common and useful conceptual model involves viewing mental health adjustment in terms of both: (1) discrete classes of complaints, symptoms, or behaviors; and, (2) the degree to which an individual's presentation represents the construct of interest (e.g., severity of symptoms, severity of associated stressors, level of adaptive functioning). It is appropriate that this classification model has been termed a class-quantitative system (Skinner, 1984).

The two most widely used diagnostic classification systems on a world-wide basis are: (1) the tenth edition of the *International Classification of Diseases* (ICD-10), classification of Mental and Behavioral Disorders (World Health Organization, 1992); and (2) the fourth edition of the *Diagnostic and Statistical Manual of Mental Disorders* (APA, 1994). Both systems are based upon a class-quantitative conceptualization of human adjustment. Both systems provide a basis for identifying discrete classes of presenting problems (e.g., depression, substance abuse, personality disorders). In addition, both systems attempt to account for aspects of human functioning along a continuum. As an example

**Table 1. Mental Health Problems Attributable
to Environmental Stressors (ICD-10)**

F43.0 Acute Stress Reaction
A transient, severe condition that may develop following exposure to an overwhelming traumatic event. Symptoms are not a function of a preexisting disorder and typically resolve within hours or days of the causative event.
F43.1 Posttraumatic Stress Disorder
A severe and persistent condition that may develop following exposure to an overwhelming traumatic event. Symptom onset ranges from immediate to delayed (rarely exceeds 6 months following event onset). Typically symptoms include intrusive memories, emotional numbness, withdrawal, avoidance, and a state of hyperarousal and anxiety.
F43.2 Adjustment Disorders
Emotional distress and functional impairment that usually arise within 1 month of a stressful event. The duration of symptoms rarely exceeds 6 months. Typical presentations include depressive reactions, mixed depressed and anxious features, disturbance of other emotion, dusturbance of conduct, and mixed disturbance of emotions and conduct.
F62.0 Enduring Personality Change after Catastrophic Experience
The personality change is profound, lasting, and in response to an extreme traumatic event. In some cases (not all), PTSD may precede the personality changes. Otherwise, the personality changes do not emanate from sources other than the traumatic event (e.g., prior psychopathology). Typical features include hostility and mistrust, social withdrawal, feeling empty or hopeless, feeling constantly anxious and threatened, and estrangement.

of the continuum concept, both the ICD-10 and DSM-IV systems recognize the existence of adjustment disorders and PTSD (APA, 1994; WHO, 1992). Whereas both conditions involve an identifiable stressor followed by a debilitating pattern of adjustment (e.g., feeling anxious, cognitive disturbances), it is clear that stressful events and subsequent adjustment patterns are viewed as more intense, threatening, or debilitating (in both the short and long term) in the case of PTSD.

The ICD-10 classification of mental and behavioral disorders does a particularly excellent job of incorporating both qualitative and quantitative aspects of adjustment to traumatic events. These two diagnostic codes are dedicated to describing adjustment to traumatic events: (1) reaction to severe stress, and adjustment disorders (F43); and, (2) enduring personality changes, not attributable to brain damage and disease (F62). Table 1 provides a brief description of the mental health disorders specified within these two diagnostic codes. This material is presented to give the reader an appreciation of the range of adjustment difficulties that may follow encounters with traumatic events (WHO, 1992).

It is important to appreciate the range of adjustment patterns that may follow exposure to traumatic events. Victims of trauma may manifest mental health disturbances immediately (within minutes, hours, or days) or at some time following (weeks, months, or years later) event exposure. The intensity of symptoms and associated functional impairment range from mild to severe. The duration of symptoms may be time-limited (hours to days) or chronic (months or years). It is also entirely possible for some people to suffer little if any lasting impairment from trauma exposure. It has even been suggested that traumatic stressors may provide an opportunity for positive outcomes, including personal growth (Lyons, 1991).

Posttraumatic Stress Disorder

Although a range of adjustment patterns may occur, PTSD is probably the most common and severe type of posttrauma mental health problem that can occur. Given the central importance of the PTSD diagnosis, further attention will be given to exploring the development and utility of this diagnostic category. Given our familiarity with the DSM-III, DSM-III-R, and DSM-IV descriptions of PTSD, our presentation will concentrate on these diagnostic systems (APA, 1980; APA, 1987; APA, 1994). A high degree of similarity between the DSM and ICD systems with regard to the PTSD diagnosis suggests that our comments apply to cases identified using either diagnostic system.

In 1980, the first operational definition of PTSD was provided in the third edition of the *Diagnostic and Statistical Manual* for the American Psychiatric Association (APA, 1980). This initial description was derived from a consideration of over a century of research and clinical work concerned with documenting typical mental health effects stemming from exposure to traumatic events (Saigh, 1993). Since this seminal diagnostic description, there has been a steady growth in the number of citations concerning PTSD (e.g., less than 25 citations in 1980, approximately 200 citations in 1990) (Saigh, 1993). The operational defining of PTSD has encouraged the development of important knowledge concerning the mental health needs of trauma victims.

Two revisions of the PTSD diagnosis have occurred since 1980. The first

Table 2. Key Findings from the DSM-IV PTSD Field Trial

Traumatic events occur frequently across the life span.

The onset (first occurrence) of a traumatic event is often before the age of 18.

Traumatic events were almost always associated with strong feelings of fear, helplessness, and horror.

The broadness or narrowness of the traumatic event definition did not greatly influence PTSD prevalence rate in the field trial sample.

Symptom level changes (e.g., reclassifying physiological reactivity from an arousal symptom to a reexperiencing symptom) did not greatly impact PTSD prevalence rates in the field trial sample.

Among field trial participants experiencing PTSD ($n = 207$), the majority (70.8%) experienced symptoms lasting 3 months or more.

Although delayed symptom onset is possible, it was not the norm among the field trial sample. A few PTSD sufferers (11.0%) reported symptom onset 6 months or longer following exposure to a traumatic event.

revision was contained in the revised third edition of the *Diagnostic and Statistical Manual* (DSM-III-R) (APA, 1987). The DSM-III-R PTSD diagnosis contained the following revisions: (1) clearer specification of the type of stressful event that might produce symptoms; (2) elaboration of symptom criteria; and, (3) the dropping of an acute subtype of the PTSD diagnosis (APA, 1980; APA, 1987; Saigh, 1993). The most recent revision of the PTSD diagnosis appears in the fourth edition of the *Diagnostic and Statistical Manual* of the American Psychiatric Association (DSM-IV) (APA, 1994). Unlike previous versions of the PTSD diagnosis, the DSM-IV revision is based upon a consideration of field trial data collected to assess the adequacy of diagnostic categories.

Several changes appear in the DSM-IV version of the PTSD diagnosis. Any changes were based upon committee deliberations informed by data from field trial results. The PTSD field trial for DSM-IV ($n = 528$ adults; $n = 400$ adults in treatment, $n = 128$ adults not in treatment) yielded a number of interesting findings (Kilpatrick et al., 1992). Table 2 provides highlights of some of the more interesting findings from the PTSD field trial data.

The DSM-IV PTSD diagnosis requires exposure to a traumatic event (". . . experienced, witnessed, or confronted with . . .") that is associated with intense feelings of fear, helplessness, or horror. Three types of symptoms are required, including: (1) one reexperiencing symptom (e.g., recurrent and intrusive recollections, recurrent distressing dreams, flashbacks); (2) three avoidance or numbing symptoms (e.g., avoiding thoughts, feelings, or talk associated with the trauma, avoiding activities, places, or people that arouse recollections of the trauma, feelings of detachment or estrangement); and, (3) two arousal symptoms (e.g., difficulty falling or staying asleep, irritability or anger, exaggerated startle response). These symptoms must follow a traumatic event and persist for at least 1 month. Additional specifications concern whether the PTSD symptoms are: (1) acute (less than 3-months' duration); (2) chronic (more than 3-months' duration); (3) or delayed in onset (onset at least 6-months' following the traumatic event) (APA, 1994).

Event Quality and Mental Health

Available research is based upon earlier versions of the PTSD diagnosis (DSM-III and DSM-III-R). It should be noted that each version of the PTSD diagnosis (DSM-III, DSM-III-R, and DSM-IV) has much in common in terms of the basic symptoms of reexperiencing of the trauma; avoidance or numbing related to the trauma; and, physiological arousal to reminders of the trauma (APA, 1980; APA, 1987; APA, 1994). In addition, the DSM-IV PTSD criteria are very consistent with the ICD-10 description of PTSD (WHO, 1992). Therefore, results based upon DSM-III or DSM-III-R PTSD criteria should be relevant for understanding PTSD as defined by either DSM-IV or ICD-10. It is likely that a new generation of research studies will appear based upon the updated PTSD criteria.

Research findings have demonstrated a clear relationship between the qualities of traumatic events and the risk for mental health problems. The relationship between event qualities and PTSD risk is especially clear in the study of combat veterans (Foy & Card, 1987; Foy, Resnick, Sipprell, & Carroll, 1987; Laufer et al., 1984). Table 3 presents a summary of the types of event characteristics that have been associated with increased mental health risk among combat veterans (Foy & Card, 1987; Grady, Woolfolk, & Budney, 1989; Jordan et al., 1991; Lund, Foy, Sipprelle, & Strachan, 1984; Solomon et al., 1986; Solomon, Mikulincer, & Hobfoll, 1987; Yehuda, Southwick, & Giller, 1992). Much of this research was based upon the responses of Vietnam veterans. Some of this research was based upon samples of Israeli war veterans.

Beyond studies of combat veterans, research indicates clear associations between event qualities and mental health functioning. One review of combat, crime, and disaster research noted that the following factors increased the risk of negative mental health outcomes: threat of death or physical injury, physical injury, receiving intentional harm, experiencing grotesque sights, violent or sudden death to valued people, and receiving information about exposure to a noxious substance (Green, 1990). One community-based study of adult female crime victims found that certain crime characteristics (a completed rape, physical injury, perceiving threat to life) were associated with an 8.5-fold increase in the risk for developing PTSD (Kilpatrick et al., 1989). Following natural or technological disasters, these characteristics have been associated with additional mental health problems: strong exposure to the elements, death of a loved one, high death rates, being blocked from escape, being injured, property loss, and proximity to the source of the disaster (Baum, 1987; Green et al., 1990; Rubonis & Bickman, 1991; Shore, Tatum, & Vollmer, 1986a,b).

A number of studies have appeared that document the prevalence of PTSD among various groups. One review noted that prevalence rates range widely, in part because of methodology differences and in part because of the

Table 3. Elements of Combat Experience Associated with an Increased Risk of Mental Health Problems

Length of combat duty
Service within a war zone
Participation in combat
Perceiving a threat to life
Being wounded
Witnessing death
Responsibility for the deaths of enemy military
Participating in or witnessing abusive violence (atrocities)
Physical deprivation
Perceiving a loss of control or meaning
Extreme intensity of battle conditions

fact that different studies concern samples with unique characteristics (Saigh, 1993). This chapter focuses on studies that, in the authors' judgment, use a strong research methodology. The focus is on large, representative samples that are recruited in a systematic (i.e., minimally biased) fashion. Standardization in the measurement of traumatic events and PTSD symptoms has been required. Regarding event measurement, preference is given to studies that probe for the presence of a range of events. This latter approach may lead to more accurate reporting of true rate of traumatic experiences and by extension the more accurate assessment of possible PTSD symptomatology associated with traumatic events.

Published PTSD prevalence rates vary as a function of the population studied. Based on sound epidemiologic research, it has been estimated that 30.6% of male and 26.9% of female Vietnam veterans suffered from PTSD at some point following their service (Kulka et al., 1991). Breslau et al. (1991) found that 9.2% of their random sample of health maintenance organization members had experienced PTSD during their lives. The PTSD rate was 23.6% among people exposed to a traumatic event in this sample. Norris (1992) studied the prevalence of PTSD during the past year and found a rate of 7.0% among individuals previously exposed to a violent event. In a large national probability sample of adult women, the following lifetime PTSD rates were found: 12.3% overall and 25.8% among crime victims (rape, molestations or attempted sexual assault, physical assault, homicide of a close friend or relative) (Resnick et al., 1993). Similarly, Kilpatrick et al. (1987) found that 27.8% of a community sample of adult female crime victims (a range of crimes) had ever experienced PTSD.

Time Course of PTSD Symptoms

The development of the PTSD syndrome represents an unfortunate outcome that may follow tragic experiences. Evidence is available to suggest that PTSD symptoms can develop into a chronic, debilitating condition. For example, it has been suggested that as many as 15.2% of male and 8.2% of female Vietnam veterans currently suffer from PTSD (Kulka et al., 1991). The existence of substantial current PTSD rates supports the possibility of ongoing mental health problems. It is also the case that Vietnam veterans with high levels of war-related stress suffer from substantial current rates of other mental health disorders (e.g., depression, alcohol abuse) (Jordan et al., 1991).

Additional reports are available concerning the longevity of posttrauma mental health problems. For example, high rates of PTSD and depressive symptoms have been documented among prisoners of war (POWs) from World War II (Kluznick, Speed, Van Valkenburg, & Magraw, 1986; Page, Engdahl, & Eberly, 1991). Among POWs who had developed PTSD, only 29% had "fully recovered" by 40 years following imprisonment. One study reported elevated psychological complaints 33 years following the Holocaust when a random community sample of survivors was contrasted to a control sample (Eaton,

Sigal, & Weinfeld, 1982). Another study found that crime-related PTSD could persist 15 years or longer among a nontreatment-seeking sample (Kilpatrick, Saunders, Veronen, Best, & Von, 1987). Green et al. (1991) noted the persistence of PTSD symptoms as long as 14 years following a major dam collapse at the Buffalo Creek Dam in West Virginia. Clearly, intense psychological distress and functional impairment may persist for many years following extreme forms of traumatic stress.

Comorbidity

The question can be raised as to whether PTSD is the only mental health problem experienced following traumatic events. If associated mental health problems arise, they would certainly be relevant for treatment provision. Empirical reports of co-occurring diagnoses are largely limited to studies concerning Vietnam combat veterans (see Eisenbruch, 1991, for an exception). Among Vietnam veterans seeking treatment, two studies found that over one-half of respondents had experienced at least one additional mental health disorder during their lifetime (Boudewyns, Albrecht, Talbert, & Hyer, 1991; Sierles, Chen, McFarland, & Taylor, 1983). The following mental health problems were common: alcohol or drug abuse, depression, antisocial personality disorder, and psychotic conditions.

Other studies are based entirely or largely on community-based samples. Green, Lindy, Grace, and Gleser (1989) reported on a sample of 200 male Vietnam veterans (33% treatment seekers, 67% non-treatment seekers). PTSD was the most frequent diagnosis (29.0%) among this sample, but it rarely occurred alone. Frequent comorbid conditions included: major depression, panic disorder, phobia, and alcohol problems. One study used a large national sample of Vietnam veterans ($n = 3016$) to determine the rate of mental health diagnoses other than PTSD (Jordan et al., 1991). Male and female veterans exposed to high levels of war-related stress (e.g., exposure to combat, exposure to abusive violence) were particularly prone to develop mental health problems. Common mental health problems included: depression, alcohol abuse or dependence, and antisocial personality disorder (men only).

Although less extensive than those investigations examining comorbidity with PTSD in veteran samples, some of the work examining prevalence of other Axis I disorders following traumatic events in the nonveteran population has been equally provocative. In one large household, probability sample of adults ($n = 3,132$), the occurrence of sexual assault was found to be a risk factor for several mental disorders (Burnam et al., 1988). In particular, sexual assault was related to the later onset of depression, substance abuse (alcohol or other drugs), and several anxiety disorders (phobia, panic disorder, and obsessive–compulsive disorder). Earlier-onset sexual assault was associated with an increased risk to mental health.

Breslau and Davis (1992) examined a random sample of 1,007 members of a large health maintenance organization. Of this sample, 394 reported having experienced a traumatic event during their lifetime (39.1%), 93 of whom even met criteria for PTSD (9.2%). In sufferers of both chronic (symptom lasting for more than 1 year in duration) and nonchronic PTSD, there were notably high lifetime rates of a variety of other Axis I disorders including: major depression, any anxiety disorder, alcohol abuse or dependence, and substance abuse or dependence. Finally this study found that in the sample of respondents with PTSD (n = 93), a total of 77 persons (82.8% of PTSD cases) met criteria for some other type of psychiatric illness (Breslau et al., 1991).

Comorbidity findings based upon veteran samples await further replication with other trauma-impacted groups. Since other trauma victims may differ in important ways (e.g., rape victims are more likely to be female, noncombat groups may be studied sooner after the traumatic event allowing for the passage of less time in which additional problems might develop), it is still not clear to what extent comorbidity poses a substantial issue in other groups of trauma victims. Based on clinical observations, however, (and the preliminary work of several authors), it is clear that other mental health diagnoses are a relevant issue for victims of traumatic experiences other than combat. Later chapters in this volume attempt to address the clinical implications of the possible comorbid mental health problems in those individuals who have lived through various traumatic experiences.

CONCEPTUAL MODELS

Psychological Models

Two psychological explanations for the development of mental health problems following traumatic events have been forwarded. The first explanation is based upon learning theory principles. The second explanation focuses on the relevance of cognition and perception in the development of mental health difficulties. Given the wide usage of learning theory and cognitive models, a brief overview of both psychological models is provided. The application of psychological models to specific traumatic events is addressed in subsequent chapters.

A learning theory explanation for the development of anxiety has been proposed with regard to combat trauma (see Keane, Zimering, & Caddell, 1985) and crime-related trauma (see Kilpatrick, Veronen, & Resick, 1979). These explanations are based upon principles of Mowrer's (1960) two-factor theory. From this viewpoint, fear is considered classically conditioned (first factor). As an example, during a sexual assault a woman is exposed to an array of threatening cues (e.g., threatening or degrading words, violent or painful acts) that can serve as unconditioned stimuli (UCS) for a strong fear response (unconditioned response [UCR]). Through associative learning, additional cues may acquire the capacity to elicit a strong fear. Therefore, situations such as sexual intimacy with a caring partner or going to an area near the sexual assault may remind the woman of the traumatic experience. These learned cues or conditioned stimuli (CS) develop the capacity to elicit an intense, often debilitating fear response (conditioned response [CR]).

The second factor operating in the learning theory model concerns instrumental avoidance behavior. Trauma victims may avoid certain cues in order to minimize experiencing overwhelming memories and fears. As an example, a sexual assault victim may avoid talking about her assault, may avoid sexual intimacies (or find such activities extremely unpleasant), or avoid public areas for fear of seeing the perpetrator (or someone that resembles the perpetrator). Although the purpose of avoidance behavior appears to be the management of painful feelings and memories, in the long run, avoidant coping strategies perpetuate feelings of fear, social isolation, and perceiving a loss of control over one's life.

A learning theory model provides an adequate explanation for the etiology of a subset of PTSD symptoms. Namely, the development of certain arousal symptoms (e.g., exaggerated startle response) and avoidance symptoms (e.g., avoidance of thoughts and feelings related to the trauma) that appear are addressed within the learning theory framework (APA, 1994). However, the development and maintenance of reexperiencing symptoms are not addressed by a learning theory approach. In particular, the problem of reexperiencing symptoms of PTSD (e.g., recurrent and distressing memories of the trauma, recurrent distressing dreams) is not addressed by learning theory. The development and maintenance of intrusive cognitive symptoms require a theoretical explanation that extends beyond principles of classical and operant conditioning (Foa & Kozak, 1986; Foa, Steketee, & Olasov-Rothbaum, 1989).

Cognitive processing models have been suggested to explain reexperiencing symptoms that are characteristic of the PTSD syndrome. An early model (described in psychodynamic terms) was forwarded by Horowitz (1986). He proposed that memory processes contain a motivational component. He noted that humans seek to understand the meaning of various life experiences. Thus, images of an event are held in "active memory" as the individual seeks to determine the personal relevance of an experience. In the case of life-threatening trauma, the individual's basic biological and emotional existence are threatened. This state of affairs presents huge challenges to typical patterns of thinking (i.e., psychological defenses) about the self and the world. From this perspective, repetitive recollections of traumatic memories alternating with avoidance behavior and feelings of numbness represent an effort to integrate traumatic memories into an acceptable view of the self (e.g., worthwhile, competent) and the world (e.g., controllable, predictable).

Other cognitive processing models have been proposed. One approach proposes the importance of a fear-based memory network (Foa et al., 1989). This approach suggests that a fear-based memory network develops following trauma and contains information regarding: trauma-related stimuli, responses to the trauma (thoughts, feelings, behaviors), and the meaning of trauma stimuli and subsequent responses. PTSD is proposed as developing when previously safe situations or people are associated with extreme danger during the trauma. Reexperiencing phenomena (e.g., memories, nightmares) reflect the inability to activate the fear network long enough to modify elements of the memory. Activation of the memory network and the incorporation of accurate information regarding the trauma (e.g., no one deserves to be raped) are made difficult by the naturally occurring avoidance of thinking about or discussing the trauma. For modification of the fear structure to occur, the memory must be activated, and new information incompatible with the perception of pervasive and chronic danger must be integrated. Cognitive–behavioral psychotherapy may be required to help the trauma victim accomplish this goal.

An additional information-processing approach was proposed by Resick and is derived from the work of McCann and her colleagues (McCann & Pearlman, 1990; McCann, Sakheim, & Abrahamson, 1988; Resick & Schnicke, 1993). This approach suggests that traumatic experiences confront the victim with information that is highly discrepant from typical beliefs (cognitive schema) about the self and the world. Typical schema include issues such as: safety, trust, power, esteem, intimacy, hope, causality, and control. This viewpoint suggests that suffering in the aftermath of traumatic events largely involves wrestling with the meaning of the event in terms of issues defined by existing beliefs. The meaning attributed to the trauma and one's role in the trauma will largely determine the course of adjustment (positive or negative) in the aftermath of the traumatic event. This approach broadens other information-processing view points by identifying a range of schemata (i.e., beyond beliefs concerning safety) that can be challenged by traumatic experiences.

Biological Models

Recent empirical work has examined the possibility that biological factors may underlie the etiology or maintenance of PTSD symptoms. Much of this work has involved the study of animal models (for example, investigations concerning animals subjected to inescapable shocks) (van der Kolk, Greenberg, Boyd, & Krystal, 1985; Vogel, 1985). In addition, biological aspects of human responses to trauma have also been examined (Blanchard, Kolb, Gerardi, Ryan, & Pallmeyer, 1986; Blanchard, Kolb, Pallmeyer, & Gerardi, 1982; Pitman et al., 1990; Pallmeyer, Blanchard, & Kolb, 1986). Most scholars acknowledge that biological factors are one of several important factors influencing the nature and course of posttrauma adjustment. The scope of this chapter does not allow for a complete review of the relevant literature; the interested reader is directed to available reviews (e.g., Charney, Deutch, Krystal, Southwick, & Davis, 1993; Pitman, 1993).

As mentioned, studies of animals may provide a model for understanding biological factors underlying posttrauma adaptation in humans. For example, it has been suggested that the inability to escape shock may lead to identifiable biological changes. Animals exposed to inescapable shock demonstrate a transient depletion of certain neurotransmitters (e.g., norepinephrine, epinephrine, and dopamine). The depletion of these neurotransmitters has been shown to produce symptoms that appear to parallel the negative symptoms of PTSD in humans; these symptoms include the constriction of affect, social withdrawal, and a decrease in goal-oriented behavior (van der Kolk et al., 1985).

Along with the reduction of the availability of these neurotransmitters, subjecting an animal to repeated and inescapable shock causes the release of endogenous opiates thereby creating a state of analgesia (van der Kolk et al., 1985). Over time, these opiates can have an addictive effect on the organism; in the absence of the opiate-releasing stressor, the animal goes through a form of opioid withdrawal leading to the exhibition of a number of PTSD like symptoms: anxiety, startle responses, difficulty sleeping, hyperalertness, impulsivity. This withdrawal paradigm has also been used to explain the high incidence of substance abuse among combat veterans with PTSD, thrill-seeking behavior, and the compulsive reexposure to trauma frequently observed in these populations (Charney et al., 1993).

Also utilizing results from animal studies of inescapable shock, Kolb (1988) has proposed a conditioned emotional response (CER) model. In essence, this model suggests that prolonged exposure to a painful, inescapable threat may produce an alteration in the neurological structures within the brain, particularly within the limbic system. According to the CER model, traumatic events may lead to an excessive stimulation of particular areas within the limbic system, particularly the locus coeruleus. The neurons of the locus coeruleus are activated by external threatening stimuli; and when stimulated, the organism displays behaviors typifying fear and alarm. The pairing of nonthreatening with threatening stimuli may lead to an overactivation of the locus coeruleus, producing fear behavior in response to otherwise neutral stimuli. Over time, this prolonged overstimulation leads to a generalized hyperactivity of the locus coeruleus and the resulting conditioned alarm state that characterizes PTSD.

To date, research on human subjects has primarily focused on the role of the autonomic nervous system in posttrauma adjustment. Several studies have demonstrated that combat veterans with PTSD have significantly higher resting heart rates and systolic blood pressures than do comparison groups (Blanchard et al., 1982, 1986). In addition, combat veterans with PTSD show reliable patterns of physiological reactivity when exposed to combat-relevant cues (visual and auditory combat-related stimuli such as slides of battle scenes or audio tapes of combat) in comparison to non-PTSD veterans, generalized anxiety disorder patients, and normal subjects (Pallmeyer et al., 1986; Pitman et al., 1990). These findings suggest that the autonomic nervous system plays a key role in posttrauma adaptation. However, it is not clear whether autonomic elevations and reactivity precede the development of PTSD. It is possible that autonomic elevations and reactivity represent a consequence of trauma exposure.

It has also been proposed that posttrauma adaptation may be related to an inherited biological predisposition to experience anxiety (Barlow, 1988; Jones & Barlow, 1990). This model suggests that people may inherit an autonomic nervous system with two characteristics: (1) a high resting rate (e.g., heart rate, blood pressure); and (2) a high rate of reactivity to threatening stimuli. It is proposed that this biological vulnerability in combination with an intense and/or prolonged stressor may result in debilitating levels of anxiety. This model suggests that stressor may be either environmental (e.g., a serious car accident) or internal (e.g., thoughts about environmental threats or internal sensations). This model also suggests that certain individual factors (e.g., social support, coping responses) may raise or lower the probability of a stressor combining with the inherited biological vulnerability to produce debilitating anxiety. At present, this biological vulnerability model is speculative as it lacks firm empirical validation. However, the emphasis on the integration of biological and psychological factors reflect an appealing trend in theoretical models of symptom development.

Integrative Models

Early models concerning the etiology of PTSD tended to focus on the role of single factors (e.g., conditioned anxiety, cognitive processes, biological vulnerability) in determining adjustment. The merit of such approaches lies in their potential for clear explanatory power. Despite this potential clarity, subsequent clinical observation and the absence of empirical data to completely support or reject a particular theoretical model have lead to the proposal of more complex etiological models. Such models attempt to integrate the potential importance of a variety of psychological, social, and biological factors in the etiology and maintenance of PTSD.

One excellent prototype of an integrative model of PTSD etiology and maintenance was proposed by Foy and his colleagues (Foy, Osato, Houskamp, & Neumann, 1993). The core of this model concerns the idea that trauma exposure may lead to conditioned emotional reactions that become either acute or chronic PTSD. The model proposes three routes by which the conditioning of posttrauma anxiety may occur: (1) direct personal experience (e.g., being raped); (2) observation (e.g., witnessing death or severe injury); or, (3) vicarious experience (e.g., learning of harm to another person).

The Foy model also proposes that other factors may mediate between trauma exposure and the conditioning of acute or chronic PTSD symptoms (Foy et al., 1993). These psychological, social, and biological factors are referred to as risk factors when their presence increases the probability of PTSD developing. Alternatively, these factors are termed resilience factors when their presence decreases the probability of PTSD emerging. The Foy model suggests that it is an empirical matter to determine the existence of risk or resilience factors in PTSD development and maintenance of PTSD. The emphasis upon the empirical validation of proposed etiological mechanisms is an appealing feature of the Foy model. In addition, the explicit recognition of the potential importance of psychological, social, and biological factors in the etiology and maintenance of PTSD is useful. The future advancement in conceptual understanding of PTSD will rely on models that attempt to integrate psychological, social, and biological mechanisms.

INTERVENTION PRINCIPLES

This section of the current chapter focuses on general features that characterize successful mental health treatment for trauma victims. Neither the specific types of treatment available nor the implementation of these psychosocial or biological treatments are described. Such "nuts and bolts" descriptions of treatment approaches are provided by subsequent chapters in this volume. The current goal is the presentation of underlying characteristics inherent in the types of treatments presented later in this volume. The presentation of these general characteristics is intended to provide an overall framework for the consideration of treatment approaches presented later in this volume.

Prevention

Prevention is one concept that is too seldom mentioned with regard to the treatment of posttrauma mental health problems. In particular, the concept of primary prevention is relevant. Technically speaking, primary prevention refers to efforts directed at minimizing the occurrence of new disorders within a population (Bloom, 1984). With regard to trauma, the idea is to do what is necessary to reduce the risk of posttrauma mental health difficulties within the general population. Norris and Thompson (Chapter 3, this volume) address the importance of primary prevention efforts related to traumatic events in greater detail.

Two types of primary prevention efforts may be relevant to mental health professionals interested in reducing posttrauma mental health problems. First, it may be possible to reduce the incidence of some traumatic events. Examples of such efforts include: crime prevention programs, fire prevention programs, transportation industry regulations, or political activism directed at lessening the incidence of violence and oppression (e.g., domestic violence, child abuse, war). Second, even if a traumatic event cannot be averted, it may be possible to limit the traumatic impact of the event upon individuals. Examples of these efforts include: emergency shelters for battered women (and children), foster-home programs, immediate mental health and legal services for other victims of violent crime, or shelters/camps designed to provide basic goods and services to the victims of mass community traumas (e.g., natural disasters, war).

Beyond the concept of primary prevention, many writers have considered potential forms of psychosocial and pharmacological treatments for the victims of traumatic events. These approaches typically intervene at the level of the individual, although some approaches involve group or family-based treatment approaches. Two principles generally underlie discussions of treatment. Secondary prevention refers to efforts directed at reducing the longevity of a disorder based on early case finding and appropriate intervention. Tertiary prevention, also known as rehabilitation, involves reducing the severity of functional impairment associated with a disorder (Bloom, 1984). In some cases, it is possible to resolve PTSD symptoms and additional trauma related problems (secondary treatment). On occasion, however, impairments become chronic. Then, efforts may be directed at helping the individual function at an optimal level despite unremitting physical or emotional effects (rehabilitation).

Trauma-Focused Treatment

The content of successful psychological treatments in this area must remain trauma-focused. For the mental health professional with modest experience in working with trauma victims, it may feel uncomfortable (e.g., intimidating, frightening) to talk with a trauma victim. What can one say to an angry combat veteran, disaster victim, the family member of a homicide victim, a rape victim, an accident victim, or a refugee who has been tortured? There seems to be an implicit desire to make such unpleasant aspects of society go away. As treatment professionals, we may worry about saying something that is insensitive, that somehow creates more emotional pain for the trauma victim. However, there is nothing so painful as silence in the face of trauma-induced suffering. Talking about traumatic experiences with a sympathetic listener is generally less emotionally painful than the original trauma.

Several currently practiced treatment modalities clearly require the treated person to focus on traumatic memories. Such treatment approaches range from implosive therapy (flooding) to cognitive therapies that encourage thinking about and talking about the personal meaning of traumatic experiences (Lyons & Keane, 1989; Resick, 1992; Rothbaum & Foa, 1993). Although controlled treatment studies concerning PTSD are relatively rare, the few available studies are supportive of the general efficacy of approaches requiring a specific focus on the consideration of traumatic memories (Solomon, Gerrity, & Muff, 1992). Such approaches have been found to be successful with groups as diverse as male combat veterans and female victims of violent crime (Fairbank & Keane, 1982; Keane, Fairbank, Caddell, & Zimering, 1989; Keane & Kaloupek, 1982; Resick & Schnicke, 1992; Rothbaum & Foa, 1992).

Skills Building

A focus on the content of traumatic memories is a necessary, but not sufficient, condition for the successful treatment of trauma victims. This assertion is based on the idea that requiring a trauma victim to consider a traumatic memory can generate extreme, sometimes debilitating levels of anxiety. Indeed, debilitating levels of anxiety are among the hallmark symptoms of PTSD. Trauma-focused treatment approaches that fail to build appropriate stress-management skills for the management of anxiety have been criticized on the grounds of creating further emotional harm to the trauma victim (Kilpatrick & Best, 1984). Indeed, it is possible that some trauma victims will prematurely terminate treatment if they are not provided with the means to manage their heightened sense of anxiety.

Many approaches to the treatment of trauma victims contain skills-building components. An illustrative example is found in the application of stress inoculation training (SIT) to the treatment of adult crime victims (Resnick & Newton, 1992). Examples of stress-management skills provided in this standard SIT treatment package include: controlled breathing exercises, deep muscle relaxation, cognitive restructuring, thought stopping, guided self-dialogue, role playing, and covert modeling. Research to date has not indicated the relative importance of each of the aforementioned skills-building modules to the general efficacy of SIT in the treatment of adult crime victims. Nevertheless, it remains important to teach the victims of all types of trauma anxiety-management skills that will allow for more effective coping with trauma-related symptoms.

Resource Enhancement

In the second chapter of this volume, Hobfoll and colleagues (Chapter 2, this volume) describe the conservation of resources (COR) stress model (see also Hobfoll, 1988, 1989). The COR model describes a range of internal (e.g., sense of control, sense of meaning) and external (e.g., social support, employment) resources that individuals may possess. According to the COR model, the loss or lack of resources contributes to the development and maintenance of psychological distress. In addition, the loss or lack of important internal and external resources will limit coping options and the efficacy of coping efforts. This is not difficult to imagine. Sensing a lack of control, lacking trustworthy companions, or being unemployed all could make it difficult to meet various life demands.

In working with trauma victims, it is important to remember that their needs will extend beyond affective and cognitive states. Trauma victims may lack certain internal and external resources based upon their life experiences. Failure to consider such resource-based needs may lead to poorer adjustment on the part of the trauma victim. As an example, combat veterans with PTSD may require housing assistance or job training and placement as part of a comprehensive treatment plan. Disaster victims or refugees may require the provision of basic goods and services (e.g., food, water, shelter, medicines) to facilitate adjustment. Holocaust survivors may benefit from religious observances or group affiliation as such experiences provide a sense of belonging and meaning that was severely challenged by the nature of their traumatic experiences.

Developmental Level

Traumatic events may occur at various times during the life span. Based on a developmental perspective, it can be assumed that individuals achieve increasingly sophisticated cognitive and affective skills as a function of meeting age-appropriate environmental demands. Internal and external resources are accrued as a function of successfully meeting environmental demands. Children meet friends or succeed in school. Adolescents work part-time, date, and eventually graduate. Young adults complete their education, start careers, marry, or start families. Limits on subsequent development are, to some extent, determined by prior successes or failures in meeting environmental demands. Traumatic events may create limits on the cognitive and affective capacity of victims to succeed in meeting ongoing environmental demands. This may limit the internal and external resources available to an individual.

Treatment approaches should consider the potential influence of traumatic events upon normal developmental processes. Particularly early or severe traumatic experiences may distort or delay developmental processes. Acquired capacities such as trust, self-esteem, self-efficacy, optimism, or sustained motivation to achieve goals may become impaired. One goal of treatment with trauma victims may be to facilitate further development of such capacities.

Integrative Approaches

One major criticism of PTSD treatment research involves the idea that such studies do not accurately reflect standard clinical practice. McFarlane (1989) noted that combinations of treatment are typically applied within clinical settings. However, treatment research typically describes the application of singular treatment approaches. In support of his position, McFarlane (1989) described the "eclectic treatment" of 51 trauma victims. About one-quarter (27.5%) were treated with psychotherapy alone, whereas most (72.5%) were treated with some combination of psychotherapy and medication. Psychotherapy approaches were described as either: dynamic, behavioral, brief, or supportive. Medications included: tricyclic antidepressants, monoamine oxidase inhibitors, benzodiazepines, lithium, or antipsychotic medications.

Comments on the importance of integrating treatment approaches are not meant to suggest that "anything goes" in terms of treatment provision. Indeed, the coming chapters reveal that certain treatment approaches have demonstrated efficacy in relieving PTSD symptoms, whereas other treatment approaches do not. The point remains, however, that treatment providers need to be creative and flexible in approaching the clinical problems presented by trauma victims. Some combination of treatment approaches (e.g., individual therapy, group therapy, medications) may be required to produce optimal results. Issues of comorbid mental health problems should be carefully considered and addressed when necessary. The roles of social and economic conditions in exacerbating and/or maintaining symptomatology should be considered and addressed.

SUMMARY

This chapter and book are based on a simple premise: good clinical practice must be guided by state-of-the-art knowledge concerning the topic of interest. This chapter has attempted a broad overview of the area of traumatic stress. Armed with this base of knowledge, the reader will be more prepared to appreciate the potential role of traumatic stress in determining mental health adjustment. Subsequent chapters in this volume provide additional information and insight regarding the topic of traumatic stress.

Key ideas have been proposed and supported by information presented in this chapter. These key concepts include the following:

- There has been a substantial and growing interest in the topic of traumatic stress over the past century.
- Traumatic events are neither rare nor unusual across the life span.
- A range of adjustment patterns, from no mental health disorders through severe mental health disorders, may follow exposure to traumatic events.
- PTSD is the most common and severe type of mental health problem that may follow exposure to a traumatic event.
- More intense traumatic events (e.g., involve physical injury, threat to life, deaths) are associated with an increased risk for developing PTSD.
- PTSD symptomatology can be chronic (lasting for years).
- PTSD often co-occurs with other mental health problems, although further research with representative samples is needed in this area.
- Several conceptual models (psychological, biological, and integrative) concerning the etiology and maintenance of PTSD symptoms have been forwarded.
- Learning theory, cognitive processing, and biological models of PTSD provide partial explanations for the etiology and maintenance of PTSD symptoms.
- The current trend is toward conceptual models that attempt to integrate psychological, social, and biological factors contributing to the etiology and maintenance of PTSD.
- Optimal mental health interventions for trauma victims are characterized by a number of general features.
- Optimal interventions focus on preventing trauma exposure and/or limiting negative mental health effects resulting from trauma exposure.
- Optimal interventions remain focused on the expression and discussion of traumatic experiences, memories, and associated thoughts and feelings.
- Optimal interventions teach needed anxiety management and other skills (e.g., social skills, job related skills) to trauma victims.
- Optimal interventions seek to assess and enhance a range of internal (e.g., sense of control, self-esteem) and external resources (e.g., employment, social support) available to the trauma victim.

- Optimal interventions assess and attempt to correct developmental problems created by earlier trauma exposure.
- Optimal interventions attempt to integrate psychological, social, and medical approaches to symptom management and resolution.

REFERENCES

American Psychiatric Association. (1980). *Diagnostic and statistical manual of mental disorders* (3rd ed.). Washington, DC: Author.

American Psychiatric Association. (1987). *Diagnostic and statistical manual of mental disorders* (3rd ed.-rev.). Washington DC: Author.

American Psychiatric Association. (1994). *Diagnostic and statistical manual of mental disorders* (4th ed.). Washington, DC: Author.

Archibald, H. C., Long, D. M., Miller, C., & Tuddenham, R. D. (1962). Gross stress reaction in combat—a 15 year follow-up. *American Journal of Psychiatry, 119,* 317–322.

Barlow, D. H. (1988). *Anxiety and its disorders: The nature and treatment of anxiety and panic.* New York: Guilford Press.

Baum, A. (1987). Toxins, technology, and natural disasters. In G. R. VandenBos & B. K. Bryant (Eds.), *Cataclysms, crises, and catastrophes: Psychology in action* (pp. 9–53). Washington, DC: American Psychological Association.

Blake, D. D., Albano, A. M., & Keane, T. M. (1992). Twenty years of trauma: Psychological abstract 1970–1989. *Journal of Traumatic Stress, 5*(3), 477–484.

Blanchard, E. B., Kolb, L. C., Gerardi, R. J., Ryan, P., & Pallmeyer, T. P. (1986). Cardiac response to relevant stimuli as a tool for diagnosing post-traumatic stress disorder in Vietnam veterans. *Behavior Therapy, 12,* 592–606.

Blanchard, E. B., Kolb, L. C., Pallmeyer, T. P., & Gerardi, R. J. (1982). A psychophysiological study of post-traumatic stress disorder in Vietnam veterans. *Psychiatric Quarterly, 54,* 220–229.

Bloom, B. L. (1984). *Community mental health: A general introduction* (2nd ed.). Monterey, CA: Brooks/Coles Publishing.

Boudewyns, P. A., Albrecht, J. W., Talbert, F. S., & Hyer, L. A. (1991). Comorbidity and treatment outcomes of inpatients with chronic combat-related PTSD. *Hospital and Community Psychiatry, 42*(8), 847–849.

Breslau, N., & Davis, G. C. (1992). Post-traumatic stress syndrome in an urban population of young adults: Risk factors for chronicity. *American Journal of the American Academy of Child Psychiatry, 149,* 336–345.

Breslau, N., Davis, G. C., Andreski, P., & Peterson, E. (1991). Traumatic events and post-traumatic stress disorder in an urban population of young adults. *Archives of General Psychiatry, 48,* 216–222.

Burkle, F. M. (1983). Coping with stress under condition of disaster and refugee care. *Military Medicine, 148,* 800–803.

Burnam, M. A., Stein, J. A., Golding, J. M., Siegel, J. M., Sorenson, S. B., Forsythe, A. B., & Telles, C. A. (1988). Sexual assault and mental disorders in a community population. *Journal of Consulting and Clinical Psychology, 56,*(6), 843–850.

Butcher, J. N., & Hatcher, C. (1988). The neglected entity in air disaster planning: Psychological services. *American Psychologist, 43*(9), 724–729.

Charney, D. S., Deutch, A. Y., Krystal, J. H., Southwick, S. M., & Davis, M. (1993). Psychobiologic mechanisms of posttraumatic stress disorder. *Archives of General Psychiatry, 50,* 294–305.

Chodoff, P. (1963). Late effects of the concentration camp syndrome. *Archives of General Psychiatry, 8,* 323–333.

Eaton, W. W., Sigal, J. J., & Weinfeld, M. (1982). Impairment in holocaust survivors after 33 years: Data from an unbiased community sample. *American Journal of Psychiatry, 139*(6), 773–777.

Eisenbruch, M. (1991). From post-traumatic stress disorder to cultural bereavement: Diagnosis of southeast asian refugees. *Social Science Medicine, 33*(6), 673–680.

Etinger, L. (1961). Concentration camp survivors in the postwar world. *American Journal of Orthopsychiatry, 32,* 367–375.

Fairbank, J. A., & Keane, T. M. (1982). Flooding for combat related stress disorders: Assessment of anxiety reduction across traumatic memories. *Behavior Therapy, 13,* 499–510.

Foa, E. B., & Kozak, M. J. (1986). Emotional processing of fear: Exposure to corrective information. *Psychological Bulletin, 99,* 20–35.

Foa, E. B., Steketee, G., & Olasov-Rothbaum, B. (1989). Behavioral/cognitive conceptualizations of post-traumatic stress disorder. *Behavior Therapy, 20,* 155–176.

Foy, D. W., & Card, J. J. (1987). Combat-related post-traumatic stress disorder etiology: Replicated findings in a national sample of Vietnam-era men. *Journal of Clinical Psychology, 43*(1), 28–31.

Foy, D. W., Osato, S. S., Houskamp, B. M., & Neumann, D. A. (1993). Etiology of posttraumatic stress disorder. In P. A. Saigh (Ed.), *Posttraumatic stress disorder: A behavioral approach to assessment and treatment* (pp. 28–49). New York: Pergamon Press.

Foy, D. W., Resnick, H. S., Sipprelle, R. C., & Carroll, E. M. (1987). Premilitary, military, and postmilitary factors in the development of combat-related posttraumatic stress disorder. *The Behavior Therapist, 10*(1), 3–9.

Freedy, J. R., Kilpatrick, D. G., & Resnick, H. S. (1993). Natural disasters and mental health: Theory, assessment, and intervention. *Journal of Social Behavior and Personality, 8*(3), 49–103.

Gibbs, M. S. (1989). Factors in the victim that mediate between disaster and psychopathology: A review. *Journal of Traumatic Stress, 2*(4), 489–514.

Grady, D. A., Woolfolk, R. L., & Budney, A. J. (1989). Dimensions of war zone stress: An empirical analysis. *The Journal of Nervous and Mental Disease, 177*(6), 347–350.

Green, B. L. (1990). Defining trauma: Terminology and generic stressor dimensions. *Journal of Applied Social Psychology, 20,* 1632–1642.

Green, B. L., Korol, M., Grace, M. C., Vary, M. G., Leonard, A. C., Gleser, G. C., & Smitson-Cohen, S. (1991). Children and disaster: Age, gender, and parental effects on PTSD symptoms. *Journal of the American Academy of Child and Adolescent Psychiatry, 30*(6), 945–951.

Green, B. L., Lindy, J. D., Grace, M. C., & Glesser, G. C. (1989). Multiple diagnosis in post-traumatic stress disorder. The role of war stressors. *The Journal of Nervous and Mental Disease, 177*(6), 329–335.

Green, B. L., Lindy, J. D., Grace, M. C., Gleser, G. C., Leonard, A. C., Korol, M., & Winget, C. (1990). Buffalo Creek survivors in the second decade: Stability of stress symptoms. *American Journal of Orthopsychiatry, 60*(1), 43–54.

Hobfoll, S. E. (1988). *The ecology of stress.* New York: Hemisphere Publishing.

Hobfoll, S. E. (1989). Conservation of resources: A new attempt at conceptualizing stress. *American Psychologist, 44*(3), 513–524.

Hobfoll, S. E., Lomranz, J., Eyal, N., Bridges, A., & Tzemach, M. (1989). Pulse of a nation: Depressive mood reactions of Israelis to the Israel–Lebanon War. *Journal of Personality and Social Psychology, 56*(6), 1002–1012.

Hobfoll, S. E., & London, P. (1986). The relationship of self concept and social support to emotional distress among women during war. *Journal of Social and Clinical Psychology, 12,* 87–100.

Horowitz, M. J. (1986). *Stress response syndromes* (2nd ed.). Northvale, NJ: Jason Aronson.

Jacobs, G. A., Quevillon, R. P., & Stricherz, M. (1990). Lessons from the aftermath of Flight

232: Practical considerations for the mental health profession's response to air disasters. *American Psychologist, 45*(12), 1329–1335.

Jones, J. C., & Barlow, D. H. (1990). The etiology of posttraumatic stress disorder. *Clinical Psychology Review, 10,* 299–328.

Jordan, B. K., Schlenger, W. E., Hough, R., Kulka, R. A., Weiss, D., Fairbank, J. A., & Marmar, C. R. (1991). Lifetime and current prevalence of specific psychiatric disorders among Vietnam veterans and controls. *Archives of General Psychiatry, 48,* 207–217.

Keane, T. C., & Kaloupek, D. J. (1982). Brief reports: Imaginal flooding in the treatment of PTSD. *Journal of Consulting and Clinical Psychology, 50*(1), 138–140.

Keane, T. M., Fairbank, J. A., Caddell, J. M., Zimering, R. T. (1989). Implosive (flooding) therapy reduces symptoms of PTSD in Vietnam combat veterans. *Behavior Therapy, 20,* 245–260.

Keane, T. M., Zimering, R. T., & Caddell, J. M. (1985). A behavioral formulation of posttraumatic stress disorder in Vietnam veterans. *The Behavior Therapist, 8,* 9–12.

Kilpatrick, D. G., & Best, C. L. (1984). Some cautionary remarks on treating sexual assault victims with implosion. *Behavior Therapy, 15,*(4), 421–423.

Kilpatrick, D. G., Best, C. L., Veronen, L. J., Amick, A. E., Villeponteaux, L. A., & Ruff, G. A. (1985). Mental health correlates of criminal victimization: A random community survey. *Journal of Consulting and Clinical Psychology, 53*(6), 866–873.

Kilpatrick, D. G., Edmunds, C. N., & Seymour, A. K. (1992). *Rape in America: A report to the nation.* Arlington, VA: National Victim Center and Medical University of South Carolina.

Kilpatrick, D. G., & Resnick, H. S. (1993). Posttraumatic stress disorder associated with exposure to criminal victimization in clinical and community populations. In J. R. T. Davidson & E. B. Foa (Eds.), *Post-traumatic stress disorder in review: Recent research and future directions* (pp. 113–146). Washington, DC: American Psychiatric Press.

Kilpatrick, D. G., Saunders, B. E., Amick-McMullan, A., Best, C. L., Veronen, L. J., & Resnick, H. S. (1989). Victim and crime factors associated with the development of crime-related post-traumatic stress disorder. *Behavior Therapy, 20,* 199–214.

Kilpatrick, D. G., Saunders, B. E., Veronen, L. J., Best, C. L., & Von, J. M. (1987). Criminal victimization: Lifetime prevalence, reporting to police, and psychological impact. *Crime and Delinquency, 33*(4), 479–489.

Kilpatrick, D. G., Veronen, L. J., & Resick, P. A. (1979). Assessment of the aftermath of rape: Changing patterns of fear. *Journal of Behavioral Assessment, 1,* 133–148.

Kinzie, J. D. (1989). Therapeutic approaches to traumatized Cambodian refugees. *Journal of Traumatic Stress, 2*(1), 75–91.

Kinzie, J. D., Sach, W. H., Angell, R. H., Clark, G., & Ben, R. (1989). A three year follow-up of Cambodian young people traumatized as children. *Journal of the American Academy of Child and Adolescent Psychiatry, 28,* 501–504.

Kluznick, J. C., Speed, N., Van Valkenburg, C., & Magraw, R. (1986). Forty-year follow-up of United States prisoners of war. *American Journal of Psychiatry, 143*(11), 1443–1446.

Kolb, L. C. (1988). A critical survey of hypotheses regarding PTSD in light of recent research findings. *Journal of Traumatic Stress, 1,* 291–304.

Kuch, K., Swinson, R. P., & Kirby, M. (1985). Post-traumatic stress disorder after car accidents. *Canadian Journal of Psychiatry, 30,* 426–427.

Kulka, R. C., Schlenger, W. E., Fairbank, J. A., Jordan, B. K., Hough, R. L., Marmar, C. R., & Weiss, D. S. (1991). Assessment of posttraumatic stress disorder in the community: Prospects and pitfalls from recent studies of vietnam veterans. *Psychological Assessment, 3*(4), 547–560.

Laufer, R. S., Gallops, M. S., & Frey-Wouters, E. (1984). War stress and trauma: The Vietnam veteran experience. *Journal of Health and Social Behavior, 25,* 65–85.

Lewis, A. (1942). Incidence of neurosis in England under war conditions. *Lancet, 2*, 175–183.

Lomranz, J., Hobfoll, S. E., Johnson, R., Eyal, N., & Zemach, M. (1994). A nation's response to attack: Israelis' depressive reactions to the Gulf War. *Journal of Traumatic Stress, 7*(1), 55–69.

Lund, M., Foy, D. W., Sipprelle, C., & Strachan, A. (1984). The combat exposure scale: A systematic assessment of trauma in the Vietnam war. *Journal of Clinical Psychology, 40*(6), 1323–1328.

Lyons, J. A. (1991). Strategies for assessing the potential for positive adjustment following trauma. *Journal of Traumatic Stress, 4*(1), 93–111.

Lyons, J. A., & Keane, T. M. (1989). Implosive therapy for the treatment of combat related PTSD. *Journal of Traumatic Stress, 2*(2), 137–152.

McCann, L., & Pearlman, L. A. (1990). *Psychological trauma and the adult survivor: Theory, therapy, & transformation.* New York: Brunner/Mazel.

McCann, I. L., Sakheim, D. K., & Abrahamson, D. J. (1988). Trauma and victimization: A model of psychological adaptation. *The Counseling Psychologist, 16*(4), 531–594.

McFarlane, A. C. (1989). The treatment of post-traumatic stress disorder. *British Journal of Medical Psychology, 62*, 81–90.

Mowrer, O. H. (1960). *Learning theory and behavior.* New York: John Wiley & Sons.

Norris, F. H. (1992). Epidemiology of trauma: Frequency and impact of different potentially traumatic events on different demographic groups. *Journal of Consulting and Clinical Psychology, 60*(3), 409–418.

Page, W. F., Engdahl, B. E., & Eberly, R. E. (1991). Prevalence and correlates of depressive symptoms among former prisoners of war. *The Journal of Nervous and Mental Disease, 179*(11), 670–677.

Pallmeyer, T. P., Blanchard, E. B., & Kolb, L. C. (1986). The psychophysiology of combat-induced post-traumatic stress disorder in Vietnam veterans. *Behavioral Research and Therapy, 24*(6), 645–652.

Pitman, R. K. (1993). Biological findings in posttraumatic stress disorder: Implications for DSM-IV classification. In J. R. T. Davidson and E. B. Foa (Eds.), *Posttraumatic stress disorder: DSM-IV and beyond* (pp. 173–189). Washington, DC: American Psychiatric Press.

Pitman, R. K., Orr, S. P., Forgue, D. F., Altman, B., de Jong, J. B., & Herz, L. R. (1990). Psychophysiologic responses to combat imagery of Vietnam veterans with Posttraumatic Stress Disorder versus other anxiety disorders. *Journal of Abnormal Psychology, 99*(1), 49–54.

Resick, P. A. (1992). Cognitive treatment of crime-related post-traumatic stress disorder. In R. J. McMahon and V. L. Quinsey (Eds.), *Aggression and violence throughout the life span* (pp. 171–191). Newbury Park, CA: Sage Publications.

Resick, P. A., & Schnicke, M. K. (1992). Cognitive processing therapy for sexual assault victims. *Journal of Consulting and Clinical Psychology, 60*(5), 748–756.

Resick, P. A., & Schnicke, M. K. (1993). *Cognitive processing therapy for sexual assault victims: A treatment manual.* Newbury Park, CA: Sage.

Resnick, H. S., Kilpatrick, D. G., Dansky, B. S., Saunders, B. E., & Best, C. L. (1993). Prevalence of civilian trauma and posttraumatic stress disorder in a representative sample of women. *Journal of Consulting and Clinical Psychology, 61*(6), 984–991.

Resnick, H. S., & Newton, T. (1992). Assessment and treatment of post-traumatic stress disorder in adult survivors of sexual assault. In D. Foy (Ed.), *Treating PTSD.* New York: Guilford Press.

Rothbaum, B. O., & Foa, E. B. (1992, October). Exposure therapy for rape victims with posttraumatic stress disorder. *Behavior Therapist*, 219–222.

Rothbaum, B. O., & Foa, E. B. (1993). Cognitive-behavioral treatment of post-traumatic stress disorder. In P. A. Saigh (Ed.), *Posttraumatic stress disorder: A behavioral approach to assessment and treatment* (pp. 85–110). New York: Pergamon Press.

Rubonis, A. V., & Bickman, L. (1991). Psychological impairment in the wake of disaster: The disaster–psychopathology relationship. *Psychological Bulletin, 109*(3), 384–399.

Saigh, P. A. (1993). History, current nosology, and epidemiology. In P. A. Saigh (Ed.), *Posttraumatic stress disorder: A behavioral approach to assessment and treatment* (pp. 1–27). New York: Pergamon Press.

Shore, J. H., Tatum, E., & Vollmer, W. M. (1986a). Evaluation of mental health effects of disaster: Mount St. Helen's eruption. *American Journal of Public Health Supplement, 76,* 76–83.

Shore, J. H., Tatum, E. L., & Vollmer, W. M. (1986b). Psychiatric reactions to disaster: The Mount St. Helens experience. *American Journal of Psychiatry, 143*(5), 590–595.

Sierles, F. S., Chen, J., McFarland, R. E., & Taylor, M. A. (1983). Posttraumatic stress disorder and concurrent psychiatric illness: A preliminary report. *American Journal of Psychiatry, 140*(9), 1177–1179.

Skinner, H. A. (1984). Models for the description of abnormal behavior. In H. E. Adams & P. B. Sutker (Eds.), *Comprehensive handbook of psychopathology* (pp. 141–159). New York: Plenum Press.

Solomon, S. D., Gerrity, E. T., & Muff, A. M. (1992). Efficacy of treatment for posttraumatic stress disorder: An empirical review. *Journal of the American Medical Association, 268*(5), 633–638.

Solomon, Z. (1988). The effects of combat-related posttraumatic stress disorder on the family. *Psychiatry, 51,* 323–329.

Solomon, Z., Mikulincer, M., & Hobfoll, S. E. (1986). Effects of social support and battle intensity on loneliness and breakdown during combat. *Journal of Personality and Social Psychology, 51*(6), 1269–1276.

Solomon, Z., Mikulincer, M., & Hobfoll, S. E. (1987). Objective versus subjective measurement of stress and social support: Combat-related reactions. *Journal of Consulting and Clinical Psychology, 55*(4), 577–583.

van der Kolk, B., Greenberg, M., Boyd, H., & Krystal, J. (1985). Inescapable shock, neurotransmitters, and addiction to trauma: Toward a psychobiology of posttraumatic stress. *Biological Psychiatry, 20,* 314–325.

Vogel, W. H. (1985). Coping, stress, stressors and health consequences. *Neuropsychobiology, 13,* 129–135.

Williams, C. L., Solomon, S. D., & Bartone, P. (1988). Primary prevention in aircraft disasters: Integrating research and practice. *American Psychologist 43*(9), 730–739.

Wolf, S., & Ripley, H. (1947). Reactions among Allied prisoners of war subjected to three years of imprisonment and torture by the Japanese. *American Journal of Psychiatry, 104,* 180–192.

World Health Organization. (1992). *The ICD-10 classification of mental and behavioral disorders: Clinical descriptions and diagnostic guidelines.* Geneva: Author.

Yehuda, R., Southwick, S. M., & Giller, E. L. (1992). Exposure to atrocities and severity of chronic posttraumatic stress disorder in Vietnam combat veterans. *American Journal of Psychiatry, 149*(3), 333–336.

2

Conservation of Resources and Traumatic Stress

STEVAN E. HOBFOLL, CARLA A. DUNAHOO, and JEANNINE MONNIER

OVERVIEW

Conservation of resources (COR) theory has been developed as a general stress theory that helps delineate both why certain circumstances are stressful and the process of people's reactions to stressful circumstances (Hobfoll, 1988, 1989; Hobfoll & Lilly, 1993). As a general theory of stress, it can help us understand both the similarities and differences inherent in traumatic stress as compared to major stressors, everyday stressors, and minor hassles. If the theory is truly helpful, it can further aid in informing interventions aimed at benefiting victims of traumatic stress. This chapter focuses on COR theory as it applies to traumatic stress and emphasizes how it helps us to understand stress reactions, recovery, and lifelong sequelae. Hopefully, it will also help the reader frame other chapters in this volume and provide a general guide for understanding the nature and treatment of traumatic stress.

This volume focuses on the particular family of stressors called traumatic events. Although traumatic stress is not a clearly defined area, it has tended to include stressful events and circumstances that are both extreme and outside of the realm of everyday experiences. Stressors are best seen as lying on a continuum, however, so there is no absolute point at which, say, major stressors end and extreme stressors begin. Thus, we must settle for a somewhat vague definition of extreme stress as those events and circumstances that, because of their

STEVAN E. HOBFOLL, CARLA A. DUNAHOO, and JEANNINE MONNIER · Applied Psychology Center, Department of Psychology, Kent State University, Kent, Ohio 44242.

Traumatic Stress: From Theory to Practice, edited by John R. Freedy and Stevan E. Hobfoll. Plenum Press, New York, 1995.

objective nature, place massive demands on individuals' abilities to maintain psychological wellness, behavioral and cognitive functioning, and physical integrity (see also American Psychiatric Association, 1987, 1994). Norris (1990) referred to traumatic stress as the population of events involving "violent encounters with nature, technology, or humankind." In this chapter, the terms traumatic stress and extreme stress are used interchangeably.

Individuals are unlikely to be confronted with extreme stressors on any given day. However, extreme stressors occur more than one might think. Approximately 683,000 women in the United States are raped annually, and one out of every eight adult women (approximately 12.1 million American women) has been the victim of forcible rape at some time during her lifetime (Kilpatrick & Edmunds, 1992). House fires occur all the time, and we can hardly watch the evening news without hearing of the plight of such fires' victims, some of whom escape, and some of whom escape having seen loved ones perish. Major auto accidents are another frequent source of traumatic stress, whereby the victims are transported from an everyday ride in the car to a scene of blood, metal, and carnage. Natural disasters, plane crashes, and war are constantly occurring and many of these extreme events impact hundreds, thousands, and even millions of people. In addition to the direct victims of these events, emergency service workers, such as police, fire fighters, and emergency medical teams are repeatedly exposed to accidents, fires, and crime scenes. They must witness the horrible realities and live with the memories that accompany and follow these events. Breslau, Davis, Andreski, and Peterson (1991) estimate that 39% of all individuals living in the United States experience a traumatic stressor at some time in their lives (see also Chapter 1, this volume).

From the clinician's standpoint, it would be impossible to have a practice in psychology, psychiatry, or social work without encountering victims of traumatic stress. These victims are seen at many different posttrauma phases, ranging from years after a childhood occurrence to immediately following traumatic victimization. Sometimes the stress event is the precipitating issue, but often it emerges more subtly as a troubling shadow that the individual finds difficult to discuss or even to remember in its details. In work with families, clinicians often find it as a "skeleton in the closet"; no one talks about it, and not everyone necessarily knows about it. But the fear of the secret escaping the closet is quite palpable when the topic is approached.

Despite the enormity of the impact and the frequency of the problem, few mental health professionals receive specific training in working with victims of traumatic stress. The training that is received tends to focus on work with individual victims and is reactive in nature, waiting for victims to seek mental health treatment. Proactive, preventive, and community intervention with victims of traumatic stress is a field still in its infancy. In a sense, this suggests that clinical training programs see traumatic stressors as more uncommon than they truly are.

Most germane to this chapter, there is limited theoretical discussion of traumatic stress that can serve as a blueprint for understanding and intervention. Instead, most models of traumatic stress are descriptive in nature and detail the symptoms and treatment of traumatic stress rather than the psychosocial mechanisms by which it occurs. In particular, prevalent models of traumatic stress (1) tend to emphasize outcome without relating well to why particular outcomes occur, (2) seldom consider factors that mediate the event–distress relationship and hence fail to explain people's differential responding, and (3) do not encompass the developmental nature of the stress process (see Chapter 1 for a more in-depth theoretical critique). Such descriptions are clinically very helpful. However, they do not suggest a priori how people will respond to traumatic stressors and why responses vary among victims. Perhaps COR theory can serve this blueprint function. In this chapter, we present COR theory in stages. At each stage of the theory, we illustrate that facet of the theory using both research and clinical examples focusing on traumatic stress events. This discussion leads to an ecological adaptation of COR theory that considers individuals in their social context in order to predict the extent of the impact of traumatic stress.

CONSERVATION OF RESOURCES THEORY

A COR theory has been presented as a model for understanding the nature and influence of all levels of stress (Hobfoll, 1988, 1989) and, in particular, to traumatic stress (Hobfoll, 1991). In essence, COR theory is based on the premise that individuals strive to obtain, retain, and protect their resources. Resources, in turn, are defined as those things that are highly valued by individuals or that serve as a means of obtaining those things that are highly valued. Four major kinds of resources have been outlined. These include: (1) object resources (e.g., car, home, clothing), (2) condition resources (e.g., tenure or seniority at work, a good marriage), (3) personal resources (e.g., occupational skills, sense of self-esteem), and energy resources (e.g., money, credit, insurance).

Given that individuals are motivated to obtain, retain, and protect resources, it follows that stress will ensue under any of three conditions:

1. First, stress occurs when there is the threat of significant resource loss.
2. Second, stress occurs when there is actual resource loss.
3. Third, stress occurs when resources are invested without resulting in significant resource gain, hence producing a net loss of resources since more resources were lost in the process of investment than were gained as an outcome of investment.

What Resources Are Key?

A potential criticism of COR theory is that almost anything that is in any way valued could be called a resource. However, there are some key resources, and there is reason to believe that these are valued widely. There is remarkably strong agreement, even across cultures, concerning many values. Health, children, the family, work, love, honor, and sense of control are universally valued (Schwartz & Bilsky, 1990), even if their rank order or interpretation are more culturally specific. Moreover, since the context of most stress research is to compare people within a given culture, not between cultures, there is even more reason to believe that a common set of resources is valued when victims of traumatic stress are viewed within one culture.

The list of resources that our work has developed is presented in Table 1. Altogether, 74 resources are listed. The list includes object resources ("housing that suits my needs"), condition resources (e.g., "status/seniority at work"), personal resources (e.g., "sense of optimism"), and energy resources (e.g., "financial resources"). The list has been incorporated into a flexible instrument called the COR-Evaluation or COR-E. Respondents indicate the importance they ascribe to the resources on a scale from 1 (little importance) to 7 (great importance). This can be done for all items or for only those resources for which losses and gains have occurred in the period in which the researcher or clinician is interested. Next, respondents indicate the degree of loss and gain they have experienced in the period of interest from 1 to 7 (little loss or gain to great loss or gain, respectively). We have typically been interested in three time periods, past year, past month, and time since a specific event (e.g., "since the hurricane").

It is important to highlight that both loss and gain may occur together in the same time period, or even as part of the same event. For example, being exposed to war may paradoxically reduce hope and increase sense of personal mastery for having survived and brought one's family to safety. Also, COR theory predicts that since people strive to protect their resources, attempts at gain will actually increase amidst loss. The experience of being assaulted may cause a person to begin an escort service at his college campus or to demand that her employer place better lighting in the parking lot and fence the area. These efforts may increase sense of efficacy. Similarly, ruin of one's home in a fire may result in increased family closeness, on one hand, and family conflict, on the other hand, as the family must live in a motel while repairs or reconstruction is completed. Ozer and Bandura (1990) found that participating in a highly aggressive self-defense course increased previously raped women's sense of self-efficacy. We would underscore not only the increase in the self-efficacy, but also the very fact that women sought such groups (perhaps a form of bolstering social resources) following their traumatic experience.

The COR-E also helps researchers and clinicians to focus on different kinds of resources than they might typically have considered. Mental health professionals in both applied and research settings tend to put greatest emphasis on psychological variables. However, in addition to personal resources that are more strictly psychological, such as sense of mastery and optimism, there are many more concrete resources, such as home, employment, and transportation. Problems in these resource domains are generally relegated to the realm of social casework. However, loss of these resources may be the central concerns

Table 1. Resources from COR Evaluation

1. Personal transportation (car, truck, etc.)
2. Feeling that I am successful
3. Time for adequate sleep
4. Good marriage
5. Adequate clothing
6. Feeling valuable to others
7. Family stability
8. "Free time"
9. Clothing that is more than what I need
10. Sense of pride in myself
11. Intimacy with one or more family members
12. Time for work
13. Feeling that I am accomplishing my goals
14. A good relationship with my children
15. Time with loved ones
16. Necessary tools for work
17. Hope
18. Children's health
19. Stamina/endurance
20. Necessary appliances for home
21. Feeling my future success depends on me
22. A positively challenging routine
23. Personal health
24. Housing that suits my needs
25. Sense of optimism
26. Status/seniority at work
27. Adequate food
28. Home that is more than what I need
29. Sense of humor
30. Stable employment
31. Intimacy with spouse or partner
32. Adequate furnishings for home
33. Feeling that I have control over my life
34. A role as a leader
35. Ability to communicate well
36. Essentials for children
37. Feeling that my life is peaceful
38. Acknowledgement for accomplishments
39. Ability to organize tasks
40. "Extras" for children
41. Sense of commitment
42. Intimacy with at least one friend
43. Money for "extras"
44. Self-discipline
45. Understanding from my employer/boss
46. Savings or emergency money
47. Motivation to get things done
48. Spouse/partner's health
49. Support from co-workers
50. Adequate income
51. Feeling that I know who I am
52. Advancement in my education or training
53. Adequate credit (financial)
54. Feeling independent
55. Companionship
56. Financial assets (stocks, property, etc.)
57. Knowing where I am going with my life
58. Affection from others
59. Financial stability
60. Feeling that my life has meaning/purpose
61. Positive feelings about myself
62. People I can learn from
63. Money for transportation
64. Help with tasks at work
65. Medical insurance
66. Involvement with church, synagogue, etc.
67. Retirement security (financial)
68. Help with tasks at home
69. Loyalty of friends
70. Money for advancement or self-improvement (education, starting a business, etc.)
71. Help with child care
72. Involvement in organizations with others who have similar interests
73. Financial help if needed
74. Health of family/close friends

following exposure to natural or technological disasters or regional warfare. Indeed, we have found that when mental health professionals emphasize psychological variables and perceptions of events in such circumstances, the clients flee treatment in search of "real answers to their real concerns." For example, in a postdisaster area, a major set of concerns involve cost gouging of victims by the construction industry and underhanded dealings by insurance companies who pressure for quick settlements at lower than the true value and who withhold monies if parties seek what they consider fair settlement. Imagine how someone might react to a psychologist pressing the individual to grieve for his or her losses and "to reframe the events." More effective, perhaps, would be a coalition of mental health professionals, attorneys, and local political leaders joining to move proactively to protect the local population against these follow-up loss events. Individual mental health workers might similarly need to form closer alliances with attorneys or other community resources that can help empower individuals who are being exploited. By combatting these concrete resource losses, psychological resources are actually gained in the process as those affected move from victim roles to protagonist roles. Similar arguments regarding the need for advocacy by mental health professionals can be made with regard to other types of traumatic events (e.g., community violence, sexual assault, violence in the schools).

The focus on broader resources does not mean that mental health professionals should ignore more traditionally psychological resources. Rather, it possibly would be more beneficial if they incorporated these with more of an action orientation that recognizes the real and immediate nature of people's resource losses and act accordingly. Unfortunately, there is little training for most mental health professionals to prepare them for these efforts. Indeed, much of the focus of traditional care is biased against discussion of practical problems as being somehow part of a less prestigious realm of difficulties (Caplan & Caplan, 1993).

COR Theories Principles and Corollaries

Until this point, we have focused on only the basic emphasis of COR theory—its attention to a broad range of resources. However, COR theory further posits a number of key principles. It is necessary to detail these if we are to understand how traumatic stress affects people.

Principle 1: The Primacy of Loss

Critical to COR theory is the principle that *loss is more heavily weighted by individuals than is gain.* Clinicians should be especially watchful of losses people encounter. The preeminence of loss over gain in cognitive psychology is well established (Tversky & Kahneman, 1981). Here it has been repeatedly found that, in the process of decision making, outcomes framed in terms of loss are weighted more strongly than outcomes framed in terms of gain. In medical research, Tymstra (1989) similarly finds that people will invest significant resources to limit the possibility of future loss, even if they must undergo difficult and even painful medical procedures. In our own work, we have found that resource loss is highly correlated with psychological distress (Hobfoll, Lilly, & Jackson, 1992).

In contrast to the influence of resource loss, resource gain has limited effect on psychological distress (Hobfoll & Lilly, 1993). Even when people make gains, clinicians should be cautious not to overestimate gain's positive impact. The effect that resource gain does have occurs in the context of offsetting loss. For example, when a child is ill, improvements in health (gains) become significant, but hearing that one's child is well when he or she has not been ill has little or no effect on well-being.

In Darwinian terms, it is possible to outline how a bias toward loss could develop. For most of evolutionary history, loss would threaten survival. People needed object, condition, personal, and energy resources for existence. Any loss of an important resource, and certainly a spiral of loss, would be critical. In contrast, the main contribution of gain was to offset the consequences of such loss. For example, extra food (gain) would be stored for the winter, a time when there was a loss of new food supplies. Likewise, more members of the group were needed to protect against group size diminishing below a critical threshold, because of inevitable loss of life. Gain also adds comfort, but comfort has no survival value per se.

This Darwinian view of stress also suggests an explanation of why traumatic stressors are accompanied by deeply etched memories in the victims and witnesses of these events. For traumatic stressors, the occurrence of loss should have special meaning because traumatic losses are most clearly and closely linked to survival. The nearly indelible images do not occur for any other class of stressors. The purpose of such detailed, long-term images may be to enhance survival (Hobfoll, 1991), as they afford greater sensitivity to the occurrence of similar circumstances. This sensitivity contributes to a hair-trigger alarm system. Psychology and psychiatry have focused on the dysfunctional aspects of this hair trigger (Horowitz, 1986), since it can interfere greatly with everyday life and functioning. However, this perceptual sensitivity is essential for future survival, and the survival value may outweigh the distressful aspects for a number of trauma survivors.

By stating that loss is the essence of stress, COR theory argues that change per se is not stressful. This is a most contentious issue that deserves clarification. In studies that, at first, indicated that change itself was stressful, both positive and negative changes were mixed by presentation of ambiguous events. For example, stress was found in early research to follow changes at work, changes in marital life, and financial change (Holmes & Rahe, 1967). However, subsequent research found that these negative consequences of change only occurred when change entailed loss or threat of loss (Thoits, 1983). Thus, when change was rephrased to ask, "Was the change positive or negative?" only those who indicated negative change showed deleterious reactions. In fact, positive changes actually buffer against negative changes (Cohen &

Hoberman, 1983). Thus, positive change makes one more resistant to negative stress reactions. This does not mean that times of change are not times to be watchful. Many changes that on their surface are positive can have negative aspects. For example, a job move may mean higher pay and prestige, but loss of friends. Although COR theory sees both losses and gains as important, it would emphasize the impact of the loss events. Given that losses outweigh gains, it should also be underscored that a few significant losses may produce more extreme effects than either individuals or mental health professionals might anticipate.

This brings us to question the very term "event" as inadequate. Clearly, events must be unpacked in terms of their components. Early research on stress depicted stressors as individual events, in the sense of being static occurrences. As such, exposure to an earthquake, fire, or flood was depicted as uniform. More recently, Dohrenwend, Raphael, Schwartz, Stueve, and Skodol (1993) presented a method for unpacking events into their many components. Hence, a disaster consists of possible financial loss, increased child-care burden, loss of home, and loss of mutual friends. The same disaster might result in gains in other resources, such as increased self-esteem and independence if one were to master disaster-related challenges. Such unpacking of event components is critical if we are to decompose the losses and gains that together comprise the changes that occurred.

Principle 2: Resource Investment

A second principle of COR theory is that *individuals must invest resources in order to obtain, retain, and protect resources.* This might sound circular, but becomes clear and straightforward with a few examples. For instance, to protect against loss of self-esteem, people must invest their self-esteem. If one is threatened with a failure experience, it is often possible to offset the loss of self-esteem by convincing oneself that one has greater worth than this and that this single failure is not so significant in light of many past accomplishments. Alternatively, people often invest one resource to protect a second resource. For instance, social support may be used to offset the loss of sense of self-esteem, as others convey to us messages of our worth amidst some difficult circumstance that threatens self-evaluation.

How are resources invested? Schönpflug (1985) has illustrated that coping demands the use of resources. Energy resources, for example, are often needed, as when survivors invest time in rebuilding their homes. It is obvious how money is invested to produce other resources such as more money, sense of success, or even self-esteem. Other, less concrete, resources must also be invested to be of value. For example, we must call on friends following exposure to a serious stressor (e.g., serious accident) if we are to receive support from them. At times, we must search deeply inside ourselves to call on our inner resources when confronting extreme stressful events (e.g., physical assault) or chronic major stressors (e.g., community violence) that have worn us down over time. Similarly, in our attempts to develop intangible resources such as love, we must invest time, energy, trust, and self-esteem. Even after all this investment, we risk the loss of all our investment if our attempts are rejected. In our research, we have repeatedly found that those who are able to invest their resources more successfully resist the more negative impact of stressful circumstances than those who either lack or misuse resources (Hobfoll, Nadler, & Leiberman, 1986; Hobfoll & Lerman, 1989). Clinicians can often aid people prior to or after trauma by helping them (1) identify their resources and (2) invest them appropriately.

Loss and Investment of Resources Following Traumatic Stress

Loss is even more germane to traumatic stress than to other types of stress. It is the nature of traumatic stress that loss is rapid, extensive (i.e., many resources lost), and deep (i.e., many losses are major in proportion). This often means that the sense of how much is lost is overwhelming to the individual. The losses typically cross all resource domains; object resources, condition resources, personal resources, and energy resources are all affected. Further, since resources are needed to offset further secondary loss, the depleted resource reservoir is found emptied of the necessary tools for successful stress management (Hobfoll, 1991). Again, because resources have been cut rapidly, broadly, and deeply, the usual arsenal of coping responses is damaged in a way that leaves people much less capable of responding to stress.

An excellent example of the primacy of loss and the tendency to invest resources following loss is provided in a study of victims of Hurricane Hugo, which struck Charleston, South Carolina, in September of 1989. The hurricane caused tremendous property damage and 13 local deaths. It was the largest physical devastation by a hurricane in U.S. history to that time. Freedy, Shaw, Jarrell, and Masters (1992) inquired into victims' resource loss, coping behavior, and personal characteristics (gender, marital status, and household income). Levels of subsequent psychological distress were also assessed. Personal characteristics explained 9.5% of the variance in psychological distress, and the aggregate of all coping behaviors explained 7.9% of the variance in psychological distress. Resource loss, in contrast, explained 34.1% of the variance in psychological distress! Looked at another way, women and men with high loss had from four to eight times the likelihood of experiencing clinically significant psychological distress than men and women who experienced low levels of resource loss, respectively. These findings strongly support the central role of resource loss in disaster responding.

Freedy et al. (1992) also examined the COR-based hypothesis that loss would motivate more coping behavior. This prediction contrasts with the assumption that negative events paralyze victims or that victims become helpless. They found that both favorable (e.g., problem-focused coping) and unfavorable coping (e.g., disengagement) were positively related to greater loss. This finding provides insight into the process of responding to stress by suggesting that victims become active in initiating whatever patterns of coping behaviors are contained within their repertoire. Some of this responding produces beneficial outcomes and some creates further difficulties, but underlying both mechanisms is the attempt to cope. When we examine their data more closely, it is of further interest that although women reported more losses than men, men with high levels of resource loss were more likely to report clinically significant levels of psychological distress. This suggests that examining resource loss may circumvent problems with males' traditional underreporting of psychologically relevant symptoms, as their reports of loss reveal a fuller picture of the extent of potential impact following a traumatic event.

Principle 3: Loss and Gain Spirals

It is important to introduce another theoretical step that follows from the preceding assumptions and principles. If (1) stress follows loss, threat of loss, or failure to gain; (2) loss is more heavily weighted than gain; and (3) people must rely on resources to offset resource loss, then it follows that *initial loss will make individuals more vulnerable to further loss*. Thus, when we speak of unpacking event components, it should be underscored that the sequences of events follows specific patterns, the first of which is a loss spiral. Loss spirals can begin very quickly. They also may have a long-term course, affecting individuals for years after the original event.

Resource Loss and Resource Gain Spirals

After confronting initial resource loss, people have fewer or less potent resources for the additional challenges that come in the wake of the first loss circumstance. Self-esteem or sense of mastery may be lower, favors may have been used up, and such resources as money and insurance may have been fully or partially depleted. Now, with the exposure to secondary stressors, further loss occurs, each loss resulting in an increasing level of vulnerability as resources are further and further depleted.

Gain spirals follow a similar process. Initial gain creates a system more resistant to stress and more capable of further gain. However, since loss is weighted greater than gain, there are two attributes of loss cycles that differentiate them from gain cycles. Specifically, loss cycles are more potent than gain cycles and occur at greater acceleration. This difference becomes critical when considering traumatic stress, as the initial stressor is, by definition, one that threatens or creates major resource loss. Following initial loss, many traumatic stressors may contribute to a sequence of further losses, each attacking the individual, group, or community, which has ever-decreasing resources.

We would also highlight a number of intervention principles that follow from a theoretical understanding of the mechanism of loss and gain spirals. If loss spirals occur with a steeply increasing slope of speed and ever greater impact, then it follows that it is critical to intervene early, before momentum is gained. Intervention should be mobilized in a matter of hours after impact of the extreme stress. The later intervention occurs, the harder it is to offset the spiral's damaging impact. Early intervention, while still difficult, can often offset loss cycles and either stabilize stress reactions or even set the stage for a gain cycle (Hobfoll & Jackson, 1991).

Gain cycles, on the other hand, occur more slowly. For many important areas of gain, meaningful milestones are only accomplished in terms of months and years. A fire can destroy a home or business in moments. To build a business or save enough to purchase a home may, in contrast, require years of investment. More intangible resources operate similarly. For example, trust can be destroyed by a single failure of supporters to come to a survivor's aid following victimization, whereas building a trusting relationship can require years. These insights help underscore the consequences of exposure to traumatic stressors, as they influence loss cycles and interfere with long-term gain cycles.

Research on Resource Loss Cycles

There are a number of disaster reports that support the importance of loss cycles. If resources are used to offset the effects of loss, we would expect that individuals and communities would be rather resistant to disasters' effects if the disasters did not produce major resource loss and if community resources were left more or less intact.

McFarlane (1992) has studied bush fires in Australia. Consistent with this aspect of COR theory, rather major fires did not produce severe, prolonged psychological distress. However, if the fire devastated the critical community resources, then there was a massive psychological effect. These findings were quite similar to the response of rape victims (Ruch & Leon, 1986). Women who were raped a second time actually coped better after this incident than women who were raped once (although clearly all of these rape survivors were deeply distressed). The authors attributed this to their increased coping resources gained after having undergone this traumatic victimization experience. However, women who were raped yet again showed the most severe effects of all. It would seem that their resource threshold was overburdened and that the subsequent consequences were psychologically very severe. Together, these very different kinds of studies support the contention that after the resource threshold is substantially overburdened, the loss cycle accelerates as evidenced by virtue of the great increase in impact and momentum of psychological effects.

The importance of resource loss is a repeated theme in traumatic stress studies and discussion. Parker (1977) found that following a cyclone, most individuals returned to normal levels of functioning. However, those victims who experienced continued losses such as loss of home and dislocation from support systems experienced more serious, long-term psychological sequelae. Similarly, in the long-term studies of survivors of the Buffalo Creek flood (Green & Gleser, 1983), the loss of community support, loss of support of neighbors and friends, loss of familiar surroundings, and the length of the dislocation period combined to contribute to widespread negative psychological outcomes among almost all of the survivors. Freedy and his colleagues have documented that level of resource loss was a crucial determinant of clinically significant levels of psychological distress following a hurricane and an earthquake (Freedy et al., 1992; Freedy, Saladin, Kilpatrick, Resnick, & Saunders, 1994). Interestingly, Butcher and Dunn (1989) have attributed separation from other victims as one of the central losses affecting airline disaster victims. Because they come from different communities, they are separated from one another and thereby lose the possible support they might receive from others who underwent this intensive experience with them.

Perhaps the best illustration of the cycle of resource loss is depicted in a highly insightful study by Kaniasty and Norris (1993). They followed a group of older-adult flood victims for a period of years after the initial disaster. Victims reported on both the changes in their emotional well-being and in their social support. COR theory predicts that chronic stress will deplete resources both because stress will cause resource loss and because resources will be repeatedly invested and eventually partially or fully depleted. The findings strongly support this contention. Over time, victims' social support waned. Moreover, as social support waned, psychological distress increased. These findings mirror what Hobfoll and Lerman (1988, 1989) found in studies of parents of chronically ill children. For these parents, initial social resources were depleted over time, and the resources that were initially effective in offsetting the deleterious effects of stress became increasingly scarce.

Weak versus Strong Resources: A Modification of Resource Fit Theory

Resources have different value and utility. Some resources can be used in a wide variety of circumstances (we call such resources **robust**), whereas others are quite **circumscribed** in their domain of use. In addition, some resources have strong effects, defined by their powerful effects in combating stress or aiding in the maintenance and building of other resources. In contrast, other resources are rather weak and only have an effect under relatively low-stress conditions.

We have concentrated on two separate distinctions between: (1) robust and circumscribed resources (i.e., how broadly the resource can be used) and (2) strong versus weak resources (i.e., how powerful the resource is in a given instance). We have found a few personality resources to be quite robust. For example, in both our own work and in reviews of the literature, we find that individuals who have high self-esteem and a strong sense of mastery (i.e., perception of the ability to influence their environment successfully) do well across a variety of stressful circumstances (Kobasa, 1987; Schwarzer, 1992); hence these resources are robust. These internal resources can be called upon in a variety of circumstances to aid the individual. Their robustness may be due, in part, to their being central to the two major challenges of stress: (1) "What is my worth if I have failed or had this happen to me?" and (2) "How likely am I to overcome this ordeal?" Second, their robustness may be a product of their being characteristics of the individuals and thereby available at all times.

We can compare these key internal resources to certain aspects of social support. Advice is one kind of social support, but it is not a robust type of support. It is likely to be useful specifically when the kind of problem being confronted demands information that is not in the repertoire of the individuals involved. Similarly, instrumental support (i.e., help in completing a task) is extremely useful when it fits the stress challenge. For example, when one's home is destroyed in a fire, help in removing debris and advice about contractors might be important. When the challenge is a more emotional one, such as in the pain of loss of a loved one, advice and instrumental aid may be totally irrelevant. Cutrona and Russel (1990) have developed a schema of social support fit consistent with this analysis. They suggest that the better the kind of support fits the specific task, the more likely that support is to be successful in limiting deleterious stress reactions. However, both our and their analyses suggest that the importance of fit is only the case for circumscribed resources.

Strong resources are effective under high-stress conditions. Mastery has been found to be not only a robust resource but also a strong resource. In one study, it was noted that as stress increased for women, mastery had an increasingly powerful effect (Hobfoll, Shoham, & Ritter, 1991). Emotional support has also been found to be a strong resource. Unlike many of the other aspects of social support (e.g., advice, instrumental aid), emotional support continues to have a strong effect under high-stress conditions (Vaux, 1988).

The robust positive impact of emotional support may stem from the fact that high-stress conditions tend to overwhelm people's internal resources. Even the strongest individuals have lapses in their sense of self-esteem and mastery. At such times, emotional support is extremely helpful, perhaps because it carries important messages of both self-worth and ability to master the stress at hand (Caplan, 1974). Cutrona and Russel (1990) found emotional support to have a meaningful impact across varied types of circumstances, indicating once again that fit is not as important as the robustness of the resource.

Weak resources also tend to be beneficial, but mainly in low-stress circumstances. In one study, we examined the influence of level of discomfort with seeking help. We found almost everyone had difficulty asking for help, but some people were less uncomfortable than others. We found that those people who were *less un*comfortable asking for help fared better under low-stress conditions in that they were able to receive more everyday assistance (Hobfoll et al., 1991). Under high-stress conditions, in contrast, those who had this resource were no more likely to receive help than others who were very uncomfortable seeking help. We interpreted this finding to indicate that low discomfort in seeking help acted as a weak resource, having its main positive effect under everyday situations rather than high-stress circumstances.

More recently we have turned to research on coping behavior in order to study its strength as a resource. Coping behavior can be defined as the things people do in reaction to stressful situations in order to alleviate the potential negative effects of stress. Somewhat surprisingly our preliminary work (Hobfoll, Dunahoo, Ben-Porath, & Monnier, 1994) has noted that coping behaviors are only weak resources. They tend to have their strongest beneficial effect under low-stress circumstances. Under higher-stress circumstances, we found that coping strategy has little effect. This suggests that clinicians should not rely on people's normal coping repertoire with the expectation that good everyday coping will translate to good coping in the face of traumatic events.

It might also be helpful to examine disaster events with specific reference to evaluation of the weak-versus-strong resource prediction for coping. Freedy et al. (1992) directly examined coping behaviors in the aftermath of Hurricane Hugo. Consistent with the weak resource model, coping behavior was only weakly related to psychological outcomes. The one aspect of coping that was more strongly related to psychological outcomes was disengagement. However, many see disengagement as a product of the poor coping that often follows severe emotional distress (Stone, Greenberg, Kennedy-Moore, & Newman, 1991) and not as coping behavior per se. The more proactive forms of coping, best typified by what has been called problem-focused coping, explained only 1% of the variance, even when examined cross-sectionally (which tends to inflate correlations).

Green, Grace, and Gleser (1985) also compared the effects of coping be-haviors to the effects of stressful events, social support, and personal variables on psychological outcomes. Their sample consisted of survivors of the Beverly Hills Supper Club fire, an event that caused panic among 2,500 patrons and resulted in the deaths of 165 people. As COR theory would predict, objective aspects of the event were by far the strongest predictors of the outcome. Objec-tive stress was a total of loss of loved ones, threat of loss during the event, and the witnessing of others' loss. Subjective stress had a small effect after 1 year, but had dissipated by 2-year follow-up. Neither coping style, nor social support, had appreciable impact on outcomes. These findings once again suggest that coping behaviors are only weak resources.

CONCLUSIONS: ECOLOGICAL CONSIDERATIONS

Traumatic stress research has been offered a number of models of trau-matic stress (Figley, 1978; Horowitz, 1986; see also Chapter 1, this volume). COR theory provides an additional model that may have the advantage of being grounded in more general stress theory, while at the same time showing promise in understanding the critical function of resource loss in traumatic stress. Early research using COR theory in the study of extreme stress has been promising and has tended to be more theory-driven than is typical in this field. By focusing on the full array of people's resources, attention is extended be-yond an individual psychology. Instead, COR theory's resource emphasis high-lights the need to understand the individual in an ecological context, owning many personal resources, sharing some social resources, and having possible access to the resources of the larger social system.

The posttraumatic resource ecology is viewed in Figure 1. The model illustrates that resources may be lost on various ecological levels, ranging from

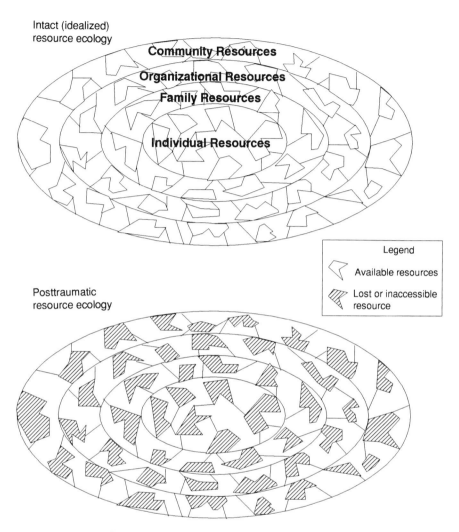

Figure 1. Resource ecology at different social levels.

the individual and family to the organization and community. A number of predictions follow from the model.

Prediction 1

The closer the loss is to the individual and family level, the more powerful the impact of loss will be. We found, for example, that surviving soldiers' combat losses were still psychologically and functionally debilitating to them well after their female loved ones had recovered from the threat of loss that the women experienced while their male loved ones were at war (Hobfoll, London, & Orr, 1988). For the soldier, then, the loss was primary.

Prediction 2

Loss at the higher level of the ecology inhibits successful coping at the lower levels. For example, Zafrir (1982) described the use of community level resources to aid families and individuals stricken in a terrorist attack. This attack involved two buses being attacked, with the result that 16 passengers were killed and 24 wounded. The authorities coordinated efforts to provide a full range of assistance to the victims and their families (e.g., providing information quickly and sensitively, providing assistance with the grief process). In contrast, in the Buffalo Creek Flood discussed earlier, the community's resources were devastated along with individuals' and families' resources. This led to more severe and long-term traumatic reactions than might otherwise have been predicted.

Prediction 3

Figure 1 illustrates that the individual and family spheres are joined at their borders with the organizational and community spheres. *Border resources are defined as resources that join the different levels.* For example, the individual's willingness to seek help is a resource that we can depict as lying on the border between individual or family resources and organizational or community resources. Resources that interface or connect different levels of resources are necessary to support optimal functioning. Another border resource is having a large social network that consists of both family and colleagues, hence being a resource between family resources and organizational resources. Hence, Prediction 3 is that loss of support at one level (e.g., organizational level) may be compensated for, in part, by support resources at the other level (e.g., family level). Loss at both levels of support, in contrast, would have the most severe impact on well-being.

Prediction 4

Finally, Prediction 3 leads to Prediction 4. Specifically, as more border resources are lost, the ability of the lower-level entity to benefit from the higher-level entity is lost. This occurs because the "connective tissue" between the various levels is necessary for cross-border resource utilization. Rather than being interconnected, marked border loss results in a disassociation of the individual from the family, the family from the organization, or the organization from the community. This isolation of available resource increases vulnerability to ongoing levels of loss and associated psychological distress. The aforementioned situation may result following exposure to particularly chronic forms of traumatic stress (e.g., domestic violence, community violence, violence within the schools).

We hope that this ecological model will help both clinicians and researchers, as it leads to insights regarding how to categorize where losses have occurred and how to identify the best level of intervention. Individual models of traumatic stress suggest that only the most internal of the resources can be addressed (e.g., self-esteem). Conservation of resources theory adds the insight that enabling resources (sense of mastery and social support) can be targeted. The ecological adaptation of COR theory further suggests that border resources will be critical.

This ecological framework further illustrates how COR theory also differs from other stress theories in its emphasis on objective stressors and its relative minimization of the importance of perceptions. This is not to say that perceptions are not one component of the trauma experience, but that their place has been overemphasized relative to objective events and the objective resources of individuals. It is not that one perceives trauma to be threatening; rather, it *is* threatening. Likewise, imagined resources (e.g., a false sense of self-esteem, perceived but with little real depth or strength) will be quickly vanquished in the face of traumatic stress experiences. Traumatic stress research and practice have tended to be descriptive, observational, and reactive; COR theory might provide one framework for promoting a more a priori approach to the conceptualization of the traumatic experience, providing a guide for clinicians, service delivery managers, researchers, and policy makers.

REFERENCES

American Psychiatric Association. (1987). *Diagnostic and statistical manual of mental disorders* (3rd ed.-rev.). Washington, DC: Author.

American Psychiatric Association. (1994). *Diagnostic and statistical manual of mental disorders* (4th ed.). Washington, DC: Author.

Breslau, N., Davis, G., Andreski, P., & Peterson, E. (1991). Traumatic events and posttraumatic stress disorder in an urban population of young adults. *Archives of General Psychiatry, 48*(3), 216–222.

Butcher, J. N., & Dunn, L. A. (1989). Human responses and treatment needs in airline disasters. In R. Gist & B. Lubin (Eds.), *Psychosocial aspects of disasters* (pp. 86–119). New York: John Wiley & Sons.

Caplan, G. (1974). *Support systems and community mental health.* New York: Behavioral Publications.

Caplan, G., & Caplan, R. B. (1993). *Mental health consultation and collaboration.* San Francisco: Jossey-Bass.

Cohen, S., & Hoberman, H. M. (1983). Positive events and social supports as buffers of life change stress. *Journal of Applied Social Psychology, 13*(2), 99–125.

Cutrona, C. E., & Russell, D. W. (1990). Type of social support and specific stress: Toward a theory of optimal matching. In B. R. Sarason, I. G. Sarason, & G. R. Pierce (Eds.), *Social support: An interactional view* (pp. 319–366). New York: John Wiley & Sons.

Dohrenwend, B. P., Raphael, K. G., Schwartz, S., Stueve, A., & Skodol, A. (1993). The structured event probe and narrative rating method for measuring stressful life events. In L.

Goldberg & S. Breznitz (Eds.), *Handbook of stress: Theoretical and clinical aspects* (pp. 174–199). New York: The Free Press.

Figley, C. R. (1978). *Stress disorders among Vietnam veterans: Theory, research, and treatment.* New York: Brunner/Mazel.

Freedy, J. R., Saladin, M. E., Kilpatrick, D. G., Resnick, H. S., & Saunders, B. E. (1994). Understanding acute psychological distress following natural disaster. *Journal of Traumatic Stress, 7*(2), 257–273.

Freedy, J. R., Shaw, D. L., Jarrell, M. P., & Masters, C. R. (1992). Towards an understanding of the psychological impact of natural disasters: An application of the conservation resources stress model. *Journal of Traumatic Stress, 5*(3), 441–454.

Green, B. C., & Gleser, G. C. (1983). Stress and long term psychopathology in survivors of the Buffalo Creek disaster. In D. Ricks & B. S. Dohrenwend (Eds.), *Origins of psychopathology* (pp. 73–90). New York: Cambridge University Press.

Green, B. L., Grace, M. C., & Gleser, G. C. (1985). Identifying survivors at risk: Long term impairment following the Beverly Hills Supper Club fire. *Journal of Consulting and Clinical Psychology, 53,* 672–678.

Hobfoll, S. E. (1988). *The ecology of stress.* Washington, DC: Hemisphere Publishing.

Hobfoll, S. E. (1989). Conservation of resources: A new attempt at conceptualizing stress. *American Psychologist, 44*(3), 513–524.

Hobfoll, S. E. (1991). Traumatic stress: A theory based on rapid loss od resources. *Anxiety Research, 4,* 187–197.

Hobfoll, S. E., Dunahoo, C. L., Ben-Porath, Y., & Monnier, J. (1994). Gender and coping: The dual-axis model of coping. *American Journal of Community Psychology, 22,* 49–82.

Hobfoll, S. E., & Jackson, A. P. (1991). Conservation of resources in community intervention. *American Journal of Community Psychology, 19*(1), 111–121.

Hobfoll, S. E., & Lerman, M. (1988). Personal relationships, personal attributes and stress resistance: Mothers' reactions to their child's illness. *American Journal of Community Psychology, 16*(4), 565–589.

Hobfoll, S. E., & Lerman, M. (1989). Predicting receipt of social support: A longitudinal study of parents' reaction to their child's illness. *Health Psychology, 8*(1), 61–77.

Hobfoll, S. E., & Lilly, R. S. (1993). Resource conservation as a strategy for community psychology. *Journal of Community Psychology, 21,* 128–148.

Hobfoll, S. E., Lilly, R. S., & Jackson, A. P. (1992). Conservation of social resources and the self. In H. O. F. Veiel & U. Baumann (Eds.), *The meaning and measurement of social support: Taking stock of 20 years of research* (pp. 125–141). Washington, DC: Hemisphere Publishing.

Hobfoll, S. E., London, P., & Orr, E. (1988). Mastery, intimacy, and stress resistance during war. *Journal of Community Psychology, 16*(3), 317–331.

Hobfoll, S. E., Nadler, A., & Leiberman, J. (1986). Satisfaction with social support during crisis: Intimacy and self-esteem as critical determinants. *Journal of Personality and Social Psychology, 51*(2), 296–304.

Hobfoll, S. E., Shoham, S. B., & Ritter, C. (1991). Women's satisfaction with social support and their receipt of aid. *Journal of Personality and Social Psychology, 61*(2), 332–341.

Holmes, T. H., & Raye, R. H. (1967). The social readjustment rating scale. *Journal of Psychosomatic Research, 11*(2), 213–218.

Horowitz, M. (1986). *Stress response syndromes* (2nd ed.). Northvale, NJ: Jason Aronson.

Kaniasty, K., & Norris, F. H. (1993). A test of the social support deterioration model in the context of natural disaster. *Journal of Personality and Social Psychology, 64*(3), 395–408.

Kilpatrick, D. G., & Edmunds, C. N. (1992). *Rape in America: A report to the nation.* Charleston, SC: Crime Victims Research and Treatment Center.

Kobasa, S. C. O. (1987). Stress response and personality. In R. C. Barnett, L. Biener, & G. R. Baruch (Eds.), *Gender and stress* (pp. 308–329). New York: The Free Press.

McFarlane, A. H. (1992). Avoidance and intrusion in posttraumatic stress disorder. *Journal of Nervous and Mental Disease, 180*(7), 439–445.

Norris, F. (1990). Screening for traumatic stress: A scale for use in the general population. *Journal of Applied Social Psychology, 20,* 1704–1718.

Ozer, E. M., & Bandura, A. (1990). Mechanisms governing empowerment effects: A self efficacy analysis. *Journal of Personality and Social Psychology, 58,* 472–486.

Parker, G. (1977). Cyclone Tracy and Darwin evacuees: On the restoration of the species. *British Journal of Psychiatry, 130,* 548–555.

Ruch, L. O., & Leon, J. J. (1986). The victim of rape and the role of life change, coping and social support during the rape trauma syndrome. In S. E. Hobfoll (Ed.), *Stress, social support, and women* (pp. 137–152). Washington, DC: Hemisphere Publishing.

Schönpflug, W. (1985). Goal directed behavior as a source of stress: Psychological origins and consequences of inefficiency. In M. Frese & J. Sabini (Eds.), *Goal directed behavior: The concept of action in psychology* (pp. 172–188). Hillsdale, NJ: Lawrence Erlbaum.

Schwartz, S. H., & Bilsky, W. (1990). Toward a theory of the universal content and structure of values: Extensions and cross-cultural replications. *Journal of Personality and Social Psychology, 58*(5), 878–891.

Schwarzer, R. (Ed.). (1992). *Self-efficacy: Thought control of action.* Washington, DC: Hemisphere Publishing.

Stone, A. A., Greenberg, M. A., Kennedy-Moore, E., & Newman, M. G. (1991). Self-report, situation-specific coping questionnaires: What are they measuring? *Journal of Personality and Social Psychology, 61*(4), 648–658.

Thoits, P. A. (1983). Dimensions of life events that influence psychological distress: An evaluation and synthesis of the literature. In H. B. Kaplan (Ed.), *Psychological stress: Trends in theory and research* (pp. 33–103). New York: Academic Press.

Tversky, A., & Kahneman, D. (1981). The framing of decisions and the psychology of choice. *Science, 24,* 453–458.

Tymstra, T. (1989). The imperative character of medical technology and the meaning of "anticipated decision regret." *International Journal of Technology Assessment in Health Care, 5,* 207–213.

Vaux, A. (1988). *Social support: Theory, research and intervention.* New York: Praeger.

Zafrir, A. (1982). Community therapeutic intervention in treatment of civilian victims after a major terrorist attack. In C. D. Spielberger & I. G. Sarason (Eds.), & N. A. Milgram (Guest Ed.), *Stress and Anxiety: Vol. 8* (pp. 303–315). New York: Hemisphere Publishing.

3

Applying Community Psychology to the Prevention of Trauma and Traumatic Life Events

FRAN H. NORRIS and MARTIE P. THOMPSON

The practice of psychology usually takes the form of clinical psychology; that is, it occurs at the individual or small-group level, begins after a mental health problem has developed, and aims to correct that problem, thus restoring mental health. Assessment and treatment are of undeniable value for victims of trauma, yet to focus solely on clinical practice would be to neglect a myriad of other opportunities to aid individuals who have been victimized by trauma, to build resistance resources among those at risk for exposure or, better still, to prevent individuals from becoming victims in the first place. "Practice" toward these ends often takes the form of *community psychology*, meaning it occurs at the community or systems level, begins earlier in the etiology of the focal problem, and has a resource-building rather than deficit-correcting orientation.

THE IMPORTANCE OF PREVENTION

Community psychology's complementary forms of practice all strive to reduce the prevalence or incidence of psychosocial problems in the population. It is traditional to talk about three types of prevention (Caplan, 1964). *Tertiary*

FRAN H. NORRIS and MARTIE P. THOMPSON · Department of Psychology, Georgia State University, Atlanta, Georgia 30303.

Traumatic Stress: From Theory to Practice, edited by John R. Freedy and Stevan E. Hobfoll. Plenum Press, New York, 1995.

prevention resembles individual rehabilitation in that it is initiated after damage has occurred, but it differs from individual rehabilitation in being large enough in scale to reduce the prevalence of disorder in the population. *Secondary prevention* is initiated at the early stages of disturbance and targets those most at-risk for disorder. The assumption of secondary prevention is that by identifying problems early, more serious psychosocial problems can be avoided. Secondary prevention programs generally attempt to expand the reach of the mental health system by using both individual-based and system-based resources effectively. *Primary prevention* aims to lower the rate of *new* cases of mental disorder by counteracting harmful situational circumstances before they have had a chance to produce illness or by strengthening individual-based resources. It does not seek to prevent a specific person from becoming sick but seeks to reduce the risk for a whole population. Caplan noted that primary prevention requires attention to identifying helpful environmental factors as well as harmful ones. Caplan's model of primary prevention focused on *supplies* (i.e., resistance resources) and *crises*, the turning points of either a developmental or accidental nature. Mental health was viewed by Caplan as the product of a successful history of crisis resolution, which in turn rested upon the individual's problem-solving skills, past experience, cultural norms, and support from family and community. The continuing relevance of Caplan's (1964) writings is striking.

Despite this long-standing emphasis on crisis, little early attention was directed toward trauma per se. Preventionists assumed traumatic events were too rare and unpredictable for population-based approaches to have much value. We now know that this is not the case. Recent evidence shows that most people will experience a traumatic event at some point during their lives, often while they are still quite young (Breslau, Davis, Andreski, & Peterson, 1991; Kilpatrick & Resnick, 1993). In one community sample of 1,000 adults, 21% had experienced a potentially traumatic event, such as an assault or injury producing accident, in the past year alone, and 69% had experienced a traumatic event at some point during their lives (Norris, 1992). The frequency of traumatic events is reason enough for seeking population-level solutions because even if only a fraction of victims develop psychological problems, there will never be enough mental health professionals to provide each stricken individual with quality remedial care (Albee, 1959).

A Resource Orientation

Underlying community psychology's advocacy of prevention are its resource orientation and ecological perspective. Hobfoll (1988) classified resources into four distinct types: *objects* (e.g., car, adequate housing), *conditions* (e.g., job, stable marriage), *personal resources* (e.g., self-esteem, mastery), and *energies* (e.g., time, money, knowledge). Enhancing resources has been a goal of community psychology since its beginnings (Kelly, 1966; Murrell, 1973; Rappaport, 1977). As Hobfoll and Lilly (1993) also pointed out, community psychology is fundamentally concerned with the fair distribution of and access to resources. Community psychologists view resources as the bedrock of mental health.

If resources are vital even under the most ordinary of circumstances, they are especially so under conditions of stress. Stress, in fact, may be conceptualized as the *loss* of resources (Hobfoll, 1988), and traumatic stress is distinctive because of the *rapidity* of resource loss that ensues. According to Hobfoll (1991), resource loss is rapid following a traumatic event because the traumatic stressor (1) undermines peoples' basic values, (2) occurs unexpectedly, (3) makes excessive coping demands, (4) is outside the realm of typical experience, and (5) leaves a mental image that is readily evoked when one is reminded of the event. Thus trauma is very likely to involve continued, multiple losses. For example, a family member of a homicide victim has not only forever lost a loved one to murder but has likely lost his or her role vis-a-vis the homicide victim (e.g., spouse, parent), a source of social support, a sense of trust in the world, and feelings of personal control.

Psychosocial interventions, then, must aim to help people amass or replace valued resources. The accrual of resources is a fundamental purpose of primary prevention efforts because individuals must invest resources in order to obtain and protect them (Hobfoll & Jackson, 1991). Therefore people who lack resources prior to stressful life events are more vulnerable to psychological distress following a traumatic event than those who have invested resources available. Similarly, the rapid replacement of resources can be viewed as the fundamental purpose of secondary prevention. The assertion that early intervention is critical is justified by Hobfoll and Lilly's (1993) concept of *loss spiral*, which is used to describe situations where initial loss begets future loss especially when preloss resources are weak. Because resource loss occurs rapidly under conditions of trauma, initial loss leaves people more vulnerable to further loss because they have depleted their resource supply. Hobfoll and Lilly contend that the speed of the downward spiral demands quick attention. Logically, the longer a loss cycle is allowed to generate momentum, the greater the resources required to halt it. As resources become more depleted, there are too few remaining resources to invest toward their replacement, making positive responses to interventions exceedingly difficult to achieve. Thus, ideally, interventions should boost resources before exposure or replace them as soon as possible after exposure. Any later may be too late for some people.

An Ecological Perspective

Complementing its resource orientation is community psychology's ecological perspective. The concept of ecology includes the assumption that people and their environments mutually influence one another and cannot be understood alone; people are part of an interconnected whole and not isolated entities. An appealing feature of Hobfoll's conceptualization of resource loss as key to understanding stressful life events is his explicit acknowledgment that traumatic stress occurs within an ecological context. Consequently, a traumatic event cannot be fully understood without attending to what is occurring outside of the individual as well as within the individual. In other words, resources need to be conceptualized as residing at different levels, from the intrapsychic level to the societal level. Obtaining and retaining resources on all levels is necessary to achieve maximum psychological health.

To be successful, then, interventions must take place at the appropriate level or even at multiple levels. Decisions as to where to intervene are fundamentally tied to interventionists' assumptions regarding the etiology of traumatic stress generally and the focal event specifically. Whereas the consequences of various potentially traumatic events appear to be markedly similar, the causes of those events are markedly different. Thus a plan for preventing exposure to fire will differ in meaningful ways from a plan for preventing exposure to interpersonal violence, although protocols for treating victims of these events may share common elements. Further complicating the issue of when and where to intervene are disagreements among mental health professionals regarding the etiology of a given stressful event. Westhues (1989), for example, distinguished between psychological and sociocultural explanations of wife battery and showed how they entailed different implications for prevention. Psychological theories tend to see the functioning of the husband or wife or both as the source of the abuse and point to the need for psychotherapy. In contrast, sociocultural theories emphasize the general acceptance of violence in the culture and men's need to assert power or domination over women. Of course, there are also integrated theories that account for abuse using a combination of psychological, sociological, political, and economic factors. The important point here is that to the extent sociocultural explanations are valid, the problem of wife battering will never be solved by treating the pathology of individual perpetrators and victims. To solve the problem, structural factors such as sex-role socialization and distribution of power have to be addressed.

A FRAMEWORK FOR TRAUMA INTERVENTION

In searching for a framework to organize the various potential points of intervention, we initially turned to Barbara Dohrenwend's (1978) model of psychosocial stress, presented as part of her presidential address to the Community Psychology Division of the American Psychological Association. The heart of Dohrenwend's model is the idea of the transient stress reaction, a reaction that resembles disorder but is inherently transient. Three possible outcomes followed the natural stress reaction: (1) growth, in which the individual used the event to develop further psychologically; (2) status quo, in which the individual returned to preevent psychological state; and (3) disorder, in which the stress reaction persisted and appeared to become self-sustaining. The next layer of the model consisted of the various personal and situational mediators that come into play at various stages of the stress sequence, potentially influencing the very occurrence of stress as well as the final outcome. Dohrenwend's resource mediation hypothesis was that these personal and situational constraints determined which outcome followed the transient stress reaction. In the presence of strong resources, growth or at least status quo was likely. In the presence of weak resources, disorder became more probable. The final layer of Dohrenwend's model illustrated potential points of intervention, ranging from political action to corrective therapy. One of the appealing features of this model was how seemingly disparate activities took on, in Dohrenwend's words, "a satisfying coherence and directedness." The prevention/intervention activities were all directed at undermining the process whereby stress generates psychopathology, but *they tackled it at different points.*

We present a simplified framework (see Figure 1) that summarizes the when and where of trauma intervention. Like Dohrenwend's, this model revolves around the course of reactions to trauma. In accord with some objective definition, a potentially *traumatic event* occurs. Typically, the event leads to a state of crisis or *traumatic stress,* subjectively defined and experienced. Often this state of stress is short-lived, but sometimes it leads to a more lasting *psychological disorder.* The next layer of the model portrays our assumptions that risk and resilience vary and are malleable. As a function of their *personal attitudes and practices* as well as *societal attitudes and practices,* individuals differ from one another in their probability of being exposed to trauma (risk). As a function of both their *personal resources* and access to *societal resources,* individuals also differ from one another in their probability of recovering from trauma if they are, in fact, exposed (resilience). The final layer of the model again highlights the potential points of intervention, organized along two dimensions. The first dimension is the *timing of the intervention.* We distinguish between interventions taking place before the crisis (*primary prevention*), during the crisis (*secondary prevention*), or after the crisis (*tertiary prevention*). The second dimension is the *level of the intervention:* Here, we distinguish between interventions targeting individual-level resources or societal-level resources.

As shown in Figure 1, our framework encompasses five intervention strategies. As in Dohrenwend's model, the endpoint is *corrective therapy,* the intervention required when psychopathology has emerged. This particular strategy constitutes prevention only if done on a very large scale. Intervention in the form of *crisis counseling* is a common secondary prevention strategy that aims to expedite the recovery (boost the resilience or replace the resources) of individuals who have recently experienced a particular stressor. *Community development* is also a form of secondary prevention, but it aims to restore or provide access to system-level resources. It should be noted that one program might use more than one strategy, i.e., crisis counseling and community development are not mutually exclusive choices. Moving backwards in the stress sequence, *general education* is a primary prevention strategy that attempts to reduce individuals' risk of experiencing trauma, whereas *political action* is a primary prevention strategy that attempts to reduce societal causes of particular traumatic events. All of these approaches are worthwhile, and it is not the aim of this

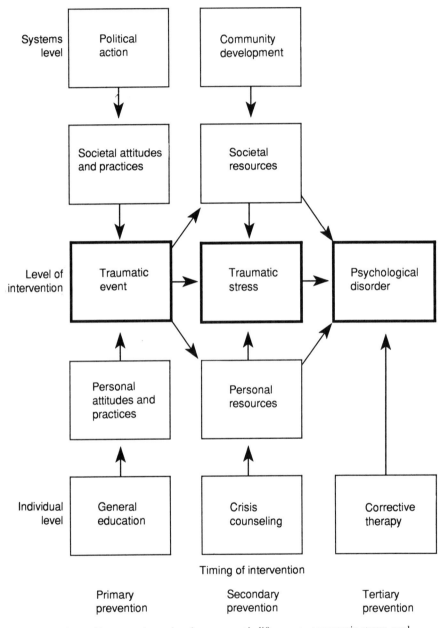

Figure 1. Points of intervention related to traumatic life events, traumatic stress, and psychopathology.

chapter to say that any of these approaches to intervention are more effective than others. Yet we would like to make the case that many of these strategies have been neglected by mental health professionals, who more readily adopt an individually based treatment stance when addressing traumatic stress. Proceeding in reverse order from corrective therapy to political action, we use Figure 1 to organize our descriptions of these various forms of practice.

Corrective Therapy

As Dohrenwend (1978) also noted in describing her framework, corrective therapy is extremely important for those persons who have developed self-sustaining psychopathology. Following traumatic events, various adverse outcomes have been observed, including but not limited to posttraumatic stress disorder (PTSD) (APA, 1994). Numerous options now exist for treating trauma-related distress. Many psychological treatments emphasize reexposure to the event and the integration of the event into existing meaning structures (Schwarz & Prout, 1991). Examples of current techniques include imaginal (Keane & Kaloupek, 1982) or prolonged (Foa, Rothbaum, Riggs, Murdock, & Walsh 1991) exposure and stress inoculation training (Meichenbaum, 1985). In their review of the efficacy of current treatments for PTSD, Solomon, Gerrity, and Muff (1992) concluded that cognitive, behavioral, psychodynamic, and pharmacological therapies all hold promise but that further research is needed to identify the most effective combinations of treatment approaches. Community psychologists view corrective therapy as a last resort for those individuals whom primary and secondary prevention strategies have failed to protect.

Crisis Counseling

Although crisis intervention encompasses a wide range of activities directed toward persons experiencing acute distress, it most often takes the form of making individual or group counseling quickly and easily available to victims. The goal is to lower situational distress to prevent the development of psychopathology. As a strategy for prevention, crisis intervention is particularly appropriate when (1) the event cannot be prevented and (2) the at-risk population is readily identified and available for interventions. Disasters, by their collective and uncontrollable nature, provide an ideal setting for crisis intervention.

A large body of literature has accumulated documenting that there is typically an immediate, short-lived, negative psychological reaction to both natural and human-caused disasters. Under certain situational and psychological conditions, this transient stress reaction may develop into more severe or chronic emotional problems (see Chapter 7, this volume). Numerous authors (e.g., Bailey, Hallinan, Contreras, & Hernandez, 1985; Cohen, 1985; Faberow, 1978; Frederick, 1981; Gist & Stolz, 1982; Hartsough, Zarle, & Ottinger, 1976; Myers, 1989) have advocated the use of crisis intervention following disasters to prevent the development of psychopathology and have offered useful guidelines for such services.

One such guideline is that crisis counseling programs should assume a proactive posture rather than a reactive one in identifying persons in need of services. This posture involves active casefinding and outreach services in the community (Okura, 1975; Richard, 1974). Outreach is needed because many people who need help may not seek it. The elderly, for example, tend to rely upon informal support structures such as family, friends, and religious organizations (Bell, Kara, & Batterson, 1978; Poulshock & Cohen, 1975). This reluctance to use formal assistance may reflect a generational emphasis on independence and "carrying one's own weight" and the stigma against utilizing "public welfare." For groups who are reluctant to request assistance, a traditional "office" approach in which the clients are self-referred may not be effective (Faberow, 1978).

Sometimes, crisis counseling differs from corrective therapy more in timing and scope than in orientation. One lesson that appears to be very difficult to learn is the irrelevance of mental health programs to persons who have more immediate and basic needs. Low utilization rates of one-on-one counseling services are commonly reported. Though not unique (e.g., Berren, Santiago, Beigel, & Timmons, 1989; Fraser & Spicka, 1981), Lois Gibbs' (1982) story is illustrative. Following the first crisis at Love Canal, New York (an infamous case of residential toxin exposure), the local mental health clinic arrived on site and set up a display to offer services. According to Gibbs, a resident and grassroots organizer, the "beaming" Mental Health Center sign alienated most of the residents. People avoided these professionals to protect their self-images and social reputations. Gibbs believed the professionals were desperately needed but that they should have been more sensitive to community attitudes and needs. As others (e.g., Faberow, 1978; Chapter 2, this volume; Seroka, Knapp, Knight, Siemon, & Starbuck, 1986) have also noted, outreach efforts to victims are most effective when they take the form of assisting them with the variety of practical problems that arise during the impact period, such as needs for housing, insurance settlement, medical care, material aid, and social services. Some people are more likely to accept help for such "problems in living" than to accept help for "mental health problems." And, we would argue, such practical resource-oriented help may be every bit as important for the preservation or restoration of mental health.

Though retaining a focus on mental health, Gist and Stolz's (1982) intervention following the Hyatt disaster differed greatly from the provision of on-the-spot brief psychotherapy that has characterized many crisis counseling programs. Following the dramatic skywalk disaster at the Hyatt Regency Hotel in Kansas City, Missouri, these authors, along with others in their community, enacted a "three-fold community-wide response" (p. 1137): First, support groups were initiated by community mental health centers in every part of the metropolitan area. Second, trauma-related training was provided to both psychologists and natural caregivers (e.g., ministers) in the area. Third, the media were engaged to publicize the availability of services, to describe typical psychological reactions to disaster, and to communicate that these reactions were normal reactions to abnormal situations that should be accepted and discussed with friends and colleagues. In the month following the skywalk's collapse, 500 persons participated in support groups, and 200 professionals attended training programs. Gist and Stolz believed that the aggressive media campaign freed those at risk from the stigma of seeking psychological help. Hard data are lacking, but the authors built a good case for the success of the intervention.

In many ways, the Kansas City program could stand as a model for crisis counseling initiatives. Particularly appealing was the effort to normalize rather than to pathologize distress. Unfortunately, it is our impression that the media do not sufficiently emphasize this. Note also that the fit between the goals of the program and the community's needs and resources was excellent. Psychological interventions seem well suited to the needs of bereaved and traumatized victims but not always to the needs of natural disaster victims, who initially are more concerned with finding shelter, water, and food. As for the generalizability of the model, it is important to recognize that Kansas City's communication and general infrastructure of goods and services were left intact. The media would be more difficult to exploit in settings where electricity is lacking and communication systems are impaired.

Another point to consider is the possibility that victims' psychological distress may emerge later than crisis counseling programs allow. One or 2 months following the disaster—after more immediate needs are met, after energy reserves and social supports begin to wear down (Kaniasty, Norris, & Murrell, 1990), and, unfortunately, after public interest has dissipated—is when psychological intervention may be needed the most (McFarlane, 1986). Rather than adding to the chaos of the emergency period, mental health workers in disaster-stricken settings might direct their energies toward planning, underwriting, and advertising later services for distressed, resource-depleted individuals. Gist and Stolz's (1982) three-fold model would seem broadly applicable in these situations.

Finally, it should be noted that crisis workers themselves experience considerable trauma. This observation has led some practitioners to develop intervention strategies especially tailored for emergency service personnel. Though not the only approach (e.g., Raphael, 1986; Talbot, Manton, & Dunn, 1992), the best-known intervention strategy may be critical incident stress debriefing (CISD; Mitchell, 1983). A critical incident is defined as "any situation faced by emergency service personnel that causes them to experience unusually strong emotional reactions which [sic] have the potential to interfere with their ability to function either at the scene or later" (Mitchell, 1983, p. 36). To defuse the stress, group meetings and structured discussions are held that emphasize normal responses to abnormal events. Typically, these meetings take place within 1 to 3 days after the incident. Over the past decade, variations of Mitchell's original technique have begun to appear, showing evidence of the technique's flexibility and appeal. Following the 1989 San Francisco earthquake, for example, Armstrong, O'Callahan, and Marmar (1991) modified and expanded CISD into a multiple stressor debriefing model for use with Red Cross volunteers and personnel. Clearly, CISD has found wide acceptance by the professional mental health community, but well-controlled studies regarding its effectiveness are generally lacking.

Community Development

Community development and crisis intervention overlap in many ways, but like Dohrenwend (1978), we feel it is useful to distinguish between community supports and therapeutic crisis interventions even though both might be provided in the context of a stressful life event. When community development is the goal, the mental health professional's role is to help community members build their own strengths. Dohrenwend's example of community development fits nicely into this chapter's theme. She described Bard's (1975) work with the New York City Police Department, the New York City Housing Authority Police, and a suburban police department. Each training project was designed to train police to change their orientations and procedures so that they would function as effective agents of social support as well as social control when they were called on to deal with familial and other interpersonal conflicts.

Mary Harvey (1990) may be among the most vocal advocates for the use of an ecological or systems-level perspective in the aftermath of disaster. In her view, trauma emanates from profound powerlessness. The emphasis for interventions, then, should be on empowerment, meaning they need to emphasize strengths, mobilize the community's capabilities, and help the community to become self-sufficient. She also believes that too much reliance on outside professionals can amplify a community's trauma. According to Harvey, one of the major tasks of a community crisis response is to identify existing resources and resource gaps: What's there? What isn't? Can we fill the gap? It is critical to make use of existing resources, that is, to include any individual, setting, and hidden resource that can be affirmed and integrated into the response plan.

Quite consistent with Harvey's opinions, Norris, Phifer, and Kaniasty (1994) made recommendations for crisis intervention that would entail mobilization of natural rather than professional supports. As they stated, "Professionals and outsiders are important sources of assistance when the level of need is high, but they must not and cannot supplant natural helping networks" (p. 396). In their study of two floods in Kentucky, levels of support received from family and friends were very low, and victims' subsequent expectations of help from those sources sharply declined (Kaniasty et al., 1990). Families and friends were presumably attending to their own needs and unable to provide these victims with sufficient help. In addition, interruptions in routine activities were quite common, thereby interfering with normal social transactions. Subsequent analyses (Kaniasty & Norris, 1993) showed that this deterioration of social support was one path through which these floods exerted their lasting effects on mental health. Though levels of helping following Hurricane Hugo were much higher, certain groups, such as African Americans and less educated persons, received far less help than their more advantaged counterparts (Kaniasty & Norris, in press). Possibly, inadequate availability of support on the community level leads to inequities on the individual level.

These findings suggest that our time as mental health professionals would be well spent in exploring ways to provide the resources that help victims help each other. Crisis teams, for example, should encourage people *not* to abandon their routine social activities, as they so often do when crisis strikes. Such activities keep people informed about the relative needs of network members, and these are undoubtedly the best forums for the sharing of experiences and feelings that is believed to be so important for disaster victims. As noted earlier, one of the basic tenets of crisis counseling is that people need to recognize that some distress is a normal reaction to an abnormal event. What better way to recognize this than through the social comparisons provided by routine social interactions? More importantly, such activities may serve to preserve both a sense of social embeddedness and the quality of community life. The direct result should be a maintenance of perceptions of social support. The indirect result should be improved mental health.

Until now, this discussion of secondary prevention strategies has focused on collective crises, such as natural or technological disasters. Whereas community-level crises are generally unpredictable, certain individual-level crises occur at predictable rates. In these cases, community members can build or strengthen their support systems so that services are in place when trauma occurs. Rape crisis centers and battered-women shelters are examples of services that are now commonly available thanks to the vision and hard work of many feminists and community activists in earlier years.

Cameron (1989) likewise has advocated for the application of community development principles in planning victim services. Though Cameron's concern was spouse abuse, the same broad principles could be applied when developing programs for other victims of violence such as rape victims or residents of disenfranchised communities. Among Cameron's most important points are these: (1) An emphasis on individual or case approaches may blame the victim by the implicit or explicit message that such difficulties can be overcome by a more competent performance by the person experiencing them. (2) People learn by doing for themselves; nonreciprocal services do not develop esteem. Helping the victimized requires assisting them to build their own power. (3) Collective responses such as mutual aid organizations and social action organizations are essential components of overcoming the inferiorization of a community of people. (4) Positions of privilege and power are seldom, if ever, willingly given up. This is as true for professional helpers as for any other group enjoying their relative advantages. One of Cameron's major contentions was that the dominant treatment paradigm and political explanations of spouse abuse are not compatible. It is very difficult for therapists, even feminist therapists, to attribute problems presented by individual women to broader societal conditions because it is not in their best interest to do so (i.e., therapists need paying customers to utilize services). Thus Cameron believes the professional-ization of spouse abuse services evident over the past few years is not without its costs. Whether one agrees with all his views or not, Cameron does provide important food for thought.

A recent and excellent example of the application of community develop-ment principles is provided by Sullivan, Tan, Basta, Rumptz, and Davidson's (1992) advocacy intervention program for women with abusive partners. This study is worth describing in some detail because it illustrates a number of principles associated with the practice of community psychology: the use of "action research," a resource orientation, and the use of paraprofessionals to expand the reach of mental health professionals. Battered women frequently lack a number of important resources, such as employment, money, housing, education, legal assistance, and social support. Yet the Sullivan et al. (1992) search of the literature over a 17-year period failed to uncover even one inter-vention designed to increase the availability of such resources to battered women.

Based on the speculation that a lack of resources played a key role in the perpetuation of domestic violence, these researchers conducted a 10-week in-tervention designed to test three hypotheses: (1) that battered women need numerous resources upon shelter exit; (2) that working with advocates would increase women's effectiveness in obtaining needed resources; and (3) that success in obtaining resources would increase the women's level of life satisfac-tion and decrease their risk of further abuse. The study involved 141 women interviewed within a week of leaving a battered women's shelter. Half were randomly assigned to receive an advocate. The 69 advocates were female un-dergraduates trained in listening skills, facts about spouse abuse, and strategies for "generating, mobilizing, and accessing" community resources.

The intervention itself involved five phases: *Assessment* was the process by which the advocate and client became acquainted and decided upon goals. *Intervention* was the actual process of brainstorming possible resources, locating resources, and devising strategies to access resources that would meet an identi-fied need. *Monitoring* refers to those efforts directed at determining if the resource had been obtained and was satisfactory in meeting the unmet need. If not, *secondary advocacy* was initiated with the goal of meeting the client's need more adequately. *Termination,* which began at about week 7 of the 10-week intervention, was the transferring to the client of knowledge regarding how to mobilize and access community resources.

Data collected from the women at the conclusion of the 10 weeks indicated that participants and advocates spent an average of 7 hours together each week. Almost all participants were very satisfied with the program and found it to have been very helpful to them. After the intervention, women in both the experimental and control conditions were asked to rate their own effectiveness in obtaining resources in 11 areas (e.g., housing, health, child care). The differ-ence was highly significant with women in the advocacy group rating them-selves as more effective.

A comparison of pre- and postintervention scores showed that *both* groups were experiencing lower levels of abuse and distress and higher levels of personal control, social support, and quality of life 10 weeks after leaving the shelter. However, women who had received an advocate improved to a significantly greater degree than others in only two areas: social support and quality of life. Over the 10-week study period, 40% of these women reported physical abuse compared to 51% of the control group, and 42% reported psychological abuse, compared to 56% of the control group. These differences were not statistically significant. Six months post-shelter, 93% of the women were reinterviewed (Campbell, Sullivan, Rumptz, Tan, & Davidson, 1993). Further abuse was reported by about 44% of the women, although 88% said they were no longer involved with their assailants. There were no significant differences in abuse between groups during this interval either. Although these data do not show strong differences between the treatment and comparison groups, it is difficult not to interpret them as showing some promise for interventions of this kind. That is, it may be the right medicine but the wrong dose.

General Education

Thus far we have discussed secondary prevention—interventions that take place *after* the traumatic event but *before* trauma-induced disorder has set in. This next approach, general education, constitutes primary prevention in that it occurs prior to a traumatic event. Educational interventions target the "person in event" by attempting to change behaviors and attitudes that make people more susceptible to experiencing trauma. Programs that attempt to educate citizens to change those behaviors that place them at risk undoubtedly constitute the most widely used prevention approach. Indeed this chapter cannot do justice to the numerous programs that have encouraged people to use safety belts, to avoid drinking while driving, to equip their homes with special locks and other crime-prevention devices, to install smoke alarms, to test for radon, to secure bookcases, and to evacuate when threatened by floods or hurricanes, (see Baker, 1979; Centers for Disease Control, 1991; Geller, 1990; Mulilis, Duval, & Lippa, 1990; Rosenbaum, 1986; Sims & Baumann, 1983; Weinstein, 1988, 1989).

Unquestionably, the area where citizen behavior has received the most attention is crime prevention. During the 1970s and 1980s, the U.S. Department of Justice funded a variety of crime- and fear-reducing programs. As for the effectiveness of these interventions, somewhat favorable evidence has been presented by Lindsay and McGillis (1986), Schneider (1986), and Fowler and Mangione (1986) based on evaluations of community-level prevention programs in Seattle, Washington, Portland, Oregon, and Hartford, Connecticut, respectively. However, Rosenbaum, Lewis, and Grant (1986) reported overall bleak results from an intervention involving eight Chicago neighborhoods (four experimental and four control). Other neighborhood-level interventions have produced even less convincing evidence that crime was reduced (Bennet &

Lavrakas, 1989; Garofalo & McLeod, 1989). There is a tendency to explain negative findings in terms of implementation difficulties (Was precaution really increased?) or research difficulties (Was the control group equally cautious?) rather than to question the underlying program model. Yet recent evidence has begun to challenge the widely accepted assumption that individual behavior is an important factor in explaining who does or does not become a victim of crime. Our prior research in this area focused on crime prevention practices as they occur naturally at the individual or household level. In two separate longitudinal studies (Norris & Johnson, 1988; Norris & Kaniasty, 1992), no evidence emerged that these practices reduced the actual probability of criminal victimization, measured 1 year after precaution was assessed. Similar results have been reported by Meithe, Stafford, and Sloane (1990) based on analyses of crimes within a sample of 19,000 households.

Our studies also failed to provide any evidence that crime prevention practices make people *feel* more safe. In the study of Chicago neighborhoods mentioned earlier (Rosenbaum et al., 1986), fear of crime actually increased in three of the four experimental neighborhoods. In a large-scale evaluation of the Eisenhower Foundation's Neighborhood Program, Bennett and Lavrakas (1989) found that fear decreased slightly in six experimental neighborhoods, increased in one, and showed no change in three. Two smaller scale interventions (Harel & Broderick, 1980; Norton & Courlander, 1982) that attempted to reduce fear among the elderly likewise failed to produce any evidence that crime prevention activities (home security surveys, safer locks) could reduce fear of crime.

In light of these studies, Kidder and Cohn's (1979) writings seem particularly perceptive. They argued that strictly individualized precautionary measures do little to promote a sense of security. They may make the home secure but leave the locality full of danger. Rather than reduce the fear, they may actually remind the occupants of the danger that lurks outside. More recently, Taylor and Shumaker (1990) explained these dynamics in terms of "perceptual adaptation." They proposed that individuals adapt to the presence of crime much as they do to chronic noise or other environmental hazards. Perceptual adaptation is a potentially useful concept for explaining the fact that as crime rates increase, fear first increases but then levels off. From this perspective, precaution would be expected to precipitate fear as it resensitizes individuals to the threat of violence around them.

The results from these studies suggest the need to seek societal-level solutions to the problems of crime and fear. This is not to say that people should quit locking their doors. Yet it needs to be recognized that crime is not going to be solved simply by encouraging citizens to be more cautious. For primary prevention to be effective, accurate understanding of the etiology of traumatic life events is necessary. Victim behavior is but one small contributor to the problem of crime.

These crime-related conclusions do not mean that people are altogether powerless to prevent accidents, injuries, or other sources of trauma. For example, individual behavior is undeniably important in the prevention of injury from motor vehicle crashes. The National Highway Traffic Safety Administration in the United States (1990) estimated that safety belts saved more than 4,800 lives in 1990 and could have saved 3,800 more if only 70% of vehicle occupants had used them. Geller's (1990) informative review of various approaches to "encouraging belts and discouraging booze" shows that educational, person-centered approaches do have merit. However, one has to judge the effectiveness of campaigns that try to motivate individuals relative to other approaches. For example, what appears to have had the greatest impact on use of safety belts are laws requiring their use (e.g., Campbell & Campbell, 1990; Centers for Disease Control, 1991; Williams & Lund, 1988). Similarly, alcohol and drugs continue to play a significant role in motor vehicle injuries and fatalities. Whereas increases in public awareness of the problem are necessary, efforts to create attitudinal change are most likely to be effective when accompanied by the adoption and enforcement of license suspension laws and changes in practices related to the availability and promotion of alcoholic beverages (Centers for Disease Control, 1991). As these examples show, prevention efforts need to address not only individual factors but also structural factors. Political action can hardly be avoided if one is serious about the prevention of traumatic life events.

Political Action

Political action seeks to change the *situation* that causes an event rather than to change individuals' risk or resilience. Like community development, political action is a system-level approach, but it constitutes primary prevention in that it takes place before the occurrence of a specific life event. Political action is the strategy that is most consistent with Caplan's original call to eliminate harmful circumstances before they occur. For example, a panel on the prevention of violence convened by the Centers for Disease Control (1991) concluded that a reduction in the access to and availability of firearms would be the single step most likely to prevent mortality from interpersonal violence. Note that the strategy of eliminating firearms is quite different from a strategy of encouraging people to avoid dangerous places after dark.

Dohrenwend (1978) considered political action to be the practice of community psychology that had moved as far away as possible from clinical psychology. Community psychologists are socialized to value social change as a professional activity, and there may be no single feature that more clearly distinguishes their training from others. Though psychologists are understandably wary of assuming the responsibility for righting society's wrongs, Dohrenwend notes that such activities should be less controversial when they are directed explicitly at reducing the incidence of stressful life events.

A practitioner who adopts a resource orientation will eventually come to see social change as essential in that many barriers to possessing adequate resources are structural ones (e.g., poverty, racism, sexism) that will never be overcome with person-centered or small-scale interventions (Hobfoll & Lilly, 1993). According to Kessler and Albee (1975), the prevention of psychosocial problems requires the abolition of social injustices such as unemployment, bad housing, discrimination, and poverty. This notion is akin to Maslow's (1954) theory of a hierarchy of needs, in which certain basic needs must be satisfied before higher-level needs such as self-esteem can be fulfilled. It is hard for a mental health professional to work on bolstering a client's self-esteem, for example, when the situational determinants of esteem, such as having employment, are not in place.

Violence is the area of trauma where calls for societal-level solutions have been most prominent to date. Koss and Harvey (1991), for example, explained that rape is a community issue (i.e., that the relationship between the victim and her community can have a profound effect upon her psychological experience and recovery). Rape victims interpret their experiences in light of community values and traditions. Like others in their communities, they may have previously held beliefs that encourage underreporting and self-blame. Observations such as these have led many communities to initiate programs aimed at educating citizens about rape. These programs attempt to demystify the crime, challenge stereotyped beliefs that blame victims while excusing perpetrators, and promote safety through rape awareness and self-defense skills. (See Koss and Harvey [1991] for some specific program descriptions.) Still needed are longer-term educational interventions that help boys and girls learn more egalitarian sex roles and nonviolent ways of resolving interpersonal conflict.

Koss and Harvey (1991) differentiate between two major approaches to rape prevention. One approach is *rape avoidance*. Like many of the crime prevention programs referenced earlier, these programs educate prospective victims about strategies for avoiding, resisting, or lessening the brutality of rape. These programs provide skills but do not eliminate the causes of rape. Though clearly oriented toward prevention, interventions with such aims carry with it the danger of perpetuating the view that women who are raped have been careless and are to some extent responsible for the rape (see also Corcoran, 1992). Koss and Harvey cogently remind us that "an unlocked window is not an invitation to rape and that the woman who invites her date in for a cup of coffee or a glass of wine has not enticed him into sexual assault" (p. 268). Again, be reminded that prevention programs are based on assumptions regarding etiology. And, logically, it can thus be inferred that programs implicitly if not explicitly communicate assumptions regarding etiology, and thus responsibility, to the public. That is, interventions can send unintended messages, can give participants unintended labels, and can have unintended consequences unless all such issues are carefully thought through in advance.

The second approach, *rape elimination*, describes programs that attempt to confront beliefs and values that support rape by condoning violence toward women. As reviewed by Koss and Harvey (1991), research findings suggest that "risk of and vulnerability to rape lies neither in the idiosyncratic and deviant characteristics of offenders, nor in the risk-taking behavior or heightened passivity of victims but in widespread cultural acceptance of given beliefs and values" (p. 269). As evidence, they cite Goodchilds and Zellman's (1984) study of high school students' opinions regarding whether it was okay to force sex in various situations, such as "she says she's going to have sex with him and then changes her mind" or "she has had sexual intercourse with other guys." Only 24% of the males and 44% of the females objected to rape in all nine circumstances provided. Clearly, studies such as this indicate that rape-prevention activities must focus on attitudinal and behavior change in the general population.

Violence against women has been seen as a social problem with possible societal-level solutions since the 1970s. More recently, violence against gay men and lesbians has come to be recognized as another shockingly frequent source of trauma whose roots lie in societal-level attitudes and structures. On the basis of their survey, the National Gay and Lesbian Task Force (NGLTF, 1984) estimated that over 90% of gays and lesbians have experienced some type of victimization (e.g., verbal abuse, physical assault) at least once in their lives because of their sexual orientation. (See also Comstock, 1991; Herek & Berrill, 1992). Berrill and Herek (1992) explained that hate crimes victimize lesbians and gay men on several levels. The *primary victimization* is that perpetrated by the assailant. The *secondary victimization* is the result of others responding negatively to the victim because of his or her sexual orientation. Herek (1992) contended that violence directed at gay men and lesbians stems from heterosexism, "an ideological system that denies, denigrates and stigmatizes any non-heterosexual form of behavior, identity, relationship or community" (p. 89). Like other forms of oppression (e.g., racism, sexism), heterosexism is manifested in two ways: *cultural heterosexism*, which is manifested in societal customs (religion) and institutions (the legal system); and *psychological heterosexism*, which is manifested in individual attitudes and behavior.

Berrill and Herek (1992) offered several policy recommendations for addressing violence against gay men and lesbians. They called for a broad-based governmental response that includes the enactment of appropriate legislation, criminal justice system reform, and extensive community education programs. Recommendations included enacting legislation that facilitates the arrest and prosecution of those who commit hate crimes, as well as abolishing the institutional barriers that inhibit reporting hate crimes and foster secondary victimization. Sensitivity training for criminal justice personnel and active outreach by police and district attorneys to the gay and lesbian community are critical. Finally, community education should be instituted to change the cultural climate in which victimization of gay men and lesbians is tolerated. Note this is virtually the identical point made by feminist activists regarding the prevention of rape—that rape-prevention activities must focus on attitudinal and behavior change in the general population. Westhues (1989) made similar comments regarding the prevention of wife battering.

The importance of political action was eloquently summarized by Barbara Pressman in the preface to her book (Pressman, Cameron, & Rothery, 1989) on assaulted women. We believe Pressman's thinking applies not only to practitioners coping with family violence but also to practitioners helping victims of community violence and other forms of trauma. Thus we would like to conclude this section with this quote:

> Unless we comprehend the social, economic, and political dimensions, and the legitimized power differentials intrinsic to violence against women and children, we will be ineffective in treating wife abuse and abuse of children. The real therapy, ultimately, is not in our offices . . . . It is for this reason, I recommend front-line therapists become involved in activist work. By so doing, they will be addressing the source of violence in the family and will mitigate the sense of helplessness and ongoing grief and rage when continuously treating family violence. . . . Only by emerging from our offices and speaking out collectively in public forums for a humane society that does not justify and legitimize inequality of women, minorities, and the poor—only then will we be working toward eradicating violence against our clients. (viii–ix)

SUMMARY

The goal of this chapter has been to apply a community psychology perspective to the design of interventions for trauma victims. Broadly speaking, this discipline of psychology directs us to develop *resource-building, multilevel,* and *timely* methods of intervening with or on behalf of trauma victims. Using Dohrenwend's (1978) model of psychosocial stress for guidance, we developed an organizing framework for thinking about practice that places trauma prevention strategies along two dimensions. The first dimension reflects whether the intervention is to be initiated after the crisis (tertiary prevention), during the crisis (secondary prevention) or before (primary prevention). The second dimension reflects whether the intervention is primarily targeting psychopathology, individual-level resources, or system-level resources. In addition to *corrective therapy,* the four strategies outlined were *crisis counseling* (secondary, individual-level), *community development* (secondary, systems-level), *general education* (primary, individual-level), and *political action* (primary, systems-level).

We believe that all of these approaches are worthwhile, and it is not the aim of this chapter to say that any one of these approaches to intervention is more effective than others. Nonetheless, in closing this chapter, we would like to reemphasize two points. The first is simply that there are many different opportunities for helping victims of trauma of which corrective individual therapy is but one. The second point is that whether we choose to become involved in the process or not, trauma is inextricably linked to social policy. Laws concerning gun control, automobile safety, helmet wearing, and abuse reporting—even issues as seemingly mundane as local building codes and land-use laws—directly influence who and how many people will be exposed to trauma. This does not mean that all practitioners will see eye to eye, but it does mean that they should be part of the debate.

Acknowledgments

The authors would like to thank Gary Uhl, Julia Perilla, and Jim Emshoff for their comments on previous drafts of this chapter.

REFERENCES

Albee, G. (1959). *Mental health manpower trends.* New York: Basic Books.

American Psychiatric Association. (1994). *Diagnostic and statistical manual of mental disorders* (4th ed.). Washington, DC: Author.

Armstrong, K., O'Callahan, W., & Marmar, C. (1991). Debriefing Red Cross disaster personnel: The multiple stressor debriefing model. *Journal of Traumatic Stress, 4,* 581–594.

Bailey, B., Hallinan, M., Contreras, & Hernandez, A. G. (1985). Disaster response: The need for community mental health center preparedness. *Journal of Mental Health Association, 12,* 42–46.

Baker, E. J. (1979). Predicting response to hurricane warnings: A reanalysis of data from four studies. *Mass Emergencies, 4,* 9–24.

Bard, M. (1975). Collaboration between law enforcement and the social sciences. *Professional Psychology, 6,* 127–134.

Bell, B., Kara, G., & Batterson, C. (1978). Service utilization and adjustment patterns of elderly tornado victims in an American disaster. *Mass Emergencies, 3,* 71–81.

Bennett, S., & Lavrakas, P. (1989). Community-based crime prevention: An assessment of the Eisenhower Foundation's neighborhood program. *Crime and Delinquency, 35,* 345–364.

Berren, M. R., Santiago, J. M., Beigel, A., & Timmons, S. (1989). A classification scheme of disasters. In R. Gist & B. Lubin (Eds.), *Psychosocial aspects of disaster* (pp. 40–58). New York: John Wiley & Sons.

Berrill, K., & Herek, G. (1992). Primary and secondary victimization in anti-gay hate crimes: Official response and public policy. In G. Herek & K. Berrill (Eds.), *Hate crimes: Confronting violence against lesbians and gay men* (pp. 289–305). Newbury Park, CA: Sage.

Breslau, N., Davis, G., Andreski, P., & Peterson, E. (1991). Traumatic events and posttraumatic stress disorder in an urban population of young adults. *Archives of General Psychiatry, 48,* 216–222.

Cameron, G. (1989). Community development principles and helping battered women: A summary chapter. In B. Pressman, G. Cameron, & M. Rothery (Eds.), *Intervening with assaulted women: Current theory, research, and practice* (pp. 157–166). Hillsdale, NJ: Lawrence Erlbaum Associates.

Campbell, B. J., & Campbell, F. A. (1990). Injury reduction and belt use associated with occupant restraint laws. In J. D. Graham (Ed.), *Preventing automobile injury: New findings from evaluation research* (pp. 24–50). Dover, MA: Auburn House.

Campbell, R., Sullivan, C., Rumptz, M., Tan, C., & Davidson, W. (1993, June). *Provision of advocacy services to women with abusive partners: A six month follow-up evaluation.* Presented at the Fourth Biennial Conference on Community Research and Action, Williamsburg, VA.

Caplan, G. (1964). *Principles of preventive psychiatry.* New York: Basic Books.

Centers for Disease Control. (1991). *Setting the National Agenda for Injury Control in the 1990's. The Third National Injury Control Conference.* Atlanta: Department of Health and Human Services.

Cohen, R. (1985). Crisis counseling principles and services. In M. Lystad (Ed.), *Innovations in mental health services to disaster victims* (pp. 151–160). Rockville, MD: National Institute of Mental Health.

Comstock, G. (1991). *Violence against lesbians and gay men.* New York: Columbia University Press.

Corcoran, C. B. (1992). From victim control to social change: A feminist perspective on campus rape prevention programs. In J. Chrisler & D. Howard (Eds.), *New directions in feminist psychology* (pp. 130–140). New York: Springer Press.

Dohrenwend, B. S. (1978). Social stress and community psychology. *American Journal of Community Psychology, 6*, 1–14.

Faberow, N. (1978). *Training manual for human service workers in major disasters* (DHEW Publication No. ADM 77–538). Washington, DC: U.S. Government Printing Office.

Foa, E. B., Rothbaum, B. O., Riggs, D., Murdock, T., & Walsh, W. (1991). Treatment of posttraumatic stress disorder in rape victims: A comparison between cognitive-behavioral procedures and counseling. *Journal of Consulting and Clinical Psychology, 59*, 715–723.

Fowler, F., & Mangione, T. (1986). A three-pronged effort to reduce crime and fear of crime: The Hartford experiment. In D. Rosenbaum (Ed.), *Community crime prevention: Does it work?* (pp. 87–108). Beverly Hills, CA: Sage.

Fraser, J., & Spicka, D. (1981). Handling the emotional response to disaster: The case for American Red Cross/community mental health collaboration. *Community Mental Health Journal, 17*, 255–264.

Frederick, C. J. (1981). *Aircraft accidents: Emergency mental health problems.* Rockville, MD: National Institute of Mental Health.

Garofalo, J., & McLeod, M. (1989). The structure and operations of neighborhood watch programs in the United States. *Crime and Delinquency, 35*, 326–344.

Geller, S. (1990). Preventing injuries and deaths from vehicle crashes. In J. Edwards, R. S. Tindale, L. Heath, & E. Posavac (Eds.), *Social influence and processes and prevention (Vol 1).* New York: Plenum Press.

Gibbs, L. (1982). Community response to an emergency situation: Psychological destruction and the Love Canal. *American Journal of Community Psychology, 11*, 116–125.

Gist, R., & Stolz, S. B. (1982). Mental health promotion and the media: Community response to the Kansas City hotel disaster. *American Psychologist, 37*, 1136–1139.

Goodchilds, J., & Zellman, G. (1984). Sexual signaling and sexual aggression in adolescent relationships. In N. Malamuth & E. Donnerstein (Eds.), *Pornography and sexual aggression.* New York: Academic Press.

Harel, Z., & Broderick, K. (1980, March). Victimization and fear of crime among the urban aged. *The Police Chief*, 34–36.

Hartsough, D. M., Zarle, T. H., & Ottinger, D. R. (1976). Rapid response to disaster: The Monticello tornado. In I. Parad, H. J. Resnik, & H. L. P. Parad (Eds.), *Emergency and disaster management: A mental health sourcebook* (pp. 363–374). Bowie, MD: The Charles Press Publishers, Inc.

Harvey, M. (1990). *An ecological view of psychological trauma and recovery from trauma.* Paper presented at the meeting of the International Society of Traumatic Stress Studies, New Orleans, LA.

Herek, G. (1992). The social context of hate crimes: Notes on cultural heterosexism. In G. Herek & K. Berrill (Eds.), *Hate crimes: Confronting violence against lesbians and gay men* (pp. 89–104). Newbury Park, CA: Sage.

Herek, G., & Berrill, K. (1992). *Hate crimes: Confronting violence against lesbians and gay men.* Newbury Park, CA: Sage.

Hobfoll, S. (1988). *The ecology of stress.* New York: Hemisphere Publishing Corporation.

Hobfoll, S. (1991). Traumatic stress: A theory based on rapid loss of resources. *Anxiety Research, 4*, 187–197.

Hobfoll, S., & Jackson, A. (1991). Conservation of resources in community intervention. *American Journal of Community Psychology, 19*, 111–121.

Hobfoll, S., & Lilly, R. (1993). Resource conservation as a strategy for community psychology. *Journal of Community Psychology, 21,* 128–148.

Kaniasty, K., & Norris, F. (1993). A test of the social support deterioration model in the context of natural disaster. *Journal of Personality and Social Psychology, 64,* 395–408.

Kaniasty, K., & Norris, F. (in press). Mobilization and deterioration of social support following natural disasters. *Current Directions in Psychological Science.*

Kaniasty, K. Z., Norris, F. H., & Murrell, S. A. (1990). Received and perceived social support following natural disaster. *Journal of Applied Social Psychology, 20,* 85–114.

Keane, T. M., & Kaloupek, D. G. (1982). Imaginal flooding in the treatment of posttraumatic stress disorder. *Journal of Consulting and Clinical Psychology, 50,* 138–140.

Kelley, J. (1966). Ecological constraints on mental health services. *American Psychologist, 21,* 535–539.

Kessler, M., & Albee, G. (1975). Primary prevention. *Annual Review of Psychology, 26,* 557–591.

Kidder, L. H., & Cohn, E. S. (1979). Public views of crime and prevention (pp. 237–264). In I. Frieze, D. Bar-Tal, & J. Carroll (Eds.), *New* approaches to social problems. San Francisco: Jossey-Bass.

Kilpatrick, D., & Resnick, H. (1993). Posttraumatic stress disorder associated with exposure to criminal victimization in clinical and community populations. In J. Davidson & E. Foa (Eds.), *Posttraumatic stress disorder: DSM-IV and beyond* (pp. 113–143). Washington, DC: American Psychiatric Press.

Koss, M., & Harvey, M. (1991). *The rape victim: Clinical and community interventions.* Newbury Park: Sage.

Lindsay, B., & McGillis, D. (1986). Citywide community crime prevention: An assessment of the Seattle program. In D. Rosenbaum (Ed.), *Community crime prevention: Does it work?* (pp. 46–67). Beverly Hills, CA: Sage.

Maslow, A. (1954). *Motivation and personality.* New York: Harper & Row.

McFarlane, A. C. (1986). Posttraumatic morbidity of a disaster: A study of cases presenting for psychiatric treatment. *The Journal of Nervous and Mental Disease, 174,* 4–14.

Meichenbaum, D. (1985). *Stress inoculation training.* New York: Pergamon Press.

Meithe, T., Stafford, M., & Sloane, D. (1990). Lifestyle changes and risks of criminal victimization. *Journal of Quantitative Criminology, 6,* 357–376.

Mitchell, J. (1983). When disaster strikes . . . The critical incident stress debriefing process. *Journal of Emergency Medical Services, 8,* 36–39.

Mulilis, J., Duval, T., & Lippa, R. (1990). The effects of a large destructive local earthquake on earthquake preparedness as assessed by an earthquake preparedness scale. *Natural Hazards, 34,* 357–371.

Murrell, S. (1973). *Community psychology and social systems: A conceptual framework and intervention guide.* New York: Behavioral Publications.

Myers, D. (1989). Mental health and disasters: Preventive approaches to intervention. In R. Gist & B. Lubin (Eds.), *Psychosocial aspects of disaster* (pp. 190–228). New York: John Wiley & Sons.

National Gay and Lesbian Task force (NGLTF). (1984). *Anti-Gay/Lesbian Victimization: A Study by the National Gay Task Force in Cooperation with Gay and Lesbian Organizations in Eight U.S. Cities.* Washington, DC: Author.

National Highway Traffic Safety Administration. (1990). *1990 Traffic Fatality Facts.* Washington, DC: US Department of Transportation.

Norris, F. H. (1992). Epidemiology of trauma: Frequency and impact of different potentially traumatic events on different demographic groups. *Journal of Consulting and Clinical Psychology, 60,* 409–418.

Norris, F. H., & Johnson, K. W. (1988). The effects of self help precautionary measures on criminal victimization and fear: Implications for crime-prevention policy. *Journal of Urban Affairs, 10,* 161–181.

Norris, F. H., & Kaniasty, K. (1992). A longitudinal study of the effects of various crime prevention strategies on criminal victimization, fear of crime, and psychological distress. *American Journal of Community Psychology, 20,* 625–647.

Norris, F. H., Phifer, J. F., & Kaniasty, K. Z. (1994). Individual and community reactions to the Kentucky floods: Findings from a longitudinal study of older adults. In R. J. Ursano, B. G. McCaughey, & C. S. Fullerton (Eds.), *Individual and community responses to trauma and disaster: The structure of human chaos* (pp. 378–400). London: Cambridge University Press.

Norton, L., & Courlander, M. (1982). Fear of crime among the elderly: The role of crime prevention programs. *The Gerontologist, 22,* 388–393.

Okura, K. (1975). Mobilizing in response to a major disaster. *Community Mental Health Journal, 11,* 136–144.

Poulshock, S. W., & Cohen, E. S. (1975). The elderly in the aftermath of a disaster. *The Gerontologist, 15,* 357–361.

Pressman, B., Cameron, G., & Rothery, M. (1989). *Intervening with assaulted women: Current theory, research, and practice.* Hillsdale, NJ: Lawrence Erlbaum Associates.

Raphael, B. (1986). *When disaster strikes.* New York: Basic Books.

Rappaport, J. (1977). *Community psychology: Values, research, and action.* New York: Holt, Rinehart, & Winston.

Richard, W. (1974). Crisis intervention services following natural disaster: The Pennsylvania Recovery Project. *Journal of Community Psychology, 2,* 211–219.

Rosenbaum, D., Lewis, D., & Grant, J. (1986). Neighborhood-based crime prevention: Assessing the efficacy of community organizing in Chicago. In D. Rosenbaum (Ed.), *Community crime prevention: Does it work?* (pp. 109–133). Newbury Park, CA: Sage.

Schneider, A. (1986). Neighborhood-based antiburglary strategies: An analysis of public and private benefits from the Portland Program. In D. Rosenbaum (Ed.), *Community crime prevention: Does it work?* (pp. 68–86). Beverly Hills, CA: Sage.

Schwarz, R. A., & Prout, M. F. (1991). Integrative approaches in the treatment of posttraumatic stress disorder. *Psychotherapy, 28,* 364–373.

Seroka, C. M., Knapp, C., Knight, S., Siemon, C. R., & Starbuck, S. (1986). A comprehensive program for postdisaster counseling. *Social Casework: The Journal of Contemporary Social Work, 67,* 37–45.

Sims, J. H., & Baumann, D. D. (1983). Educational programs and human response to natural hazards. *Environment and Behavior, 15,* 165–189.

Solomon, S. D., Gerrity, E. T., & Muff, A. M. (1992). Efficacy of treatments for posttraumatic stress disorder. *Journal of the American Medical Association, 268,* 633–638.

Sullivan, C. M., Tan, C., Basta, J., Rumptz, M., & Davidson, W. S. (1992). An advocacy intervention program for women with abusive partners: Initial evaluation. *American Journal of Community Psychology, 20,* 309–332.

Talbot, A., Manton, M., & Dunn, P. (1992). Debriefing the debriefers: An intervention strategy to assist psychologists after a crisis. *Journal of Traumatic Stress, 5,* 45–62.

Taylor, R. B., & Shumaker, S. A. (1990). Local crime as a natural hazard: Implications for understanding the relationship between disorder and fear of crime. *American Journal of Community Psychology, 18,* 619–641.

Weinstein, N. (1988). The precaution adoption process. *Health Psychology, 7,* 355–386.

Weinstein, N. (1989). Effects of personal experience on self-protective behavior. *Psychological Bulletin, 105,* 31–50.

Westhues, A. (1989). What we know about preventing wife assault. In B. Pressman, G. Cameron, & M. Rothery (Eds.), *Intervening with assaulted women: Current theory, research, and practice* (pp. 137–156). Hillsdale, NJ: Lawrence Erlbaum Associates.

Williams, A. F., & Lund, A. K. (1988). Mandatory seat belt use laws and occupant crash protection in the United States: Present status and future prospects. In J. D. Graham (Ed.), *Preventing automobile injury: New findings from evaluation research* (pp. 51–72). Dover, MA: Auburn House.

4

General Principles of Biological Intervention Following Trauma

HAROLD KUDLER and JONATHAN R. T. DAVIDSON

INTRODUCTION

This chapter presents our view of state of the art biological principles for the evaluation and treatment of traumatic stress disorders. The lion's share of the biological literature on traumatic stress deals with patients suffering from chronic posttraumatic stress disorder (PTSD) (APA, 1987, 1994). There are a range of mental health problems that may follow traumatic events, and it is not clear that each problem shares the same biological characteristics. Therefore, these recommendations may not be generalizable to all patients dealing with the aftermath of a traumatic event.

Not everyone will agree with our reasoning or practices. Such is the state of the art. Our approach is practical, internally consistent, and, whenever possible, substantiated by research. Although there is no magic bullet for traumatic stress, these biological strategies can be combined with the other modalities described in this volume to inform and enhance clinical care.

MODELS FOR ASSESSMENT AND TREATMENT

Dimensions of Posttraumatic Pathology

Traumatic stress disorders begin when a catastrophic life event is transduced into biological, psychological, and social dimensions of pathology. It is

HAROLD KUDLER · Psychiatry Service, Durham VA Medical Center, and Department of Psychiatry and Behavioral Sciences, Duke University Medical Center, Durham, North Carolina 27705.   JONATHAN R. T. DAVIDSON • Department of Psychiatry and Behavioral Sciences, Duke University Medical Center, Durham, North Carolina 27710.

Traumatic Stress: From Theory to Practice, edited by John R. Freedy and Stevan E. Hobfoll. Plenum Press, New York, 1995.

difficult to isolate a symptom in any single dimension. The somatic features of PTSD (racing heart, disturbed sleep, exaggerated startle response, impaired memory and concentration) may be intrapsychic reactions to stressful events. The cognitive aspects (intrusive memories, recurrent nightmares, psychological distress on encountering reminders) may represent damage to biological arousal and memory systems. Changes in social behavior may reflect biological or psychological dysfunction. Each dimension of pathology complicates and sustains the others. As such, posttraumatic disorders present a serious challenge to theory about mind and brain and provide a natural meeting place for the many disciplines working in the field of mental health.

The Biological Concept of Traumatic Stress

The concept of traumatic stress evolves with our understanding of human nature. Each successive view of mind and brain engenders new theories: Each new approach determines its own treatment recommendations.

Historical Review

Da Costa (1871), who treated American Civil War veterans, observed their shortness of breath, racing pulse, and dizziness. Because he was a cardiologist, he assumed that they had heart problems and prescribed cardiac medicines. His contemporary, the neurologist, Weir Mitchell (1877), attributed the same symptoms to neurological illness caused by malnutrition and exhaustion. His prescription included bed rest, isolation, and a nourishing diet.

Neurologically oriented physicians of the late 19th and early 20th centuries held that the anxiety symptoms of train-wreck survivors resulted from a rapid deceleration of the central nervous system ("railway spine") (Erichsen, 1882) and that World War I "shell shock" (Mott, 1919) reflected vibration of the molecules of the brain.

Some World War I clinicians believed that acute combat reactions were a form of hysteria and applied painful electric jolts (a contemporary treatment for hysteria) (Freud, 1920/1955a). Freud (1920/1955b) was so impressed by the repetitive nightmares of World War I veterans that he qualified his dictum that all dreams were wish fulfillments. His proposed concepts of stimulus barrier, death instinct, and the repetition compulsion were meant to explain *both* the biological and the psychological levels of trauma response.

By the end of World War II, psychoanalytic principles informed practitioners about psychological issues in combat trauma. Kardiner (1941), who had been analyzed and trained by Freud, understood combat stress as a physioneurosis in which both body and mind were disturbed. Because there was no organizing theory of traumatic stress, clinicians pursued an eclectic program of biological interventions including sodium amytal infusion, carbon dioxide inhalation, insulin shock (Sargant & Slater, 1972) and electroconvulsive therapy (Grinker & Spiegel, 1945). The charts of World War II combat veterans disclose successive strata of diagnoses ("nerves," neurosis, depression, bipolar illness, panic disorder) and medications (phenobarbital, meprobamate, chlorproma-zine, diazepam).

More recently, monoamine oxidase inhibitor (MAOIs) and tricyclic anti-depressants (TCAs) have been shown to be helpful in treating PTSD (Kosten, Frank, Dan, & Giller, 1990). Because these agents markedly affect the neuro-transmitter noradrenaline, the findings encouraged an understanding of trau-matic stress as an instability of the noradrenergic system (Kolb, 1987; South-wick et al., 1993). Recent experience with selective serotonin reuptake inhibiting antidepressants (SSRIs) led researchers to view PTSD as a se-rotonergic phenomenon (Davidson, Roth, & Newman, 1991).

Still other approaches have been suggested: van der Kolk, Greenberg, Boyd, and Krystal (1985) likened the autonomic instability of PTSD to that of opiate withdrawal and described PTSD as a dysregulation of endogenous opiates. Lipper et al. (1986) conceptualized PTSD as a kindling phenomenon (in which a subthreshold stimulus, repeated over time, generates massive out-flow response) and reported a treatment trial with the antikindling agent, carbamazepine. Some sleep researchers (Ross, Ball, Sullivan, & Caroff, 1989) have dubbed PTSD a sleep disorder and suggest corresponding treatment. Others suggest that PTSD is a disorder of memory (Pitman, 1989).

The Need for Practical Models

Scientific speculation is logical, but so were the blind men who hypothe-sized about the elephant. Researchers do not know enough about the biology of psychological trauma (and the disorders that follow it) to offer more than tentative recommendations for its biological assessment and treatment. Clini-cians are practical people who forego ultimate answers in favor of safe and effective guidelines. What follows is an attempt at such guidelines.

APPROACHES TO ASSESSMENT

Standardized Instruments

A number of biological assessment techniques have been applied in cases of PTSD. There has been less research on the application of biological assess-ment techniques to other posttraumatic mental health problems. Among the most basic and accessible indicators of a survivor's symptom state are responses to standardized history-taking tools. Examples of structured interviews include the *Structured Clinical Interview for Diagnosis* (SCID) (Spitzer, Williams, & Gib-bon, 1987), the *Anxiety Disorders Interview Schedule* (ADIS) (Blanchard, Gerardi, Kolb, & Barlow, 1986), and the *Clinician Administered PTSD Scale* (CAPS-1) (Blake et al., 1990). The standardized, patient-rated questionnaires include the *Mississippi Scale for Combat-Related PTSD* (Keane, Caddell, & Taylor, 1988), the *Impact of Event Scale* (Horowitz, Wilner, & Alvarez, 1979) and the *Symptom Checklist 90*, revised edition (SCL-90-R) (Derogatis, 1983). Clinicians should pay careful attention to core PTSD symptoms, such as fitful sleep, impaired concentration, hypervigilance, exaggerated startle, extreme physiological reactivity, distressing memories or dreams, flashbacks (includes a dissociative quality), and intense distress at exposure to reminders of a traumatic event.

Talking with the Family

One way of demonstrating that a disorder has a biological basis is to conduct a family history study. No linkage has been established between PTSD and any family history of psychiatric illness (Davidson, Smith, & Kudler, 1989). On a practical note, family members are often the best source of information about the patient's posttraumatic problems, even if the patient insists that the family knows nothing about his or her traumatic experience or complaints. Family members know if the patient fights in his or her sleep, tears up the bed at night, has to sleep in a separate bed or a separate room, or refuses to go to supermarkets, theaters, church, or funerals. They are sensitive to changes in the patient's relationships and can provide a third-party report on substance-abuse problems. They are also key elements of the patient's support system. If you enlist their help in the assessment stage of treatment, you may have a better chance of enlisting their help in the work that follows.

Medical Evaluation

It is important to remember that a number of physical disorders can mimic or exacerbate posttraumatic pathology. These include reactions to drugs (prescribed or abused), endocrine disorders (including hypothalamic, pituitary, thyroid, adrenal, and diabetic dysfunction), neurological disorders (including acute or chronic brain injury endured in the trauma), cardiac, hepatic, and respiratory problems. Thorough medical history, physical examination, and laboratory evaluation (including screens for substance abuse) are important elements of comprehensive patient assessment.

Laboratory Tests

Researchers are attempting to develop specific laboratory tests for posttraumatic disorders based on biological markers.

Psychophysiological Measures

Patients with PTSD can be distinguished from normal controls by the former's higher resting heart rate and increased cardiac responsivity to combat reminders (Blanchard, Kolb, Gerardi, Ryan, & Pallmeyer, 1986). Ornitz and Pynoos (1989) found that children with PTSD suffer from an exaggerated startle reaction and that this tendency fails to habituate. Testing for a habituation-resistant startle response may eventually become a component of a biological PTSD assessment battery.

Sleep researchers (Ross et al., 1989) have documented dramatic abnormalities in trauma survivors but have yet to establish a sleep pattern so characteristic of PTSD as to comprise a diagnostic test.

Pitman's group (Pitman et al., 1990) found that PTSD patients exposed to a narrative retelling of their own traumatic experiences exhibit a marked increase in psychophysiological reactivity (heart rate, galvanic skin response, and muscle tension). The magnitude of their response successfully distinguished PTSD patients from controls. This assessment can be conducted in most biofeedback laboratories and may provide a reliable and practical diagnostic measure of PTSD.

Neuroendocrine Measures

Lactic acid infusion, which provokes anxiety attacks in patients with panic disorder, can generate flashbacks in PTSD patients (Rainey et al., 1987), as can intravenous yohimbine, an adrenergic agonist (Southwick et al., 1993). These results have implications for the nosology of the anxiety disorders and the catecholaminergic basis of PTSD, but neither agent can be advocated as a diagnostic test.

The West Haven VA group (Mason, Giller, Kosten, & Harkness, 1988) reported that patients with PTSD have a higher proportion of norepinephrine to cortisol (as reflected in 24-hour urine collections) than most other psychiatric patients. This test has yet to be developed for routine diagnostic use. A multidimensional hormone assessment of PTSD may provide greater discriminant power. It has also been suggested that adult survivors of childhood trauma may be marked by residual abnormalities in thyroid metabolism (Gillette & Robertson, 1989).

Normal subjects suppress morning cortisol production after a nighttime, 1-mg dose of dexamethasone. Patients suffering from melancholic depression tend to be nonsuppressors on this dexamethasone suppression test (DST) (Carroll et al., 1981). Kudler, Davidson, Meador, Lipper, and Ely (1987) found that patients with PTSD are normal suppressors of cortisol on the DST unless they are also melancholically depressed (in which case they were nonsuppressors). Yehuda et al., (1993) later demonstrated that patients with PTSD may be "super-suppressors" of cortisol on the dexamethasone suppression test. This research may lead to a reliable laboratory test to diagnose PTSD.

Table 1 summarizes strategies for the biological assessment of PTSD.

Future Directions

To date, most research on assessment has involved patients with chronic PTSD. More study is needed to determine if these tools are useful in assessing acute PTSD or other posttraumatic states. Researchers may eventually succeed in combining structured interviews, self-assessment questionnaires, and laboratory tests into practical batteries for assessing the full range of posttraumatic disorders.

Table 1. Biological Assessment Strategies

I. Current, validated assessments
    A. Structured questions about somatic problems
        1. Procedures
            a. Clinical interview
            b. Standardized interview
            c. Self-rated questionnaires
            d. Interview family members about patient's
                1) Sleep
                2) Breathing
                3) Tendency to jump or startle
                4) Behavior in crowds and public places
        2. Advantages
            a. Well validated instruments
            b. Easily accessible
        3. Disadvantages
            a. These methods may be sensitive in eliciting data but the findings could represent any of a number of problems, not just posttraumatic disorders
            b. Potentially vulnerable to exaggeration, malingering
    B. Physiologic hyperarousal in response to personalized trauma "scripts"
        1. Procedure
            a. Construct script from patient's report
            b. Measure response to reexposure
                1) Heart rate
                2) Skin galvanic response
                3) Muscle tension
        2. Advantage
            a. Can be performed in most biofeedback laboratories
        3. Disadvantages
            a. Requires
                1) Comprehensive staff training
                2) Calibration of instruments
                3) Adherence to technique
II. Laboratory findings that may be developed as diagnostic tests
    A. Demonstration of nonhabituating startle response
    B. Provocation of flashbacks by infusion of
        1. Lactic acid
        2. Yohimbine
    C. Increased 24-hour norepinephrine-cortisol ratio
    D. "Super-suppression" of cortisol on the dexamethasone suppression test
    E. Advantages
        1. Less subjective
        2. Results can be combined to establish a multidimensional biological assay for PTSD
    F. Disadvantages
        1. Few of these findings have been replicated
        2. Unclear if specific for PTSD or helpful in assessing other posttraumatic disorders
        3. Comorbid disorders that may confound interpretation of these tests include:
            a. Major depression
            b. Substance abuse/withdrawal
            c. Panic disorder

APPROACHES TO TREATMENT

General Principles

Since we do not fully understand the biological basis of traumatic stress, we can not direct our efforts toward a fundamental level of pathology. Instead, we are governed by a clinical principle: What treatment is most likely to make this patient feel or function better? The answer will be different for different patients. Most treatment research has involved combat veterans with chronic PTSD. These findings may not be generalizable to other patient groups. They do, however, offer the best foundation for new clinical trials.

The Medications

Antidepressants

Not long ago, anxiety was treated with tranquilizers and insomnia with sleeping pills. Then it was discovered that antidepressants can also decrease anxiety. Antidepressants are less likely to be abused than tranquilizers or sleeping pills and can be taken less often. They seem to decrease anxiety symptoms directly instead of just quieting the patient (i.e., by impacting biological mechanisms underlying core PTSD symptoms). Antidepressants are now first-line drugs in the treatment of anxiety disorders, including PTSD (Friedman, 1988; Lydiard, Roy-Byrne, & Ballenger, 1988).

Choosing an Antidepressant

The general classes of antidepressants, their side effects, special considerations, and representative members, are summarized in Table 2. They include the tricyclic antidepressants, the monoamine oxidase inhibitors, the selective serotonin reuptake inhibitors, and one triazolopyridine antidepressant, trazodone. The choice of antidepressant depends on the patient's symptom pattern: Does he or she need to sleep more or less? Does the patient take other medicines that might interact with antidepressants? Does his or her work demand alertness, concentration, balance? Is he or she susceptible to dizziness and falls? Is the patient easily sedated or constipated? Failure with a particular class of antidepressants may indicate trial with a different class. If a patient is acutely suicidal, one can choose an agent that is less toxic in overdose situations. Finally, a patient will not take a drug that he or she cannot afford.

Managing Patients on Antidepressants

Antidepressant doses and maintenance levels are believed to be much the same in PTSD as in other applications. As always, the very young, the medically infirm, and the elderly are most vulnerable to side effects. Clinicians must be aware of possible interactions between these agents and other drugs, including drugs of abuse. Antidepressants may also provide benefits for patients with comorbid major depression. Depressed patients usually respond to antidepressants within 2 to 4 weeks, but patients with PTSD may take longer.

Table 2. Antidepressants and PTSD

Class	Examples	Advantages	Disadvantages
1. Tricyclic (TCAs)	Amitriptyline Imipramine Nortriptyline Desipramine	Promote sleep, calming, affordable	Can cause fainting, sedation, confusion, constipation
2. Selective serotonin reuptake inhibitors (SSRIs)	Fluoxetine Sertraline Paroxetine	Less sedating, fewer side effects, safer in overdose	Can cause insomnia, agitation, sexual dysfunction; may disrupt metabolism of other drugs
3. Monoamine oxidase inhibitors (MAOIs)	Phenelzine	Less sedating, effective in several studies	Restrictive diet, can cause dizziness
4. Triazolopyridine	Trazodone	Promotes sleep, calming, safer in overdose	No good support for role as a single agent in PTSD

Research findings (Kudler, Davidson, Stein, & Erickson, 1989) and extensive clinical experience suggest that an antidepressant be continued for at least 8 weeks before moving on to another antidepressant.

Adverse Effects

Clinicians should provide patients with a brief description of possible adverse effects before treatment begins and review these at every visit. It is important to ask about dry mouth, weight changes, racing heart, skipped heartbeats, dizziness, fainting, falls, sedation, agitation, gastrointestinal distress, headaches, glaucoma, and decreased sexual drive or ability. Older patients should have a recent electrocardiogram (ECG) on record prior to beginning an antidepressant trial. This will assure that the physician is aware of any cardiac rhythm or conduction problems that might contraindicate a particular antidepressant trial. This ECG will also provide a baseline measure in case it is later suspected that the antidepressant has affected cardiac function. Women of childbearing age should be screened for pregnancy and advised on the risks and benefits of their medication in light of actual or potential pregnancy.

Patients taking monoamine oxidase inhibitors must be especially careful about what they eat. Consumption of aged food (such as ripened cheeses) and drink (especially red wines), foods naturally rich in the amino acid, tyramine (e.g., broad bean pods, chicken liver), certain over-the-counter and prescription drugs (including many cold remedies, narcotics, and anesthetic preparations) may lead to severe attacks of hypertension and should be avoided. New, more selective, quickly reversible monoamine oxidase inhibitors, such as moclobemide, produce fewer side effects and allow a freer diet (Dingemanse, 1993).

These are important advantages over the older MAOIs. However, while the new MAOIs have proven helpful in the treatment of major depression, researchers have yet to establish their efficacy in the treatment of posttraumatic disorders. At this time, moclobemide is not available in the United States, but it can be obtained in many other countries.

Special Considerations with Antidepressants

It is sometimes difficult to distinguish the adverse effects of antidepressants from PTSD, itself. Both can cause anxiety, restlessness, confusion, insomnia, and nightmares. The clinician should choose an agent carefully and proceed slowly. He or she should start one drug at a time and only change one at a time. Each time a new problem arises, the last step should be undone to see if things improve. When side effects interfere with treatment, a decrease in dose often decreases or eliminates the problem. Occasionally, a patient will experience an adverse effect that suggests he or she cannot tolerate the drug. If it is reasonably safe, a subsequent drug "rechallenge" may establish whether the drug was the culprit.

Often PTSD patients are sensitive to bodily stimuli, not all of which come from medication. They often somaticize their anxiety and tend to be less trusting than other patients. If they believe that their discomfort is coming from their prescribed medicine, they may quit both it and the treatment. A physician who is thoughtful, practical, and collaborative in managing medication issues is modeling a coping strategy that patients and their families can employ when problems occur between visits. Open communication diminishes anxiety, builds rapport, and supports compliance.

Other Medications

When antidepressants fail or only partially succeed, the clinician should consider other strategies. Each new situation requires its own risk/benefit analysis. Circumstances sometimes call for a combination of agents. At other times, one drug should be substituted for the other. There is a broad palette of medications from which to choose. What follows is a sampling of potentially helpful drugs and some provisional guidelines on their use.

Anxiolytics

Benzodiazepine tranquilizers such as diazepam, lorazepam, and clonazepam can help control free-floating anxiety, startle, hypervigilance, and panic attacks (Tyrer, 1983). Their long-term use can be problematic because of potential tolerance, abuse, and addiction. This concern leads some centers to refuse to treat patients with these agents. In our experience, the benefits of benzodiazepines sometimes outweigh the disadvantages. We favor case-by-case management over inflexible policy. Among the benzodiazepines, clonazepam has the advantage of being relatively nonsedating and having a longer duration of action. Shorter-acting agents, such as alprazolam, have been associated with "rebound" effects (sudden return of symptoms such as insomnia and anxiety as medication levels subside).

Buspirone, a predominantly serotonergic, nonbenzodiazepine anxiolytic, can also reduce anxiety without sedation. It should be considered for substance abusers suffering from traumatic stress because it does not usually produce a "high" and does not appear to be addictive. Unfortunately, some patients familiar with other tranquilizers miss the "high" and decide that buspirone doesn't work. In addition, because buspirone's therapeutic effects may not be evident for 2 weeks or more, some patients quit before they have given it a fair chance. It's often the patient's family that first notices that the patient is less jumpy and irritable on buspirone. Patient education and collaboration with the family improve the chances for success with buspirone.

Sleep Aids

Nightmares and disturbed sleep are probably the most frequent complaints among trauma survivors (Ross et al., 1989). It is important to assess sleep history and provide practical advice about sleep. Patients should be advised to avoid alcohol and caffeine and to establish a regular sleep schedule. Antidepressants often promote sleep, if not at the outset, then once their therapeutic effect takes hold. One practical strategy is to start with an antidepressant alone. If, after 2 weeks, the patient still has severe sleep problems that compromise his or her function, it may be helpful to provide 2 to 4 weeks of sleep medication with the understanding that this will be discontinued once the antidepressant has reached its full effect. Even then, some patients will still have severe sleep problems. These patients can be prescribed a limited supply of a sleep medication each month to be used only on the worst nights. Flurazepam, chloral hydrate, or diphenhydramine may improve sleep. Like most sedatives, they can also be abused. Many clinicians frown on any long-term use of sleep agents. On the other hand, sleep medicines can be helpful in the context of a positive treatment alliance.

It has been suggested that cyproheptadine, an antihistamine with serotonergic properties, is specifically helpful in reducing PTSD nightmares (Brophy, 1991; Harsch, 1986). Our clinical experience with this agent has been disappointing. We cannot, at present, recommend its use.

Decreasing Autonomic Hyperarousal

Etiologic theories about the noradrenergic system led to experiments with the α_2-adrenergic agonist, clonidine, and the β-adrenergic blocker, propranolol (Kinzie & Leung, 1989; Kolb, Burns, & Griffiths, 1984). Clonidine has not found its way into general use, although Marmar, Foy, Kagan, and Pynoos (1993) suggest it could help PTSD patients with comorbid opiate dependence, since clonidine attenuates opiate withdrawal (Gold, Pottash, Sweeney, & Kleber, 1980). Clonidine can produce dizziness and fainting spells. Propranolol is sometimes useful in decreasing PTSD symptoms including intrusive memories, exaggerated startle, and hyperalertness (Famularo, Kinscherff, & Fenton,

1988; Kolb et al., 1984). Potential side effects include depression and organic brain syndrome. Another β-adrenergic blocker, atenolol, may be just as useful and has the advantage of once- or twice-a-day dosing (Lydiard et al., 1988). Clinicians should remember that β-adrenergic blockers can potentiate the effects of other agents including the adverse cardiac effects of antidepressants.

Mood Stabilizers

Lithium, carbamazepine, and sodium valproate, drugs that are useful in treating bipolar mood swings, may also have application in the treatment of PTSD (Keck, McElroy, & Friedman, 1992; Lipper et al., 1986; van der Kolk, 1983). Dosage is the same as in other applications. All three require regular monitoring of blood levels, and all can produce serious adverse effects when therapeutic levels are exceeded. Patients on lithium should be monitored at baseline and throughout treatment for renal insufficiency, hypothyroidism, and cardiac conduction problems. Carbamazepine can suppress white blood cell count, a rare but potentially lethal problem (Elphick, 1989). Carbamazepine can also produce sedation and clumsiness. Sodium valproate is often well tolerated but can, on rare occasions, produce severe liver problems. Despite these precautions, each of these agents can be helpful and should be considered when other measures fail.

Antipsychotics

Antipsychotic agents, such as haloperidol and chlorpromazine, are sometimes prescribed for trauma survivors. These agents promote sleep and may reduce impulsive behavior but carry the risk of severe side effects including tardive dyskinesia, a movement disorder that is often permanent. Their use may be justified when paranoia approaches delusional levels, when intrusive or dissociative symptoms progress toward frank psychosis, or when a patient exhibits marked borderline personality and self-destructive features (Friedman, 1988). Psychotherapeutic procedures (e.g., supportive, thought-stopping, stress-management, and problem-solving techniques) may offer an alternative or a complement to antipsychotic medication. Pervasive psychosis suggests a serious comorbid disorder such as schizophrenia, affective illness, substance abuse, or trauma-induced organic brain disorder.

TREATMENT STRATEGIES

Treatment plans begin with careful assessment. If you do not have a good appraisal of pretreatment status, it is impossible to define treatment goals or know if you have reached them. Once the diagnosis is verified, and symptoms and signs are mapped out, the clinician should pick the agent that best matches the patient's needs and vulnerabilities. It is helpful to begin with simple questions like: "What most bothers this patient?" "Is there a reason not to prescribe this particular medicine?" or "Is the patient better than he or she was before taking this medicine?"

We customarily begin treatment with an antidepressant. No one of these will be best for all patients. Phenelzine (an MAOI), imipramine and amitriptyline (both TCAs), and fluoxetine (an SSRI) have all been effective in controlled studies (Solomon, Gerrity, & Muff, 1992). Sertraline and paroxetine (also SSRIs) can also help, and some patients report less agitation with these than with fluoxetine. On the other hand, many patients prefer doxepin, an older TCA, that deepens sleep, calms, and costs less.

The recent review by Solomon et al. (1992) supports the use of antidepressants as first-line treatment for PTSD but points out that many so-called drug responders still met criteria for PTSD at the end of the studies. Patients who respond well to amitriptyline note improved sleep, decreased frequency of nightmares, decreased anxiety (both during nightmares and throughout the following day), and decreased need to avoid trauma reminders or other surroundings including crowds, public places, and family gatherings (Davidson et al., 1993). Still other benefits may accrue over time as patients improve in self-confidence, self-esteem, and social interaction.

When faced with inadequate response to an antidepressant, our first thought is to try an antidepressant of a different class. We may choose to begin treatment with one of the tricyclics because they promote sleep, are reasonably priced, and their use is supported by the largest body of research. If the patient fails to respond or cannot tolerate the TCA, we switch to a selective serotonergic reuptake inhibitor such as fluoxetine, paroxetine, or sertraline. We may begin treatment with an SSRI if the initial history and examination suggest that the patient will have difficulty tolerating TCA side effects. Some clinicians have suggested that patients with PTSD may require relatively high doses of fluoxetine to realize significant treatment effects (Nagy, Morgan, Southwick, & Charney, 1993). Recent discoveries about the effects of fluoxetine on the metabolism of the other antidepressants (Feighner, Boyer, Tyler, & Neborsky, 1990) have led to the recommendation to wait as long as 2 weeks before stopping an SSRI antidepressant and beginning a tricyclic. Some patients changing between fluoxetine and an MAOI develop a severe, potentially lethal serotonergic syndrome manifested by confusion, coma, marked fever, and/or dangerous hypertension (Beasley, Masica, Heiligenstein, Wheadon, & Zerbe, 1993). Patients changing from MAOIs to fluoxetine should wait at least 2 weeks to allow MAOI activity to subside between drug trials. Patients changing from fluoxetine to MAOIs should wait 5 weeks because of fluoxetine's slower rate of elimination (Dista Products Company, 1993; Sternbach, 1988).

If a patient feels that the antidepressant helps but remains anxious or cannot sleep, we may add a tranquilizer or a sedative (see above). Benzodiazepines, such as clonazepam, can be added to an antidepressant if there are marked symptoms of hypervigilance or startle, but, again, the potential for abuse should be considered. Although we generally discourage prescribing two antidepressants simultaneously, trazodone can be an excellent sleep aid for patients taking a specific serotonin reuptake inhibitor. Clinicians need to be aware that some patients may experience adverse interactions when trazodone is added to SSRIs (Metz & Shader, 1990).

There is no body of research to instruct clinicians how to proceed when antidepressants fail to help patients with posttraumatic disorders. A first step is to check if the patient has reached therapeutic blood levels. Inadequate dosing, excessive dosing, or poor compliance may be involved. Some clinicians add lithium to an antidepressant in hopes of potentiating its action. This strategy has been helpful in treatment-resistant depression (Nemeroff, 1991). Others (Kolb et al., 1984) prefer to add a β-adrenergic blocker such as propranolol or atenolol to the antidepressant. Dosage is titrated upwards until the patient's resting pulse hovers around 60 beats per minute (reflecting adequate β-adrenergic blockade), or until side effects intervene. It is probably better to taper and discontinue an antidepressant for at least 2 weeks before beginning a trial of carbamazepine or sodium valproate. Some patients will respond to a mood-stabilizing drug alone, but others will require the combination of a mood stabilizer and an antidepressant. Because of the complex and overlapping metabolism of mood-stabilizing drugs and antidepressants, we suggest adding carbamazepine or sodium valproate to an antidepressant only if the patient fails to respond to more conservative trials.

Although electroconvulsive therapy (ECT) may be indicated for some patients with PTSD who are also suffering from major depression, there is no research to support a role for ECT in the treatment of PTSD, itself.

THE ROLE OF THE MENTAL HEALTH TEAM

Many patients are treated by a mental health team. Whereas the psychiatrist bears primary responsibility for the management of the patient's medication and supervision of the patient's overall medical care, the entire team needs to be alert to medical issues. This is especially important in that the patient's primary clinician is often a nonmedical mental health professional. Of all team members, the primary clinician is most likely to know the patient's current status and is in the best position to collaborate with the psychiatrist, the patient, and the patient's family on day-to-day treatment issues. Sometimes nonmedical team members observe evidence of medical problems: For instance, an activities therapist might note that the patient almost fell while rising from a chair. Every person working on the team must recognize the need to share his or her concerns with the psychiatrist. The psychiatrist, in turn, has a responsibility to educate the team about potential medical problems, including medication side effects.

The treatment team also needs to realize the crucial importance of integrating biological and psychotherapeutic approaches toward the patient. If a nonmedical psychotherapist notes that a patient is unable to develop therapeutic rapport or make progress in therapy because of overwhelming symptoms, the psychiatrist should be asked if a medication adjustment might help control those symptoms. If the patient complains to the psychiatrist about worsening symptoms, the physician may want to ask the primary clinician if the increase in symptoms might be related to issues coming up in therapy, responses to the anniversary of a traumatic event, a return to substance abuse, or important changes in the patient's environment. This kind of teamwork places medical decision making in a practical context and is often key in deciding whether to change a dose, add a second agent, or give up on a particular medication. Treatment teams work best in a culture of free communication and shared responsibility. Each member of the team has a unique perspective on the patient and each plays a part in developing and maintaining positive team attitudes.

FACTORS COMPLICATING TREATMENT

Clinicians should always inquire about substance abuse and must be prepared to discover such abuse in midtreatment, even when it has been denied (Jelinek & Williams, 1987). Many patients are concerned enough about mixing illicit drugs with medications that they give up medication for weeks at a time during drug-abuse binges. Clinicians should consider the possibility of covert substance abuse if the patient's symptoms seem unusually treatment-resistant or if they follow an erratic course. Long-term alcohol abuse may alter the patient's metabolism of antidepressants and other drugs. In our experience, substance abuse or dependence can also lead to tolerance to the sedative and tranquilizing effects of antidepressants. The possibility of concurrent physical and psychiatric illness has been noted above.

Traumatic events with attendant physical injury can result in acute or chronic pain that may increase the survivor's sense of being damaged and helpless. Prompt, sufficient pain control may reduce psychiatric morbidity. On the other hand, pain medications can cause confusion, sedation, and constipation (especially when combined with psychotropic agents) and may predispose to substance abuse. Medical and psychological consultation on pain control can reduce both the patient's suffering and his or her pain medication requirement (Yost, 1987).

Our strategy for medication management is summarized in Table 3.

THE BIOLOGICAL TREATMENT OF ACUTE TRAUMA

Military experts generally advise against the use of medication in the acute posttraumatic state. Their philosophy is not to medicalize acute stress reactions. Soldiers are not to think of themselves as patients: they are undergoing a normal, transient reaction. Every effort is made to keep them in uniform, on some kind of duty, and near the front. Most soldiers suffering from combat

Table 3. Approaches to Treatment

I. Some practical questions to keep in mind
  A. What bothers this patient most?
  B. Can this problem be controlled through psychotherapeutic or environmental interventions?
  C. Is there a reason *not* to prescribe this particular medicine?
  D. Is the patient any better on medicine than before?
II. Start with an antidepressant
  A. Select the specific antidepressant by
    1. The nature of the patient's complaints
    2. The agent's side-effect profile
      a. Can this patient stand these side effects?
    3. The patient's past experience with medicines
      a. What has worked?
      b. What hasn't?
    4. The patient's suicide potential
      a. Is the patient likely to overdose on a prescribed drug?
    5. The patient's ability to pay for the medicine
III. Add specific agents for specific reasons
  A. Anxiolytics for anxiety
  B. Hypnotics or sedating antidepressants for sleep
  C. Antiadrenergic agents or benzodiazepines for hyperarousal
  D. Antipsychotics for psychosis, marked thought disorder, dissociation or bizarre behavior
IV. When all else fails
  A. Check the antidepressant blood level
  B. Consider and address complicating factors
    1. Substance abuse
    2. Underlying physical illness
    3. Comorbid psychiatric illness
    4. Pain
  C. Add lithium to the antidepressant, *or*
  D. Try an antidepressant of a different class, *or*
  E. Discontinue antidepressants and try either carbamazepine or sodium valproate
  F. Consider a combined trial of an antidepressant and carbamazepine or sodium valproate

stress seem to do well without medication (Stokes, 1990). On the other hand, Friedman, Southwick, and Charney (1993) have described a broad range of medication strategies that may have application in the midst of acute combat reactions. Herman (1992), writing about acute posttraumatic states in the general population, suggests that medication be considered when patients are unable to reestablish normal patterns of eating and sleeping, or when intrusive and hyperarousal symptoms overwhelm the patient's capacity to cope.

Could medication given immediately after exposure to a traumatic event avert a chronic posttraumatic illness? Turchan, Holmes, and Wasserman (1992) describe an air-disaster survivor who developed severe posttraumatic complaints (including nightmares, flashbacks, and exaggerated startle) within 8 days after the crash. They felt this patient was likely to meet full criteria for PTSD once the 1-month duration criterion was satisfied. Amitriptyline therapy was initiated, and, within 2 weeks, the patient improved substantially. He did not develop PTSD. Of course, this patient might have improved without medication.

Friedman et al. (1993) urge that, even when extreme psychiatric symptoms appear, it is best to withhold all medications for at least 48 hours. They reason that this will allow some patients to respond to a safer, more structured environment and catch up on badly needed sleep. It also allows time to evaluate and treat complicating physical problems such as acute brain injury and severe pain. Even in acute postcombat situations, many patients will respond to psychosocial interventions such as critical incident debriefing (Solomon & Benbenishty, 1989) and not require medication.

The literature on survivors of rape (Kilpatrick, Veronen, & Resick, 1979) indicates that, in their natural course, most intrusive symptoms diminish after 3 to 6 months. On the other hand, most of these same subjects still reported significant anxiety and fear 1 year after the rape. Burgess and Holstrom (1979) reported that three-fourths of the rape victims they recontacted between 4 and 6 years after the event considered themselves to have recovered, but only one-third of them reported that it took less than 1 year to recover. Could medical intervention have made a difference? Given the lack of controlled studies on this issue, it is difficult to answer whether early and aggressive pharmacological treatment of trauma survivors will help avert PTSD. It is also difficult to disallow a role for medication.

We agree with Herman (1992) that time-limited use of tranquilizers and sleep aids can help certain patients in the acute posttraumatic period. Like Friedman et al. (1993), we would manage extremely dangerous, agitated, or psychotic reactions aggressively (but in a time-limited trial) with a short-acting benzodiazepine, such as lorazepam, or, if necessary, a nonsedating antipsychotic such as haloperidol. In such cases, it is important to remain alert to the possibility that these agents may further complicate an underlying physical disorder.

We recommend postponing antidepressant trials until at least 1 month after the traumatic event. We would begin antidepressants only if the patient were so disabled by posttraumatic symptoms as to be unable to reestablish relatively normal patterns of nutrition, rest, and social interaction. Our reasoning is that, for such patients, antidepressants may provide assistance in decreasing intrusive symptoms and hyperarousal (some of which may be primarily biological in origin) that inhibit the survivor's ability to feel safe, cope, and return to his or her former lifestyle. Some will not agree with this suggestion, and we have no research evidence to back it up; however, we see few, if any, serious medical contraindications to such trials in otherwise healthy patients. When we weigh the academic uncertainty on this point against the clinical reality that many patients suffer severe symptoms in the first weeks and months after a traumatic event, symptoms that have responded to antidepressant treatment in patients with chronic PTSD (Solomon et al., 1992), we would rather err on the side of alleviating suffering. Some clinicians may choose to put off antidepressant trials until 3 months after the event because they believe that many patients will recompensate without medication and that medication trials will only muddy the waters. This is a perfectly reasonable approach, but, until research offers conclusive evidence, the question of when to begin an antidepressant trial should be based on clinical issues (the patient's condition, coping ability, and choice), not academic ones.

If the decision is to proceed with a medication trial, the benefit of pharmacological treatment should be reevaluated at least monthly. Medication should be used at the lowest effective dose and tapered or, if possible, discontinued soon after the patient returns to normal function.

The decision to use medication in the acute posttraumatic period requires a collaborative effort between the treatment team and the patient. Whereas medication may help some survivors rest and feel more in control, other patients feel that taking medication means giving up control. This highly individual matter needs to be addressed at the outset of treatment. Education and support can make the difference between promoting confidence and autonomy or fostering insecurity and dependence.

KEY FACTORS IN SUCCESSFUL TREATMENT

A Confusion of Tongues

The posttraumatic disorders are a markedly heterogeneous group. They can affect any individual at any life phase. Many people endure multiple traumas over the course of their lives. Sequelae may be acute, chronic, or phasic. Posttraumatic states are often complicated by comorbid disorders including depression, substance abuse, and pain. Trauma may also cause organic mental disorders, disfigurement, and physical disability. While theorists argue about the relationship between trauma history and personality (Gunderson & Sabo, 1993; Kudler, 1993), it is clear that trauma survivors can experience profound and lasting changes in temperament and social function. The International Classification of Diseases (World Health Organization, 1992) recognizes the diagnosis of Enduring Personality Change after Catastrophic Experience. These long term sequelae complicate treatment at many levels by interfering with the patient's ability to trust a clinician, hold a job, or establish a satisfying life style.

Predicting Treatment Response

It would be useful to be able to predict which treatment is best for which person. In an 8-week, double-blind study of 62 veterans with combat-induced PTSD (Davidson et al., 1993), we found that the more severe a patient's PTSD, depression, and anxiety were at the outset, the less that patient improved on amitriptyline. These same baseline measures did not predict who would respond to placebo. Neither age nor overall number of comorbid psychiatric disorders predicted who improved on amitriptyline. Patients with significant problems with memory, concentration, somatic anxiety (physical complaints like racing heart, gastrointestinal distress, dizziness, etc.), chronic worry, fear of the future, and feelings of guilt also did less well on amitriptyline. Guilt, which was dropped as a PTSD symptom in the DSM-III revision (APA, 1987), was a powerful predictor of poor response to amitriptyline among our combat veterans. These findings suggest that baseline Hamilton anxiety (Hamilton, 1959) and depression (Hamilton, 1960) ratings may help clinicians predict treatment response or, at least, gauge treatment effects.

Another widely used measure that had predictive value in our study was the Impact of Event Scale (IES) (Horowitz et al., 1979). This brief, self-rated instrument measures intrusive and avoidant symptoms. We found five items that, when strongly endorsed at the start of the study, predicted poor response to amitriptyline. Four of these were avoidant symptoms ("I tried to remove it from my memory," "I tried not to talk about it," "I was aware that I still had a lot of feelings about it, but I didn't deal with them," and "I tried not to think about it") and one was intrusive ("I had waves of strong feelings about it"). Better outcomes might be achieved by combining antidepressant therapy with treatments aimed specifically at avoidant behaviors such as stress management, social skills training, or direct therapeutic exposure.

GUIDELINES FOR SUCCESSFUL TREATMENT

Medications neither take precedence over nor preclude the use of other treatment modalities. A good pretreatment baseline assessment is essential. If you cannot demonstrate improvement by the end of a trial, it's time to consider a new approach. Successful therapy can be cautiously continued with an eye to the risks and benefits of ongoing treatment. It is not yet possible to predict which treatment will be best for a given patient or which patients are most likely to respond to treatment.

Clinicians must accept the limitations of psychopharmacological treatments. Biological intervention cannot take away a painful memory or make a bad experience into a good one. It *can* improve the survivor's ability to cope with posttraumatic symptoms. This margin of relief is all that most patients expect of their doctor: it is a success in itself.

CASE EXAMPLES

The following case examples are offered to illustrate our principles in clinical terms. Table 2 (Antidepressants and PTSD) and Table 3 (Approaches to

Treatment) will guide the reader through the reasoning behind our treatment choices.

Case 1

A 72-year-old veteran presented to his Veterans Administration Mental Health Clinic in the company of his daughter. He complained of feeling depressed and "all tied up inside." Symptoms included poor sleep with frequent midnight awakenings, loss of interest in church programs, and increasing irritability. He now avoided the grandchildren he used to take fishing. He recently started taking shots at stray dogs in the field behind his home. These features were, for the most part, an intensification of what his daughter called his "normal personality." He had always been "stand-offish" and somewhat irritable. He had put his guns up some years before after "getting hotheaded and shooting out the television."

Things had gotten progressively worse since his wife's death, 5 months earlier. He felt "jumpy." He woke up at night with his heart racing and his pajamas soaked in sweat. He had no memory of dreaming. He stopped attending church functions because of "all the bother there." His daughter added that, even when he used to attend church, he always sat in the back row. He had given up yard work, but the house was still clean.

The patient denied hallucinations and had no suicidal or homicidal intention. He did feel that "life isn't likely to get much better." His cognitive examination was remarkable for difficulty with serial calculations. He could only recall two of three words after 5 minutes. He had "a little trouble coming up with people's right names" and recently left a kettle on the stove long after its contents had evaporated.

Review of the patient's record revealed discharge from the Army in 1945 with a diagnosis of "nerves." He had three past psychiatric admissions: 1948, 1953, and 1958. The first illness was probably the most severe. Complaints at that time included poor energy, irritability, and reclusiveness. He had lost almost 10% of his normal body weight. He responded to a course of electroconvulsive therapy. During the later admissions, he was successfully treated with antianxiety agents. He had been taking 5 mg of diazepam, three times a day for over 20 years as prescribed by his local medical doctor. On closing the chart, the reviewer noted a sticker identifying the patient as an ex-prisoner of war, a fact that did not figure in any of the discharge summaries and that had not been mentioned by the patient.

When asked about his POW experience, he denied that this was "much of an issue." He had dreamed about it in the first years after the war and still thought about it sometimes. His daughter knew little about her father's war history: "We didn't talk about it at home." The patient reluctantly began a terse recitation of dates and events. While describing the death of a friend, he became hoarse, and he looked down at the floor, overwhelmed with emotion.

Over the next several interviews it became clear that not a single day passed in which the patient did not think about combat and imprisonment. Certain events, such as his friend's death, were relived almost daily. Although he claimed no memory for most dreams, he recalled his wife saying that he was "fighting the war in his sleep." They had stopped sleeping in the same room over 20 years ago because of his swinging, kicking, and yelling. He once broke her nose in his sleep.

Psychological testing, including Minnesota Multiphasic Personality Inventory and Hamilton depression scale, suggested that the patient was dysphoric but not clinically depressed. Both the IES and the Mississippi Scale confirmed problems with intrusive war memories and an insistence on avoiding anything that might trigger these memories.

The treatment team suspected that the patient was suffering from chronic PTSD exacerbated by his wife's recent death. His confusion might be part of the PTSD but could also represent an early dementing process. Although diazepam might have been responsible for his mild concentration and memory problems, it also seemed to control his anxiety ("It's the one thing that's held me together."). The team decided to continue diazepam because of the patient's great faith in it. They reserved the option of discontinuing anxiolytics altogether or switching to a less sedating agent (clonazepam or buspirone) depending on the patient's response to further treatment. They educated him about the potential hazards of anxiolytics (especially sedation, confusion, and addiction/withdrawal problems) and contracted with him to make whatever changes in medication made the most sense over the course of time. Both the patient and his daughter were recruited to observe for any sedation or confusion as new medication was added.

Baseline biological assessment included a medical history, physical examination, complete blood count, serum electrolytes, glucose, calcium, B_{12}, and folate levels, kidney, liver, and thyroid function tests, and an electrocardiogram. Physical and laboratory examination revealed the patient to be in good health. Besides his diazepam, his only regular medication was an idiosyncratic regimen of laxatives and antidiarrheal agents. These, he willingly tapered. A consultation with a dietician helped in this regard.

After much discussion, the patient began a trial of nortriptyline. This medication was chosen because it is relatively free of anticholinergic and adrenergic effects (especially orthostatic hypotension) and would promote sleep better than selective serotonin reuptake inhibitors. Unfortunately, the patient developed severe dry mouth and constipation on the starting dose of 10 mg at bedtime. The patient was told to discontinue nortriptyline and wait 2 weeks for the medication to clear his system. His anticholinergic complaints cleared. He then began a trial of paroxetine. This SSRI was chosen because it has no active metabolites. The patient was begun on 10 mg each morning. Diazepam was continued at 5 mg three times a day but only as needed for control of overwhelming anxiety.

The patient lived too far from the medical center to allow for a course of hospital-based psychotherapy visits. The team social worker worked in concert with the patient and the local Veterans Outreach Center to locate an ex-POW group in his area. This team was led by one of the Veterans Outreach staff who offered to act as a liaison between the group program and the hospital treatment team. The patient agreed to meet with the team psychologist to discuss stress-management skills and went home with a series of relaxation tapes that, with practice, helped him manage day-to-day anxiety with less and less diazepam.

At telephone follow-up 1 week after beginning paroxetine, the patient denied any adverse effects of treatment. His evolving trust in the treatment team seemed to have improved his self-confidence. He was allowing his daughter to take him out shopping (he still stayed in the car most of the time). At a clinic visit, 3 weeks after beginning paroxetine, the patient noted that he was sleeping a bit sounder and "tore up the bed a lot less." When he did wake up in the middle of the night, he found it easier to fall back asleep, and he was less tense the following day. He noted that his ex-POW group provided him with an outlet he had badly needed: For the first time, he could talk about combat, imprisonment, and their sequelae without fearing that no one would believe, much less understand, him.

The dose of paroxetine was gradually increased to 30 mg over the course of 6 weeks. The patient found that he was able to get by with an average of just 5 mg of diazepam a day. He took this at bedtime, and it helped him fall asleep. There were no signs of undue sedation or confusion. His ability to perform serial calculations had improved.

An increase in paroxetine dosage to 40 mg per day was followed by complaints of mild agitation. Attempts at split dosing of paroxetine, morning and evening, failed to relieve the problem. The dose was reduced to 30 mg, and the agitation subsided.

By 10 weeks on paroxetine, the patient was again taking part in church activities. He spoke with pride about a successful church fund raiser in which he had participated. He spent some afternoons with his grandchildren at a local park and felt that things were "getting back on track." He still struggled with painful memories of the war and his captivity. He ruefully acknowledged, "I'm never going to forget them." On the other hand, he felt "less haunted by them."

The patient (and his daughter) were seen at progressively longer intervals. He continued to meet with the ex-POWs regularly and from time-to-time sought counseling at the Veterans Outreach Center. Despite occasional "rough times," including the anniversaries of his capture and of his wife's death, he felt able to cope.

Case 2

A 26-year-old operating room nurse presented to the outpatient psychiatric clinic because she no longer "felt comfortable" at work after surviving an attempted rape in the parking deck of her hospital. At the time of the event, she had brushed away offers of help. She took a few days off and returned to work with apparent good adjustment. Only later did she realize how apprehensive she felt in the parking lot. Three months passed, and the assailant had not been captured. She began having recurrent nightmares that replayed the crime. She found herself thinking about her assailant. Was he coming back for her? Would he appear at her home? Her sleep suffered, and she was so easily startled that people at work were beginning to comment. Although she was talking about her fears with her sister, she felt no closer to mastering them.

Following a thorough medical examination, including a pregnancy test and discussion of the importance of contraceptive techniques during medication trials, the patient was begun on a trial of nortriptyline. This tricyclic antidepressant was chosen because of her young age, good health, need for sleep, and limited insurance benefits for prescription drugs. She felt that she could not afford selective serotonin reuptake inhibitors.

Her dose was increased by 25 mg every fifth day to 75 mg each evening, and then in 25-mg increments per week to a total daily dose of 125 mg at bedtime. No serious side effects developed, and, 2 weeks after beginning medication, she was falling asleep sooner and sleeping more soundly. She was noticeably less anxious and jumpy. When anxiety became severe during the day, she found that 25 mg nortriptyline calmed her. She would then take the balance of her daily dose at bedtime with good effect. The clinic psychologist suggested a course of exposure therapy, but the patient declined because she felt she was making sufficient progress in a weekly rape support group. She also said that she did not feel ready to confront her feelings on a one-to-one basis. As her anxiety diminished, she agreed to begin a course of weekly meetings with the psychologist. They began with a focus on desensitization to cues recalling the traumatic incident and continued with supportive and insight-oriented meetings. After 4 months, the patient chose to terminate her regular meetings with the psychologist. She was still attending her rape support group. The patient asked if she might call on the psychologist again if she felt she needed her help. The psychologist encouraged her to do so.

After 6 months, the patient collaborated with her physician on a plan to taper and discontinue the nortriptyline. At 2 years follow-up she is working and remains symptom-free with the exception of occasional nightmares and manageable anxiety in parking decks.

CONCLUSIONS

Each of these patients presented with PTSD symptoms, but their complaints, needs, and abilities to collaborate in treatment reflected their different ages, states of health, support systems, stressors, and personalities. In both cases, we took a thorough history, conducted standardized baseline assessments of symptoms and assured ourselves that there were no absolute medical contraindications to biological intervention. Our first patient was a bit frail. He could not tolerate a TCA at all and had to be maintained at a fairly low dose of an SSRI. Our younger patient tolerated her TCA well but was initially less open to talking about her concerns with the treatment team. Her response to medication seemed to support her ability to engage in psychotherapy.

We have tried to emphasize the importance of collaborating with patients and their families on treatment plans and the need to integrate biological and psychosocial interventions in developing a comprehensive treatment plan. At follow-up, neither patient was cured. Each still suffered from intrusive memories, intermittent anxiety and sensitivity to environmental triggers, especially when new events resembled the original stressor in form or theme. On the other hand, each of the patients (1) experienced a reduction in symptoms, (2) established a more satisfactory lifestyle, (3) gained a better understanding of his or her problem, and (4) developed a broader support system. We are satisfied that these four changes constitute reasonable goals for any therapeutic intervention for patients suffering from trauma-related mental health problems.

ACKNOWLEDGMENTS

Drs. Kudler and Davidson wish to acknowledge support from VA Merit Review Grants for the study of posttraumatic stress disorder.

REFERENCES

American Psychiatric Association. (1987). *Diagnostic and statistical manual of mental disorders* (3rd ed., revised). Washington, DC: Author.

American Psychiatric Association. (1994). *Diagnostic and statistical manual of mental disorders* (4th ed.). Washington, DC: Author.

Beasley, C. M., Masica, D. N., Heiligenstein, J. H., Wheadon, D. E., & Zerbe, R. L. (1993). Possible monoamine oxidase inhibitor–serotonin uptake inhibitor interactions: Fluoxetine clinical data and preclinical findings. *Journal of Clinical Psychopharmacology, 13*, 312–320.

Blake, D. D., Weathers, F. W., Nagy, L. M., Kaloupek, D. G., Klauminzer, G., Charney, D. S., & Keane, T. M. (1990). A clinician rating scale for assessing current and lifetime PTSD: The CAPS-1. *The Behavior Therapist, 9*, 187–188.

Blanchard, E. B., Gerardi, R. J., Kolb, L. C., & Barlow, D. H. (1986). The utility of the Anxiety Disorders Interview Schedule (ADIS) in the diagnosis of post-traumatic stress disorder (PTSD) in Vietnam veterans. *Behaviour Research and Therapy, 24*, 577–580.

Blanchard, E. B., Kolb, L. C., Gerardi, R. J., Ryan, P., & Pallmeyer, T. P. (1986). Cardiac response to relevant stimuli as an adjunctive tool for diagnosing post-traumatic stress disorder in Vietnam veterans. *Behavior Therapy, 17*, 592–606.

Brophy, M. H. (1991). Cyproheptadine for combat nightmares in post-traumatic stress disorder and dream anxiety disorder. *Military Medicine, 156*, 100–101.

Burgess, A. W., & Holmstrom, L. L. (1979). Adaptive strategies and recovery from rape. *American Journal of Psychiatry, 136*, 1278–1282.

Carroll, B. J., Feinberg, M., Greden, J. F., Tarika, J., Albala, A. A., Haskett, R. F., James, N. M., Kronfol, Z., Lohr, N., Steiner, M., de Vigne, J. P., & Young, E. (1981). A specific laboratory test for the diagnosis of melancholia. *Archives of General Psychiatry, 38,* 15–22.

Da Costa, J. M. (1871). On irritable heart: A clinical study of a form of functional cardiac disorder and its consequences. *American Journal of Medical Science, 61,* 17–52.

Davidson, J. R. T., Kudler, H. S., Saunders, W. B., Erickson, L., Smith, R. D., Stein, R. M., Lipper, S., Hammett, E. B., Mahorney, S. L., & Cavenar, J. O. (1993). Predicting response to amitriptyline in post-traumatic stress disorder. *American Journal of Psychiatry, 150,* 1024–1029.

Davidson, J. R. T., Roth, S., & Newman, E. (1991). Treatment of post-traumatic stress disorder with fluoxetine. *Journal of Traumatic Stress, 4,* 419–423.

Davidson, J. R. T., Smith, R. D., & Kudler, H. S. (1989). Familial psychiatric illness in chronic Post-traumatic Stress Disorder. *Comprehensive Psychiatry, 30,* 1–7.

Derogatis, L. R. (1983). *The SCL-90-R: Administration, scoring and procedures manual II.* Baltimore: Clinical Psychometric Research.

Dingemanse, J. (1993). An update of recent moclobemide interaction data. *International Clinical Psychopharmacology, 7,* 167–180.

Dista Products Company (1993). Fluoxetine (Prozac) package insert. Indianapolis: Dista Division of Eli Lilly and Company.

Elphick, M. (1989). Clinical issues in the use of carbamazepine in psychiatry: A review. *Psychological Medicine, 19,* 591–604.

Erichsen, J. E. (1882). *On concussion of the spine: Nervous shock and other obscure injuries of the nervous system in their clinical and medico-legal aspects.* London: Longmans, Green and Company.

Famularo, R., Kinscherff, R., & Fenton, T. (1988). Propranolol treatment for childhood post-traumatic stress disorder, acute type. *American Journal of Diseases of Children, 142,* 1244–1247.

Feighner, J. P., Boyer, W. F., Tyler, D. L., & Neborsky, R. J. (1990). Adverse consequences of fluoxetine–MAOI combination therapy. *Journal of Clinical Psychiatry, 51,* 222–225.

Friedman, M. J. (1988). Towards rational pharmacotherapy for post-traumatic stress disorder: An interim report. *American Journal of Psychiatry, 145,* 281–285.

Friedman, M. J., Southwick, S. M., & Charney, D. S. (1993). Pharmacotherapy for recently evacuated military casualties. *Military Medicine, 158,* 493–497.

Freud, S. (1955a). *Beyond the pleasure principle.* In J. Strachey (Ed.), *Standard edition 18* (pp. 1–64). London: Hogarth Press. Original work published 1920.

Freud, S. (1955b). Memorandum on the electrical treatment of war neurotics. In J. Strachey (Ed.), *Standard edition* (pp. 211–215). London: Hogarth Press. Original work published 1920.

Gillette, G. M., & Robertson, K. R. (1989). *TSH response to TRH in depressed women as related to severity of childhood incestuous abuse.* Presented at the 142nd annual meeting of the American Psychiatric Association, San Francisco.

Gold, M. S., Pottash, A. C., Sweeny, D. R., & Kleber, H. D. (1980). Opiate withdrawal using clonidine: A safe, effective, and rapid nonopiate treatment. *Journal of the American Medical Association, 243,* 343–346.

Grinker, R. R., & Spiegel, J. P. (1945). *Men under stress.* New York: McGraw-Hill.

Gunderson, J. G., & Sabo, A. N. (1993). The phenomenological and conceptual interface between borderline personality disorder and PTSD. *American Journal of Psychiatry, 150,* 19–27.

Hamilton, M. (1959). The assessment of anxiety states by rating. *British Journal of Medical Psychology, 32,* 50–55.

Hamilton, M. (1960). A rating scale for depression. *Journal of Neurology, Neurosurgery and Psychiatry, 23,* 56–62.

Harsch, H. H. (1986). Cyproheptadine for recurrent nightmares. *American Journal of Psychiatry, 143,* 1491–1492.

Herman, J. L. (1992). *Trauma and recovery.* New York: Basic Books.
Horowitz, M. J., Wilner, N., & Alvarez, W. (1979). Impact of event scale: A measure of subjective distress. *Psychosomatic Medicine, 41,* 207–218.
Jelinek, J. M., & Williams, T. (1987). Post-traumatic stress disorder and substance abuse: Treatment problems, strategies and recommendations. In T. Williams (Ed.), *Post-traumatic stress disorders: A handbook for clinicians* (pp. 103–117). Cincinnati: Disabled American Veterans.
Kardiner, A. (1941). *The traumatic neuroses of war.* New York: Paul Hoeber.
Keane, T. M., Caddell, J. M., & Taylor, K. T. (1988). Mississippi scale for combat-related post-traumatic stress disorder: Three studies in reliability and validity. *Journal of Consulting and*

2). Valproate and carbamazepine in the
rders, withdrawal states, and behavioral
harmacology, 12 (supplement), 36S–41S.
(1979). The aftermath of rape: Recent
hiatry, 49, 658–669.
Cambodian patients with posttraumatic
sease, 177, 546–550.
s explaining post-traumatic stress disor-
)5.
ranolol and clonidine in the treatment of
er Kolk (Ed.), *Posttraumatic stress disorder:*
). Washington, DC: American Psychiatric

L. (1990). Treating post-traumatic stress
E. L. Giller (Ed.), *Biological assessment and*
–202). Washington, DC: American Psychi-

der and PTSD [letter]. *American Journal of*

er, S., & Ely, T. (1987). The DST and post-
Psychiatry, 144, 1068–1071.
Erickson, L. (1989). Measuring results of
f Psychiatry, 146, 1645–1646.
J. D., Hammett, E. B., Mahorney, S. L., &
rbamazepine in post-traumatic stress disor-

1988). Recent advances in the psychophar-
Hospital and Community Psychiatry, 39, 1157–

Marmar, C. R., Foy, D., Kagan, B., & Pynoos, R. S. (1993). An integrated approach for treating post-traumatic stress. *Review of Psychiatry, 12,* 239–272.
Mason, J. W., Giller, E. L., Kosten, T. R., & Harkness, L. (1988). Elevation of urinary norepinephrine/cortisol ration in post-traumatic stress disorder. *Journal of Nervous and Mental Disease, 176,* 498–502.
Metz, A., & Shader, R. I. (1990). Adverse interactions encountered when using trazodone to treat insomnia associated with fluoxetine. *International Clinical Psychopharmacology, 5,* 191–194.
Mitchell, S. W. (1877). *Fat and blood and how to make them.* Philadelphia: J. B. Lippincott & Co.
Mott, F. W. (1919). *War neuroses and shell shock.* London: Oxford Medical Publications.
Nagy, L. M., Morgan, C. A., Southwick, S. M., & Charney, D. S. (1993). Open prospective trial of fluoxetine for post-traumatic stress disorder. *Journal of Clinical Psychopharmacology, 13,* 107–113.

Nemeroff, C. B. (1991). Augmentation regimens for depression. *Journal of Clinical Psychiatry*, *52*, (Supplement), 21–27.

Ornitz, E. M., & Pynoos, R. S. (1989). Startle modulation in children with post-traumatic stress disorder. *American Journal of Psychiatry*, *146*, 866–870.

Pitman, R. K. (1989). Post-traumatic stress disorder, hormones, and memory [editorial]. *Biological Psychiatry*, *26*, 221–223.

Pitman, R. K., Orr, S. P., Forgue, D. F., Altman, B., de Jong, J. B., & Herz, L. R. (1990). Psychophysiologic responses to combat imagery of Vietnam veterans with posttraumatic stress disorder versus other anxiety disorders. *Journal of Abnormal Psychology*, *99*, 49–54.

Rainey, J. M., Aleem, A., Ortiz, A., Yergani, V., Pohl, R., & Berchou, R. (1987). A laboratory procedure for the induction of flashbacks. *American Journal of Psychiatry*, *144*, 1317–1419.

Ross, R. G., Ball, W. A., Sullivan, K. A., & Caroff, S. N. (1989). Sleep disturbance as the hallmark of post-traumatic stress disorder. *American Journal of Psychiatry*, *146*, 697–707.

Sargant, W. W., & Slater, E. (1972). *An introduction to physical methods of treatment in psychiatry.* New York: Science House.

Solomon, S. D., Gerrity, E. T., & Muff, A. M. (1992). Efficacy of treatments for posttraumatic stress disorder: An empirical review. *Journal of the American Medical Association*, *268*, 633–638.

Solomon, Z., & Benbenishty, R. (1989). The role of proximity, immediacy, and expectancy in frontline treatment of combat stress reaction among Israelis in the Lebanon war. *American Journal of Psychiatry*, *143*, 613–617.

Southwick, S. M., Krystal, J. H., Morgan, C. A., Johnson, D., Nagy, L. M., Nicolaou, A., Heninger, G. R., & Charney, D. S. (1993). Abnormal noradrenergic function in post-traumatic stress disorder. *Archives of General Psychiatry*, *50*, 266–274.

Spitzer, R. L., Williams, J. B. W., & Gibbon, M. (1987). *Structured clinical interview for DSM-III-R (SCID).* New York: Biometrics Research Department, New York State Psychiatric Institute.

Sternbach, H. (1988). Danger of MAOI therapy after fluoxetine withdrawal. *Lancet*, *2*, 850–851.

Stokes, J. (1990). *Psychopharmacotherapy in a theater of operations.* Presented at Veterans Affairs/Department of Defense Joint Contingency Planning Meeting, Fort Benjamin Harrison, Indianapolis, IN, December 17–21, 1990.

Turchan, S. J., Holmes, V. F., & Wasserman, C. S. (1992). Do tricyclic antidepressants have a protective effect in post-traumatic stress disorder? *New York Journal of Medicine*, *92*, 400–402.

Tyrer, P. (1983). The place of tranquilizers in the management of stress. *Journal of Psychosomatic Research*, *27*, 385–390.

van der Kolk, B. A. (1983). Psychopharmacological issues in post-traumatic stress disorder. *Hospital and Community Psychiatry*, *34*, 683–691.

van der Kolk, B., Greenberg, M., Boyd, H., & Krystal, J. H. (1985). Inescapable shock, neurotransmitters, and addiction to trauma: Toward a psychobiology of posttraumatic stress. *Biological Psychiatry*, *20*, 314–325.

World Health Organization. (1992). *The ICD-10 Classification of Mental and Behavioural Disorders: Clinical Descriptions and Diagnostic Guidelines.* Geneva: Author.

Yehuda, R., Southwick, S. M., Krystal, J. H., Bremner, J. D., Charney, D. S., & Mason, J. W. (1993). Enhanced suppression of cortisol following dexamethasone administration in post-traumatic stress disorder. *American Journal of Psychiatry*, *150*, 83–86.

Yost, J. F. (1987). The psychopharmacologic management of post-traumatic stress disorder (PTSD) in Vietnam veterans and in civilian situations. In T. Williams (Ed.), *Post-traumatic stress disorders: A handbook for clinicians* (pp. 93–101). Cincinnati: Disabled American Veterans.

II

Defining the Nature
of Traumatic Events

This section contains five chapters concerning the following categories of common traumatic events: war-related trauma, violent crime, natural and technological disasters, accidental injury, and torture. The chapters are written by authors having substantial research and clinical expertise regarding the particular traumatic event considered. The overall goal of each chapter in this section is to provide the reader with a broad base of knowledge concerning each category of traumatic event. A concise overview of each chapter follows.

Chapter 5, *Military Trauma,* is written by Frank W. Weathers, Terrence M. Keane, and Brett T. Litz. Their chapter begins with a historical review of war-related trauma. This retrospective is useful as it reminds us of the continuity of trauma-based mental health problems across different time periods (i.e., we are dealing with a very reliable, if tragic, phenomenon). The remainder of their chapter addresses four key issues regarding war-related stress. These issues are: (1) defining the nature of war, including elements that make war psychologically traumatic; (2) documenting immediate and long-term consequences of war-related stress; (3) discussing the prevalence of war-related mental health problems; and, (4) discussing factors that increase or decrease the risk of developing war-related psychological problems. Two particular strengths stand out in this chapter. First, the chapter is well grounded in existing scientific literature. Second, the authors provide several narrative and clinical examples that clearly document the clinical importance of their ideas. One cannot read this chapter without becoming well informed regarding war-related trauma.

Chapter 6, *Violent Crime and Mental Health,* is written by Rochelle F. Hanson, Dean G. Kilpatrick, Sherry A. Falsetti, and Heidi S. Resnick. This chapter is also remarkable in that it is well grounded in scientific research. It too takes rather complex ideas and illustrates their practical implications, an essential task for a clinical handbook. One unique contribution of this chapter is in the emphasis of factors that determine possible exposure to violent crime. Similar to Norris and Thompson in Chapter 3, Hanson and colleagues emphasize the potential to lessen exposure to violent crime in various ways. This preventive thrust is a powerful idea that is too often overlooked in the allocation of mental health resources. Hanson and colleagues also discuss the more often considered issues of trauma prevalence, risk and resilience factors, and negative mental health outcomes.

Chapter 7 is titled *The Mental Health Impact of Natural and Technological Disasters*. It is written by two leading experts, Bonnie L. Green and Susan D. Solomon. These authors offer a heuristic model that integrates the role of both individual and environmental factors in determining adjustment following both natural (e.g., hurricanes, earthquakes) and technological (e.g., airplane crashes, nuclear accidents) disasters. Throughout the chapter, the authors illustrate the potential utility of this model by citing relevant research. A number of startling statistics are offered. They document that thousands of disasters have occurred world wide in recent decades, producing millions of deaths and various other forms of suffering. Such statistics argue for viewing disasters (and other traumatic events) as major threats to public health. The authors end by suggesting implications for mental health practice. They emphasize the necessity of assessing the level of mental health risk among various populations within disaster-impacted communities. They suggest the importance of a range of formal and informal sources of help. Particular emphasis is placed on the potential role of social relationships in reducing mental health risk. Implicit in their suggestions is that mental health services must be multifaceted and flexible, changing in response to the needs of individual survivors.

Chapter 8, *The Psychological Impact of Accidental Injury: A Conceptual Model for Clinicians and Researchers*, is written by Joseph R. Scotti and colleagues. Similar to Solomon and Green, Scotti and colleagues offer a number of statistics to document the high base rate of accidental injury (e.g., 57 million Americans suffered an accident injury in one recent year). The authors emphasize the multidetermined and potentially idiographic nature of adjustment following accidental injury, an important point that can be lost when clinical practice is based too heavily upon statistics from group-level data (e.g., population means or prevalence rates). Through a combination of clinical examples and the citation of relevant research, the authors illustrate the potential utility of their structured, behavioral approach to understanding the role of individual and environmental factors in determining posttrauma adjustment. A range of accident cases are considered, including: motor vehicle accidents, other transportation mishaps, occupational accidents, fires or burns, and falls. Developmental issues (both children and elderly adults) and other special issues (head injuries and compensation seeking) are also discussed. The chapter ends on a strong note, with the application of the proposed behavioral model to a complex clinical case.

Chapter 9 is written by Peter Vesti and Marianne Kastrup and addresses perhaps the least familiar type of trauma within this volume. Their chapter is titled *Refugee Status, Torture, and Adjustment*. The authors are psychiatrists who work at the International Rehabilitation and Research Center for Torture Victims in Copenhagen, Denmark. This center is one of approximately 60 similar centers world wide. The purpose of such centers is to provide mental health and rehabilitation services to the victims of political or state-sanctioned torture. In Chapter 9, the authors describe the nature and prevalence of torture practices. They emphasize the clandestine—and thus difficult to document—nature of this activity. Thus, this chapter cites some research statistics. However, the ideas in the chapter are heavily influenced by clinical experience and observation. Similar to other chapters in Part II, mental health risk and resilience factors are discussed. In addition, a range of psychological, social, physical, and legal outcomes are considered.

5

Military Trauma

FRANK W. WEATHERS, BRETT T. LITZ, and TERENCE M. KEANE

INTRODUCTION AND HISTORICAL PERSPECTIVE

In the last 25 years, the scientific study of the psychological aftermath of war has flourished. A burgeoning clinical and empirical literature has provided incontrovertible evidence that war exacts a heavy toll in terms of human suffering, not only for combatants but also for military support personnel and affected civilians. Clinical investigators have delineated the symptoms that characterize war-related stress reactions and have devised etiological models that explain the onset and course of these symptoms. In addition, they have developed increasingly sophisticated assessment instruments and clinical interventions to evaluate and treat combat veterans.

In many ways the study of war-related trauma has served as a paradigm for the study of other types of traumatic stress such as rape and natural disasters. In 1980, the American Psychiatric Association, spurred in large part by reports documenting a distinct pattern of psychological problems among Vietnam combat veterans, adopted posttraumatic stress disorder (PTSD) as an official diagnostic category for the first time in the third edition of the *Diagnostic and Statistical Manual* (DSM-III) (APA, 1980). This recognition of PTSD as a distinct diagnostic entity stimulated even greater interest in attempting to understand and treat the war-related stress reactions, and it legitimized those veterans whose lives had been so profoundly disrupted by the lingering effects of their combat experiences.

What is remarkable about this energetic, sustained commitment to the

FRANK W. WEATHERS, BRETT T. LITZ, and TERENCE M. KEANE · Boston VA Medical Center, Boston, Massachusetts 02130.

Traumatic Stress: From Theory to Practice, edited by John R. Freedy and Stevan E. Hobfoll. Plenum Press, New York, 1995.

study of war-related trauma is not its magnitude but the fact that it has emerged so recently. After all, since earliest times war has been a terrible but undeniable fact of human existence. Indeed, as a noted military historian recently concluded, "the written history of the world is largely a history of war" (Keegan, 1993, p. 386). Moreover, the adverse, often devastating psychological impact of war has long been recognized, and throughout history rich descriptions of war-related stress reactions abound. For example, in his discussion of Homer's *The Iliad*, Shay (1991) identified a number of themes that sound remarkably contemporary to those familiar with the difficulties facing Vietnam veterans. In *The Iliad* Achilles feels betrayed by his superiors and becomes mistrustful of everyone around him. He suffers profound grief and guilt over the loss of a beloved comrade. Enraged over this death he goes "berserk," and with reckless disregard for his own safety, he savagely attacks the enemy, committing atrocities in his desire for revenge. Finally, he complains of feeling emotionally numb, that he is "already dead."

Another striking illustration occurs in an often-cited passage from Shakespeare's *Henry IV*, Part I. In it Lady Percy expresses her concern over Hotspur's recent behavior, and in doing so, eloquently depicts a number of classic symptoms of war-related PTSD, including (in order) estrangement from others, restricted range of affect, difficulty sleeping, exaggerated startle, dysphoria, nightmares, and strong anxiety:

> O my good lord, why are you thus alone?
> For what offense have I this fortnight been
> A banished woman from my Harry's bed?
> Tell me, sweet lord, what is't that takes from thee
> Thy stomach, pleasure, and thy golden sleep?
> Why dost thou bend thine eyes upon the earth,
> And start so often when thou sit'st alone?
> Why hast thou lost the fresh blood in thy cheeks
> And given my treasures and my rights of thee
> To thick-eyed musing and cursed melancholy?
> In thy faint slumbers I by thee have watched,
> And heard thee murmur tales of iron wars,
> Speak terms of manage to thy bounding steed,
> Cry 'Courage! to the field!'...
> Thy spirit within thee hath been so at war,
> And thus hath so bestirred thee in thy sleep,
> That beads of sweat have stood upon thy brow
> Like bubbles in a late-disturbed stream,
> And in thy face strange motions have appeared,
> Such as we see when men restrain their breath
> On some great sudden hest. O, what portents are these? . . . (Act II, scene *iii*)

Other evidence of war-related PTSD can be found in more recent history. Hendin and Haas (1984a) presented two case examples of Civil War veterans, Lewis Paine, a conspirator in the plot to assassinate President Lincoln, and Ambrose Bierce, a well-known journalist and author. Paine fought for several years in the Confederate army, and his war experiences had a dramatic impact on his behavior. Good-natured and well-liked growing up, he became temperamental and increasingly violent, and he completely withdrew from family members. After he was arrested following Lincoln's death, he tried to commit suicide. These changes were obvious to all who knew him, and his lawyer defended him by arguing that he suffered from war-related mental illness. Bierce fought for the North throughout the war, seeing heavy action and sustaining severe wounds. In their analysis of Bierce's private life and written work, Hendin and Haas (1984a) identified a pattern of symptoms commonly found in veterans with PTSD, including nightmares, emotional numbing, hypervigilance, heavy drinking, and a preoccupation with violence.

As these examples demonstrate, throughout history the symptoms of war-related PTSD have been readily apparent to anyone with the opportunity to observe an afflicted veteran. Nonetheless, prior to World War I, the medical profession generally ignored the adverse impact of war on psychological functioning, and even the preeminent psychopathologists of the late 19th and early 20th centuries (e.g., Kraepelin, 1913; Bleuler, 1924) gave little consideration to war-related stress syndromes. A growing awareness of such syndromes was apparent as early as the Civil War, when the term "nostalgia" was used to refer to a mix of severe depression and loneliness thought to result from prolonged absence from home (Kentsmith, 1986). However, the systematic investigation of war-related stress was first compelled by the horror of World War I, when millions fought and died in the first war conducted on a global scale and staggering rates of psychiatric casualties began to occur (see Herman, 1992; Kentsmith, 1986; Trimble, 1981).

In World War I, soldiers initially were thought to be suffering from the physical symptoms of constant exposure to the blast of artillery shells, and the diagnosis of "shell shock" was coined. Eventually, however, the psychological nature of the symptoms of shell shock was recognized, and the syndrome was conceptualized as a form of neurosis. Battlefield psychiatrists learned much about the phenomenology of war-related stress reactions and discovered the ingredients of effective intervention that became codified as the principles of *proximity, immediacy,* and *expectancy:* That is, that treatment should be initiated quickly, very close to the front lines, and with the expectation that the affected soldier will return to duty (Salmon, 1919).

The end of World War I eliminated the immediate press of treating psychiatric casualties in order to maintain an adequate fighting force, and interest in veterans and their problems quickly waned. Insights that had been gained were ignored, only to be rediscovered as if brand new during World War II. As Kardiner and Spiegel (1947) saw it:

> Somewhere the superstition was started that data collected from World War I had nothing to do with World War II. This war was going to be different. Perhaps it was anticipated that modern implements of warfare would create a new disease entity, or that a fresh point of view might add new information. Both of these proved to be untrue. The syndromes described in the last war are precisely the same as those in World War I. (p. 3)

However, these earlier lessons were quickly relearned and significant advances in the conceptualization and treatment of war-related stress ensued.

Some of the most powerful new insights appeared in the classic texts of Kardiner and Spiegel (1947) and Grinker and Spiegel (1945). These seminal works provided compelling explications of the phenomenology, nosology, and treatment of war-related stress, thereby anticipating virtually every aspect of contemporary research on PTSD.

Two conceptual breakthroughs are particularly noteworthy. The first was that the meaning of the term neurosis needed to be broadened well beyond the traditional psychoanalytic sense: Although anxiety was still a useful organizing principle, the anxiety and terror experienced in battle derives primarily not from the activation of underlying personality conflicts but from the very real, present danger in the war-zone environment. The second was that a war-stress reaction is not a static entity but an unfolding process, with acute and chronic phases, that must be observed over time if it is to be adequately understood.

Despite these gains, the end of the war once again brought about a rapid decline in interest in the problems of veterans, and the study of war trauma was all but abandoned until the Vietnam war. Why has the study of war trauma waxed and waned, and what can account for the renewed surge of interest in the topic over the last 25 years? In her landmark work on psychological trauma, Herman (1992) argued that this "familiar process of amnesia" typifies the study of trauma in general, and that:

> The systematic study of psychological trauma therefore depends on the support of a political movement. Indeed, whether such study can be pursued or discussed in public is itself a political question. The study of war trauma becomes legitimate only in a context that challenges the sacrifice of young men in war. (p. 9)

In Herman's view, the impetus for the current period of investigation that began in the Vietnam era came from the indignation of the veterans themselves and was bolstered by the antiwar movement: "The moral legitimacy of the antiwar movement and the national experience of defeat in a discredited war had made it possible to recognize psychological trauma as a lasting and inevitable legacy of war" (p. 27).

In a similar vein, Solomon (1993), in her extensive investigation of combat stress reactions in Israeli soldiers, identified powerful cultural forces at work to disavow the long-term psychological sequelae of war. One such force was the resistance of the military to acknowledging that war can inflict lasting psychological damage. Another potent force was the denial of any weakness or vulnerability that might undermine Israel's new national identity:

> The idea that participation in combat might leave a searing imprint clashed with the image of the Israeli superman so assiduously cultivated by Israel's founders and pioneers and so eagerly adopted by subsequent generations. . . . In this collective belief system, weakness had no place. (pp. 51–52)

However, this reluctance eventually was overcome by the necessity of understanding the psychological problems of soldiers, given the potential impact of such problems in a small country with a large number of citizens serving in the military.

Undoubtedly, other factors also have facilitated the investigation of the effects of war, including the emergence of increasingly sophisticated models of psychopathology and the development of innovative research methods. But whatever the reasons may be, the study of war trauma is now firmly established as a legitimate scientific endeavor, and a consistent body of knowledge has been established. Regardless of whether the observations have been informal or scientific, ancient or modern, two conclusions have been confirmed repeatedly. First, exposure to war-zone stress is associated with a variety of acute and chronic psychological problems. Second, this relationship is not perfect: That is, not everyone exposed to war develops a clinically significant stress reaction. The overarching question now has shifted from "Does war have a negative impact on psychological functioning?" to "Why do some individuals develop significant psychological problems, while some appear to make a good adjustment and function effectively?"

In our view, an individual's unique adaptation to war-zone stress is best understood in terms of complex interactions among the aspects of the trauma, aspects of the individual, and aspects of the recovery environment (see Green, Wilson, & Lindy, 1985). In the remainder of this chapter, we review the existing literature in an effort to address several key questions:

1. What is the nature of war, and what makes it traumatic?
2. What are the psychological consequences of exposure to war-zone stress?
3. How prevalent are war-zone stress reactions?
4. What are the risk factors for developing a war-zone stress reaction? What are the resilience factors?

Because of space constraints, this chapter is limited to a discussion of combatants and does not discuss the closely related literature on prisoners of war (see Hunter, 1993; Sutker, Winstead, Galina, & Allain, 1991; Ursano, 1985) or on the effects of war on civilians and refugees (see Kinzie, 1993; Mollica, Wyshak, & Lavelle, 1987).

THE NATURE OF WAR-ZONE STRESS

War involves prolonged exposure to a staggering array of extreme stressors, ranging from various physical privations to the pervasive threat of death. Each war poses its own hardships that color the experience of combatants and produce unique effects on long-term psychological adjustment. Wars differ with respect to climate (e.g., tropical, desert, Arctic), terrain (e.g., mountains, forest, plains), methods of warfare (e.g., conventional, guerilla), and types of weapons used. Also, wars may be fought on domestic or foreign soil, and they may be popular or unpopular. Finally, the experience of war may be very different depending on combatants' branch of service (e.g., Marines, Air Force) and specific duties (e.g., infantry, artillery, pilot).

However, although each war is different, the core traumatic experience in any war is a profound and sustained degree of life threat or threat of serious injury and excruciating pain:

> The paramount stress is the actual danger of destruction, complete or partial. And it is this factor that predominates all others in importance and to which most reactions are oriented. All others are contributory. The danger of death is real, actual, immediate, inescapable; from it no flight is possible. When we study war neuroses we are studying essentially men's reactions to this real and immediate danger of destruction. (Kardiner & Spiegel, 1947, pp. 20–21)

The fear of being injured or killed is compounded by other experiences with death, including the horror and grief of witnessing the injury or death of fellow soldiers; killing the enemy, or even more psychologically damaging, killing a fellow soldier; and witnessing or participating in atrocities, or behaviors considered excessively brutal even for a war zone. Lifton (1974) has referred to the fallout of this inundation with death and dying as the "death imprint," which he views as the most significant and disturbing sequela of war.

Wars share other common traumatic elements as well. As shown in Table 1, investigators have developed conceptual schemes for delineating the dimensions underlying the vast array of experiences combatants may encounter. These schemes overlap substantially, but each emphasizes somewhat different aspects of war-zone stress. For example, Grinker and Spiegel (1945) and Kardiner and Spiegel (1947) identified three types of war-related stressors: (1) demands on physical resources, which comprise the contextual stressors of

Table 1. Dimensions of War-Zone Stress

Source	Dimensions	Examples
Grinker & Spiegel (1945), Kardiner & Spiegel (1947)	1. Demands on physical resources	Inadequate food, water, shelter, hygiene; physical exertion; fatigue; auditory irritation
	2. Demands on emotional resources	Threat of personal injury or death; injury or death of friend; engaging in hostile, destructive activity
	3. Loss of cohesion/morale in combat unit	Poor relations with peers; loss of trust in leaders; perception of "losing"
Laufer, Gallops, & Frey-Wouters (1984)	1. Level of combat exposure	Served in forward areas; participated in firefights; received incoming fire; being wounded
	2. Witnessing abusive violence	Torture of prisoners; physical mistreatment of civilians; mutilation of bodies
	3. Participation in abusive violence	

(continued)

Table 1. *(Continued)*

Source	Dimensions	Examples
Schlenger et al. (1992): dimensions applicable to both male and female Vietnam veterans	1. Exposure to combat/ exposure to dead and wounded	Receiving fire; firing weapon at enemy; being wounded or injured; exposure to wounded/dying/dead; caring for casualties
	2. Exposure to or participation in abusive violence	Torturing prisoners; harming civilians; mutilation of bodies
	3. Deprivation	Lack of shelter, food, water supplies; fatigue; exposure to insects and disease
	4. Loss of meaning and control	Sense of purposelessness; feeling out of touch with the world
King, King, Gudanowski, & Vreven (1995)	1. Traditional combat events	Receiving fire; firing weapon at enemy; being wounded or injured; exposure to wounded/dying/dead
	2. Atrocities/episodes of extraordinarily abusive violence	Torturing prisoners; harming civilians; use of cruel weaponry or chemicals; mutilation of bodies
	3. Subjective or perceived threat	Perception of imminent danger/life threat; belief that one would not survive
	4. Harsh or malevolent environment	Lack of food, water; poor living arrangements; harsh climate; unpredictable/extended work schedule
Wolfe, Brown, Furey, & Levin (1993): dimensions applicable to female Vietnam veterans	1. Quality of care provided	Triage decisions; unnecessary death from inadequate equipment/personnel; life-threatening errors as a result of fatigue
	2. Discriminatory experiences	Sexual harassment; coercive sexual experiences; gender-based discrimination
	3. Environmental stressors	Receiving fire; imminent danger; uncomfortable environment; lack of time off
	4. Exposure to catastrophic death and dying	Viewing stream of casualties/ severely mutilated; attending to someone dying

inadequate food, water, and living conditions, as well as exhaustion resulting from sleep deprivation and physical exertion; (2) demands on emotional resources, consisting primarily of constant exposure to death; and (3) loss of cohesion and morale in the combat unit. These authors are unique among those cited in Table 1 in their emphasis on the stress associated with a breakdown in group cohesion in the combat unit. This is a crucial dimension, the power of which should not be underestimated: Strong attachments to fellow soldiers provide a potent buffer against fear, whereas a lack of cohesion, or worse, open dissension, can be a significant source of distress.

Laufer, Gallops, and Frey-Wouters (1984) distinguished three key aspects of war-zone stress: exposure to combat and witnessing or participating in abusive violence. Their emphasis on abusive violence as a separate dimension stemmed from reports of atrocities committed in the Vietnam war. However, atrocities are an ancient fact of war. As noted above, Homer described such savage violence in Achilles, attributing it to a mix of frustration, grief, and rage. The link between rage and dehumanizing violence was also clear to O'Brien (1993), who recognized uncanny similarities between his combat experiences in Vietnam and the experiences of the British troops who committed atrocities in the retreat from Lexington and Concord during the Revolutionary War:

> I identified with those British troops. The parallels struck me as both obvious and telling. A civil war. A powerful world-class army blundering through unfamiliar terrain. A myth of invincibility. Immense resources of wealth and firepower that somehow never produced definitive results. A sense of bewilderment and dislocation. A tough, skilled, zealous enemy that for years had been grossly underestimated. Growing frustration and rage at guerilla tactics—the constant sniping, the deadly little ambushes, an enemy that refused to fight conventional battles . . . Men died, then more men died, and after a time the enemy became "devils" and "demons" and "savages"—dinks, slopes, gooks. Houses were burned. Rumors of atrocity justified other atrocities. A kind of wildness invaded our spirits—animal desperation, animal fury—and gradually the entire universe seemed to condense into a fierce struggle for personal sanity. (p. 66)

It must be emphasized that most combatants do not deliberately participate in atrocities. However, since the Vietnam war, a number of clinical and empirical reports have shown that those who do participate in or witness acts of excessively brutal violence are at greater risk for developing severe, intractable symptoms of PTSD (e.g., Breslau & Davis, 1987; Gallers, Foy, Donahoe, & Goldfarb, 1988; Haley, 1974; Yager, Laufer, & Gallops, 1984; Yehuda, Southwick, & Giller, 1992).

Schlenger et al. (1992) factor-analyzed data on exposure to war-zone stress drawn from the National Vietnam Veterans Readjustment Study (NVVRS) (Kulka et al., 1990), a study widely recognized as the most methodologically rigorous epidemiological investigation of PTSD to date. The NVVRS included an extensive inventory of items intended to provide an exhaustive assessment of the aspects of combat exposure described in the literature as being important. Analyzing the data separately for men and women, Schlenger et al. (1992) found some slight differences in the factors that emerged, but the dimensions in Table 1 essentially apply to either gender. Their conceptual scheme distinguishes "high magnitude" stressors such as life threat and exposure to death and dying from "low magnitude" stressors such as various physical deprivations.

Like Laufer et al. (1984), Schlenger et al. (1992) also found a dimension of exposure to or participation in abusive violence, as well as a new dimension, loss of meaning and control. This latter dimension refers to existential conflicts triggered by war, such as a sense of purposelessness and inability to find meaning in the experience. The circumstances of the Vietnam conflict were particularly conducive to the loss of meaning and control: It was an unpopular war that lacked clear objectives, making it difficult for some combatants to justify their own behavior, or to justify the death and destruction around them.

King, King, Gudanowski, and Vreven (1995) also analyzed the NVVRS data, supplying rationally derived categories for the same items used by Schlenger et al. (1992). They arrived at similar dimensions, distinguishing between traditional combat and harsh or malevolent environment and identifying a separate dimension of atrocities. But they also added a dimension of subjective or perceived threat, which speaks to the issue of whether stressors can be specified in completely objective terms, or whether an individual's subjective appraisal of the stressor must be considered.

Finally, Wolfe, Brown, Furey, and Levin (1993), recognizing that women in a war-zone may face a very different set of stressors, proposed several key dimensions of war-zone stress for women. Two of the dimensions they outlined are similar to those identified for men, including environmental stressors, consisting primarily of traditional combat experiences, and exposure to catastrophic death and dying. A third dimension, quality of care provided, is more centrally related to the experience of female Vietnam veterans, although it also is applicable to many male veterans, especially medical corpsmen and doctors. They also identified a fourth dimension, discriminatory experiences, that is much more specific to women. However, this dimension also may apply to at least some males who are raped or sexually coerced in the military, and if it were expanded to include racial or ethnic discrimination, it would apply broadly to all minority personnel (see Parson, 1985; Pina, 1985).

The conceptual schemes outlined in Table 1 are helpful in understanding the trauma of the war zone, but they don't address the question of how war compares with other types of traumatic events. Green (1993) proposed eight generic dimensions of trauma that are helpful in contextualizing war-zone stressors. These are: (1) threat to life and limb, (2) severe physical harm or injury, (3) receipt of intentional harm or injury, (4) exposure to the grotesque, (5) violent or sudden loss of someone close to you, (6) witnessing or learning of violence to someone close to you, (7) learning of exposure to a noxious agent, and (8) causing death or severe harm to another. Clearly, a soldier in any war zone is at risk for being exposed to *all* of these types of events, and combatants with moderate to high degrees of exposure typically experience multiple incidents reflecting the full gamut of psychological trauma.

War-zone trauma is characterized not only by exposure to a broad range of stressors, but by the frequency and duration of exposure, and by the unique demands of being a victim as well as a perpetrator of traumatic violence. Since military duty in a war zone typically lasts over months or even years, there is a much greater likelihood of repeated and sustained traumatic exposure. Also, unlike many other victims of interpersonal trauma, combatants have the training and the means to aggress against the attacker, killing or maiming the enemy in the context of being victimized and threatened. This conflict often leads to the use of coping strategies such as aggression and violence and emotional numbing, which further colors the traumatic conditioning that takes place in a war zone.

SYNDROMES OF WAR-ZONE STRESS

Symptom Picture

As noted earlier, a variety of labels have been used to describe the psychological problems that can develop as an result of exposure to war-zone stress. In addition to nostalgia and shell shock, war-zone stress reactions have been classified as traumatic neurosis, war neurosis, combat exhaustion, or battle fatigue (see Kentsmith, 1986). Historically, however, this terminological confusion has arisen from a failure to recognize the distinction between acute and chronic phases of war-zone stress reactions, and from a failure to appreciate fully the diversity of symptoms that can appear during the acute phase. Acute stress reactions occur either during combat or shortly after, whereas chronic reactions persist over time. Chronic reactions may represent a crystallization of an acute reaction but also may develop in combatants who did not break down in combat. According to Kardiner and Spiegel (1947):

> The simple fact is that the stresses of war create only one syndrome which, though not unique to war conditions, is extremely frequent . . . a syndrome which is variously identified as traumatic neurosis, shell shock, battle fatigue, combat exhaustion, and any number of variations of nomenclature. All these terms mean the same thing. They all refer to the common acquired disorder consequent on war stress . . . It is a process and it changes, becomes organized and consolidated, and in each of these time phases different phenomena appear. (p. 2)

The first two editions of the Diagnostic and Statistical Manual of Mental Disorders (DSM) perpetuated the lack of recognition of a chronic war-related stress syndrome, classifying reactions to combat either as "gross stress reaction" (APA, 1952) or "transient situational disturbance" (APA, 1968). Both of these designations implied that reactions to combat were relatively brief in nature and could be expected to resolve quickly. Clinicians were directed to make a diagnosis of another disorder should symptoms endure. Only with the inclusion of PTSD in DSM-III was there official acknowledgment that the symptoms of traumatic stress can persist for months or years (APA, 1980).

Recently, Solomon (1993), drawing on her thorough examination of psychiatric casualties in the Israeli army, proposed a useful distinction between what she calls "combat stress reaction" (CSR), which refers to the acute syndrome of war-zone stress occurring on the battlefield, and PTSD, which refers to the lasting effects of war (see Chapter 10, this volume). Like Kardiner and Spiegel nearly half a century earlier, Solomon (1993) was struck by the bewildering variety and instability of symptoms characteristic of acute reactions, which make CSR especially difficult to define:

> A major cause of the lack of clear definition is the polymorphous and labile quality of CSR, that is, the variability and rapid changes of its somatic, emotional, cognitive, and behavioral manifestations. Some casualties become apathetic and withdrawn; others rant and rage. Some freeze on the spot or hide in a trench, while others run amok or charge against a hidden enemy. Moreover, whatever the predominant symptom, it can be rapidly replaced by others that, in turn, can yield to yet others. (pp. 27–28)

In order to delineate the essential features of CSR, Solomon and her colleagues interviewed Israeli soldiers, collecting and analyzing first-person accounts of CSRs. Six primary dimensions were identified: (1) distancing, which refers to the use of psychic numbing or fantasy to reduce the staggering sensory overload of the battlefield; (2) anxiety, ranging from apprehension to incapacitating terror, in conjunction with sleeplessness and intrusive images of death; (3) guilt and exhaustion, which are related in that CSR casualties often feel guilty about their loss of functioning; (4) loneliness and vulnerability; (5) loss of control, including impulsive behaviors such as running amok, as well as the inability to regulate emotional states or bodily functions; and (6) disorientation, including confusion, loss of concentration, and fainting. As Solomon (1993) noted, these dimensions are largely consistent with other accounts of acute war-zone stress reactions (e.g., Grinker & Spiegel, 1945; Kardiner & Spiegel, 1947).

In contrast to CSR, PTSD is a more clearly discernible syndrome comprising three clusters of symptoms: (1) reexperiencing the trauma, (2) numbing and avoidance, (3) and hyperarousal (APA, 1980, 1987, 1994). In PTSD, frightful and horrific images of traumatic war experiences force their way into consciousness in the form of intrusive thoughts, nightmares, and flashbacks. These symptoms, which many investigators regard as the hallmark of the disorder (e.g., Brett & Ostroff, 1985), may appear suddenly and without warning, unbidden and apparently uncued. Alternatively, they may be triggered by reminders of combat, including overt, obvious cues (e.g., war movies; hearing firecrackers or helicopters) as well as cues such as emotional states (e.g., sadness, anger, longing for intimacy) that have a more subtle association with the trauma.

Closely linked with the reexperiencing symptoms are a class of symptoms characterized by heightened states of physiological arousal, including exaggerated startle, irritability and anger, hypervigilance, sleep disturbance, and difficulty concentrating. These hyperarousal symptoms may be viewed as manifestations of conditioned emotional responses (e.g., Keane, Fairbank, Caddell, Zimering, & Bender, 1985) or as the sequelae of the chronic overstimulation of the "fight or flight" response (Kardiner & Spiegel, 1947; Kolb, 1987). The myriad dangers of a war zone demand of combatants a perpetual state of vigilance, leaving the sympathetic nervous system in a state of permanent "overdrive."

In order to reduce the painful impact of intrusions and arousal, veterans with PTSD employ a variety of avoidance strategies. They avoid situations reminiscent of combat (e.g., parades, veterans activities, hunting) and suppress trauma-related thoughts and feelings. Some succeed in blocking out painful memories altogether, leaving them with psychogenic amnesia for at least some portion of a traumatic event. In addition, they often evidence significant signs of psychic numbing similar to those seen in CSR. They are less interested in daily activities, feel distant or cut off from other people, and complain of feeling emotionally "shut down." Many veterans turn to the powerful numbing effects of alcohol and other drugs. They also may channel their emotional energy strategically, using rage to displace fear and vulnerability, or profound depression to preclude feeling anything at all. However, although these avoidance strategies can consume enormous energy, they are seldom completely successful, and traumatic memories continually threaten to break through into awareness. Herman (1992) has designated this ongoing struggle between intrusion and constriction as the central dialectic of trauma.

In addition to these cardinal symptom clusters, combat veterans with PTSD often suffer from a variety of associated problems. At the symptom level, one of the most important collateral features of war-zone-related PTSD is guilt (e.g., Glover, 1984; Kubany, 1994). Frequently PTSD patients feel guilty about their behavior in the war-zone (acts of commission), or about their failure to act at a crucial moment (acts of omission). They also may feel guilty simply about surviving when others around them were killed. Other associated symptoms include homicidal or suicidal ideation, verbal or physical aggression, and dissociative symptoms such as amnesia, depersonalization, derealization, and identity disturbance (Bremner, Steinberg, Southwick, Johnson, & Charney, 1993).

At the diagnostic level, one of the best-replicated findings regarding the clinical picture of PTSD is a high rate of comorbidity: That is, combat veterans with PTSD typically meet the criteria for at least one other psychiatric disorder (e.g., Keane & Wolfe, 1990; Kulka et al., 1990). For example, in the NVVRS (Kulka et al., 1990), veterans with PTSD had higher current and lifetime prevalence of every disorder assessed, relative to veterans without PTSD. Particularly high rates of alcohol abuse, generalized anxiety disorder, depression, and antisocial personality disorder were found among PTSD veterans. An astonishing 99% of the PTSD group met the lifetime criteria for at least one additional disorder, as compared to 41% of the non-PTSD group.

Data from our clinic (Orsillo, Weathers, Litz, Steinberg, & Keane, 1993) substantiates these results: Virtually every PTSD veteran in our sample had at least one other lifetime diagnosis, and relative to non-PTSD veterans, PTSD veterans had significantly higher rates of current and lifetime depression, panic, and social phobia. The PTSD veterans also had very high rates of alcohol and drug abuse, but they did not differ from control subjects in this regard, probably because most of the non-PTSD subjects also were seeking clinical services, many of them for substance use disorders.

Given the powerful, pervasive nature of the symptoms of PTSD, it is not surprising that this syndrome can have a deleterious effect on virtually every aspect of psychological functioning. In order to fully appreciate the impact of PTSD on the lives of afflicted veterans, it is crucial to look beyond a tally of symptoms and consider the functional impairment these symptoms cause. Such a view has been incorporated into the newly released diagnostic criteria for PTSD in the Diagnostic and Statistical Manual of Mental Disorders IV (DSM-IV) (APA, 1994), which include the new requirement that symptoms either cause significant distress or cause marked impairment in an important area of functioning.

A growing number of research studies have documented the disrupting effect of PTSD on veterans' lives. For example, Keane, Scott, Chavoya, Lamparski, and Fairbank (1985) found that Vietnam veterans with PTSD suffered a steep decline in the size and quality of their social support networks after the war, reporting significantly lower levels of support relative to veterans without PTSD. In a study of marital adjustment in Vietnam combat veterans, Carroll, Rueger, Foy, and Donahoe (1985) found that veterans with PTSD reported significantly more problems in self-disclosure, emotional expressiveness, and physical aggression with their spouses and partners, and poorer overall adjustment in their relationships, than did veterans without PTSD. Nezu and Carnavale (1987) found that PTSD in Vietnam veterans was associated with poorer interpersonal problem solving and greater emotion-focused versus problem-focused coping.

Jordan et al. (1992) recently completed a comprehensive investigation of the impact of PTSD on family and marital functioning conducted as part of the NVVRS. They found that relative to control groups veterans with PTSD were younger, less well-educated, less likely to be employed, and less likely to be married. Of the veterans who had been married, veterans with PTSD were more likely to be divorced. They also found that veterans with PTSD and their spouses and partners report more marital problems, more parenting problems, more family violence, and poorer overall family adjustment. Such findings demonstrate that the repercussions of PTSD are manifested in every sphere of afflicted veterans' social and occupational functioning.

Course

Although the cross-sectional symptom pictures of CSR and PTSD have been well documented, much less is known about the course of war-zone stress reactions. As discussed above, observations to date suggest that CSR represents the acute phase and PTSD represents the chronic phase of a disorder that unfolds over time. However, the relationship between these phases is not well understood. Prospective, longitudinal data are rare, and much of what is known is based on retrospective reports. Understanding the course of war-zone stress reactions requires the consideration of at least three key questions:

1. Do war-zone stress reactions constitute an acute or a chronic syndrome?
2. Does the onset of symptoms occur immediately or after a significant delay?
3. Are symptoms relatively stable over time, or is there evidence of a phasic disorder?

Regarding the first question, converging evidence from extensive clinical observations (e.g., Kardiner & Spiegel, 1947), epidemiological studies (e.g., Kulka et al., 1990), and long-term follow-up studies (e.g., Archibald & Tuddenham, 1965) clearly point to a chronic syndrome of war-zone stress. Virtually every study indicates that years and even decades after exposure to war, a significant proportion of veterans still suffer from what is now known as war-zone-related PTSD. For example, data from the NVVRS indicated that half of all Vietnam veterans who ever had PTSD still had it nearly two decades after the war. A 3-year follow-up of Israeli veterans with and without CSR (Solomon, 1993) revealed that 75% of CSR casualties were diagnosed with PTSD in at least 1 of the years and 28% had PTSD for all 3 years. In contrast, only 28% of the non-CSR group had PTSD at some point, and just 3% had PTSD for all 3 years. In our clinic, as in other Department of Veterans Affairs Medical Centers throughout America, we routinely assess and treat Vietnam veterans, and even Korean and WW II veterans, whose symptoms have persisted relatively unabated since discharge from the military.

More difficult to answer is the question of the timing of the onset of symptoms. The clinical and empirical evidence regarding CSR clearly indicates that at least in some veterans the onset of symptoms is immediate. However, during the Vietnam war, considerable controversy arose around this issue. Initial reports suggested that the rates of psychiatric casualties were much lower than in previous wars: about 1.2%, compared to 6% during the Korean conflict and 23% during WW II (see Bourne, 1970). Nonetheless, this optimistic outlook began to fade after it was discovered that following homecoming many veterans began to show significant impairment in functioning and symptoms of war-zone stress. Some investigators took this as evidence of a delayed stress syndrome (e.g., Figley, 1978). Indeed, we have seen a number of cases in our clinic in which the veteran returned from Vietnam and apparently functioned at a very high level, holding down steady employment, marrying, raising children, only to have an apparently abrupt onset of symptoms as many as 10 to 15 years later.

Still, such cases do not necessarily provide conclusive evidence of a true delayed stress response. There are a number of possible explanations for a delay in symptom reporting. One is that there is a true delayed stress syndrome in which the onset of symptoms occurs well after the end of the war—after an interval of months or even years in some cases. However, a second possibility is that symptoms do begin immediately, but some afflicted individuals postpone seeking treatment, perhaps because they have adequate coping responses, or because their symptoms initially are relatively mild. Whatever the reason, even though they are symptomatic all along, they do not come to the attention of mental health workers until well after the war. A third possibility is that for some combatants the initial symptom picture may consist primarily of negative symptoms (i.e., avoidance and emotional numbing), so that the full stress-response syndrome may go undetected.

Solomon (1993) presented data directly addressing this issue. In an examination of 150 Israeli veterans who sought treatment for PTSD at least 6 months after combat, she found that: ". . . genuinely delayed onset was quite rare in our sample. In the vast majority of the cases, there was no true latency period: The veterans had approached the mental health services following protracted, often unremitted suffering (p. 213)." In this sample only 10% were classified as genuine cases of delayed-onset PTSD. For the rest of the sample, the apparent delay in symptom onset could be accounted for by delayed help-seeking for chronic PTSD (40%), exacerbation of subclinical PTSD (33%), or reactivation of an earlier CSR from a previous war (13%). For a few veterans, the presenting symptoms turned out to be related to a psychiatric disorder other than PTSD (4%).

The last issue to be considered is whether the symptom picture shows variability over time. Some have argued that PTSD is a phasic disorder, characterized by phases of intrusive symptoms alternating with phases of avoidance and numbing symptoms (e.g., Horowitz, 1986). This may be the case for some combatants, although there is scant evidence bearing directly on this issue. In a similar vein, Solomon (1993) reported that a significant proportion of Israeli veterans showed apparent fluctuation of symptoms over time. Nearly one-half of the CSR group and one-fourth of the non-CSR subjects had some variability in diagnostic status across the 3 years of her follow-up study. However, the PTSD veterans we see in our clinic typically present with significant numbers of both intrusive and avoidance symptoms, and based on their retrospective accounts, they appear to have had the same symptom configuration for extended periods of time. The issue of symptom variability over time clearly merits further investigation.

Prevalence

In the last 15 years, investigators have conducted a number of epidemiological studies designed both to determine the prevalence of PTSD and other psychological problems in combat veterans and to identify risk factors associated with an increased likelihood of developing a stress-related syndrome (for a review, see Keane, 1990; Kulka et al., 1991). The available studies have focused almost exclusively on Vietnam veterans, and with few exceptions they have included only male veterans as subjects.

Estimates of the prevalence of PTSD and other stress-related syndromes vary widely from study to study. This is in large part the result of methodological differences across studies, particularly regarding the methods used to select subjects and to determine "caseness," or the presence or absence of a disorder in a given individual. Some studies have investigated samples that either are too small or are unrepresentative of the population of all veterans, and most studies have relied on assessment instruments that are inadequate for identifying PTSD (Keane, 1990; Kulka et al., 1991). Early studies were conducted prior to the publication of official diagnostic criteria and prior to the development of psychometrically sound diagnostic instruments. Thus, the data that were collected did not necessarily correspond directly to PTSD as currently conceptualized, and the measures used had unknown validity (see Kulka et al., 1991).

In one of the earliest studies, Egendorf, Kadushin, Laufer, Rothbart, and Sloan (1981) used a probability sampling procedure to survey a total of 1,340 Vietnam theater veterans, Vietnam era veterans, and nonveteran control subjects. Because the study was conducted in the late 1970s, the survey did not include questions corresponding directly to the criteria for PTSD developed for the DSM-III (APA, 1980). Rather, the investigators determined the prevalence of significant stress reactions based on a 22-item symptom checklist that overlapped with PTSD symptoms. Depending on the region of the country being sampled, they estimated that 21% to 26% of theater veterans had a current stress reaction, as compared to 17% to 18% of era veterans and 14% to 19% of nonveterans. Veterans exposed to heavy combat had an even greater risk for having a current stress reaction (34%–35%). Also, ethnic minority status was a significant risk factor: Both blacks (39%–41%) and Chicanos (38%) were more likely to have a current stress reaction relative to whites (17%–20%).

In another early study, Card (1983) surveyed 481 Vietnam theater veterans, 502 Vietnam era veterans, and 487 nonveterans, all of whom were first studied as ninth graders in 1960 as a part of Project TALENT, a longitudinal study of achievement. Again, the survey did not include questions specifically designed to measure PTSD symptoms. Instead, a diagnosis of PTSD was derived by fitting questionnaire items, including modified items from the Brief Symptom Inventory (BSI) (Derogatis & Spencer, 1982), to PTSD criteria. The current prevalence of PTSD for theater veterans was 19.3%, which was significantly higher than the prevalence for era veterans (12.9%) or nonveterans (12.1%). As in the Egendorf et al. (1981) study, veterans with high levels of combat exposure were at increased risk for PTSD, with a current prevalence of 27%. Card (1983) also found that exposure to war-zone stress was the strongest contributor to PTSD. Of 10 specific combat exposure variables, 8 were significantly associated with PTSD symptomatology, as opposed to only 1 of 14 premilitary sociodemographic and personality variables (low self-confidence at age 15) and only 1 of 11 military adjustment variables (high alcohol consumption in the military).

Two additional studies employed survey instruments containing questions that more directly assessed PTSD symptoms. Snow, Stellman, Stellman, and

Sommer (1988) surveyed 2,858 male Vietnam veterans identified from American Legion membership lists. The PTSD measure was a symptom checklist based on DSM-III criteria. Although prevalence estimates varied depending on how exposure to combat was defined, as many as 15% of veterans were found to have current PTSD. Goldberg, True, Eisen, and Henderson (1990) examined 715 monozygotic male twin pairs who were discordant for service in the Vietnam theater. Again, the PTSD measure was a symptom checklist based on PTSD criteria. The current prevalence rate of PTSD for twins who were Vietnam theater veterans was 16.8% as compared to 5% for their cotwins who served in the military but not in Southeast Asia. Also, for the twins exposed to the Vietnam theater, the prevalence of PTSD increased as the degree of combat exposure increased: At the lowest levels of combat exposure these twins were up to three times more likely to have PTSD relative to their cotwins, but at the highest levels of combat, they were more than nine times more likely to have PTSD.

More recently, in order to estimate the lifetime prevalence of PTSD in the general population, Helzer, Robins, and McEvoy (1987) administered the PTSD module of the Diagnostic Interview Schedule (DIS) (Robins, Helzer, Croughan, & Ratcliff, 1981) to respondents at the St. Louis site of the Epidemiological Catchment Area (ECA) study. Of the total sample of 2,493 subjects, 64 were male Vietnam theater veterans. The investigators found that the lifetime prevalence of PTSD was 4% among combat-exposed veterans who had not been wounded, 20% among wounded veterans, and 6.3% for all veterans combined. Relative to an estimated 1% lifetime prevalence of PTSD in the general population, these rates suggest that Vietnam theater veterans are at increased risk for developing PTSD. However, the small sample size does not allow for stable estimates of prevalence and makes it difficult to generalize to Vietnam veterans in general.

In the Vietnam Experiences Study (VES), the Centers for Disease Control (1988) used the PTSD module of the DIS to determine current and lifetime PTSD diagnostic status in 2,490 Vietnam veterans. The lifetime prevalence of PTSD was found to be 14.7%, and the current prevalence (previous month) was 2.2%. This current prevalence estimate is significantly lower than in other studies, and this discrepancy has been a target of criticism. In particular, the VES has been criticized for reliance on the DIS to assess PTSD. The authors of the NVVRS have argued that the version of the DIS PTSD module used in the VES has very low sensitivity for diagnosing PTSD, meaning that it fails to detect true cases of PTSD, and thus it substantially underestimates the actual prevalence of the disorder (Kulka et al., 1991).

The NVVRS (Kulka et al., 1990) surpassed all other epidemiological studies of combat-related PTSD conducted to date. This study had several unique advantages, including the use of a national probability sample to ensure representativeness, the use of multiple measures of PTSD in recognition of the fallibility of any single measure, and the inclusion of both male and female veterans and controls. Kulka et al. (1990) found that among Vietnam theater veterans the current prevalence of PTSD was 15.2% for males and 8.5% for females, with a lifetime prevalence of 30.9% for males and 26.9% for females. In addition, 11.1% of males and 7.8% of females had current partial PTSD, meaning that they had a significant number of PTSD symptoms but did not meet all the criteria for the disorder. These data indicate that more than a quarter of all Vietnam theater veterans currently have PTSD or high levels of PTSD symptomatology. The current prevalence of PTSD was much lower for Vietnam era veterans (2.5% for males and 1.2% for females) and civilian controls (1.1% males and 0.3% females).

As in other studies, veterans with the greatest exposure to combat were at significantly elevated risk for developing PTSD. For those with high levels of combat exposure, the current prevalence of PTSD was 35.8% for males and 17.5% for females, whereas for those with low to moderate levels of combat exposure, the prevalence was 8.5% for males and 2.5% for females. Also, ethnicity was again an important risk factor for PTSD. The current prevalence of PTSD was 20.6% for blacks and 27.8% for Hispanics, as compared to 13.7% for white/other veterans.

RISK AND RESILIENCE

A large number of empirical studies, including the epidemiologic studies described above, point to the unambiguous conclusion that the level of exposure to war-zone trauma is the best predictor of PTSD, with greater exposure leading to greater symptomatology. Nonetheless, clinical investigators have identified other risk factors that may render certain individuals particularly susceptible to the psychological impact of war-zone stress. In addition to the risk factors noted earlier, studies have focused primarily on genetic influences and developmental experiences. In addition, a few studies have identified resilience factors that may buffer the effects of war-zone stress for some veterans.

Genetic Factors

Recent family studies and twin studies have investigated the possibility of a genetic contribution to adjustment to war-zone trauma. According to the logic of the family-study approach, if there is a genetic predisposition for combat-related PTSD, then close relatives of veterans with PTSD should be at increased risk for PTSD, or perhaps at increased risk for disorders commonly found to be comorbid with PTSD such as depression and panic disorder. In the first study of psychiatric disorders in the families of veterans with PTSD, Davidson, Swartz, Storck, Krishnan, and Hammett (1985) interviewed 36 World War II, Korean, and Vietnam veterans with PTSD, asking them to report psychopathology in their first degree relatives. For purposes of comparison, these investigators also reported data previously collected on nonveterans diagnosed with either depression or generalized anxiety disorder.

They found that the rate of anxiety disorders among the relatives of the

PTSD subjects was higher than among the relatives of depressed subjects and comparable to that found in the relatives of subjects with generalized anxiety. Also, in both the PTSD and generalized anxiety groups, relatives had roughly equal rates of anxiety and depression, whereas in the depression group, relatives had much higher rates of depression than of anxiety disorders. Although this pilot study had several important methodological limitations, including small sample size, lack of matched control groups, and reliance on the family-history method, it provided some evidence that PTSD may be more closely related to other anxiety disorders than to depression.

Davidson, Smith, and Kudler (1989) conducted a second study designed to address some of the limitations of the first. To determine family history of psychiatric disorders, they conducted family-history interviews with 108 World War II, Korean, and Vietnam veterans with PTSD, all but two of whom had been in combat. They also interviewed subjects in three different control groups, including 21 nonpsychiatric controls, 24 subjects with major depression, and 15 alcoholics. Overall, very few differences were found among the four groups. When compared to the families of the three control groups, the families of veterans with PTSD were not found to be at increased risk for any of the psychiatric disorders assessed. In fact, only two significant differences were found between the PTSD group and any of the control groups. First, the siblings and parents of depressed subjects were at greater risk both for chronic depression and for a category combining both chronic and remitting depression, relative to the siblings and parents of PTSD subjects. Second, the children of depressed subjects were at greater risk for generalized anxiety disorder than were the children of PTSD subjects.

An intriguing finding involving the families of PTSD subjects emerged when the investigators compared the 106 PTSD subjects who had been in combat with the 31 control subjects who also had been in combat (Davidson et al., 1989). The siblings and parents of PTSD subjects were at increased risk for a category combining all anxiety disorders assessed (generalized anxiety, phobic/panic, and PTSD). Overall, this study suggests that PTSD does not have a familial association with depression but may have a familial association with other anxiety disorders.

Although family studies are suggestive of genetic influences, they cannot isolate the impact of genetic influences from the impact of shared environment. Twin studies and adoption studies provide much clearer evidence of an independent contribution of heredity to the development of psychopathology. To date, no adoption studies of PTSD have been conducted, but in a recent twin study, investigators attempted to disentangle the relative contributions of genetic factors and environmental factors to the development of PTSD symptoms.

True et al. (1993) measured the degree of combat exposure and the severity of PTSD symptoms in 4,042 pairs of male twins from the Vietnam Era Twin (VET) Registry. Both members of all twin pairs served on active duty at some point during the Vietnam era. Fifty-five percent of the twin pairs were monozygotic (MZ) or identical twins, and the rest were dizygotic (DZ) or fraternal twins. The logic of the twin study approach is that if genetic factors are important in the development of a disorder, then MZ twins, who are genetically identical, should have greater similarity of symptoms relative to DZ twins, who on average share only half of their genes. Thus, if heredity is an important etiological factor in combat-related PTSD, then MZ twins should be more similar than DZ twins in terms of PTSD symptoms.

However, as True et al. (1993) point out, a complicating factor in applying the twin study methodology to combat-related PTSD is that MZ twins are more likely to be concordant for exposure to combat. This leaves open the possibility that any greater similarity of PTSD symptoms in MZ twins relative to DZ twins could result from this higher concordance for exposure to combat. Therefore, they conducted an analysis allowing them to estimate the genetic contribution to PTSD symptoms above and beyond the genetic contribution to combat exposure. They concluded that "heritability contributes substantially to the susceptibility for nearly all symptoms of PTSD, even after taking into account differences in concordance for combat exposure between MZ and DZ twins" (p. 261). Estimates of the amount of variance in PTSD symptoms caused by genetic influences ranged from 13% to 30% for reexperiencing symptoms, 30% to 34% for avoidance symptoms, and 28% to 32% for hyperarousal symptoms. Although these estimates indicate a significant impact of heredity on the development of PTSD, they can also be seen as indicating that two-thirds or more of the variability in PTSD symptoms is attributable to environmental factors such as exposure to combat and various developmental risk factors.

Developmental Factors

A number of investigations have focused on the role of premilitary vulnerability in the development of PTSD, including variables such as unstable families, childhood physical and sexual abuse, the presence of conduct disorder or other psychiatric problems, and having a father who had been in combat. Fontana and Rosenheck (1993) recently reviewed studies examining the contribution of these and other factors to the development of PTSD. They noted that these studies suffer from a variety of methodological problems, making it difficult to ascertain the actual degree of impact of developmental history. Using a sophisticated statistical approach, they evaluated the causal contribution of a number of variables from several domains, including premilitary vulnerabilities, military entry conditions (e.g., age of entry and drafted versus enlisted), war-zone experiences, and dissociative reactions during combat.

Although several premilitary variables had an indirect effect on PTSD, Fontana and Rosenheck (1993) found that only one, having a father who had been in combat, made a direct contribution to the development of PTSD. They concluded that:

[The sons of combat veterans] joined the military at a younger age and were more prone to participate in abusive violence than others. . . . We believe that an idealization of combat and war as extension of the father may be an important mechanism involved in these paths. Such an idealization may either prime young soldiers to engage in destruction as a fulfillment of the heroic image for themselves, or it may result in severe disillusionment in the face of the unromantic realities of war. It is also possible that fathers who were damaged psychologically in combat passed their traumatization on to some of their sons. For these sons, simply being in a war zone may have been sufficient to reactivate the secondary traumatization from their childhood. (p. 492)

Several very recent studies have examined more closely the role of childhood abuse in the development of PTSD. Bremner, Southwick, Johnson, Yehuda, and Charney (1993) found that Vietnam veterans with PTSD had significantly higher rates of childhood physical abuse and higher overall rates of early trauma than did veterans without PTSD. This finding was replicated by Zaidi and Foy (1994) who found a strong positive correlation between early physical abuse and combat-related PTSD. In general, childhood trauma as a risk factor for combat-related PTSD has been largely ignored in previous investigations. However, these new findings suggest that the systematic evaluation of early abuse experiences should be a standard part of any assessment of PTSD in combat veterans.

Resilience Factors

Relatively few studies have attempted to identify the characteristics of combat veterans who make a positive adjustment following their war experiences. Hendin and Haas (1984b) summarized their findings from intensive interviews with 10 Vietnam combat veterans who did not evidence PTSD. They identified the following characteristics that this group of veterans seemed to have in common: (1) the ability to function calmly under pressure; (2) the use of understanding and judgment; (3) the acceptance of fear in themselves and in others; (4) a lack of participation in excessive violence; and (5) an absence of guilt. In a second study Wolfe, Keane, Kaloupek, Mora, and Wine (1993) examined 152 Vietnam combat veterans, identifying a subset of veterans with high levels of combat exposure who seemed to have adjusted well to life after the military. In this study, the most powerful predictor of positive adjustment was the use of nonavoidant, problem-focused methods of coping with stress. Although these studies offer only preliminary evidence, they clearly point to the need to better understand how some veterans are able to adapt favorably to their war-zone experiences.

WOMEN IN THE WAR ZONE

A pressing issue in the investigation of military trauma is the impact of war-zone stress on women. Until recently, women have not been recognized sufficiently for their roles in the military in general, nor for their direct contributions to war-zone operations in particular. Thus, the literature on the unique psychological impact of war-zone stress on women is still quite limited (Wolfe, 1993). Historically, two factors account for this lack of attention to women veterans. First, war-zone-related PTSD has been stereotyped as stemming from extreme and direct life-threatening combat events, thus implicitly excluding women who served in combat-support and service-support roles (see King et al., 1995). Second, women have tended not to seek services at Department of Veterans Affairs Medical Centers, fostering the erroneous conclusion that they have not suffered from PTSD and other psychosocial problems stemming from war-zone exposure.

Recently, there has been a positive shift in the manner in which policy makers in America perceive women veterans' contributions to the military. There is growing recognition that women in a war zone can experience a wide range of potentially traumatic stressors and can develop PTSD and other psychological problems requiring treatment (Baker, Menard, & Johns, 1989; Schnaier, 1986). As a result of the greater support and validation women veterans have received on a societal level, more of them have begun to disclose memories of their war-zone experiences. As women play an increasingly active role in the military, serving in greater numbers and in roles that expose them to greater levels of combat, gender differences in response to war-zone stress will become a crucial focus for research.

SUMMARY AND CONCLUSIONS

War is a terrifying, horrifying experience that taxes every physical and psychological resource and leaves an indelible imprint on the psyche long after the fighting stops. It differs from many other traumatic life events in its prolonged intensity and its blurring of the distinction between victim and perpetrator. War leads to a characteristic stress response known in its acute phase as combat stress reaction and in its chronic phase as posttraumatic stress disorder. The degree of combat exposure consistently has been shown to be the most powerful predictor of war-related psychological problems, but individual differences in genetics, developmental history, and personality factors may shape an individual's unique adaptation to trauma. Although much progress has been made in understanding the long-term effects of exposure to war-zone stress, many questions involving the etiology, assessment, and treatment of war-related stress syndromes remain unanswered. Unfortunately, although war may not be an inevitability, there is every indication that future military conflicts will continue to provide opportunities to investigate all of the issues raised in this chapter regarding the impact of war-zone stress on psychological functioning.

REFERENCES

American Psychiatric Association. (1952). *Diagnostic and statistical manual of mental disorders.* Washington, DC: Author.

American Psychiatric Association. (1968). *Diagnostic and statistical manual of mental disorders* (2nd ed.). Washington, DC: Author.

American Psychiatric Association. (1980). *Diagnostic and statistical manual of mental disorders* (3rd ed.). Washington, DC: Author.

American Psychiatric Association. (1987). *Diagnostic and statistical manual of mental disorders* (3rd ed.-rev.). Washington, DC: Author.

American Psychiatric Association. (1994). *Diagnostic and statistical manual of mental disorders* (4th ed.). Washington, DC: Author.

Archibald, H. C., & Tuddenham, R. D. (1965). Persistent stress reaction after combat. *Archives of General Psychiatry, 12,* 475–481.

Baker, R. R., Menard, S. W., & Johns, L. A. (1989). The military nurse experience in Vietnam: Stress and impact. *Journal of Clinical Psychology, 45,* 736–744.

Bleuler, E. (1924). *Textbook of psychiatry.* New York: Macmillan.

Bourne, P. G. (1970). Military psychiatry and the Vietnam experience. *American Journal of Psychiatry, 127,* 481–488.

Bremner, J. D., Southwick, S. M., Johnson, D. R., Yehuda, R., & Charney, D. S. (1993). Childhood physical abuse and combat-related posttraumatic stress disorder in Vietnam veterans. *American Journal of Psychiatry, 150,* 235–239.

Bremner, J. D., Steinberg, M., Southwick, S. M., Johnson, D. R., & Charney, D. S. (1993). Use of the structured clinical interview for DSM-IV dissociative disorders for systematic assessment of dissociative symptoms in posttraumatic stress disorder. *American Journal of Psychiatry, 150,* 1011–1014.

Breslau, N., & Davis, G. C. (1987). Posttraumatic stress disorder: The etiologic specificity of wartime stressors. *American Journal of Psychiatry, 144,* 578–583.

Brett, E. A., & Ostroff, R. (1985). Imagery and posttraumatic stress disorder: An overview. *American Journal of Psychiatry, 142,* 417–424.

Card, J. J. (1983). *Lives after Vietnam.* Lexington, MA: Lexington Books.

Carroll, E. M., Rueger, D. B., Foy, D. W., & Donahoe, C. P. (1985). Vietnam combat veterans with posttraumatic stress disorder: Analysis of marital and cohabiting adjustment. *Journal of Abnormal Psychology, 94,* 329–337.

Centers for Disease Control. (1988). Health status of Vietnam veterans: I. Psychosocial characteristics. *Journal of the American Medical Association, 259,* 2701–2707.

Davidson, J., Smith, R., & Kudler, H. (1989). Familial psychiatric illness in chronic posttraumatic stress disorder. *Comprehensive Psychiatry, 30,* 339–345.

Davidson, J., Swartz, M., Storck, M., Krishnan, R. R., & Hammett, E. (1985). A diagnostic and family study of posttraumatic stress disorder. *American Journal of Psychiatry, 142,* 90–93.

Derogatis, L. R., & Spencer, P. M. (1982). *The Brief Symptom Inventory administration, scoring, and procedures manual-I.* Baltimore: Clinical Psychometric Research Institute.

Egendorf, A., Kadushin, C., Laufer, R. S., Rothbart, G., & Sloan, L. (1981). *Legacies of Vietnam: Comparative adjustment of veterans and their peers.* New York: The Center for Policy Research.

Figley, C. R. (1978). Symptoms of delayed combat stress among a college sample of Vietnam veterans. *Military Medicine, 143,* 107–110.

Fontana, A., & Rosenheck, R. (1993). A causal model of the etiology of war-related PTSD. *Journal of Traumatic Stress, 6,* 475–500.

Gallers, J., Foy, D. W., Donahoe, C. P., & Goldfarb, J. (1988). Post-traumatic stress disorder in Vietnam combat veterans: Effects of traumatic violence exposure and military adjustment. *Journal of Traumatic Stress, 1,* 181–192.

Glover, H. (1984). Survival guilt and the Vietnam veteran. *Journal of Nervous and Mental Disease, 172,* 393–397.

Goldberg, J., True, W. R., Eisen, S. A., & Henderson, W. G. (1990). A twin study of the effects of the Vietnam war on posttraumatic stress disorder. *Journal of the American Medical Association, 263,* 1227–1232.

Green, B. L. (1993). Identifying survivors at risk: Trauma and stressors across events. In J. P. Wilson & B. Raphael (Eds.), *International handbook of traumatic stress syndromes* (pp. 135–144). New York: Plenum Press.

Green, B. L., Wilson, J. P., & Lindy, J. D. (1985). Conceptualizing PTSD: A psychosocial framework. In C. R. Figley (Ed.), *Trauma and its wake: The study and treatment of posttraumatic stress disorder* (pp. 53–69). New York: Brunner/Mazel.

Grinker, R. R., & Spiegel, J. P. (1945). *Men under stress.* Philadelphia: Blakiston.

Haley, S. A. (1974). When the patient reports atrocities. *Archives of General Psychiatry, 30,* 191–196.

Helzer, J. E., Robins, L. N., & McEvoy, L. (1987). Post-traumatic stress disorder in the general population: Findings of the Epidemiological Catchment Area Survey. *New England Journal of Medicine, 317,* 1630–1634.

Hendin, H., & Haas, A. P. (1984a). Posttraumatic stress disorders in veterans of early American wars. *Psychohistory Review, 25,* 25–30.

Hendin, H., & Haas, A. P. (1984b). Combat adaptations of Vietnam veterans without posttraumatic stress disorders. *American Journal of Psychiatry, 141,* 956–960.

Herman, J. L. (1992). *Trauma and recovery.* Basic Books.

Horowitz, M. J. (1986). *Stress response syndromes* (2nd ed.). Northvale, NJ: Jason Aronson.

Hunter, E. J. (1993). The Vietnam prisoner of war experience. In J. P. Wilson & B. Raphael (Eds.), *International handbook of traumatic stress syndromes* (pp. 297–303). New York: Plenum Press.

Jordan, B. K., Marmar, C. R., Fairbank, J. A., Schlenger, W. E., Kulka, R. A., Hough, R. L., & Weiss, D. S. (1992). Problems in families of male Vietnam veterans with posttraumatic stress disorder. *Journal of Consulting and Clinical Psychology, 60,* 916–926.

Kardiner, A., & Spiegel, H. (1947). *War stress and neurotic illness.* New York: Harper.

Keane, T. M. (1990, Fall). The epidemiology of post-traumatic stress disorder: Some comments and concerns. *PTSD Research Quarterly,* pp. 1–3.

Keane, T. M., Fairbank, J. A., Caddell, J. M., Zimering, R. T., & Bender, M. E. (1985). A behavioral approach to assessing and treating post-traumatic stress disorder in Vietnam veterans. In C. R. Figley (Ed.), *Trauma and its wake (vol. 1)* (pp. 257–294). New York: Brunner/Mazel.

Keane, T. M., Scott, W. O., Chavoya, G. A., Lamparski, D. M., & Fairbank, J. A. (1985). Social support in Vietnam veterans with posttraumatic stress disorder: A comparative analysis. *Journal of Consulting and Clinical Psychology, 53,* 95–102.

Keane, T. M., & Wolfe, J. (1990). Comorbidity in post-traumatic stress disorder: An analysis of community and clinical studies. *Journal of Applied Social Psychology, 20,* 1776–1788.

Keegan, J. (1993). *A history of warfare.* New York: Alfred A. Knopf.

Kentsmith, D. K. (1986). Principles of battlefield psychiatry. *Military Medicine, 151,* 89–96.

King, D. W., King, L. A., Gudanowski, D. M., & Vreven, D. L. (1995). Alternative representations of war zone trauma: Relationships to posttraumatic stress disorder and other outcomes in male and female Vietnam veterans. *Journal of Abnormal Psychology, 104,* 184–196.

Kinzie, J. D. (1993). Posttraumatic effects and their treatment among Southeast Asian refugees. In J. P. Wilson & B. Raphael (Eds.), *International handbook of traumatic stress syndromes* (pp. 311–319). New York: Plenum Press.

Kolb, L. C. (1987). A neuropsychological hypothesis explaining posttraumatic stress disorders. *American Journal of Psychiatry, 144,* 989–995.

Kraepelin, E. (1913). *Lectures on clinical psychiatry* (3rd English ed.). New York: William Wood.

Kubany, E. S. (1994). A cognitive model of guilt typology in combat-related PTSD. *Journal of Traumatic Stress, 7,* 3–19.

Kulka, R. A., Schlenger, W. E., Fairbank, J. A., Hough, R. L., Jordan, B. K., Marmar, C. R., & Weiss, D. S. (1990). *Trauma and the Vietnam War generation: Report of findings from the National Vietnam Veterans Readjustment Study.* New York: Brunner/Mazel.

Kulka, R. A., Schlenger, W. E., Fairbank, J. A., Jordan, B. K., Hough, R. L., Marmar, C. R., & Weiss, D. S. (1991). Assessment of posttraumatic stress disorder in the community: Prospects and pitfalls from recent studies of Vietnam veterans. *Psychological Assessment: A Journal of Consulting and Clinical Psychology, 3,* 547–560.

Laufer, R. S., Gallops, M. S., & Frey-Wouters, E. (1984). War stress and trauma: The Vietnam experience. *Journal of Health and Social Behavior, 25,* 65–85.

Lifton, R. J. (1974). "Death imprints" on youth in Vietnam. *Journal of Clinical Child Psychology, 3,* 47–49.

Mollica, R. F., Wyshak, G., & Lavelle, J. (1987). The psychosocial impact of war trauma and torture on Southeast Asian refugees. *American Journal of Psychiatry, 144,* 1567–1572.

Nezu, A. M., & Carnevale, G. J. (1987). Interpersonal problem solving and coping reactions of Vietnam veterans with posttraumatic stress disorder. *Journal of Abnormal Psychology, 96,* 155–157.

O'Brien, T. (1993, April). Ambush! *Boston Magazine,* pp. 62–106.

Orsillo, S. M., Weathers, F. W., Litz, B. T., Steinberg, H. R., & Keane, T. M. (1993, November). *Current and lifetime prevalence of comorbid psychiatric disorders in combat-related PTSD.* Paper presented at the annual meeting of the Association for Advancement of Behavior Therapy, Atlanta, GA.

Parson, E. R. (1985). The intercultural setting: Encountering black Viet Nam veterans. In S. M. Sonnenberg, A. S. Blank, & J. A. Talbott (Eds.), *The trauma of war: Stress and recovery in Viet Nam veterans* (pp. 359–387). Washington, DC: American Psychiatric Press.

Pina, G. (1985). Diagnosis and treatment of post-traumatic stress disorder in Hispanic Viet Nam veterans. In S. M. Sonnenberg, A. S. Blank, & J. A. Talbott (Eds.), *The trauma of war: Stress and recovery in Viet Nam veterans* (pp. 389–402). Washington, DC: American Psychiatric Press.

Robins, L. N., Helzer, J. E., Croughan, J., & Ratcliff, K. S. (1981). National Institute of Mental Health diagnostic interview schedule: Its history, characteristics, and validity. *Archives of General Psychiatry, 38,* 381–389.

Salmon, T. W. (1919). The war neuroses and their lesson. *New York State Journal of Medicine, 51,* 993–994.

Schlenger, W. E., Kulka, R. A., Fairbank, J. A., Hough, R. L., Jordan, B. K., Marmar, C. R., & Weiss, D. S. (1992). The prevalence of post-traumatic stress disorder in the Vietnam generation: A multimethod, multisource assessment of psychiatric disorder. *Journal of Traumatic Stress, 5,* 333–363.

Schnaier, J. A. (1986). A study of women Vietnam veterans and their mental health adjustment. In C. R. Figley (Ed.), *Trauma and its wake. Vol. II: Traumatic stress theory, research, and intervention* (pp. 97–132). New York: Brunner/Mazel.

Shay, J. (1991). Learning about combat stress from Homer's *Iliad. Journal of Traumatic Stress, 4,* 561–579.

Snow, B. R., Stellman, J. M., Stellman, S. D., & Sommer, J. F. (1988). Post-traumatic stress disorder among American Legionnaires in relation to combat experience in Vietnam: Associated and contributing factors. *Environmental Research, 47,* 175–192.

Solomon, Z. (1993). *Combat stress reaction: The enduring toll of war.* New York: Plenum Press.

Sutker, P. B., Winstead, D. K., Galina, Z. H., & Allain, A. N. (1991). Cognitive deficits and psychopathology among former prisoners of war and combat veterans of the Korean conflict. *American Journal of Psychiatry, 148,* 67–72.

Trimble, M. (1981). *Post-traumatic neurosis.* New York: John Wiley & Sons.

True, W. R., Rice, J., Eisen, S. A., Heath, A. C., Goldberg, J., Lyons, M. J., & Nowak, J. (1993).

A twin study of genetic and environmental contributions to liability for posttraumatic stress symptoms. *Archives of General Psychiatry, 50,* 257–264.

Ursano, R. J. (1985). Viet Nam era prisoners of war: Studies of U.S. Air Force prisoners of war. In S. M. Sonnenberg, A. S. Blank, & J. A. Talbott (Eds.), *The trauma of war: Stress and recovery in Viet Nam veterans* (pp. 339–358). Washington, DC: American Psychiatric Press.

Wolfe, J. (1993, Winter). Female military veterans and traumatic stress. *PTSD Research Quarterly,* pp. 1–4.

Wolfe, J., Brown, P. J., Furey, J., & Levin, K. B. (1993). Development of a wartime stressor scale for women. *Psychological Assessment, 5,* 330–335.

Wolfe, J., Keane, T. M., Kaloupek, D. G., Mora, C. A., & Wine, P. (1993). Patterns of positive readjustment in Vietnam combat veterans. *Journal of Traumatic Stress, 6,* 179–193.

Yager, T., Laufer, R., & Gallops, M. (1984). Some problems associated with war experience in men of the Vietnam generation. *Archives of General Psychiatry, 41,* 327–333.

Yehuda, R., Southwick, S. M., & Giller, E. L. (1992). Exposure to atrocities and severity of chronic posttraumatic stress disorder in Vietnam combat veterans. *American Journal of Psychiatry, 149,* 333–336.

Zaidi, L. Y., & Foy, D. W. (1994). Childhood abuse experiences and combat-related PTSD. *Journal of Traumatic Stress, 7,* 33–42.

6

Violent Crime and Mental Health

ROCHELLE F. HANSON, DEAN G. KILPATRICK,
SHERRY A. FALSETTI, and HEIDI S. RESNICK

OVERVIEW

Violent crime has become one of the most significant concerns among people today (Kilpatrick, Seymour, & Boyle, 1991), and rates of violent crime have risen substantially in America as well as in other countries around the world (Reiss & Roth, 1993; Rosenberg & Fenley, 1991). Many Americans have been victims of violent crime sometime during their lives, and many other Americans, who have not yet been victimized, fear becoming violent crime victims in the future (Kilpatrick et al., 1991). This fear of crime among Americans is not unfounded. In 1990, more than 23,000 people in the United States were homicide victims (Reiss & Roth, 1993), and over 6 million violent crimes were disclosed to interviewers from the National Crime Victimization Survey (Bureau of Justice Statistics, 1990). As a consequence, violent crime and fear of violent crime have become important antecedents of fear and anxiety in America. Moreover, violent crime is a predominant contributing factor to the development of mental health problems, most commonly, posttraumatic stress disorder (PTSD) (Breslau, Davis, Andreski, & Peterson, 1991; Kilpatrick et al., 1989; Resnick, Kilpatrick, Dansky, Saunders, & Best, 1993).

ROCHELLE F. HANSON · Center for Sexual Assault/Abuse Recovery and Education (CARE), Student Health Care Center, University of Florida, Gainesville, Florida 32611.   DEAN G. KILPATRICK, SHERRY A. FALSETTI, and HEIDI S. RESNICK · National Crime Victims Research and Treatment Center, Department of Psychiatry and Behavioral Sciences, Medical University of South Carolina, Charleston, South Carolina 29425.

Traumatic Stress: From Theory to Practice, edited by John R. Freedy and Stevan E. Hobfoll. Plenum Press, New York, 1995.

Violent crime is not limited to the United States, but the United States has the dubious distinction of having the highest violent crime rate of any industrialized nation (Reiss & Roth, 1993; Rosenberg & Mercy, 1991). Because the bulk of extant research focuses primarily on violent crime and its mental health impact in the United States, this chapter emphasizes work done in the United States. The extent to which findings from the United States can be generalized to other parts of the world is an empirical question, but what has been learned about the violent crime and its mental health consequences in the United States has substantial relevance to other industrialized nations.

Our goals for this chapter are to (1) discuss key conceptual and methodological issues involved in measuring violence and its mental health impact; (2) present prevalence data for violent crime and for crime-related mental health problems; (3) describe and present supporting evidence for a hypothetical model addressing risk factors for exposure to violent crime; (4) describe violence-related mental health problems following exposure to violent crime; (5) discuss factors that increase or decrease the risk of developing violence-related mental health problems; and (6) highlight some implications for prevention and mental health treatment.

CONCEPTUAL AND METHODOLOGICAL ISSUES IN MEASURING VIOLENT CRIME AND MENTAL HEALTH IMPACT

Obtaining an accurate understanding of the scope and nature of violent crime as well as the mental health impact of such victimization requires some knowledge of important conceptual and methodological issues. Elsewhere, Kilpatrick, Resnick, Saunders, and Best (in press) identified several such issues. First, violent crime history, particularly that involving highly stigmatized crimes such as sexual assault, is difficult to measure. Second, the violent crime history of a given individual is often complex. Many individuals have experienced several different violent crimes occurring throughout their lifetimes. As Kilpatrick et al. (in press) note, much extant research suffers from one or more of the following problems: (1) exclusive focus on only one type of violent crime, occurring at only one time of life, and perpetrated by only one type of assailant; (2) failure to consider the potential impact of multiple violent crime events; (3) use of nonrepresentative samples; (4) use of univariate data analytic models that do not examine for complex relationships between violent crime risk factors and mental health risk factors; and (5) failure to establish the temporal sequence of violent crime, mental health functioning, and further violent crime victimization.

Our major purpose in delineating these conceptual and methodological problems is not to denigrate existing research efforts. Rather, we raise such problems hoping that the reader will consider the conceptual and methodological adequacy of research studies when considering the extent to which the research can inform clinical practice.

THE SCOPE OF VIOLENT CRIME

Perceptions of the Violent Crime Problem

Violent crime is perceived to be a major problem by most Americans. In 1991, the National Victim Center commissioned a public opinion survey in which telephone interviews were conducted with a national household probability sample of 1,000 adult Americans (Kilpatrick et al., 1991). When asked how concerned they were about a series of social problems, more Americans said they were more concerned about violent crime and drug abuse than about unemployment, pollution, the deficit, and educational quality. More than four out of five Americans (82%) said they were very concerned about violent crime, and more than half (54%) said that violent crime was more of a problem now in their community than it was 10 years ago (Kilpatrick et al., 1991).

How Does Violent Crime in America Compare to That in Other Countries?

Comparing the rates of most types of violent crimes across nations is hindered by differences in legal definitions of crime and lack of access to information about crimes that aren't reported to police. If the legal definition of a crime such as rape differs in two countries or if the proportion of rape cases that are reported to police differ, then any comparisons of rape rates in the two countries are likely to be misleading. However, criminal homicide, commonly referred to as murder, is an exception to this general rule because it is legally defined similarly in most nations and rarely goes unreported.

Using the crime of homicide as a benchmark, it is clear that the United States leads industrialized nations of the world both with respect to homicide rates and mortality rates due to homicide. In 1984 in the United States, the *homicide rate* (i.e., the number of homicides per 100,000 people) was over five times greater than the rate in Western Europe: 7.9 homicides per 100,000 people compared to an average rate of 1.5 in European countries. As discussed by Reiss and Roth (1993), the *homicide mortality rate* (i.e., the number of homicide deaths per 100,000 people) in the United States (8.3 per 100,000 population in 1984) was nearly twice that of any European nation.

Although subject to the limitations described above, reported rates of other crimes also appear to be higher in the United States than in other countries. Reported rapes were more than six times as common in the United States (35.7 versus 5.4 per 100,000 in Europe) and robberies four times as common (205 versus 49 per 100,000) (Gurr, 1989). A 1988 survey of 17 industrialized countries indicated that the United States had the highest prevalence rates for serious sexual assault and all other assaults, including threats of physical harm (Reiss & Roth, 1993). More detailed discussions of international comparisons on violent crime rates are provided by Reiss and Roth (1993) and Gurr (1989).

Crime Trends in America

Rates of violent crime in America have varied over the course of the 20th century. As discussed by Reiss and Roth (1993), population-adjusted homicide rates in the 20th century have two peaks followed by declines. The first peak occurred in the 1930s, followed by a steady decline, reaching a low in the 1960s. The second peak occurred in 1980, following a steady rise over the 1960s and 1970s. Although many people believe that contemporary homicide rates are higher than at any other time in history, in fact, "the 1990 homicide rate as reported by the Uniform Crime Reports (9.4 per 100,000 population) is somewhat lower than the two previous peaks in the 20th century (a mean of 9.5 in 1931–1934 and 10.4 in 1979–1981)" (Reiss & Roth, 1993, p. 50). However, in line with people's perceptions, the 1990 rate for aggravated assaults is higher than the 1980 rate in all American cities. Thus, rates of homicide may be slightly lower than in the past, but rates of nonfatal acts of violence may have reached an all-time high. To examine this more fully, we turn to a discussion of incidence and prevalence rates for different types of crime within the United States.

Prevalence of Violent Crime

Overview

Violent crime estimates generate a surprising amount of debate and controversy, probably because there are substantial political consequences attached to crime rates. Local governments with much higher crime rates than their neighboring communities are often unpopular with the voters. In contrast, advocates for increased police or other criminal justice system services might use high crime rates to support their cause. Given the highly politicized treatment that crime statistics often receive, it is important to understand where crime estimates come from, limitations of major data-gathering systems, and how some key crime estimates are defined. Careful consideration of how a crime estimate was obtained and what it is measuring can help reduce confusion about what the estimate means and how it compares to other estimates.

Some estimates of violent crime include only crimes reported to police. Other estimates attempt to provide data on all crimes, including those that were not reported to police. Obviously, the latter estimates should be higher than the former because they should include all crimes, not just those reported to police. Another important distinction is whether a statistic addresses the *prevalence of crime victims* within a population of interest (i.e., the proportion of population members who have been victimized in a given time frame) or the *incidence of crime cases* (i.e., the number of discrete violent crime cases that occur to members of a population during a given time frame). Following this distinction, the *lifetime prevalence* of violent crime victims is defined as the proportion of the population that has ever been a violent crime victim. The *past year prevalence* is defined as the proportion of the population who were violent crime victims in the past year. Most crime incidence data is based on crimes that occurred during a 1-year period, so *violent crime incidence* is defined as the number of violent crimes occurring within a 1-year period. *Violent crime rates* are usually calculated by taking crime incidence data and adjusting them for population size (i.e., the number of violent crimes per 100,000 people). *Note:* There are generally more crime incidents than crime victims because many crime victims are victimized more than once.

National Estimates

The Federal Bureau of Investigation Uniform Crime Report (UCR) relies on incident reports made by American police departments of crimes reported to police and provides national incidence rates for homicide as well as three types of nonfatal violent crimes (i.e., forcible rape, robbery, and aggravated assault). Because the UCR is based on police reports, it only collects data on crimes that have been reported to the police. In recording data on crime, the UCR only records information on the most serious crime committed. In other words, if a physical assault occurs during a household burglary, only the physical assault is recorded. In 1990, the UCR recorded 2 million violent crimes. The UCR provides no information about crimes that were not reported to police or about crimes that occurred prior to the year statistics were gathered.

The National Crime Victimization Survey (NCVS) is an annual survey of a representative sample of approximately 50,000 American households and is designed to collect information on unreported as well as reported crimes. Persons aged 12 and over are asked to provide information concerning crime occurring during a 6-month period prior to interview. The NCVS classifies crimes as either personal or household victimizations. *Personal victimizations* include crimes of violence (forcible rape, robbery, and aggravated assault) or crimes of theft (personal larceny with contact and personal larceny without contact). *Household victimizations* include burglary, household larceny, and motor vehicle theft. In 1990, the NCVS reported that more than 34 million personal and household crime victimizations occurred. Slightly more than half of these victimizations (nearly 19 million) were attempted or completed personal victimizations, and about one-third of these (6 million) were violent crimes (Bureau of Justice Statistics, 1992). The NCVS does not collect information about murders or about violent crimes occurring to children under age 12.

As has been noted by several researchers (Reiss & Roth, 1993; Sparks, 1982; Von, Kilpatrick, Burgess, & Hartman, 1991), there are several limitations to both the UCR and the NCVS with respect to their ability to provide good national data on crime rates (i.e., number of crimes adjusted for population in a given period of time) and the prevalence of crime victims (i.e., the proportion of persons who have been victimized during a given time period). First, neither of the two national crime data-base systems provides information about the lifetime prevalence of crime victimization because they measure crime rates per year—not the proportion of people who have ever been crime victims. Second, both the UCR and NCVS are limited in their ability to detect certain types of violent crimes that are either not stereotypic street crimes and/or that are highly stigmatized such as rape or various forms of family violence (Bachman, 1994; Kilpatrick, 1993; Koss, 1993; Reiss & Ross, 1993; Von et al., 1991). Third, the UCR and NCVS provide limited information on the outcome of crime and violence. Neither of the existing national systems collects any data on the mental health impact of the traumatic event on the victim.

Epidemiologic Studies

Several recent epidemiologic studies have used victimization surveys to obtain information on the prevalence of violence exposure. These surveys ask respondents to provide information concerning their lifetime history of victimization, including crime-related events such as physical and sexual assault, robbery, witnessing violence, and homicide of a family member or close friend, as well as other types of traumatic events (e.g., natural disasters, serious accidents) (Breslau et al., 1991; Kilpatrick, Saunders, Veronen, Best, & Von, 1987; Norris, 1992; Resnick et al., 1993). Although lifetime prevalence rates for exposure to violence vary across studies, a consistent finding is that such events occur to a substantial number of people. For example, the lifetime prevalence of exposure to crime-related events varies from 8% reported by Breslau et al. (1991) in a community sample of young adults, to 75% reported by Kilpatrick et al., (1987) in their community sample of adult females. Kilpatrick et al. (1987) also found that over half (53.7%) of the women in their sample had experienced more than one crime during their lives.

Data from the National Women's Study (NWS), which included a national household probability sample of 4,008 adult women, indicated that a substantial proportion of American women experienced violence. More than one-third of respondents (36%) reported that they had experienced at least one crime-related traumatic event in their lifetime, including completed rape, molestation, attempted sexual assault, aggravated physical assault, or homicide of a family member or close friend (Resnick et al., 1993). Based on the 1989 U.S. Census Bureau estimate of 96,056,000 U.S. adult women (age 18 or older), it is estimated that more than 34 million women have experienced some type of crime during their lifetime, with more than 12 million experiencing a completed rape, and nearly 10 million experiencing serious physical assault. Importantly, over half of all crime victims (51.8%) had either experienced more than one type of crime or more than one crime of the same type (Resnick et al., 1993).

A study of the 1992 Los Angeles Civil disturbances (the L.A. County Study) conducted by our research group also found high rates of exposure to violence (Hanson, Kilpatrick, Freedy, & Saunders, in press). This study involved a telephone survey of a household probability sample of 1,200 adult residents of Los Angeles County conducted 6 months after the 1992 civil disturbances. Of the 1,200 residents, 400 resided in South Central, Los Angeles, the area most heavily impacted by the rioting. The other 800 respondents lived in other areas of Los Angeles County. In the year prior to the survey, 6.9% of respondents indicated that they had been direct victims of a violent crime (e.g., physical assault, sexual assault, robbery, shooting, and mugging), nearly one in five (19.0%) had witnessed someone being injured or killed, and 7.9% reported the homicide death of a family member or close friend (Hanson, Freedy, Kilpatrick, & Saunders, 1993).

Reasons for Variability in Prevalence Rates across Studies

In examining prevalence and incidence rates of violent assault across studies, there is considerable variability in findings. This variability results from a variety of factors including differences in the type of samples as well as differences in the definitions of violence and victimization. First, studies on prevalence of violence differ in the type of sample. Some studies have only included women (Kilpatrick et al., 1987; Resnick et al., 1993), and data indicate that there are gender differences in exposure to violent assault (Breslau et al., 1991; Gelles & Straus, 1988; Hanson et al., 1993; Norris, 1992) with women being more likely to be rape or domestic violence victims and men being more likely to be victims of aggravated assault, robbery, and murder. The majority of studies rely on community samples, and the characteristics of different communities may vary widely, contributing to differences in crime prevalence rates. The only study to date that used a nationally representative sample included adult women (Resnick et al., 1993). While the findings of this study are certainly important, they do not provide us with national data on violence exposure for men.

A second explanation for variability of findings is differences in definitions used for eliciting information concerning exposure to violent and traumatic events. Studies have documented that the use of behaviorally specific questions to detect trauma history produces significantly higher prevalence rates (and presumably more accurate) than single-item screening questions. For sexual assault, studies find that asking respondents if they have been "raped" elicits much lower prevalence rates than if behaviorally specific structured questions are used to define sexual assault (Koss, 1983; 1993). One reason for this is that people do not always perceive a sexual assault incident to be a rape. If the assailant was a family member, a friend, or a dating partner, some individuals may not label the incident as a rape. If the assault did not involve vaginal penetration, but did involve some other type of sexual penetration (i.e., oral or anal), individuals may not categorize the event as a rape. As a consequence, clear, specific questions concerning the identity of the offender, and behaviorally specific questions concerning the nature of the assault typically elicit higher prevalence rates for sexual assault (Chapter 11, this volume; Resnick et al., 1993).

In summary, methodological variations across studies and inherent difficulties in measurement of emotionally stressful and stigmatizing events such as violent crime probably account for much of the conflicting information about the extent and nature of violent crime. However, by any measure, violent crime is not rare. It effects the lives of many Americans and their loved ones. Next, we consider what is known about factors that increase the risk for violent crime.

RISK FACTORS FOR EXPOSURE TO VIOLENT ASSAULT

A Theoretical Model for Exposure to Violent Assault

Although the major focus of the chapter is understanding the mental health impact of violent crime, crime cannot have an impact on mental health unless a person is victimized by crime. Thus, exposure to crime is a necessary but not sufficient condition for development of crime-related mental health problems, so it is important to review what is known about factors that increase

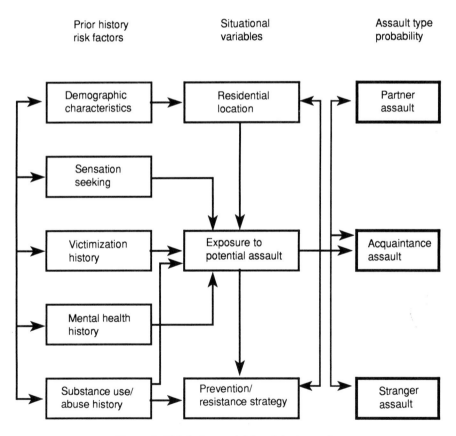

Figure 1. Risk factor model for violent assault.

exposure to violent crime. The model itself, which is depicted in Figure 1, is a simplified version of a model developed by Kilpatrick, Resnick, and Weaver (1994) to predict risk of violent sexual or physical assaults of women. However, this simplified model attempts to address factors increasing risk of violent assaults for people of both genders.

The model distinguishes among three different types of violent assaults: (1) partner assaults (i.e., those committed by the victim's romantic partner), (2) acquaintance assaults (i.e., assaults committed by assailants other than romantic partners who are known well by the victim), and (3) stranger assaults (i.e., assaults perpetrated by strangers). This distinction is important and is based on the belief that there is no logical reason to assume that the same factors predict violent assaults by partners, by acquaintances, and by strangers. Similarly, there is little reason to assume that the same prevention strategies are effective in reducing risk of violent assault across these three types of potential assailants. For example, risk of street crime perpetrated by strangers might be higher in inner-city, high-crime areas, and typical crime prevention approaches (e.g., community policing, neighborhood watch programs) might be expected to reduce risk of stranger assault. But risk of assault by a romantic partner such as a spouse, boyfriend, or girlfriend is probably less dependent on whether you live in a high-crime area than on other factors (e.g., alcohol usage, social isolation). Likewise, typical street crime prevention efforts are unlikely to influence risk of assault by romantic partners or acquaintances.

Five prior history risk factors are included in the model: demographic characteristics, the personality variable of sensation seeking, victimization history, mental health history, and substance abuse history. Three situational factors are in the model: residential location, prevention/resistance strategy, and exposure to potential assailants. The latter factor is viewed as being a necessary, but obviously not sufficient, condition for assault to occur. Even if a potential victim has numerous risk factors for assault, he or she cannot become an assault victim unless a potential attacker has the opportunity to assault them. For example, a woman without a partner has no risk of partner assault, although she might be at risk for being assaulted by a stranger as she returns home from shopping at the mall.

Risk Factors for Violent Assault

Demographic Characteristics

There is considerable evidence that risk of becoming a crime victim varies as a function of demographic variables such as gender, age, race, and socioeconomic class (Adler et al., 1994; Bachman, 1994; Breslau et al., 1991; Bureau of Justice Statistics, 1992; FBI Uniform Crime Reports, 1992; Hanson et al., 1993; Kilpatrick et al., 1991, in press; Norris, 1992; Reiss & Roth, 1993; Rosenberg & Mercy, 1991). With the exception of sexual assault and domestic violence, data consistently show that men have higher risk of assault than women (Gelles & Straus, 1988; Hanson et al., 1993; Norris, 1992). Lifetime risk of homicide is three to four times higher for men and women (Bureau of Justice Statistics, 1992).

Age is inversely related to risk of violent assault, with adolescents having substantially higher rates of assault than young adults or older Americans (Bureau of Justice Statistics, 1992; Hanson et al., 1993; Kilpatrick et al., in press; Kilpatrick, Edmunds, & Seymour, 1992; Reiss & Roth, 1993; Whitaker & Bastian, 1991). For example, data from the National Women's Study indicate that 62% of all forcible rape cases occurred when the victim was under 18 years of age (Kilpatrick et al., 1992), and data from the National Crime Victimization Survey indicate that 12- to 19-year olds are two to three times more likely than those over 20 to become victims of personal crime each year (Whitaker & Bastian, 1991).

Most studies indicate that racial and ethnic minorities have higher rates of assault than other Americans (FBI Uniform Crime Report, 1991; Hanson et al., 1993; Kilpatrick et al., 1991; Reiss & Roth, 1993). In 1990, African Americans were six times more likely than white Americans to be homicide victims (FBI Uniform Crime Report, 1992). Rates of violent assault are approximately twice as high for African and Hispanic Americans compared to white Americans (Reiss & Roth, 1993). With respect to the lifetime prevalence of violent crime victimization, Kilpatrick et al. (1991) found that African Americans (28%) and Hispanic Americans (30%) were significantly more likely than white Americans (19%) to have been violent victims of crime. Hanson et al. (1993) reported that there were no significant differences in lifetime prevalence rates of violent victimization from racial status but that African Americans and Hispanic Americans in Los Angeles had higher rates of past-year exposure to violence than their white American counterparts.

Some data indicate that violence disproportionately affects those from lower socioeconomic classes (U.S. Bureau of the Census, 1991). Family income has been found to be related to rates of violence and victimization, with lower-income families at a higher risk than those from higher-income brackets (Reiss & Roth, 1993). For example, in 1988, the risk of victimization was 2.5 times greater for families with the lowest incomes (under $7,500) compared to those with the highest ($50,000 and over) (Reiss & Roth, 1993). Using longitudinal data from the National Women's Study, Kilpatrick et al. (in press) found that women with household incomes less than $10,000 had odds 1.8 times greater than those with incomes of $10,000 or more of becoming a rape or aggravated assault victim in the 2-year follow-up period. Poverty increased assault risk even after controlling for the effects of prior victimization and sensation seeking.

Other studies report that family income is a less important predictor of victimization than gender, age, or ethnicity (Reiss & Roth, 1993). For example, in the L.A. County Study, household income was not significantly related to lifetime or past-year violence exposure, whereas gender and age were significant predictors (Hanson et al., 1993).

Some of the conflicting findings about demographic characteristics as risk factors for violent crime are attributable to methodological variations across studies. However, an important source of the conflicting findings is the extent to which many demographic variables are confounded. For example, the demographic variables of age, gender, and racial status all tend to be confounded with income: young people tend to be poorer than older people; women tend to have less income than men, and African Americans have less income than white Americans. Given these confounding variables, the need for multivariate analysis, which controls for the effects of potentially confounding variables, is apparent.

Sensation Seeking

As described by Zuckerman, "sensation seeking is a personality trait defined by the need for varied, novel, and complex sensations and experiences and the willingness to take physical and social risks for such experiences" (1979, p. 10). There is some evidence that the sensation-seeking trait is heritable (Eysenck, 1983) and that heritability contributes approximately two-thirds of the variance for this trait. Sensation seeking tends to be inversely related to age and to be higher among men than among women (Zuckerman, 1983).

In two reviews of research findings regarding the sensation-seeking trait, Zuckerman (1979, 1983) identifies characteristics of high-sensation seekers that we might expect to make them more vulnerable to violent attack by others. First, high-sensation seekers are more likely than low-sensation seekers to engage in risk-taking behaviors. As Zuckerman notes (1979), they tend to appraise most situations as less risky than low-sensation seekers. They are also more likely to engage in risky activities and are more adventuresome in phobic situations that make low-sensation seekers anxious, fearful, and avoidant. If we assume that at least some risky situations involve increased contacts with potential assailants, then a greater propensity for risk taking would also increase risk of assault.

Second, a number of studies have shown that significant relationships exist between sensation seeking and the extent of substance use and abuse (Brill, Crumpton, & Grayson, 1971; Carrol & Zuckerman, 1977; Kilpatrick, McAlhaney, McCurdy, Shaw, & Roitzsch, 1982; Kilpatrick, Sutker, & Smith, 1976; Zuckerman, Bone, Neary, Mangelsdorff, & Brustman, 1972). Findings from these studies indicate that high-sensation seekers are more likely to use or abuse a wide variety of substances than are low-sensation seekers. This could increase risk of violent assault in several ways: (1) visibly intoxicated people might be targeted by potential assailants because of their presumed lessened ability to protect themselves; (2) those using illicit substances might have increased contact with potentially violent members of the drug trade; and (3) substance use to the point of intoxication might reduce a potential victim's judgment about the degree of risk posed by given situations.

Kilpatrick et al. (in press), found that adult women who were at or above the median in sensation-seeking scores were more likely than those below the median to sustain a rape or aggravated assault within the 2-year follow-up period in the National Women's Study (5.4% versus 2.9%). Results of multivariate logistic regression analysis indicated that odds of new assault increased with higher-sensation seeking after controlling for the effects of poverty and prior victimization.

Victimization History

Data from several sources indicate that risk of violent assault is higher among people with a history of prior assault than among people without such a history (Kilpatrick et al., in press; Koss & Dinero, 1989; Wyatt, Gutherie, and Notgrass, 1992). Longitudinal data from the National Crime Victimization Survey (NCVS) suggest that assault rates are higher among those who reported assaults in previous assessments than their nonassaulted counterparts (Zawitz, 1988). At least some of this repeat victimization is probably attributable to regional and locational differences in crime rates (i.e., persons living in high-crime cities and neighborhoods are more likely to be attacked than those residing in low-crime areas). Also, certain types of crimes afford perpetrators considerable continuing access to victims (e.g., child physical and sexual assault, marital rape, or physical assault). Perpetrators in these types of partner or acquaintance assaults have increased opportunity to commit repeated assaults, and this factor probably accounts for the relatively high rates of repeat victimization in such cases.

Some of the most relevant research examining the issue of victimization history as a risk factor for new assault has focused on sexual assault. Two good studies using probability samples of adult women found that the biggest risk factor for sexual assault as an adult was a history of child sexual assault (Koss & Dinero, 1989; Wyatt et al., 1992).

Using longitudinal data from the National Women's Study (NWS), Kilpatrick et al. (in press) evaluated several risk factors for new rapes and aggravated assault that occurred during a 2-year follow-up period after initial assessment. At the initial assessment, 80% of women had no prior assaults; 13.4% had one assault; 4.6% had two prior assaults, and 2.1% had three or more prior assaults. During the 2-year follow-up period, 4.3% of this national probability sample of adult women experienced a new assault. Even after controlling for the effects of poverty and sensation seeking, results of multivariate logistic regression analysis indicated that the number of prior assaults increased the odds for new assaults. Compared to women with no prior assault, odds for new assault were 2.3 times greater for women with one prior assault, 5.3 times greater for women with two prior assaults, and 13.2 times greater for women with three or more prior assaults. These findings provide compelling support for the hypothesis that victimization history is an important risk factor for future assault.

Mental Health History

The research addressing this topic is underdeveloped, particularly longitudinal research that is able to determine whether a person had a mental health problem prior to the *first* time she or he was ever victimized. However, there is little question that the prevalence of violent assault history is higher among persons with mental health problems than among those without such problems. For example, Saunders, Kilpatrick, Resnick, and Tidwell (1989) reviewed intake records at a community mental health center and found that 28.9% of intakes had documentation that clients had been victims of sexual assault, physical assault, or were the family members of homicide victims. After brief training and implementation of a victimization screening form, 72.2% of clients were found to have been victims of these same three crimes. This study indicated that people seeking treatment for mental health problems were likely to have been crime victims. However, the study was unable to address the important issue of whether the violent crime preceded the mental health problem, the mental health problem preceded the violent crime, or whether both these factors were at work in establishing the relationship.

There are reasons to hypothesize that some people with mental health problems might be more vulnerable to violent assault than those without such problems. First, individuals with some types of mental health disorders may be particularly vulnerable to attack by predatory assailants. For example, some reports suggest that a large proportion of homeless Americans have untreated major mental disorders. Potential attackers have substantial access to such individuals because the homeless have limited ability to protect themselves on the streets. Second, persons with mental disorders who are *not* homeless may exhibit certain behavioral cues of vulnerability that may result in their being identified as potential targets for attack. Third, some persons with mental disorders are frustrating to deal with because of their lack of behavioral inhibitions, dementia, or other abnormalities. It is reasonable to assume that some relatives or other acquaintances might use unusual behavior as an excuse to assault or otherwise mistreat a mentally ill acquaintance.

Substance Abuse History

The relationship between substance abuse history and violent assault history has been found in several studies and involves most of the same issues that were just discussed with respect to mental health problems. A higher prevalence of violent assault history among substance users and/or those with substance abuse-related problems than among nonproblematic substance users has been found by several investigators, as will be described in a subsequent section of this chapter. However, an important issue that is seldom addressed in such studies is the temporal sequence of substance abuse and violent assault. Does substance abuse occur prior to violent assault? Does violent assault increase risk of substance abuse? Is the violent assault–substance abuse relationship a vicious cycle in which both events foster the development of the other?

Cottler, Compton, Mager, Spitznaggel, and Janca (1992) argue that substance abusers are more likely than those without substance abuse problems to experience events (including violent crime) that can produce PTSD. There are technical problems with the Cottler et al. (1992) study that make it impossible to examine whether traumatic events and PTSD influence the development of substance abuse, however.

Data from the National Women's Study (NWS) support the vicious cycle theory (Kilpatrick, Resnick, Saunders, Best, & Epstein, 1994). Among this national probability sample of adult women, there was a significant relationship between past-year substance use and risk of sustaining a violent assault in a 2-year follow-up period. Rates of new assault (3.9%) were lowest among women with no heavy or problematic alcohol use and no drug use. Women with alcohol dependence had slightly higher new assault rates (6.1%). Those with marijuana use but no hard drug use had still higher new assault rates (9.6%), and women with polydrug use had the highest new assault rates (28.1%). As will be discussed in a subsequent section, however, the Kilpatrick et al. (1994) study also found that history of violent assault was a risk factor for alcohol dependence even after controlling for the effects of family history of substance abuse problems, sensation seeking, and PTSD. Among assault victims with alcohol dependence, only 29.6% reported having ever become intoxicated prior to their first assault. This suggests that substance abuse does increase risk of assault, but that this may well be because many adult women began using substances in the first place following a violent assault.

Residential Location

Where you live influences your risk of becoming a violent crime victim. Using FBI Uniform Crime Report (UCR) data on violent crimes reported to police from 1973 to 1990 for cities of different sizes, Reiss and Roth (1993) report that violent crime rates increased as a function of community size. For example, the violent crime rate was 359 per 100,000 residents in cities of less than 10,000 but 2,243 in cities with over a million in population (Reiss & Roth, 1993, p. 79). Data including nonreported crimes from the National Crime Victimization Survey (NCVS) also indicate that violent crime rates are highest in central cities, somewhat lower in suburban areas, and lowest in rural areas (Bureau of Justice Statistics, 1992). As was noted previously, the UCR and the NCVS are better at measuring street crime than at measuring violent crimes perpetrated by acquaintances or partners. Thus, the increased risk of violent assault associated with residential location most likely results from stranger attacks, not necessarily from attacks by family members or romantic partners.

Exposure to Potential Assailants

No violent assault can occur unless a potential assailant has access to a potential victim. Someone could have *every* previously discussed risk factor for violent assault and be completely safe from assault unless approached by a potential assailant. Like many profound truths, this fact is so simple that it is often overlooked or discounted.

One of the most prominent theories attempting to predict risk of criminal victimization is the routine activities theory. As described by Laub (1990), this theory states that risk of victimization is related to a person's lifestyle, behavior, and routine activities. In turn, lifestyles and routine activities are generally related to demographic characteristics (e.g., age, marital status) and other personal characteristics (e.g., sensation seeking). If a person's lifestyle or routine activities place him or her in frequent contact with potential assailants, then that individual is more likely to be assaulted than if routine activities and lifestyle do not bring him or her into as frequent contact with such predatory individuals. For example, young men have higher rates of assaultive behavior than any other age-gender group (Reiss & Roth, 1993; Rosenberg & Mercy, 1991). Thus, routine activities or lifestyles that involve considerable contact with young men should have higher rates of victimization. Likewise, people who are married, who never leave their houses after dark, and who never take public transportation should have limited contact with young men and reduced risk of assault.

Although some have argued that routine activities theory has substantial support in the empirical literature (Gottfredson, 1981; Laub, 1990), most of the crime victimization data used to evaluate assault risk measure stranger assaults much better than partner or acquaintance assaults. Thus, the theory is probably much more relevant to stranger assaults than to other assaults. Still, it does have some value because it emphasizes the obvious—you can't be assaulted unless some assailant has access to you.

THE IMPACT OF VIOLENT CRIME ON MENTAL HEALTH AND LIFE STYLE

Overview

Violent crime exacts a heavy toll on the mental health and lifestyles of many Americans. This section provides a brief summary of what is known about the mental health impact of violent crime with particular emphasis on posttraumatic stress disorder (PTSD). It also addresses the issue of how violent crime and fear of same have caused Americans to change their lifestyles.

Crime-Related PTSD

Posttraumatic stress disorder is one of the most common psychological disorders associated with violence exposure (Breslau et al., 1991; Green, 1994; Kilpatrick & Resnick, 1993; Kilpatrick et al., 1989; Resnick et al., 1993). Resnick et al. (1993) estimated that the lifetime PTSD prevalence rate for a representative national sample of 4,008 adult women was 12.3%. The lifetime prevalence rate of PTSD increased dramatically for women who had experienced violent crimes, with 30% of the sexual assault victims and almost 40% of the physical assault victims meeting criteria for lifetime PTSD. In the L.A. County Study, 12.1% of the 1,200 male and female respondents met criteria for lifetime

PTSD, whereas 20.5% of assault victims had lifetime PTSD (Hanson, Freedy, & Kilpatrick, 1994). Although rates for current PTSD (exhibiting symptoms within the past 6 months) among violence victims have typically been lower, they are still substantial. For example, the current PTSD prevalence rate for the entire sample in the NWS was 4.6% compared to 9.7% among assault victims (Resnick et al., 1993). Thus, assault victims were more than twice as likely as nonvictims to have PTSD. In the L.A. County Study, 4.1% of all adults had current PTSD (Hanson et al., in press).

Other Mental Health Problems

Substance Abuse

Several studies indicate that substance use disorders are more prevalent in individuals who have a history of criminal victimization (Burnam et al., 1988; Cottler et al., 1992; George & Winfield-Laird, 1986; Helzer, Robins, & McEvoy, 1987; Kilpatrick, 1990; Kulka et al., 1990; Sorenson, Stein, Siegel, Golding, & Burnam, 1987). For example, in a study of 3,125 Los Angeles residents, as part of the NIMH Epidemiologic Catchment Area project, rates of substance abuse or dependence (both alcohol and other drug) were significantly higher among sexual assault victims compared to nonvictims (Sorenson et al., 1987). Resnick et al. (1993) found that 80% of women who reported having sought treatment for a substance use disorder at some point during their lives also reported having experienced a sexual assault, physical assault, or the death of a family member due to homicide.

As was previously discussed, Kilpatrick et al. (1994) found that history of violent assault increased risk of alcohol dependence even after controlling for family history of substance abuse problems, sensation seeking, and PTSD. In another paper based on NWS longitudinal data, Epstein, Saunders, Kilpatrick, and Resnick (1994) used path analytic techniques to clarify the extent to which psychological distress mediated the impact of childhood rape on women's substance use as adults. Women's alcohol and drug use were monitored during a 1-year follow-up period, and they were classified into one of four mutually exclusive groups: nonusers, heavy alcohol consumers or problem drinkers, marijuana users, or polydrug users. Results of the path analysis indicated that the primary influence of child rape on adult substance use was mediated by depression and PTSD.

Depression

Longitudinal studies of sexual assault victims consistently find more depression among victims compared to controls immediately following the assault and at postassault follow-ups (Atkeson, Calhoun, Resick, & Ellis, 1982; Ellis, Calhoun, & Atkeson, 1980; Frank & Stewart, 1984; Kilpatrick, Veronen, & Resick, 1979). Sorenson et al. (1987) found higher rates of major depression, mania, antisocial personality, and three other anxiety disorders (phobia, panic, and obsessive–compulsive) among the sexually assaulted compared to non-assaulted participants. Studies have indicated that victims of other types of crime also evidence symptoms of depression. In the NWS more than half of aggravated assault victims (54.7%), and 41.4% of victims who had experienced the homicide of a family member or friend met criteria for lifetime major depressive episode.

Sexual Dysfunction

Studies of sexual dysfunction most commonly report that rape victims avoid sexual activities and experience less sexual satisfaction (Becker, Abel, & Skinner, 1979; Becker, Skinner, Abel, & Treacy, 1982; Burgess & Holmstrom, 1979; Kilpatrick et al., 1987; Orlando & Koss, 1983; Resick, 1986; Saunders, Villeponteaux, Lipovsky, Kilpatrick, & Veronen, 1992). For example, Ellis et al. (1980) investigated the frequency of sexual activity in female rape victims who reported being sexually active prior to the rape. At a 2-week postrape assessment, nearly one-third of the women (29%) reported that they were not sexually active, and another one-third (32%) reported a decrease in sexual activity. For women who reported frequent sexual activity prior to the rape, sexual activity had returned to these levels at a 1-year postrape follow-up. However, avoidance of sex was still common at the 1-year follow-up among women who reported low levels of sexual activity prior to the rape.

Becker, Skinner, Abel, and Cichon (1986) investigated sexual dysfunction among sexual assault victims and nonvictims. They found that 59% of the sexual assault victims reported at least one sexual dysfunction, compared to only 17% of the nonvictims. In addition, 69% of the victims who reported a sexual dysfunction viewed their assault as the cause of their problems. Although studies have reported relationships between rape and sexual dysfunction, sexual problems among victims of other types of crime have not been adequately studied. Future research needs to examine whether victims of nonsexual crimes evidence higher base rates of sexual dysfunctions compared to nonvictims.

Life-Style Changes and Social Adjustment

Several changes in life style have also been noted following victimization, including changes of residence, decreases in work productivity, and decreased participation in social activities. Williams and Holmes (1981) reported that one in four rape victims moved following the rape, and one in five changed their phone numbers to new, unlisted numbers. Veronen and Kilpatrick (1980) also found that rape victims moved significantly more often than nonvictims. Resick, Calhoun, Atkeson, and Ellis (1981) found impairment in the place of work up to 8 months postrape. With respect to social activities, Kilpatrick et al. (1987) found that completed rape was associated with an impairment in social and leisure activities. Ellis et al. (1980) found no differences between rape victims and victims of other types of assaults in the frequency of engaging in social activities. However, in comparison to victims of other types of crimes, rape victims reported less satisfaction engaging in these types of activities.

Violence Exposure and Fear of Crime

Previous studies have indicated that exposure to violence (both chronic and acute) has a significant impact on fears of crime and crime-related changes in life style. In the National Victim Center-funded survey of 1,000 Americans (Kilpatrick et al., 1991), a substantial number of Americans indicated that they were very or somewhat fearful of being attacked or robbed in a number of situations, including at home, when traveling, when alone at night in their neighborhood, when in their neighborhood in the daytime, and with others at night. In all cases, women's fears were greater than men's.

A further illustration of the toll that crime has played is that many Americans report changes or restrictions in their life style because of their fears of victimization. More than half of Americans (60%) indicated that they limit places they will go to by themselves; almost one-third (32%) limit times or places they will go shopping; and more than one in five (22%) limit the times or places they will work. Fear of crime as well as crime-related restrictions on lifestyles and behavior were found to be substantially higher for women than for men and for racial and ethnic minorities than for whites. For example, women were far more likely than men to limit places they will go by themselves (73% versus 45%) and to limit the places or times they shop (45% versus 18%). Overall, these data indicate that fears of crime and the consequent restrictions in life style affect a substantial proportion of Americans.

FACTORS RELATED TO THE DEVELOPMENT OF VIOLENCE-RELATED MENTAL HEALTH PROBLEMS

Overview

Exposure to violence increases the risk for a myriad of mental health and adjustment problems. It is important to note that exposure to some factors substantially increases the risk of adverse mental health outcomes (e.g., physical injury, perceptions of threat to life). Alternatively, the presence of additional factors may reduce the likelihood of adverse mental health outcomes following exposure to violence (e.g., adequate social ties). In this section, we briefly review knowledge concerning known risk and protective factors. For the sake of clarity, we conceptualize risk and protective factors at three levels: individual, family, and community.

Individual Factors

The first group of individual level factors serve a protective function and are derived from research in the field of developmental psychopathology. These studies conceptualize children to be at mental health risk because of factors such as parental psychopathology, poverty, or warfare. Additional factors such as temperament, gender, or IQ are proposed as mediating the relationship between stressors and adjustment. For example, children with difficult temperaments appear to adjust more poorly to environmental stressors (Rutter, 1989; Werner & Smith, 1982). In contrast, children with higher IQs appear to respond more adaptively to stress (Garmezy & Masten, 1986). Dispositional attributes, such as activity level, sociability, intelligence, communication skills, self-esteem, hardiness, autonomy, and internal locus of control appear to be important protective factors against the development of psychological adjustment problems (Garmezy & Masten, 1986; Werner, 1989, 1992; Werner & Smith, 1982). Being female and high socioeconomic status have also been found to moderate the effects of stress (Garmezy & Masten, 1986).

Perceptions are a second type of individual level factor that may impact adjustment to violent events. Cognitive processes of appraisal and attribution are relevant here. For example, Gold (1986) investigated the relationship between sexual victimization and adjustment among adults using the learned helplessness model of depression as a framework. She found that victims were more likely than nonvictims to attribute the causes for bad events to internal, stable, and global factors, whereas good events were more likely to be attributed to external factors. More recently, Falsetti and Resick (1990) reported differences in causal attributions of sexual assault victims experiencing symptoms of depression and/or PTSD and nonvictims. Victims rated the causes of hypothetical positive events as more unstable than nonvictims. Victims also viewed the causes of hypothetical negative events as more internal than nonvictims. When victims and nonvictims were compared in their attributions for actual traumatic events, victims rated the cause of their victimization as more stable than nonvictims. These findings suggest that victims are more likely to make attributions that reflect a lack of control over both positive and negative events.

Perceiving extreme threat for serious injury or death substantially increases the risk for developing PTSD (Kilpatrick et al., 1989; Kilpatrick et al., in press; Kilpatrick & Resnick, 1993). For example, crime victims from the NWS were classified into four groups on the basis of their life threat or injury experiences during the crime: no life threat or injury, life threat only, injury only, or both life threat and injury (Resnick et al., 1993). The lifetime PTSD rates for these four groups were 19% (no life threat or injury), 26.6% (life threat only), 30.6% (injury only), and 45.2% (both life threat and injury) respectively.

Participation in the criminal justice system is an additional factor that may impact the mental health impact of violent crime. Intuitively, we would expect involvement in court proceedings to increase stress for crime victims; however, criminal justice system involvement is generally viewed as facilitating emotional recovery (Calhoun, Atkeson, & Resick, 1982; Kilpatrick & Otto, 1987; Kilpatrick et al., 1979). For example, Cluss, Boughton, Frank, Stewart, and West (1983) found that there were no differences in social adjustment or depressive symptoms in rape victims based on whether or not they wished to prosecute. In addition, Resick (1988) found that crime victims who participated in the criminal justice system reported greater self-esteem at 6 months post-crime than individuals who did not participate because their assailant could not be found. Alternatively, it is possible that nonparticipants evidenced higher levels of distress because their assailants were not apprehended.

One study of recent crime victims and their family members found that approximately one-half of the participants met criteria for PTSD at some point during their lifetime (Freedy, Resnick, Kilpatrick, Dansky, & Tidwell, 1994). Although these findings may seem at odds with the research previously discussed, it is important to note that respondents were assessed for a lifetime history of PTSD; thus, participation in the criminal justice system did not *cause* the development of PTSD. On the basis of this study, it is difficult to conclude whether the victimization, involvement in the criminal justice system, or some combination of these two factors presented a risk for PTSD. This study also found that a substantial number of the participants did not receive adequate access to a variety of services that might be expected to reduce the distress associated with victimization and criminal justice system involvement (e.g., psychological counseling, legal assistance). Overall, these findings suggest that the lack of services provided to crime victims may contribute to mental health problems, whereas involvement in the criminal justice system may actually help to empower victims. Clearly, further research is needed in this area before any firm conclusions can be made.

Chronic exposure to violence is the final factor that we will consider as a potential individual level determinant of mental health risk. It is reasonable to assume that repeated victimization desensitizes individuals to violence. Research has not generally supported the notion of desensitization. Instead, multiple victimizations seem to present a significant risk factor for the development of adjustment problems. For example, in the NWS, women who experienced multiple traumatic events were more likely to meet criteria for PTSD than women who reported a single trauma or no trauma history. Kilpatrick et al. (in press) found that the number of prior rapes or aggravated assaults increased risk of current PTSD even after controlling for the effects of having experienced a new assault during the 2-year follow-up period. Among women who never had a prior assault or one in the follow-up period, the current PTSD rate was 3.2%. Women with no prior assault and an assault during the follow-up period had a current PTSD rate of 19.4%. Women with one prior assault and one new assault had a similar current PTSD rate of 18.3%. However, women with two prior assaults and a new assault had a current PTSD rate of 52.9%. The rate of current PTSD among women with three prior assaults and no new assaults was 21.5%, and women with three prior assaults and one new assault had a current PTSD rate of 51.8%.

In our L.A. County Study, we examined whether exposure to violence during the 1992 civil disturbances would be related to symptoms of distress after taking into account lifetime victimization experiences. In a series of regression analyses, we found that disturbance-related violence was significantly predictive of current PTSD, even after statistically controlling for the effects of lifetime and past-year victimization (e.g., physical assault, sexual assault, witnessing violence). Thus, although people had been exposed to previous violence, an acute traumatic event of extreme magnitude (i.e., the civil disturbances) was still associated with substantial levels of distress (Hanson et al., in press).

Family Factors

Family cohesion, supportive family members, absence of familial discord and neglect, and good parent–child relationships appear to be important factors in protecting mental health (Garmezy & Masten, 1986; Werner, 1989, 1992; Werner & Smith, 1982). Jenkins and Smith (1990) found that close sibling relationships reduced distress symptoms in children from conflicted homes. Studies with adults, particularly women, have identified a supportive spousal relationship as being an important buffer against stress (Brown, Bhrolchai, & Harris, 1975; Husaini, Neff, Newbrough, & Moore, 1982; Paykel, Emms, Fletcher, & Rassaby, 1980). Other findings have suggested that, particularly for women, spousal ties may place excessive demands on women in times of extreme stress leading to more negative psychological and physical outcomes (Solomon, Smith, Robins, & Fischbach, 1987). In particular, chronic stressors (e.g., living in a high-crime neighborhood), may make supportive relationships difficult to maintain such that requesting and receiving support becomes a burden both for the giver and recipient (Hobfoll, Freedy, Lane, & Geller, 1990).

Other family factors such as a history of mental health and substance abuse problems might also be associated with adjustment following victimization. It is likely that a mental health problem would interfere with a family member's ability to provide needed support to a victim. Further, having a family member with these types of problems introduces additional stressors that may impede recovery.

Community Factors

Few studies have identified community level variables that may serve to protect mental health. However, it is clear that broader environmental conditions (e.g., police protection, fire and rescue services, adequate schools, adequate health care facilities, shopping facilities, public transportation, churches, community centers, etc.) should have a powerful influence on positive mental health (Hobfoll, Dunahoo, & Monnier, Chapter 2, this volume). Research indicates that neighborhood disorganization is associated with higher rates of violence (Reiss & Roth, 1993). It is also plausible to assume that lower levels of neighborhood disorganization, characterized by a sense of neighborhood community (i.e., involvement in community activities, availability of community support networks, availability and satisfaction with community services) would help to reduce the adverse consequences of violence exposure. Alternatively, the poor physical condition of the neighborhood and high levels of neighborhood disorganization could have an additive effect, meaning that these community-level variables exacerbate problems associated with violence exposure.

Additional research findings can be interpreted as suggesting the potential importance of community-level factors in promoting mental health. For example, Jenkins and Smith (1990) found that close relationships with adults outside the family were associated with less distress in children from homes characterized by high rates of marital conflict. Also, Garmezy (1985, 1987) similarly found that external support, whether from an adult (e.g., a teacher) or an institution (e.g., a church) moderated the effects of stress in poverty-stricken families. From the perspective of conservation of resources (COR) stress theory, organizational and community-level resources are complementary to individual and family-level resources. According to COR stress theory, the lack or depletion of such resources is predicted to diminish coping options and result in feelings of emotional distress (Chapter 2, this volume).

The impact of within-family social ties upon mental health was previously discussed as a family-level factor. Social ties beyond the level of the family can now be discussed as a community-level factor with potential relevance to determining mental health outcome. A considerable amount of research has been conducted in the area of social support. Findings generally conclude that social support is associated with fewer symptoms of distress and less psychopathology. The data on social support as a protective factor, however, are mixed, with some studies indicating that social support reduces the adverse affects of a stressor, whereas other studies find that social support can exacerbate stress or, in some circumstances, introduce a new set of problems (for a review, see Cohen & Wills, 1985). Under conditions of stress, it is often difficult to maintain existing relationships or to have the resources and ability to seek needed support (Hobfoll et al., 1990).

Positive social support is associated with fewer symptoms following victimization (Atkeson et al., 1982; Frank & Anderson, 1987; Gerrol & Resick, 1988; Moss, Frank, & Anderson, 1987; Norris & Feldman-Summers, 1981; Ruch & Chandler, 1980; West, Frank, Anderson, & Stewart, 1987). Kaniasty and Norris (1992) investigated the buffering effects of social support among victims of violence or property crimes and found that perceived support was related to a reduction in symptoms of depression, anxiety, hostility, and fear among victims of violent crime. In contrast, received support was only associated with a reduction in fear of crime among violent-crime victims.

IMPLICATIONS FOR PREVENTION AND MENTAL HEALTH TREATMENT

Implications for Prevention of Violent Assault

Americans are generally concerned about violent crime, and it has a large impact on their mental health as well as their freedom. The same is true for citizens of many other industrialized nations. Mental health professionals have a stake in learning more about violence prevention because it pertains to the well-being of their clients, and because they themselves wish to live in an environment where they and their family members are safe from the threat of violent attack. Therefore, a brief overview of prevention approaches is provided (also see Chapter 3, this volume).

When most people think about violent crime prevention, they think about ways they can reduce their risk of becoming a violent-crime victim. This goal is the essence of one primary prevention strategy called opportunity reduction, which has been defined as "making a potential target of attack inaccessible or unattractive by making the attack itself dangerous or unprofitable to the criminal" (National Crime Prevention Institute, 1986). Opportunity reduction has three main assumptions: (1) potential crime victims must do things that reduce their vulnerability to crimes and that reduce the likelihood that they will be injured if attacked; (2) the actions victims can take are limited by their control over their environment; and (3) the environment that we are attempting to control is that of the potential victim, not that of the potential criminal. Examples of opportunity-reduction approaches would be neighborhood watch programs, installation of home security systems, or taking crime prevention/self-defense training courses.

As a primary prevention technique, opportunity reduction has three major problems. First, even if a person is successful in making her- or himself a "hard target" who is unattractive to potential attackers, the potential attacker may well turn his attention to a "soft target." Thus, even if effective in particular instances, opportunity-reduction approaches do not prevent crimes—they merely redistribute them. Second, as has been pointed out by McCall (1993) and Sparks and Bar On (1985), opportunity reduction focuses on control of potential victims, not of potential criminals. This focus on victims makes it the potential victim's responsibility to avoid attack and contributes to victim blame when an attack does occur (i.e., "that woman wouldn't have gotten raped if she hadn't been out by herself at night"). One victim addressed this problem in her testimony to the President's Task Force on Victims of Crime: "To blame victims for crime is like analyzing the cause of World War II and asking, "What was Pearl Harbor doing in the Pacific, anyway?'" (1982, p. 2). Third, opportunity-reduction approaches may reduce an individual's risk of being assaulted, but they do so by reducing the individual's freedom to go where and when he or she pleases. Living alone in a bank vault would clearly reduce one's risk of being assaulted but at a very high price.

Despite its limitations as a primary prevention approach, we are not suggesting that opportunity-reduction techniques be ignored. Indeed, learning how to become a "hard target" is one of the few things an individual can do to reduce his or her risk of becoming a crime victim. However, we also think it is important to recognize that "opportunity reduction is not enough" if our goal is actual crime prevention.

Another primary prevention strategy is what has been called legislative prevention (Gladstone, 1980; McCall, 1993). The essence of this strategy is to enact laws that will either deter potential criminals from committing crimes in the first place or that will ensure long periods of incarceration if they commit crimes. Advocates of this approach suggest that society must "get tough" on criminals. Typical suggestions include: having lengthy mandatory sentences, abolishing parole, or enacting "three strikes and you're out" laws that provide for mandatory life sentences for those convicted of three violent crimes. Proponents of this legislative prevention strategy say it could prevent crime in two ways: (1) it could deter potential criminals from committing crimes because they fear stiff penalties; or (2) it could incapacitate violent criminals by separating them from potential victims.

How well has this approach worked? Reiss and Roth (1993) described the results of a study commissioned by the National Research Council that examined the relationship between the number of incarcerated prisoners and violent crime rates. Between 1975 and 1989, the prison population in the United States nearly tripled; there was no change in the probability of arrest per violent crime, and the average time served in prison per violent crime nearly tripled. Throughout this 15-year period, the violent crime rate showed negligible changes. Reiss and Roth (1993) concluded that increasing sentences has little effect on violent crime rates but that increasing the likelihood that a violent criminal will receive some incarceration would have much more deterrent value than the length of a sentence. In essence, it appears more important to ensure that a criminal receive some jail time than to increase the amount of jail time that criminal receives.

A major limitation of the "get tough on crime" approach as a primary prevention technique is that most violent criminals are never arrested and convicted for the crimes they commit. According to data from the NCVS, fewer than half of all violent crimes were reported to police from 1982–1984 (Zawitz, 1988). Data from the NWS indicated that 71% of forcible rapes and 56% of aggravated assaults experienced by adult women were not reported to police (Kilpatrick et al., 1994). Of crimes reported to police, only 25% of robberies, 54% of rapes, 62% of aggravated assaults, and 72% of murders resulted in arrests (Zawitz, 1988). Clearly, not all arrests result in successful prosecutions, so it is apparent that only a minority of violent assailants ever get convicted, much less are incarcerated. One implication of these data on the extent to which violent crimes go unreported is that encouraging crime victims to report crimes to police is a type of crime prevention. Kilpatrick et al., (1992) described the importance of getting rape victims to report in the following terms:

> Unreported rapes are a threat to public safety in America . . . rapists cannot be apprehended, indicted, prosecuted, and incarcerated if the criminal justice system does not know that a rape has occurred. Such undetected rapists remain invisible to the criminal justice system. If rape victims are reluctant to report, then rapists will remain free to continue raping America's women, men, and children. (p. 6)

McCall (1993) notes that early identification and intervention with potential offenders is a type of secondary crime prevention and that treatment and rehabilitation of convicted offenders is tertiary crime prevention. Thus, getting victims to report has the potential of facilitating these types of crime prevention.

An exciting development in the crime prevention field has been the application of public health prevention approaches to the problem of violence. Traditional public health primary prevention approaches either try to change the environment in ways that weaken or eliminate the stressor agent (e.g., attack malaria by draining the swamps that breed mosquitoes that cause the disease) or strengthen the vulnerable population (e.g., attacking polio by inoculating children). Given the broad scope of violence and the multiple biopsychosocial factors that influence violent behavior, a comprehensive discussion of public health primary prevention approaches is clearly beyond the scope of this chapter. However, potential primary prevention approaches are discussed in some detail elsewhere (McCall, 1993; Mercy, Rosenberg, Powell, Broome, & Roper, 1993; Reiss & Roth, 1993; Rosenberg & Mercy, 1991).

In summary, prevention of violent assault should be an important public policy objective because of the broad scope and devastating mental health impact of violence. Learning how to reduce personal risk of becoming an assault victim is important, but so are efforts to actually reduce the overall rate of violent assault. Because violence is such a multidimensional problem, no single approach is likely to prevent violent assault in and of itself. Because Americans are so concerned about violent crime as a public policy issue, it appears easy for some public policy makers to make political hay by advocating that society "getting tough on crime." However, it is clear that effective public policy requires that we not limit our efforts to "getting tough" or to opportunity reduction. Practicing mental health professionals have much to contribute in terms of being creative and energetic advocates for the development of more comprehensive crime prevention efforts.

Implications for Mental Health Treatment

In this closing section, we emphasize the broad issues involved in providing mental health treatment to the victims of violent crime. Specific approaches to assessment and treatment, however, are not covered. These "nuts and bolts" facets of clinical practice are covered in detail by Falsetti and Resnick (Chapter

11). Instead, our focus is on presenting six key issues that are of general relevance in the treatment of violent-crime victims.

First, as has been described elsewhere (Kilpatrick, 1983; Koss & Harvey, 1987; Saunders et al., 1989), many mental health professionals are already treating victims of rape and other types of violence without knowing it because they do not screen their clients for histories of violent assault. Without a thorough knowledge of a client's victimization history, it is difficult to assess the extent to which presenting problems are victimization related.

Kilpatrick (1983) identified four reasons that many rape victims are unwilling to disclose their rapes to mental health professionals: (1) they fear retribution by the assailant for telling anyone about the rape, desire to avoid the stigma associated with being labeled as a rape victim, and/or fear of being blamed; (2) they do not perceive there to be a relationship between the presenting problem and their victimization experience; (3) they have been "punished" when they have disclosed the rape to other people (e.g., other people have responded negatively when they have disclosed in the past); (4) they are never asked by the mental health professional if they have been victimized. These basic reasons for nondisclosure are probably as applicable to other crime victims as they are to rape victims. The key to good case finding is addressing as many of these issues as possible. Kilpatrick (1983) described two major case-finding techniques for doing so: (1) gathering routine, systematic data about victimization experiences from all clients; and (2) examining presenting problems that are particularly prevalent among victims and hypothesizing that an undisclosed victimization experience may play some etiological role in the problem. For example, if a female client presents with a great deal of fear and anxiety of record onset, if she reports substantial restrictions in her behavior and lifestyle because of fear, if she reports drinking considerably more alcohol than she has in the past, a clinician might reasonably wonder if she might have been sexually assaulted recently.

A second key point is that therapists should recognize that many people have traumatic event histories that are complex and involve several different traumatic events occurring throughout the life span. It is important to screen comprehensively for such events (see Chapter 11, this volume; Resnick, Kilpatrick, & Lipovsky, 1991, for specific suggestions on how to conduct comprehensive victimization screening).

Third, mental health professionals should also routinely screen for PTSD among clients who have experienced crimes or other potential traumatic events. It is clear that crime victims with PTSD are considerably more distressed than crime victims without PTSD. It is also clear that crime victims with PTSD are much more likely than crime victims without PTSD to have a host of other mental health problems including substance use/abuse, depression, suicidal ideation, suicide attempts, bulimia, and panic disorder. Therefore, it is extremely useful clinically to know whether a crime victim has PTSD (see Chapter 11, this volume, for discussion of how to assess for PTSD).

Fourth, mental health professionals should learn about and network with other agencies and professionals that provide services to crime victims. Over the past 20 years, a crime victims' rights movement has grown substantially in the United States and throughout the world (Andrews, 1992; Kilpatrick & Otto, 1987; Lurigio, Skogan, & Davis, 1990). An important consequence of the victims' rights movement has been the development of numerous rape crisis centers, battered women's shelters, Mothers Against Drunk Drivers chapters, and criminal justice systems-based victim/witness assistance programs (Davis & Henley, 1990; Geis, 1990; Kelly, 1990; Kilpatrick et al.). These programs, and the victims they serve, can benefit greatly from collaborative relationships with mental health professionals.

In 1982, the Presidents' Task Force on Victims of Crime recommended that the mental health community should "establish and maintain direct liaison with other victim service agencies." Not only can agencies benefit from the involvement of mental health professionals, but mental health professionals can get a great deal of help for their clients from these agencies. Violent-crime victims involved with the criminal justice system have higher rates of PTSD than violent-crime victims in general (Freedy et al., 1994), and many such victims state that they lack access to mental health services. Thus, this partnership between mental health professionals and victim service professionals must be cultivated.

Fifth, mental health professionals should recognize that they have an important role to play in crime prevention and substance abuse prevention. Because violent assault victims have an increased risk of revictimization, of developing PTSD, and developing substance use/abuse problems, there are several things mental health professionals can do with respect to prevention. They can work with crime prevention and self-protection training specialists to make sure their clients with histories of violence get training that might reduce their risk of subsequent attack. They can try to ensure that victims of violence get exposed to substance abuse prevention training because such victims are at higher risk of developing substance abuse problems. They can make sure that clients with substance abuse problems receive self-protection and crime prevention training because such clients, particularly those who use hard drugs, are at particularly high risk of being attacked. And they ought to focus on providing treatment for crime-related PTSD as an important aspect of substance abuse treatment.

Finally, mental health professionals should consider that their training and expertise place them in a unique position to understand and assist crime victims in a broader sense. Over a decade ago, the Presidents' Task Force on Violent Crime (1982) provided a clear statement of what is needed from the mental health community:

> Property damage and physical injury are readily apparent, easily understood consequences of violent crime. The psychological wounds sustained by victims of crime, and the best means of treating such injuries, are less well understood. If this severe suffering is to be relieved mental health professionals must lead the way. (p. 105)

Although considerable progress has been made since 1982, this statement, and its challenge to the mental health community, is as applicable today as it was then. We must press forward with our best clinical and research efforts on behalf of crime victims.

REFERENCES

Adler, N. E., Boyce, T., Chesney, M. A., Cohen, S., Folkman, S., Kahn, R. L., & Syme, S. L. (1994). Socioeconomic status and health. *American Psychologist, 49*, 15–24.

Andrews, B. A. (1992). *Victimization and survivor services: A guide to victims assistance.* New York: Springer Publishing Company.

Atkeson, B. M., Calhoun, K. S., Resick, P. A., & Ellis, E. M. (1982). Victims of rape: Repeated assessment of depressive symptoms. *Journal of Consulting and Clinical Psychology, 50*, 96–102.

Bachman, R. (1994). *Violence against women. A national crime victimization survey report.* Washington, DC: U.S. Department of Justice.

Becker, J. V., Abel, G. G., & Skinner, L. J. (1979). The impact of a sexual assault on the victim's sexual life. *Victimology: An International Journal, 4*, 229–235.

Becker, J. V., Skinner, L. J., Abel, G. G., & Cichon, J. (1986). Level of postassault sexual functioning in rape and incest victims. *Archives of Sexual Behavior, 15*, 37.

Becker, J. V., Skinner, L. J., Abel, G. G., & Treacy, E. (1982). Incidence and types of sexual dysfunctions in rape and incest victims. *Journal of Sex and Marital Therapy, 8*, 65–74.

Breslau, N., Davis, G. C., Andreski, P., & Peterson, E. (1991). Traumatic events and post-traumatic stress disorder in an urban population of young adults. *Archives of General Psychiatry, 48*, 216–222.

Brill, N. C., Crumpton, E., & Grayson, H. M. (1971). Personality factors in marijuana use. *Archives of General Psychiatry, 24*, 163–165.

Brown, G. W., Bhrolchai, M. N., & Harris, T. (1975). Social class and psychiatric disturbance among women in the urban population. *Sociology, 9*, 225–254.

Bureau of Justice Statistics. (1990). *Criminal victimization in the United States, 1988.* Washington, DC: U.S. Government Printing Office.

Bureau of Justice Statistics. (1992). *Criminal victimization in the United States, 1990.* Washington, DC: U.S. Government Printing Office.

Burgess, A. W., & Holstrom, L. L. (1979). Adaptive strategies and recovery from rape. *American Journal of Psychiatry, 136*, 1278–1282.

Burnam, M. A., Stein, J. A., Golding, J. M., Siegel, J. M., Sorenson, S. B., Forsythe, A. B., & Telles, C. A. (1988). Sexual assault and mental disorders in a community population. *Journal of Consulting and Clinical Psychology, 56*, 843–850.

Calhoun, K. S., Atkeson, B. M., & Resick, P. A. (1982). A longitudinal examination of fear reactions in victims of rape. *Journal of Counseling Psychology, 29*, 655–661.

Carrol, E. N., & Zuckerman, M. (1977). Psychopathology and sensation seeking in 'downers,' 'speeders,' and 'trippers': A study of the relationship between personality and drug choice. *International Journal of Addictions, 12*, 591–601.

Cluss, P. A., Boughton, J., Frank, L. E., Stewart, B. D., & West, C. (1983). The rape victims: Psychological correlates of participants in the legal process. *Criminal Justice and Behavior, 10*, 342–357.

Cohen, S., & Wills, T. A. (1985). Stress, social support, and the buffering hypothesis. *Psychological Bulletin, 98*, 310–357.

Cottler, L. B., Compton, W. M., Mager, D., Spitznagel, E. L., & Janca, A. (1992). Posttraumatic stress disorder among substance users from the general population. *American Journal of Psychiatry, 149*, 664–670.

Davis, R. C., & Henley, M. (1990). Victim service programs. In A. J. Lurigion, W. G. Skogan, &

R. C. Davis (Eds.), *Victims of crime: Problems, policies, and programs* (pp. 157–169). Newbury Park: Sage Publications.

Ellis, E. M., Atkeson, B. M., & Calhoun, K. S. (1981). An assessment of long-term reaction to rape. *Journal of Abnormal Psychology, 90,* 263–266.

Ellis, E. M., Calhoun, K. S., & Atkeson, B. M. (1980). Sexual dysfunction in victims of rape. *Women and Health, 5,* 39–47.

Epstein, H. J., Saunders, B. E., Kilpatrick, D. G., & Resnick, H. S. (1994). *The assessment of psychological distress as a possible mediator between childhood rape and subsequent substance use among women.* Unpublished manuscript, Medical University of South Carolina, Charleston, South Carolina.

Eysenck, H. J. (1983). A biometrical–genetical analysis of impulsive and sensation seeking behavior. In M. Zuckerman (Ed.), *Biological bases of sensation seeking, impulsivity, and anxiety.* Hillsdale, NJ: Lawrence Erlbaum Associates.

Falsetti, S. A., & Resick, P. A. (1990). *Causal attributions, self-blame and perceived responsibility in victims of crime.* Unpublished manuscript, University of Missouri-St. Louis.

Federal Bureau of Investigation. (1991). *Uniform crime reports for the United States: 1990.* Washington, DC: United States Government Printing Office.

Federal Bureau of Investigation. (1992). *Uniform crime reports: Crime in the United States, 1991.* Washington, DC: U.S. Government Printing Office.

Frank, E., & Anderson, B. P. (1987). Psychiatric disorders in rape victims: A revisit. *Journal of Affective Disorders, 7,* 77–85.

Frank, E., & Stewart, B. D. (1984). Depressive symptoms in rape victims: A revisit. *Journal of Affective Disorders, 7,* 77–85.

Freedy, J. R., Resnick, H. S., Kilpatrick, D. G., Dansky, B. S., & Tidwell, R. P. (1994). The psychological adjustment of recent crime victims in the criminal justice system. *Journal of Interpersonal Violence, 9,* 450–468.

Garmezy, N. (1985). Stress-resistant children: The search for protective factors. In J. E. Stevenson (Ed.), *Recent research in developmental psychopathology* (pp. 213–233). Oxford: Pergamon Press.

Garmezy, N. (1987). Stress, competence, and development: Continuities in the study of schizophrenic adults, children vulnerable to psychopathology, and the search for stress-resistant children. *American Journal of Orthopsychiatry, 57,* 159–174.

Garmezy, N., & Masten, A. S. (1986). Stress, competence, and resilience: Common frontiers for therapist and psychopathologist. *Behavior Therapy, 17,* 500–521.

Geis, G. (1990). Crime victims: Practices and prospects. In A. J. Lurigion, W. G. Skogan, & R. C. Davis (Eds.), *Victims of crime: Problems, policies, and programs* (pp. 251–267). Newbury Park: Sage Publications.

Gelles, R. J., & Straus, M. A. (1988). *Intimate violence: The consequences of abuse in the American family.* New York: Simon & Schuster.

George, L. K., & Winfield-Laird, I. (1986). *Sexual assault: Prevalence and mental health consequences.* A final report submitted to NIMH for supplemental funding to the Duke University epidemiological catchment area.

Gerrol, R., & Resick, P. A. (1988, November). *Sex differences in social support and recovery from victimization.* Paper presented at the 22nd Annual Meeting of the Association for the Advancement of Behavior Therapy, New York.

Gladstone, F. J. (1980). *Co-ordinating crime prevention efforts (Home Office Research Study No. 62).* London: Her Majesty's Stationery Office.

Gold, E. R. (1986). Long-term effects of sexual victimization in childhood: An attributional approach. *Journal of Consulting and Clinical Psychology, 54,* 471–475.

Gottfredson, M. R. (1981). On the etiology of criminal victimization. *Journal of Criminal Law and Criminology, 77,* 714–726.

Green, B. L. (1994). Psychosocial research in traumatic stress: An update. *Journal of Traumatic Stress, 7,* 341–357.

Gurr, T. R. (1989). Historical trends in violent crime: Europe and the United States. In T. R. Gurr (Ed.), *Violence in America (Vol. 1)* (pp. 21–54). Newbury Park, CA: Sage .

Hanson, R. F., Freedy, J. R., & Kilpatrick, D. G. (1994). *Impact of urban violence on psychosocial functioning, Final report.* Washington, DC: National Institute of Mental Health.

Hanson, R. F., Freedy, J. R., Kilpatrick, D. G., & Saunders, B. E. (1993, November). *Civil unrest in Los Angeles: Diversity in community, race/ethnicity and gender.* Poster presented at the Annual Meeting of the Association for the Advancement of Behavior Therapy, Atlanta.

Hanson, R. F., Kilpatrick, D. G., Freedy, J. R., & Saunders, B. E. (in press). Los Angeles County following the 1992 civil disturbances: Degree of exposure and impact on mental health. *Journal of Consulting and Clinical Psychology.*

Helzer, J. E., Robins, L. N., & McEvoy, L. (1987). Post-traumatic stress disorder in the general population. *New England Journal of Medicine, 317,* 1630–1634.

Hobfoll, S. E., Freedy, J., Lane, C., & Geller, P. (1990). Conservation of social resources: Social support resource theory. *Journal of Social and Personal Relationships, 7,* 465–478.

Husaini, B. A., Neff, J. A., Newbrough, J. R., & Moore, M. C. (1982). The stress-buffering role of social support and personal confidence among the rural married. *Journal of Community Psychology, 10,* 409–426.

Jenkins, J. M., & Smith, M. A. (1990). Factors protecting children living in disharmonious homes: Maternal reports. *Journal of the American Academy of Child Adolescent Psychiatry, 29,* 60–69.

Kaniasty, K., & Norris, F. H. (1992). Social support and victims of crime: Matching event, support, and outcome. *American Journal of Community Psychology, 20,* 211–241.

Kelly, D. P. (1990). *Victims of crime: Problems, policies, and programs.* Newbury Park, CA: Sage Publications.

Kilpatrick, D. G. (Ed.). (1983). Special feature: Assessment and treatment of rape victims [special issue]. *The Clinical Psychologist, 36*(4).

Kilpatrick, D. G. (1990, October). The epidemiology of potentially stressful events and their traumatic impact: Implications for prevention. In C. Dunning (chair), *Trauma studies: Contributions to prevention.* Plenary session conducted at the 6th Annual Meeting of the International Society for Traumatic Stress Studies, New Orleans, LA.

Kilpatrick, D. G. (1993). Introduction [special section on rape]. *Journal of Interpersonal Violence, 8*(2), 193–197.

Kilpatrick, D. G., Edmunds, C. N., & Seymour, A. K. (1992). *Rape in America: A report to the nation.* Arlington, VA: National Victim Center.

Kilpatrick, D. G., McAlhaney, D. A., McCurdy, R. L., Shaw, D. A., & Roitzsch, J. C. (1982). Aging, alcoholism, anxiety, and sensation seeking: An exploratory investigation. *Addictive Behaviors, 7,* 139–142.

Kilpatrick, D. G., & Otto, R. K. (1987). Constitutionally guaranteed participation in criminal proceedings for victims: Potential effects on psychological functioning. *Wayne State Law Review, 34*(1), 7–28.

Kilpatrick, D. G., & Resnick, H. S. (1993). PTSD associated with exposure to criminal victimization in clinical and community populations. In J. R. Davidson & E. B. Foa (Eds.), *Post-traumatic stress disorder in review: Recent research and future directions* (pp. 113–143). Washington, DC: American Psychiatric Press.

Kilpatrick, D. G., Resnick, H. S., Saunders, B. E., & Best, C. L. (in press). Rape, other violence against women, and posttraumatic stress disorder: Critical issues in assessing the adversity–stress–psychopathology relationship. In B. P. Dohrenwend (Ed.), *Adversity, stress, and psychopathology,* Washington, DC: American Psychiatric Press.

Kilpatrick, D. G., Resnick, H. S., Saunders, B. E., Best, C. L., & Epstein, J. (1994, June). *Violent assault and alcohol dependence among women: Results of a longitudinal study.* Poster presented at the annual meeting of the Research Society on Alcoholism, Maui, Hawaii.

Kilpatrick, D. G., Resnick, H. S., & Weaver, T. (1994). *Risk and prevention factors in violence in women.* Unpublished manuscript.

Kilpatrick, D. G., Saunders, B. E., Amick-McMullan, A., Best, C. L., Veronen, L. J., & Resnick, H. S. (1989). Victim and crime factors associated with the development of crime-related post-traumatic stress disorder. *Behavior Therapist, 20,* 199–214.

Kilpatrick, D. G., Saunders, B. E., Veronen, L. J., Best, C. L., & Von, J. M. (1987). Criminal victimization: Lifetime prevalence, reporting to police, and psychological impact. *Crime and Delinquency, 33,* 479–489.

Kilpatrick, D. G., Seymour, A. K., & Boyle, J. (1991). *America speaks out: Citizens attitudes about victims' rights and violence.* Arlington, VA: National Victim Center.

Kilpatrick, D. G., Sutker, P. B., & Smith, A. D. (1976). Deviant drug and alcohol use: The role of anxiety, sensation seeking, and other personality variables. In M. Zuckerman and C. Speilberg (Eds.), *Emotions and anxiety: New concepts, methods, and applications.* New York: Lawrence Earlbaum Associates.

Kilpatrick, D. G., Veronen, L. J., & Resick, P. A. (1979). The aftermath of rape: Recent empirical findings. *American Journal of Orthopsychiatry, 49*(4), 658–669.

Kilpatrick, D. G., Saunders, B. E., Veronen, L. J., Best, C. L., & Von, J. M. (1987). Criminal victimization: Lifetime prevalence, reporting to police, and psychological impact. *Crime and Delinquency, 33*(4), 479–489.

Koss, M. P. (1983). The scope of rape: Implications for the clinical treatment of victims. *The Clinical Psychologist, 36,* 88–91.

Koss, M. P. (1993). Detecting the scope of rape: A review of prevalence research methods. *Journal of Interpersonal Violence, 8,* 198–222.

Koss, M. P., & Dinero, T. E. (1989). Discrimination analysis of risk factors for sexual victimization among a national sample of college women. *Journal of Consulting and Clinical Psychology, 57,* 242–250.

Koss, M. P., & Harvey, M. R. (1987). *The rape victims: Clinical and community approaches to treatment.* Lexinton, MA: Stephen Greene.

Kulka, R. A., Schlenger, W. E., Fairbank, J. A., Hough, R. L., Jordan, B. K., Marmar, C. R., & Weiss, D. S. (1990). *Trauma and the Vietnam war generation.* New York: Brunner/Mazel.

Laub, J. H. (1990). Patterns of criminal victimization in the United States. In A. J. Lurigion, W. G. Skogan, & R. C. Davis (Eds.), *Victims of crime: Problems, policies, and programs* (pp. 23–46). Newbury Park, CA: Sage Publications.

Lurigio, A. J., Skogan, W. G., & Davis, R. C. (1990). *Victims of crime: Problems, policies and programs.* Newbury Park, CA: Sage Publications.

McCall, G. J. (1993). Risk factors and sexual assault prevention. *Journal of Interpersonal Violence, 8,* 277–295.

Mercy, J. A., Rosenberg, M. L., Powell, K. E., Broome, C. V., & Roper, W. L. (1993). Public health policy for preventing violence. *Health Affairs: The Quarterly Journal of the Health Sphere, 12,* 7–25.

Moss, M., Frank, E., & Anderson, B. (1987). *The effects of marital status and partner support on emotional response to acute trauma: The example of rape.* Unpublished manuscript, University of Pittsburgh, Pittsburgh, PA.

Murphy, S. M., Kilpatrick, D. G., Amick-McMullan, A. E., Veronen, L. J., Paduhovich, J., Best, C. L., Villeponteaux, L. A., & Saunders, B. E. (1988). Current psychological functioning of child sexual assault survivors: A community study. *Journal of Interpersonal Violence, 3*(1), 55–79.

National Crime Prevention Institute. (1986). *Understanding crime prevention.* Boston: Buttersworths.

Norris, F. H. (1992). Epidemiology of trauma: Frequency and impact of different potentially traumatic events on different demographic groups. *Journal of Consulting and Clinical Psychology, 60,* 409–418.

Norris, J., & Feldman-Summers, S. (1981). Factors related to the psychological impacts of rape on the victim. *Journal of Abnormal Psychology, 90,* 562–567.

Orlando, J. A., & Koss, M. P. (1983). The effect of sexual victimization on sexual satisfaction: A study of the negative association hypothesis. *Journal of Abnormal Psychology, 92,* 104–106.

Paykel, E. S., Emms, E. M., Fletcher, J., & Rassaby, E. S. (1980). Life events and social support in puerperal depression. *British Journal of Psychology, 136,* 339–346.

President's Task Force on Victims of Crime. (1982). *President's task force on victims of crime final report.* Washington, DC: U.S. Government Printing Office.

Reiss, A. J., & Roth, J. A. (1993). *Understanding and preventing violence.* Washington, DC: National Academy Press.

Resick, P. A. (1986, May). *Reactions of female and male victims of rape or robbery.* Final report of NIMH Grant No. MH 37296.

Resick, P. A. (1988). *Reactions of female and male victims of rape or robbery.* Final report of NIJ Grant No. 85-IJ-CX-0042.

Resick, P. A., Calhoun, K. S., Atkeson, B. M., & Ellis, E. M. (1981). Social adjustment in victims of sexual assault. *Journal of Consulting and Clinical Psychology, 49,* 705–712.

Resnick, H. S., Kilpatrick, D. G., Dansky, B. S., Saunders, B. E., & Best, C. (1993). Prevalence of civilian trauma and post-traumatic stress disorder in a representative national sample of women. *Journal of Consulting and Clinical Psychology, 61,* 984–991.

Resnick, H. S., Kilpatrick, D. G., & Lipovsky, J. A. (1991). Assessment of rape-related post-traumatic stress disorder. Stressor and symptom dimensions. *Psychological Assessment: A Journal of Consulting and Clinical Psychology, 3,* 561–572.

Rosenberg, M. L., & Fenley, M. A. (1991). *Violence in America: A public health approach.* New York: Oxford University Press.

Rosenberg, M. L., & Mercy, J. A. (1991). Assaultive violence. *Violence in America, 2,* 14–50.

Ruch, L. O., & Chandler, S. M. (1980, September). *The impact of sexual assault on three victim groups receiving crisis intervention services at a rape treatment center: Adult rape victims, child rape victims and incest victims.* Paper presented at the American Sociological Meeting, New York, New York.

Rutter, M. (1989). Isle of Wight revisited: Twenty-five years of child psychiatric epidemiology. *Journal of the American Academy of Child Adolescent Psychiatry, 28,* 633–653.

Saunders, B. E., Kilpatrick, D. G., Resnick, H. S., & Tidwell, R. P. (1989). Brief screening for lifetime history of criminal victimization at mental health intake: A preliminary study. *Journal of Interpersonal Violence, 4,* 267–277.

Saunders, B. E., Villeponteaux, L. A., Lipovsky, J. A., Kilpatrick, D. G., & Veronen, L. J. (1992). Child sexual assault as a risk factor for mental disorders among women: A community survey. *Journal of Interpersonal Violence, 7,* 189–204.

Solomon, S. O., Smith, E. M., Robins, L. N., & Fischbach, R. L. (1987). Social involvement as a mediator of disaster-induced stress. *Journal of Applied Social Psychology, 17,* 1092–1112.

Sorenson, S. B., Stein, J. A., Siegel, J. M., Golding, J. M., & Burnam, M. A. (1987). The prevalence of adults sexual assault: The Los Angeles Epidemiological Catchment Area Project. *American Journal of Epidemiology, 126,* 1154–1164.

Sparks, C. H. (1982). *Community action strategies to stop rape* (Final Report, grant #R18MH29049). Washington, DC: National Institute of Mental Health, National Center for the Prevention and Control of Rape.

Sparks, C. H., & Bar On, B. A. (1985). *A social change approach to the prevention of sexual violence against women,* unpublished manuscript, Stone Center for Developmental Service and Studies, Wellesley College, Wellesley, MA.

U.S. Bureau of the Census (1991). *Statistical abstract of the United States: 1991 (111th ed.)*. Washington, DC: Author.

Veronen, L. J., & Kilpatrick, D. G. (1980). Self-reported fears of rape victims: A preliminary investigation. *Behavior Modification, 4,* 383–396.

Von, J. M., Kilpatrick, D. G., Burgess, A. W., & Hartman, C. R. (1991). Rape and sexual assault. In M. L. Rosenberg & M. A. Fenley (Eds.), *Violence in America: A public health approach* (pp. 95–122). New York: Oxford University Press.

Werner, E. E. (1989). High-risk children in young adulthood: A longitudinal study from birth to 32 years. *American Journal of Orthopsychiatry, 59,* 72–81.

Werner, E. E. (1992). The children of Kauai: Resiliency and recovery in adolescence and adulthood. *Journal of Adolescent Health, 13,* 262–268.

Werner, E. E., & Smith, R. S. (1982). *Vulnerable but invincible: A longitudinal study of resilient children and youth*. New York: McGraw-Hill.

West, D. G., Frank, D., Anderson, B., & Stewart, B. D. (1987). *Social support and postrape symptomatology*. Unpublished manuscript, Western Psychiatric Institute, Pittsburgh, PA.

Whitaker, C. J., & Bastian, L. D. (1991). *Teenage victims: A national crime survey report (NCJ-128129)*. Washington, DC: U.S. Department of Justice.

Williams, J. E., & Holmes, K. A. (1981). *The second assault: Rape and public attitudes*. Westport, CT: Greenwood Press.

Wyatt, G. E., Guthrie, D., & Notgrass, C. M. (1992). Differential effects of women's child sexual abuse and subsequent sexual revictimization. *Journal of Consulting and Clinical Psychology, 3,* 561–572.

Zawitz, M. W. (Ed.). (1988). *Report to the nation on crime and justice* (2nd ed.). Washington, DC: U.S. Department of Justice.

Zuckerman, M. (1979). *Sensation seeking: Beyond the optimal level of arousal*. Hillsdale, NJ: Lawrence Erlbaum.

Zuckerman, M. (Ed.). (1983). *Biological bases of sensation seeking, impulsivity, and anxiety*. Hillsdale, NJ: Lawrence Erlbaum.

Zuckerman, M., Bone, R. N., Neary, R., Mangelsdorff, D., & Brustman, B. (1972). What is the sensation seeker? Personality trait and experience correlates of the sensation seeking scales. *Journal of Consulting and Clinical Psychology, 39,* 308–321.

7

The Mental Health Impact of Natural and Technological Disasters

BONNIE L. GREEN and SUSAN D. SOLOMON

INTRODUCTION

Unfortunately, disasters are quite common occurrences in the United States and elsewhere. Because of the frequency of these events, it is important to understand their long-term consequences, as well as which aspects of these events, and the people and communities exposed to them, predict better and worse adjustment over time. Such information is potentially helpful in targeting individuals and groups for mental health interventions and in developing strategies for outreach to affected populations. In the present chapter, we review the literature with regard to the overall impact of disaster (i.e., does disaster have negative mental health effects?) along with the types of symptoms that have been shown empirically to be associated with these events. We also summarize what is presently known about the longitudinal course of responses to disaster events. Next, we discuss risk factors for the development of psychological symptoms, including stressor characteristics, individual characteristics, and social–environmental characteristics. Factors contributing to positive outcomes are also addressed in this section. Finally, implications for prevention and intervention drawn from these studies are noted.

This review is guided by a model, developed earlier, of factors influencing positive and negative outcomes following a traumatic event (Green, Wilson, &

BONNIE L. GREEN · Department of Psychiatry, Georgetown University School of Medicine, Washington, D.C. 20007.   **SUSAN D. SOLOMON** · Violence and Traumatic Stress Research Branch, National Institute of Mental Health, Rockville, Maryland 20857.

Traumatic Stress: From Theory to Practice, edited by John R. Freedy and Stevan E. Hobfoll. Plenum Press, New York, 1995.

Lindy, 1985). This model starts with exposure to specific aspects of the event (in this case, disaster) such as violent loss, threat to life, and exposure to grotesque aspects of death and injury. The exposure triggers the mental/psychological processing of the event along the lines proposed by Horowitz and others (e.g., Horowitz, 1986), including intrusion or reexperiencing phenomena, and avoidance and denial responses. This processing takes place in the context of personal characteristics and social or recovery factors. Personal characteristics include such factors as past history of trauma, past psychological problems, and coping and defense styles. Social/recovery factors include the community response to the event, the strength and availability of one's social networks (including indigenous and professional helpers), the socioeconomic and cultural context, and similar factors. Together these factors affect whether or not the individual is able to process the event successfully by him- or herself, the nature of the outcomes, and the length of the recovery process. Outcomes may be negative, neutral, or positive, and may change over time as additional stresses and resources are brought to bear (see Figure 1).

As we review studies in this chapter, we sometimes distinguish natural from technological disaster events; however, they are probably more alike than different. Disasters are conceptualized as environmental stressors that happen to a community. Traditionally, disasters have been seen as sudden, unexpected events that potentially endanger life and property. Tornadoes, hurricanes, floods, and earthquakes are examples of "natural" disasters, whereas plane crashes, explosions, structure collapses and collisions are examples of "human-caused" or "technological" disasters. The latter are usually a result of accident or mishap, but they may also result from negligence, and may be affected by natural environmental phenomena (e.g., a plane crash related to bad weather). Similarly, natural disasters may be mitigated by human intervention (e.g., hurricane warnings and evacuation). Thus the distinction between natural and technological disasters is not completely clear-cut. The two types have in common the immediate threat and danger and the potential for ongoing disruption. However they may differ with regard to whether there is someone to "blame" for the event and whether it could have been prevented. The conceptual differences between these two types of events were most clearly drawn by Baum and colleagues (Baum, Fleming, & Davidson, 1983). They argued that we "expect" natural disasters to some extent, since we do not have, and do not expect to have, control over nature. In contrast, we expect to be able to control technology, and thus it may be more of a blow to suffer a technological catastrophe (a loss of control), since, by definition, it could have been prevented. "Silent" disasters, such as radiation leaks or chemical toxin exposure, have no "low point" when the damage done is clearly over and can be assessed, since risk for cancer, later birth defects, or similar problems may continue for decades.

DISASTER OCCURRENCE

As is the case with other types of traumatic events, natural and technological disasters are more common than we would like to think. Excluding the

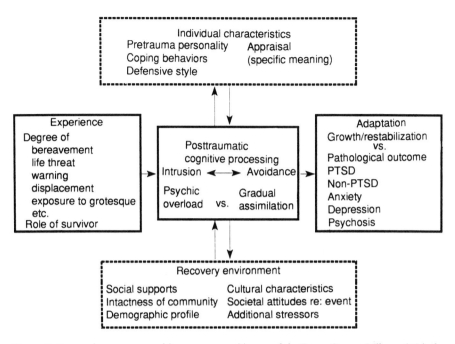

Figure 1. Processing a catastrophic event: a working model. (From Green, Wilson, & Lindy, 1985, with permission.)

United States, there have been nearly 2,400 disasters worldwide since 1900 (through 1986) (U.S. Agency for International Development, 1986), producing 42 million deaths, and disrupting the lives of 1.4 billion people. Further, these events are not randomly distributed among the populations of the world. The report noted above found that 86% of the reported disasters and 78% of all deaths occurred in developing countries. Thus, each disaster in a developing country leaves more exposed individuals in need of disaster relief and other services, most likely under conditions of fewer resources to bring to bear. A more recent report by the International Federation of Red Cross and Red Crescent Societies (1993) showed similar trends. Between 1967 and 1991, 7,766 disasters world wide were reported, with over 7 million people killed and nearly 3 trillion people *affected* (defined as those needing immediate [life sustaining] or long-term [social or economic] assistance as a direct consequence of the disaster), with, again, the poorer countries and those with the largest populations sustaining the most losses.

In the United States in 1989, Hurricane Hugo and the Loma Prieta earthquake killed 90 people. Direct economic losses were about $15 billion, and thousands were homeless for over a year (U.S. National Committee for the Decade of National Disaster Reduction, 1991). Based on a random national survey of telephone-owning households in which people were questioned concerning their disaster experience during the 10-year period 1970–1980, an estimate was made that almost 2 million households per year (24.5 per 1,000) experienced injuries or damages from either household fires or one of the four most common natural hazards (floods, hurricanes, and severe tropical storms, tornadoes and severe windstorms, earthquakes, and severe tremors) (Rossi, Wright, Weber-Burdin, & Perina, 1983).

Human-made disasters such as chemical pollution, transportation accidents, explosions, structural failures, terrorism, and the like, pose an ever-increasing threat to physical and mental health. Although the extent of exposure to technological disaster is difficult to estimate, a 1980 Senate Subcommittee concerned with only one such hazard, chemical dumps, noted that as many as 30,000 sites may be capable of causing significant health problems from their proximity to public ground water supplies for drinking (Cohn, 1980).

Recently, mental health investigators have assessed exposure to disaster and other traumatic events in the general population at an individual level. A study by Norris (1992) assessed exposure more systematically and found that 69% of her community sample, drawn from four communities in the southeastern United States, had experienced at least one traumatic event. The effects of Hurricane Hugo were specifically assessed as part of that study; however, individual exposure to other disasters was also evaluated. Norris found that over 13% of her total sample reported lifetime exposure to a natural or man-made disaster (excluding Hugo), and about 2% reported past-year exposure. For "other hazard" (causing evacuation from one's home, or an environmental danger), the rates were 14% lifetime and 6% past year.

Other general population studies have examined the lifetime prevalence of exposure to natural disasters. One household probability sample of adults ($n = 1,009$) impacted by the Loma Prieta earthquake (San Francisco, California area; October, 1989) was interviewed approximately 2 years following the earthquake. It was discovered that 82.9% had experienced another earthquake either before or after the Loma Prieta earthquake! In addition, 27.8% had experienced a natural disaster other than another earthquake. Another household probability sample of adults ($n = 776$) impacted by Hurricane Hugo (Charleston, South Carolina area; September, 1989) was interviewed about 2 years following the storm. One-third (31.6%) reported having experienced another natural disaster (J. R. Freedy, personal communication, 1994). Clearly, over the course of a lifetime, the risk for exposure to a natural disaster may be considered substantial.

PSYCHOSOCIAL OUTCOMES OF DISASTER

Overall Impact

The most common area of investigation in the disaster literature has been disaster's mental health impact. We do not have the space to review all such studies here, but we do review a number of the most methodologically sound studies to date in addressing this question. Although the studies focus on different types of outcomes, in general they indicate that there are significant mental health effects associated with disasters when survivors are compared to people not exposed to these events.

Although the studies that follow have tended to focus on more pathological outcomes, and particularly on diagnoses following disaster events, it is certainly the case that not all outcomes constitute diagnosable pathology, or even more negative affects or behaviors. As mentioned in the model described earlier, extreme stress situations may also produce more neutral outcomes, or under certain circumstances, even promote personal growth. Further, although initial reactions to disaster may include surprise, helplessness, shock, anger, and confusion, many of these reactions resolve in most survivors within a few months (e.g., Freedy, Kilpatrick, & Resnick, 1993), and long-term negative reactions are present in many fewer individuals. Those individuals who are more vulnerable, and the circumstances leading to more risk, are described later in this chapter.

With regard to natural disasters, Shore, Tatum, and Vollmer (1986) studied over 500 community survivors of the Mount St. Helen's Volcano, which killed 62 people. They found higher lifetime rates (since the disaster) of depression, anxiety, and posttraumatic stress disorder (PTSD) diagnoses in the survivors than in an unexposed control sample. Murphy (1984) studied individuals from the same disaster and stratified them on extent of bereavement. At 11 months, bereaved subjects had higher depression and somatic symptoms than nonbereaved controls, although no differences in physical health were noted. McFarlane (1987) studied 235 families in Australia, by mail survey, who had been exposed to bushfires that had killed 14 people and destroyed a great deal of property and hundreds of thousands of livestock. At 8 and 26 months, the fire-exposed sample reported more "irritable distress" (irritability among family members, fighting, not enjoying activities together) than the unexposed sample.

Since disasters happen unexpectedly, we rarely have knowledge about the condition of exposed individuals prior to the event. However, several recent disaster studies involved investigators who were already in the field collecting data for another purpose, and found themselves with "predisaster" data that allowed them to assess increases in symptoms that were specifically tied to the event. Canino, Bravo, Rubio-Stipec, & Woodbury (1990) had collected epidemiologic data in Puerto Rico about 1 year before floods and mud slides there killed 180 people. They were able, following the disaster, to reevaluate 375 of the initial respondents and over 500 new respondents at about 2 years postdisaster. They found significantly increased symptoms of depression, from predisaster levels, among those exposed to the disaster, but did not find increased panic or alcohol abuse. In the postdisaster wave, they also assessed PTSD, drug abuse, and generalized anxiety through retrospective reports. They found significantly increased generalized anxiety symptoms, and new PTSD cases. The exposed group showed higher use of health care services as well (retrospectively evaluated).

Phifer and Norris (1989) also collected prospective data following floods in Kentucky that occurred while they were collecting epidemiologic data on 200 older adults. Controlling for preflood levels of distress, exposed flood victims with personal losses were more depressed and anxious than nonvictims 3 to 6 months after the first flood. Adams and Adams (1984) studied community records for the period from 7 months before to 7 months after the Mount St. Helen's eruption and found disaster-related increases in mental health visits, substance abuse visits, medical visits, court cases, and domestic violence reports. However, decreases were noted in divorce rates and child abuse. The meaning of these latter findings is not clear.

With regard to technological disaster, Green, Grace, et al. (1990) compared 120 former litigant survivors of a dam collapse disaster that killed 125 people to a nonlitigant group and a group not exposed to the disaster at 14 years postdisaster. The exposed litigant and nonlitigant groups did not differ from each other, but the exposed groups differed significantly from the unexposed group, showing higher rates of depression, anxiety, and lifetime PTSD.

Holen (1991) studied Norwegian survivors of an oil rig collapse in the North Sea, in which 123 workers (of 212 on the rig) died. They were compared to workers on another rig that did not collapse over a period of several years. Psychiatric diagnoses were eight times higher in the survivors than those unexposed. Sick leave was also used twice as much by survivors than by nonexposed workers. These differences in use of sick leave continued throughout the 8-year follow-up of these survivors.

A number of studies have been conducted on survivors of "silent" disasters, most of them on the Three Mile Island (TMI) nuclear leak disaster. For example Baum and his colleagues (Baum, Schaeffer, Fleming, & Collins, 1986; Davidson, Fleming, & Baum, 1987) studied about 40 TMI residents within 5 miles of the plant and compared them to nonexposed respondents at approximately 17 months following the original TMI incident. The TMI group was significantly higher on overall distress, as well as somatic complaints, anxiety, alienation symptoms, and sleep disturbance. Further signs of distress were indicated by their lower performance on a proofreading task used to assess concentration, and higher levels of epinephrine, norepinephrine, and urinary cortisol than unexposed residents. Further, medical records of the TMI group showed elevations in systolic and diastolic blood pressure from pre- to post-TMI, as well as more physician-rated problems and more prescriptions given. Thus the effects of these events can be seen not only in self-reported distress and other indicators dependent upon the subject's reporting (e.g. diagnoses) but are reflected in performance tasks and physical indicators as well. A 5-year follow-up showed that many of these problems continued to persist over the long-term for the TMI residents (Davidson, Fleming, & Baum, 1986).

A cross-sectional study of the St. Louis, Missouri (Times Beach) disasters, which included dioxin exposure, floods, tornadoes, and radioactive exposure (Smith, Robins, Przybeck, Goldring, & Solomon, 1986), found direct exposure to be associated with significantly higher levels of new PTSD and depression symptoms. Whereas the increase in depression symptoms occurred only among those with prior symptoms, the increase in PTSD symptoms occurred whether or not individuals had prior symptoms. New symptoms of other disorders were not associated with exposure.

These studies of both natural and technological disasters clearly indicate that disasters have a negative impact on mental health. Consistent effects were reported in the areas of PTSD symptoms, other anxiety symptoms, somatization, and depression. Findings regarding alcohol abuse were less clear-cut. In addition, the distress symptoms also had physiological manifestations that could be shown to be associated with the disaster, were measurable in individuals, and were reflected in visits to physicians and to mental health clinics, and in use of sick leave. Since a number of these studies were prospective in nature, new symptoms appearing after disaster exposure could be evaluated. Thus the evidence for negative mental health effects of disaster is quite compelling.

Severity of Impact

Although some impact of disasters was noted in all studies, the absolute levels of these effects, and their clinical significance, are more difficult to judge. Investigators do not often use the same instruments to measure outcome, and cutoff levels used to determine "rates" of impairment may be arbitrary. However, even if everyone were using the same instrument with the same cutoff, differences among events would be expected, since disasters vary among themselves in the extent of death, injury, and property destruction. Further, studies may select greater or lesser exposed subsamples to evaluate and may define "exposure" in different ways. A more liberal definition of exposure will lead to lower reported rates of symptoms and disorders, whereas study of more severely exposed individuals will give higher estimates. This is true because as exposure increases, so do symptoms (see below).

Only one study of which we are aware compared level of current symptoms of PTSD across different event types. That study (Norris, 1992) found that, relatively speaking, symptoms associated with disaster exposure were somewhat fewer than those associated with other types of traumatic events, such as crime victimization. Current PTSD rates for crime victims were 8.5%, those for accident victims were 8.6%, and those for victims of hazards (disasters) were 5.8%. These findings indicate that disaster has a noteworthy impact on current mental health, although this impact may be somewhat less than that for other traumatic events.

For purposes of "getting a feel" for the extent of diagnosable psychopathology that can occur following a disaster, we report on rates of PTSD from several studies that used a structured interview to make the diagnosis. Although PTSD is clearly not the only diagnosis to arise from disaster exposure, it is the most common. Therefore, its assessment gives us some idea of the number of people who might be significantly affected.

With regard to natural disasters, the Shore et al. (1986) study reported earlier, of the Mt. St. Helen's eruption showed that 11% of men with high exposure (property loss of $5000 or more, *or* death of a family member or close relative) developed depression, generalized anxiety, or PTSD (they did not separate the disorders), whereas 21% of women with high exposure developed these disorders. The disorders all arose within the first 2 years after the disaster and had abated by 3 years. Canino et al. (1990) found a PTSD rate of only 4% at 2 years following the mud slides in Puerto Rico. Steinglass and Gerrity (1990) studied a flood in one community and a tornado in another, and found different rates of PTSD across the two communities (excluding bereaved subjects) about 1 1/2 years after the disasters, with the flooded community showing a rate of 5% and the tornado-hit community, a rate of 21%.

In technological events, the rates vary even more widely. The St. Louis studies showed PTSD rates of 5.2% after 1 year in subjects directly exposed to flooding and dioxin (Smith et al., 1986). Smith, North, McCool, and Shea (1990) found 22% new PTSD cases in hotel employees at 1 month following the crash of a plane into their hotel. Fifty-four percent of these employees had at least one diagnosable disorder. Green, Grace, et al. (1990) showed a PTSD rate of 23% in litigants and nonlitigants 14 years following a dam collapse; however, this was not a representative sample of the community.

Clearly, the use of mental health diagnoses to describe disaster effects does not capture all of the distress that is clinically significant, so it gives us a conservative estimate of who might be in need of services. Even so, although the reported rates vary a great deal, they do indicate that disaster may produce rates of impairment that are clinically noteworthy. Those studies specifying rates do not provide much evidence for the differential impact of natural versus technological events. Further, since the time frame varies from one study to the next, comparisons are made more difficult. Most of the studies reported were conducted over a year after the event, so early impacts are not well documented. In the next section, we examine studies that followed survivors longitudinally.

Longevity and Course of Impact

It is important to know the period and course of time during which survivors of disaster are at risk for purposes of mental health planning. There are now a number of longitudinal studies that have followed survivors for various periods, some for many years post-disaster. These studies, generally speaking, indicate that the negative effects of disasters tend to decrease over time, although they do not necessarily disappear. Chronic adjustment problems are a possibility following exposure to particularly severe disasters.

It is in the realm of longevity of responses that there was some indication of differences between natural and technological events. Studies of natural disasters tended to show declines in symptoms over a 1- to 2-year period, with functioning often returning to normal ranges (Adams & Adams, 1984; Murphy, 1986; Phifer & Norris, 1989; Shore et al., 1986), although there are exceptions (McFarlane, 1987). Technological disasters have been followed for longer periods and also tend to indicate decreases in symptoms over time. However, the return to "normal" is not as clearly demonstrated. Green, Grace, Lindy, Titchener, and Lindy (1983) found that although some symptoms following a nightclub fire decreased between 1 and 2 years, symptoms of hostility actually increased. Studies by Davidson et al. (1986) of Three Mile Island showed elevated symptoms and physiological problems extending for 5 years, and Holen's study of the oil rig collapse showed effects to 8 years. Green, Lindy, et al. (1990) showed continued PTSD in a quarter of dam-collapse survivors as long as 14 years post-event. Symptoms in these studies sometimes lasted as long as the follow-up period studied. This set of findings indicates that responses to disasters may be quite persistent. Further, there is some evidence, particularly in technological events, that symptoms related to anger and irritability may not decline, but may continue or even increase post-disaster.

The comparison between natural and technological disasters is intriguing but needs to be interpreted cautiously. The physical severity of the natural and the technological events studied so far is not necessarily equivalent, i.e., more deaths occurred in the latter events, and it is possible that the longevity of impacts actually relates more to the severity than to the type of event (see below). Nevertheless, the possibility of differences between the two types of events needs to continue to be explored, since psychologically, being the victim of an "Act of God" may be perceived very differently by individuals than being a victim when another person or persons caused the victimization, even accidentally through oversight or negligence. The importance of hostility or anger symptoms associated with technological events may be related to this distinction. In the studies cited in this chapter, some of the high-death-rate natural disasters (e.g., Puerto Rican mud slides) showed relatively low disorder rates several years post-event, whereas the TMI disaster, for example, showed impacts (compared to controls) for at least 5 years, although no one was even injured. Studies of other types of human-caused events such as war or child abuse have shown impacts for three or more decades (e.g., Saunders, Villeponteaux, Lipovsky, Kilpatrick, & Veronen, 1992; Speed, Engdahl, Schwartz, & Eberly, 1989), suggesting that deliberately perpetrated events may be on the upper end of a dimension of event causality that puts people at risk for more chronic negative impacts (Green, 1993). However, this notion needs to be expressed as a hypothesis since direct comparisons have not been made.

RISK FACTORS AND MEDIATORS OF PSYCHOLOGICAL OUTCOMES FOLLOWING DISASTER

Mediators are aspects of the situation that play a central role in determining how victims react to disaster, and what physical and mental health consequences these reactions produce. Studies of the effects of mediators help identify those victims likely to develop prolonged effects.

Individual Exposure Severity

The degree of exposure to the disaster itself, via life threat, loss of loved ones, property loss, community disruption, and exposure to grotesque death, has been shown repeatedly to relate to the risk for psychological problems following disasters. These aspects of traumatic events may be conceptualized along the lines of the present volume as resource losses that occur to the individuals exposed to the event (see Chapter 2, this volume). They also have an element of exposure to death or to threat of death (Green, 1993). Other authors have suggested that such traumatic events cause individuals to question basic assumptions about their vulnerability (Janoff-Bulman, 1992). In conservation of resources (COR) theory, such assumptions regarding world view would fall under the specific category of personal characteristics, as a subset of resources (Hobfoll, 1989). Not surprisingly, the presence and severity of life-threatening aspects of events increase the risk for negative psychological consequences. This association has been demonstrated in natural disasters (see Bravo, Rubio-Stipec, Canino, Woodbury, & Ribera, 1990; Freedy, Shaw, Jarrell, & Masters, 1992; Phifer & Norris, 1989; Shore et al., 1986) and in technological disasters (see Bromet, Parkinson, & Dunn, 1990; Green, Grace, & Gleser, 1985; Smith et al., 1986). Not all exposure differences were associated with all outcomes, but a very consistent pattern exists. The few studies that do not show this trend tend to have all high-exposure subjects. Therefore, knowing which subjects were more exposed to a disaster event gives the clinician a starting point in identifying those survivors who are most at risk for developing problems.

In addition to the more immediate impacts of disasters such as threat to life and loss of loved ones and property, there are often more chronic or ongoing disruptive circumstances associated with these events. Since those with the greatest initial impact are likely to have the most ongoing strain, it is difficult to separate these aspects empirically. However, these ongoing circumstances are likely to take a psychological toll as well. For example, in the Buffalo Creek disaster described earlier, those individuals who had to move the farthest and the most times as a result of the disaster were at higher risk for negative mental health outcomes at both 2 years and 14 years (Gleser, Green, & Winget, 1981; Green, 1992). Conversely, those men who were able to go back to their homes and clean them up following the dam collapse (an active coping mode that likely led to feelings of control) were at reduced risk for mental health problems (Gleser et al., 1981). These two types of stressors, the acute threat, and the more chronic "strain," are likely explained by somewhat different processes and may be associated with somewhat different types of effects (e.g., PTSD is likely associated primarily with the former). However both are important and contribute to long-term risk.

Personal Characteristics

Findings with regard to gender and adjustment following disasters are mixed. Whereas some studies have found women to be at higher risk, others have found men at higher risk, or no differences. A simple count might suggest that women are more vulnerable; however, gender differences may depend upon the nature of the event or which particular adjustment outcome is examined. For example, a number of studies have found that women have higher rates of anxiety and depression (e.g., Gleser et al., 1981; Shore et al., 1986), whereas men may have more physical complaints and may abuse alcohol more (e.g., Gleser et al., 1981; Logue, Hansen, & Struening, 1979).

Age-related comparisons are difficult, since studies tend to include different age groups and use different cut-offs. However, taken together, studies examining the effects of age suggest that middle-aged subjects are most at risk for psychological problems (Green, Gleser, Lindy, Grace, & Leonard, in press). This group tends to be responsible for both children and for parents in the event of a crisis, which may make them more vulnerable. Older subjects may be relatively protected because of a history of experiences with similar events, which they have survived (Norris & Murrell, 1988). Race and ethnicity have not often been investigated in the context of disaster (Green, in press) and when it has, the findings are mixed, and usually do not take social class into account. It appears that the extent to which ethnic and cultural differences affect outcome may depend upon the nature of the disaster event and the meaning of that event and its losses to particular subpopulations (Green, in press; Norris, 1992). Education level, prior psychological problems, and prior disaster exposure all have mixed findings in the disaster literature, and few studies have been done that address these issues. More research is needed in these areas.

Social Mediators

The victim's social network includes kin, friends, neighbors, and community gatekeepers (see Solomon, 1986, for an extensive discussion of this topic). The immediate social environment can be an important mediator of individual outcomes following exposure to disaster.

Children may be particularly vulnerable to social mediators. For example, a study by McFarlane, Policansky, and Irwin (1987) indicated that the mother's response to disaster (Australian bush fires) was a better predictor of the child's response than was the child's exposure to the disaster. This relationship was particularly affected by the extent of intrusive symptoms experienced by the mother and by her changed pattern of parenting (overprotection). The initial reactions of other family members may also serve to define the severity of the event for the child. Family members may disagree about what actions, if any, to take, thereby prolonging the uncertainty, particularly about events that are intrinsically ambiguous (e.g., exposure to toxic waste, radon contamination of the home). Along these lines, a study of the TMI nuclear disaster by Handford et al. (1986) found that the reactions of children did *not* relate to the *intensity* of their parents' response. However, children of parents who *disagreed* in their immediate reactions to the event were significantly more upset than children of parents who responded consistently, even when both parents were highly distressed. Another study of TMI sheds some light on these findings. Bromet,

Hough, and Connell (1984) found that there was no relationship between adverse TMI experiences and the child's adjustment (social competence, self-esteem, behavioral problems) in families with a good milieu, but more adverse experiences *did* predict adjustment problems in families with a poor milieu.

A study by Green et al. (1991) found that both individual parental pathology and family atmosphere in the home contributed to PTSD symptoms in children 2 years following a dam-collapse disaster. After mothers' and fathers' overall severity of pathology had been accounted for statistically, an irritable or depressed family atmosphere (rated by trained raters) contributed significant additional variance to the prediction of PTSD symptoms.

Research on the topic of social support suggests that social involvement can be a mixed blessing in times of trouble (see Solomon, 1986, for a review). Both support availability and support provision have been examined for their effects as mediators of victims' responses. Although providing support under normal conditions may benefit the provider as well as the recipient, Shumaker and Brownell (1984) point out that large-scale emergencies force providers to give support at a time when they too need help, thereby making the supportive role in itself a source of stress.

A study directly examining these issues in the St. Louis flood and dioxin-exposed individuals described earlier found that for women, midrange levels of support availability were associated with the most favorable outcomes, whereas those women with high-support availability did more poorly (Solomon, Smith, Robbins, & Fischbach, 1987). For females in particular, then, too much involvement has its cost, perhaps because of the obligation to reciprocate implied by accepting informal help (Shumaker & Brownell, 1984). Because women are more often called upon to provide emotional support than are men (Fischer, 1982; Gove & Hughes, 1984), household exposure to disaster may serve to overload the capacity of women to provide the nurturance asked of them. Perhaps it is for this reason that the Solomon et al., 1987 study found that women with *excellent* spouse relationships had worse outcomes following disaster than those with weaker spouse ties. This finding was in direct contrast to that for disaster-exposed males, whose outcomes positively related to the strength of the spouse relationship. Similarly, Gleser et al. (1981) found that married women victims of the Buffalo Creek disaster showed higher psychopathology than women victims who lived alone; further, a spouse's anxiety or depression more seriously distressed women than men. Gleser et al.'s results (1981) suggest that women may respond as much or more to their husbands' mental health problems as to the disaster that precipitates them. These findings, taken together, suggest the possibility that, for some, strong family ties may be more burdensome than supportive in times of extreme stress (see Hobfoll & London, 1986; Solomon, 1986; Solomon et al., 1987).

Further study of the St. Louis disaster population suggests that single parents may be at particularly high risk for losing access to emotional support following a disaster, and access to at least moderate levels of emotional support may be an important mediator of disaster's effect on psychiatric distress (Solomon, Bravo, Rubio-Stipec, & Canino, 1993). It may be the level of social support, rather than simply the family role per se, that places individuals at particularly high risk following disaster impact. If so, levels of available support should be assessed by mental health workers, since disaster exposure has been found to be associated with declines in both perceptions of support and social participation (Kaniasty, Norris, & Murrell, 1990).

Community Mediators

A final important class of mediators of psychological responses to disaster relates to the community context of the event. Community-level factors that potentially affect individual response include the extent of community disruption, the scope and centrality (what proportion of the total community is affected and whether the event affects only specific subgroups; see Green, 1982, for a discussion), the setting of the community (e.g., rural versus urban), and the nature of the community response (e.g., solidarity versus conflict).

Golec (1983) argues that community-level variables may be even more critical than the disaster event itself in predicting individual outcomes. Her analysis of the 1976 Teton Dam collapse in Wyoming suggests that an unusually positive community response to the disaster resulted in remarkably rapid recovery. Despite substantial material loss and social disruption (70% of the homes in the county were severely damaged or totally destroyed), several community characteristics optimized recovery: adequate warning, a low death and injury rate, a highly integrated and homogeneous (Mormon faith) population, effective local disaster response, maintenance of social networks, adequate financial compensation, and a surplus of resources for immediate needs.

Findings by Phifer and Norris (1989) further illuminate the effect of the community as a mediator of disaster's effect on mental health. These investigators found that whereas personal losses were most closely associated with persistent (2-year post-disaster) increases in negative affect (e.g., sadness, anxiety, discouragement, worry, and agitation), extent of community destruction was more closely associated with declines in positive affect (e.g., feeling less enthusiasm, less energy, and less enjoyment of life). Thus, although being singled out for disaster losses may serve to increase psychiatric symptomatology, widespread community destruction may rob even those without personal losses of the qualities that make living in their community a worthwhile experience.

CONCLUSIONS AND IMPLICATIONS

Taken as a whole, these studies offer some intriguing implications for both victim assistance and further research. They show that exposure to disaster is an all too common experience, and that such exposure is capable of having a negative effect on mental health for a sizable proportion of those so exposed, and that for some victims, disaster can have lingering effects.

A number of factors influence the likelihood and extent of the emotional problems that victims may face in the aftermath of disaster. Of primary importance is the severity of the exposure itself, but many personal characteristics and social and community mediators can affect psychological outcomes as well.

Disasters that destroy the community's natural social networks may be among the most psychologically devastating, regardless of the extent of objective damage or relief efforts. Further, since disaster tends to disrupt the role of family provider, those with the expectation of fulfilling this role may find the disaster experience most directly debilitating. Individuals expecting to fulfill a nurturant role may experience negative psychological effects when disaster intensifies nurturance demands beyond the supporter's capacity to satisfy. Because single parents fulfill both these roles, experiencing a disaster may be most stressful of all for these kind of victims. However, objective indicators such as demographics may not be sufficient to identify disaster victims in need of counseling, since perceived levels of available emotional support may importantly modify the effects of disaster exposure, regardless of family role.

The above findings suggest that preventive interventions for disaster victims should target the most severely exposed individuals in terms of life threat, loss of loved ones, and other resource loss. These individuals should then be assessed for their perceptions of community cohesion, available emotional support, and the realistic levels of these social resources. When diagnostic indicators suggest the presence of psychiatric problems, victims may need to be encouraged or assisted in locating resources for emotional support other than the nuclear family. These might consist of self-help groups tailored to particular victim subgroups, such as groups for single parents, or individual counseling sessions with professionals. Although individuals may seek out these services themselves, it may be necessary to mobilize more informal resources to help survivors link up with more of these traditional sources of professional support.

Informal social networks can be used to disseminate information about an agency and to generate referrals. Indigenous paraprofessionals may be recruited for postdisaster case-finding (Bowman, 1975; Duffy, 1978; Zarle, Hartsough, & Ottinger, 1974). The efficacy of these indigenous workers stems in part from their status as reference group members who transmit norms sanctioning the use of professional services. This is especially important because experiencing obvious psychological or physical disaster aftereffects may not in itself be sufficient for victims to seek professional help. They must also perceive the symptoms as interfering with effective functioning, and they must perceive help-seeking as sanctioned by their support group (Zola, 1973; see also Lieberman, 1982; Wallston, Alagna, DeVellis, & DeVellis, 1983).

Because social networks serve as major sources of information about and referral to professional services, informal community caregivers and neighborhood leaders can be identified and used to publicize mental health programs. For example, a disaster might affect a neighborhood of low-income elderly who are relatively isolated and unaware of existing formal resources. If network analysis suggested frequent church attendance, the clergy could be a helpful source for disseminating information about the available mental health programs (Mitchell & Trickett, 1980). Along these lines, Leutz (1976) found that providing information about formal resources to nonmental health and informal caregivers (such as clergy, bartenders, and merchants) increased the number of referrals made by these individuals to social service agencies.

For networking strategies to be effective, program staff must learn to identify network leaders and provide them with (1) consultation for the psychological and health problems that come before them, (2) information about existing community resources, and (3) backup services for problems beyond the capacity of the informal support system (Cohen & Sokolovsky, 1979).

In addition to providing strategies for linking individuals with community resources, social support networks can also be effectively activated to target larger groups of people for educational information through public service announcements by the media. Newspaper, radio, and television personnel should be encouraged to go beyond fragmented dramatization of a disaster event. They may help activate citizenry toward creation of support resources for themselves, as well as help victims to identify existing formal resources and available options for rebuilding their community. Mental health professionals can provide a coordinated flow of therapeutic messages and information to the local media in four areas: (1) Certain distressing reactions are to be expected following a disaster. (2) These are normal responses to an abnormal event. (3) It is important to be accepting of one's own as well as others' feelings and to share one's feelings with others. (4) Help is available.

ACKNOWLEDGMENTS

This work was supported in part by contract number 91MF17504001D to B. L. Green from the National Institute of Mental Health. The authors wish to acknowledge Ms. Susan Weigert for her help in summarizing the articles reviewed in this chapter.

REFERENCES

Adams, P., & Adams, G. (1984). Mount Saint Helen's ashfall. *American Psychologist, 39,* 252–260.

Baum, A., Fleming, R., & Davidson, L. (1983). Natural disaster and technological catastrophe. *Environment and Behavior, 15,* 333–354.

Baum, A., Schaeffer, M., Lake, R., Fleming, R., & Collins, D. (1986). Psychological and endocrinological correlates of chronic stress at Three Mile Island. *Perspectives on Behavioral Medicine, 2,* 201–217.

Bowman, S. (1975, August). *Disaster intervention from the inside.* Paper presented at the annual meeting of the American Psychological Association, Chicago, IL.

Bravo, M., Rubio-Stipec, M., Canino, G., Woodbury, M., & Ribera, J. (1990). The psychological sequelae of disaster stress prospectively and retrospectively evaluated. *American Journal of Community Psychology, 18,* 661–680.

Bromet, E., Hough, L., & Connell, M. (1984). Mental health of children near the Three Mile Island reactor. *Journal of Preventive Psychiatry, 2,* 275–301.

Bromet, E., Parkinson, D., & Dunn, L. (1990). Long-term mental health consequences of the accident at Three Mile Island. *International Journal of Mental Health, 19,* 48–60.

Canino, G., Bravo, M., Rubio-Stipec, M., & Woodbury, M. (1990). The impact of disaster on mental health: Prospective and retrospective analyses. *International Journal of Mental Health, 19,* 51–69.

Cohen, C. I., & Sokolovsky, J. (1979). Clinical use of network analysis for psychiatric and aged populations. *Community Mental Health Journal, 15*(3), 203–213.

Cohen, V. (1980, June 7). Waste sites may invade water supply, subcommittee told. *The Washington Post,* A2.

Davidson, L., Fleming, I., & Baum, A. (1986). Post-traumatic stress as a function of chronic stress and toxic exposure. In C. Figley (Ed.), *Trauma and its wake: Vol. 2* (pp. 57–77). New York: Brunner/Mazel.

Davidson, L., Fleming, R., & Baum, A. (1987). Chronic stress, catecholamine, and sleep disturbance at Three Mile Island. *Journal of Human Stress, 13,* 75–83.

Duffy, J. C. (1978). Emergency mental health services during and after a major aircraft accident. *Disasters, 2*(213), 159–162.

Fischer, C. S. (1982). *To dwell among friends: Personal networks in town and city.* Chicago: University of Chicago Press.

Freedy, J. R., Kilpatrick, D. G., & Resnick, H. S. (1993). Natural disasters and mental health: Theory, assessment, and intervention. *Journal of Social Behavior and Personality, 8*(5), 49–103.

Freedy, J., Shaw, D., Jarrell, M., & Masters, C. (1992). Towards an understanding of the psychological impact of natural disasters: An application of the Conservation of Resources stress model. *Journal of Traumatic Stress, 5,* 441–454.

Gleser, G. C., Green, B. L., & Winget, C. N. (1981). *Prolonged psychosocial effects of disaster: A study of Buffalo Creek.* New York: Academic Press.

Golec, A. (1983). A contextual approach to the social psychological study of disaster recovery. *International Journal of Mass Emergencies and Disasters, 1*(2), 255–276.

Gove, W. R., & Hughes, M. (1984). *Overcrowding in the household.* New York: Academic Press.

Green, B. L. (1982). Assessing levels of psychosocial impairment following disaster: Consideration of actual and methodological dimensions. *The Journal of Nervous and Mental Disease, 17*(9), 544–552.

Green, B. L. (1992, August). *PTSD following a disaster: Comparison of first and second decade predictors.* Presented at the annual meeting of the American Psychological Association. Washington, DC.

Green, B. L. (1993). Identifying survivors at risk: Trauma and stressors across events. In J. P. Wilson & B. Raphael (Eds.), *International handbook of traumatic stress syndromes* (pp. 135–144). New York: Plenum Press.

Green, B. L. (in press). Cross-national and ethnocultural issues in disaster research. In A. Marsella, M. Friedman, E. Gerrity, & R. Scurfield (Eds.), *Ethnocultural aspects of posttraumatic stress disorders.* Washington, DC: American Psychological Association.

Green, G., Gleser, G., Lindy, J., Grace, M., & Leonard, A. (in press). Age-related reactions to the Buffalo Creek Dam Collapse: Second decade effects. In P. E. Ruskin & J. A. Talbott (Eds.), *Aging and posttraumatic stress disorder.* Washington, DC: American Psychiatric Press.

Green, B., Grace, M., & Gleser, G. (1985). Identifying survivors at risk: Long-term impairment following the Beverly Hills Supper Club fire. *Journal of Consulting and Clinical Psychology, 53,* 672–678.

Green, B., Grace, M., Lindy, J., Gleser, G., Leonard, A., & Kramer, T. (1990). Buffalo Creek survivors in the second decade: Comparison with unexposed and nonlitigant groups. *Journal of Applied Social Psychology, 20,* 1033–1050.

Green, B., Grace, M., Lindy, J., Titchener, J., & Lindy, J. (1983). Levels of functional impairment following a civilian disaster: The Beverly Hills Supper Club fire. *Journal of Consulting and Clinical Psychology, 51,* 573–580.

Green, B. L., Korol, M., Grace, M. C., Vary, M. G., Leonard, A. C., Gleser, G. C., & Smitson-Cohen, S. (1991). Children and disaster: Age, gender, and parental effects on PTSD symptoms. *Journal of the American Academy of Child and Adolescent Psychiatry, 30,* 945–951.

Green, B., Lindy, J., Grace, M., Gleser, G., Leonard, A., Korol, M., & Winget, C. (1990). Buffalo Creek survivors in the second decade: Stability of stress symptoms. *American Journal of Orthopsychiatry, 60,* 43–54.

Green, B. L., Wilson, J. P., & Lindy, J. D. (1985). Conceptualizing post-traumatic stress disorder: A psychosocial framework. In C. Figley (Ed.) *Trauma and its wake: Vol. I* (pp. 53–69). New York: Brunner/Mazel.

Handford, H., Mayes, S., Mattison, R., Humphrey, F., Bagnato, S., Bixler, E., & Kales, J. (1986). Child and parent reaction to the Three Mile Island nuclear accident. *Journal of the American Academy of Child Psychiatry, 25,* 346–356.

Hartsough, D. (1983). *Mitigating the emotional consequences of disaster work: A guide for training and debriefing.* Unpublished manuscript, Purdue University, Lafayette, IN.

Hobfoll, S. E. (1989). Conservation of resources: A new attempt at conceptualizing stress. *American Psychologist, 44,* 513–524.

Hobfoll, S. E., & London, P. (1986). The relationship of self-concept and social support to emotional distress among women during war. *Journal of Social and Clinical Psychology, 4,* 189–203.

Holen, A. (1991). A longitudinal study of the occurrence and persistence of posttraumatic health problems in disaster survivors. *Stress Medicine, 7,* 11–17.

Horowitz, M. J. (1986). *Stress response syndromes (2nd ed.).* Northvale, NJ: Jason Aronson.

International Federation of Red Cross and Red Crescent Societies. (1993). *World disaster report 1993.* Dordrecht, The Netherlands: Martinus Nijoff.

Janoff-Bulman, R. (1992). *Shattered assumptions.* New York: The Free Press.

Kaniasty, K. Z., Norris, F. H., & Murrell, S. A. (1990). Received and perceived social support following natural disaster. *Journal of Applied Social Psychology, 20*(2), 85–114.

Leutz, W. N. (1976). The informal community caregiver: A link between the health care system and local residents. *American Journal of Orthopsychiatry, 46,* 678–688.

Lieberman, M. A. (1982). The effects of social supports on responses to stress. In L. Goldberger, & S. Breznitz (Eds.), *Handbook of stress: Theoretical and clinical aspects* (pp. 764–783). New York: Free Press.

Logue, J., Hansen, H., & Struening, E. (1979). Emotional and physical distress following Hurricane Agnes in Wyoming Valley of Pennsylvania. *Public Health Reports, 94,* 495–502.

McFarlane, A. (1987). Family functioning and overprotection following a natural disaster: The longitudinal effects of post-traumatic morbidity. *Australian and New Zealand Journal of Psychiatry, 21,* 210–218.

McFarlane, A., Policansky, S., & Irwin, C. (1987). A longitudinal study of the psychological morbidity in children due to a natural disaster. *Psychological Medicine, 17,* 727–738.

Mitchell, R. E., & Trickett, E. J. (1980). Task force report: Social networks as mediators of social support: An analysis of the effects and determinants of social networks. *Community Mental Health Journal, 16,* 27–44.

Murphy, S. (1984). Stress levels and health status of victims of a natural disaster. *Research in Nursing and Health, 7,* 205–215.

Murphy, S. (1986). Status of natural disaster victims health and recovery 1 and 3 years later. *Research in Nursing and Health, 9,* 331–340.

Norris, F. (1992). Epidemiology of trauma: Frequency and impact of different potentially traumatic events on different demographic groups. *Journal of Consulting and Clinical Psychology, 60,* 409–418.

Norris, F., & Murrell, S. (1988). Prior experience as a moderator of disaster impact on anxiety symptoms in older adults. *American Journal of Community Psychology, 16,* 665–683.

Phifer, J., & Norris, F. (1989). Psychological symptoms in older adults following natural disaster: Nature, timing, duration, and course. *Journal of Gerontology: Social Sciences, 44,* S207–S217.

Rossi, P. H., Wright, J. D., Weber-Burdin, E., & Perina, J. (1983). Victimization by natural hazards in the United States, 1970–1980; survey estimates. *International Journal of Mass Emergencies and Disasters, 1*(3), 467–482.

Saunders, B. E., Villeponteaux, L. A., Lipovsky, J. A., Kilpatrick, D. G., & Veronen, L. J. (1992). *Journal of Interpersonal Violence, 7,* 189–204.

Shore, J., Tatum, E., & Vollmer, W. (1986). Psychiatric reactions to disaster: The Mount St. Helens experience. *American Journal of Psychiatry, 143,* 590–595.

Shumaker, S. A., & Brownell, A. (1984). Toward a theory of social support: Closing conceptual gaps. *Journal of Social Issues, 40*(4), 11–36.

Smith, E., North, C., McCool, R., & Shea, J. (1990). Acute postdisaster psychiatric disorders: Identification of persons at risk. *American Journal of Psychiatry, 147,* 202–206.

Smith, E. M., Robins, L. N., Pryzbeck, T. R., Goldring, E., & Solomon, S. D. (1986). Psychosocial consequences of a disaster. In J. H. Shore (Ed.), *Disaster stress studies: New methods and findings.* Washington, DC: American Psychiatric Press.

Solomon, S. D. (1986). Mobilizing social support networks in times of disaster. In C. Figley (Ed.), *Trauma and its wake: Vol. 2* (pp. 232–263). New York: Brunner/Mazel.

Solomon, S. D., Bravo, M., Rubio-Stipec, M., & Canino, G. (1993). Effect of family role on response to disaster. *Journal of Traumatic Stress, 6*(2), 255–269.

Solomon, S. D., Smith, E. M., Robins, L. N., & Fischbach, R. L. (1987). Social involvement as a mediator of disaster-induced stress. *Journal of Applied Social Psychology, 17*(2), 1092–1112.

Speed, N., Engdahl, B. E., Schwartz, J., & Eberly, R. (1989). Posttraumatic stress disorder as a consequence of the prisoner of war experience. *Journal of Nervous and Mental Disease, 177,* 147–153.

Steinglass, P., & Gerrity, E. (1990). Natural disasters and post-traumatic stress disorder: Short-term versus long-term recovery in two disaster-affected communities. *Journal of Applied Social Psychology, 20,* 1746–1765.

United States Agency for International Development, Office of U.S. Foreign Disorder Assistance. (1986). *Disaster history: Significant data on major disasters worldwide, 1900 to present.* Washington, DC: Author.

United States National Committee for the Decade for Natural Disaster Reduction. (1991). *A safer future: Reducing the impact of natural disaster.* Washington, DC: National Academy Press.

Wallston, B. S., Alagna, S. W., DeVellis, B. M., & DeVellis, R. F. (1983). Social support and physical health. *Health Psychology, 2*(4), 367–391.

Zarle, T. H., Hartsough, D. M., & Ottinger, D. R. (1974). Tornado recovery: The development of a professional–paraprofessional response to a disaster. *Journal of Community Psychology, 2*(4), 311–320.

Zola, I. K. (1993). Pathways to the doctor—from person to patient. *Social Science and Medicine, 7,* 677–689.

8

The Psychological Impact of Accidental Injury

A Conceptual Model for Clinicians and Researchers

JOSEPH R. SCOTTI, BEVERLEY K. BEACH,
LYNN M. E. NORTHROP, CHERYL A. RODE,
and JOHN P. FORSYTH

OVERVIEW

Although much attention, in terms of clinical and research efforts, has been given to the psychological effects of various traumatic events, systematic study of trauma following accidents has been virtually ignored until recently. This omission is striking given that some of the earliest descriptions of what is now referred to as posttraumatic stress disorder (PTSD) were related to traumatic accidental injury. For instance, in 1871, Rigler described the effects of injuries caused by railroad accidents (e.g., passenger car derailments, train crashes), labeling the resultant outcome "compensation neurosis" (Trimble, 1985). This term captured the intermingled effects of having incurred a traumatic injury and the seeking of compensation (e.g., legal, medical, and financial) for such injuries. The possibility of malingering was recognized early on, particularly in the case of individuals seeking compensation for psychological distress (Trimble, 1985).

In this chapter, we address the psychological effects of accidental injury by

JOSEPH R. SCOTTI, BEVERLEY K. BEACH, LYNN M. E. NORTHROP, CHERYL A. RODE, and JOHN P. FORSYTH • Department of Psychology, West Virginia University, Morgantown, West Virginia 26506.

Traumatic Stress: From Theory to Practice, edited by John R. Freedy and Stevan E. Hobfoll. Plenum Press, New York, 1995.

presenting a conceptual framework that links the multiple factors involved in the development and maintenance of PTSD—a framework that can be used to guide clinical practice and research in this area. We outline a number of these effects as described in the clinical and research literature in relation to a variety of factors that may require special consideration in interventions with cases of accidental injury. We must note at the outset that the effects of accidental injury are not restricted to PTSD-related symptoms. Rather, such events can have a broad impact on the psychological adjustment of the victim. We begin by providing a definition of accidental injury, along with summary statistics that elucidate the extent of the problem. We then describe several typical motor vehicle accident (MVA) cases to demonstrate the range of severity of both the characteristics of accidents and their psychological and behavioral consequences.

DEFINITION AND RATES OF ACCIDENTAL INJURY

Accidental injury here refers to unintentional harm incurred to self, others, or property as the result of human error, technological failure, or other unforeseen circumstances. It does not include acts of war, nature, or crime (including homicide and suicide or other self-inflicted harm). Transportation accidents, be they in cars, trucks, trains, buses, planes, or ships, are a major cause of accidental injury, with human error being implicated in over 85% of vehicle collisions (see Massie, Campbell, & Blower, 1993). Such events as falls, drownings, sports injuries, occupational injuries, and home injuries may also be included within the realm of accidental injuries that result from human error. Alcohol use appears to play a major role in accidents, increasing both the risk and severity of accidents of all types (Hingson & Howland, 1993; Honkanen, 1993). Events such as construction failures (e.g., hotel walkway collapse, Wilkinson, 1983), explosions (Realmuto, Wagner, & Bartholow, 1991), and radiation exposures (e.g., Baum, Gatchel, & Schaeffer, 1983) constitute another category of accidents in which human error may be involved. Although the distinction may be arbitrary, such "technological disasters" are covered elsewhere in this text (see Chapters 7 and 12, this volume).

The yearly incidence of injuries is staggering. In their report to Congress on the cost of injury in the United States, Rice, MacKenzie, and Associates (1989) noted that approximately 57 million Americans were injured during 1985 alone. This figure included 143,000 deaths, 2.3 million hospitalizations, and 54 million injuries not resulting in hospitalization. Approximately two-thirds of the fatalities and 84% of the hospitalized injuries were judged to be unintentional in nature, thus qualifying here as accidental. Rice et al. (1989) report that MVAs (32.2%) and firearms (22.1%) were the leading causes of fatal injuries. However, as one-third of injury deaths were related to intentional acts (e.g., homicide or suicide), MVAs comprised about 51% of deaths resulting from *un*intentional injuries. Falls (33.4%) were the leading cause of injury resulting in hospitalization, followed by MVAs (22.3%). A review of 1986 accident rates by Sosin, Sacks, and Sattin (1992) provides comparable data.

The Rice et al. (1989) study indicated that males accounted for 72% of injuries resulting in death, and 56% of nonfatal injuries (hospitalized and nonhospitalized). Age was also related to injury (Rice et al., 1989), with persons aged 25 to 44 years and 15 to 24 years accounting for approximately one-third and one-fifth of all injuries (fatal and nonfatal), respectively. Persons aged 45 to 64 years ranked third in the receipt of fatal and hospitalized injuries, and children aged 5 to 14 years were third in the number of nonhospitalized injuries. Persons aged 75 years and older, although comprising some 5% of the U.S. population, accounted for 14% of fatal and hospitalized injuries (Rice et al., 1989). Risk of injury by ethnic group or region of the country was not presented in the otherwise extensive analyses presented by Rice and colleagues.

Rice et al. (1989) estimated that the total lifetime cost for injuries sustained in 1985 alone will exceed $158 billion, with three-fourths of that cost being incurred within 1 year of the injury. These figures exceed those of all other leading causes of death (e.g., heart disease, cancer), and include medical and disability costs, and lost work productivity. Yet, these figures do not include direct mental health costs nor the inestimable cost of suffering and reduced quality of life for accident victims and their families. More important to the focus of this chapter, these figures fail to address the short- and long-term psychological sequelae of accidental injury. This omission may reflect the lag in the clinical and research literature regarding the psychological impact of accidental injury. Thus, we attempt to summarize the available evidence of the impact of accidental injury, beginning with several case descriptions.

MOTOR VEHICLE ACCIDENT CASE DESCRIPTIONS

In order to highlight the multiple factors involved in outcome following a traumatic accident, we describe several actual cases that vary in the severity of the event and in the psychological impact upon the individuals involved. To standardize the type of traumatic accident, each case concerns a motor vehicle accident.

Case Descriptions

Case 1

Daniel and Ellen were a married couple in their early 30s. While Ellen was driving their car, with Daniel in the passenger seat, they were struck from behind at an intersection in a three-car, chain-reaction accident. Their car received only minor, repairable damage to the rear bumper, and none of the five persons involved in the accident received any physical injuries beyond minor and short-lived neck pain. This was the third minor accident (the second as a passenger) that Daniel had experienced. Some 10 years earlier, Ellen had been in a severe accident resulting in hospitalization for a traumatic head injury. For several months after the accident, both Daniel and Ellen were hypervigilant while driving, frequently checked the rearview mirror, and were more cautious in traffic. Although this reaction dissipated over time for both Daniel and Ellen, it lasted significantly longer for Ellen. Four years later, Daniel was in another accident when a drunk driver failed to yield at a traffic light, totaling Daniel's car and resulting in a knee injury that required surgery. He again became hypervigilant, particularly at intersections, had a number of dreams about the accident, and felt angry about the loss of his car, the physical injury, and insurance company's management of the claim.

Case 2

Francine, a woman in her mid-30s and a native of Africa, experienced a motor vehicle accident while living in the United States. Her vehicle had been forced off the road into a tree by a truck that had crossed the midline on a rain-slick curve. Both Francine and her two young daughters, aged 4 and 8, received minor physical injuries, and the car was substantially damaged. For several months following the event, Francine experienced nightmares of the accident, was fearful of driving, and avoided the accident site when she did drive. The two daughters were also fearful of riding in a car, particularly when their mother was driving, and engaged in repetitive play scenarios concerning the accident. The younger daughter also evidenced anxiety over separation from her mother and sister.

Case 3

Gordon, a male in his early 20s, was a member of the armed forces stationed in Germany (see Scotti & Lyons, in press, for a full case description). While he was driving a 2½-ton truck on a local access road, he struck a car exiting the *autobahn* at a high rate of speed. The truck drove over the car, decapitating its occupants. Gordon was physically uninjured; however, some 20 years post-event, he continued to evidence severe psychopathology, including PTSD (e.g., avoidance of driving, nightmares, flashbacks, and hypervigilance), obsessive–compulsive disorder (e.g., hand-washing related to blood on his hands from pulling the decapitated victims from their car), and alcohol dependence.

Case 4

Harvey was a male in his mid-20s who was diagnosed with moderate mental retardation. He had been in a minor MVA, had witnessed the fatal beating of his older brother, and had witnessed the fatal fall of a co-worker into an industrial cooking vat at a food factory. Although physically uninjured in each of these events, Harvey reported frequent distressing dreams and intrusive thoughts about the events, and he was hyperaroused and easily angered. He complained of being anxious much of the time, and he exhibited an overconcern for the safety of his fellow workers at a sheltered workshop.

Case Features and Diagnostic Criteria

The above case examples illustrate the range of traumatic events and their psychological sequelae. They also challenge the first criterion for a diagnosis of

PTSD as specified in the *Diagnostic and Statistical Manual of Mental Disorders* (3rd edition-revised) (DSM-III-R) (American Psychiatric Association, 1987). According to the DSM-III-R, to be viewed as traumatic, an event must be "outside the range of usual human experience and . . . be markedly distressing to almost anyone" (APA, 1987, p. 250). Clearly, given the previous statistics, accidents are not beyond the range of usual human experience—they are, in fact, a rather common occurrence. However, accidents that involve extreme injury and loss of life may be sufficiently infrequent and distressing to almost anyone that they can be considered traumatic according to this definition. This definitional requirement has been amended in the newer DSM-IV (APA, 1994), requiring that ". . . the person experienced, witnessed, or was confronted with an event or events that involved actual or threatened death or serious injury, or a threat to the physical integrity of self or others . . .," and ". . . the person's response involved intense fear, helplessness, or horror" (pp. 427–428). However, there is still the assumption that the event must in some way be "extreme," a feature that is not easily quantified.

Within a class of events, such as MVAs, there are factors, such as intensity, duration, and frequency, that may have a differential impact upon a person. This may be seen in the different intensities and frequencies of the accidents experienced by each of the four cases described above (e.g., minor injury vs. loss of life; one vs. multiple accidents). Important factors in the individual response to trauma may also include (1) history of other forms of trauma (e.g., the case of Harvey), (2) developmental stage (e.g., the case of Francine's two daughters), and (3) deficient skills repertoires (e.g., Harvey's mild mental retardation).

Although we most often associate trauma with a diagnosis of PTSD, additional or alternate symptoms and diagnoses are possible following an event. These responses to trauma include: (1) adjustment disorders in the cases of Ellen and Daniel, (2) phobia and separation anxiety in the cases of Francine's two young daughters, (3) severe PTSD in the case of Harvey caused by multiple extreme stressors, and finally, (4) as in the case of Gordon, PTSD complicated by a comorbid diagnosis of obsessive–compulsive disorder and alcohol dependence. How then do aspects of the traumatic event, combined with the previous histories of the victims, lead to the idiosyncratic symptom patterns described above? To answer this question, we briefly turn to a framework for conceptualizing the interaction of multiple factors involved in individual responses to environmental stressors such as accidents. We provide this framework to link a number of lines of evidence in PTSD and other responses to trauma and to give the clinician and researcher a workable model for practice and research.

A PARADIGMATIC FRAMEWORK OF RESPONSE
TO TRAUMATIC EVENTS

As noted by Freedy and Donkervoet (Chapter 1, this volume), single-factor theories cannot adequately explain the role of multiple-response domains in the symptomatic presentations of trauma victims. Further, such theories do not explain sufficiently the differential or idiographic response to events. In order to satisfy these theoretical requirements, a comprehensive, multifactor framework that incorporates both environmental and individual factors, all three response domains (affective/physiological, cognitive, and motoric), and a developmental perspective (i.e., pre-, within-, and postevent variables), is necessary. Such a comprehensive framework would serve two primary functions: (1) It would aid researchers in integrating and extending current knowledge bases from a variety of fields (e.g., physiology, genetics, psychology, neurology) and from a variety of theoretical perspectives (e.g., psychodynamic, behavioral, cognitive). (2) It would assist clinicians in utilizing the amassed knowledge base in the development of idiographic functional analyses and the development of comprehensive treatment strategies that may be tailored to the client's idiosyncratic presentation in a function–treatment matching approach (see Eifert, Evans, & McKendrick, 1990; Evans, 1985; Haynes & O'Brien, 1990; Staats, 1993; Staats & Heiby, 1985). Such a function–treatment approach, though a hallmark of behavior therapy, is rarely taken in practice, at least as judged by models published in the intervention literature (see Scotti, Evans, Meyer, & Walker, 1991; Scotti, McMorrow, & Trawitzki, 1993).

Integrated Models

Recently proposed models of PTSD have begun to integrate biological, psychological, and social variables into a comprehensive framework (see Chapter 1, this volume; and Chapter 2, this volume). The present section outlines a dynamic heuristic model of PTSD, that is based upon the paradigmatic behavioral framework (Heiby & Staats, 1990; Staats, 1993; Staats & Burns, 1992; see also Eifert & Evans, 1990). This model's utility is in its movement beyond static descriptions of potentially relevant variables to a dynamic, process-oriented developmental framework. As such, this heuristic model allows for an understanding of the etiological and maintaining processes involved in PTSD, and it serves to inform comprehensive assessments that in turn may give rise to more efficacious treatment planning. Many of the factors in this framework are derived primarily from the combat and rape literature—where available, research on accident-related PTSD is included.

Figure 1 presents the six critical elements of this model, including: (1) original learning, (2) accident/trauma learning, (3) unlearned/genetic biological vulnerability, (4) present situation, (5) acquired/learned biological vulnerability, (6) psychological vulnerability, and (7) present symptomatic responses. The model proposes that multiple factors (behavioral, biological, and environmental) reciprocally interact with each other over time, such that deficient and inappropriate skills repertoires in the motor, cognitive, and affective/physiological response domains evolve continuously and interact with biological vulnerabilities and environmental stressors to produce the symptomatic presentations labeled PTSD. The model is in some respects an elaboration of the old stimulus-organism-response-contingency-consequence model (SORKC) (Kanfer & Phil-

S_1

*Original Learning
(Historical antecedents)*
- sexual, physical, emotional abuse
- neglect/abandonment
- alcoholic home
- conflictual home
- family psychiatric history (particularly anxiety disorders, alcoholism, and drug abuse)
- unsignaled/ noncontingent punishment

S_2

Accident/Trauma Learning
- nature of the accident: suddenness, unpredictability, breadth of effect
- extent of personal injury
- exposure to injury of others/vicarious conditioning
- blame by self and others
- low social support

O_1

Unlearned/Genetic Biological Vulnerability
- genetic predisposition
- high autonomic resting levels
- hyper-arousability/ physiological reactivity
- somatic complaints

S_3 *Present Situation (Current antecedents)*
- stimulus triggers, that is, stimuli (visual, auditory/ semantic, olfactory) reminiscent of the accident
- interpersonal or physical anxiety provoking situation
- low social support

O_2 *Acquired/Learned Biological Vulnerability*
- conditioned autonomic arousal
- high basal blood pressure and heart rate
- increased autonomic and neurochemical (norepinephrine, epinephrine and dopamine) reactivity and locus ceruleus function
- increased endogenous opioids
- low urinary cortisol levels
- depleted norepinephrine levels

Psychological Vulnerability: Deficient and Inappropriate Personality Repertoires

EMOTIONAL-MOTIVATIONAL
- intense emotional arousal

LANGUAGE-COGNITIVE
- selective attention to threat cues
- interpretation/perception of traumatic event
- hypervigilance to threat cues
- problem-solving deficits

SENSORY-MOTOR
- avoidance of threat situations
- deficient social skills
- deficient social support seeking skills
- learned helplessness/passivity

R ⟶ s ⟶ C

Symptomatic responses (R), their stimulus properties (s), and consequences (C)

EMOTIONAL-MOTIVATIONAL AND PHYSIOLOGICAL
- emotional avoidance, "numbing"
- irritability, hostility, anger
- sympathetic hyperarousal, inability to relax

LANGUAGE-COGNITIVE/COVERT BEHAVIOR
- hypervigilance to threat cues
- avoidance of aversive memories
- intrusive thoughts (state dependent cued retrieval of traumatic memories)
- concentration difficulties
- survival guilt, negative self-statements

SENSORY-MOTOR
- restlessness
- avoidance of stimuli/situations reminiscent of traumatic event
- fight/flight behavior

Figure 1. Outline of the paradigmatic framework model for PTSD.

lips, 1970) and social learning models (Adams & Cassidy, 1993; Bandura, 1968; Kanfer & Saslow, 1969) providing a greater recognition of biological/organismic variables, and cumulative hierarchical learning that occurs over time—essentially what might be called "personality" or what Staats has referred to as basic behavioral repertoires (Staats, 1975, 1990, 1993).

Outline of the Model

Original Learning/Historical Antecedents (S₁)

This component represents the individual learning history before the traumatic accident. Research on combat and rape trauma reveals the importance of the following pretrauma variables: (1) socioeconomic status (Cordray, Polk, & Britton, 1992), (2) childhood physical abuse (Bremner, Southwick, Johnson, Yehuda, & Charney, 1993), (3) exposure to other traumatic events (Bremner et al., 1993), and (4) preexisting psychopathology (Green, Grace, Lindy, Gleser, & Leonard, 1990; Schnurr, Friedman, & Rosenberg, 1993). However, there are negative findings on these characteristics as well (see Foy, Carroll, & Donahoe, 1987, for a review). Ethnicity has been shown to be related to response to trauma; although this relation may be confounded by increased exposure to many of the other factors outlined above (Penk et al., 1989). The limited studies on accident-related PTSD provide evidence for the relationship between prior psychopathology (especially substance abuse which itself may lead to accidents) (Honkanen, 1993) and prior trauma and the subsequent response to accidental injury (Blanchard, Hickling, Taylor, Loos, & Gerardi, 1994a; Scotti et al., 1992).

These factors are evident in the previous case examples. For instance, a previous trauma history is present in the cases of Daniel, Ellen, and Harvey; a previous psychiatric history and developmental delays (suggestive of deficient and inappropriate behavioral repertoires) are noted in Harvey's case; and a family history of parental conflict and substance abuse is present in the case of Gordon. Finally, we are concerned with the developmental level of Francine's two daughters, this being a reflection of age-related accumulation of hierarchical skills.

Biological Vulnerability

Biological vulnerability may be divided into unlearned (O₁) and acquired (O₂) vulnerabilities that correspond to genetically based, inherited characteristics and perhaps predispositions, and those that result from traumatic conditioning and long-standing patterns of behavior. As Freedy and Donkervoet (Chapter 1, this volume; see also Foy, Resnick, Sipprelle, & Carroll, 1987) have presented a review of biological findings, only two major points will be noted here. First, genetic factors, possibly related to heightened autonomic resting levels and physiological reactivity, have been associated with posttrauma symptomatology (Davidson, Swartz, Storck, Krishnan, & Hammett, 1986; True et al., 1993). Second, exposure to traumatic events has been associated with altered autonomic functioning (Malloy, Fairbank, & Keane, 1983; McFall, Murburg,

Roszell, & Veith, 1989; van der Kolk, Greenberg, Boyd, & Krystal, 1985), and with altered neurochemical (epinephrine, norepinephrine, and dopamine) and endogenous opioid functioning (Charney, Deutch, Krystal, Southwick, & Davis, 1993; Southwick et al., 1993; van der Kolk et al., 1985).

It should be noted that much of the biological research is fraught with methodological difficulties (e.g., small sample sizes, reliance on posttrauma measures) and may overstate the role of biological factors in accident-related PTSD. As is typical in clinical work, information regarding pretrauma biological vulnerabilities was not available for the four sample cases, and information on posttrauma biological vulnerabilities was only available for Gordon (e.g., high blood pressure, autonomic arousal, possible depleted monoamines related to severe depression). Thus, it is difficult to know if biological abnormalities preceded or followed the accidents.

Characteristics of the Traumatic Event (S_2)

Even the most extreme traumatic event does not invariably lead to the development of PTSD or related symptoms (Davidson & Foa, 1991). This prompts the question "What aspects of an event give rise to PTSD or other pathology?" Important characteristics of traumatic events include: (1) physical harm to self; (2) witnessing the death of others, especially a grotesque death (e.g., dismemberment, decapitation); (3) active participation in the event (e.g., war atrocities); (4) the death of close family members; (5) extreme loss or threat of loss of personal property and other resources; and (6) frequency and duration of events (see Chapters 1 & 2, this volume; Foy, Sipprelle, Rueger, & Carroll, 1984; Green, Grace, Lindy, & Gleser, 1990; Lyons, 1991; Scotti, 1992; but see also Kilpatrick, Veronen, & Best, 1985). Similarly, characteristics of MVAs that are related to trauma response include: (1) injury to self (e.g., bruises, open wounds, time to heal) or others (i.e., injuries or death of others), and (2) extent of vehicle damage (Scotti et al., 1992).

These aspects of accident/trauma learning are evident in a number of the sample cases. Specifically, multiple events occurred in the cases of Daniel, Ellen, and Harvey. Severe injury to self or death of others was present for Ellen, Gordon, and Harvey. Two of the cases demonstrate deficient environmental resources for postaccident coping. Francine's extended family was located in Africa, and so she had few local resources, whereas Gordon's accident precipitated a medical discharge from the military and a subsequent divorce.

Present Situation (S_3)

A central feature of Mowrer's two-factor model as it relates to PTSD (see Keane, Fairbank, Caddell, Zimering, & Bender, 1985; Scotti, 1992) and current information-processing models (Foa & Kozak, 1986; Litz & Keane, 1989) is that current stimuli may activate symptoms and trigger memories of the traumatic event through stimulus generalization or the activation of fear networks and schema. For example, sights, sounds, and smells reminiscent of the accident (e.g., screeching brakes and gasoline in the case of a MVA) may exacerbate symptoms. Numerous laboratory studies document the physiological arousal experienced upon exposure to pictures, films, words, or even odors related to the original trauma (e.g., McCaffrey, Lorig, Pendrey, McCutcheon, & Garrett, 1993; McNally, Kaspi, Riemann, & Zeitlin, 1990; Pallmeyer, Blanchard, & Kolb, 1986), and we may assume similar effects in the natural environment (Breslin, Craig, Streisand, & Baum, 1993). These situational triggers were evident in each of the four sample cases (e.g., Francine's daughters were more fearful when their mother was driving).

Other environmental stressors appear to be related to an exacerbation of symptoms, including job loss, death of family members, loss of social support, and physical illness. This literature is rather large, and there have been inconsistent findings regarding the relationship between social support and posttrauma functioning (see for instance Barrett & Mizes, 1988; Golding, Siegel, Sorenson, Burnam, & Stein, 1989; Kaniasty & Norris, 1992; Lyons, 1991; Solomon, Bravo, Rubio-Stipec, & Canino, 1993). However, it is generally either social isolation or excessive social demands that adversely impacts psychological adjustment.

Psychological Vulnerability

This aspect of the model represents the deficient and inappropriate behavioral repertoires of the individual in each of the three domains (i.e., emotional-motivational, language-cognitive, and sensory-motor). These skills repertoires represent the cumulative learning history of the individual and constitute the individual coping resources available during traumatic events. Such learned behavioral patterns may include avoidance of threat situations, deficient social skills and thus deficits in acquiring and maintaining social support, hypervigilance to threat-relevant cues, and poor problem-solving and coping skills (Blake, Cook, & Keane, 1992; Fairbank, Hansen, & Fitterling, 1991; Gibbs, 1989; Lyons, 1991; Wolfe, Keane, Kaloupek, Mora, & Wine, 1993). Higher levels of perceived threat (Green, Grace, & Gleser, 1985), suffering (Speed, Engdahl, Schwartz, & Eberly, 1989), perceived low level of controllability (Frye & Stockton, 1982; Mikulincer & Solomon, 1988), and the use of denial and avoidance (Green et al., 1985; Solomon, Mikulincer, & Flum, 1988) also may exacerbate PTSD or increase its likelihood following accidents. High rates of domestic violence and divorce, substance abuse, alcohol abuse, and unemployment among veterans with PTSD may be indicative of maladaptive patterns of behavior (Abueg & Fairbank, 1992; Harkness, 1993; Keane, Gerardi, Lyons, & Wolfe, 1988; Watson, Kucala, Manifold, Juba, & Vassar, 1988; see also Foy et al., 1984).

The relevance of deficient and inappropriate personality repertoires is seen in the four case studies. For example, hypervigilance, caution, and avoidance of trauma-related cues were evident in all four cases. Developmentally (because of age or mental retardation), Francine's children and Harvey may have had fewer coping skills, such as ability to seek support or solve problems. Finally, Gordon used alcohol as a maladaptive coping strategy.

Present Symptomatic Responses (R)

These symptomatic responses, diagnosable as PTSD or other disorders, constitute the result of the interactions among the previously described components of the framework. When exposed to situational triggers, the biological dysregulations and deficient/inappropriate behavioral response patterns may result in symptoms in the emotional-motivational and physiological response domain (e.g., irritability and hyperarousal), the language-cognitive domain (e.g., intrusive thoughts of the trauma), and the sensory-motor domain (e.g., restlessness and active avoidance of threat-related situations). Notably, these symptoms interact with, reinforce, and set the occasion for each other. For example, intrusive thoughts may occasion concentration difficulties and poor job performance that in turn could lead to stressful interactions with the supervisor and subsequent behavioral avoidance. Additionally, hypervigilance for threat-relevant stimuli and misperception of environmental cues may lead to inappropriate aggressive behavior and subsequent social punishment. This could set the occasion for social avoidance, thereby preventing the availability of social support and compounding preexisting social skills deficits.

In this hypothetical situation (which is not discrepant from what may be seen clinically and is clearly evident in the case of Gordon), multiple factors within the model interact and feed into each other resulting in new learning that compounds the disorder. In the next section, we outline the multiple psychological effects, that is the symptomatic responses, that have been documented as outcomes of accidental injury. Keeping the above framework in mind, the reader should begin to see the multiple factors that determine individual response to events.

LITERATURE SURVEY ON SYMPTOMATIC RESPONSES TO ACCIDENTAL INJURY

An Overview and a Caution

In this section, we provide an overview of the psychological and behavioral impact of accidents and related traumatic events. One caveat must be acknowledged at the outset, however. As has been noted by Adams-Tucker (1984) and actually cataloged by Kurkjian and Scotti (1990) in regard to adult survivors of sexual abuse, the effects of trauma are many and varied, and they range from an extreme response to none at all. As indicated by the cases described above and the studies discussed below, similar conclusions may be made regarding the psychological effects of accidents. It is important to realize that PTSD is not the sole clinical outcome of trauma. Rather there is likely a continuum of responses along which PTSD is not even the endpoint. Multiple personality and other dissociative disorders, and perhaps even psychosis, are more extreme responses to trauma (Braun, 1993; Horowitz, 1993; March, 1990; Scotti & Lyons, 1990). Adjustment disorders are less extreme responses. The variety and variable intensity of individual responses make it important to keep in mind that research in this area largely discusses group responses to trauma (e.g., 30% of the victims exhibit one symptom or another) and rarely deals with the individual case. Yet, it is the individual who is of greatest concern in clinical practice. As we demonstrate below, the model presented earlier can be utilized in the performance of idiographic functional analyses and function–treatment matching.

Epidemiologic Data on PTSD and Accidents

Before moving to specific types of accidents and responses, we note a number of studies that provide epidemiologic data on PTSD in the general population. Although Helzer, Robins, and McEvoy (1987) provide perhaps the earliest general population study, they also report the lowest lifetime prevalence rate (1%) of all studies to date. Breslau and Davis (1992), in an urban population survey, found a 9.2% lifetime rate of PTSD. They also found that 39% of the respondents had experienced a traumatic event, with chronic PTSD being exhibited in 13.4% of these persons. Similarly, Resnick, Kilpatrick, Dansky, Saunders, and Best (1993) found a lifetime exposure to noncrime traumatic events (e.g., accidents, disasters) to be 33% among a nationwide sample of women, with a 9% lifetime rate for PTSD. Finally, Norris (1992), in a sample of 1,000 adults from the southeastern United States, found that 69% had never experienced a traumatic event, with 21% receiving such exposure in the prior year. The events included crime (e.g., robbery, rape), combat, and disasters, with 7% of the sample meeting criteria for PTSD. Norris (1992) judged MVAs to be ". . . the single most significant event . . ." (p. 416) of those in her study. A full 23% of the participants had experienced an MVA, with 12% of them meeting criteria for PTSD (Norris, 1992). These studies help document the general prevalence of exposure to traumatic events and the resulting rates of PTSD. However, they generally fail to clearly specify the categories of trauma, especially the types of accidents, and reactions other than PTSD. For that information, we now turn to studies on specific accident types.

Accident Types and Responses

Transportation Accidents or "Planes, Trains and Automobiles"

As noted earlier, MVAs comprise the largest class of accidental deaths, with 22.3% of hospitalized injuries related to MVAs (Rice et al., 1989). The psychological literature on car and truck accidents is fairly small but is rapidly growing. There is, however, a rather large literature on the classification (i.e., by type of collision and injury), epidemiology, and prevention of transportation accidents in such journals as *Accident Analysis and Prevention* and *Transportation Research Record*.

Two recent studies have looked at train accidents. Boman (1979) examined the behavioral responses to the Granville, Australia, train derailment in which 83 people died. His cataloging of symptoms in the survivors at 18 months post-accident included fear of train travel, hypervigilance (especially to train sounds), anxiety, irritability, insomnia, nightmares, depression, guilt, anger, poor concentration, headaches, and conversion symptoms. Theorell et al. (1992) approached train accidents from a different point of view, that of subway-train drivers who had experienced a "person under train incident"— that is, the injuring or killing of persons who had fallen in front of a moving train. This group of researchers found transitory (i.e., up to 3 weeks post-event) psychophysiological reactions (e.g., sleep disturbance, elevated prolactin levels), and longer-term (i.e., up to the 1-year course of the study) increases in absenteeism that were associated with depression. Greater symptomatic response was associated with serious injury to the victim (i.e., the person under the train) as compared to the mild injury or death of the victim.

Plane crash survivors have also been shown to exhibit traumatic stress responses. Sloan (1988) studied 30 survivors of the crash of a chartered plane up to 1-year post-event, finding that initially 93% of the survivors reported at least four symptoms of PTSD, and 54% met full criteria for PTSD. After 1 year, 41% of the survivors exhibited one or more symptoms of PTSD, and 10% to 15% still met criteria for PTSD. In general, the survivors showed increased depression, anxiety, intrusive thoughts, avoidance, and somatization, which waned (rapidly in some cases) over the 1-year period of the study. Older survivors were reported to be somewhat less effected by the crash. A major concern in relation to airplane disasters is the effect not only on the survivors but on airline personnel and rescue workers (Williams, Solomon, & Bartone, 1988). As Butcher and Hatcher (1988) point out, "airplane crashes are seldom neat and tidy accidents" (p. 725). The enormity of such events, in terms of destruction to persons, aircraft, and property, impacts large numbers of individuals well beyond the crash survivors themselves. McCaffrey and Fairbank (1985) discuss the assessment and treatment of PTSD in a male veteran who was involved in two helicopter crashes, the first as a guard at a crash site and the second as one of the mechanics having performed a preflight maintenance check on a helicopter that crashed shortly after take-off. Despite such studies, additional research in this area is needed.

A number of major ship disasters have also been reported, including the *Herald of Free Enterprise* ferry, which capsized and killed 200 passengers and crew (Joseph, Brewin, Yule, & Williams, 1991; Joseph, Williams, Yule, & Walker, 1992), the *Jupiter* cruise ship, which capsized and killed four persons (Joseph, Andrews, Williams, & Yule, 1992; Joseph Williams, et al., 1992; Yule & Udwin, 1991), the *Southern Star*, which sank at sea and whose survivors were adrift for 13 days (Henderson & Bostock, 1977), and a boating accident at the Pittsburgh (PA) Regatta (Martini, Ryan, Nakayama, & Ramenofsky, 1990). The child and adult survivors of the two capsized crafts showed: intrusive thoughts and images; avoidance of thoughts, feelings, and images; depression; anxiety; and increased levels of general psychiatric symptomatology (Joseph, Andrews, et al., 1992; Joseph et al., 1991; Joseph, Williams, et al., 1992; Yule & Udwin, 1991). Importantly, Joseph, Andrews, et al. (1992) demonstrated a relationship between higher levels of social support and better long-term outcome. Symptoms in the adult shipwreck survivors at 12 to 24 months post-event included depression, insomnia, anxiety (especially in bad weather—a present situational cue in the conceptual model), irritability, poor concentration, nightmares, guilt, and impotence (Henderson & Bostock, 1977).

Motor vehicle accidents comprise the largest portion of the transportation accident literature. There is a large literature simply on the classification of car, motorcycle, and truck accident types, grouping accidents by severity of injury (e.g., type of wounds, number of fatalities, etc.), type of collision (e.g., same direction, opposite direction, fixed versus moving objects, etc.), and other characteristics such as seatbelt usage, time of day, and degree of intoxication (see for example Blower, Campbell, & Green, 1993; Kraus et al., 1993; Massie et al., 1993; Rutledge & Stutts, 1993). More germane to this chapter, a typology of the psychiatric reactions of MVA survivors also has been compiled (Goldberg & Gara, 1990).

In their analysis of 55 adult MVA patients, Goldberg and Gara (1990) found major depression to be evident in 43.6% of the survivors, diagnosable PTSD in 14.5%, chronic pain in 20%, and symptoms suggestive of postconcussive syndrome (e.g., memory or concentration disturbance, irritability) in 21.8%. Blanchard et al. (1994a) found that 46% of a sample of 50 victims of MVAs met full criteria for PTSD, with 20% meeting partial criteria, and all experiencing some reluctance to drive. Hickling and Blanchard (1992), in a separate analysis of 20 MVA victims, found somewhat different rates of pathology, with 50% to 65% exhibiting PTSD with concurrent driving phobia, and 45% exhibiting major depression. Other symptoms described by Hickling and Blanchard (1992) included pain, headache, dysthymic disorder, panic disorder, obsessive–compulsive disorder, alcohol abuse, and organic brain syndrome. Similar diagnoses and symptoms (including sleep disturbances, flashbacks, guilt, and psychophysiological reactivity to accident-related cues) have been reported for MVA survivors in a number of other assessment and treatment studies (Blanchard, Hickling, Taylor, Loos, & Gerardi, 1994b; Burstein, 1989; Foeckler, Garrard, Williams, Thomas, & Jones, 1978; Kuch, 1987; Lyons & Scotti, in press; McCaffrey & Fairbank, 1985; Platt & Husband, 1987; Scotti et al., 1992).

Work by Scotti et al. (1992) demonstrates that victims of severe MVAs report fear of driving and score significantly higher on traditional measures of PTSD symptomatology, such as the Impact of Event Scale (Horowitz, Wilner, & Alvarez, 1979; Zilberg, Weiss, & Horowitz, 1982), the Keane PTSD Scale of the Minnesota Multiphasic Personality Inventory (MMPI) (Keane, Malloy, & Fairbank, 1984; Koretzky & Peck, 1990; Lyons & Keane, 1992; Lyons & Scotti, 1994), and a modified version of the Mississippi Scale for Combat-Related PTSD (Keane, Caddell, & Taylor, 1988; Scotti et al., 1992). Accident characteristics contributing to the designation of "mild" versus "severe" accidents include having totaled the vehicle, sustaining injuries (including bruises and open wounds), and injury severity (i.e., time to heal). Scotti et al. (1992) also reported that those persons exposed to severe accidents were more likely to have experienced a greater number of other forms of trauma, including floods, death of a significant other, physical or sexual abuse, or physical assault. These findings are echoed by those of Blanchard et al. (1994a).

Occupational Accidents

Beyond a discussion of workman's compensation and disability costs, and absenteeism, our review of the occupational injury literature revealed little that addressed the psychological impact of on-the-job injury. Indeed, this literature primarily focuses on types of accidents and fatality rates, such as agricultural-related fatalities (e.g., falling objects, electrocutions, and tractor and other equipment accidents; Bobick & Jenkins, 1992; To, Wacker, & Dosman, 1993); construction worker electrocutions (Centers for Disease Control, 1992); chain-saw and other logging accidents in forestry workers (Slappendel, Laird, Kawachi, Marshall, & Cryer, 1993); and fatal and nonfatal injuries among health care workers (Stout, 1992).

In the United States, approximately 7,000 persons died each year during the period 1980–1985 from occupational injuries (Bell et al., 1990). Assumedly, there are also many survivors of such occupational accidents, and these individuals are likely to experience the full range of psychological and behavioral symptoms described previously in relation to other types of accidents. For example, Cassiday, Scotti, and Lyons (1990) described PTSD, depression, and agoraphobia in the case of a maintenance man who had been electrocuted several times in the course of his work. In a study of the factors involved in disability after an industrial injury, Magrega, Spencer, and McDaniel (1993) found that 13 demographic variables (e.g., age, gender, number of dependents, type of injury) accounted for less than 1% of the variance in amount of time taken to return to work. As is typical of the research in this field, the Magrega et al. (1993) study did not include the severity of injury or psychological factors such as premorbid personality or social support. Clearly, additional work is needed in this area to elaborate the psychological impact of traumatic occupational injuries.

Fires and Burns

Among the most studied fire disasters is the Beverly Hills Supper Club fire of 1977, in which 165 persons died of burns or smoke inhalation (Green et al., 1985; Green, Grace, Lindy, Titchener, & Lindy, 1983). At 1- and 2-years post-event, survivors continued to exhibit high levels of anxiety and depression (Green et al., 1983). Jones and Ribbe (1991) have also documented fear, anxiety, depression, and avoidant and intrusive symptoms of PTSD in survivors of residential fires (homes and a boarding school dormitory). Similarly PTSD has been documented in hospitalized burn patients (Silva, Leong, & Ferrari, 1991), with prevalence rates increasing following discharge from hospital (Roca, Spence, & Munster, 1992). In a review by Patterson and colleagues (1993), psychological responses to burns included PTSD and other anxiety responses, depression, psychosis, and behavioral problems. Patterson et al. (1993) also noted that premorbid characteristics appear related to risk for burns, including preexisting depression and suicidality, substance abuse, and character disorders.

Falls

Although many people experience falls, heavy users of alcohol (Honkanen, 1993) and older adults are particularly vulnerable to this type of accident. Thirty percent of people over 65 years of age fall each year, and that figure increases to 40% for persons over age 80 (Tinetti, Speechly, & Ginter, 1988). Falling constitutes a major health hazard for older adults, being the sixth leading cause of death among older adults, and accounting for the majority of injury-related deaths in the elderly (Baker & Harvy, 1985).

In addition to the significant impact on morbidity and mortality, older adults sometimes experience psychological problems following a fall. Several studies have documented a cluster of symptoms, including excessive fear of standing erect or of ambulating, disturbance in balance and gait, a tendency to clutch and grab at near-by objects when standing or walking, reluctance to walk without assistance, avoidance of situations that would necessitate walking, and increased dependence on significant others (Bhala, O'Donnel, & Thoppil, 1982; Murphy & Issacs, 1982; Tinetti & Powell, 1993; Walker & Howland, 1990). When the presence or extent of these symptoms cannot be accounted for by neurological or orthopedic abnormalities, they can be classified as postfall syndrome (Murphy & Isaacs, 1982).

A number of historical and accident variables appear to increase the probability of developing psychological problems following a fall. For example, the victim's level of independence prior to the fall, a history of previous falls, length of time spent on the ground before help arrived, and the extent of physical injury and related disability incurred from the fall all have been shown to predict the development of postfall syndrome (Bhala et al., 1982; Murphy & Isaacs, 1982; Tinetti & Powell, 1993; Walker & Howland, 1990).

Rescue Workers and Other Professionals

Where there are accidents, there are invariably rescue workers and other helping professionals. Consequently, stress responses, including vivid reexperiencing, intrusive thoughts, feelings of helplessness and guilt, and physiological reactions have been documented in fire fighters (Fullerton, McCarroll, Ursano, & Wright, 1992), disaster workers, and other emergency personnel (Genest, Levine, Ramsden, & Swanson, 1990; Wilkinson, 1983; see also Mitchell & Dyregrov, 1993, for a review). One of the authors (JRS) assessed a classic case of PTSD in an emergency medical technician who responded to the scene of a devastating air show disaster in which a plane crashed directly into the viewing stands.

Clearly the above events constitute exposure to traumatic events as a *witness*, and may result in PTSD or other psychological symptoms even though the person was not himself at risk of serious injury or death. The DSM-IV criteria A for PTSD includes being *confronted* with an event that involved serious injury to *others*, and responding with *horror* (APA, 1994). This new definition of PTSD may therefore incorporate the vicarious traumatization experienced by mental health professionals as a result of repeatedly hearing the graphic and distressing stories of trauma survivors (McCann & Pearlman, 1990).

DEVELOPMENTAL FACTORS IN RESPONSE TO TRAUMA

The largest share of trauma research deals with adult populations. We wish to acknowledge here the impact of trauma on the young child and the older adult, an impact that may reflect the level of development of basic behavioral repertoires, such as (1) the relative lack of abundance of life experiences and coping skills as a function of age, and (2) the experience of multiple traumas over the life span having either an inoculating or a cumulative effect on the individual. Other complications of aging may play a role in trauma response, including physical health problems or concerns, diminished social support, and diminished cognitive functioning.

The Child Victim

Studies on trauma experienced by children have included abuse (Wolfe, Gentile, & Wolfe, 1989), violent crime (Malmquist, 1986; Terr, 1983), war survivors (Arroyo & Eth, 1985), and natural disasters (Galante & Foa, 1986; McFarlane, 1987). Less well known are the effects of accidental injury on children. As discussed above, children are the victims of mild to life-threatening accidents on a daily basis, including transportation accidents, structural collapse, falls, explosions, drownings, and technological failure. Statistics from the field of pediatrics suggest that accidental injury poses the single greatest threat to child physical well-being (Methany, 1988). Emerging evidence indicates that significant numbers of child accident victims experience behavioral and emotional difficulties similar to adult victims of accidental injury. Considering the potential for long-term negative psychological impact that has been documented here, understanding the distress and resiliency of child accident victims would seem of paramount importance to preventative psychology.

A number of the studies discussed above document the effects of accidental trauma on children. Contrary to early theorizing (Garmezy & Rutter, 1985), these effects include PTSD and suggest that the disorder is likely to persist for an extended period of time if untreated. Given that the long-term effects on adults of having experienced sexual or physical abuse as a child are well documented (Kurkjian & Scotti, 1990; Rowan & Foy, 1993), there is cause to believe that the effects of accidental injury could also persist into adulthood. In keeping with the paradigmatic framework model, the developmental stage at which the trauma occurs is critical as the child's age is related to coping strategies (Compas & Epping, 1993), ability to deal with death and loss (Gudas, 1993), and the perception or recognition of the extent of danger to which the child has been exposed. Potentially, trauma experienced at a young age could lead to further behavioral deficits in these areas and may increase the psychological vulnerability to future events (see Lyons, 1987).

The Older Adult Victim

The bulk of PTSD research addresses the psychological impact of trauma on young and middle-aged adults to the neglect of studies addressing the impact on older adults (Bell, 1978; Phifer & Norris, 1989). There are an increasing number of studies dealing with the elderly as long-term survivors of traumatic events that occurred in their youth (primarily World War II combat, POW and concentration camp survivors—see Wilson & Raphael, 1993). Yet there are no published studies exclusively addressing the psychological impact of accidental traumas that occur to older adults, with the exception of falls. Albeit mixed, some information regarding the older adult trauma victim is available in the natural disaster literature.

Bell (1978), and Huerta and Horton (1978) found that older adults reported lower levels of emotional and physical stress than did younger disaster victims. They accounted for these age differences by showing that older adults perceived less deprivation (Bell, 1978) and disruption to their lives and well-being (Huerta & Horton, 1978) as a function of the disaster than did younger adults, regardless of objective ratings of actual disruption. Bell (1978) found that following a devastating tornado, older adult victims were less likely to endorse being afraid, nervous, tense, or worried, and more likely to endorse being secure, happy, friendly, and content than were their younger adult counterparts.

No studies comparing the responses of older and younger adult victims have shown older survivors to fair worse than younger survivors. In fact, Norris (1992) suggests that older adults may actually have lower rates of PTSD, especially following crime and accidents. Several noncomparative studies have found that older adults do experience significant negative psychological impact following natural disasters (such as Phifer & Norris, 1989). Factors that may be important in the response of older persons to trauma, as derived from the paradigmatic model, might include poor physical health (and other biological changes), decreased social support because of age-related death of friends and family, lowered socioeconomic status (SES) with retirement, decreased opportunities for work or recreational activity (psychological vulnerability), and more frequent exposure to trauma over the course of the life span. In fact, one of the authors (LMEN) has a 72-year-old client who recently discontinued driving following an accident 2 years prior because he was fearful that he was too old to continue driving. He since has become dependent upon others for transportation and is now considerably more isolated and depressed. By delineating the multiple determinants of the psychological impact of accidental injury, the proposed framework may provide a useful guide for clinical work with accident victims.

FURTHER COMPLICATING FACTORS IN THE RESPONSE TO ACCIDENTAL INJURY

Several factors complicate the diagnosis of a psychological response to traumatic accidental injury. These include the presence of head injury and related symptoms, and monetary compensation that may result in malingering. We briefly address each in turn.

Head Injury and Trauma

In short, an accident severe enough to cause physical injuries, such as open-head wounds or closed-head concussions, may also be severe enough to cause PTSD and related disorders. Head trauma has been associated with PTSD (Horton, 1993), as well as a number of other psychiatric complications (Kwentus, Hart, Peck, & Kornstein, 1985; Middelboe, Birket-Smith, Andersen, & Friis, 1992; Prigatano, 1992). Clinicians and researchers are advised to be aware of the overlap in symptomatology between postconcussive head injury and PTSD, including memory problems, attention difficulties, emotional lability, disinhibition, avoidance, and loss of interest (Davidoff, Laibstain, Kessler, & Mark, 1988). The time course of these two conditions differs, such that mild postconcussive head injury is of relatively brief duration (i.e., several days to several months), whereas PTSD symptoms are considered chronic after 3 months. The differences are again blurred in cases of severe head injury in which there may be a loss of higher cortical functions and thus more long-term or even permanent effects (Davidoff et al., 1988). It is strongly advised that the clinician screen for postconcussive syndrome whenever a case of accidental injury involves physical trauma to the head.

Compensation Issues

Clinicians may play a useful role in advocating for victims of accidents via assessing the extent of psychological impairment and vocational capability, education about compensation issues, and assistance to legal representatives. In addition, as is discussed in other chapters in this text, treatment of the accident victim must be conducted within the context of a trusting, supportive, and collaborative therapeutic relationship. However, given today's litigious atmosphere where media advertisements abound from lawyers willing to help file suit for compensation of accident-related injuries, the clinician should be aware of the possibility of the patient malingering for compensatory gains. In one study on worker's compensation, Hester, Decelles, and Gaddis (1986; cited in Magrega et al., 1993) reported that injured workers were less likely to return to work if their disability income was at least 75% of their regular wages. Lees-Haley (1990) found that untrained, nontraumatized volunteers could produce an Impact of Event Scale profile that was a believable response to distress caused by exposure to toxins from a hazardous waste site. Burstein (1986), on the other hand, found no differences in *acute* PTSD symptoms between trauma victims who might have been eligible for compensation and those who were not. Thus, although more evidence is needed to answer the question about the relationship between compensation and symptomatology, it would be prudent to consider possible sources of compensation when assessing for trauma-related disorders.

USE OF THE MODEL IN THE FUNCTIONAL ANALYSIS OF CLINICAL CASES

Summary Comments

We have attempted in the above sections to present the major effects that have been documented in response to traumatic accidental injury. Persons familiar with the PTSD literature or who review the other chapters in this volume will realize that the same range of symptom patterns result from an incredible variety of events that may be classified as traumatic. It is important to recall that these results have largely been obtained from group studies in which heterogenous groups of individuals are diagnosed with PTSD on the basis of meeting criteria within the three symptom clusters. This approach fails to adequately recognize the wide variation in individual symptomatology within that single diagnostic category (see for instance Norris, 1992).

Our goal in outlining the psychological impact of accidents has been to identify the commonly presented symptoms toward which we need to direct our assessment and treatment strategies for the individual client. Additionally, we have provided a framework that may guide clinicians and researchers in a multifactor assessment of potentially relevant individual and environmental factors. In this way we can design more comprehensive and focused assessments and ultimately provide more efficacious individualized treatments. The use of such models may also help clarify the individual response to trauma, and thus it may lead to prediction and eventually prevention of disorders.

We have proposed that PTSD and related responses to trauma involve a complex interplay of environmental events (historical, trauma-related, and present situations), physiological and neurochemical dysregulations (both inherited and acquired), and inappropriate and deficient behavioral repertoires in the physiological/affective, cognitive, and motoric response domains. Consequently, proficient assessment and treatment of these responses requires an idiographic, multivariate approach. The paradigmatic behavioral framework outlined here may be employed to develop such idiographic evaluations and treatment plans. The clinician may use the general framework to guide a comprehensive assessment interview by addressing each subdomain within the framework (e.g., gathering historical information on family history and upbringing, specifying the characteristics of the trauma, determining current comorbid disorders and deficient behavioral repertoires, and delineating situational stressors and trauma-relevant cues). Through this process, client-irrelevant components may be eliminated from the framework, leaving only idiographically relevant or critical areas that are then further assessed and incorporated into a treatment strategy. As recommended by Staats and Heiby (1985), environmental and personal resources should also be identified and developed to displace maladaptive repertoires and to serve a preventative function. Thus the framework can provide sufficient specificity to allow for the precise matching of treatment to individual needs (Eifert, Evans et al., 1990). The efficacy of such a deficit-treatment matching model has already been demonstrated in the depression literature (Heiby, 1986; McKnight, Nelson, Hayes, & Jarrett, 1984).

Use of the Framework in a Case Example

We previously provided a number of MVA case descriptions, one of which we would now like to elaborate upon to demonstrate the use of the framework. An individualized model for the case of Gordon is presented in Figure 2. As is depicted in the figure, prior history may already have created a predisposition for an extreme response to a traumatic event. Gordon was raised in an isolated, rural community where he engaged in minor juvenile offenses and just managed to obtain a high school degree. His father was an alcoholic and was abusive to Gordon's mother and perhaps Gordon as well. The use of alcohol by his father may have set the stage for Gordon engaging in substance abuse as an adolescent and during the time of his military service. This behavioral response pattern may have impeded the learning of appropriate coping skills, ones that may have been more useful to Gordon than continued substance abuse following the traumatic accident. We speculate that biological vulnerabilities may have been innately present as Gordon described himself as a "nervous child," or may have been acquired in his conflict-ridden and abusive family environment.

Aspects of the single, traumatic MVA also are outlined in Figure 2 and include the gruesome scene of bloody and decapitated bodies with which Gordon had physical contact in his desperate attempt to provide aid. The multiple stimuli associated with this event formed a highly complex conditioned stimulus (see Levis, 1985; Scotti, 1992) that became generalized and in the present situation evokes symptomatic responses. For instance, certain smells (e.g., radiator fluid, cooking meat) and sounds (e.g., grinding metal, squealing tires) evoke autonomic arousal, intrusive thoughts, and images of the accident. These stimuli were important in treatment as they provided the central cues used in a course of implosive therapy (Lyons & Scotti, in press).

Information contained in the skills repertoire subdomains also is directly relevant to constructive treatment planning. In Gordon's case, it would appear that training in appropriate ways to solicit social support (a factor that appears to moderate the response to trauma) is warranted, as is treatment for substance abuse (a problem that may exacerbate symptoms or impede treatment). Relaxation skills might also be taught, and use of exposure-based therapies or cognitive restructuring may decrease hypervigilance and selective attention to threat cues (see Chapter 13, this volume). As demonstrated in this model, inter-

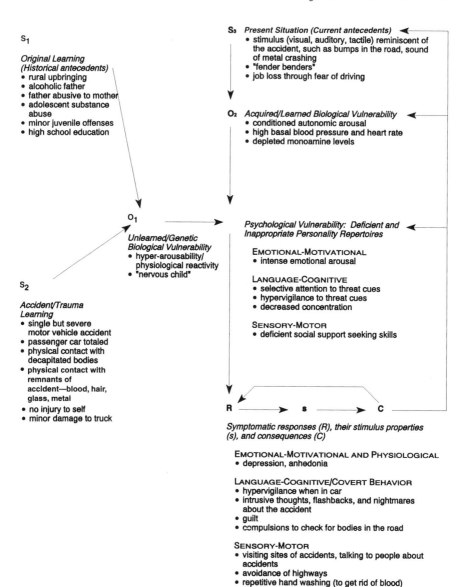

Figure 2. Application of paradigmatic framework model in the case of Gordon.

disciplinary treatment planning is also warranted here. Depression, autonomic arousal, and high blood pressure may be viewed as aspects of the biological vulnerability and symptomatology, in part acquired as a result of the traumatic event. Thus, treatment with antidepressant and antihypertensive medication may be warranted (see Chapter 4, this volume). Finally, the individualized listing of symptomatic responses in each of the three response domains is also useful in treatment planning. As described earlier, these symptomatic responses have their own stimulus properties and consequences that may feed back on themselves and exacerbate situational stressors and biological and psychological vulnerabilities.

CONCLUSIONS

Such a framework model provides clinicians with the flexibility to fit the multiple aspects of the individual case by altering the details of the general model, thereby creating an idiographic and dynamic case formulation. The basic framework directs attention to the assessment of the multivariate factors of which the symptoms are a function. Although, by definition, the symptoms of PTSD are common across victims of trauma, the details of the events, historical factors, current stressors, and behavioral repertoires are idiosyncratic. For instance, in the case of Harvey, his mild mental retardation becomes part of the historical antecedents to trauma and is also implicated in psychological vulnerability caused by deficient repertoires (such as in the cognitive and motor domains). Analysis of the case of Harvey must include his prior exposure to multiple traumatic events. We have already discussed the important differences in the four case studies with regard to characteristics and severity of the trauma.

Ultimately, the utility of this conceptual framework will have to be demonstrated by both clinicians and researchers alike. Our aim has been to provide more than another cataloging of responses to a typology of event characteristics and to suggest, instead, how those event characteristics interact with numerous other factors to produce the psychological impact of accidental injury. The relevance of this framework to clinical practice and research in other forms of trauma (e.g., combat, sexual abuse, incest; see Scotti, Forsyth, Beach, Northrop, & Thompson, 1993), as well as other areas of psychopathology (e.g., depression, personality disorders; see Beach & Eifert, 1994; Eifert & Evans, 1990), suggests promise for more comprehensive and evolving conceptions of the causes of human suffering.

ACKNOWLEDGMENTS

Preparation of this manuscript was supported by a Mini-Grant from the Eberly College of Arts and Sciences, West Virginia University, which is gratefully acknowledged. Portions of this paper were presented at the 1993 (May) conference of the Association for Behavior Analysis, Chicago, IL. The authors thank Linda Beeler, Kimberly Cornell, Risa Thompson, and Seth Brown for their assistance in the preparation of this manuscript and acknowledge the participation of Dr. Judith Mathews in the case of Francine.

REFERENCES

Abueg, F. R., & Fairbank, J. A. (1992). Behavioral treatment of posttraumatic stress disorder and co-occurring substance abuse. In P. A. Saigh (Ed.), *Posttraumatic stress disorder: A behavioral approach to assessment and treatment* (pp. 111–146). Boston: Allyn & Bacon.

Adams, H. E., & Cassidy, J. F. (1993). The classification of abnormal behavior. In P. B. Sutker & H. E. Adams (Eds.), *Comprehensive handbook of psychopathology* (2nd ed., pp. 3–25). New York: Plenum Press.

Adams-Tucker, C. (1984). Early treatment of child incest victims. *American Journal of Psychotherapy, 38,* 505–516.

American Psychiatric Association. (1987). *Diagnostic and statistical manual of mental disorders* (3rd ed.-revised). Washington, DC: Author.

American Psychiatric Association. (1994). *Diagnostic and statistical manual of mental disorders* (4th ed.). Washington, DC: Author.

Arroyo, W., & Eth, S. (1985). Children traumatized by Central American warfare. In S. Eth & R. S. Pynoos (Eds.), *Post-traumatic stress disorder in children* (pp. 101–120). Washington, DC: American Psychiatric Press.

Baker, S. P., & Harvy, A. H. (1985). Fall injuries in the elderly. *Clinical Geriatric Medicine, 1,* 501–512.

Bandura, A. (1968). A social learning interpretation of psychological dysfunctions. In P. London & P. Rosenhan (Eds.), *Foundations of abnormal psychology* (pp. 293–344). New York: Holt, Rinehart & Winston.

Barrett, T. W., & Mizes, J. S. (1988). Combat level and social support in the development of posttraumatic stress disorder in Vietnam veterans. *Behavior Modification, 12,* 100–115.

Baum, A., Gatchel, R. J., & Schaeffer, M. A. (1983). Emotional, behavioral, and physiological effects of chronic stress at Three Mile Island. *Journal of Consulting and Clinical Psychology, 51,* 565–572.

Beach, B. K., & Eifert, G. H. (1994). *An expanded paradigmatic behavioral model of depression.* Unpublished manuscript, Department of Psychology, West Virginia University, Morgantown, West Virginia.

Bell, B. D. (1978). Disaster impact and response: Overcoming the thousand natural shocks. *The Gerontologist, 18,* 531–540.

Bell, C. A., Stout, N. A., Bender, T. R., Conroy, C. S., Crouse, W. E., & Myers, J. R. (1990). Fatal occupational injuries in the United States, 1980 through 1985. *Journal of the American Medical Association, 263,* 3047–3050.

Bhala, R. P., O'donnel, J., Thoppil, E. (1982). Ptophobia. *Physical Therapy, 62,* 187–190.

Blake, D. D., Cook, J. D., & Keane, T. M. (1992). Post-traumatic stress disorder and coping in veterans who are seeking medical treatment. *Journal of Clinical Psychology, 48,* 695–704.

Blanchard, E. B., Hickling, E. J., Taylor, A. E., Loos, W. R., & Gerardi, R. J. (1994a). Psychological morbidity associated with motor vehicle accidents. *Behaviour Research and Therapy, 32,* 283–290.

Blanchard, E. B., Hickling, E. J., Taylor, A. E., Loos, W. R., & Gerardi, R. J. (1994b). The psychophysiology of motor vehicle accident related posttraumatic stress disorder. *Behavior Therapy, 25,* 453–467.

Blower, D., Campbell, K. L., & Green, P. E. (1993). Accident rates for heavy truck-tractors in Michigan. *Accident Analysis and Prevention, 25,* 307–321.

Bobick, T. G., & Jenkins, E. L. (1992). Agricultural-related fatalities: 1986–1988. In S. Kumar (Ed.), *Advances in industrial ergonomics and safety IV* (pp. 121–128). Bristol, PA: Taylor & Francis.

Boman, B. (1979). Behavioural observations on the Granville train disaster and the significance for psychiatry. *Social Science and Medicine, 13A,* 463–471.

Braun, B. G. (1993). Multiple personality disorder and posttraumatic stress disorder: Similarities and differences. In J. P. Wilson & B. Raphael (Eds.), *International handbook of traumatic stress syndromes* (pp. 35–47). New York: Plenum Press.

Bremner, J. D., Southwick, S. M., Johnson, D. R., Yehuda, R., & Charney, D. S. (1993). Childhood physical abuse and combat-related posttraumatic stress disorder in Vietnam veterans. *American Journal of Psychiatry, 150,* 235–239.

Breslau, N., & Davis, G. C. (1992). Posttraumatic stress disorder in an urban population of young adults: Risk factors and chronicity. *American Journal of Psychiatry, 149,* 671–675.

Breslin, F. C., Craig, K., Streisand, R., & Baum, A. (1993, August). *Environmental triggers and distress in motor vehicle accident victims.* Paper presented at the 101st Annual Meeting of the American Psychological Association, Toronto, Canada.

Burstein, A. (1986). Can monetary compensation influence the course of a disorder? *American Journal of Psychiatry, 143,* 112.

Burstein, A. (1989). Posttraumatic stress disorder in victims of motor vehicle accidents. *Hospital and Community Psychiatry, 40,* 295–297.

Butcher, J. N., & Hatcher, C. (1988). The neglected entity in air disaster planning: Psychological services. *American Psychologist, 43,* 724–729.

Cassiday, K. L., Scotti, J. R., & Lyons, J. A. (1990, November). *A case of PTSD following severe electric shock: Treatment outcome and return of fear.* Paper presented at the 24th Annual Convention of the Association for Advancement of Behavior Therapy, San Francisco, CA.

Centers for Disease Control. (1992, March). Electrocutions in the construction industry involving portable ladders: United States, 1984–1988. *Morbidity and Mortality Weekly Report, 41,* 187–189.

Charney, D. S., Deutch, A. Y., Krystal, J. H., Southwick, S. M., & Davis, M. (1993). Psychobiologic mechanisms of posttraumatic stress disorder. *Archives of General Psychiatry, 50,* 294–305.

Compas, B. E., & Epping, J. E. (1993). Stress and coping in children and families: Implications for children coping with disaster. In C. F. Saylor (Ed.), *Children and disasters* (pp. 11–28). New York: Plenum Press.

Cordray, S. M., Polk, K. R., & Britton, B. M. (1992). Premilitary antecedents of posttraumatic stress disorder in an Oregon cohort. *Journal of Clinical Psychology, 48,* 271–280.

Davidoff, D. A., Laibstain, D. F., Kessler, H. R., & Mark, V. H. (1988). Neurobehavioral sequelae of minor head injury: A consideration of post-concussive syndrome versus posttraumatic stress disorder. *Cognitive Rehabilitation, 6,* 8–13.

Davidson, J. R. T., & Foa, E. B. (1991). Diagnostic issues in posttraumatic stress disorder: Considerations for the DSM-IV. *Journal of Abnormal Psychology, 100,* 346–355.

Davidson, J. R. T., Swartz, M. S., Storck, M., Krishnan, K. R. R., & Hammett, E. B. (1986). A diagnostic and family study of posttraumatic stress disorder. *American Journal of Psychiatry, 142,* 121–123.

Eifert, G. H., & Evans, I. M. (Eds.). (1990). *Unifying behavior therapy: Contributions of paradigmatic behaviorism.* New York: Springer.

Eifert, G. H., Evans, I. M., & McKendrick, V. G. (1990). Matching treatments to client problems not diagnostic labels: A case for paradigmatic behavior therapy. *Journal of Behavior Therapy and Experimental Psychiatry, 21,* 163–172.

Evans, I. M. (1985). Building systems models as a strategy for target behavior selection in clinical assessment. *Behavioral Assessment, 7,* 21–32.

Fairbank, J. A., Hansen, D. J., & Fitterling, J. M. (1991). Patterns of appraisal and coping across different stressor conditions among former prisoners of war with and without posttraumatic stress disorder. *Journal of Consulting and Clinical Psychology, 59,* 274–281.

Foa, E. B., & Kozak, M. J. (1986). Emotional processing of fear: Exposure to corrective information. *Psychological Bulletin, 99,* 20–35.

Foeckler, M. M., Garrard, F. H., Williams, C. C., Thomas, A. M., & Jones, T. J. (1978). Vehicle drivers and fatal accidents. *Suicide and Life-Threatening Behavior, 8,* 174–182.

Foy, D. W., Carroll, E. M., & Donahoe, C. P., Jr. (1987). Etiological factors in the development of PTSD in clinical samples of Vietnam combat veterans. *Journal of Clinical Psychology, 43,* 17–27.

Foy, D. W., Resnick, H. S., Sipprelle, R. C., & Carroll, E. M. (1987). Premilitary, military, and postmilitary factors in the development of combat-related posttraumatic stress disorder. *Behavior Therapist, 10,* 3–9.

Foy, D. W., Sipprelle, R. C., Rueger, D. B., & Carroll, E. M. (1984). Etiology of posttraumatic stress disorder in Vietnam veterans: Analysis of premilitary, military, and combat exposure influences. *Journal of Consulting and Clinical Psychology, 52,* 79–87.

Frye, J. S., & Stockton, R. A. (1982). Discriminant analysis of posttraumatic stress disorder among a group of Vietnam veterans. *American Journal of Psychiatry, 139,* 52–56.

Fullerton, C. S., McCarroll, J. E., Ursano, R. J., & Wright, K. M. (1992). Psychological response of rescue workers: Fire fighters and trauma. *American Journal of Orthopsychiatry, 62,* 371–378.

Galante, R., & Foa, D. (1986). An epidemiological study of psychic trauma and treatment effectiveness for children after a natural disaster. *Journal of the American Academy of Child Psychiatry, 25,* 357–363.

Garmezy, N., & Rutter, M. (1985). Acute reactions to stress. In M. Rutter & L. Hersov (Eds.), *Child and adolescent psychiatry: Modern approaches* (2nd ed., pp. 152–176). Oxford: Blackwell.

Genest, M., Levine, J., Ramsden, V., & Swanson, R. (1990). The impact of providing help: Emergency workers and cardiopulmonary resuscitation attempts. *Journal of Traumatic Stress, 3,* 305–313.

Gibbs, M. S. (1989). Factors in the victim that mediate between disaster and psychopathology: A review. *Journal of Traumatic Stress, 2,* 489–514.

Goldberg, L., & Gara, M. A. (1990). A typology of psychiatric reactions to motor vehicle accidents. *Psychopathology, 23,* 15–20.

Golding, J. M., Siegel, J. M., Sorenson, S. B., Burnam, M. A., & Stein, J. A. (1989). Social support sources following sexual assault. *Journal of Community Psychology, 17,* 92–107.

Green, B. L., Grace, M. C., & Gleser, G. C. (1985). Identifying survivors at risk: Long-term impairment following the Beverly Hills Supper Club fire. *Journal of Consulting and Clinical Psychology, 53,* 672–678.

Green, B. L., Grace, M. C., Lindy, J. D., & Gleser, G. C. (1990). War stressors and symptom persistence in posttraumatic stress disorder. *Journal of Anxiety Disorders, 4,* 31–39.

Green, B. L., Grace, M. C., Lindy, J. D., Gleser, G. C., & Leonard, A. (1990). Risk factors for PTSD and other diagnoses in a general sample of Vietnam veterans. *American Journal of Psychiatry, 147,* 729–733.

Green, B. L., Grace, M. C., Lindy, J. D., Titchener, J. L., & Lindy, J. G. (1983). Levels of functional impairment following a civilian disaster: The Beverly Hills Supper Club fire. *Journal of Consulting and Clinical Psychology, 51,* 573–580.

Gudas, L. J. (1993). Concepts of death and loss in childhood and adolescence: A developmental perspective. In C. F. Saylor (Ed.), *Children and disasters* (pp. 67–84). New York: Plenum Press.

Harkness, L. L. (1993). Transgenerational transmission of war-related trauma. In J. P. Wilson & B. Raphael (Eds.), *International handbook of traumatic stress syndromes* (pp. 635–643). New York: Plenum Press.

Haynes, S. N., & O'Brien, W. H. (1990). Functional analysis in behavior therapy. *Clinical Psychology Review, 10,* 649–668.

Heiby, E. M. (1986). Social versus self-control skills deficits in four cases of depression. *Behavior Therapy, 17,* 158–169.

Heiby, E. M., & Staats, A. W. (1990). Depression: Classification, explanation, and treatment. In G. H. Eifert & I. M. Evans (Eds.), *Unifying behavior therapy: Contributions of paradigmatic behaviorism* (pp. 220–246). New York: Springer.

Helzer, J. E., Robins, L. N., & McEvoy, L. (1987). Post-traumatic stress disorder in the general population: Findings of the epidemiologic catchment area survey. *New England Journal of Medicine, 317,* 1630–1634.

Henderson, S., & Bostock, T. (1977). Coping behaviour after shipwreck. *British Journal of Psychiatry, 131,* 15–20.

Hickling, E. J., & Blanchard, E. B. (1992). Post-traumatic stress disorder and motor vehicle accidents. *Journal of Anxiety Disorders, 6,* 285–291.

Hingson, R., & Howland, J. (1993). Alcohol and non-traffic unintended injuries. *Addiction, 88,* 877–883.

Honkanen, R. (1993). Alcohol in home and leisure injuries. *Addiction, 88,* 939–944.

Horowitz, M. J. (1993). Stress-response syndromes: A review of posttraumatic stress and adjustment disorders. In J. P. Wilson & B. Raphael (Eds.), *International handbook of traumatic stress syndromes* (pp. 49–60). New York: Plenum Press.

Horowitz, M., Wilner, N., & Alvarez, W. (1979). Impact of Event Scale: A measure of subjective stress. *Psychosomatic Medicine, 41,* 209–218.

Horton, A. M., Jr. (1993). Posttraumatic stress disorder and mild head trauma: Follow-up of a case study. *Perceptual and Motor Skills, 76,* 243–246.

Huerta, F., & Horton, R. (1978). Coping behavior of elderly flood victims. *The Gerontologist, 18,* 541–546.

Jones, R. T., & Ribbe, D. P. (1991). Child, adolescent, and adult victims of residential fire: Psychological consequences. *Behavior Modification, 15,* 560–580.

Joseph, S. A., Andrews, B., Williams, R., & Yule, W. (1992). Crisis support and psychiatric symptomatology in adult survivors of the Jupiter cruise ship disaster. *British Journal of Clinical Psychology, 31,* 63–73.

Joseph, S., Brewin, C. R., Yule, W., & Williams, R. (1991). Causal attributions and psychiatric symptoms in survivors of the Herald of Free Enterprise disaster. *British Journal of Psychiatry, 159,* 542–546.

Joseph, S. A., Williams, R., Yule, W., & Walker, A. (1992). Factor analysis of the Impact of Events Scale with survivors of two disasters at sea. *Personality and Individual Differences, 13,* 693–697.

Kanfer, F. H., & Phillips, J. S. (1970). *Learning foundations of behavior therapy.* New York: John Wiley & Sons.

Kanfer, F. H., & Saslow, G. (1969). Behavioral diagnostics. In C. M. Franks (Ed.), *Behavior therapy: Appraisal and status* (pp. 417–444). New York: McGraw-Hill.

Kaniasty, K., & Norris, F. H. (1992). Social support and victims of crime: Matching event, support, and outcome. *American Journal of Community Psychology, 20,* 211–241.

Keane, T. M., Caddell, J. M., & Taylor, K. L. (1988). Mississippi Scale for Combat-Related Posttraumatic Stress Disorder: Three studies in reliability and validity. *Journal of Consulting and Clinical Psychology, 56,* 85–90.

Keane, T. M., Fairbank, J. A., Caddell, J. M., Zimering, R. T., & Bender, M. E. (1985). A behavioral approach to assessing and treating post-traumatic stress disorder in Vietnam veterans. In C. R. Figley (Ed.), *Trauma and its wake: The study and treatment of post-traumatic stress disorder* (pp. 257–294). New York: Brunner/Mazel.

Keane, T. M., Gerardi, R. J., Lyons, J. A., & Wolfe, J. (1988). The interrelationship of substance abuse and posttraumatic stress disorder: Epidemiological and clinical considerations. In M. Galanter (Ed.), *Recent developments in alcoholism* (Vol. 6, pp. 27–48). New York: Plenum Press.

Keane, T. M., Malloy, P. F., & Fairbank, J. A. (1984). Empirical development of an MMPI subscale for the assessment of combat-related posttraumatic stress disorder. *Journal of Consulting and Clinical Psychology, 52,* 888–891.

Kilpatrick, D. G., Veronen, L. J., & Best, C. L. (1985). Factors predicting psychological distress among rape victims. In C. R. Figley (Ed.), *Trauma and its wake: The study and treatment of post-traumatic stress disorder* (pp. 113–141). New York: Brunner/Mazel.

Koretzky, M. B., & Peck, A. H. (1990). Validation and cross-validation of the PTSD subscale of the MMPI with civilian trauma victims. *Journal of Clinical Psychology, 46,* 296–300.

Kraus, J. F., Anderson, C. L., Arzemanian, S., Salatka, M., Hemyari, P., & Sun, G. (1993). Epidemiological aspects of fatal and severe injury urban freeway crashes. *Accident Analysis and Prevention, 25,* 229–239.

Kuch, K. (1987). Treatment of PTSD following automobile accidents. *Behavior Therapist, 10,* 224, 242.

Kurkjian, J. A., & Scotti, J. R. (1990). *The representation of psychology in the child sexual abuse literature: An analysis and bibliography.* (ERIC Document Reproduction Service No. ED 312 529).

Kwentus, J. A., Hart, R. P., Peck, E. T., & Kornstein, S. (1985). Psychiatric complications of closed head trauma. *Psychosomatics, 26,* 8–17.

Lees-Haley, P. R. (1990). Malingering mental disorder on the Impact of Event Scale (IES): Toxic exposure and cancerphobia. *Journal of Traumatic Stress, 3,* 315–321.

Levis, D. J. (1985). Implosive therapy: A comprehensive extension of conditioning theory of fear/anxiety to psychopathology. In S. Reiss & R. R. Bootzin (Eds.), *Theoretical issues in behavior therapy* (pp. 49–82). New York: Academic Press.

Litz, B. T., & Keane, T. M. (1989). Information processing in anxiety disorders: Application to the understanding of post-traumatic stress disorder. *Clinical Psychology Review, 9,* 243–257.

Lyons, J. A. (1987). Posttraumatic stress disorder in children and adolescents: A review of the literature. *Developmental and Behavioral Pediatrics, 8,* 349–356.

Lyons, J. A. (1991). Strategies for assessing the potential for positive adjustment following trauma. *Journal of Traumatic Stress, 4,* 93–111.

Lyons, J. A., & Keane, T. M. (1992). Keane PTSD Scale: MMPI and MMPI-2 update. *Journal of Traumatic Stress, 6,* 111–117.

Lyons, J. A., & Scotti, J. R. (1994). Comparability of two administration formats of the Keane Posttraumatic Stress Disorder Scale. *Psychological Assessment, 6,* 209–211.

Lyons, J. A., & Scotti, J. R. (in press). Behavioral treatment of a motor vehicle accident survivor: An illustrative case of direct therapeutic exposure. *Cognitive and Behavioral Practice.*

Magrega, D. J., Spencer, W. A., & McDaniel, R. S. (1993). Factors involved in time taken in returning to work after an industrial injury. *Journal of Rehabilitation, 59,* 13–17.

Malloy, P. F., Fairbank, J. A., & Keane, T. M. (1983). Validation of a multimethod assessment of posttraumatic stress disorders in Vietnam veterans. *Journal of Consulting and Clinical Psychology, 51,* 488–494.

Malmquist, C. P. (1986). Children who witness parental murder: Post-traumatic aspects. *Journal of the American Academy of Child Psychiatry, 25,* 320–325.

March, J. S. (1990). The nosology of posttraumatic stress disorder. *Journal of Anxiety Disorders, 4,* 61–82.

Martini, D. R., Ryan, C., Nakayama, D., & Ramenofsky, M. (1990). Psychiatric sequelae after traumatic injury: The Pittsburgh regatta accident. *Journal of the American Academy of Child and Adolescent Psychiatry, 29,* 70–75.

Massie, D. L., Campbell, K. L., & Blower, D. F. (1993). Development of a collision typology for evaluation of collision avoidance strategies. *Accident Analysis and Prevention, 25,* 241–257.

McCaffrey, R. J., & Fairbank, J. A. (1985). Behavioral assessment and treatment of accident-related posttraumatic stress disorder: Two case studies. *Behavior Therapy, 16,* 406–416.

McCaffrey, R. J., Lorig, T. S., Pendrey, D. L., McCutcheon, N. B., & Garrett, J. C. (1993). Odor-induced EEG changes in PTSD Vietnam veterans. *Journal of Traumatic Stress, 6,* 213–224.

McCann, I. L., & Pearlman, L. A. (1990). Vicarious traumatization: A framework for understanding the psychological effects of working with victims. *Journal of Traumatic Stress, 3,* 131–149.

McFall, M., Murburg, M., Roszell, D., & Veith, R. (1989). Psychophysiologic and neuroendocrine findings in posttraumatic stress disorder: A review of theory and research. *Journal of Anxiety Disorders, 3,* 243–257.

McFarlane, A. C. (1987). Post-traumatic phenomena in a longitudinal study of children following a natural disaster. *Journal of the American Academy of Child and Adolescent Psychiatry, 26,* 764–769.

McKnight, D. L., Nelson, R. O., Hayes, S. C., & Jarrett, R. B. (1984). Importance of treating individually-assessed response classes in the amelioration of depression. *Behavior Therapy, 15,* 315–335.

McNally, R. J., Kaspi, S. P., Riemann, B. C., & Zeitlin, S. B. (1990). Selective processing of threat cues in post-traumatic stress disorder. *Journal of Abnormal Psychology, 99,* 398–402.

Methany, A. P. (1988). Accidental injuries. In D. K. Routh (Ed.), *Handbook of pediatric psychology* (pp. 108–134). New York: Guilford Press.

Middelboe, T., Birket-Smith, M., Andersen, H. S., & Friis, M. L. (1992). Personality traits in patients with postconcussional sequelae. *Journal of Personality Disorders, 6,* 246–255.

Mikulincer, M., & Solomon, Z. (1988). Attributional style and combat-related posttraumatic stress disorder. *Journal of Abnormal Psychology, 97,* 308–313.

Mitchell, J. T., & Dyregrov, A. (1993). Traumatic stress in disaster workers and emergency personnel: Prevention and intervention. In J. P. Wilson & B. Raphael (Eds.), *International handbook of traumatic stress syndromes* (pp. 905–914). New York: Plenum Press.

Murphy, J., & Isaacs, B. (1982). The post-fall syndrome. *Gerontology, 28,* 265–270.

Norris, F. H. (1992). Epidemiology of trauma: Frequency and impact of different potentially traumatic events on different demographic groups. *Journal of Consulting and Clinical Psychology, 60,* 409–418.

Pallmeyer, T. P., Blanchard, E. B., & Kolb, L. C. (1986). The psychophysiology of combat-induced post-traumatic stress disorder in Vietnam veterans. *Behaviour Research and Therapy, 24,* 645–652.

Patterson, D. R., Everett, J. J., Bombardier, C. H., Questad, K. A., Lee, V. K., & Marvin, J. A. (1993). Psychological effects of severe burn injuries. *Psychological Bulletin, 113,* 362–378.

Penk, W. E., Robinowitz, R., Black, J., Dolan, M., Bell, W., Dorsett, D., Ames, M., & Noriega, L. (1989). Ethnicity: Post-traumatic stress disorder (PTSD) differences among black, white, and Hispanic veterans who differ in degrees of exposure to combat in Vietnam. *Journal of Clinical Psychology, 45,* 44–50.

Phifer, J. F., & Norris, F. H. (1989). Psychological symptoms in older adults following natural disaster: Nature, timing, duration, and course. *Journal of Gerontology, 44,* 207–217.

Platt, J. J., & Husband, S. D. (1987). Posttraumatic stress disorder and the motor vehicle accident victim. *American Journal of Forensic Psychology, 35,* 35–42.

Prigatano, G. P. (1992). Personality disturbances associated with traumatic brain injury. *Journal of Consulting and Clinical Psychology, 60,* 360–368.

Realmuto, G. M., Wagner, N., & Bartholow, J. (1991). The Williams pipeline disaster: A controlled study of a technological accident. *Journal of Traumatic Stress, 4,* 469–479.

Resnick, H. S., Kilpatrick, D. G., Dansky, B. S., Saunders, B. E., & Best, C. L. (1993). Prevalence of civilian trauma and posttraumatic stress disorder in a representative national sample of women. *Journal of Consulting and Clinical Psychology, 61,* 984–991.

Rice, D. P., MacKenzie, E. J., & Associates. (1989). *Cost of injury in the United States: A report to Congress.* San Francisco: Institute for Health and Aging, University of California and Injury Prevention Center, The Johns Hopkins University.

Roca, R. P., Spence, R. J., & Munster, A. M. (1992). Posttraumatic adaptation and distress among adult burn survivors. *American Journal of Psychiatry, 149,* 1234–1238.

Rowan, A. B., & Foy, D. W. (1993). Post-traumatic stress disorder in child sexual abuse survivors: A literature review. *Journal of Traumatic Stress, 6,* 3–20.

Rutledge, R., & Stutts, J. (1993). The association of helmet use with injury outcome of motorcycle crash injury when controlling for crash/injury severity. *Accident Analysis and Prevention, 25,* 347–353.

Schnurr, P. P., Friedman, M. J., & Rosenberg, S. D. (1993). Premilitary MMPI scores as predictors of combat-related PTSD symptoms. *American Journal of Psychiatry, 150,* 479–483.

Scotti, J. R. (1992). An analysis of several parameters of conditioned fear in combat-related post-traumatic stress disorder: Serial cues, contexts, conditioning trials, and avoidance behaviors. Doctoral dissertation, State University of New York at Binghamton. *Dissertation Abstracts International, 53*(2), 1076B–1077B (University Microfilms No. DA 9217704).

Scotti, J. R., Evans, I. M., Meyer, L. H., & Walker, P. (1991). A meta-analysis of intervention research with problem behavior: Treatment validity and standards of practice. *American Journal on Mental Retardation, 96,* 233–256.

Scotti, J. R., Forsyth, J. P., Beach, B. K., Northrop, L. M. E., & Thompson, J. (1993, May). Paradigmatic behavioral framework model for combat-related post-traumatic stress disorder. In G. H. Eifert (Chair), *A paradigmatic behavioral bridge from infrahuman to human behavior: Theory, clinical applications, and philosophical underpinnings.* Symposium presented at the 19th Annual Convention of the Association for Behavior Analysis, Chicago.

Scotti, J. R., & Lyons, J. A. (1990, November). The relationship between post-traumatic stress disorder and dissociative experiences. In R. J. McNally (Chair), *Cognition and trauma: New research on post-traumatic stress disorder.* Symposium conducted at the 24th Annual Convention of the Association for Advancement of Behavior Therapy, San Francisco.

Scotti, J. R., McMorrow, M. J., & Trawitzki, A. L. (1993). Behavioral treatment of chronic psychiatric disorders: Publication trends and future directions. *Behavior Therapy, 24,* 527–550.

Scotti, J. R., Wilhelm, K. L., Northrop, L. M. E., Price, G., Vittimberga, G. L., Ridley, J., Cornell, K., Stukey, G. S., Beach, B. K., Mickey, G. H., & Forsyth, J. (1992, November). *An investigation of post-traumatic stress disorder in vehicular accident survivors.* Paper presented at the 26th Annual Convention of the Association for Advancement of Behavior Therapy, Boston.

Silva, J. A., Leong, G. B., & Ferrari, M. M. (1991). Posttraumatic stress disorder in burn patients. *Southern Medical Journal, 84,* 530–531.

Slappendel, C., Laird, I., Kawachi, I., Marshall, S., & Cryer, C. (1993). Factors affecting work-related injury among forestry workers: A review. *Journal of Safety Research, 24,* 19–32.

Sloan, P. (1988). Post-traumatic stress in survivors of an airplane crash-landing: A clinical and exploratory research intervention. *Journal of Traumatic Stress, 1,* 211–229.

Solomon, S. D., Bravo, M., Rubio-Stipec, M., & Canino, G. (1993). Effect of family role on response to disaster. *Journal of Traumatic Stress, 6,* 255–269.

Solomon, Z., Mikulincer, M., & Flum, H. (1988). Negative life events, coping responses, and combat-related psychopathology: A prospective study. *Journal of Abnormal Psychology, 97,* 302–307.

Sosin, D. M., Sacks, J. J., & Sattin, R. W. (1992). Causes of nonfatal injuries in the United States, 1986. *Accident Analysis and Prevention, 24,* 685–687.

Southwick, S. M., Krystal, J. H., Morgan, A., Johnson, D., Nagy, L. M., Nicolaou, A., Heninger, G. R., & Charney, D. S. (1993). Abnormal noradrenergic function in posttraumatic stress disorder. *Archives of General Psychiatry, 50,* 266–274.

Speed, N., Engdahl, B., Schwartz, J., & Eberly, R. (1989). Posttraumatic stress disorder as a consequence of the POW experience. *Journal of Nervous and Mental Disorders, 177,* 147–153.

Staats, A. W. (1975). *Social behaviorism.* Homewood, IL: Dorsey Press.

Staats, A. W. (1990). Paradigmatic behavior therapy: A unified framework for theory, research, and practice. In G. H. Eifert & I. M. Evans (Eds.), *Unifying behavior therapy: Contributions of paradigmatic behaviorism* (pp. 14–54). New York: Springer.

Staats, A. W. (1993). Personality theory, abnormal psychology, and psychological measurement: A psychological behaviorism. *Behavior Modification, 17,* 8–42.

Staats, A. W., & Burns, L. G. (1992). The psychological behaviorism theory of personality. In G. V. Caprara & G. L. van Heck (Eds.), *Modern personality psychology: Critical reviews and new directions* (pp. 161–199). New York: Harvester-Wheatsheaf.

Staats, A. W., & Heiby, E. M. (1985). Paradigmatic behaviorism's theory of depression: Unified, explanatory, and heuristic. In S. Reiss & R. R. Bootzin (Eds.), *Theoretical issues in behavior therapy* (pp. 279–330). New York: Academic Press.

Stout, N. A. (1992). Occupational injuries and fatalities among health care workers in the United States. *Scandinavian Journal of Work Environment and Health, 18*(Suppl. 2), S88–S89.

Terr, L. C. (1983). Chowchilla revisited: The effects of psychic trauma four years after a school-bus kidnapping. *American Journal of Psychiatry, 140,* 1543–1550.

Theorell, T., Leymann, H., Jodko, M., Konarski, K., Norbeck, H. E., & Eneroth, P. (1992). "Persons under train" incidents: Medical consequences for subway drivers. *Psychosomatic Medicine, 54,* 480–488.

Tinetti, M. E., & Powell, L. (1993). Fear-of-falling and low self-efficacy: A cause of dependence in elderly persons. *The Journals of Gerontology, 48*(special issue), 35–38.

Tinetti, M. E., Speechly, M., & Ginter, S. F. (1988). Risk factors for falls among elderly persons living in the community. *New England Journal of Medicine, 319,* 1701–1707.

To, T., Wacker, K., & Dosman, J. A. (1993). A pilot study of farm accidental injuries in Aberdeen, Saskatchewan. *Canadian Journal of Public Health, 84,* 153–154.

Trimble, M. R. (1985). Post-traumatic stress disorder: History of a concept. In C. R. Figley (Ed.), *Trauma and its wake: The study and treatment of post-traumatic stress disorder* (pp. 5–14). New York: Brunner/Mazel.

True, W. R., Rice, J., Eisen, S. A., Heath, A. C., Goldberg, J., Lyons, M. J., & Nowak, J. (1993). A twin study of genetic and environmental contributions to liability for posttraumatic stress symptoms. *Archives of General Psychiatry, 50,* 257–264.

van der Kolk, B., Greenberg, M., Boyd, H., & Krystal, J. (1985). Inescapable shock, neurotransmitters, and addiction to trauma: Toward a psychobiology of posttraumatic stress. *Biological Psychiatry, 20,* 314–325.

Walker, J. E., & Howland, J. (1990). Falls and fear-of-falling among elderly persons living in the community: Occupational therapy interventions. *American Journal of Occupational Therapy, 45,* 119–122.

Watson, C. G., Kucala, T., Manifold, V., Juba, M., & Vassar, P. (1988). The relationships of post-traumatic stress disorder to adolescent illegal activities, drinking, and employment. *Journal of Clinical Psychology, 44,* 592–598.

Wilkinson, C. B. (1983). Aftermath of a disaster: The collapse of the Hyatt Regency Hotel skywalks. *American Journal of Psychiatry, 140,* 1134–1139.

Williams, C. L., Solomon, S. D., & Bartone, P. (1988). Primary prevention in aircraft disasters: Integrating research and practice. *American Psychologist, 43,* 730–739.

Wilson, J. P., & Raphael, B. (Eds.). (1993). *International handbook of traumatic stress syndromes.* New York: Plenum Press.

Wolfe, J., Keane, T. M., Kaloupek, D. G., Mora, C. A., & Wine, P. (1993). Patterns of positive readjustment in Vietnam combat veterans. *Journal of Traumatic Stress, 6,* 179–193.

Wolfe, V. V., Gentile, C., & Wolfe, D. A. (1989). The impact of sexual abuse on children: A PTSD formulation. *Behavior Therapy, 20,* 215–228.

Yule, W., & Udwin, O. (1991). Screening child survivors for post-traumatic stress disorders: Experiences from the "Jupiter" sinking. *British Journal of Clinical Psychology, 30,* 131–138.

Zilberg, N. J., Weiss, D. S., & Horowitz, M. J. (1982). Impact of Event Scale: A cross-validation study and some empirical evidence supporting a conceptual model of stress response syndromes. *Journal of Consulting and Clinical Psychology, 50,* 407–414.

9

Refugee Status, Torture, and Adjustment

PETER VESTI and MARIANNE KASTRUP

INTRODUCTION

Among traumatic events caused by humans, torture is unique as an activity devoted to the confinement, control, and destruction of other people. Torture is reviewed as a concept in this chapter, and torture methods as they are used today will be described, together with the prevalence of torture practices. Furthermore, the consequences for the individual and for society are considered. The review is based on research findings reported in the professional literature and on the clinical experience gained at the International Rehabilitation and Research Center for Torture Victims (RCT) in Copenhagen, Denmark. Symptoms related to torture practices have received increasing attention over the past 25 years. At the time when the RCT was established in 1984, interest was focused on the aims of torture, its physical and psychological methods, its aftereffects, and treatment of the individual survivor. The focus of the RCT has gradually enlarged to address the needs of the family and friends surrounding the torture survivor. At the same time it was recognized that, when torture is practiced in a society, the state of health throughout the whole society suffers. Thus attention has little by little shifted from the individual survivor to society at large in recognition of the fact that torture is an effective weapon against the social freedoms found in democratic societies.

THE SCOPE OF THE TRAUMATIC EVENT

Torture as a Concept

The concept of torture can be defined in several ways. The Concise Oxford Dictionary (1984) defines torture as follows: "The infliction of severe

PETER VESTI and **MARIANNE KASTRUP** · Rehabilitation and Research Centre for Torture Victims, Borgergade 13, DK-1300 Copenhagen K, Denmark.

Traumatic Stress: From Theory to Practice, edited by John R. Freedy and Stevan E. Hobfoll. Plenum Press, New York, 1995.

bodily pain, especially as a punishment or as a means of persuasion." More complete definitions have been introduced in some of the declarations and conventions that are available to the health professions. An example is the Tokyo Declaration of the World Medical Association (WMA) (Doctors, ethics, and torture, 1987), which states:

> For the purpose of this Declaration, torture is defined as the deliberate, systematic or wanton infliction of physical or mental suffering by one or more persons acting alone or on the orders of any authority, to force another person to yield information, to make a confession, or for any other reason.

The American Psychological Association unconditionally condemned torture in the Joint Resolution Against Torture of the American Psychological Association and the American Psychiatric Association (International Union of Psychological Science, 1976/1985). A specific definition is not given in this resolution, but the participating associations cited the definition given in the United Nations Convention Against Torture and Other Cruel, Inhuman, or Degrading Treatment or Punishment, and the United Nations (UN) Principles of Medical Ethics. According to the UN Declaration, torture is defined as follows:

> Any act by which severe pain or suffering, whether physical or mental, is intentionally inflicted on a person for such purposes as obtaining from him or a third person information or confession, punishing him for an act he has committed or is suspected of having committed, or intimidating him or a third person, or for any reason based on discrimination of any kind, when such pain or suffering is inflicted by or at the instigation of or with the consent or acquiescence of a public official or other person acting in an official capacity. It does not include pain or suffering arising only from—inherent in or incidental to—lawful sanctions.

The nursing profession also condemns torture and any form of participation in it, as outlined in the Role of the Nurse in the care of Detainees and Prisoners (International Council of Nurses [ICN], 1975) and the statement on the Nurse's Role in Safeguarding Human Rights (ICN, 1983, Jacobsen & Vesti, 1992).

The ethical duties with respect to torture have been outlined for all health professionals in the principles of medical ethics (Council for International Organizations of Medical Sciences, 1983). Torture is defined in these principles as in the UN declaration on the protection of all persons from being subjected to torture and other cruel, inhuman, or degrading treatment or punishment. The UN declaration of torture (see above) will be used for the current chapter and Chapter 14 in this volume. The UN definition is being employed as it is perhaps the most comprehensive and widely cited definition of torture available. In addition, as an organization, the United Nations is widely recognized and sanctioned throughout the world to work for the establishment of human rights. The practice of torture is obviously an egregious violation of basic human rights.

Torture is usually seen as one end of a continuum, beginning at cruel, inhuman, and/or degrading treatment and leading up to outright torture. There is no specific cutoff point between the two extremes, and this will always vary with the actual circumstances; for example, an act that may constitute torture in an elderly person might not be regarded as such in a healthy, young adult. It is noteworthy that the above definitions are conceptual, indicating that the perpetrator is functioning in some capacity or other as a government agent. It is considered implicit in the above definitions of torture that health professionals should in no way directly or indirectly participate in or condone such practices. That these conventions are necessary bears witness to the fact that health professionals, both present and past, have applied their skills in the practice of torture, an issue dealt with elsewhere (Vesti, 1990; Bloche, 1987).

A key difference between torture and other types of traumatic events is the complete control of the perpetrator over the victim, a condition described by total dependency and helplessness. The purpose of torture furthermore is to disrupt the humanity and individuality of the victim (i.e., to break down his or her will) and to make the victim conform to the wishes of the torturer. This breaking down of the humanity of the victim distinguishes torture from other violent acts. When torture is broken down into its components, similarities with other types of trauma will be found. The injuries follow traumatological principles (e.g., bone fractures, the sequelae of the application of electricity or burns). However, whereas trauma in the form of domestic violence or combat trauma contains some predictable factors, the torture victim is usually alone; the whole situation is largely unpredictable, and this loss of predictability is further exploited in the extreme by the torturer. The victim often goes through the ordeal without social support.

Torture is not a legal concept and is absent from most national legal codes. There are a few exceptions. For example, Cyprus has incorporated the concept of torture into law as a consequence of the European Convention for the Prevention of Torture (European Committee for the Prevention of Torture and Inhuman or Degrading Treatment or Punishment, 1993). Also, Chile has incorporated the concept of torture along the lines of the declarations and conventions of the UN. A person who has allegedly perpetrated torture will be charged in most countries with willful injury, rape, assault with intent to do bodily harm, or similar aggressive acts. Torture is still used as a judicial form of punishment, for instance in Pakistan and Sudan. For example, detailed instructions are given in the Whipping Ordinance of Pakistan (The Execution of the Punishment of Whipping Ordinance, 1987), in which the whip is specified and the conditions and mode of its use are described in detail. To mention some of the points that are outlined in the ordinance, it is specified that the convict is medically examined, that the stripes must be applied so that death does not result, that the punishment of a pregnant woman must be postponed until after delivery, and that the stripes shall be spread over the body and not applied to delicate parts of the body.

It is implicit in the concept of torture that the infliction of pain is at a maximum at a certain point, but this does not imply that emotions such as fear and sadness are maximal at the same moment. Torture may thus be conceptualized as a process that spans from the time of arrest until the release or death of the victim (Basoglu & Mineka, 1992).

Torture Methods

Torture may be described as a methodical process that uses both physical and psychological methods to injure victims (Bøjholm et al., 1992). Currently used torture methods are well described in several publications, for example, by Amnesty International and the RCT in Copenhagen (Amnesty International, 1992; Jacobson & Vesti, 1992). Examples of physical torture methods include beating and shoving, squeezing/pressure techniques, pinching (particularly on sensitive areas of the body), insertion of objects into bodily orifices, exposing the victims to extreme or prolonged physical exertion, strangulation, obstruction of the airway, drowning/near drowning, exposure to chemicals (e.g., corrosives, poisons, drugs), exposure to extremes of heat or cold, exposure to electricity, bright light torture, and noise torture (e.g., loud continuous noise or intermittent bursts of loud noise). Examples of psychological torture include sensory or perceptual deprivation, social deprivation, nutrition being withheld or made contingent on compliance, withholding physical examination and treatment of illness, denying access to personal and environmental hygiene, verbal and physical threats, efforts to humiliate, nonconventional sexual acts, communication techniques (e.g., withholding communication, promising special access to communication in exchange for compliance), and intentional misuse of medical methods for treatment on healthy or ill persons.

Prevalence of Torture and Torture Survivors

Because of the secret nature of torture, no government openly admits that it is practiced. Therefore, all prevalence figures presented in this chapter represent rough estimates. According to Amnesty International, more than 60 nations, including several European countries, are still using state-sanctioned or -condoned torture (Amnesty International, 1992). Most of the states that perpetrate torture suffer from poor economic circumstances and have a governmental system that is influenced or dominated by strong authoritarian rule, if not frank dictatorship. Such governmental systems have insufficient insight into or control over the working of the police or military forces. The state is frequently under some form of siege from civil unrest along the lines of economic or ethnic division. This is not to say that the better organized states of the world are free from torture. In the latter cases, however, most of the known cases of torture relate to the investigations of the police force. Several such cases are known from European countries, and the alleged ill treatment occasionally leads to disciplinary action against the involved personnel (Amnesty International, 1991).

Available estimates of prevalence are all summaries of indirect measurements. These indications of torture may be through bibliographical accounts of torture survivors (e.g., Jacobo Timermans [1982] from Argentina and Dr. Simion Gluzman [1989] from Ukraine), or reports from mass media (e.g., in the ongoing war in Bosnia, where newspaper teams uncover and point to cases of torture). Other indications of torture may be seen indirectly in the applications for financial and technical support for rehabilitation programs for torture survivors, such as are received by the UN Voluntary Fund, or by the RCT in Copenhagen. There are now more than 60 centers or treatment facilities for torture survivors all over the world, and the sheer growth in this activity also points to a pressing need for treatment, which is further reflected in the size of waiting lists at centers dedicated to the psychological and social needs of torture survivors. Publications from organizations such as the American Association for the Advancement of Science (AAAS) and the French organization Médecins du Monde also provide valuable information about the prevalence of torture. A reasonable estimate is that more than one-third of the world's nations employ torture today. With ongoing torture in such a large number of countries, it is likely that the vast majority of the survivors live in their home countries after the torture and that only a minority manage to escape.

Torture survivors may also be found among people who are refugees (Agger & Jensen, 1990; Mollica, Wyshak, & Lavelle, 1987; Kinzie, 1989). However, refugee statistics are notoriously uncertain, and the concept of refugee status is itself problematic. It was estimated in 1992 that there were more than 14 million refugees worldwide, refugees being defined as persons who for political reasons have been or are at high risk of becoming persecuted by the government of their country. This figure, however, did not include internal refugees (i.e., people forced to live in restricted areas of their own country). When compiling reports from several groups involved in rehabilitation of torture survivors, the proportion of refugees who are also torture survivors is estimated between 5% to 35%, excluding the proportion of criminals who have been tortured during their investigation (Baker, 1992).

Geographical Distribution of Torture

Torture, as a state-sponsored activity, yet clandestine and illegal, occurs mostly in the economically deprived parts of the world, and particularly in nations struggling for development. Whereas it is evident that the number of cases of torture in developed countries is far less than in underdeveloped countries, the verified cases point to the risk of falling back to old practices, particularly in times of stress or unrest. Thus, Spain and Portugal were regularly accused of torture before their dictatorships ended. During the period of dictatorship in Greece (1967–1975), numerous cases of torture were perpetrated and documented, and today Turkey has repeatedly been accused of perpetrating torture, particularly in the struggle against the Kurdish population (European Committee for the Prevention of Torture and Inhuman or Degrading Treatment or Punishment, 1993).

A prime example of torture in a developed country occurred in the United Kingdom (UK). During the struggle in Northern Ireland against the Irish Republican Army (IRA) in the 1970s, the UK employed interrogation techniques that included sensory deprivation and inducing physical exhaustion. These interrogation procedures were reported to the European Commission of Human Rights, which labeled them as torture. However, when the case was taken to the European Court of Human Rights, the practices were labeled as cruel, inhuman, and degrading treatment (rather than outright torture); nevertheless, the case led to the abolition of these practices (Compton, Fay, & Gibson, 1971).

All extremist political regimes, whether left- or right-wing, may try to justify the use of torture. In essence, the practice of torture becomes a means of exerting social control. However, it is important to recognize that even though the reason for torture may be political, in the broadest sense of the word, the consequences are injuries of individuals, so that torture becomes also a health care problem with ramifications for mental and physical well-being.

A Typical Torture Victim

There are no consensus data yet on the demographic and psychological backgrounds of the torture survivors prior to their torture. However, it is evident that, insofar as the purpose of torture is the control of society, the victims will be those who are in a position to struggle against the government. Examples of typical torture victims include: political leaders, union leaders, poets and authors, or people in positions within movements for the rights of indigenous people. Such individuals are visible in society, and their actions and appearances may be of public interest. Thus, they are the targets of repressive governments and at risk of state-sanctioned or condoned torture. Examples of the above may be seen in the biographies of Alexander Solzhenitsyn (author) from the former USSR, Mikis Theodorskis (composer) from Greece, Victor Padar Jarré (musician) from Chile, and Eva Forest (author and psychiatrist) from Spain. Men appear more frequently in the statistics than women, primarily because of the traditional male role. Nevertheless, women and even children can become torture victims (Acuna, 1987). Some individuals are tortured because the authorities may wish to find or punish a third party (e.g., children being tortured to reach their parents).

The Purpose of Torture

Torture is intended to destroy the ability of the individual to function physically and psychologically (Agger, 1989). The torture is delivered in an unpredictable and inescapable way, and even if information or confessions are extracted, the torturer does not necessarily stop. Torture may be conducted with several goals in mind. One purpose of torture is to elicit information. This is the case when individuals do not wish to volunteer this information, be they criminals, suspected or guilty, or any human being in opposition to, or perceived as a threat to, a totalitarian government. Another purpose of torture is to obtain a confession. This was particularly important in previous judicial cases because a confession was a prerequisite for a guilty verdict. It has even been claimed that opposition to torture in Europe was brought about not by humanitarian principles but by the abolition of the need for a confession in order to sentence criminals (Langbein, 1977). Torture can also be used to punish. Throughout the history of society, the breaking of rules has led to sanctions by society and even to state-sanctioned torture such as flogging or public dismemberment. Torture may also be used to demonstrate power. Leaders of authoritarian regimes need to induce terror into the society they wish to control, and the torture of individuals, caught more or less at random, serves to induce this terror in the rest of the population. Finally, torture may be aimed at bringing about forcible indoctrination. After the Second World War, a number of dissidents, particularly in former East European countries, were tortured before they were brought to one of the show trials, often to denounce friends, families, and even themselves. For many years this procedure was labeled brainwashing (Hinkle & Wolff, 1956).

During the last two decades, following the study of an increasing number of torture survivors, some points of relevance have emerged about the purpose of torture. Torture often continues far beyond when the victim has given up, for example even after all information has been given. Torture is often perpetrated for months, even after the information has lost its value. It is known from the resistance movements of the Second World War that the groups were organized in cells, and that if anyone was captured they would try to avoid giving information during the first 24 hours, so that their cell would have time to reorganize. Military authorities undergoing civil strife have stated that torture as such is a poor source of information, and that the use of modern information technology is a far better method.

Based on the above observations, the authors and many of their colleagues have concluded that torture is not currently perpetrated for rational reasons (e.g., to elicit information, to punish). Rather, it is more likely that torture is fueled by efforts to destroy the individuality and humanity of the victims (Somnier & Genefke, 1986). Following torture experiences, victims are often unable to function in routine psychological and social roles. Their lives are ruined, and they live as deterrents to other people. This latter fact is particularly striking when personalities who were outspoken and visible appear as subdued persons broken in spirit and body following torture.

ADJUSTMENT RISK FACTORS

Environmental Factors

Torture is such a monstrous attack on the individual that, irrespective of individual or social factors, it will cause symptoms in the great majority of human beings. Nevertheless, some factors do influence the emergence of psychological sequelae. The torturers can achieve the effects they want by using torture in a methodical fashion. They know that individuals differ, and by alternating physical and psychological torture methods, practically all individuals can be broken. The torturers also consider the psychological mechanisms of the victim, and they exploit these mechanisms, for example by isolating the victims after the torture and by meting out the torture in a random fashion in order to increase unpredictability. High levels of unpredictability during traumatic experiences may worsen psychological symptoms (Steketee & Foa, 1987).

In addition to the torture itself, several factors directly relating to the torture and controllable by the authorities may worsen later individual adjustment. Among such factors may be the prison conditions. Sometimes the victims are kept isolated, preventing attachment to other human beings, and the uncertainty continues as to when the torture will resume. In addition, the rules of the prison system may be changed intentionally or made unpredictable. One of the functions of the psychologist in the Liberated Prison in Uruguay seems to have been the changing of prison regulations to heighten the state of unpredictability for the prisoners (Bloche, 1987). This state of disorientation could be maintained over long periods (e.g., days, weeks). The prisoners only realized that the rules had been changed when they were punished for acts that were previously not punishable. Furthermore, in order to decrease the likelihood that political prisoners might combine their efforts against the prison regulations and authorities, their sleep was interrupted by loud irregular noises and the prisoners were studied individually and in groups to identify any leaders, who were then removed. Well-functioning leaders would occasionally be placed with severely disturbed psychiatric patients as an additional source of stress.

Emotions, including guilt and anxiety, are also induced in the survivors, making readjustment more difficult. Survivors are frequently forced to sign statements, perhaps even on blank paper, that they were well-treated in the prison. Sometimes survivors are made aware of all the names they allegedly may have betrayed, and torturers may suggest their days are numbered if they survive and are released. Torture survivors may become stigmatized, dangerous to associate with, or even forgotten by family and associates. This is now reported in the former Soviet Union, where thousands of human beings were forcefully sent away to camps in remote areas and tortured, only to be stigmatized and forgotten should they return to society. It is only now that many of these torture survivors are able to speak publicly about what they have been through and how they are still suffering. The same phenomenon is recognized in most of the former communist countries and demonstrates how the official psychology and psychiatry have not recognized the mental and physical sequelae of torture.

Individual Factors

Even though few human beings are able to cope with the stress induced by torture, different reactions are experienced. A dose–response effect is observed following torture, but this also applies to rape, combat, and proximity to disastrous events (Centers for Disease Control, 1988; Steketee & Foa, 1987;

Pynoos et al., 1987). The dose–response relationship is further seen in animal experiments, in which duration, repetitiveness, and severity of the trauma influence the measured outcome (Anisman & Sklar, 1981). As a conceptual point, it is important to recognize that more extreme forms of stress (of which torture is one form) are likely to minimize individual differences in stress reactions. With more moderate stressors, it is anticipated that individual differences play a greater role in determining psychological adjustment.

Because of a sparsity of quantitative research concerning the impact of individual variables on posttorture adjustment, we focus attention on clinical observations and on applying selected findings from related areas of trauma research. Several factors predating experiences with torture may be relevant to subsequent adjustment. In one study, female sex and lower education correlated with higher scores of anxiety (Paker, Paker, & Yüksel, 1992). Other factors that have received attention include parental poverty (Davidson, Smith, & Kudler 1989), childhood conduct problems (Kulka et al., 1988), neuroticism, and previous psychiatric disorder (McFarlane, 1989). Age is also likely to be important, because the younger the person when tortured, the more profound the potential effect on the formation of the personality. Previous trauma exposure has also been suggested as a vulnerability factor (Freedy, Resnick, & Kilpatrick, 1992). Other potential vulnerability factors suggested from animal studies are maternal deprivation and repeated separations (Saporta & van der Kolk, 1992).

Several individual factors existing at the time of the torture may impact subsequent adjustment. The psychology of the individual is obviously of importance, but this area has not yet been sufficiently researched. However, from a clinical point of view, a positive effect with respect to readjustment has been observed when the victim is able to "make sense of" the torture and understand why he or she was tortured, as opposed to not understanding the situation. For example, victims may be tortured because of a third party; but at first they may not realize this, thinking perhaps that they were in the hands of criminals. Some victims understand the ordeal through religious or political beliefs, or as an experience to be observed introspectively. Both defense mechanisms will probably have a positive influence on the outcome of the torture (Bettelheim, 1943). Additional stress may relate to the uncertainty as to the whereabouts of the family, or even the knowledge that significant numbers of others are themselves being subjected to torture. Such added burdens undoubtedly have considerable, though as yet unproven, negative influence on the outcome.

Several posttorture factors may impact adjustment following torture. Prime among the several factors that may relate to the outcome of the adjustment are the availability of help and support from family and peer groups. Evidence that the whole family, and not just the torture survivor, is under stress is provided by the increased divorce rate, another example of negative adjustment (Gonsalves, 1990).

Some torture survivors manage to flee their country. By becoming refugees, numerous other problems are faced. First, before fleeing, torture survivors all too often have to eke out a meager existence in their home countries after release from prison, being forced for example into unemployment and thereby being deprived of the possibility of sustaining their lives and those of their families. They may be under constant harassment by the authorities. A substantial proportion are also forced to live underground for long periods. The flight itself is often dangerous. It entails economic hardship and personal danger, for example in crossing borders illegally, not only for the torture survivor but also for their families. Even after crossing the border, the stress continues in the form of the risk of being sent back, finding a country of exile, learning a new language, settling in a new country and a new culture, and hoping to find some form of employment. In the new country, treatment resources may be scarce. Many individuals with torture sequels never come to the attention of the available organizations, or there may be long waiting lists. At the same time, the torture survivor may live in a world of nonrecognition because of political or racial/ethnic prejudices of his or her new society.

RESILIENCE FACTORS

Environmental Factors

It has occasionally been suggested that torture survivors have become more human and mature as a result of their ordeal. Sometimes the term "successful survivor" has been applied, suggesting that torture may promote some level of personal growth and strength (Gill, 1988; Miller, 1992). Such a statement is a paraphrasing of Nietzsche's "If it does not kill you—it is good for you." This phenomenon of torture-induced growth has not been observed in clinical work at the RCT Copenhagen. It is hard to imagine any potential benefit from a method devised to control, humiliate, and injure human beings. Perhaps the so-called positive effects represent individuals whose coping mechanisms were able to deal with the level of stress to which they were subjected. On the other hand, apparently well-adjusted torture survivors may simply be hesitant to express the actual level of their suffering for continuing fear, shame, or other negative emotions. Indeed, the phenomena of numbing and the avoidance of fear-evoking topics are hallmarks of PTSD (APA, 1994). It is important to recognize that torture survivors have been seen to function for years following torture and then suddenly break down and even commit suicide (Solkoff, 1992).

As an additional point, the question of selection is of importance. Clients who come to rehabilitation centers will obviously be suffering psychological and physical symptoms and hope for an amelioration. This motivation, of course, excludes people who suffer few negative consequences. An unknown proportion of torture survivors are apparently capable of surviving with their symptoms. They may suffer nightmares or other symptoms for many years and yet manage to live on; this is also seen in prisoners of war, a proportion of whom have been tortured (Miller, 1992).

Some factors relating to the trauma of torture have a marked positive impact on the later adjustment of the survivors. As the aim of torture is to destroy the person through the psychological and physical pain, the state of hyperarousal may be somewhat lessened by the victims being together with other victims after the torture. Human beings need to form attachments, especially in times of danger; turning to others is a major coping strategy (Rajecki, Lamb, & Obmascher, 1978). Torture survivors tell of the positive effect of being with fellow human beings, of being able to talk about the ordeal directly afterwards, and of being comforted. A regular prison with rules and regulations that are being observed, even though strict, is preferable to the constant changing or arbitrary rules in the torture center. Family visits are important to dissipate relatives' fear—as is news from the outside. Once the survivor is released, obtaining a job and being able to support and protect one's family is of prime importance for adjustment. Only few previously tortured refugees manage to achieve these conditions relatively quickly, and most do not before the lapse of several years after the torture.

Individual Factors

Individuals with well-developed coping mechanisms and good understanding of why the torture is taking place stand a better chance of getting through the ordeal without major functional impairment. From the psychodynamic perspective, such individuals will typically use defense mechanisms of a mature level, such as humor and sublimation, and be capable of gaining a subjective meaning and making sense of the event (Bettleheim, 1943). Other important coping mechanisms employed during the torture may be dissociation and daydreaming. However, once the survivors are back in society, it is necessary for them to readjust their means of coping with their internal psychological states (i.e., cognition and affect). From a clinical perspective, readjustment following torture experiences is a complex process. However, it appears that several individual and environmental factors (e.g., prior positive adjustment, absence or low levels of prior trauma exposure, a supportive family and extended social network, the recognition of the torture sequelae, and the availability of rehabilitation programs) in combination impact the rate and extent of individual recovery.

PSYCHOSOCIAL OUTCOME

Overview

Evaluation of the psychosocial outcome of torture for the individual and his or her family is carried out using standard mental health assessment procedures. The study of the psychosocial outcome of torture is largely based on the symptoms presented and the demographic background (e.g., marital status, employment status). However, it is well-known that methods developed for one area of mental health practice are not automatically equally well-suited to other areas and that great care should be taken in avoiding a priori assumptions (Mollica, 1992). Work has begun on developing assessment procedures with normative data specific to torture (Mollica & Caspi-Yavin, 1991; Mollica et al., 1992). The selection of particular measures and interviewing techniques will necessarily need to be adjusted based upon local standards of practice (see Chapter 14, this volume).

Precautions

The accuracy of the reporting of torture sequelae is influenced by several factors. First, a portion of torture victims are killed under torture, and the psychological outcome of this group is by definition unavailable. Second, most survivors stay in their country of origin, and for obvious reasons it is not possible to interview them directly. Some indirect attempts to investigate this area have been made (e.g., examining the general psychopathology of prison inmates when it is suspected that some of the victims are torture survivors) (Eleazar, Obillo, & Lopez, 1992). Third, the extreme selection of torture survivors as refugees must be taken into consideration. The victims have survived the torture and managed to stay alive after release from jail, often underground or under other hard circumstances. They have managed to escape, to obtain asylum, and to present themselves at some treatment facility. Forth, torture survivor refugees often have a poor command of the new language, and they may distrust the interpreters, perhaps because they belong to different ethnic groups within the same country. It also has to be recognized that different cultures contain different verbal expressions of emotion, and that the ease with which symptoms of a psychological nature are volunteered may also be different. Fifth, when refugees are questioned about the ordeal, a certain overreporting may be expected because being a torture survivor may facilitate obtaining refugee status (Cathcart, Berger, & Knazan, 1979). At the same time underreporting also comes into play because recounting the torture may be painful (e.g., by revealing various forms of sexual abuse that perhaps not even the spouse is aware of). Furthermore, the torture survivor has often told part of the torture on earlier occasions and been accused of lying. Sixth, it is well-known that torture survivors may change the details of their story as therapy progresses; this may be related to the amount of tension and anxiety released during the therapy (Mollica & Caspi-Yavin, 1992). Finally, most investigations have been carried out at treatment centers for torture survivors, and most of the clients have been young single males, without severe psychiatric diseases with or without relation to the torture.

The Interview

Information is obtained in various ways. Some investigators use open-ended interviews, whereas others use semistructured or structured interview forms such as the SCID, ADIS, or SADS (Bøjholm et al., 1992). Both groups, however, have to be sure that all relevant topics are covered. More than one interview with the survivor may be necessary in order to build up trust and to evaluate the many individual and environmental aspects relevant to determining adjustment. Several of the traditional methods may be very well developed with respect to our population (e.g., the MMPI-2), but new instruments have now been developed out of a recognition that transcultural factors are important in assessing psychological symptoms in clients from a diversity of cultures (e.g., the Hopkins Symptom Checklist, Indochinese Version) (see Chapter 14, this volume).

Psychological Symptoms at the Time of Examination

In reviewing the literature and clinical experiences, one becomes aware of a set of symptoms that appears regularly in torture survivors. Most commonly, these symptoms can be fit under the diagnostic category of Posttraumatic Stress Disorder (PTSD) (APA, 1994; WHO, 1992). However, other mental health problems such as depression or psychosis may occur (Kinzie & Boehnlein, 1989; Kinzie et al., 1990; Mollica et al., 1987). We now turn attention to describing some of the commonly observed psychological outcomes of torture.

Posttraumatic Stress Disorder

One manifestation of torture may be to reexperience images related to the mistreatment. This may be in the form of recurrent nightmares in which the torture, either in its totality or in some particular details, is replayed. This may contribute to sleeping disorders and a chronic state of tiredness and exhaustion. Reexperiencing in the form of flashbacks also occurs during waking hours and may be triggered by uniforms, sirens, airplane noise, or even people resembling persons from the torture center. It is not unheard of to have former torture victims react with flashbacks to standard medical examinations. Upon exploration, it is commonly noted that some feature of the examination (e.g., a lab coat, the request to disrobe, examination of a particular body area) is in some way similar to some detail of a previous torture experience. Sudden unprovoked recollections may also occur. This attachment to the trauma was noted as early as 1889 by Janet and has been described as an almost compulsive tendency to reexperience and repeat the painful traumatic experience (Saporta & van der Kolk, 1992).

Avoidance and numbing constitute an additional class of symptoms. Torture survivors learn that certain activities provoke intrusive cognitive states or intense states of physiological arousal. Thus, as an adaptive strategy, the individual may make numerous attempts to minimize contact with people, places, things, or activities that generate painful symptomatology. Torture survivors may take a different route when confronted with armed personnel, or they may avoid news from home. They have frequently become more sensitive to violence and film scenes with a strong emotional content. One aspect of torture is a shutting down of the emotional life during the torture in order to survive, and afterwards it may be extremely difficult to permit oneself to enter into emotional relationships again. This emotional numbing may be one of the prices of survival for some (Baker, 1992).

Increased arousal symptoms are also observed. The level of physiological and emotional arousal is raised to a maximum level during torture, which seems to be an outgrowth of surviving in a hopeless situation. However, this level of arousal continues, and the survivors will constantly be plagued by its manifestations. Poor sleep, which has been reported frequently, has been verified by several studies that have now demonstrated a decreased level of stage 4 sleep (Åstrøm, Lunde, Ortmann, Trojaborg, & Boysen, 1989; Vesti, Somnier, & Kastrup, 1992). Concentration and memory are affected, making the comprehension of new information more difficult. A natural outgrowth of such difficulties in cognitive processing is the fact that the individual has a difficult time in learning that some (or many) parts of his or her current environment may actually be much more safe and supportive of his or her well-being than that individual is able to perceive. Often, torture survivors are easily startled and are frequently tense, sometimes feeling a need to scan the surroundings for signs of threat. Furthermore, the whole symptom complex may fluctuate with time, and reemergence of symptoms may be triggered by events reminiscent of or associated with the original trauma.

It is evident from the above that many of the symptoms of torture survivors fall under the category of PTSD of the American Psychiatric Association (APA, 1994) and now of the International Classification of Diseases (ICD-10) by the World Health Organization (WHO, 1992). Nevertheless, several other patterns of adjustment (e.g., depression, substance abuse, reactive psychosis, or personality changes) are sometimes observed. These other patterns of adjustment may be observed in isolation, but it is often the case that PTSD or other anxiety-based symptoms form the core of the clinical presentation with other clinical problems occurring in addition. Attention is now turned toward considering some of these additional patterns of adjustment that may occur at some point in time (even months or years) following victimization by torture.

Depression

Substantial elevations in depressed affect have been noted among torture survivors (Kinzie, 1989; Mollica et al., 1990; Mollica et al., 1987). Depression may be diagnosed according to standard procedures, and symptoms are often seen as reactive. Torture survivors frequently live under very complex circumstances. After having been severely injured, they have somehow managed to leave the prison, but the ensuing lack of employment possibilities, the shunning by neighbors, or even hatred by the families of those the victim was forced to betray, all set the stage for depressive symptoms. In some cases in which victims have managed to escape, the authorities may have arrested another family member and perhaps even tortured that person in order to recapture the escaped person. Living with such a burden in a foreign country, with poor contact to the new society and in cultural isolation, may pave the way for the emergence of a reactive depression. Others develop depression of a more existential nature in response to the understanding of human brutality and a disbelief that our species will ever be able to change. In other people, depression may simply emerge as a secondary issue concerning frustration over functional losses resulting from prolonged anxiety-based symptoms.

Reactive Psychosis

A small percentage (perhaps less than 10%) of torture survivors may experience psychotic episodes (Kinzie & Boehnlein, 1989). Such experiences may involve flashbacks of scenes from the torture chamber. This reaction may be elicited by or during psychotherapy, or during routine somatic investigations, or it may be precipitated by the drugs used for anesthesia before an operation (e.g., Pentothal). Clients have been referred regularly to the RCT after a severe reaction when they were to undergo an operation. The reaction is often referred to as a hysterical reaction by the stall until the trauma-based content of the reaction is realized. The waking-up phase after an operation is another danger point. Torture survivors may believe themselves back in the torture chamber, regaining consciousness after torture, and staff members may be seen as torturers. It is typically helpful to try to calm and reassure torture victims experiencing such extreme reactions. Simple strategies aimed at reorienting the person to personnel, place, and time are often quite helpful (e.g., stating names, stating location, stating time and date, reassuring regarding safety; see Chapter 14, this volume, for additional suggestions).

Comorbidity

This topic has not yet been studied in torture survivors alone. To get a glimpse of what might emanate, we have to turn to other groups, including members of the armed forces who have been tortured. Reviewing veteran studies, the comorbid diagnoses particularly included alcoholism and antisocial personality disorder (Sierles, Chen, McFarland, & Taylor, 1983). Lifetime comorbidity includes alcohol abuse, depression, and generalized anxiety, and panic disorder. It is interesting to note that the ICD diagnostic manual has noted the possibility of enduring personality changes following catastrophic circumstances (WHO, 1992; see Chapter 1, this volume). The comorbidity should be seen in the light of an ongoing exposure to acute and chronic stressors. Such factors extend from the actual torture experiences through subsequent experiences with trying to survive (e.g., asylum-seeking, refugee status).

Some health care professionals have noted that the recognition of the symptoms of torture survivors is a medicalization of a political problem. From this perspective, it is possible to argue that political involvement and advocacy by treatment professionals is a necessary component to appropriate mental health prevention and treatment efforts. Other professionals have cautioned that regardless of political circumstances, no human beings should be denied treatment access. In the opinion of the current authors, it is important for health care professionals to act in order to promote human welfare, regardless of social and political pressures. Indeed, health care professionals may carry a moral or social authority that may persuade governmental authorities to act in minimizing the root causes of human suffering. However, political advocacy efforts cannot replace the need for treatment and support services for individual torture survivors. Norris and Thompson (Chapter 3, this volume) discuss some similar ideas concerning preventing several sources of traumatic events within community settings.

Physical Sequelae at the Time of Examination

The psychiatric and psychological symptoms of torture survivors may also be seen in the light of organic brain damage. Many concentration camp survivors were investigated after the Second World War, and it was concluded that the concentration camp syndrome was an organic syndrome (Thygesen, Hermann, & Willanger, 1970). Later investigations have also concluded that a strong predictor of PTSD in prisoners of war is loss of body weight (Beebe, 1975; Eitinger, 1971). Today, however, starvation is not regularly part of torture. There is no consensus as to the relative effects of hunger and torture on the development of the symptomatology, and no study has yet demonstrated unequivocal brain damage in torture survivors of the last two decades.

Torture that is purely psychological in nature is confined to the most developed countries. Less sophisticated forms of torture are used by the vast majority of nations employing torture. This means that the body is attacked in order to affect the mind, and it is therefore not surprising that torture survivors have many somatic symptoms. The most common findings are changes in the ligaments, joints, and muscles, particularly in the back, from the neck to the pelvis, and in the feet (Skylv, 1992). Despite most of the findings being of musculoskeletal origin, other diseases and conditions must not be overlooked, and thorough investigations are necessary. Dental decay represents a special problem, not only because of pain, but also because several missing teeth may cause social embarrassment and prolong adjustment problems. Concomitant diseases must be considered. They include infections, such as tuberculosis, that may have developed in the primitive prison conditions. Because of the reactions of torture survivors, it is important that the medical and psychological personnel dealing with these problems are well informed about the sequelae of torture (see Chapter 14, this volume).

Social Sequelae at the Time of Examination

The psychological and physical sequelae of torture cause severe impairment in the social function of the torture survivor and his or her family. In addition, many social difficulties are related to the refugee status. The asylum phase is a time of bewilderment, frustration, and anger, forming one part of the triad; the effect of torture on the victim; the effect of asylum seeking, and the effects of being a refugee (Baker, 1992) constitute the others. After asylum is granted, torture survivors have difficulty in learning the new language, in particular because of decreased concentration and memory, as well as symptoms of increased arousal. These difficulties, together with the often great differences between the cultures of the survivors and the new country, further isolate the survivors and their families. Negative consequences for interpersonal relationships are seen, including an increased divorce rate (Gonsalves, 1990). This may be caused by many factors, but the new cultural environment, with a more independent role for the female, may be one important factor. Another more speculative reason is that defense mechanisms of displacement may turn the anger from the torturers to the spouse. Problems may be compounded by the role confusion that arises when the income of the male family head no longer provides the necessary means for the family. Older children, for example, when their father was in prison or living underground, have sometimes had to take over many of his roles in the family.

Most refugees encounter economic hardship and have to live on social benefits for some time. Nonrecognition of educational degrees adds to the burden. Highly trained professionals are forced to see their educational efforts ruined and may have to take nonskilled jobs or go on living on unemployment benefits. Based on clinical work at the RCT, it has been noted that there is a range in the pattern of social adjustment achieved by torture survivors. Some torture survivors are able to improve their circumstances, gradually achieving more tolerable living circumstances. Other torture survivors continue to be plagued by difficult circumstances that they seem unable to improve upon to any appreciable degree.

Legal Considerations

Torture survivors may also face legal problems. These may be related to several sources, including: (1) proof that they are torture survivors in order to obtain asylum or compensation, or to take the torturers to court; (2) obtaining permission of entry for their families into the new country; or (3) general legal matters concerning welfare benefits, housing, and other concerns in their new countries.

More attention should be given to the possibility that refugees coming to our countries may have been tortured, because by international law torture survivors have certain rights. The foremost is the right not to be sent back if they are at risk of being tortured again. It is necessary to recognize the fluctuating symptomatology of the torture survivors and that there may be delayed help-seeking and delayed onset of symptoms. The stories of the survivors are frequently disbelieved, and other explanations for the symptoms, frequently in the form of alternative diagnoses, are given. Typical alternative explanations include personality problems (e.g., antisocial personality, pathological liar, histrionic personality disorder); ordinary mental illnesses (e.g., anxiety disorders,

depressive disorders, and particularly somatoform disorders such as hypochondriasis); organic brain syndrome (e.g., dementia); malingering and factitious disorders; and adjustment disorders, particularly when stress has been
experienced (Somnier, Vesti, Kastrup, & Genefke, 1992). Even today, understanding of the symptoms and signs caused by torture is not widespread in the
medical and psychological community. Since the burden of proof lies with the
survivors, it is the duty of the health professionals to provide the best possible
care, including recognition of the potential causative relationship between torture experiences and subsequent psychological and physical functioning.

One service that health care professionals may provide to torture survivors
is to refer them to competent legal representatives. As mentioned, the legal
issues faced may be varied and complex, changing depending on the particular
individual and circumstances. The obtaining of legal advice is often complicated by symptomatology (e.g., hyperarousal) that makes it difficult for the
torture survivor to tolerate various stressors, particularly experiences that serve
as reminders of previous maltreatment. However, as is the case for the survivors of other forms of traumatic stress (e.g., violent crime), legal representation may lead to the safeguarding of basic human rights and the reestablish-
ment of a sense of personal control and dignity (see Chapter 1, this volume).
Thus, in combination with attention to physical, psychological, and social
needs, referral for legal advice and assistance can be beneficial (see Chapter 14,
this volume).

THE COURSE OF ADJUSTMENT

It is clinically informative to consider typical patterns of adjustment as
these patterns unfold over time. Comments in this regard rely largely on clinical observations based upon work with torture survivors. Where relevant, research literature based upon responses of either torture survivors or the victims of other traumatic events is cited. For the sake of the current discussion, it
is convenient to divide symptom development into three time periods. These
time periods include: (1) the first few months following torture; (2) adjustment
during the following decade; and (3) long-term adjustment.

Symptoms During the First Months after Torture

The majority of torture survivors have psychological symptoms, and many
may suffer from PTSD or other serious mental health problems (McNally,
1992). As stated, torture is a concept, and studying the adjustment after torture
will include studying the various subgroups that may be included in the torture
process. Examining data from rape victims may help to inform a discussion of
what to expect from torture victims. For example, more than 95% of rape
victims report symptoms within 2 weeks after the rape; however, the percentage of these symptoms will taper off during the following months to about 42%

6 months later (Rothbaum & Foa, 1989). Possibly, ideal conditions (e.g., adequate social support, little prior or subsequent trauma experience, lack of prior psychopathology) allow some torture survivors to recover from debilitating psychological symptoms relatively soon. At the RCT, however, it has been a common clinical observation that symptomatology may be phasic. That is, symptomatology can be suppressed to subclinical levels for some length of time. However, at a later point in time, it is not unusual for reminders to lead to the contemporary worsening of mental health symptoms (Vesti & Kastrup, 1992).

Adjustment during the Following Decade

During this phase, the survivors who have managed to escape have arrived in their new countries. The modifying effects of the refugee experience typically color the symptomatology of the torture. In the years following the torture, the psychological symptomatology is primarily that of an anxiety disorder (although depressive symptoms are often noted). The symptoms may be persistent; no major improvement in symptomatology had occurred when Greek torture survivors were examined in Greece 10 years after their release (Petersen et al., 1985). Similarly, it has been observed that torture victims from Southeast Asia suffer persistent mental health problems (Kinzie et al., 1990; Mollica et al., 1987).

The effects of torture appear to be relatively unaffected by other factors such as emigration. Evidence of this is found in studies comparing torture survivors with nontortured refugees from the same country (Hougen, Kelstrup, Petersen, & Rasmussen, 1988). This fact is of importance when considering that the refugee experience, as such, increases vulnerability to mental illness, on top of that induced by emigration (Hitch & Rack, 1980; Odegaard, 1932). However, adjustment should not be conceptualized as a smooth process. The symptoms may fluctuate, torture victims remaining free of symptoms for months or even years (Miller, 1992; Solkoff, 1992), and the symptomatology may not even be detected in the years following the trauma. Several explanations for this may be forwarded, including: delayed help-seeking, exacerbation of subclinical symptoms, reactivation of symptoms, and delayed onset of symptoms.

Long-Term Adjustment

Long-term follow-up studies have been carried out, particularly of concentration camp survivors and prisoners of war. Concentration camp survivors have been studied extensively. They had undergone torture, but they had also been starved, thus confounding the effects of torture on adjustment. Their symptomatology persisted for decades and was even passed on to the next generation (Solkoff, 1992). Prisoners of war have also been examined long after they were repatriated. Anxiety symptoms were demonstrated in 50% to 67% of soldiers at homecoming, some of whom had been tortured. The per-

roughly halved 40 years later (Kluznik, Speed, van Valkenburg, & Magraw, 1986). There seems to be a shift in the symptomatology in old survivors from anxiety to depressive symptoms, which are persistently found after many years (Tennant, Goulston, & Dent, 1986).

CONCLUSIONS

Torture is a devastating experience for the individual in the psychological, physical, and social sense. It is an experience that is so overwhelming that few individuals possess coping mechanisms that can handle such an experience. In addition, the symptoms affect the families involved as well as the surrounding society. The symptoms are of long duration, and only knowledge and awareness of this tragic dimension of human existence will ensure adequate recognition and treatment of the victims. During the last decade, many publications have emerged on the topic of torture survivors, and whereas this particular field within medicine and psychology is gradually finding its place, there is still the need for enhanced awareness and action within groups of health care professionals. It seems evident that a substantial proportion of survivors develop a symptomatology close to the entity of PTSD, but others do not, and we are only at the beginning of describing this latter group. It is hoped that the current chapter will have sensitized the reader to the existence of torture as a particularly severe form of trauma. Clinical assessment and treatment of torture survivors are considered in Chapter 14 of this volume.

REFERENCES

Acuna, J. E. (1987). *Children of the storm: Experiences of the Children's Rehabilitation Center.* Manila: Children's Rehabilitation Center.

Agger, I. (1989). Sexual torture of political prisoners: An overview. *Journal of Traumatic Stress, 2*(3), 305–318.

Agger, I., & Jensen, S. B. (1990). Testimony as ritual and evidence in psychotherapy for political refugees. *Journal of Traumatic Stress, 3*(1), 115–130.

American Psychiatric Association. (1994). *Diagnostic and statistical manual of mental disorders* (4th ed.). Washington, DC: Author.

Amnesty International. (1991). *Amnesty International report.* London: Author.

Amnesty International. (1992). *Amnesty International report.* London: Author.

Anisman, H. L., & Sklar, L. S. (1981). Social housing conditions influence escape deficits produced by uncontrollable stress: Assessment of the contribution of norepinephrine. *Behavioral Neural Biology, 32,* 406–427.

Åstrøm, C., Lunde, I., Ortmann, J., Trojaborg, W., & Boysen, G. (1989). Sleep disturbances in torture survivors. *Acta Neurologica Scandinavica, 79,* 150–154.

Baker, R. (1992). Psychosocial consequences for tortured refugees seeking asylum refugee status in Europe. In M. Basoglu (Ed.), *Torture and its consequences: Current treatment approaches* (pp. 83–106). Cambridge: Cambridge University Press.

Basoglu, M., & Mineka, S. (1992). The role of uncontrollable and unpredictable stress in posttraumatic stress responses in torture survivors. In M. Basoglu (Ed.), *Torture and its conse-*

quences: Current treatment approaches (pp. 182–225). Cambridge: Cambridge University Press.

Beebe, G. W. (1975). Follow-up studies of World War II and Korean War prisoners: II. Morbidity, disability, and maladjustments. *American Journal of Epidemiology, 101,* 400–422.

Bettelheim, B. (1943). Individual and mass behavior in extreme situations. *Journal of Abnormal Social Psychology, 38,* 417–452.

Bloche, M. G. (1987). *Uruguay's military physicians: Cogs in a system of state terror.* Washington, DC: American Association for the Advancement of Science, Committee on Scientific Freedom and Responsibility.

Bøjholm, S., Foldspang, A., Juhler, M., Kastrup, M., Skylv, G., & Somnier, F. (1992). *Monitoring the health and rehabilitation of torture survivors: A management information system for a rehabilitation and research unit for torture victims.* Copenhagen: International Rehabilitation Council for Torture Victims.

Cathcart, L. M., Berger, P., & Knazan, B. (1979). Medical examination of torture victims applying for refugee status. *Canadian Medical Association Journal, 121,* 179–184.

Centers for Disease Control. (1988). Health status of Vietnam veterans: I. Psychosocial characteristics. *Journal of the American Medical Association, 259,* 2701–2707.

Compton, E., Fay, E. S., & Gibson, R. (1971). *Report of the inquiry into allegations against the security forces of physical brutality in Northern Ireland arising out of events on the 9th of August 1971.* London: Her Majesty's Stationery Office.

Concise Oxford Dictionary. (1984). Oxford: Clarendon Press.

Council for International Organizations of Medical Sciences. (1983). *Principles of medical ethics relevant to the protection of prisoners against torture.* Geneva: Author.

Davidson, J., Smith, R., & Kudler, H. (1989). Validity and reliability of the DSM-III criteria for posttraumatic stress disorder: Experience with structured interview. *Journal of Nervous and Mental Disorders, 177,* 336–341.

Doctors, ethics, and torture. (1987, August). Proceedings of an international meeting, Copenhagen. *Danish Medical Bulletin, 34,* 185–216.

Eitinger, L. (1971). Acute and chronic psychiatric reactions in concentration camp survivors. In L. Levin (Ed.), *Society, stress, and disease* (pp. 219–230). New York: Oxford University Press.

Eleazar, J., Obillo, E., & Lopez, J. P. (1992). The psychiatric morbidity patterns among Filipino political prisoner. *Progress Notes, 6,* 4–5.

European Committee for the Prevention of Torture and Inhuman or Degrading Treatment or Punishment (CPT). (1993, December). Public statement on Turkey adopted on 15 December 1993. *Human Rights Law Journal, 14,* 49–54.

The Execution of the Punishment of Whipping Ordinance. (1987). *New Islamic laws.* Lahore: Mansoor Book House.

Freedy, J. R., Resnick, H. S., & Kilpatrick, D. G. (1992). Conceptual framework for evaluating disaster impact: Implications for clinical intervention. In L. S. Austin (Ed.), *Responding to disaster: A guide for mental health professionals* (pp. 3–23). Washington, DC: American Psychiatric Press.

Gill, A. (1988). *The journey back from Hell.* London: Grafton Books.

Gluzman, S. (1989). *On Soviet totalitarian psychiatry.* Amsterdam: International Association on the Political Use of Psychiatry.

Gonsalves, C. J. (1990). The psychological effects of political repression on Chilean exiles in the US. *American Journal of Orthopsychiatry, 60,* 143–154.

Hinkle, L. E., & Wolff, H. G. (1956). Communist interrogation and indoctrination of "enemies of the states." *Archives of Neurology and Psychiatry, 76,* 115–174.

Hitch, P., & Rack, P. (1980). Mental illness among Polish and Russian refugees in Bradford. *British Journal of Psychiatry, 37,* 206–211.

Hougen, H. P., Kelstrup, J., Petersen, H. D., & Rasmussen, O. V. (1988). Sequelae to torture: A controlled study of torture victims living in exile. *Forensic Science International, 36,* 153–160.

International Union of Psychological Science. (1985). Statement by the International Union of Psychological Science. In Amnesty International (Comp.), *Ethical codes and declarations relevant to the health professions* (pp. 22–23). London: Amnesty International. Original work published July, 1976.

Jacobsen, L., & Vesti, P. (1992). *Torture survivors—A new group of patients* (2nd ed.). Copenhagen: Danish Nurses' Organization.

Kinzie, J. D. (1989). Therapeutic approaches to traumatized Cambodian refugees. *Journal of Traumatic Stress, 2*(1), 75–91.

Kinzie, J. D., & Boehnlein, J. K. (1989). Post-traumatic psychosis among Cambodian refugees. *Journal of Traumatic Stress, 2*(2), 185–198.

Kinzie, J. D., Boehnlein, J. K., Leung, P. K., Moore, L. J., Riley, C., & Smith, D. (1990). *American Journal of Psychiatry, 147*(7), 913–917.

Kluznik, J. C., Speed, N., van Valkenburg, C., & Magraw, R. (1986). Forty-year follow-up of United States prisoners of war. *American Journal of Psychiatry, 143,* 1443–1446.

Kulka, R. A., Schlenger, W. E., Fairbank, J. A., Hough, R. L., Jordan, B. K., Marmar, C. R., & Weiss, D. S. (1988). *National Vietnam Veterans Readjustment Study (NVVRS): Description, current status, and initial PTSD prevalence estimates.* Research Triangle Park, NC: Research Triangle Institute.

Langbein, J. H. (1977). *Torture and the law of proof: Europe and England in the Ancien regime.* Chicago: University of Chicago Press.

McFarlane, A. C. (1989). The aetiology of post-traumatic morbidity: Predisposing, precipitating, and perpetuating factors. *British Journal of Psychiatry, 154,* 221–228.

McNally, R. (1992). Psychopathology of post-traumatic stress disorder (PTSD): Boundaries of the syndrome. In M. Basoglu (Ed.), *Torture and its consequences: Current treatment approaches* (pp. 229–252). Cambridge: Cambridge University Press.

Miller, T. W. (1992). Long-term effects of torture in former prisoners of war. In M. Basoglu (Ed.), *Torture and its consequences: Current treatment approaches* (pp. 107–135). Cambridge: Cambridge University Press.

Mollica, R. (1992). The prevention of torture and the clinical care of survivors: A field in need of a new science. In M. Basoglu (Ed.), *Torture and its consequences: Current treatment approaches* (pp. 23–37). Cambridge: Cambridge University Press.

Mollica, R. F., & Caspi-Yavin, Y. (1991). Measuring torture and torture-related symptoms. *Psychological Assessment, 3*(4), 581–587.

Mollica, R. F., & Caspi-Yavin, Y. (1992). Overview: The assessment and diagnosis of torture events and symptoms. In M. Basoglu (Ed.), *Torture and its consequences: Current treatment approaches* (pp. 253–274). Cambridge: Cambridge University Press.

Mollica, R. F., Caspi-Yavin, Y., Bollini, P., Truong, T., Tor, S., & Lavelle, J. (1992). Validating a cross-cultural instrument for measuring torture, trauma, and posttraumatic stress disorder in Indochinese refugees. *Journal of Nervous and Mental Disease, 180*(2), 111–116.

Mollica, R. F., Wyshak, G., & Lavelle, J. (1987). The psychosocial impact of war trauma and torture on Southeast Asian refugees. *American Journal of Psychiatry, 144*(12), 1567–1572.

Mollica, R. F., Wyshak, G., Lavelle, J., Truong, T., Tor, S., & Yang, T. (1990). Assessing symptom change in Southeast Asian refugee survivors of mass violence and torture. *American Journal of Psychiatry, 147,* 83–88.

Odegaard, O. (1932). Immigration and insanity. *Acta Psychiatrica Neurologica Scandinavica, Supplement 4.*

Paker, M., Paker, Ö, & Yüksel, S. (1992). Psychological effects of torture: An empirical study of tortured and non-tortured non-political prisoners. In M. Basoglu (Ed.), *Torture and its consequences: Current treatment approaches* (pp. 72–82). Cambridge: Cambridge University Press.

Petersen, H. D., Abildgaard, U. Daugaard, G., Jess, P., Marcussen, H., & Wallach, M. (1985). Psychological and physical long-term effects of torture: A follow-up examination of 22 Greek persons exposed to torture 1967–1974. *Scandinavian Journal of Social Medicine, 13,* 89–93.

Pynoos, R. S., Frederick, C., Nader, K., Arroyo, W., Steinberg, A., Eth, S., Nunez, F., & Fairbanks, L. (1987). Life threat and posttraumatic stress in school-age children. *Archives of General Psychiatry, 44,* 1057–1063.

Rajecki, D. W., Lamb, M. E., & Obmascher, P. (1978). Toward a general theory of infantile attachment: A comparative review of aspects of the social bond. *Behavioral Brain Sciences, 3,* 417–464.

Rothbaum, B. O., & Foa, E. B. (1989). *Subtypes of PTSD and duration of symptoms.* Paper prepared for the DSM-IV workgroup of post-traumatic stress disorder.

Saporta, J. A., & van der Kolk, B. A. (1992). Psychobiological consequences of severe trauma. In M. Basoglu (Ed.), *Torture and its consequences: Current treatment approaches* (pp. 151–181). Cambridge: Cambridge University Press.

Sierles, F. S., Chen, J. J., McFarland, R. E., & Taylor, M. A. (1983). Posttraumatic stress disorder and concurrent psychiatric illness: A preliminary report. *American Journal of Psychiatry, 140,* 1177–1179.

Skylv, G. (1992). The physical sequelae of torture. In M. Basoglu (Ed.), *Torture and its consequences: Current treatment approaches* (pp. 38–55). Cambridge: Cambridge University Press.

Solkoff, N. (1992). The Holocaust: Survivors and their children. In M. Basoglu (Ed.), *Torture and its consequences: Current treatment approaches* (pp. 136–148). Cambridge: Cambridge University Press.

Somnier, F. E., & Genefke, I. K. (1986). Psychotherapy for victims of torture. *British Journal of Psychiatry, 149,* 323–329.

Somnier, F., Vesti, P., Kastrup, M., & Genefke, I. (1992). Psychosocial consequences of torture: Current knowledge and evidence. In M. Basoglu (Ed.), *Torture and its consequences: Current treatment approaches* (pp. 56–71). Cambridge: Cambridge University Press.

Steketee, G., & Foa, E. B. (1987). Rape victims: Post-traumatic stress responses and their treatment: A review of the literature. *Journal of Anxiety Disorders, 1,* 69–86.

Tennant, C. C., Goulston, K. J., & Dent, O. F. (1986). The psychological effect of being a prisoner of war: Forty years after release. *American Journal of Psychiatry, 143,* 618–621.

Thygesen, P., Hermann, K., & Willanger, R. (1970). Concentration camp survivors in Denmark: Persecution, disease, disability, compensation. *Danish Medical Bulletin, 17,* 65–108.

Timermans, J. (1982). *Preso sin nombre, celda sin numero.* Barcelona: El Cid.

van der Kolk, B. A., & Ducey, C. P. (1989). The psychological processing of traumatic experience: Rorschach problems in PTSD. *Journal of Traumatic Stress, 2,* 259–274.

Vesti, P. (1990). Extreme man made stress and anti-therapy: Doctors as collaborators in torture. *Danish Medical Bulletin, 37,* 466–468.

Vesti, P., & Kastrup, M. (1992). Psychotherapy for torture survivors. In M. Basoglu (Ed.), *Torture and its consequences: Current treatment approaches* (pp. 348–362). Cambridge: Cambridge University Press.

Vesti, P., Somnier, F., & Kastrup, M. (1992). *Psychotherapy with torture survivors: A report of practice from the Rehabilitation and Research Centre for Torture Victims (RCT), Copenhagen, Denmark.* Copenhagen: International Rehabilitation Council for Torture Survivors.

World Health Organization. (1992). *The international classification of mental and behavioral disorders* (10th ed.). Geneva: Author.

III

Assessment and
Treatment Issues

The chapters in Part III translate material presented in Parts I (i.e., core issues to the traumatic stress field) and II (i.e., a broad knowledge base regarding five specific traumatic events) into applied terms. Thus, the chapters in this section most clearly embody the theme of translating theoretical ideas and empirical facts into clinical practice. To gain the fullest appreciation of material in this section, the reader is encouraged to refer to earlier chapters in this volume as appropriate. We now turn to a brief summary of each of the six chapters in this section.

Chapter 10 is titled *Helping the Victims of Military Trauma* and is written by Zahava Solomon and Arieh Y. Shalev. A primary strength of this chapter lies in the fact that the authors are Israeli citizens with extensive experience in research and clinical work with the victims of war-related trauma. The ongoing occurrence of conflict in the Middle East is certainly tragic. It also provides, however, a natural laboratory for assessing and treating stress-related conditions. The authors refer to both acute and chronic psychosocial impairment related to war. They also consider intervention approaches ranging from stress debriefing to more formal and elaborate forms of clinical intervention. Concerning the latter, Solomon and Shalev review extant research support for both biological and psychosocial forms of treatment. A range of psychosocial approaches are reviewed (behavioral, cognitive, psychodynamic). The authors also point out that treatment must address the needs of family members, who suffer along with the combat survivor. The authors end with the realistic conclusion that no one form of treatment is sufficient to address the needs of all trauma victims. They call for eclectic approaches and a commitment to the development of new forms of intervention.

Chapter 11, *Helping the Victims of Violent Crime,* is written by Sherry A. Falsetti and Heidi S. Resnick. These authors do a particularly excellent job in integrating extant theory (e.g., crisis theory, learning theory, cognitive theories) with assessment and treatment practice. Their consideration of assessment is notable for the attention to standardization and breadth. Falsetti and Resnick clearly instruct the reader regarding the taking of a careful trauma history, a practice that is often ignored in clinical practice. They also emphasize assessing and treating a range of mental health outcomes, including posttraumatic stress disorder (PTSD), major depression, substance abuse, and panic disorder. The authors describe available behavioral and cognitive–behavioral approaches to treatment, cite supporting research, and refer the reader to additional materials as needed. The chapter ends with a clinical case example that clearly applies the issues outlined within the chapter.

Alexander C. McFarlane wrote Chapter 12, *Helping the Victims of Disaster.* The chapter begins with a discussion of the impact of trauma upon clinical judgment and personal well-being of the professional. This is an issue for all clinical work with trauma victims. McFarlane emphasizes the complex and evolving nature of disasters by recommending that interventions can occur at five phases in time ranging from before to following the disaster (planning, threat, inventory and rescue, remedy, recovery). He states that the nature of intervention will change in each time phase. He also discusses a biopsychosocial model for individual mental health risk or resiliency that can be considered in light of the five stages of intervention. Appropriate assessment (interview and self-report) and treatment strategies are considered. Regarding intervention, McFarlane emphasizes both prevention and treatment. He does a particularly excellent job of discussing the common elements in successful mental health treatment, emphasizing a flexible clinical approach that integrates biological and psychosocial approaches. The author ends with a series of fascinating case examples that illustrate a range of clinical concerns (e.g., brief interventions, control issues, death, family issues, depression, emergency service personnel, and dissociative symptoms).

Chapter 13, *Accidental Injury: Approaches to Assessment and Treatment,* is written by Connie L. Best and David P. Ribbe. These authors offer a very pragmatic approach that is illustrated with two clinical case examples. A major strength of this chapter lies in the emphasis upon the art of clinical practice (e.g., establishing and maintaining rapport and trust in addition to using specific assessment and treatment techniques). A standardized cognitive–behavioral approach to both assessment and treatment is presented. The authors rely upon Lang's three-channel model for fear responses (physical, cognitive, and behavioral). A series of intervention techniques corresponding to each physical, cognitive, and behavioral aspect of fear are suggested. Based on their extensive clinical experiences, the authors discuss several special issues that may require clinical attention (perceptions of life threat, physical injury, immediate versus long-term reactions, and advocacy).

Chapter 14, *Treatment of Torture Survivors: Psychosocial and Somatic Aspects,* is written by Peter Vesti and Marianne Kastrup. This chapter represents a follow-up to the broad overview of torture provided by the same authors in Chapter 9. Vesti and Kastrup approach this topic primarily based upon clinical experience. Their clinical perspective, in contrast to that of several others presented in this volume, is primarily psychodynamic in nature. Given the global scope and political nature of torture, the authors emphasize remaining sensitive to cultural traditions of torture survivors, as these traditions may impact the type and course of treatment. It is also unique that their chapter discusses contraindications to intensive, uncovering forms of therapy (e.g., distorted sense of normalcy, severe substance abuse). Their assessment procedures are brief, structured, and repeated at regular intervals. They broadly discuss the following aspects of treatment: practical issues, general phases of treatment, treatment techniques, and key elements in successful treatment. They also discuss a range of services to supplement individual treatment (e.g., somatic treatment, social services, legal problems, and spiritual guidance). Two case histories are discussed to illustrate the authors' approach to clinical work.

The final chapter, *Traumatic Stress: A Blueprint for the Future,* is written by John R. Freedy and Stevan E. Hobfoll. The chapter is an integrative summary of previous chapters. Summary statements are provided, integrating common themes that apply to different trauma populations across different settings. When possible, appropriate courses of action for professionals are suggested. Encouraging meaningful, collective action by mental health professionals is a major goal for this volume. It is hoped that the final chapter—combined with the earlier chapters—provide mental health professionals with the knowledge base, technical skills, and motivation necessary to transform *Traumatic Stress: From Theory to Practice.*

10

Helping Victims of Military Trauma

ZAHAVA SOLOMON and ARIEH Y. SHALEV

OVERVIEW

Active participation in combat exposes the soldier to extreme stress, which may result in both immediate and long-term impairment in his mental health. The most prevalent effects that are associated with combat-related stress are combat stress reaction (CSR) and posttraumatic stress disorder (PTSD) (APA, 1987, 1994; Solomon, 1993).

This chapter surveys the available treatment approaches for CSR and PTSD. Although PTSD can develop from CSR, it need not, and the chapter treats them separately. It begins with reviews of two approaches taken by the military itself within, or shortly following, the combat situation: (1) debriefing, a preventive approach used to reduce the risk of long-term psychological injury; and (2) frontline treatment, the prevalent mode of dealing with acute CSR in most western armies. Following this, we present four major models of PTSD: the biological, the behavioral, the psychodynamic, and the cognitive. In each case, we discuss the basic theory and assumptions of the treatment modes that follow from them, as well as the research that has examined the effectiveness of the therapies. The chapter concludes with the observation that treatment results have been partial at best, sometimes alleviating the symptoms but rarely ever effecting a cure. We suggest that pharmacotherapy, based on the biological model of PTSD, may be used to facilitate the patient's participation in psycho-

ZAHAVA SOLOMON · Bob Shapell School of Social Work, Tel Aviv University, Ramat Aviv, 69 978, Israel.   **ARIEH Y. SHALEV** · Department of Psychiatry, Center for Traumatic Stress, Hadassah University Hospital, Jerusalem 91120, Israel.

Traumatic Stress: From Theory to Practice, edited by John R. Freedy and Stevan E. Hobfoll. Plenum Press, New York, 1995.

therapy. We call for the development of new treatment approaches and controlled studies of their effectiveness.

COMBAT STRESS REACTION

The condition known today as combat stress reaction (CSR) (Solomon, 1993) has been called by a variety of names: "nostalgia," "soldier's heart," "shell shock," "combat neurosis," "battle fatigue," and "combat exhaustion," to name but a few. Typically, CSR is characterized by a reduction of the person's capacity to function as a soldier (Kormos, 1978) and by the subjective experience of overwhelming distress and inescapable anxiety.

Classical descriptions (e.g., Grinker & Spiegel, 1945) suggest that CSR often follows a phase of physical and mental exhaustion. Beyond its essential element of dysfunction, CSR is a heterogenous condition that may include dissociative states, confusion, disorientation, overreaction or inappropriate responses to minor threats, restlessness, agitation, stupor, motor retardation, uncontrolled affects (anxiety, panic, terror, sadness, guilt, shame), perplexity, and conversion symptoms (paralysis, blindness, mutism). Soldiers may suffer from symptoms of hyperarousal, emotional dyscontrol, diminished interest in things that were commonly meaningful to them, reduced social interaction, sustained criticism and mistrust, and somatic manifestations of anxiety (e.g., diarrhea, nausea, tremulousness, fatigue, cold sweats, headaches, heart palpitation).

During the acute phase, it is sometimes difficult to distinguish between CSR and reactions of fear and anxiety that are common during combat. Many soldiers are, at times, tense, restless, anxious, and frightened. The identification threshold, or the level of dysfunction and distress that can be borne by both the individual and the unit without labeling the soldier as a CSR casualty, varies with personal, social, and situational factors (Moses & Cohen, 1984).

Some cues, however, may suggest that the soldier's reaction is extreme. The principal indicators are: emotions that are strong enough to interfere with task accomplishment; distress that is significantly more intense than that of other soldiers exposed to the same conditions; tension that is beyond the soldier's control and does not decrease during periods of relief; and behavior or responses that seem to others different from the individual's usual character.

COMBAT STRESS REACTION AND POSTTRAUMATIC STRESS DISORDER

With the end of the war, or even within 48 to 72 hours of the onset of the stress, the debilitating effects of combat stress may abate in some cases, whereas in others, profound and prolonged psychological sequelae in the form of PTSD, characterized by intrusive recollections of the traumatic event, psychic numbing, and symptoms of autonomic arousal (APA, 1987, 1994) may follow.

Recent research shows, however, that many trauma survivors develop

PTSD without presenting disability symptoms during combat. Solomon (1993) found that 1, 2, and 3 years after the 1982 Lebanon war, 16%, 19%, and 9% of groups of several hundred Israeli combat veterans who had not been identified as CSR casualties suffered from diagnosable PTSD.

Similarly, the discrepancy between reports of low numbers of stress casualties during the Vietnam war (Bourne, 1969; Ingraham & Manning, 1986) and the large number of veterans who developed PTSD in the subsequent years (e.g., Kulka et al., 1989) suggest that many of those who developed PTSD had not been so identified during their terms of service. Data on delayed referral for treatment (e.g., Solomon, Kotler, Shalev, & Lin, 1989) suggests that veterans may suffer from PTSD for prolonged periods of time without seeking professional help.

A comparison of the clinical pictures of CSR and PTSD revealed some similarities and some distinctive features. Some of the symptoms appear in both CSR and PTSD, others in one but not in the other. The clinical picture of CSR is generally more complex, entails more symptoms, and is polymorphic. In comparison, PTSD is by definition composed of a given set of symptoms. Yet, even symptoms common to both CSR and PTSD may take different forms in these two entities. For example, the anxiety feelings aroused during battle by the fear of death are crystallized after the war into anxiety that is not specifically related to death but is generalized to every potential threat. This emphasizes the continuity between immediate and long-term sequelae, yet it also demonstrates the different forms they take. Similarly, dissociation, psychic numbing and depression may characterize CSR, yet whereas psychic numbing is a distinct PTSD symptom, depression is considered a possible associated feature.

Attention is now turned to treatment modalities aiming at: (1) prevention or reduction of the risk for CSR/PTSD, (2) curing CSR, and (3) curing and rehabilitating PTSD casualties.

COMBAT STRESS REACTION: PREVENTION AND COMBAT-INDUCED PSYCHOPATHOLOGY

Debriefing

A widely shared notion suggests that primary intervention, that is reducing the risk of CSR/PTSD in soldiers exposed to combat, is most effective and thus most desirable (Solomon & Benbenishty, 1986). New stress-management methods involving entire groups of survivors, not necessarily casualties, have, therefore, been developed and implemented (Griffin, 1987; Raphael, 1986; Birenbaum, Copolon & Scharff, 1976; Cohen, 1976; Cohen & Ahearn, 1980). Debriefing has been especially recommended for survivors of group trauma such as combat (Dunning & Silva, 1980; Jones, 1985; Mitchell, 1981; Bergman & Queen, 1986).

Debriefing is a group-oriented intervention in which the major elements of an event are reviewed by participants shortly after its termination. Debriefing addresses all the survivors of the event regardless of their immediate reaction. It uses the group's natural resources and existing institutional structures, and does not label any individual reaction as deviant or pathological. Implied in the practice of debriefing are the assumptions that peers can support individual healing and that traumatic experiences (like grief) are better worked through in natural groups.

Debriefing interviews follow a variety of protocols, but they usually entail a systematic review of the event and of the participants' reactions and an application of a "stress management" technique (e.g., working-through, abreaction, sharing, psychoeducation, or teaching coping skills).

Debriefing may have any of a variety of goals. These include: (1) working-through emotional overload (e.g., Mitchell, 1981, 1983), (2) improvement of group cohesion (e.g., Griffin, 1987), (3) teaching coping skills (e.g., Bergman & Queen, 1986), and (4) detection of symptomatic individuals (e.g., Mitchell, 1983).

Accordingly, various aspects of the exposure have been suggested as focal points for debriefing sessions. Among them are the factual reality of the event (Marshall, 1944), the emotional reactions of exposed individuals (e.g., Mitchell, 1983), reframing the meaning or implications (e.g., Bergman & Queen, 1986), and residual symptoms (e.g., Mitchell, 1983).

Similarly, a range of techniques has been employed, including cognitive rehearsal, ventilation, "resource mobilization" (Mitchell, 1983), sharing and education (Raphael, 1986), and active counseling and teaching (e.g., Wagner, 1979). Dunning (1990) distinguished between two distinct types of structured debriefing: *educational debriefing*, which informs participants of the psychological and behavioral reactions of other people in similar situations, and *psychological debriefing*, which includes ventilation of feelings about the event and exploration of signs of distress.

During combat, however, psychological debriefing has obvious limitations. There are inevitably few mental health professionals at the front, and those that are there are often regarded by the troops as outsiders and intruders. Moreover, military groups have their own psychological leaders, whose authority has been to encourage functioning for the next action. These considerations suggest that debriefing protocols that can be carried out by natural leaders are more appropriate for wars than those conducted by professionals.

The effectiveness of debriefing has received only limited attention. In a recent study, Shalev, Rogel-Fuchs, and Peri (in press) have conducted Marshall debriefing sessions in six infantry units of the Israel Defense Forces (IDF) shortly after fire fights on the Lebanese border. Debriefing sessions were followed by a significant decrease in anxiety and a significant increase in self-efficacy. Unfortunately, the long-term effects of debriefing have not yet been studied in a systematic manner (Bloom, 1985).

Frontline Treatment of CSR Casualties

Casualties of CSR may be treated anywhere, from the combat zone itself through to the rear echelons. The closer the treatment to the front, the shorter is its duration, and the more effective it is considered to be. Only when there is no significant improvement is the soldier transferred to treatment installation further away from the battlefield.

Treatment of CSR usually involves a deliberate effort to reestablish preexisting psychological homeostasis by providing the soldier with temporary relief from stress and with biological and social support. Today, the prevailing military approach to the treatment of CSR casualties is frontline treatment. Developed by Salmon (1919) and later rephrased by Artiss (1963), frontline treatment is based on the principles of proximity, immediacy, and expectancy. These principles stipulated that afflicted soldiers should be treated in close proximity to the combat zone, as soon as possible after the onset of symptoms, and with the expectation of a quick return to combat. Most western armies observe the following guidelines:

1. Meet the casualty's physiological needs (e.g., food, sleep).
2. Provide temporary relief from source of stress (e.g., removal from fire).
3. Use human contact to reassure, clarify, and share emotions; humanize, and legitimize fears; allow expressions of grief, guilt, and shame, but challenge self-depreciation.
4. Convey to the patient expectation of full recovery and return to duty.
5. Promote social support that will allow reintegration of the casualty in his or her unit.
6. Treat the casualty as soon as possible.
7. Do not change the soldier's status as a member of the combat team until appropriate efforts to reverse the traumatic effects of the stress have been made and have been proven unsuccessful.

As a rule, the treatment should be given at the first station where temporary protection from direct stress can be effected. This may be on the field itself, in the battalion's first aid station, or in the field hospital. One of the aims of the treatment at this phase is preventing isolation, loneliness, and detachment.

When CSR symptoms erupt during active combat, attention should be paid to the casualties' potentially dangerous behavior stemming from disorientation, agitation, or a possible dissociative state. The afflicted soldier should be restrained and prevented from both unnecessarily exposing himself to fire and from losing contact with his unit. This is an important task of the medic.

The battalion medical aid station is the last treatment facility. The soldier is still within his unit and is able to enjoy the support of peers, and from which he can rapidly resume his duties. In several western armies (e.g., the IDF), CSR patients can remain in the battalion medical aid station for 24 to 48 hours. Such patients are transferred to treatment installations further away from the battlefield when there is no significant improvement in their condition within this brief time frame.

The field hospital is the first station in which the soldier is separated from his group. He loses contact with his comrades and commanders, in many cases is deprived of his personal belongings, and has his personal weapon taken away.

He has to cope within circumstances for which he was never trained, and is handled by professionals who must still gain his confidence. Moreover, evacuation from his unit officially marks the soldier as a "mental patient," with the associated stigma. The psychological impact of such an act is tremendous, and such changes may aggravate the CSR casualty's preexisting difficulties.

On the other hand, the field hospital is often the first place where professional help can be provided. The mental health unit in the field hospital has a double mission: (1) to enable psychological reintegration; and (2) to convey the message of healing and return to military duty. These are difficult tasks, and the professional team should be aware of them. The time allowed in the field hospital may vary from 48 hours to 7 days, according to the state of the combat and the availability of staff. Treatment may include both individual and group therapy. It has been postulated that maintaining military discipline is beneficial.

The base hospital in the rear echelon generally receives CSR casualties from three different sources: CSR casualties who did not improve in previous stations, casualties who were air-evacuated without previous intervention, and soldiers whose CSR was first manifested, or was aggravated, when they were away from the front. Since the base hospital should not attempt to function as a primary care facility, it has been argued that soldiers not yet treated should be sent back to frontline treatment facilities. However, the logistics of such transfer are difficult if not impossible, and there are no data supporting its efficacy. In fact, although frontline treatment is the preferred treatment for CSR in many armies, it is apparently rarely given to all the casualties. For example, in the Lebanon War only 7% of the Israeli CSR casualties received frontline care. Both logistic conditions and moral dilemmas on the part of the treatment professionals have presented obstacles.

The advantage of the base hospital is that it can provide skilled professional help and that there is more time to address the relevant issues. At such hospitals, highly skilled professionals may try to get the patients to recall events and express emotions related to these events (abreaction). They may employ a range of interventions: interpersonal and group therapy, behavioral psychotherapy, and pharmacotherapy. The long-term effect of each of these interventions with combat stress casualties has not yet been systematically studied.

Consistent clinical impressions of several armies support the effectiveness of frontline treatment. Yet, to the best of our knowledge, it has been empirically assessed only among Israeli soldiers in the Lebanon War (Solomon & Benbenishty, 1986). A study of all the identified Israeli CSR casualties in that war examined the effectiveness of the prevailing frontline doctoring, stressing the principles of proximity, immediacy, and expectancy. This quasiexperimental study examined two treatment outcomes: return to the military unit and the presence of PTSD. All three treatment principles were associated with a higher rate of return to the military unit. The beneficial effect of frontline treatment was also evidenced by lower rates of PTSD. These encouraging results were observed at the 1-year follow-up.

HELP FOR COMBAT VETERANS WITH
POSTTRAUMATIC STRESS DISORDER

The Clinical Picture

Posttraumatic stress disorder is a complex disorder that includes a variety of biopsychosocial impairments. To be diagnosed with PTSD, a person must evince a set of intrusive, avoidance, and hyperarousal symptoms (APA, 1987, 1994). However, clinical studies show both variations within the syndrome and a large variety of symptoms above and beyond those included in the formal PTSD diagnosis. Some casualties compulsively reexperience the traumatic event in nightmares or in waking scenes and recollections. Casualties in extreme, dissociative states act as if they are reexperiencing the traumatic event concretely in the present. Other expressions of PTSD include emotional numbing, feelings of alienation, inhibited relations with others, and lack of interest in previously enjoyed activities. Some people endeavor to avoid stimuli related to the traumatic event, whereas others are strongly drawn to such stimuli. In addition, PTSD can be accompanied by anxiety and depression, obsessive–compulsive symptoms, anger, or hostility (Helzer, Robins, & Hesselbock, 1987; Solomon, 1993).

Biological Models of PTSD

Research into the psychobiology of PTSD has followed two paths. The first has been a search for the biological mechanisms common to PTSD and other mental disorders. The second has been a quest for specific biological attributes of PTSD. Both trends have implications for treatment (for review see McFarlane, 1989; Friedman, 1988; Davidson, 1992; also see Chapter 4, this volume).

Biological Components of PTSD and Other Mental Disorders

Clinical findings suggest a comorbidity of PTSD and several other disorders. Panic disorder was diagnosed in 13% to 19% of PTSD patients (Bleich, Siegel, Garb, & Lerer, 1986; McFarlane, 1992). Symptoms of phasic arousal in PTSD (e.g., flashbacks, intrusive recollections) may resemble panic attacks. Anxiety, dissociation, and flashbacks can be elicited in PTSD patients by the same experimental procedures that elicit panic attacks in panic disorder patients (e.g., yohimbine or lactate infusion) (Morgan et al., 1990).

Theoretical formulations based on these findings assign a role to the locus ceruleus–norepinephrine (LC-NE) "alarm" system in PTSD and predict a positive effect of antipanic medication and of clonidine in this disorder. Both types of medication have been studied in clinical trials.

Major depression is frequently diagnosed in PTSD patients. Depressive symptoms resemble PTSD symptoms of "diminished interest," "restricted range of affect," and a "sense of a foreshortened future" (APA, 1987, 1994), and PTSD patients have been found to respond positively to antidepressants and MAO inhibitors such as amitriptyline, imipramine, and desipramine.

Finally, there are reports of comorbidity between PTSD and obsessive–compulsive disorder (OCD) (Helzer et al., 1987; Escobar et al., 1983; Davidson, Roth, & Newman, 1991). Also PTSD symptoms such as obsessive "rumination" and obsessions have been interpreted as suggesting a common neurobiological mechanism with OCD. Controlled studies of drugs that are effective in OCD (the selective serotonin reuptake inhibitors [SSRIs]) are reviewed below (see also Chapter 4, this volume).

Biological Attributes Specific to PTSD

Specific biological models of PTSD include: (1) dysregulation of opioid neuromodulation; (2) imprinting and consolidation of memories (Pitman, 1989; Shalev, Rogel-Fuchs, & Pitman, 1992); and (3) hypothalamic–pituitary–adrenal (HPA) axis dysregulation (Yehuda, Giller, Southwick, Lowy, & Mason, 1991; Mason, Giller, Kosten, & Yehuda, 1990).

The opioid model suggests that spontaneous repetition of distressful memories, self-inflicted injuries, repeated self-exposure and sensation seeking in traumatized patients, may result from "addiction to trauma," mediated by a dysfunctional brain opioid system. This hypothesis is partially supported by a study showing that naloxone, an opiate antagonist, could reverse stress-induced analgesia in PTSD veterans during exposure to combat scenes (Pitman, van der Kolk, Orr, & Greenberg, 1990).

The memory-imprinting model assumes that the "etching" of traumatic scenes onto the person's neuronal network plays a major role in the etiology of PTSD. Stress hormones, present during the traumatic event, may mediate the consolidation of traumatic memories into brain structures such as the amygdala and the hippocampus (Pitman, 1989). A recent development of this model further suggests, by analogy with fear-conditioning experiments in animals, that traumatic memories are normally stored "forever" at a subcortical level (Shalev, Rogel-Fuchs, et al., 1992) and that problems in their extinction over time, observed in PTSD, result from decreased inhibitory control by cortical structures.

A variant of the memory-imprinting theme is the kindling model of PTSD (van der Kolk, Greenberg, Boyd, & Krystal, 1985; Krystal, 1990), which suggests that the repeated processing of distressful recollections in the brain lowers the threshold for neuronal transmission, thereby "biasing" the brain toward fear and arousal. Importantly, this model extends the time interval during which "traumatic imprinting" takes place into the past exposure period. It suggests that intense arousal experienced during some critical period following the trauma is pathogenic. Interventions aimed at reducing hyperarousal among recent trauma survivors (e.g., by early use of tranquilizers, relaxation, withdrawal from sources of stress, interpersonal interventions) are, accordingly, conceived as having the potential to prevent PTSD development. The model also predicts an association between secondary stressors (that follow the impact phase of traumatic events) and long-term psychopathology.

Finally, studies of the HPA stress axis in PTSD have revealed a hypersensitive feedback loop (e.g., increased dexamethasone suppression), elevated urinary catecholamine, and decreased epinephrine/cortisol ratios (Charney et al., 1993; Yehuda, Giller, & Mason, 1993). Findings of hyperresponsiveness of the HPA stress axis in PTSD are diametrically opposed to findings of blunted response of the HPA axis in depression.

Pharmacotherapy

The impact of several classes of medicine have been examined. Studies of antidepressants suggest that these drugs may have a significant effect on core symptoms of PTSD and on associated depression, insomnia, and anxiety. The magnitude of the response, however, is far from that obtained in major depression or panic disorder in which good remission is the rule. Moreover, two placebo-controlled double-blind studies (Shestazki, Greenberg, & Lerer, 1988; Riest, Kauffman, & Haier, 1976) and an uncontrolled trial (Lerer et al., 1987) failed to show that antidepressants have a significant effect on core PTSD symptoms. Similarly, a recent placebo-controlled study of amitriptyline on Vietnam veterans (Davidson et al., 1993) revealed only a trend toward improvement in anxiety and depression. The patients' age, the intensity of their exposure to trauma, and the presence of concurrent depression and concurrent anxiety were inversely correlated to the drug effect.

Comparisons of antidepressants (e.g., Bleich et al., 1986; Kosten, Frank, Dan, McDougle, & Giller, 1991) failed to find differences in their therapeutic effect. Recent trials of the SSRI fluoxetine (van der Kolk et al., 1995; Nagy, Southwick, & Charney, 1993; Shay, 1991) suggest that this third generation antidepressant may specifically affect core PTSD symptoms. Two uncontrolled studies suggest that the effect of antidepressants on PTSD may be enhanced, as in resistant depression, by lithium (Irwin, Van-Putten, Guze, & Marder, 1989) and clonidine (Kinzie & Leung, 1989). Several reviewers of this field (Solomon, Gerrity, & Muff, 1992; Friedman, 1988, Davidson et al., 1993) suggest that effective treatment of PTSD takes a long period of time, and that this might explain the negative results of some of these studies (i.e., time allocated for taking a medication may have been insufficient to achieve a therapeutic effect).

Studies of anxiolytic benzodiazepines (alprazolam, clonazepam) have yielded mixed findings. One controlled study (Braun, Greenberg, Dasberg, & Lerer, 1990) failed to show a specific effect of alprazolam on core PTSD symptoms, despite a modest effect on anxiety. An uncontrolled study of clonazepam (Loewenstein, Hornstein, & Farber, 1988) describes improved sleep and a reduction in nightmares, flashbacks, and panic attacks. Finally Wells et al. (1991) reported beneficial effects of the atypical sedative buspirone. However, severe withdrawal symptoms were described in patients taking alprazolam (Risse et al., 1990).

Mood stabilizers such as lithium, valproate, and carbamazepine have been studied in open trials. The results suggest that these drugs may have beneficial effects on irritability, impulse control, hyperactivity, and some core PTSD symptoms. By virtue of their antikindling effect (i.e., their ability to prevent the facilitation of synaptic transmission), carbamazepine and valproate have been thought to have particular promise in treating PTSD, since synaptic facilitation may play a crucial role in this disorder. This claim has not been confirmed empirically, however, and it is also possible that chronic PTSD patients would not benefit from an antikindling effect years after the event.

Pharmacological studies of PTSD suffer from numerous shortcomings (Solomon, Gerrity, et al., 1992). Very few of the studies are controlled, and their results are inconsistent. Moreover, the effect of early pharmacological treatment has not been studied, even though theoretical considerations, outlined above, suggest that early treatment may help prevent PTSD. Surprisingly, no study has evaluated the effect of drugs beyond several weeks of treatment, despite the fact that many PTSD patients are on medication for years. Finally, variations in daily doses, in the duration of treatment, and the outcome criteria used in these studies undermine their ability to provide clinical guidelines.

Overall, one may conclude that the effect of pharmacological agents on PTSD is at best palliative. Pharmacotherapy alone is rarely sufficient for complete remission of PTSD (Friedman, 1988). Moreover, nonspecific effects have been documented more often than specific effects. On the other hand, many PTSD patients find their symptoms so intolerable that they use other CNS-active agents, engage in life-threatening behavior, and in some cases even attempt suicide. The risks and limited effects of pharmacotherapy of PTSD should, therefore, be weighed against the dangers of drug abuse, uncontrolled violence, and suicide. Symptom relief provided by medication may also facilitate the patient's participation in individual, behavioral, or group psychotherapy (Friedman, 1988; see also Chapter 4, this volume).

Psychological Dimensions of PTSD

The Behavioral Model of PTSD

A current view of PTSD identifies classical conditioning as the mechanism linking the symptoms of PTSD to the precipitating trauma (e.g., Kolb & Multipassi, 1982). According to this model, cues associated with the traumatic event become conditioned stimuli (CS) for the trauma and evoke conditioned emotional responses (CR) in the form of PTSD symptoms. Consistent with this view are findings of elevated physiological arousal produced by trauma-related cues in individuals with PTSD (Pitman et al., 1987). Contrary to classical conditioning, however, the learned avoidance in PTSD does not diminish with time, despite the obvious lack of reinforcement (i.e., no further exposure to combat). A dual-conditioning model has, therefore, been found appropriate for PTSD (Keane et al., 1985). This model suggests that the initial classical conditioning (resulting in avoidance of cues actually present during the trauma) is followed by operant conditioning, in which avoidance of a variety of internal and external cues that are loosely associated with the trauma is negatively reinforced by reduction in distress and tension. Such avoidance behavior prevents the extinction of the conditioned response over time and expands the avoidant behavior to secondary and tertiary cues (alias "inappropriate generalization") (Keane et al., 1985). The resulting constriction in activities is illustrated by the PTSD criteria (APA, 1987, 1994).

Behavioral Therapy

Interventions based on behavioral theory are designed to undo CR to CS that have been paired with the trauma. Behavior therapy proceeds either by gradual (desensitization) or by massed exposure to the CS.

Desensitization consists of reexposure, step by step, to cues reminiscent of the CS, until unlearning occurs. Desensitization protocols often include training in skills (e.g., relaxation, thought stopping) that enable the patient to control his response (CR). Flooding consists of prolonged exposure to the CS, designed to exhaust the response (usually arousal) so that the patient may remain in contact with the CS without producing a CR. The reexposure may be in vivo (i.e., to real objects or situations) or in vitro (to internal imagery or thoughts of the aversive situation). All these methods have been used in the treatment of PTSD.

Four controlled studies (Keane, Fairbank, Caddel, & Zimmering, 1989; Boudewyns & Hyer, 1990; Cooper & Clum, 1989; Foa, Rothbaum, Riggs, & Murdock, 1991) indicate that flooding has a positive effect in PTSD symptoms. Keane et al. (1989) found a significant effect of flooding on reexperiencing, anxiety, and depression. Boudewyns and Hyer (1990) found that flooding positively affected adjustment in Vietnam veterans. Cooper and Clum (1989) describe positive interaction between flooding and interpersonal treatment. Finally, Foa et al. (1991) showed that prolonged exposure was effective in reducing PTSD symptoms in rape victims. On the other hand, in an uncontrolled study by Pitman et al. (1991), flooding was associated with exacerbation of depression, alcohol consumption, panic anxiety, and mobilization of negative appraisal. None of the above-mentioned studies claims that flooding has a curative effect on PTSD, only a palliative effect on PTSD symptoms. It has also been suggested that flooding is inappropriate if prior stress-management skills have not been targeted (Kilpatrick & Best, 1985).

In vitro desensitization has been studied in two controlled (Peniston, 1986; Brom, Kleber, & Defares, 1989) and several uncontrolled studies (Shalev, Orr, & Pitman, 1992; Vaughn & Tarrier, 1992; Mueser, Yarnold, & Foy, 1991). In Peniston's study (1986), treatment was associated with reduction in nightmares, flashbacks, muscle tension, and readmission rates. Brom et al. (1989), who compared desensitization, brief dynamic therapy, hypnosis, and waiting list controls, found that all treatment modes were associated with measurable improvement, and that desensitization and hypnotherapy affected intrusive symptoms rather than avoidance symptomatology. Shalev, Orr, et al. (1992), who measured the effect of desensitization on physiological responses, found it to be specifically related to those aspects of the subjects' trauma that were desensitized. Similar results have been reported by Fairbank and Keane (1982), where positive results of flooding did not extend to anxiety associated with other traumatic experiences. These findings suggest that desensitization to one event (e.g., one combat action) may not necessarily apply to all the memories engendered by complex events such as wars.

A comprehensive study of in vivo exposure (Solomon, Waysman, et al., 1992) involved a complex rehabilitation and training program conducted by the IDF on PTSD veterans of the Israel–Lebanon War (1982). It should be noted that these veterans suffered from chronic PTSD. The program included exposure to military cues (e.g., rifle range, artillery fire) within a military milieu, along with cognitive, behavioral, and supportive interventions. Participants of the program fared worse than control subjects; their distress, social dysfunction, and PTSD symptoms were aggravated by the program. The reasons for the negative results from this project have been discussed in detail elsewhere (Bleich, Shalev, Shoham, Solomon, & Kotler, 1992; Cooper, 1992; Solomon, Gerrity, et al., 1992). Regarding behavioral therapy, it has been suggested that the program did not present sufficient exposure to military stressors (e.g., firing a rifle) to insure a positive remedial response (Solomon, Gerrity, et al., 1992).

Schufield, Wong, and Zeeroachah (1992) report similar reactivation of traumatic memories in Vietnam veterans with PTSD after "helicopter ride therapy." The exposure to military helicopters was associated with intrusive painful memories, "in flight reactions," but it allegedly improved group cohesion and desensitized the participants to riding in a helicopter. A case report (Hytten & Herlofsen, 1989) indicated that reexposure in vivo apparently succeeded in reducing avoidance and demoralization.

All in all, studies of behavioral treatment of PTSD report significant but partial improvement. Like other forms of therapy, behavior therapy alleviates symptoms rather than cures the disorder. One may conclude, therefore, that undoing "conditioned responses" may not suffice in PTSD, where the pathophysiology certainly exceeds that in learned conditioning, and moreover, that direct exposure and incautious flooding may result in reactivation and aggravation of PTSD symptoms and behavior.

Psychodynamic Formulation of PTSD

The psychodynamic formulations of "traumatic neurosis" are complex and multifaceted. One thrust is that the neurosis involves damage to a component of the mental apparatus. The other thrust is that it involves incomplete processing of traumatic experiences, similar to that which occurs in pathological grief.

Damage to the Mental Apparatus

The oldest psychodynamic formulation (Freud, 1920/1957) suggested that war trauma creates a breach in a hypothetical "stimulus barrier" that normally protects the mental apparatus from excessive "excitation." As a result of this structural impairment, the mental apparatus abruptly modifies its rules of action, and instead of being dominated by homeostasis-based dynamics, exemplified by the "pleasure principle," adopts a hypothetical "repetition compulsion"—a more "primitive" and more "biological" set of functional rules. Individuals with traumatic neuroses, therefore, are captive to endless repetition, which can take the form of repeated nightmares, or "repetition compulsion."

Clearly the most powerful insight in Freud's formulation is that the repetitive phenomenon in the traumatic neurosis does not necessarily represent a step toward self-healing, but is rather a traumatic surrender of the psychic apparatus as a result of an injury. Freud consequently recognized that single-modality treatment strategies, including the gold standard of psychoanalysis, were insufficient for traumatic neurosis (Freud, 1919/1957). Later formulations (e.g., "shrinking of the ego," "collapse of structures") (Benyaker, Kutz, Dasberg, & Stern, 1989) also adopted the metaphor of damage to the mental apparatus and emphasized the impact of psychic trauma on the mental structure. Transposing Freud's metaphor of the "stimulus barrier" into neurophysiological language, Kolb (1987) hypothesized that "changes occur in posttraumatic stress disorder as the consequence of excessive and prolonged sensitizing stimulation leading to depression of habituation learning" (p. 989).

Recent structural formulations adapt Freud's original stance. At the heart of these formulations is the appraisal that mental trauma does not simply add content to all conflicts, but alters the rules of mental functioning (e.g., Laufer, 1988; Lifton, 1988). The practical implications of these formulations is the recognition that the PTSD patients are fundamentally impaired, and consequently the PTSD therapy must include ego-support and address the vulnerability of the patients' character structure.

A variation of the theme of "psychic destruction" has been offered by Krystal's description of "loss of affective modulation" in survivors of massive trauma. Krystal (1978) argued that psychological surrender, typical to situations of prolonged subjugation to extreme adversity, leads to a permanent impairment of the survivor's affective life (e.g., inability to make use of subtle affective cues; loss of affective modulation). This impairment resembles alexithymia, a mental condition in which the person is unable to recognize and utilize internal states of affect. Research has confirmed the presence of alexithymic traits in war veterans with PTSD (Hyer et al., 1990).

Unresolved Mental Processes

The second psychodynamic model is derived from the paradigm of loss, mourning, and "grief work," and relates to the similarities between symptoms of intrusion and avoidance observed in posttraumatic individuals and those Freud (1917/1957) and Lindermann (1944) described in the early phases of grief. Horowitz (1974) hypothesized that the "stress response syndrome"—an early equivalent of PTSD—results from incomplete mental processing of the traumatic event. Horowitz' subdivision of posttraumatic symptoms into intrusion and avoidance, which follows Lindermann's description, is clearly reflected in the first two DSM-III PTSD diagnostic criteria of reexperiencing and avoidance (APA, 1987, 1994). From a practical point of view, the concept implies that PTSD might abate if the sufferer is allowed to "work through" his or her experiences. This is the main working through thrust of psychodynamic therapy for PTSD. However, the intensity of arousal and panic associated with the reactivation of traumatic memories, the advent of dissociative reactions during exploration of the trauma, and the extent of psychic avoidance observed in most PTSD patients make the explorative approach impractical in many cases.

Psychodynamic Psychotherapy

Psychodynamic psychotherapy specifically addresses the meaning of both the traumatic event and of the trauma-related symptoms and behavior. The analytic therapist hopes that insight into the conscious and unconscious meaning of symptoms will help the survivors master their inner experiences and repair the torn fabric of their lives (Lindy, 1993). Lindy (1993) describes three stages of therapy and their corresponding tasks. The first is an opening phase aimed at gaining the patient's permission to access inner traumatic experiences, in which establishing a therapeutic alliance is the main task. The second is the middle phase, the purpose of which is to explore and work through the special configuration of the traumatic event. Interpretation of transference is an important source of insight at this stage. The third and final phase tries to create a continuity of meaning and to promote self-integration.

Therapists have consistently emphasized both the importance and the difficulties in establishing a therapeutic alliance (Marmar, Foy, Kagan, & Pynoos, 1993; Haley, 1974) with PTSD patients. Psychodynamic treatment is often quite prolonged.

Most of the literature of psychodynamic therapy of PTSD consists of case reports, and many emphasize theoretical and technical aspects of the treatment. Outcome evaluation studies are scarce. The controlled study of Brom et al. (1989) mentioned above, which compared brief dynamic psychotherapy to hypnotherapy, desensitization, and waiting-list control, found that all active treatment groups improved significantly. In another treatment project Lindy (1988), who studied the outcomes of 1-year-long individual psychoanalytic psychotherapy with 21 PTSD Vietnam veterans, found a reduction in most of the formal features of PTSD, including intrusive phenomena and depression, but not avoidance.

Cognitive Formulation of PTSD

The cognitive model (e.g., Janoff-Bulman, 1985; McCann & Pearlman, 1992), like the psychodynamic, holds that the PTSD casualty has suffered significant "mental damage." In this model, however, the damage consists of the loss of the person's previous beliefs and assumptions about life. This view is that the trauma undermined the casualties' previous world view, including beliefs about safety, trust, self-esteem, intimacy, power, and independence. The traumatic experience exposes their expectations, behavior, and experience as inaccurate, insufficient, or inadequate (McCann & Pearlman, 1992). As a result, feelings of vulnerability and feelings of mistrust and weakness are aroused and generalized, and the PTSD victim is left in a state of disarray, isolation, and pessimism. Cognitive therapists propose diagnosing and redressing specific dysfunctional schemata (i.e., set of beliefs) and helping the survivor generate more functional alternatives.

Cognitive Therapy

Cognitive therapy (e.g., Janoff-Bulman, 1985; McCann & Pearlman, 1992) attempts to challenge the overpowering control that rigid cognitive schemata have on the traumatized individual's life. Two controlled studies, both of victims of sexual assault, found that cognitive therapy was followed by significant improvement. Foa and Kozak (1985, 1986) suggested that perception of controllability and predictability, and subsequent attribution of threat, are central to the development of PTSD. A treatment condition combining behavioral and cognitive techniques, the stress inoculation treatment (SIT) was derived from these ideas (Foa et al., 1991) and was compared with prolonged exposure (PE), counseling, and waiting-list control. Stress innoculation treatment produced significant reduction of PTSD symptoms immediately after treatment. However, PE had greater efficacy in reducing PTSD symptoms at a 3-month follow-up. Resick and Shnicke (1992), who compared cognitive processing therapy with waiting-list control, found alleviation of depression in subjects in the treatment group, which was maintained for 6 months.

SECONDARY TRAUMATIZATION

Long-term effects of combat-induced psychopathology are not limited to the combatants (Maloney, 1988; Rosenheck & Nathan, 1985). The term "secondary traumatization" (Figley, 1983) has been used to indicate that others who come into close contact with a trauma victim may experience considerable emotional upset and may, over time, themselves become indirect victims of the trauma.

Both CSR and PTSD were found to be associated with increased psychiatric symptoms in the veterans' wives (Solomon, Waysman, et al., 1992). Veterans' PTSD, particularly, was found to contribute to impaired social relations among their wives in a broad range of contexts, from inner feelings of loneliness, through impaired marital and family relations, and extending to the wider social networks (Solomon, Waysman, et al., 1992).

Whereas the troubled veteran is the focus of concern for most treatment agencies, his wife, partner, or children, who suffer(s) considerable emotional and social distress, is/are often ignored. If the suffering of family members is ignored, however, the family is unlikely to respond in ways that will foster the recovery of the combat veteran. On the contrary, the family will in all likelihood reinforce or even exacerbate the veteran's own distress. Therefore, any treatment that focuses exclusively on the individual veteran and ignores his interpersonal context would have significantly reduced his chances of success. It seems more appropriate to consider family-systems treatment orientation. This would serve two purposes: (1) prevention of secondary traumatization among wives and children; and (2) improved recovery rates among the veterans themselves.

CONCLUSION

Despite the wide acceptance of the multifactorial etiology of PTSD (e.g., Figley, 1987; Green, Wilson, & Lindy, 1985), most of the literature on clinical intervention has been restricted to rather simple approaches. At the same time, many recent reports tend to express explicit discontent with treatment results (e.g., Lindy, 1988; Boudewyns & Hyer, 1990; Braun et al., 1990; Pitman et al., 1991), often reporting a high incidence of negative therapeutic outcome (Braun et al., 1990; Pitman et al., 1991; Solomon, Shalev, et al., 1992).

Recently, several clinicians have called for combined or eclectic approaches to treatment (e.g., McFarlane, 1989; Solomon, Gerrity, et al., 1992). In reality pharmacological treatment often facilitates psychotherapy. The Coach Project implemented by the IDF (Solomon, Shalev, et al., 1992), among other ambitious projects, combined behavioral, cognitive, milieu, and supportive strategies. Unfortunately, even such projects did not yield encouraging results.

In summary, PTSD is a complex disorder highly resistant to cure by any of the treatment modalities available to date. The development of new modes of intervention is called for. So is further controlled study of the efficacy of existent treatment modes. Mental health professionals in the area of traumatology still face the challenge of finding means of better alleviating the sufferings of traumatized individuals and their families, who share in the casualties' pain.

REFERENCES

American Psychiatric Association. (1987). *Diagnostic and statistical manual of mental disorders* (3rd ed.-rev). Washington, DC: American Psychiatric Press.

American Psychiatric Association. (1994). *Diagnostic and statistical manual of mental disorders* (4th ed.). Washington, DC: Author.

Artiss, K. L. (1963). Human behavior under stress: From combat to social psychiatry. *Military Magazine, 128,* 1011–1015.

Benyakar, M., Kutz, I., Dasberg, H., & Stern, M. J. (1989). The collapse of structure: A structural approach to trauma. *Journal of Traumatic Stress, 2,* 431–450.

Bergman, L. H., & Queen, T. (1986). *Critical incident stress: Part 1. Fire command.* (pp. 52–56).

Birenbaum, F., Copolon, J., & Sharff, I. (1976). Crisis intervention after a natural disaster. In R. H. Moos (Ed.), *Human adaptation: Coping with life crises* (pp. 394–404). Lexington: Health and Company.

Bleich, A., Shalev, A., Shoham, S., Solomon, Z., & Kotler, M. (1992). PTSD: Theoretical and practical considerations as reflected through Koach—An innovative treatment project. *Journal of Traumatic Stress, 5*(2), 265–271.

Bleich, A., Siegel, B., Garb, R., & Lerer, B. (1986). Post-traumatic stress disorder following combat exposure: Clinical features and psychopharmacological treatment. *British Journal of Psychiatry, 149,* 354–369.

Bloom, B. L. (1985). *Stressful life events, theory, and research: Implications for primary prevention.* Rockville, MD: NIMH/ADAMHA.

Boudewyns, P. A., & Heyr, L. (1990). Physiological response to combat memories and preliminary treatment outcomes in Vietnam, veterans PTSD patients treated with direct therapeutic exposure. *Behavior Therapy, 21,* 63–87.

Bourne, P. G. (1969). Military psychiatry and the Viet Nam War in perspective. In P. G. Bourne (Ed.), *The psychology and physiology of stress* (pp. 219–236). New York: Academic Press.

Braun, P., Greenberg, D., Dasberg, H., & Lerer, B. (1990). Core symptoms of posttraumatic stress disorder unimproved by alprazolam treatment. *Journal of Clinical Psychiatry, 51,* 236–238.

Brom, D., Kleber, R. J., & Defares, P. B. (1989). Brief psychotherapy for posttraumatic stress disorders. *Journal of Consulting and Clinical Psychology, 57,* 607–612.

Charney, D. S., Dutch, A. Y., Krystal, J. H., Soutwick, S. M., & Davis, M. (1993). Psychobiologic mechanisms of posttraumatic stress disorder. *Archives of General Psychiatry, 50,* 294–306.

Cohen, R. C. (1976). Post disaster mobilization of a crisis intervention team: The Managua experience. In H. G. Parad, H. L. P. Resnick, & L. P. Parad (Eds.), *Emergency and disaster management: A mental health handbook.* Baltimore: Charles Press.

Cohen, R. E., & Ahearn, F. L. (1980). *Handbook of mental health care for disaster victims.* Baltimore: Johns Hopkins University Press.

Cooper, N. A., & Clum, G. A. (1989). Imaginal flooding as a supplementary treatment group for PTSD in combat veterans: A controlled study. *Behavior Therapy, 20,* 381–391.

Cooper, S. (1992). Anthropological impressions of Koach: Participant observations. *Journal of Traumatic Stress, 5*(2), 247–264.

Davidson, J. (1992). Drug therapy of post-traumatic stress disorder. *British Journal of Psychiatry, 160,* 309–314.

Davidson, J., Kudler, H. S., Saunders, W. B., Erickson, L., Smith, R. D., Stein, R. M., Lipper, S., Hammett, E. B., Mahorney, S. L., & Cavenar, J.O.J. (1993). Predicting response to amitriptyline in posttraumatic stress disorder. *American Journal of Psychiatry, 150,* 1024–1029.

Davidson, J., Roth, S., & Newman, E. (1991). Fluoxetine in the post-traumatic stress disorder. *Journal of Traumatic Stress, 4,* 419–425.

Dunning, C. (1990). Mental health sequelae in disaster workers: Prevention and intervention. *International Journal of Mental Health, 19,* 91–103.

Dunning, C., & Silva, M. (1980). Disaster-induced trauma in rescue workers. *Victimology, 5,* 287–297.

Escobar, J. I., Randolph, E. T., Puente, G., Spiwak, F., Asamen, J. K., Hill, M., & Hough, R. L. (1983). PTSD in Hispanic Vietnam veterans—Clinical phenomenology and sociocultural characteristics. *Journal of Nervous and Mental Diseases, 171,* 586–569.

Fairbank, J. A., & Keane, T. M. (1982). Flooding for combat-related stress disorder: Assessment of anxiety reduction across traumatic memories. *Behavior Therapy, 13,* 499–510.

Figley, C. R. (1983). Catastrophes: An overview of family reactions. In C. R. Figley & H. I. McCubbin (Eds.), *Stress and the family, Vol. II: Coping with catastrophe* (pp. 3–20). New York: Brunner/Mazel.

Figley, C. R. (1987). Toward a field of traumatic stress. *Journal of Traumatic Stress, 1,* 3–16.

Foa, E. B., & Kozak, M. L. (1985). Treatment of anxiety disorders: Implications for psycho-
    pathology. In A. H. Turna & J. Maser (Eds.), *Anxiety and the anxiety disorders* (pp. 131–170).
    Hillsdale, NJ: Lawrence Erlbaum Associates.
Foa, E. B., & Kozak, M. L. (1986). Emotional processing of fear: Exposure to corrective
    information. *Psychological Bulletin, 99*, 20–30.
Foa, E. B., Rothbaum, B. O., Riggs, D. S., & Murdock, T. B. (1991). Treatment of posttrauma-
    tic stress disorder in rape victims: A comparison between cognitive–behavioral proce-
    dures and counseling. *Journal of Consulting and Clinical Psychology, 59*, 715–723.
Freud, S. (1957). *Mourning and melancholia. Standard edition, Vol. CIV.* London: Hogarth Press.
    Original work published 1917.
Freud, S. (1957). *Lines of advance in psychoanalytic therapy. Standard edition, Vol. 17.* London:
    Hogarth Press. Original work published 1919.
Freud, S. (1957). *Beyond the pleasure principle. Standard edition, Vol. XVIII.* London: Hogarth
    Press. Original work published 1920.
Friedman, M. J. (1988). Toward rational pharmacotherapy for posttraumatic stress disorder:
    An interim report. *American Journal of Psychiatry, 145*, 218–285.
Green, B. L., Wilson, J. P., & Lindy, J. D. (1985). Conceptualizing posttraumatic stress disor-
    der: A psychological framework. In C. R. Figley (Ed.), *Trauma and its wake, the study and
    treatment of post-traumatic stress disorder* (pp. 53–69). New York: Brunner/Mazel.
Griffin, C. A. (1987). Community disasters and post traumatic stress disorder: A debriefing
    model for response. In T. Williams (Ed.), *Post traumatic stress disorders: A handbook for
    clinicians* (pp. 293–298). Cincinnati: Disabled American Veterans Publication.
Grinker, R. R., & Spiegel, J. P. (1945). *Men under stress.* Philadelphia: Blakiston.
Haley, S. (1974). When the patient reports atrocities. *Archives of General Psychiatry, 57*, 607–
    612.
Helzer, J. E., Robins, L. N., & Hesselbrock, M. (1979). Depression in Vietnam veterans and
    civilian controls. *American Journal of Psychiatry, 136*, 412–420.
Helzer, J. E., Robins, L. N., & McEvoy, L. (1987). Post-traumatic stress disorder in the general
    population: Findings of the Epidemiologic Catchment Area survey. *New England Journal
    of Medicine, 137*:1630–1634.
Horowitz, M. J. (1974). Stress response syndromes: Character style and dynamic psycho-
    therapy. *Archives of General Psychiatry, 31*, 768–781.
Hyer, L., Woods, M., Summers, M. N., Boudewyns, P., & Harrison, W. R. (1990). Alexithymia
    among Vietnam veterans with posttraumatic stress disorder. *Journal of Clinical Psychiatry,
    51*, 243–247.
Hytten, K., & Herlofsen, P. (1989). Accident stimulation as a new therapy technique for post-
    traumatic stress disorder: A case study. *Acta Psychiatrica Scandinavica, 80*, 79–83.
Ingraham, L., & Manning, F. (1986). American military psychiatry. In R. A. Gabriel (Ed.),
    Military psychiatry (pp. 25–66). New York: Greenwood Press.
Irwin, M., Van-Putten, T., Guze, B., & Marder, S. R. (1989). Pharmacological treatment of
    veterans with posttraumatic stress disorder and concomitant affective disorder. *Annals of
    Clinical Psychiatry, 1*, 127–130.
Janoff-Bulman, R. (1985). The aftermath of victimization: Rebuilding shattered assumptions.
    In C. R. Figley (Ed.), *Traum and its wake, the study and treatment of post-traumatic stress disorder*
    (pp. 15–36). New York: Brunner/Mazel.
Jones, D. R. (1985). Secondary disaster victims: The emotional impact of recovering and
    identifying human remains. *American Journal of Psychiatry, 142*, 303–307.
Keane, T. M., Fairbank, J. A., Caddel, J. M., & Zimmering, R. T. (1989). Impulsive (flooding)
    therapy reduces symptoms of PTSD in Vietnam combat veterans. *Behavior Therapy, 20*,
    245–260.

Keane, T. M., Fairbank, J. A., Caddel, M. T., Zimmering, R. T., & Bender, M. E. (1985). A behavioral approach to assessing and treating post-traumatic stress disorders in Vietnam veterans. In C. R. Figley (Ed.), *Trauma and its wake, the study and treatment of post-traumatic stress disorder* (pp. 257–294). New York: Brunner/Mazel.

Kinzie, J., & Leung, P. (1989). Clodine in Cambodian patients with posttraumatic stress disorder. *Journal of Nervous and Mental Diseases, 177*, 546–550.

Kolb, L. C. (1987). A neuropsychological hypothesis explaining the post-traumatic stress disorder. *American Journal of Psychiatry, 144*, 989–999.

Kolb, L. C., & Multipassi, L. R. (1982). The conditioned emotional response: A subclass of the chronic and delayed post traumatic stress disorder. *Psychiatric Annals, 12*, 979–987.

Kormos, H. R. (1978). The nature of combat stress. In C. R. Figley (Ed.), *Stress disorders among Vietnam veterans*. New York: Brunner/Mazel.

Kosten, T. R., Frank, J. B., Dan, E., McDougle, C. J., & Giller, E. L. (1991). Pharmacotherapy for posttraumatic stress disorder using phenelzine or imipramine. *Journal of Nervous and Mental Diseases, 179*, 366–370.

Krystal, H. (1978). Trauma and affect. *Psychoanalytic Study of the Child, 33*, 81–116.

Krystal, J. H. (1990). Animal models for posttraumatic stress disorder. In E. L. Giller (Ed.), *Biological assessment and treatment of posttraumatic stress disorder*. Washington, DC: American Psychiatric Press.

Kulka, R. A., Schlenger, W. E., Fairbank, J. A., Hough, R. L., Jordan, B. K., Marmar, C. R., & Weiss, D. A. (1989). *Trauma and the Vietnam War generation (Psychosocial series #18)*. New York: Brunner/Mazel.

Laufer, R. S. (1988). The serial self: War trauma, identity and adult development. In J. P. Wilson, Z. Harel, & B. Kahana (Eds.), *Human adaptation to extreme stress from the holocaust to Vietnam* (pp. 33–53). New York: Plenum Press.

Lerer, B., Bleich, A., Kotler, M., Garb, R., Hertzberg, M., & Levin, B. (1987). Posttraumatic stress disorder in Israeli combat veterans: Effect of phenelzine treatment. *Archives of General Psychiatry, 44*, 976–981.

Lifton, R. J. (1988). Understanding the traumatized self: Imagery symbolization and transformation. In J. P. Wilson, Z. Harel, & B. Kahana (Eds.), *Human adaptation to extreme stress from the holocaust to Vietnam* (pp. 7–32). New York: Plenum Press.

Lindermann, E. (1944). Symptomatology and management of acute grief. *American Journal of Psychiatry, 101*, 141–148.

Lindy, J. D. (1988). *Vietnam—A casebook*. New York: Brunner/Mazel.

Lindy, J. D. (1993). Focal psychoanalytic psychotherapy of posttraumatic stress disorder. In J. P. Wilson & B. Raphael (Eds.), *International handbook of traumatic stress syndromes* (pp. 803–809). New York: Plenum Press.

Lowenstein, R. J., Hornstein, N., & Farber, B. (1988). Open trial of clonazepam in the treatment of posttraumatic stress disorder. *Dissociation, 1*, 3–12.

Maloney, L. J. (1988). Posttraumatic stresses of women partners of Vietnam veterans. *Smith College Studies in Social Work, 58*, 112–143.

Marmar, C. R., Foy, D., Kagan, B., & Pynoos, R. S. (1993). An integrated approach for treatment of post traumatic stress disorder. In J. M. Oldham, M. B. Riba, & A. Tasman (Eds.), *American Psychiatric Press review of psychiatry* (Vol. 12, pp. 230–271). Washington, DC: American Psychiatric Press.

Marshall, S. L. A. (1944). *Island victory*. New York: Penguin Books.

Mason, J. W., Giller, E. L., Kosten, T. R., & Yehuda, R. (1990). Psychoendocrine approach to the diagnosis and pathogenesis of posttraumatic stress disorder. In E. L. Giller (Ed.), *Biological assessment and treatment of posttraumatic stress disorder* (pp. 65–87). Washington, DC: American Psychiatric Press.

McCann, I. L., & Pearlman, L. A. (1992). Constructivist self-development theory: A theoretical framework for assessing and treating traumatized college students. *Journal of the American College of Health, 40,* 189–196.

McFarlane, A. C. (1989). The treatment of post traumatic stress disorder. *British Journal of Medical Psychology, 62,* 81–90.

McFarlane, A. C. (1992). Multiple diagnoses in posttraumatic stress disorder in the victims of a natural disaster. *Journal of Nervous and Mental Diseases, 180,* 498–504.

Mitchell, J. T. (1981). *Emergency response to crisis: A crisis intervention guidebook of emergency service personnel.* Bowie, MD: Brady Co.

Mitchell, J. T. (1983). When disaster strikes. *Journal of Emergency Medical Services, 8,* 36–39.

Morgan, C. A., Southwick, S., Grillon, C., et al. (1990, October). *Yohimbine potentiates acoustic startle response in humans.* Presented at the Sixth Annual Meeting of the International Society for Traumatic Stress Studies, New Orleans.

Moses, R., & Cohen, I. (1984). Understanding and treatment of combat neurosis: The Israeli experience. In H. J. Schwartz (Ed.), *Psychotherapy of the combat veteran* (pp. 269–303). New York: Spectrum Publications.

Mueser, K. T., Yarnold, P. R., & Foy, D. W. (1991). Statistical analysis for single-case designs: Evaluating outcome of imaginal exposure treatment of chronic PTSD. *Behavior Modification, 15,* 135–155.

Nagy, L., Southwick, S. M., & Charney, D. S. (1993). Open prospective trial of fluoxetine for posttraumatic stress disorder. *Journal of Clinical Psychopharmacology, 13,* 107–113.

Peniston, E. G. (1986). EMG biofeedback assisted desensitization treatment for Vietnam combat veterans post traumatic stress disorder. *Clinical Biofeedback Health, 9,* 35–41.

Pitman, R. K. (1989). Posttraumatic stress disorder, hormones and memory. *Biological Psychiatry, 26,* 221–223.

Pitman, R. K., Altman, B., Greenwald, E., Longpre, R. E., Macklin, M. L., Poire, R. E., & Steketee, G. S. (1991). Psychiatric complications during flooding therapy for posttraumatic stress disorder. *Journal of Clinical Psychiatry, 57,* 17–20.

Pitman, R. K., Orr, S. P., Frgue, D. F., DeJong, J. B., & Claiborn, J. M. (1987). Psychophysiology of PTSD imagery in Vietnam combat veterans. *Archives of General Psychiatry, 44,* 970–997.

Pitman, R. K., van der Kolk, B. A., Orr, S. P., & Greenberg, M. S. (1990). Naloxone-reversible analgesic response to combat-related stimuli in posttraumatic stress disorder. A pilot study. *Archives of General Psychiatry, 47,* 541–544.

Raphael, B. (1986). *When disaster strikes.* New York: Basic Books.

Resick, P. A., & Schnicke, M. K. (1992). Cognitive processing therapy for sexual assault victims. *Journal of Consulting and Clinical Psychology, 60,* 748–756.

Riest, C., Kauffman, C. D., & Haier, R. J. (1976). A controlled trial of desipramine in 81 men with posttraumatic stress disorder. *American Journal of Psychiatry, 146,* 513–516.

Risse, S. C., Whitters, A., Burke, J., Chen, S., Scurfield, R. M., & Raskind, M. A. (1990). Severe withdrawal symptoms after discontinuation of alprazolam in eight patients with combat-induced posttraumatic stress disorder. *Journal of Clinical Psychiatry, 51,* 206–209.

Rosenheck, R., & Nathan, P. (1985). Secondary traumatization in the children of Vietnam veterans with PTSD. *Hospital and Community Psychiatry, 36,* 538–539.

Salmon, T. (1919). The war neurosis and their lessons. *New York State Journal of Medicine, 59,* 933–944.

Schufield, R. M., Wong, L. E., & Zeeroachah, E. B. (1992). An evaluation of the impact of "helicopter ride therapy" for in-patient Vietnam veterans with war-related PTSD. *Military Medicine, 157,* 67–73.

Shalev, A. Y., Orr, S. P., & Pitman, R. K. (1992). Psychophysiologic response during script driven imagery as an outcome measure in post-traumatic stress disorder. *Journal of Clinical Psychiatry, 53,* 324–326.

Shalev, A. Y., Rogel-Fuchs, Y., & Peri, T. (in press). Debriefing combat units in the Israel Defense Force effect on anxiety and self efficacy.

Shalev, A. Y., Rogel-Fuchs, Y., & Pitman, R. K. (1992). Conditioned fear and psychological trauma. *Biological Psychiatry, 31,* 863–865.

Shay, J. (1991). Fluoxetine reduces explosiveness and elevates mood on Vietnam combat vets with PTSD. *Journal of Traumatic Stress, 5,* 97–110.

Shestatzki, M., Greenberg, D., & Lerer, B. (1988). A controlled trial of phenelzine in post-traumatic stress disorder. *Psychiatry Res, 24,* 149–155.

Solomon, S. D., Gerrity, E. T., & Muff, A. M. (1992). Efficacy of treatment for posttraumatic stress disorder. *JAMA, 268,* 633–638.

Solomon, Z. (1993). *Combat stress reaction: The enduring role of war.* New York: Plenum Press.

Solomon, Z., & Benbenishty, R. (1986). The role of proximity, immediacy, and expectancy in frontline treatment of combat stress reaction among Israelis in the Lebanon War. *American Journal of Psychiatry, 143,* 613–617.

Solomon, Z., Kotler, M., Shalev, A. Y., & Lin, R. (1989). Delayed post-traumatic stress disorder. *Psychiatry, 52,* 428–436.

Solomon, Z., Shalev, A. Y., Spiro, S., Dolev, A., Bleich, A., Waysman, M., & Cooper, S. (1992). The effectiveness of the Koach project: Negative psychometric outcome. *Journal of Traumatic Stress, 5,* 247–264.

Solomon, Z., Waysman, M., Levy, G., Fried, B., Mikulincer, M., Benbenishty, R., Florian, V., Bleich, A. (1992). From front line to home front: A study of secondary traumatization. *Family Process, 31,* 289–302.

van der Kolk, B. A., Dryfuss, D., Michaels, M., Shera, D., Berkowitz, R., Fisher, R., & Saxe, G. (1995). Fluoxetine in the treatment of post traumatic stress disorder. *Journal of Clinical Psychiatry, 55,* 517–522.

van der Kolk, B. A., Greenberg, M., Boyd, H., & Krystal, J. H. (1985). Inescapable shock, neurotransmitter and addiction to trauma: Towards a psychobiology of post traumatic stress disorder. *Biological Psychiatry, 22,* 314–325.

Vaughan, K., & Tarrier, N. (1992). The use of image habituation training with posttraumatic stress disorders. *British Journal of Psychiatry, 161,* 658–664.

Wagner, M. (1979). Airline disaster: A stress debrief program for police. *Police Stress, 2,* 16–20.

Wells, B. G., Chu, C. C., Johnson, R., Nasdahl, C., Ayubi, M. A., Sewell, E., & Statham, P. (1991). Buspirone in the treatment of posttraumatic stress disorder. *Pharmacotherapy, 11,* 340–343.

Yehuda, R., Giller, E. L., & Mason, J. W. (1993). Psychoneuroendocrine assessment of post traumatic stress disorder: Current progress and new directions. *Progress in Neuropsychopharmacology and Biological Psychiatry, 17,* 541–550.

Yehuda, R., Giller, E. L., Southwick, S. M., Lowy, M. T., & Mason, J. W. (1991). Hypothalamic pituitary adrenal dysfunction in posttraumatic stress disorder. *Biological Psychiatry, 30,* 1031–1048.

11

Helping the Victims of Violent Crime

SHERRY A. FALSETTI and HEIDI S. RESNICK

In this chapter we provide a critical overview of theory, assessment, and treatment pertaining to victims of crime. We first present the theories of victim reactions that have influenced assessment and treatment approaches. Then we examine assessment issues, including trauma assessment, diagnostic assessment of posttraumatic stress disorder (PTSD), and other comorbid disorders including depression, substance abuse, and panic disorder. Specific treatment approaches are summarized. These will include crisis intervention, stress inoculation therapy, prolonged imaginal exposure, and cognitive processing therapy. Finally, a case study of comorbid PTSD and panic disorder is presented.

THEORIES OF VICTIM REACTIONS

Several different theories have been applied to victim reactions, including crisis theory, learning theories, information-processing theories, and more recently, cognitive constructivist theories. These theories are reviewed briefly to provide an overview and framework for understanding assessment and treatment of victims of crime.

Crisis Theory

Crisis theory was one of the first theories used to explain victim reactions (Burgess & Holmstrom 1974, 1979; Sales, Baum, & Shore, 1984). Within this

SHERRY A. FALSETTI and HEIDI S. RESNICK · National Crime Victims Research and Treatment Center, Department of Psychiatry and Behavioral Sciences, Medical University of South Carolina, Charleston, South Carolina 29425.

Traumatic Stress: From Theory to Practice, edited by John R. Freedy and Stevan E. Hobfoll. Plenum Press, New York, 1995.

framework, victimization is considered to be an event that overwhelms one's coping resources, thus causing a crisis reaction. Models based on crisis theory generally propose several stages of reactions and recovery. These include models by Burgess and Holmstrom (1974, 1979) that propose stages of acute disorganization and long-term recovery, as well as a five-stage model developed by Forman (1980) that includes initial reactions, denial, symptom formation, anger, and resolution. Crisis theories have not fared well as an explanation for victim reactions because they cannot explain the specific symptoms that develop, or why some victims continue to have reactions past 6 weeks, which is the time frame that crisis theory proposes for crisis reactions (Kilpatrick & Veronen, 1984; Resick & Schnicke, 1990). However, crisis interventions that address many practical needs of victims such as replacing resources that may have been lost during a crime, providing education about the criminal justice system, arranging transportation, arranging time off from work, and making doctor's appointments are helpful in the recovery process of victims. Furthermore, it may provide a useful framework for understanding the reactions of victims who do not develop disorders such as PTSD or depression. Crisis intervention approaches are based on crisis theory and are discussed in the treatment section of this chapter.

Learning Theory

Learning theory has also been proposed to explain victim reactions (Becker, Skinner, Abel, Axelrod, & Cichon, 1984; Holmes & St. Lawrence, 1983; Kilpatrick, Veronen, & Resick, 1982; Kilpatrick, Veronen, & Best, 1985). In general, learning theory proposes that the fear and anxiety reactions of victims are acquired through classical conditioning.

At the time of a traumatic event, individuals often experience high levels of arousal and fear. When in a high state of arousal, previously neutral stimuli may become conditioned stimuli that acquire the capacity to evoke fear and anxiety. For instance, for a woman who was raped in the summer, wearing shorts, in a parking garage and parked next to a green van, the presence of any of these stimuli may later trigger fear and anxiety. In learning terms, these stimuli would now be conditioned stimuli because prior to the rape these things did not cause fear and anxiety. It is only because they were present with fear and anxiety during the crime that they now have the capacity to trigger this response. There is nothing about these stimuli in and of themselves that is dangerous.

In addition to the conditioning that takes place at the time of a traumatic event, fear may generalize to other objects or situations that are similar to stimuli present at the time of the crime. In the case above, this woman may become afraid of all parking garages, all vehicles or other objects that are of the same color green as the van that was present at the time of her assault, or of wearing any summer clothing. Furthermore, she may avoid these stimuli to reduce her anxiety. Because avoidance responses are negatively reinforced by anxiety reduction following avoidance behavior, they tend to be very difficult responses to decrease. Unfortunately, this sets up a viscous cycle because avoidance behavior only serves to reinforce the feeling of escaping danger. In reality, however, if the fear and anxiety could be tolerated long enough to engage in the feared behavior, new learning could take place that would include realizing that these conditioned stimuli are not dangerous. As a result of this new learning, the fear and anxiety response should then decrease.

Learning theory accounts for many of the symptoms of PTSD, including intense psychological distress and the physiological reactivity at exposure to events that symbolize or resemble an aspect of the traumatic event and avoidance symptoms. However, learning theory may not fully account for other symptoms. For instance, persistent reexperiencing of the event and other intrusive symptoms, such as nightmares and flashbacks, cannot be fully accounted for by learning theory. In addition, some of the reexperiencing symptoms of individuals who were not direct victims, but who lost family members by murder are not fully accounted for by learning theory. Oftentimes surviving family members suffer from intrusive images of what they imagine the scene of their loved one's death to have been, even if they were not present at the time of the death. For instance, a mother whose son was killed may keep seeing an image of him being shot, although she was not present at the time the incident took place. Furthermore, conditioning models cannot adequately account for why rape causes more psychological disturbances than many other crimes, such as robbery, even when perceived threat and injury are statistically controlled. It seems quite probable, that in addition to classical conditioning and operant avoidance, cognitive factors such as how information is processed, may also play a role in reactions to trauma.

Information-Processing Theory

Out of this need for a better understanding of victim reactions and variables that influence recovery, information processing theories have recently been applied within the victim reaction research. Chemtob, Roitblat, Hamada, Carlson, and Twentyman (1988) have developed a "cognitive action" theory of PTSD based on their work with Vietnam veterans. Chemtob et al. (1988) propose that people suffering from PTSD develop fear structures that hold images and memories of threatening events as well as information regarding emotions and plans for action. These fear structures comprise threat schema that Chemtob et al. (1988) propose are weakly activated at all times in people with PTSD. Thus, for someone with PTSD, many events that are not objectively dangerous may be interpreted as potentially dangerous. Furthermore, the generally activated threat schema can also elicit memories, emotions, and physiological reactions associated with traumatic events.

Foa, Steketee, and Olasov-Rothbaum (1989) have also proposed an information-processing theory to explain PTSD. Similar to Chemtob et al. (1988), Foa et al. (1989) conceptualize PTSD as primarily an anxiety disorder that results from the development of a fear network. Their theory is based on the work of Lang (1977) and proposes that an internal fear structure is developed that is a program for escape and avoidance behavior. Thus, stimuli that access the fear schema can cause the victim to avoid reminders of a traumatic event. Any stimuli and responses that were associated with the crime can become part of the fear schema, thus not only do certain places or objects become fear producing, but thoughts and physical sensations can also become part of the fear schema.

Cognitive Constructivist Theory

More recently, constructivist theory has been applied to understand reactions to victimization. Constructivist theorists propose that individuals actively construct their own mental representations of the world (Meichenbaum, 1993). These representations, sometimes referred to as schema, have personal meaning and are based on each individual's unique life experiences.

McCann and Pearlman (1990) proposed that there are specific schema that may be disrupted by victimization. These include safety, trust, independence, power, esteem, and intimacy schema. According to McCann and Pearlman (1990), individuals have such schema about themselves and about other people. Depending upon the individual's previous life experiences, victimization may either serve to disrupt or confirm prior beliefs. For example, for someone who has a previous victimization history, another victimization may serve to confirm negative beliefs about being able to trust others. Conversely, for someone who has never experienced any prior victimization and is perhaps very trusting of others, being victimized would disrupt positive beliefs about trusting others.

Resick and Schnicke (1993) have taken a broader approach in their investigations of rape victims by combining principles from learning, information-processing, and constructivist theories. They have suggested that victims suffer from many more negative affective reactions than simply fear. In their conceptualization of PTSD, they have proposed that rape is such a traumatic experience that victims are often unable to integrate the event successfully with prior beliefs and experiences. Instead, the event is either changed to fit prior beliefs (assimilation) or prior beliefs are altered (accommodation). They further hypothesized that symptoms of intrusion and avoidance occur because the event has not been either assimilated or accommodated successfully. In addition, their treatment approach, cognitive-processing therapy, directly addresses disruptions in the schema proposed by McCann and Pearlman (1990). Although information-processing and cognitive theories of victim reactions add substantially to our understanding of victim reactions, there is still much needed research to test these theories with rape victims as well as with victims of other crimes to determine if such theories adequately account for both the symptoms and other variables identified as important to the understanding of victim reactions.

THE ASSESSMENT OF TRAUMA AND ASSOCIATED DISORDERS

Identification of Trauma History

Currently there is a lack of sufficient emphasis on comprehensive assessment of stressor events that may lead to or exacerbate PTSD, major depressive disorder, other anxiety disorders, as well as a variety of other outcomes that may include physical illness or subclinical psychological distress. Recent data indicating the high prevalence of crime and other civilian traumatic events make it clear that efforts need to be directed towards the development of valid and reliable instruments to assess stressor event history.

Data indicate that approximately 40% to 70% of individuals within general population samples have been exposed to crime or other traumatic events included in the PTSD diagnostic criteria (Breslau, Davis, Andreski, & Peterson, 1991; Norris, 1992; Resnick, Kilpatrick, Dansky, Saunders, & Best, 1993) and that many individuals have been multiply exposed to such extreme stressors (Breslau et al., 1991; Resnick et al., 1993). In addition, some civilian crime incidents such as rape and other sexual assault require the use of sensitive behaviorally specific terms for adequate assessment, rather than legal terminology that may be poorly understood or defined idiosyncratically by respondents (Koss, 1985; Kilpatrick, 1983). Furthermore, qualities of events such as degree of injury received, relationship to the victim in cases of indirect victimization, and fear of injury or death during the event are associated with PTSD and therefore require careful assessment (Green, 1990; Kilpatrick, Saunders, et al., 1989).

The Structured Clinical Interview for Diagnostic and Statistical Manual-III-Revised (DSM-III-R) (SCID) (Spitzer, Williams, & Gibbon, 1987), and the Diagnostic Interview Schedule (DIS) (Robins, Helzer, Cottler, & Goldring, 1988) are two of the most widely used instruments for PTSD assessment. However, these instruments do not contain behaviorally specific items to assess traumatic stressor events, such as sexual assault. Detailed examples of instruments that cover a range of types of events and event characteristics are described in Kilpatrick, Saunders, et al. (1989), Resnick et al. (1993), and Falsetti, Resnick, Kilpatrick, and Freedy (1994).

Major crime events and other Criterion A events (the stressor criterion from the PTSD diagnosis) (APA, 1994) assessed with specific behavioral definitions include: homicide of a close friend or relative, direct experience of completed rape, other sexual assault, aggravated assault, disaster, accidents, other incidents involving perceived life threat, injury, or witnessing violence. The interviews allow for multiple occurrence of incidents and assess the stressor qualities included in proposed DSM-IV criteria (i.e., whether actual injury and perceived threat of serious harm occurred as part of each type of incident assessed).

The assessment of traumatic events is an area under development, and research is needed to develop standardized instruments that could be used across studies and clinical populations. For a more in-depth review of these issues as well as other published and unpublished instruments, see Resnick, Falsetti, Kilpatrick, & Freedy (in press) or Resnick, Kilpatrick & Lipovsky (1991). We close this section with a specific example of the questions from the National Women's Study PTSD Module (Kilpatrick, Resnick, Saunders, & Best, 1989) designed to assess history of completed rape using specific behavioral descriptions rather than legal terminology. These questions follow an opening preface that establishes that the interviewer will be asking questions about unwanted sexual advances that may be from individuals that the respondent knows and may occur at any age, and that also establishes the idea that knowing about these events is useful because they may affect people in terms of their functioning:

- Has a man or boy ever made you have sex by using force or threatening to harm you or someone close to you? Just so there is no mistake, by sex we mean putting a penis in your vagina.
- Has anyone ever made you have oral sex by force or threat of harm? Just so there is no mistake, by oral sex we mean that a man or a boy put his penis in your mouth or someone penetrated your vagina or anus with their mouth or tongue.
- Has anyone ever made you have anal sex by force or threat of harm?
- Has anyone ever put fingers or objects in your vagina or anus against your will by using force or threats?

Clinical Issues in Assessing Traumatic Event History

Practitioners may feel uncomfortable conducting specific assessment of trauma history, particularly in reference to sexual assault incidents. It is important to recognize that the potential impact of such events on the victim should outweigh any awkwardness experienced by the professional. Avoidance of such information can send a negative message. An important component of this type of assessment is to provide an understandable rationale for why this information is important. Thus, as Resnick et al. (1991) noted, the provision of an opening preface serves as an acknowledgment to the respondent that some incidents being asked about may be difficult to talk about, but that it is important to ask about them because they can have a significant impact on psychological adjustment. In addition, a good preface to a trauma-assessment interview provides the respondent with an awareness that the professional is aware of the range of conditions that may characterize specific types of events. These include the facts that such incidents can occur in childhood and can be perpetrated by someone known to the victim. As previously suggested, the use of structured questions allows for specific events and important event characteristics (e.g., injury, perception of threat to life) to be identified. Structured approaches can guide the inquiry and, with repeated practice, lead to reduction in interviewer apprehension.

The following introduction provides an example of an opening preface to facilitate the assessment of sexual assault history using terms that are descriptive of the behavior involved (Saunders, Kilpatrick, Resnick, & Tidwell, 1989):

> One type of event that happens to men as well as women, and boys as well as girls, is sexual mistreatment or sexual assault. Men are assaulted under the same kinds of situations as women, but it may be even more difficult for a man to report an assault because he may be ashamed or fear that others will ridicule or not believe him. When asked about sexual abuse or mistreatment, many people tend to think about incidents in which they were attacked or mistreated by a total stranger. As you answer these questions, please remember that we need to know about all incidents of sexual abuse or mistreatment, not just those involving a stranger. Thus, please don't forget to tell us about incidents that might have happened when you were a child or those in which the person who tried to abuse or mistreat you was someone you knew, such as a friend, boyfriend or girlfriend, or even a spouse or family member. Now, here are some questions about some of these experiences you might have had. (p. 274).

Posttraumatic Stress Disorder Symptoms and Diagnostic Assessment

As noted, PTSD is a disorder commonly associated with being the victim of a crime, thus the assessment of PTSD symptomatology is of utmost importance. Ideally, it is recommended that multimodal assessments that include cognitive, physiological, and behavioral modalities be conducted. However, we realize that oftentimes this is not feasible in terms of time or availability of measures and equipment. Thus, we restrict our discussion to structured interview and self-report measures that are most useful and readily available.

In conducting assessments of crime victims, it is important to consider the evaluation of symptoms within the context of the posttrauma time frame. The results of Rothbaum, Foa, Riggs, Murdock, and Walsh (1992) indicate that approximately 50% of those with initial PTSD may persist in a chronic course after 3 months post-trauma and that the remainder show a recovery pattern in terms of PTSD within the first 3 months. Thus, the 3-month time frame should be kept in mind when evaluating distress levels.

Several structured interview measures have been developed that assess diagnostic criteria for PTSD. Most frequently used interviews include the Structured Clinical Interview for DSM-III-R (SCID) (Spitzer et al., 1987) and the Diagnostic Interview Schedule (DIS) (Robins et al., 1988). The Clinician Administered PTSD Scale (CAPS), a more recently developed PTSD interview that includes assessment of symptom frequency and intensity, is described in Blake et al. (1990).

With regard to self-report instruments, there are limited data available on use of such measures as indicators of PTSD as designated by clinical interview. We note here several reports of measures for which such scoring rules and cutoff scores are available. Rothbaum et al. (1992) report data on predictive utility of cutoff scores obtained within the first few weeks post-trauma on the Impact of Events Scale (IES) (Horowitz, Wilner, and Alvarez, 1979) and Rape Aftermath Symptom Test (RAST) (Kilpatrick, 1988) in predicting chronic PTSD among rape victims. It should be noted that the

RAST, which contains items from the Symptom Checklist-90-Revised (SCL-90-R) (Derogatis, 1983) and the Modified Fear Survey (MFS) (Seidner & Kilpatrick, 1988), is relevant for administration to individuals who have experienced a wide variety of stressor events, not just rape. Saunders, Mandoki, and Kilpatrick (1990) reported results of a second scale derived from the SCL-90-R that discriminated between current PTSD-positive and -negative cases identified using structured diagnostic interviews within a large community sample. For a more in-depth review of symptom assessment issues and instruments, see Resnick et al., 1991.

Finally, there are now some promising self-report measures that cover more comprehensively all the PTSD criteria symptoms within a single instrument. These instruments include the PTSD Symptom Scale (PSS) (Foa, Riggs, Dancu, & Rothbaum, 1993) and the Modified PTSD Symptom Scale (MPSS-SR) (Resick, Falsetti, Resnick, & Kilpatrick, 1991) which was a modification of the PSS that included changing several individual items and incorporating an assessment of reported severity of symptoms as well as frequency of symptoms. Both instruments consist of 17 items that correspond to the DSM-III-R symptom criteria for PTSD. Like the PSS, the MPSS-SR is designed to assess PTSD symptoms for the 2-week period prior to the time of administration and takes about 10 to 15 minutes for most people to complete. Furthermore, in recognition of the high prevalence of multiple stressor events that may be experienced, the respondent is instructed to report symptom frequency and severity within the past 2 weeks that may relate to any of the Criterion A stressor events that have been evaluated as part of the thorough stressor event assessment. Finally, both measures may be scored as dichotomous or continuous measures of symptom distress. Further data related to reliability and validity of the MPSS-SR are presented in Falsetti, Resnick, Resick, and Kilpatrick (1993).

Prevalence and Assessment of Depression in Victims of Crime

In addition to the diagnosis of PTSD, depression is another common psychological disorder found in crime victims (Resick, 1989). In a study of short-term reactions, Frank and Stewart (1984) reported that 56% of a sample of rape victims ($n = 90$) were moderately to severely depressed within 1 month post-assault. Hough (1985) indicated that over 50% of a sample of burglary victims suffered from depression.

Ellis, Atkeson, and Calhoun (1981) investigated long-term reactions to victimization, including depression. They found that in women 1 to 16 years post-rape, 45% were moderately to severely depressed as measured by the Beck Depression Inventory (BDI) (Beck, Ward, Mendelson, Mock, & Erbaugh, 1961). More recently, Kilpatrick, Saunders, Best, and Von (1987) found that 46% of women who had experienced one rape and 80% of women who had experienced two rapes met criteria for major depressive disorder at some time in their lives. Other researchers have also reported depression in their studies of crime victims

(Atkeson, Calhoun, Resick, & Ellis, 1982; Kilpatrick & Veronen, 1984; Resick, 1988; Rothbaum, Foa, Murdock, Riggs, & Walsh, 1990).

Clearly, in addition to assessment of PTSD, the assessment of comorbid depression in clinical practice with victims of crime is very important for accurate diagnosis and treatment. The most common instruments used to assess depressive symptoms in this population include the Structured Diagnostic Interview for DSM-III-R (SCID) (Spitzer, Williams, Gibbon, & First, 1990) and the Beck Depression Inventory (BDI) (Beck, et al., 1961).

The SCID is conducted in an interview format and requires a trained clinician for administration. It is designed to assess all DSM-III-R disorders; however, it is possible to use modules only for specific diagnoses of interest. For instance, to assess depression, one may administer the specific questions that assess major depression, mania, and dysthymia. Questions follow DSM-III-R symptom criteria, and instructions for administration are provided. In order to determine if a symptom is absent, subthreshold, or threshold requires some clinical judgment.

The BDI, also frequently used to assess depression, has the advantage of being a self-report instrument, thus does not require a trained clinician for administration. Respondents are asked to complete 21 items that relate to common symptoms of depression by selecting one of four statements for each item that best describes the way the participant feels at the time. Atkeson et al. (1982) found the BDI to discriminate between rape victims and nonvictims 2 months after the assault. Although it should not be used to diagnose clinical depression, the BDI is a helpful screening instrument. Careful clinical interview can be used to determine diagnostic status.

Substance Abuse: A Further Complication in Reactions to Victimization

Substance abuse is often another common problem for victims of crime. Kilpatrick, Edmunds, and Seymour (1992) found higher rates of substance use reported by crime victims compared to individuals who did not report a victimization history in a large national probability sample of 1,000 adult women. Fifty-two percent of rape victims reported using marijuana compared to only 16% of nonvictims; almost 16% of victims reported cocaine use compared to 2.5% of nonvictims; and 12% of victims reported using other hard drugs compared to only 1% of nonvictims. Furthermore, victims who also had PTSD were five times more likely to have two or more major alcohol-related problems compared to victims who did not have PTSD. Finally, victims with PTSD were four times more likely to have two or more serious drug-related problems compared to victims without PTSD. These findings indicate a strong need to assess for substance abuse in victims of crime, particularly in victims who have been diagnosed with PTSD. Many clinicians have not formally assessed for substance abuse with victims of crime until recently. The SCID includes assessment of psychoactive substance use disorders that can be used to diagnose substance abuse disorders, as does the DIS (Helzer, Robins, & McEvoy, 1987).

Panic Attacks and Panic Disorder in Victims of Crime

As noted by Falsetti, Resnick, Dansky, Lydiard, and Kilpatrick (1995), many of the physiological symptoms in panic disorder (PD) are identical to those observed in PTSD. Shortness of breath, rapid heart rate, choking, chest pain, dizziness, nausea, feelings of unreality, numbness or tingling sensations, hot flashes or chills, sweating, and trembling or shaking are symptoms of both panic attacks and the physiological arousal of PTSD. Furthermore, researchers are beginning to question the utility of excluding panic attacks from being diagnosed in the presence of other anxiety disorders.

In fact, the DSM-IV includes a revision in which panic attacks are listed prior to the criteria for anxiety disorders, therefore allowing the specification of the absence or presence of panic attacks with other anxiety disorders (APA, 1994; Brown & Barlow, 1992). This would allow for the diagnosis of PTSD with panic attacks, thus providing a more accurate clinical description for many patients who have suffered trauma.

Although most patients do not connect their first panic attack to any prior events, if questioned carefully, approximately 80% of patients are able to describe one or more negative life events prior to their first panic attack (Uhde et al., 1985). Typically stressors such as interpersonal conflict, death of a loved one, major surgery or illness, and fairly common life events have been assessed.

Unfortunately, with the exception of case studies, traumatic life events such as rape, physical assault, and childhood sexual assault have received very little attention in individuals with PD. This is surprising given that Roy-Byrne, Geraci, and Uhde (1986) in an investigation of 44 panic-disordered patients and 44 controls matched for sex and age, reported that the quality of stressful events, specifically, whether the events were personally threatening or not, was more important than the total number of stressful life events in distinguishing patients with panic attacks from controls.

Falsetti et al. (1995) examined the prevalence of criminal victimization, panic, and PTSD among a representative community sample of women. The sample included 391 respondents, of whom 295 were crime victims. Of the full sample, 21% met criteria for lifetime PTSD, 5.6% met criteria for current PTSD, 7.9% reported panic attacks, and 4.6% met full criteria for PD. Among respondents with PD, 94.4% reported history of criminal victimization. In terms of comorbidity of PD and PTSD, 44.4% of those diagnosed with PD met lifetime criteria for PTSD, and 22.2% met criteria for current PTSD. It appears that a "true alarm," such as physical assault or rape may trigger the first panic attack in victims of crime. This may then become associated with chronic arousal that could put an individual at risk for subsequent PD.

Because PD has traditionally not been assessed in relation to victimization, there are no instruments specifically designed for use with crime victims to assess PD. However, there are several instruments designed to assess PD that have been used in general clinic and anxiety treatment settings, including the SCID Panic Disorder Module (Spitzer, Williams, & Gibbon, 1987) and the ADIS-R for DSM-III-R Panic Disorder (Di Nardo et al., 1985). Both instruments are interview formats that include instructions and require some clinical judgment for proper diagnosis. These instruments are typically brief enough to allow for routine use within clinical settings.

PSYCHOLOGICAL APPROACHES TO TREATMENT

Early treatments for crime victims were based on crisis theory and focused on helping victims deal with the immediate aftermath of victimization (Forman, 1980; Fox & Scherl, 1972; Yassen & Glass, 1984). More recently, as PTSD has become recognized as a primary disorder following victimization, the treatment for victims of crime has focused on alleviating the reexperiencing, avoidance, and arousal symptoms of PTSD. Furthermore, as research is indicating that many crime victims suffer from other disorders concurrent with PTSD, there is a need to develop treatments that can also address problems such as substance abuse, depression, and panic disorder.

In the following sections we describe crisis intervention and three treatment approaches: stress inoculation training (SIT), prolonged exposure therapy (PE), and cognitive processing therapy (CPT). Furthermore, we present a clinical case study of comorbid PD and PTSD using a combination of two treatment approaches: a modification of the Mastery of Your Anxiety and Panic (MAP; Barlow and Craske, 1988) treatment and techniques from CPT (Resick & Schnicke, 1993).

For full descriptions of SIT, PE, and CPT we refer readers to the following resources: (1) SIT: Kilpatrick et al., (1982), Foa, Rothbaum, & Steketee (1993), Resnick & Newton (1992), Resick & Jordan (1988), Veronen & Kilpatrick (1983); (2) PE: Foa, Rothbaum, Riggs, and Murdock (1991), Foa et al. (1993), and (3) CPT: Resick (1992), Resick & Schnicke (1990, 1992, 1993), Calhoun & Resick (1993).

Crisis Intervention

Crisis intervention was designed to help victims understand their reactions and to address needs such as medical care and notification of family and friends. Crisis intervention may also aid the victim in understanding legal matters, provide psychiatric referral, and address other practical concerns such as financial and safety needs. It is a common treatment approach for rape crisis centers, where women are often seen immediately after the rape and need support and information. This is also a common approach of many victim outreach programs whose goals are to identify the needs of victims and then connect them with appropriate referrals and other appropriate resources.

In general, crisis intervention is an active and direct approach that is short term. Information about the likely course of reactions is provided, and these reactions are normalized to assure victims that they are not "going crazy." Victims are encouraged to talk about what happened and to feel their feelings about it. Client concerns such as the personal meaning of the crime, whom to tell, and concerns about others' reactions should also be discussed. Resources, such as food and shelter should be assessed, and community resources to replace any lost resources should be mobilized. For instance, if someone has been robbed, he or she may need help with paying bills and obtaining food. A victim advocate can contact utility companies to delay payment without penalty and locate food through local food banks or churches. In addition, the victim may need information about what to expect in the legal process. Most people have stereotyped ideas of what court will be like and need accurate information about the length of time it may take for a case to go to trial and what the process will involve for them. They may also need to arrange for time off from work or for transportation. Crisis intervention also involves clarifying and reinforcing adaptive coping mechanisms. Social support should be assessed and mobilized as well. Finally, the need for referral for other services, including more intensive mental health or medical services should be assessed.

Burgess and Holmstrom (1976) developed a crisis intervention approach for rape victims that included help in arranging for gynecological treatment and follow-up, helping the victims to activate social support, encouraging the victim to discuss the event, and implementation of psychological therapy. Similarly, Fox and Scherl (1972) identified seven areas that a crisis counselor should address with victims. These include medical attention, legal matters and police contacts, notification of family and friends, current practical concerns, clarification of factual information, emotional responses, and psychiatric consultation.

Perl, Westin, and Peterson (1985) investigated the effectiveness of crisis intervention with 17 female rape victims and concluded that most of the women improved from such treatment. This study did not include objective measures and was instead based on subjective reports of the women and therapists' ratings, which may have biased results. Although crisis intervention is not considered state of the art psychological treatment for victims suffering from more serious problems such as PTSD and depression, it is very useful as a community support for victims in the immediate aftermath of crime. This may be the only contact many victims have with any mental health services, thus crisis intervention continues to provide an important link for referral for more comprehensive services when needed.

Stress Inoculation Training

Stress Inoculation Training (SIT), based on learning theory, was originally developed from Meichenbaum's (1974) stress inoculation and was adapted by Kilpatrick et al. (1982) and Veronen and Kilpatrick (1983) to treat the fear and anxiety experienced by rape victims; SIT consists of three treatment phases:

education, skill building, and application (Resick & Jordan, 1988). Generally treatment requires 8 to 14 sessions depending upon individual needs of the client and the specific approach. Resick and Jordan (1988), for instance, describe an 8-session group stress inoculation approach, whereas Resnick and Newton (1992) describe a 12- to 14-session individual therapy approach. The techniques used are essentially the same, however.

Educational Phase

The first session or two of treatment includes an overview of treatment, a presentation about how the fear response develops based on learning theory, information about sympathetic nervous system arousal, and instruction in progressive muscle relaxation. Clients are asked to practice progressive relaxation and to identify cues that trigger fear reactions. In the following session(s) the information previously given is reviewed, and the fear response is described in further detail as occurring in three response channels: the body (physiological reactions), the mind (thoughts), and behavior (actions). Practice of relaxation training, identification of fear cues, and identification of safety factors are practiced outside of sessions as homework.

Skill-Building Phase

This phase of treatment emphasizes the development of coping skills for the three channels described above. Most descriptions of SIT include teaching diaphragmatic breathing, thought stopping, covert rehearsal, guided self-dialogue, and role playing (Kilpatrick et al., 1982; Resnick & Newton, 1992; Resick & Jordan, 1988). In addition, Resick and Jordan (1988) include the "quieting reflex," a brief relaxation technique developed by Stroebel (1983) and problem-solving techniques as skill-building components. These techniques are described in the references provided above, thus will not be described again here.

Application phase

In the application phase of treatment, the goal is to have clients integrate and apply the skills they have learned and to use the following steps of stress inoculation: (1) assess the probability of feared event, (2) manage escape and avoidance behavior with thought stopping and the quieting reflex, (3) control self-criticism with guided self-dialogue, (4) engage in the feared behavior, and (5) self-reinforcement for using skills. Clients are asked to develop fear hierarchies to continue exposure work after therapy has ended. The final session consists of a review of the training program.

Studies that have investigated the efficacy of SIT have been promising. Veronen and Kilpatrick (1982) reported that SIT was effective in treating fear, anxiety, tension, and depression in 15 female rape victims treated with 20 hours of SIT. Unfortunately, there was not a control group in this study for comparison. Veronen and Kilpatrick (1983) did attempt a comparison study shortly after utilizing SIT, peer counseling, and systematic desensitization. In this study, participants were allowed to choose a treatment. Over half chose not to participate, no one chose systematic desensitization, 11 chose SIT, 1 did not choose and was assigned SIT, and 3 others chose peer counseling. They reported that the clients who completed SIT had improved from pre- to posttreatment, but unfortunately no comparisons among treatments could be conducted.

Resick, Jordan, Girelli, Hutter, and Marhoefer-Dvorak (1988) compared six 2-hour group sessions of SIT, assertion training, and supportive psychotherapy plus information, and a waiting-list control group. They reported that all three treatments were effective in reducing symptoms, with no significant differences between treatments. The clients on the waiting-list control did not improve. At a 6-month follow-up, improvement was maintained in relation to rape-related fears, but not on depression, self-esteem, and social fears.

Foa et al. (1991) compared SIT, exposure treatment, supportive counseling, and a no-treatment control group. All clients were seen for nine 90-minute sessions twice a week. The SIT approach in this study differed from that described by Kilpatrick et al. (1982) in that it did not include instructions for *in vivo* exposure to feared situations. Foa et al. (1991) reported that all of the treatments utilized led to some improvement in anxiety, depression, and PTSD: SIT was indicated to be the most effective treatment for PTSD at immediate follow-up, whereas at a 3.5-month follow-up, clients who had participated in the exposure treatment had less PTSD symptoms.

Prolonged Exposure Therapy

Prolonged imaginal exposure therapy, also referred to as flooding, has proven to be an effective treatment for many Vietnam veterans with PTSD (Fairbank & Keane, 1982; Keane, Fairbank, Caddell, & Zimering, 1989; Keane & Kaloupek, 1982), and more recently, it has been investigated as a treatment option for rape victims with PTSD (Foa et al., 1991). This treatment approach is based on principles of learning and information-processing theories. One of the primary goals of exposure therapy is to confront the feared stimuli in imagination so that fear and anxiety decrease. This is similar to watching a scary movie over and over. At first it may be very scary, but by the 20th viewing, it would not be as scary. Analogously, replaying a frightening memory becomes less frightening as it is recounted numerous times in an objectively safe environment.

Clients are also asked to confront fear cues that are not dangerous but that may have been paired with danger at the time of the traumatic event. In vivo exposure to fear cues is used to extinguish the fear associated with these stimuli. This involves exposure to objects or situations in real life. In our earlier example of the woman who was raped in a parking garage, in vivo exposure entailed sitting in a parking garage in her car with her therapist. She would monitor her anxiety, which decreased as she was able to learn that it was not the parking garage that was dangerous, but her assailant.

Foa et al. (1991) describe prolonged exposure treatment for rape victims with PTSD within 9 biweekly 90-minute sessions. The first two sessions of treatment were used for the initial interview, to explain the rationale of treatment, and to plan treatment. The remaining seven sessions consisted of imaginal exposure to the rape. Clients were asked to describe their rape in great detail in the present tense, as though it were really happening. They were instructed to repeat the account over and over for about an hour. Typically, during the first two imaginal exposure sessions, clients were allowed to choose the level of detail that was tolerable to them. In the remaining exposure sessions, clients were asked to describe the assault in as much detail as possible. Subjective units of distress (SUDs) ratings were assessed within and across sessions to monitor fear and anxiety levels. Exposure sessions were recorded and given to clients to take home and listen to at least once a day to provide further exposure trials. In addition, clients were encouraged to practice exposing themselves to situations that are not dangerous, but that they fear because of the rape. Examples of such situations for rape victims often include dating, going out with friends, watching the news or reading the newspaper (often avoided because of stories about similar crimes), and other situations that were specific to their experience.

In addition to the Foa et al. (1991) comparison study described under SIT that indicated PE was an effective treatment in alleviating symptoms of PTSD, several other researchers have also indicated the efficacy of flooding therapy. Haynes and Mooney (1975) describe the use of flooding as an effective treatment for physical and sexual assault victims. Rychtarik, Silverman, Van Landingham, and Prue (1984) described a case study of an incest victim successfully treated with imaginal flooding.

Despite the success of prolonged exposure treatment, it has been recommended that this treatment be used with caution as some professionals have noted the potential of severe complications including precipitation of panic disorder, exacerbation of depression, and relapse of alcohol abuse (Pitman, Altman, & Greenwald, 1991). In addition, flooding has received considerable criticism because it does not address faulty cognitions and fails to enhance the development of coping skills (Kilpatrick et al., 1982; Kilpatrick et al., 1985).

Cognitive Processing Therapy

Cognitive processing therapy was developed by Resick and Schnicke (1990, 1992, 1993) based on information processing and cognitive constructivist theory. This treatment is designed for rape victims suffering from PTSD and depression. Resick and Schnicke propose that PTSD consists of more than a fear network. Victims may also suffer from other strong feelings such as disgust, shame, and anger. As a framework for understanding how other intense emotions might develop, they have highlighted the work of Hollon and Garber (1988) who have suggested that when a person is exposed to information that is schema-discrepant, assimilation or accommodation takes place. Put simply, this means that when something unusual happens that we either don't really have a category (schema) for, or that doesn't happen in the way our schema indicates it "should" (i.e., rapes only happen to bad people who walk in dark alleys at night), then we either must alter the information (assimilation) or alter our schemas (accommodation). Examples of assimilation include self-blaming statements ("It must be my fault because I was wearing a short skirt," or "Maybe it wasn't really rape, but I really wanted it like he said"), whereas accommodation often results in extreme cognitive distortions, such as, "I never feel safe," "I trust no one," and "I have to be in control at all times."

The goal of CPT is to assist in integrating the event, with complete processing of emotions and accommodation of schema while helping the client to maintain or achieve a healthy outlook and balanced perception of the world. Furthermore, the following issues that McCann, Sakheim and Pearlman (1988, McCann and Pearlman 1990) have identified as being affected by victimization are also a focus of CPT: safety, trust, power, esteem, and intimacy.

Cognitive processing therapy provides exposure to the traumatic memory and training in challenging maladaptive cognitions. This treatment may be better than exposure alone because it also provides corrective information regarding misattributions or other maladaptive beliefs (Resick & Schnicke, 1993); CPT is focused on identifying and modifying "stuckpoints," which are inadequately processed conflicts between prior schema and new information (i.e., the traumatic event). Stuckpoints are also proposed to arise from (1) negative, conflicting schemata imposed by others (victim blame), (2) an avoidant coping style, or (3) no relevant schema in which to store the information.

As described by Resick and Schnicke, CPT can be conducted in either group or individual sessions and can be completed in 12 weekly sessions. The content of treatment includes a cognitive information-processing explanation of traumatic event reactions and writing assignments about the meaning of the event. This is followed by education regarding basic feelings and how changes in self-statements can affect emotions. Clients are also taught how to identify the connections between actions, beliefs, and consequences and are asked to write accounts of the traumatic event and to read it repeatedly. Resick and Schnicke (1993) point out that writings about the trauma are often more detailed than oral accounts and serve as exposure, which facilitates a decrease of strong negative emotions in a way similar to that described in the section on prolonged imaginal exposure. The accounts also expose stuckpoints. In addition, several of the sessions focus on developing skills to analyze and confront stuckpoints and other maladaptive self-statements regarding the traumatic event. This is followed by a series of sessions that cover the five belief areas proposed by McCann et al. (1988). The final session is devoted to review and planning for the future.

Investigations of the efficacy of CPT in treating PTSD and depression have been promising. Resick and Schnicke (1992) reported significant improvements on depression and PTSD measures pretreatment to six-months posttreatment for 19 sexual assault survivors who were at least 3 months postrape at the start of treatment. Therapy was conducted in group format over 12 weeks, and a waiting-list control group was also employed ($n = 20$). Rates of PTSD went from a pretreatment rate of 90% to a posttreatment rate of 0%. Rates of major depression decreased from 62% to 42%. Further evaluation of the treatment indicates usefulness of both group and individual formats, with somewhat higher efficacy for treatment administered in individual sessions (Resick & Schnicke, 1993).

In sum, CPT appears to be an effective treatment for PTSD, and also appears promising in treating depression in female rape victims. Investigations of utilizing this treatment with other victim groups, for instance survivors of domestic violence, victims of physical assault, or men who have been victims of crime are needed to determine if this treatment may also be useful in helping other victims. Applicability of this treatment to less-educated victims should also be investigated. The average educational levels in Resick's studies have generally been above the high school level (Resick & Schnicke, 1993), and many of the worksheets used in treatment are quite complex, thus may need to be simplified to be understandable for some clients.

A Case Presentation: Treatment of Comorbid PTSD and PD

As research in the area of trauma has progressed, it is becoming apparent that many victims who develop PTSD also develop other disorders. Thus, to effectively treat many victims, combining and adapting treatment approaches for other disorders may be necessary. In addition, many clinicians have validly noted that treatment outcome research studies often focus on the "pure" patients, whose cases are relatively straightforward, and are not complicated by factors such as multiple victimization or comorbid disorders. The complaint of many clinicians is that these "pure" cases are not the norm for the cases they see in their practices or clinics. Our aim here is to present a "messy" case; one that may be more typical and that includes multiple trauma and comorbidity of disorders.

Mr. Z

Mastery of your anxiety and panic (MAP) (Barlow and Craske, 1988), a cognitive behavioral treatment for panic, was adapted and applied to a 35-year-old male who had experienced multiple traumatic events and was suffering from both PTSD and panic disorder (PD). The MAP treatment includes exposing clients to physical sensations they may experience during a panic attack by having them practice such exercises as stair stepping, hyperventilating, and spinning in a chair. In addition, education about panic attacks is provided, and clients are taught several cognitive restructuring skills. This treatment was chosen because the patient was unable to discuss his past traumas without fear of panic attacks. Later work focused on trauma, employing many components of CPT, which was originally designed for the treatment of PTSD and depression in female rape victims. The following will provide a summary of the MAP and CPT treatment components employed in this case.

History of Mr. Z

Mr. Z is a 35-year-old white male who at the time of intake reported that he had been physically assaulted three times in the past 3 years. One attack included a nearly fatal stabbing that required three surgeries and hospitalization for 2 months. In addition, he reported that he had been physically abused by his father and stepfather as a child. Mr. Z presented with the following symptoms: intense episodes of anxiety and panic that included shortness of breath, chest pain, palpitations, trembling, nausea, fear of dying, and fear of others thinking he was crazy. Mr. Z. also reported difficulty concentrating, feeling on guard, nightmares, flashbacks, intrusive thoughts, and being easily startled.

Assessment Measures

The following assessment measures were utilized: High and Low Magnitude Events Structured Interview (Kilpatrick, Resnick, & Freedy, 1991), Structured Clinical Interview for DSM-III-R (SCID) (Spitzer et al., 1987), Modified PTSD Symptom Scale-Self Report (MPSS-SR) (Resick et al., 1991), Symptom Checklist-90-Revised (SCL-90-R) (Derogatis, 1983), and the Physical Reactions Scale (Falsetti & Resnick, 1992).

Assessment and Monitoring of Symptoms

The initial assessment indicated that Mr. Z met diagnostic criteria for both PTSD and PD. Mr. Z's panic attacks were often triggered by conditioned cues from his assaults (e.g., restaurants, knifes, news stories about violence) but had also generalized and occurred unexpectedly. Mr. Z monitored his panic attacks, anxiety, depression, and worry about panic on a daily basis. Initially, Mr. Z averaged two panic attacks a week, and on a scale of 0 = not at all anxious to 8 = extremely anxious, his average anxiety ratings ranged from 4 to 7 in the first weeks of treatment.

Course of Treatment

The adaptation of the MAP treatment consisted of 25, once weekly, 50-minute individual therapy sessions. Initial sessions focused on providing education about panic and PTSD including an explanation of physical, cognitive, and behavioral components of anxiety. During this time, Mr. Z carefully examined the sequence of his panic attacks as homework. Mr. Z was also taught breathing retraining to decrease hyperventilation. This was followed by several sessions on cognitive restructuring and thought monitoring for catastrophic thoughts and overestimations of negative outcomes. He was also taught to identify conditioned cues for panic that were related to traumatic events he had experienced. In later sessions, interoceptive exposure to somatic sensations was conducted to decrease fear of these symptoms. Final MAP sessions focused on panic were devoted to developing a hierarchy for in vivo exposure to situations that in the past had elicited panic, including sitting in a restaurant and riding a bus. Mr. Z had been stabbed in a restaurant, thus this was a conditioned cue associated with the level of fear and anxiety he had experienced at the time of the stabbing.

During the course of treatment, Mr. Z revealed that he had been sexually abused by his mother, thus he continued with treatment after the completion of MAP to focus on distress related to these traumatic memories. Many of Mr. Z's issues were similar to that of female rape victims, and he displayed numerous cognitive distortions, thus a CPT approach seemed appropriate.

Mr. Z. completed CPT exposure work, through writing about his abuse and discussing his writings in sessions. Faulty cognitions, such as "I deserved to be abused, because I was a lot of trouble," were challenged, and Mr. Z has adapted many new beliefs that are more realistic. Mr. Z has continued to work on these issues in treatment for the past year, and because of the chronicity of his abuse, is seen as a "long-term" therapy case. It is likely that he will remain in treatment for another 3 to 6 months.

Results of Treatment (Thus Far)

Mr. Z has had only one panic attack since his 24th session of therapy and has remained panic-free for 9 months prior to this one attack. Based on posttest results obtained after the MAP treatment, he no longer met criteria for either PTSD or PD. On the Physical Reactions Scale, Mr. Z reported only one set of physical symptoms: trembling and shaking. Mr. Z's SCL-90-R scores dropped dramatically. His pretest Global Severity Index T-score was 98.7, whereas his posttest score, approximately 1 year later, was 62.9. The frequency and severity of his PTSD symptoms as measured by the Modified PTSD Symptom Scale also decreased with treatment (initial sum score = 90, postsum score = 43). Mr. Z no longer reports any PTSD symptomatology in relation to the three physical assaults for which he initially sought treatment. He continues to have sporadic nightmares in association with the sexual abuse he experienced as a child, however. He is currently able to perform many activities that he had avoided, including eating in restaurants and driving a car.

REFERENCES

American Psychiatric Association. (1994). *Diagnostic and statistical manual of mental disorders* (4th ed.). Washington, DC: Author.

Atkeson, B. M., Calhoun, K. S., Resick, P. A., & Ellis, E. M. (1982). Victims of rape: Repeated assessment of depressive symptoms. *Journal of Consulting and Clinical Psychology, 50,* 96–102.

Barlow, D. H., & Craske, M. G. (1988). *Mastery of your anxiety and panic.* Manual available from the Center for Stress and Anxiety Disorders, 1535 Western Avenue, Albany, NY 12203.

Beck, A. T., Ward, C. H., Mendelson, M., Mock, J. E., & Erbaugh, J. K. (1961). An inventory for measuring depression. *Archives of General Psychiatry, 4,* 561–571.

Becker, J. V., Skinner, L. J., Abel, G. G., Axelrod, R., & Cichon, J. (1984). Sexual problems of sexual assault survivors. *Women and Health, 9,* 5–20.

Blake, D. D., Weathers, F. W., Nagy, L. M., Kaloupek, D. G., Klaumizer, G., Charney, D., & Keane, T. M. (1990). A clinician rating scale for assessing current and lifetime PTSD: The CAPS-1. *The Behavior Therapist, 13.* 187–188.

Breslau, N., Davis, G. C., Andreski, P., & Peterson, E. (1991). Traumatic events and post-traumatic stress disorder in an urban population of young adults. *Archives of General Psychiatry, 48,* 216–222.

Brown, T. A., & Barlow, D. H. (1992). Comorbidity among anxiety disorders: Implications for treatment and DSM-IV. *Journal of Consulting and Clinical Psychology, 60,* 835–844.

Burgess, A., & Holmstrom, L. (1974). Rape trauma syndrome. *American Journal of Psychiatry, 131,* 981–986.

Burgess, A. W., & Holmstrom, L. L. (1976). Coping behavior of the rape victim. *American Journal of Psychiatry, 133,* 413–418.

Burgess, A. W., & Holstrom, L. L. (1979). Adaptive strategies and recovery from rape. *American Journal of Psychiatry, 136,* 1278–1282.

Calhoun, K. S., & Resick, P. A. (1993). Treatment of PTSD in Rape Victims. In D. A. Barlow (Ed.), *Clinical handbook of psychological disorders* (pp. 48–98). New York: Guilford Press.

Chemtob, C., Roitblat, H. L., Hamada, R. S., Carlson, J. G., & Twentyman, C. T. (1988). A cognitive action theory of post-traumatic stress disorder. *Journal of Anxiety Disorders, 2,* 253–275.

Derogatis, L. R. (1983). *Symptom Checklist-90-revised: Administration, scoring and procedures manual-II* (2nd ed.). Baltimore: Clinical Psychometric Research.

Di Nardo, P. A., Barlow, D. H., Cerny, J., Vermilyea, B. B., Vermilyea, J. A., Himada, W., & Waddell, M. (1985). *Anxiety Disorders Interview Schedule—revised (ADIS-R).* Albany, NY: Phobia and Anxiety Disorders Clinic, State University of New York at Albany.

Ellis, E., Atkeson, B., & Calhoun, K. (1981). An assessment of long-term reaction to rape. *Journal of Abnormal Psychology, 90,* 263–266.

Fairbank, J. A., & Keane, T. M. (1982). Flooding for combat-related stress disorders: Assessment of anxiety reduction across traumatic memories. *Behavior Therapy, 13,* 499–510.

Falsetti, S. A., & Resnick, H. S. (1992). *Physical Reactions Scale.* Charleston, SC: Crime Victims Research and Treatment Center, Medical University of South Carolina.

Falsetti, S. A., Resnick, H. S., Dansky, B. S., Lydiard, R. B., & Kilpatrick, D. G. (1995). The relationship of stress to panic disorder: Cause or effect? In C. M. Mazure (Ed.), *Does stress cause psychiatric illness?* (pp. 111–147). Washington, DC: American Psychiatric Press.

Falsetti, S. A., Resnick, H. S., Kilpatrick, D. G., & Freedy, J. R. (1994). A review of the "Potential Stressful Events Interview": A comprehensive assessment instrument of high and low magnitude stressors. *Behavior Therapist, 17,* 66–67.

Falsetti, S. A., Resnick, H. S., Resick, P. A., & Kilpatrick, D. G. (1993). The Modified PTSD Symptom Scale: A brief self-report measure of post-traumatic stress disorder. *Behavior Therapist, 16,* 161–162.

Foa, E. B., Riggs, D. S., Dancy, C. V., & Rothbaum, B. O. (1993). Reliability and validity of a brief instrument for assessing posttraumatic stress disorder. *Journal of Traumatic Stress, 6,* 459–473.

Foa, E. B., Rothbaum, B. O., Riggs, D. S., & Murdock, T. B. (1991). Treatment of posttraumatic stress disorder in rape victims: A comparison between cognitive–behavioral procedures and counseling. *Journal of Consulting and Clinical Psychology, 59,* 715–723.

Foa, E. B., Rothbaum, B. O., & Steketee, G. S. (1993). Treatment of rape victims. *Journal of Interpersonal Violence, 8,* 256–276.

Foa, E. B., Steketee G., & Olasov-Rothbaum, B. (1989). Behavioral/cognitive conceptualizations of post-traumatic stress disorder. *Behavior Therapy, 20,* 155–176.

Forman, B. D. (1980). Cognitive modification of obsessive thinking in a rape victim: A preliminary study. *Psychological Reports, 47,* 819–822.

Fox, S. S., & Scherl, D. J. (1972). Crisis intervention with victims of rape. *Social Work, 17,* 37–42.

Frank, E., & Stewart, B. D., (1984). Depressive symptoms in rape victims: A revisit. *Journal of Affective Disorders, 7,* 77–85.

Green, B. L. (1990). Defining trauma: Terminology and generic stressor dimensions. *Journal of Applied Social Psychology, 20,* 1632–1642.

Haynes, S. N., & Mooney, D. K. (1975). Nightmares: Etiological, theoretical, and behavioral treatment considerations. *Psychological Record, 25,* 225–236.

Helzer, J. E., Robins, L. N., & McEvoy, L. (1987). Post-traumatic stress disorder in the general population. *New England Journal of Medicine, 317,* 1630–1634.

Hollon, S. D., & Garber, J. (1988). Cognitive therapy. In L. Y. Abramson (Ed.), *Social cognition and clinical psychology: A synthesis* (pp. 204–253). New York: Guilford Press.

Holmes, M. R., & St. Lawrence, J. S. (1983). Treatment of rape-induced trauma: Proposed behavioral conceptualization and review of the literature. *Clinical Psychology Review, 3,* 417–433.

Horowitz, M., Wilner, N., & Alvarez, W. (1979). Impact of Event Scale: Measure of subjective distress. *Psychosomatic Medicine, 41,* 209–218.

Hough, M. (1985). The impact of victimization: Findings from the British Crime Survey. *Victimology, 10,* 498–511.

Keane, T. M., Fairbank, J. A., Caddell, J. M., & Zimering, R. T. (1989). Implosive (flooding) therapy reduces symptoms of PTSD in Vietnam combat veterans. *Behavior Therapy, 20,* 245–260.

Keane, T. M., & Kaloupek, D. G. (1982). Imaginal flooding in the treatment of posttraumatic stress disorder. *Journal of Consulting and Clinical Psychology, 50,* 138–140.

Kilpatrick, D. G. (1983). Rape victims: Detection, assessment, and treatment. *The Clinical Psychologist, 36,* 92–95.

Kilpatrick, D. G. (1988). Rape Aftermath Symptom Test. In M. Hersen & A. S. Bellack (Eds.), *Dictionary of behavioral assessment techniques* (pp. 366–367). New York: Pergamon Press.

Kilpatrick, D. G., Edmunds, C. N. & Seymour, A. K. (1992). *Rape in America: A report to the nation.* Arlington, VA: National Victim Center.

Kilpatrick, D. G., Resnick, H. S., & Freedy, J. R. (1991). *High and low magnitude events structured interview.* Charleston, SC: Crime Victims Research and Treatment Center, Medical University of South Carolina.

Kilpatrick, D. G., Resnick, H. S., Saunders, B. E., & Best, C. L. (1989). *National women's study PTSD module.* Unpublished instrument, Crime Victims Research and Treatment Center, Department of Psychiatry, Medical University of South Carolina, Charleston.

Kilpatrick, D. G., Saunders, B. E., Amick-McCullan, A., Best, C. L., Veronen, L. J., & Resnick, H. S. (1989). Victim and crime factors associated with the development of crime-related post-traumatic stress disorder. *Behavior Therapy, 20,* 199–214.

Kilpatrick, D. G., Saunders, B. E., Best, C. L., & Von, J. M. (1987). Criminal victimization: Lifetime prevalence, reporting to police, and psychological impact. *Crime and Delinquency, 33,* 479–489.

Kilpatrick, D. G., & Veronen, L. J. (1984). *Treatment of fear and anxiety on victims of rape* (Final report, Grant No. RO1MH2902). Rockville, MD: National Institute of Mental Health.

Kilpatrick, D. G., Veronen, L. J., & Best, C. L. (1985). Factors predicting psychological distress among rape victims. In C. R. Figley (Ed.), *Trauma and its wake: Vol. 1. The study and treatment of posttraumatic stress disorder* (pp. 113–141). New York: Brunner/Mazel.

Kilpatrick, D. G., Veronen, L. J., & Resick, P. A. (1982). Psychological sequelae to rape. In D. M. Doleys, R. L. Meredith, & A. R. Ciminero (Eds.), *Behavioral medicine: Assessment and treatment strategies* (pp. 473–497). New York: Plenum Press.

Koss, M. P. (1985). The hidden rape victim: Personality, attitudinal, and situational characteristics. *Psychology of Women Quarterly, 9,* 193–212.

Lang, P. J. (1977). Imagery in therapy: An information processing analysis of fear. *Behavior Therapy, 8,* 862–886.

McCann, L., & Pearlman, L. A. (1990). *Psychological trauma and the adult survivor: Theory, therapy, & transformation.* New York: Brunner/Mazel.

McCann, L., Sakheim, D. K., & Pearlman, L. A. (1988). Trauma and victimization: A model of psychological adaptation. *Counseling Psychologist, 16,* 531–594.

Meichenbaum, D. (1974). *Cognitive behavior modification.* Morristown, NJ: General Learning Press.

Meichenbaum, D. (1993). Changing conceptions of cognitive behavior modification: Retrospect and prospect. *Journal of Consulting and Clinical Psychology, 61,* 202–204.

Norris, F. H. (1990). Screening for traumatic stress: A scale for use in the general population. *Journal of Applied Social Psychology, 20,* 1704–1718.

Norris, F. H. (1992). Epidemiology of trauma: Frequency and impact of different potentially traumatic events on different demographic groups. *Journal of Consulting and Clinical Psychology, 60,* 409–418.

Perl, M., Westin, A. B., & Peterson, L. G. (1985). The female rape survivor: Time-limited group therapy with female–male cotherapists. *Journal of Psychosomatic Obstetrics and Gynecology, 4,* 197–205.

Pitman, R. K., Altman, B., Greenwald, E., Longpre, R. E., Macklin, M. L., Poiré, R. E., & Steketee, G. S. (1991). Psychiatric complications during flooding therapy for posttraumatic stress disorder. *Journal of Clinical Psychiatry, 52,* 17–20.

Resick, P. A. (1988). *Reactions of female and male victims of rape or robbery.* Final report of NIJ Grant No. 85-IJ-CX-0042.

Resick, P. A. (1989). Victims of sexual assault. In A. Lurigio, R. C. Davis, & W. G. Skogan (Eds.), *Victims in the criminal justice system.* Newbury Park, CA: Sage Publications.

Resick, P. A. (1992). Cognitive treatment of crime-related post-traumatic stress disorder. In R. D. Peters, R. J. McMahon, & V. L. Quinsey (Eds.), *Aggression and violence throughout the life span* (pp. 171–191). Newbury Park, CA: Sage Publications.

Resick, P. A., Falsetti, S. A., Resnick, H. S., & Kilpatrick, D. G. (1991). *The modified PTSD symptom scale—self report.* St. Louis: University of Missouri; Charleston, SC: Crime Victims Treatment and Research Center, Medical University of South Carolina.

Resick, P. A., & Jordan, C. G. (1988). Group stress inoculation training for victims of sexual assault: A therapist manual. In P. A. Keller & S. R. Heyman (Eds.), *Innovations in clinical practice: A source book* (Vol. 7, pp. 99–111). Sarasota, FL: Professional Resource Exchange.

Resick, P. A., Jordan, C. G., Girelli, S. A., Hutter, C. H., & Marhoefer-Dvorak, S. (1988). A comparative outcome study of behavioral group therapy for sexual assault victims. *Behavior Therapy, 19,* 385–401.

Resick, P. A., & Schnicke, M. K. (1990). Treating symptoms in adult victims of sexual assault. *Journal of Interpersonal Violence, 5,* 488–506.

Resick, P. A., & Schnicke, M. K. (1992). Cognitive processing therapy for sexual assault victims. *Journal of Consulting and Clinical Psychology, 60,* 748–756.

Resick, P. A., & Schnicke, M. K. (1993). *Cognitive processing therapy for rape victims: A treatment manual.* Newbury Park, CA: Sage.

Resnick, H. S., Falsetti, S. A., Kilpatrick, D. G., & Freedy, J. R. (in press). Assessment of rape and other civilian trauma-related posttraumatic stress disorders: Emphasis on assessment of potentially traumatic events. In T. W. Miller (Ed.), *Stressful life events* (2nd ed.). Madison, CT: International Universities Press.

Resnick, H. S., Kilpatrick, D. G., Dansky, B. S., Saunders, B. E., & Best, C. L. (1993). Prevalence of civilian trauma and PTSD in a representative national sample of women. *Journal of Consulting and Clinical Psychology, 61,* 984–991.

Resnick, H. S., Kilpatrick, D. G., & Lipovsky, J. A. (1991). Assessment of rape-related post-traumatic stress disorder: Stressor and symptom dimensions. *Psychological Assessment, 3,* 561–572.

Resnick, H. S., & Newton, T. (1992). Assessment and treatment of post-traumatic stress disorder in adult survivors of sexual assault. In D. Foy (Ed.), *Treating PTSD*. New York: Guilford Press.

Robins, L. N., Helzer, J., Cottler, L., & Goldring, E. (1988). *NIMH Diagnostic Interview Schedule Version-III-Revised (DIS-III-R)*. Washington, DC: NIMH.

Rothbaum, B. O., Foa, E. B., Murdock, T., Riggs, D. S., & Walsh, W. (1990). *Post-traumatic stress disorder in rape victims*. Unpublished manuscript, Department of Psychiatry, Medical College of Pennsylvania, Philadelphia.

Rothbaum, B. O., Foa, E. B., Riggs, D. S., Murdock, T., & Walsh, W. (1992). A prospective examination of posttraumatic stress disorder in rape victims. *Journal of Traumatic Stress, 5*, 455–475.

Roy-Byrne, P. P., Geraci, M., & Uhde, T. W. (1986). Life events and the onset of panic disorder. *American Journal of Psychiatry, 143*, 1424–1427.

Rychtarik, R. G., Silverman, W. K., Van Landingham, W. P., & Prue, D. M. (1984). Treatment of an incest victim with implosive therapy: A case study. *Behavior Therapy, 15*, 410–420.

Sales, E., Baum, M., & Shore, B. (1984). Victim readjustment following assault. *Journal of Social Issues, 40*, 117–136.

Saunders, B. E., Kilpatrick, D. G., Resnick, H. S., & Tidwell, R. P. (1989). Brief screening for lifetime history of criminal victimization at mental health intake: A preliminary study. *Journal of Interpersonal Violence, 4*, 267–277.

Saunders, B. E., Mandoki, K. A., & Kilpatrick, D. G. (1990). Development of a crime-related post-traumatic stress disorder scale within the Symptom Checklist-90-revised. *Journal of Traumatic Stress, 3*, 439–448.

Seidner, A. L., & Kilpatrick, D. G. (1988). Modified fear survey. In M. Hersen & A. S. Bellack (Eds.), *Dictionary of Behavioral Assessment Techniques* (pp. 307–309). New York: Pergamon Press.

Spitzer, R. L., Williams, J. B., & Gibbon, M. (1987). *Structured clinical interview for DSM-III-R— Nonpatient version* (SCID-NP-V). New York: New York State Psychiatric Institute, Biometrics Research Department.

Spitzer, R. L., Williams, J. B., Gibbon, M., & First, M. B. (1990). *Structural clinical interview for DSM-III-R—Patient Edition, version 1.0 Washington, DC:* American Psychiatric Press.

Stroebel, C. F. (1983). *Quieting reflex training for adults: Personal workbook (or practitioners guide)*. New York: DMA Audio Cassette Publications.

Uhde, T. W., Boulenger J. P., Roy-Byrne, P. P., Geraci, M. P., Vittone, B. J., & Post, R. M. (1985). Longitudinal course of panic disorder: Clinical and biological consideration. *Progressive Neuro-Psychopharmacology and Biological Psychiatry, 9*, 39–51.

Veronen, L. J., & Kilpatrick (1982, November). *Stress inoculation training for victims of rape: Efficacy and differential findings*. In *Sexual Violence and harrassment*. Symposium conducted at the 16th Annual Convention of the Association for Advancement of Behavior Therapy, Los Angeles, California.

Veronen, L. J., & Kilpatrick, D. G. (1983). Stress management for rape victims. In D. Meichenbaum & M. E. Jaremko (Eds.), *Stress reduction and prevention* (pp. 341–374). New York, Plenum Press.

Yassen, J., & Glass, L. (1984). Sexual assault survivors groups: A feminist practice perspective. *Social Work, 29*, 252–257.

12

Helping the Victims
of Disasters

ALEXANDER C. MCFARLANE

OVERVIEW

This chapter examines the various ways in which mental health professionals can assist in the psychological care and rehabilitation of disaster victims. This requires an understanding of the unpredictability and uncontrollability of disasters. It is important to realize that these are situations that require considerable adaptability by the professional, confront many of the usual clinical roles, and test the capacity for empathy. On occasions, dealing with traumatized populations challenges the normal professional impartiality and demands that the clinician take on the role of community activist. In the first instance, assessing the impact of disasters is a critical process because each type of event produces novel problems and an individual profile of trauma. It is useful to conceptualize the needs of a population in the different phases that are associated with disasters, as the range of professional responses required will vary significantly with the passage of time.

A biopsychosocial model of adaptation assists in focusing on the multiple dimensions that influence the process of postdisaster adjustment. The assessment of disaster victims requires both a focus on a series of issues in relation to the individual victim but also a broader perspective of the issues being faced by the whole community. Intervention similarly should be planned at a number of levels. In the first instance, assisting in the initial containment of the disaster can be aided if a number of specific issues are addressed. The opportunities for group and individual preventive interventions are greatest in the immediate aftermath of the event but require prior planning and adequate skills in those

ALEXANDER C. McFARLANE • Department of Psychiatry, University of Adelaide, P.O. Box 17, Eastwood. 5063 South Australia.

Traumatic Stress: From Theory to Practice, edited by John R. Freedy and Stevan E. Hobfoll. Plenum Press, New York, 1995.

involved professionals. The difference between prevention and treatment needs to be recognized. Treatment that focuses on assisting the processing of the traumatic memories appears to be the most efficacious and can be assisted by the appropriate use of psychotropic medication.

THE NATURE OF DISASTERS

A disaster may confront the clinician with possibly hundreds or even thousands of victims with multiple immediate needs. This contrasts with the predictability of most other clinical settings characterized by the familiar office environment and regular appointments. Thus, the very nature of disasters emphasizes the difficulty in defining a prescribed method or single approach to intervention. Rather, flexibility and innovation are often required to deal with these events that are by their nature unpredictable and uncontrollable. Disasters confront people with overwhelming threats to their sense of safety as well as often lead to large-scale destruction of property and possessions. In the wake, many may be left bereaved. Thus, disasters tax the coping ability of even the most hardy individuals and confront people with beliefs about the safety and predictability of their lives (Raphael, 1986).

Inevitably, any clinician who deals with disaster victims is directly confronted by the enormity and unpredictability of the situation. An essential skill is the ability to take a broad and flexible approach based upon a careful and unprejudiced assessment of the issues.

Emergency service such as fire, rescue, and ambulance departments have detailed plans to manage the acute response to catastrophic events that aim to create an operational and psychological structure in the face of chaos. Frequently, such plans are developed in the light of the experience of a preceding disaster or catastrophe. Almost inevitably the next disaster will be different and, hence, inadequately prepared for. Disasters are immensely challenging to the clinician because a highly flexible response is required. Furthermore, disasters have a variety of dimensions that can not be easily separated including the practical consequences of the loss of property and employment as well as the effects of bereavement and individual trauma. Any mental health intervention must take account of the ongoing need the victims may have for safety, shelter, and food, as well as the demands created by reconstruction of homes and businesses. Thus, the short-term needs of a population may differ from the chronic problems and issues that require intervention (Freedy, Shaw, Garrell, & Masters, 1992; Freedy, Saladin, Kilpatrick, Resnick, & Saunders, 1994).

THE CHALLENGE TO PROFESSIONAL ROLES

Working in the trauma area confronts professionals in an unusually personal way because it requires the ability to accept the reality of human tragedy. In fact, history exemplifies the frequency with which the effects of trauma have been denied (van der Kolk, 1987). For example despite the enormous carnage and suffering in World War I, traumatized soldiers were often treated punitively by clinicians.

Herman (1992) has recently highlighted this issue:

> To study psychological trauma is to come face to face, both with human vulnerability in a natural world and for a capacity for evil in human nature. To study psychological trauma means bearing witness to horrible events. When these events are natural disasters or acts of God, those who bear witness sympathise readily with their victims, but when the traumatic events are of human design, those who bear witness are caught in the conflict between the perpetrator and victim. It is morally impossible to remain neutral in this conflict; the bystander is forced to take sides. (p. 7)

The experience of working in disaster settings does not confirm this view as many do not empathize readily with the victim after such events, particularly when a disaster becomes the subject of litigation. This brings to play a range of social attitudes and attributions that stereotype the victim as a person who is liable to exaggerate his or her distress and/or whose distress is the product of vulnerability thereby minimizing the reality for contribution of the traumatic experience. Herman (1992) describes the social process:

> It is very tempting to take the side of the perpetrator. All the perpetrators ask is that the bystander do nothing. . . . The victim, on the contrary, asks the bystander to share the burden or pain. . . . After every atrocity, one can expect to hear the same predictable apologies; "it never happened; the victim lies; the victim exaggerates; the victim brought it on herself; in any case, it is time to forget the past and move on." (p. 8)

Inevitably, dealing with the traumatized victim requires the therapist to empathize with and contemplate the nature of that victim's experience. This can be extremely challenging because the therapist is not protected by the host of technical skills that can be taught in psychotherapy training or the skills of clinical assessment. On one hand, such work can be extremely engaging professionally and provide a powerful sense of purpose. Some therapists may find this degree of identification unsettling and be unable to escape from their moral or judgmental perspectives. Equally, other therapists may be overwhelmed by their identification with the victim. Working in this area demands a constant examination and assessment of the internal dynamics of one's response to these issues. It emphasizes the importance of regular supervision or at least an opportunity for regular case discussions with a trusted colleague where such matters can be explored.

Dealing with traumatized populations challenges the normal professional impartiality and may demand that the clinician takes on roles of advocate and community activist. This advocacy role must counter any tendency to foster blame and seek scapegoats. Careful clinical assessment of both a patient's symptoms and past history must not be put to one side as a consequence of identifying with the victim's predicament. In individuals who inappropriately seek to attribute their misfortune to the trauma that befell them, facilitating this projection can be as destructive as denying the imprinting and disorganization caused by the traumatic experience itself.

Above all else, working with traumatized populations requires constant listening and acceptance of their attitudes and predicaments if an empathic service is to be provided. Clinicians whose experience comes from treating patients are placed in an unusual role in that they will often have contact with people of unusual resilience and strength who do not require any support or assistance. It is easy to reject such hardiness as being denial or an insensitivity to psychological issues. The need for the mental health professional to demonstrate the importance of his or her role may become unduly assertive about the need for prevention or debriefing in the light of people's independence. However, Alexander's (1993) conclusion after the "Piper Alpha" disaster in which an oil platform was destroyed in a massive fire and explosion with substantial loss of life is worth remembering:

> A major trap seems to be that helpers become pedlars of gloom and miserable statistics about the presence of post traumatic [sic] stress symptoms. However awful that the circumstances of a disaster [are], it is imperative that a positive approach be maintained. People do cope with adversity, and even in the worst tragedies one can (and should) find the positive gains.

A further issue can arise from the identification with the predicament of the victim. In a desire not to stigmatize those who develop symptoms, it can be claimed that posttraumatic stress disorder (PTSD) is a normal response to an abnormal situation (APA, 1987, 1994). Despite the intentions of such an assertion, it can have two effects. First, it can fail to identify the severity of the suffering of people who do develop major posttraumatic psychopathology and their need for very specific psychiatric treatment. Second, it can mean that a variety of important predisposing and perpetuating factors that are necessary to understand the type and severity of somebody's ongoing symptoms are ignored or not taken into account in their treatment. To the clinician, impartiality does not mean detachment in these environments.

ASSESSING DISASTER-RELATED TRAUMA

The theoretical underpinnings of early interventions into disaster were based on understandings about the effects of grief, loss and crisis theory (Raphael, 1986). Similarly Horowitz's (1986) pioneering interest into the effects of traumatic stress arose out of his clinical work with the effects of traumatic bereavement. Until the incorporation of PTSD in the Diagnostic and Statistical Manual III (DSM-III) (APA, 1980), much of the psychosocial support provided for disaster victims used this paradigm, which often meant that the recurring and intrusive nature of traumatic imagery was often misunderstood. Conversely, the increasing recognition of PTSD has meant that in more recent times the interaction between grief and PTSD has received relatively little discussion. This is an important clinical issue because the bereaved will often hold on to their recurring memories of the dead relative, and these images will have a very different meaning than the paralyzing fear that will go with traumatic remembrances. The importance of taking a broader perspective has been highlighted by Freedy et al.'s (1994) conceptualization of the impact of these events using a Hobfoll's conservation of resources stress model (Hobfoll, 1988, 1989). This highlights that the impact of a disaster may be at a variety of levels that go beyond the acute impact of the event and the losses involved.

It is important that individual disasters are carefully assessed because there are a range of possible outcomes for the communities and individuals involved (as described in Chapter 7, this volume). The nature of the health service provided needs to represent a flexible response determined by the careful assessment of the type of disaster. A variety of classifications of disasters and the victims have been proposed that focus on the highly variable outcomes (Taylor, 1989).

Firstly, some disasters affect a group of people who coincidentally happen to be at a particular point in time, such as in an aircraft accident. In the aftermath of such a disaster, the survivors will be scattered over wide geographical areas. A centrally based service designed to offer preventative and long-term follow-up would therefore be an impractical solution to the long-term needs of the victims. These disasters are characterized by their very high levels of danger and threat to the individuals exposed as well as by the substantial risk of death and being bereaved.

The above contrasts to disasters that affect circumscribed geographical regions and generally involve very substantial property loss, such as bush fires and hurricanes. The presence of mental health personnel intrusively interfering with the work of containing the immediate threat and flocking to the site of the emergency may jeopardize utilization of mental health interventions later (Berah, Jones, & Valent, 1984). It is important that somebody is clearly designated the authority to manage and ration services at this point. After such events, the services will be required for a long period, and the demand may initially be underestimated while the community deals with its distress by focusing on reconstruction.

A third type of disaster includes those where there can be very substantial property loss but because of their slow onset, there is relatively low threat to individuals and a low loss of life, such as floods and agricultural disasters. A variety of health problems tend to emerge following such disasters, and for this reason linking a prevention and intervention service with primary health care services is a particularly useful approach following such events. Finally, some disasters involve very little or no property loss or loss of life, but they entail a very high potential threat. One such example is the Three Mile Island disaster when there was a threatened melt down of a nuclear reactor (Bromet, Schulberg, & Dunn, 1982). Given that no actual harm may have occurred, focusing on the potential threat may lead to a heightened sensitivity and exaggerate people's sense of danger and lead to inappropriate litigation. On the other hand, if a population has been genuinely threatened, it is important that their experience is acknowledged, and the effects managed.

After every disaster, the role of the background psychological morbidity in a community should be taken into account. Data from a variety of epidemiologic studies such as the Epidemiological Catchment Area Study (Regier et al., 1984), would suggest that at any point, 20% of the population or more may be suffering from a psychiatric disorder and may be more likely to develop a mental health problem following such an event. For this reason, a disaster service needs to be able to deal with a full range of psychiatric illnesses and recognize that there may be a variety of groups where the disaster experience plays differing roles in determining their current pattern of disorder.

PHASES OF INTERVENTION

In planning mental health interventions after disasters, it is important to look at these events as a longitudinal process and to think about the issues at both the level of the community and the individuals. This implies, different models of intervention at different points and provides a way of conceptualizing the integration of prevention and treatment. The duration of the phases described are variable according to the nature of the disaster, for example the threat and impact phases may last for only seconds in an aircraft crash but for days or weeks in a flood.

Planning

Disasters can be anticipated with varying degrees of accuracy. Disaster plans embody the collective knowledge and risk assessment for any particular region. It is critical that in a general disaster plan, the role of mental health professionals is clearly defined. Sometimes government disaster planners are resistant to this idea as they believe the primary role of such plans is to develop strategies for dealing with the acute emergency. However, it is only if relationships are well established with mental health teams prior to disasters that proper integration will occur in the immediate aftermath. A second important aspect of planning will be to ensure the development of team and individual skills for dealing with trauma in mental health services. This has many immediate benefits. In most communities, very large numbers of people are traumatized in individual accidents that do not attract the public empathy or interest that surround disasters. The needs of these people, whether they be the victims of motor vehicle or industrial accidents, rape or crime, often are denied the same services and support available to people in mass disasters. Ideally, sophisticated services would exist for dealing with the victims of trauma on a day-to-day basis. They would then be ideally placed to be a central focus of a disaster plan. This involves training a number of other service providers as well as identifying specific strategies within their organization. The focus of such a service around an academic unit can act as a valuable source of information about lessons learned from other disasters.

An important ancillary role is to provide training for emergency service

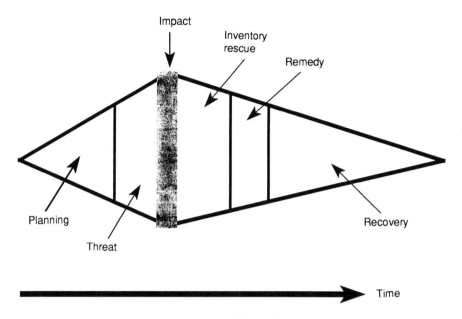

Figure 1. Phases of disaster intervention.

personnel about behavior in disasters and may include support for debriefing organizations within those structures (Mitchell & Dyregrov, 1993). If a working relationship exists prior to a disaster, the interactions in the face of an emergency will be substantially facilitated. Finally, there is a role for public education about issues of trauma.

Threat

With some disasters, no warning will exist about the tragedy (e.g., a plane crash). However, with certain natural disasters, such as hurricanes and bush fires, authorities are able to make reasonably accurate predictions of risk. Prior warnings of risk may occur minutes, hours, or days before the disaster impact. The community's response to warnings can play a very important role in improving survival-oriented behaviors. A critical element to heeding such warnings is the psychology of threat appraisal. Mental health professionals can assist in disaster management by discussing through the media at times of high risk of disaster the factors that influence people's tendency to minimize the risks and to maintain their sense of vulnerability. Access to the media depends on respected practitioners being readily available and willing to approach the press and negotiate program time. Individual journalists are often sensitive to the issues because they will have had first-hand experience of traumatic incidence as reporters. Information should be provided both about the nature of acute traumatic reactions and ways of adaptively managing the distress. Disaster planning and training can play important roles in decreasing the levels of exposure within communities.

Impact

During major disaster, there is generally little or no role to be played by the mental health professional, although useful advice can be provided about issues such as the importance of keeping families together and limiting the tours of duty of those involved in rescue and containment. A small percentage of people may require acute first aid. Accepting the clear direction of emergency workers is essential. Subsequent programs can be considerably undermined if mental health professional interfere with the immediate management of the event.

Inventory and Rescue

During this phase of the disaster, the community at large will be highly focused on the distress, loss, and suffering of the victims. It is essential that the immediate practical needs of the population are at first secured during this situation. The provision of basic services such as shelter, food, and water by a range of authorities including the military is an essential priority in major disasters. However, if a disaster has not devastated an entire community, the immediate response of the informal networks such as family and friends should not be underestimated, and these are often preferred to relief provided by disaster authority. Following the Ash Wednesday bush fire disaster in South Australia, very few families requested the provision of emergency housing (McFarlane & Raphael, 1984).

The bereaved are a group who will have special needs at this stage and should be supported through the process of body identification and encouraged to see the body to assist in the process of saying goodbye. Disasters that involve people outside their community such as the Sioux City Flight 242 crash in 1989 in which 112 died will demand that immediate care and support be provided for the victims and assistance with a variety of basic needs and psychological care offered (Jacobs, Quevillon, & Stricherz, 1990).

The priority roles for mental health professionals during this phase will be to assist in the acute debriefing of victims and emergency service personnel. As well, this is a critical stage for the development of linking with practical relief services. At times, welfare services may see themselves as equally being able to take on the role of the mental health needs of the population. It is important that clear lines of responsibility are negotiated at such a point. The need for sensitively providing guidance and debriefing for community leaders should also not be forgotten. The survivors should be encouraged to become involved in collective self-help efforts built on the interdependence of family, friends, and neighbors.

The designation of credible and well-informed media spokespersons can also play a very important role at this stage. Through the media, it may be possible to provide useful information to the victims about their reactions and the availability of future services. Similar information can be provided in group meetings at shelters, community centers, houses of worship, or other places where people congregate. In these meetings, people should be encouraged to share their experiences as well as be given useful ideas about stress management. In places with well-developed disaster plans, booklets discussing patterns of symptomatic response and ways of facilitating management of acute distress will be distributed at this stage. This is a phase when the community recovery processes can be encouraged by ceremonies of remembrance for the dead and the losses, and thanksgiving for survival and bravery during rescue. This phase of the disaster is the major opportunity for preventive interventions and will generally last for up to 2 weeks.

Remedy

Once the immediate disorganization and chaos that surrounds a disaster begins to settle and a detailed inventory of the losses has occurred, a critical planning phase is entered. On the basis of similar events, it should be possible at this point to make some predictions about the possible needs for treatment and assistance, both in terms of the numbers likely to seek such treatment and also the ideal location of services. Frequently, there is a significant delay between the occurrence of a disaster and the presentation for assistance, particularly when there are major tasks of reconstruction to attend to (McFarlane, 1986). The practical survival tasks will take precedence, and needs for treatment will only occur later in the picture. At this stage, it is important to try and provide a focused education program for primary health care workers who will have frequent and ongoing contact with the disaster victims. Often these trusted members of a local community provide an essential link to a traumatized community. Carefully appraising the needs of these primary health care providers and responding to their suggestions are important ways of winning trust. The development of these educational programs is something that can be accomplished prior to the event.

It is during this phase that much of the review of the existing disaster plans occurs. It is important that mental health service providers play an active role in this process. Frequently disaster plans are revised by internal audits within services. Often valuable information can be obtained when speaking to a range of disaster workers from other services.

At this point, the mental health professional may need to take on the role of advocate for the disaster victims. As is reflected in media reports, the overwhelming public distress and sympathy accompanying such events quickly dies and turns to indifference. In the longer term, often the mental health professional is alone in focusing on these people's ongoing predicaments from a variety of perspectives. This is an important role as often the victims come to be stigmatized and disempowered by the wider community if the process of reconstruction is difficult. The length of time in the remedy phase varies depending on the complexity of the disaster and associated relief efforts. Generally, the remedy phase requires 3 to 9 months to run its course.

The Recovery Phase

It is during this period that the majority of disaster victims will present for longer-term treatment and rehabilitation. Referral by word of mouth and reputation often plays an important role in their accepting the services that are available. A constant reappraisal of needs and outcomes is an important part of ongoing clinical work. In this regard, prior development of a quality assurance and monitoring program also needs to be an important priority. Given that each disaster is a unique event, it is essential to make sure that all victim groups receive services that are appropriate to their particular needs.

If financial compensation and litigation become involved, the mental health professional may become extensively involved as an expert witness. The traumatic stress community has provided an international focus for raising some of the issues arising out of the litigation of disasters. Frequently the compensation system focused on regional jurisdictions may not have previously had to conform a large number of litigants or complex legal questions. It is important that the mental heath professional assists lawyers in understanding some of the systems that have been used and developed to deal with litigation such as in the United Kingdom when, following the Zeebrugge ferry disaster, a group of senior counsel developed guidelines for the presentation of cases and evidence (Napier, 1991). In this disaster, a ferry that crossed the English Channel sank in 1988 when it set sail with the cargo doors open. This legal process significantly shortened the course of litigation and the risks to individual litigants of sustaining further major losses through prolonged legal battles. The possibility of being involved in litigation also emphasizes the importance of keeping careful and detailed records with an awareness that these may subsequently be subpoenaed as evidence in court proceedings.

Finally, the lessons learned from disasters may have important social and political consequences. The lessons from disasters are frequently forgotten because they do not impact in the larger elements of society. Maintaining the interest of politicians and public administrations can also be another important role played by mental health workers. Ultimately, it may be one of the few groups that act as a focal point for bearing witness to the ongoing suffering of a traumatized community.

Viewing disasters as a longitudinal process emphasizes the importance of differentiating the interventions at different stages as highlighted in Figure 1. Central to this is the concept of prevention. Primary prevention is involved in attempting to minimize the threat of disasters within the community and in teaching adaptive disaster-related behavior. As well, dealing with the acute distress of victims and emergency services workers is central to minimizing the emergence of PTSD and long-term disabilities and is focused on the impact and inventory phases. Not infrequently, the preventive interventions after disasters are not provided for some weeks, even months after the event. It is important to realize that what might be a highly effective preventive intervention in the days immediately after such a tragedy will have little effect in the longer term. This emphasizes the importance of careful assessment and diagnosis and the need to differentiate treatment and prevention. It is also important to stress that early treatment plays an important role in the prevention of secondary disabilities and emphasizes the need for active intervention in the remedy phase. In PTSD, these disabilities can be substantial, particularly because of the impact of the emotional withdrawal and numbing on family relationships. On occasions, the tragedy of a disaster is further compounded by the disruption of marital relationships because of the impact of the posttraumatic morbidity.

The receptiveness of communities to outside assistance can also change dramatically during the recovery phase. This has been called the development of "the trauma membrane" around the victims that develops within their community (Lindy, Green, Grace, & Titchener, 1983). The increasing development of avoidance and social withdrawal are also major factors that come to influence the willingness of traumatized people to go beyond their immediate social circle and community.

Within communities there can also be a range of responses. New leadership structures may arise as well as the scapegoating of some community members. Particularly, issues to do with compensation and disaster relief can prove to be extremely divisive. An awareness of these matters may only come through the ongoing contact with individual victims. Dealing with these broader matters through community leaders and community development programs is an ongoing responsibility. The recovery phase may persist from several years through a decade post-disaster. The longevity of the recovery phase is generally a function of the degree of community destruction, impoverished recovery resources, and in some cases prolonged litigation.

BIOPSYCHOSOCIAL MODEL OF INTERVENTION

Following disasters, clinicians are required to deal with a wide range of individual responses. First, information available from a range of disasters suggests that the prevalence of psychiatric disorder in a disaster-affected community will increase significantly, although the exact prevalence will vary according to the nature and severity of the disaster (see Chapter 7, this volume). Although PTSD will be the most common disorder, major depressive disorder, panic disorder, and generalized anxiety disorder will also occur with an increased prevalence and often coexist with PTSD (Green, Lindy, Grace, & Leonard, 1992; McFarlane & Papay, 1992). Alcohol abuse occurs in approximately 30% of those with a posttraumatic stress disorder and should always be assessed (McFarlane et al., 1994).

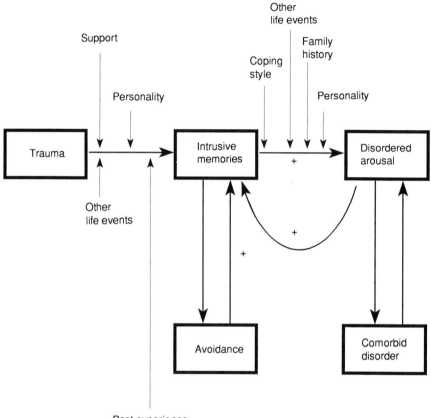

Figure 2. Biopsychosocial model of intervention.

However, a number of other victims will not have a diagnosable psychiatric disorder but will be distressed or grieving. Although distress has received remarkably little investigation within the psychological literature, diagnostic assessments and conceptual models need to differentiate between the normal distress response including grief and established psychiatric illness. Figure 2 presents a model for conceptualizing the distress response to traumatic events. Many people who do not develop long-term consequences of a traumatic experience also experience intrusive and distressing recollections and some avoidance phenomena in the period immediately after a disaster. These thoughts and feelings are not confined to the sufferers of PTSD. Rather, the intensity, associated behavioral dysfunction, and duration of these phenomena differentiate those with severe PTSD (McFarlane, 1992). The determinants of this initial distress response will be influenced by the factors listed in Figure 2. An individual's ability to modulate and contain this initial reaction plays an important role in determining whether this distress progresses to PTSD (McFarlane, 1992). This model provides a framework for assessment and intervention that should aim to focus on minimizing the role for the various vulnerability factors discussed by Green and Solomon (Chapter 7, this volume).

The acute intrusive cognitions about an event are likely to particularly reflect the attempts of the individual to come to terms with the meaning of the traumatic experience and to work through the psychological representations of the experience. The person's distress should be assessed in three areas. First, the meaning of the disaster to the individual's own self-image and behaviors should be determined. Frequently, in disasters people are confronted with their lack of control and helplessness. Second, disasters often confront individuals with reactions in other people that they otherwise would have little inkling of. This may particularly be the case if there has been contributory negligence in a disaster or somebody's behavior has jeopardized the victim's survival or contributed to the death of family members. Finally, the individual's distress may focus on that person's general feeling of the world being a changed and more dangerous place. These perceptions are influenced by a number of issues (Freedy, Kilpatrick, & Resnick, 1993) including previous life experiences, the person's coping skills, and his or her general arousability. The individual's ability to mobilize appropriate relationships and support constitutes another critical set of variables at this stage of the process of adaptation. Prevention aims to mobilize an individual's resources in the immediate postdisaster period and to minimize chance of irrational distortions in the developing meaning of the disaster.

The progression from a state of distress to more severe symptoms is influenced by range of other vulnerabilities, including a past or family history of psychiatric illness, neuroticism as a personality trait, a range of social mediators and other life events of trauma occurring after the disaster. Victims who dissociate during the disaster and also those who develop high levels of anxiety in the immediate aftermath (Cardena & Spiegel, 1993) are more likely to develop long-term disorder. For example, Weisaeth (1989) in a longitudinal study of the victims of a factory disaster indicated that the failure of insomnia, anxiety, and general agitation to settle in the first weeks was a major predictor of a posttraumatic stress disorder. This model allows the definition of high-risk groups in the aftermath of a disaster and emphasizes that the severity of exposure and the extent of losses alone are not good predictors. In a setting where only limited resources are available for prevention and acute treatment, victims with high levels of acute distress should be targeted.

It is important to emphasize that the development of chronic symptoms is the exception rather than the rule. These are circumstances that lead to opportunities for growth and increased self-respect. Many people go through a process of reassessing their values and priorities. These outcomes should be seen in the context of the large number of disaster-related factors and other individual characteristics that influence the patterns of adaptation.

ASSESSMENT

Strategic Issues

As described, major tasks of assessment following a disaster are to define the population requiring services and to develop the appropriate design of services. The initial assessment should consider the broad social and community impact of the disaster from a strategic perspective. Organizations that have had personnel in operational roles in the disaster who may require subsequent support should be identified and contact made with the appropriate leadership. The groups who are given the brief to assist in the immediate provision of relief such as the Red Cross and welfare groups should be contacted, and strategies should be developed to assist them to the structures and venues they have set up. This process of planning and assessment will mean that services complement and support each other, rather than finish up in competition that can be highly destructive for all those involved.

Regular meetings should be held with the appropriate organizations to review the ongoing relief effort and service provision to resolve any deficiencies and conflicts and to identify groups whose needs may not have been identified in the initial response phase. Frequent feedback should also be obtained from community leaders and representatives of the victims about the appropriateness of the services being provided. These meetings can also be used to identify high-risk groups according to a range of criteria (Freedy, Kilpatrick, & Resnick, 1993). After disasters many professionals will volunteer to assist. It is important to establish a register and to define their skills and qualifications; their ongoing work should also be assessed.

Against this background the remainder of this section deals with assessing the needs of individual victims.

Interview

The detail and emphasis of any assessment will depend upon the phase of the disaster—when it occurs—and whether the purpose of assessment is for prevention, treatment, or a compensation claim. Whatever the setting, a number of unusual issues arise. Many of the victims will have no previous contact with a mental health professional. Careful explanation and description of the process may be very helpful in dealing with initial issues of trust and apprehension. Greater time than is normally set aside for a clinical assessment may also be necessary. This is time well spent, as evidence suggests that the assessment process can have a significant therapeutic value (Turner, Thompson, & Rosser, 1993). Given that it is often the first occasion when the individual will give a detailed account of his or her experience and losses, in the context and examination of the individual's subsequent distress and symptoms, the assessment process can provide a very important opportunity for the ventilation of affect and the exploration of meanings. At the conclusion education and explanation are important so as to assist the development of a sense of control and the development of self-help strategies.

Assessment of the exposure to the traumatic event needs to include assessment of the severity of the perceived threat, the feelings and behavior during the event—particularly those of helplessness and terror—as well as the extent of dissociation. A detailed account of what the person actually witnessed and the most horrifying aspects of this element need to be documented. If family members or friends have died, the circumstances and attempts to render assistance should be clarified. How the news of the death was ascertained can also be a critical determinant of outcome. The extent of property loss and its consequences also have important influences upon long-term adjustment. Finally, the general context of the disaster and surrounding life events should also be clarified. These elements of the assessment interview can be critical to the development of an adequate therapeutic alliance.

The importance of hearing about the individual's experience in the disaster can distract from obtaining an adequate assessment of the individual's subsequent symptoms and preoccupations. A thorough diagnostic assessment should be completed. A personal and life history also assists in creating an understanding of the context in which the disaster experience has occurred and the matrix of protective (e.g., adequate social support) and vulnerability factors (e.g., prior psychopathology) that will influence the individual's coping. It is particularly important to document prior traumatic experiences and episodes of major loss and the subsequent patterns of adjustment as these provide insights into possible responses to current circumstances.

Psychometric Assessment

Questionnaires have a very useful role to play in the postdisaster setting. First they can be helpful in screening populations and defining those who are at particular risk and likely to benefit from interventions. This approach will be necessary in situations where the available resources mean that preventative interventions cannot be provided to all those exposed, or this might be impractical for other reasons. Second, this instrument can play a useful role in monitoring treatment. At times it can be difficult to estimate the frequency and intensity of intrusive and distressing recollections clinically. The Impact of Events Scale (Horowitz, Wilner, & Alvarez, 1979,) is a 15-item measure of intrusion and avoidance that is readily accepted because of its face validity. General levels of symptomatic distress can be measured using instruments such as the 28-item version of the General Health Questionnaire (Goldberg, 1972) or the SCL 90-R (Derogatis, 1983). There is a need to standardize assessments in these settings, and two groups have made specific recommendations that should serve as a standard (Freedy et al., 1993; Raphael, Lindin & Weisaeth, 1989).

Other Issues

Considerable research is occurring into a variety of other methods of assessment of the victims of trauma. These include laboratory measurement of the startle response and the patterns of physiological distress such as increased heart rate and skin conductors triggered by exposures to reminders of trauma (Pitman et al., 1990). A range of possibly specific biological abnormalities are being documented including patterns of cortisol, norepinephrine, and dopamine response (Yehuda, Southwick, Mason, Ma, & Giller, 1992; Yehuda, Resnick, Kahana, Giller, 1993). However, it is premature to routinely measure these in a clinical setting, particularly because of the time and cost involved.

The assessment of other family members is also an important issue in the disaster setting. Unlike many other traumas, it is frequently the case that more than one family member may have been directly exposed to the trauma. A series of important interactions can occur between individual family members that have significant bearing on adjustment. To begin with, if one person has been particularly adversely effected, this will be a constant reminder of the effects of the disaster and may prevent the family from working through the experience. Frequently, the intensity of preoccupation resonates between family members and effects many interactions such as the patterns of parenting. Children quickly pick up their parents' anxiety and react to any overprotection with an increase in their vigilance including the possibility of a recurrence of the disaster. In this way, the reexperiencing symptoms of a PTSD can be an important indicator of the family's pattern of response as well as the extent of individual traumatization. These issues will often only emerge if all the members of a family are assessed.

Many victims of disasters will primarily present with physical symptoms (Shalev, Bleich, & Ursano, 1990; Escobar et al., 1992). For this reason, it is important that general practitioners and internists who are likely to have contact with disaster-effected populations are aware of how these symptoms may be indicative of underlying PTSD. Once a detailed physical assessment has excluded any significant underlying organic pathology, it is important that the underlying psychophysiological origin of these symptoms is explained.

INTERVENTION AND TREATMENT APPROACHES

Psychosocial Interventions

The management of a disaster requires a broad psychosocial approach that addresses a range of needs and issues and does not just provide for the immediate clinical needs of the victims. The section of this chapter dealing with the phases of a disaster addresses a number of these issues. There is a primacy of needs in the aftermath of disaster, and the victims should be facilitated in dealing with issues such as shelter, clothing, and food. Similarly, in the longer term, the ongoing practical consequences of the disaster are a major cause of distress and predict chronic symptoms of distress and maladjustment (McFarlane & Papay, 1992). Any psychological service provided in the aftermath of disaster should be closely linked to the services addressing these welfare needs so that access to the available services can be facilitated.

In disasters where the victims assemble at registration points, mental health professions have important roles to play in assisting distress victims to deal with a number of immediate issues. A site coordinator should be appointed who designates roles according to the individual skills of the professionals involved, monitors their performance and ensures that their time at the disaster site is rationed appropriately (Jacobs et al., 1990). The roles may include dealing with distressed families arriving at the scene of the disaster, having to deliver a formal death notice, and assisting victims establish contact with relatives and other sources of assistance. Often in these settings, there are considerable periods of waiting, and the information available about the casualties and damage may only be sparse. Rumors often abound, and these must constantly be checked. Providing support and an opportunity for appropriate reflection and recounting of the trauma creates a sense of containment and reordering in the face of chaos.

Careful registration procedures are necessary so as to keep track of the survivors and to ensure consistent contact wherever possible. Protecting the victims from the inappropriate and intrusive interest of the media and attorneys is also an important role. The media can reasonably expect some contact with the survivors and relatives. At this stage a plan for providing information to the media should be developed with several ingredients (Gist & Stolz, 1982). The range of reactions should be described with an emphasis on the notion that these are normal reactions to abnormal circumstances and the need to share these reactions. The help available should be described. If the disaster involves an airline or similar organization, it is important to establish a formalized link for the two-way provision of information. Work in this area also may allow the establishment of contacts with organizations involved in the immediate disaster management who may subsequently require debriefing.

Prevention

Given the wide range of responses, a significant number of therapeutic skills are necessary to deal with the loss, trauma, and anxiety that arise in the aftermath of a disaster. Preventative interventions should be directed toward those who have a particularly high probability of developing symptoms. However the management of these groups requires skill and experience. High-risk groups include people who have intense exposure or who may have sustained significant injury or loss. It is also important to assess the perceived meaning of the event. These interventions are often most effective when provided in a group setting. The technique of critical-incident stress debriefing was developed in the late 1970s to provide early interventions in group settings for emergency service personnel (Mitchell & Dyregrov, 1993). The important ingredients of this approach include confrontation with the experience, education about patterns of response as well as a direct expression of thoughts and feelings about the experience. The aim is also to facilitate the development of the practical mastery of these situations. Similar techniques are used in individual interventions.

Unlike the critical-incident assessment debriefing model, which is often carried out by a respected peer, individual prevention is often provided by a trained mental health professional. This may extend over a series of sessions and be more focused than group debriefing. Early interventions are particularly helpful because they can modify the development of inappropriate guilt or perceptions about an individual's behavior during the event. The meaning of a traumatic experience will often develop in the immediate aftermath as the person learns more about the circumstances of the trauma and the experiences of other people in the disaster. Preventative interventions can play an important role in modifying misinterpretations or inappropriate guilt. Often, one of the hardest issues to confront is that a person was able to do nothing either to protect himself or save those in the near vicinity. Dealing with these issues of helplessness and powerlessness can play an important role in preventing the long-term traumatic stress response. Given the importance of using preventative approaches wherever possible, there is much evidence to suggest that some people go on to develop significant PTSD despite this approach being used (see Smith, North, McCool, & Shea, 1990). The provision of preventative interventions may lull service providers into a false sense of security that more sophisticated treatment services will not be required in the longer term.

At times, it may be necessary to extend what was initially a preventative intervention into more prolonged treatment.

Common Elements of Treatment

A variety of treatment approaches have been proposed to deal with the effects of trauma. At this stage, there is not sufficient evidence to suggest thesuperiority of one form of treatment over another (Brom, Kleber, & Defares, 1989). These treatment approaches share a number of common goals that include:

1. To develop a realistic appraisal of the threat and the opportunities for response. On one hand this may involve confronting an individual's denial of the realistic danger or on the other hand developing a sense of reassurance about the lack of opportunities to respond.
2. To encourage the focus on current safety and to assist individuals in dealing with the traumatic memories by focusing on the time when they first felt out of danger following the disaster. This may involve ensuring that the individuals do not become retraumatized by the process of treatment if they feel unable or unready to confront the traumatic memories.
3. To facilitate the progression from the sense of being a helpless victim to a sense of being a survivor. This involves shifting away from a sense of

persecution by the disaster to a sense of being able to build upon the experience and to develop a future sense of goals.
4. To assist in the development of affective modulation because the victims of disaster often fluctuate between numbing and withdrawal and hypervigilance and over arousal. This can be done both through focused activity and specific anxiety-management strategies.
5. To maintain intimate and rewarding social relationships rather than progressive withdrawal and social detachment. This often involves dealing with the sense of irritability and preoccupation associated with traumatic reminders.
6. To overcome cognitive and behavioral avoidance of both internal cues and external reminders of trauma by assisting the individual to work through the meaning of his or her traumatic exposure and to gain a sense of mastery over the individual's intrusive recollections.

There is an increasingly sophisticated literature about treatment methods in PTSD. However, many clinicians will be familiar with a number of approaches and tend to be eclectic in their management. Such flexibility is an important element of dealing with the multiple and variable needs of individual disaster victims (Marmar, Foy, Kagan, & Pynoos, 1993). It is important to match the quality of an individual patient's distress and the clustering of that person's symptoms to particular treatment approaches. For example, a patient who has extremely intense avoidance, to the point where more than a peripheral discussion of a traumatic event is impossible, may make a dynamic psychotherapy or cognitive–behavioral intervention impractical. However, after a period of treatment with an antidepressant such as fluoxetine or dothiepin, it may be possible to use one of these approaches.

A patient in whom the meaning of the experience raises a number of issues and a variety of reflections about the reactions of others during the disaster may be particularly suited to a dynamic psychotherapeutic approach. For others, a cognitive–behavioral therapy provides an opportunity to both simultaneously deal with the individual's avoidance as well as the need to rework the traumatic experience. Thus, a process of education and negotiation needs to occur with a person before embarking on a particular treatment approach. Trust is an essential ingredient of the therapeutic approach, and the patient must feel secure and confident that the therapist is not only genuine, empathic, and warm, but also able to cope with bearing witness to the trauma and understanding its significance.

Specific Methods of Treatment

The specific techniques of the different psychotherapies will be only briefly summarized. Firstly, dynamic psychotherapy for PTSD is based on understanding the conscious and unconscious meanings that develop within the traumatic event and its aftermath. The approach depends upon the retelling of the experience. The challenge for the therapist is to ensure that the associated affect does not become disorganizing and overwhelming. There needs to be a slow confrontation of the patient's feelings of helplessness, shame, and vulnerability, particularly as the conflictual meanings of the trauma begin to emerge.

The important therapeutic ingredients include the provision of support, helping the patient develop more realistic appraisals of his or her affect and responses and developing strategies to contain the trauma experience in tolerable doses. Maladaptive avoidance strategies such as compulsive work, the excessive use of alcohol and drugs or thrill-seeking behavior need to be explored and challenged. More detailed accounts of the type of treatment can be found elsewhere (Lindy, 1986; Marmar, 1991).

Several forms of cognitive–behavioral therapy exist. A combination of classical and operant conditioning has been used to explain the development and persistence of acute symptoms associated with traumatic events (Kilpatrick, Veronen, & Resick, 1979; Keane, Fairbank, Caddell, & Zimering, 1989). Consistent with this learning theory explanation, Meichenbaum's (1985) stress inoculation training (SIT) has been successfully adapted for use with the victims of violent trauma (Veronen & Kilpatrick, 1983; Best, Amick, Veronen, & Kilpatrick, 1987). More strictly cognitive therapies that focus on information processing (i.e., the meaning of traumatic memories) and issues such as control, predictability, trust, self-esteem, and intimacy have also been successfully used with trauma victims (Foa, Steketee, & Rothbaum, 1989; Resick & Schnicke, 1992). In these latter approaches, the central therapeutic modality is the use of exposure strategies to reduce the intrusions and hyperarousal. The associated maladaptive assumptions and traumatic meanings are addressed using typical cognitive restructuring strategies. The central cognitive strategies involve examining whether the catastrophic outcome could have been predicted. Second, the issue is to determine whether the trauma could have been modified by any action of the individual, and finally, the issue of individual responsibility is examined—in particular whether the individual could have behaved in any way that had significant implications on the outcomes.

The role of drug treatment should always be considered in the context of the ongoing psychological and social management of the trauma response and is discussed in detail by Kudler and Davidson (Chapter 4, this volume). Medicines are of particular use in controlling the symptoms of disordered arousal. Particularly when PTSD is complicated by major depressive disorder or panic disorder, control of these associated symptoms can assist greatly in the victim's ability to participate in psychotherapy (Friedman, 1993; van der Kolk et al., 1994). There is little evidence to suggest that the use of medication interferes with the psychotherapeutic process.

Predictors of Outcome

No intervention modality is universally effective with every case, and all forms of treatment have the capacity to worsen people's symptoms. Therefore, the constant monitoring of people's progress and restitution is an important ingredient of any program. Additionally, little information is available about the predictors of outcome from treatment, in contrast to the natural history of the trauma response. It would appear that one of the best predictors of outcome is early intervention. This prevents the development of patterns of secondary morbidity and possible may prevent the patterns of disordered arousal from becoming entrenched. Victims who develop significant levels of comorbidity, particularly phobic and anxiety disorders or bipolar disorder, seem to do particularly badly (McFarlane & Papay, 1992). It is also often the case that the disaster begins a progression of adverse life experiences compounded by the dislocation and financial strains of reconstruction. This can also serve to maintain the individual's sense of traumatization and significantly limit the effects of intervention. An individual's personality strengths are also an important issue to take into account. Hardiness and a general willingness to confront one's fears and dangers also prevent the emergence of avoidance and social estrangement. People who are naturally introverted appear to have greater difficulty managing and overcoming these symptoms of traumatic stress.

SPECIAL ISSUES

Assisting the victims of a disaster requires flexibility and a willingness to constantly reassess one's interventions. A series of examples are given of specific difficulties or issues that can arise in the treatment of disaster victims. These case examples are from patients treated after an Australian bush fire disaster that devastated large areas of rural country in 1983 with considerable threat to life. The victims often not only lost their livelihood but also their homes, which meant the complete loss of their possessions. The individual details have been changed to disguise the identity of the people.

The Value of the Single Intervention

A 29-year-old farmer had been shooting kangaroos in a sunflower crop close to a boundary fence 3 weeks prior to the disaster. He was seen by a neighboring farmer who berated him because of his conservationist ideals. At the height of the disaster, the conservationist was trapped in his vehicle trying to escape, and his neighbor discovered his charred remains.

When seen 3 years after the disaster, this man had regular nightmares and continued to be intensely distressed about his neighbor's death. On the Impact of Events Scale, which measures levels of intrusion and avoidance, he had a score of 65 out of a possible 75. It was impossible to provide any prolonged treatment because the man lived many miles from a therapist. He was seen for two interviews, one an assessment and a second therapeutic session that focused on some of the recurring intrusive memories and thoughts about the disaster. This session explored his profound sense of guilt about what he had said to his neighbor about killing the kangaroos. He had ridiculed him about not being able to cope with the necessity of killing wildlife that was damaging his crops. He was extremely distressed by what he had seen of his neighbor's body. His reaction was much more intense than he could ever have anticipated, which contributed to his sense of guilt, as their argument had partly focused on coping with being able to tolerate killing.

Clarifying this link helped this man to provide a structure for understanding why these memories had been preying so intensely on his mind. Six months after this session, the same man again completed the Impact of Events Scale and had a score of only 3. Normally a longer intervention would have been provided. This suggests that, given a framework for meaning, many victims are able to resolve distressing and preoccupying issues effectively without lengthy contact with a therapist.

Dealing with Lack of Control

People who have been successful in their lives and been able to plan effectively can find disasters difficult to reconcile. A 60-year-old man had attempted to escape the oncoming fire and at one point had turned down a road to flee the flames. Unbeknownst to him, the fire had jumped the apparent front, and he drove into a situation of extraordinary danger. He came extremely close to losing his life. He was completely unaware that had he turned in the other direction at the intersection, he would only have had to travel several hundred meters to have reached safety. The man was intensely distressed and preoccupied for many years about how his incorrect choice (and therefore stupidity, in his perception) had placed him in danger. He was unable to accept his failure in judgment.

Such cases are common, and cognitive–behavioral approaches can be useful in these instances. This man was required repeatedly to go through the events of the day of the disaster and to focus on his intense fear and distress. A critical issue in treatment was to discuss his reasoning at the intersection on the road. This made him confront the fact that if he had only had the information available to him at the time of the fire, he would have still made the decision to turn away from the fire. It was only as he came to accept that he had no way of knowing that turning in the opposite direction would have taken him to safety that he came to tolerate his sense of helplessness and lack of control. Ultimately, he came to accept his vulnerability with a sense of relief.

The Problem of Causing Another's Death

At the height of the blaze, a 36-year-old woman had panicked and left her husband in the open as the fire storm was about to hit. As a consequence, he died, having boiled to death as he attempted to find shelter in a water tank.

Her treatment posed a major problem because at one level it was undeniable that she had panicked and contributed to her husband's death. He would have survived if they had sought shelter in the car as the fire front passed. The intense distress she experienced facing this issue was further compounded because she had had a highly ambivalent marriage and had been planning to separate from her husband. She spoke of the experience of the disaster in a very rigid and inflexible way. The idea that she should discuss the trauma became so distressing that she refused to enter into treatment.

When seen 8 years later, she remained severely symptomatic but continued to reject the need for any psychotherapeutic intervention. This case emphasizes that on occasions it can be extremely difficult to establish a treatment alliance that permits the therapist to explore the trauma, and this is particularly the case when guilt is a prominent affect. In such cases, the provision of support and psychopharmacological treatment may be all that can be offered. Contact could also be maintained through an integrated health and welfare service that might permit the development of the trust necessary to accept treatment by initially addressing the person's practical needs.

The Interaction of Symptom Patterns in Families

A middle-aged couple presented for treatment following the destruction of their farm in which 7,000 sheep had been burned and a relative had been seriously injured. The husband was particularly concerned about his wife's ongoing distress. However, she stated that she was not distressed about the disaster, the only problem was that she kept on being upset when people spoke of it. Given the enormous resources involved in reconstruction and ongoing litigation surrounding the disaster, it was impossible not to frequently confront the issues. Her avoidance was initially dealt with by treating her underlying anxiety symptoms with a tricyclic antidepressant. Once her distress was less intense, she began to be able to talk about her terrifying experience. What emerged, was her rapid recognition that her husband had in fact actively encouraged her avoidance and he himself was unable to cope with his own recollections and distress. Treating this couple together provided important insights as to how their symptoms interacted and how the husband, who was more severely traumatized, had been able to distract attention from his distress by focusing on his wife's symptoms.

The Complication of Major Depression

A woman had discovered her 27-year-old son's body and had only been able to recognize him because she identified the pocket knife that lay in the ashes. She readily welcomed the offer of treatment that initially focused on dealing with her grief as well as her intense and traumatic recollections of finding her son's body. She had some difficulty initially accepting the need to control these distressing recollections as she did not want to lose the memory of her son. However, treatment became prolonged and difficult, but it increasingly emerged that she had developed a major vegetative disorder, characterized by diurnal mood variation, weight loss, and psychomotor retardation. Treatment with an antidepressant led to a significant improvement in her mood, which again allowed her to continue resolving her feelings of traumatization and grief.

In the subsequent years, she developed a recurrent depressive disorder, and at these times, she tended to have a major recurrence of her posttraumatic symptoms. Ongoing prophylaxis of her mood disorder played an important role in ensuring her long-term stabilization.

Children and Separation

After this disaster, children were often separated from their parents for several days because of the prolonged period required to contain the fires and then deal with injured livestock. Michelle was a 9-year-old at the time of the disaster and did not see her parents for 3 days. During this time she believed that they both had been killed.

As she was an only child, her parents were particularly concerned about her state. Her mother became increasingly overprotective, wishing to anticipate and prevent ongoing perceived threats. However the mother was also traumatized by the disaster, and her intrusive recollections were often triggered by her daughter's distress.

This case demonstrates the need to look at the transgenerational effects of trauma and the interaction between the symptoms of parents and children. The mother was unable to confront her ongoing sense of anxiety and protectiveness as being of any consequence, and the family dropped out of treatment. The daughter went on to develop significant disabling anxiety symptoms in late adolescence. This case emphasizes the need to deal with the issues of separation in the immediate aftermath of a disaster, when there may have been greater acceptance of the mother's distress as a problem, because of the potential for long-term disruption.

Emergency Service Personnel as Victims

A senior ambulance officer was off duty and at home when the disaster struck. At the height of the fire, he was evacuated to a safe area and required to provide first aid to many burned and injured victims. One child, the same age as his own daughter particularly played on his mind. As he was himself a victim of the event, he was unable to use his normal coping mechanisms to distance himself from the distress of his victims. He often feared that he had undertreated some of the injured and, as a consequence, lost much of his confidence at work. A major focus of this man's cognitive–behavioral treatment was to focus on the exact steps and actions that he took during the disaster and to reappraise the reality of the circumstance. In actuality, he had provided optimal treatment and first aid and, in fact, had been commended for his actions. Focusing both on his distress and accepting the fact that he was also a victim who had experienced a profound sense of helplessness in the circumstances again allowed him to return to the work environment where he could face the thought of having to deal with children who had been injured.

Dissociative Symptoms

Dissociative symptoms play a major problem in treatment because for some individuals, when arousal becomes too intense, they can no longer involve themselves in the therapeutic process but, rather, dissociate. A man had been trapped in the fire and was in the vicinity of several other vehicles in which six people died. The interior of his car was substantially damaged, indicating that the temperature had reached over 130°, although it did not ignite. He had also evacuated a seriously burned man who subsequently died in the back of his car. It was only some six sessions into a cognitive–behavioral program that he was able to describe the way he frequently dissociated both during treatment sessions and when exposed to a range of traumatic triggers. If anything, it appeared that an attempt to work through his traumatic images had intensified his distress and worsened his dissociative response. An awareness of this potential is important and possibly a negative effect of such treatment. His symptoms were better stabilized using a more supportive and interpretive approach supplemented by the use of antidepressants.

CONCLUSIONS

These case examples exemplify a number of the problems and issues that can arise in treating the victims of disasters. They emphasize (1) that there are no simple solutions in treatment with some patients and (2) the need to frequently reassess the effects of treatment and possibly adopt some alternative approach.

In conclusion, the treatment of disaster victims demands an appraisal of the broader impact of the event and the tailoring of the service to the context and phase of the disaster. This demands flexibility and renegotiation with the affected community and individual victims. Finally research can play an important role in this context because it allows an objective assessment of the needs for services and the targeting of the groups most likely to benefit from treatment.

REFERENCES

Alexander, D. A. (1993). The Piper Alpha oil rig disaster. In J. P. Wilson & B. Raphael (Eds.), *International handbook of traumatic stress syndromes* (pp. 461–470). New York: Plenum Press.

American Psychiatric Association. (1980). *Diagnostic and Statistical Manual of Mental Disorders* (3rd ed.). Washington, DC: American Psychiatric Association.

American Psychiatric Association. (1987). *Diagnostic and statistical manual of mental disorders* (3rd ed.-revised). Washington, DC: Author.

American Psychiatric Association. (1994). *Diagnostic and statistical manual of mental disorders* (4th ed.). Washington, DC: Author.

Berah, E. F., Jones, H. J., & Valent, P. (1984). The experience of a mental health team involved in the early phase of a disaster. *Australian and New Zealand Journal of Psychiatry, 18*(4), 354–358.

Best, C. L., Amick, A. E., Veronen, L. J., & Kilpatrick, D. G. (1987). Manual for stress inoculation training treatment for rape victims. Medical University Press: Charleston, SC.

Brom, D., Kleber, R. J., & Defares, P. B. (1989). Brief psychotherapy for posttraumatic stress disorders. *Journal of Consulting and Clinical Psychology, 57*(5), 607–612.

Bromet, E. J., Schulberg, H. C., & Dunn, L. O. (1982). Reactions of psychiatric patients to the Three Mile Island nuclear accident. *Archives of General Psychiatry, 39*(6), 725–730.

Cardena, E., & Spiegel, D. (1993). Dissociative reactions to the San Francisco Bay area earthquake of 1989. *American Journal of Psychiatry, 150*(3), 474–478.

Derogatis, L. R. (1983). *SCL-90-R: Administration, scoring and procedures manual-II for the revised version* (2nd ed.). Towson, MD: Clinical Psychometric Research.

Escobar, J. I., Canino, G., Rubio-Stipec, M., & Bravo, M. (1992). Somatic symptoms after a natural disaster: A prospective study. *American Journal of Psychiatry, 149*, 965–967.

Foa, E. B., Steketee, G., & Rothbaum, B. O. (1989). Behavioral/cognitive conceptualizations of post-traumatic stress disorder. *Behavior Therapy, 20*(2), 155–176.

Freedy, J. R., Kilpatrick, D. G., & Resnick, H. (1993). Natural disaster and mental health: Theory, assessment and intervention. *Journal of Social Behavior and Personality, 8*(5), 49–103.

Freedy, J. R., Saladin, M. E., Kilpatrick, D. G., Resnick, H. S., & Saunders, B. E. (1994). Understanding acute psychological distress following natural disaster. *Journal of Traumatic Stress, 7*(2), 257–273.

Freedy, J. R., Shaw, D. L., Garrell, M. P., & Masters, C. (1992). Towards an understanding of the impact of natural disasters: An application of the conservation of resources stress model. *Journal of Traumatic Stress, 5*, 441–454.

Friedman, M. J. (1993). Psychobiological and pharmacological approaches to treatment. In J. P. Wilson & B. Raphael (Eds.), *International Handbook of Traumatic Stress Syndromes* (pp. 785–794). New York: Plenum Press.

Gist, R., & Stolz, S. B. (1982). Mental health promotion and the media: Community response to the Kansas City hotel disaster. *American Psychologist, 37*, 1136–1139.

Goldberg, D. P. (1972). *The detection of psychiatric illness by questionnaire.* London: Oxford University Press.

Green, B. L., Lindy, J. D., Grace, M. C., & Leonard, A. C. (1992). Chronic posttraumatic stress disorder and diagnostic comorbidity in a disaster sample. *Journal of Nervous and Mental Disease, 180*(12), 760–766.

Herman, J. (1992). *Trauma and recovery.* New York: Basic Books.

Hobfoll, S. E. (1988). *The cology of stress.* Washington, DC: Hemisphere.

Hobfoll, S. E. (1989). Conservation of resources: A new attempt at conceptualizing stress. *American Psychologist, 44*, 513–524.

Horowitz, M. J. (1986). *Stress-response syndromes.* New York: Jason Aronson.

Horowitz, M. J., Wilner, N., & Alvarez, W. (1979). Impact of Event Scale: A measure of subjective stress. *Psychosomatic Medicine, 41*(3), 209–218.

Jacobs, G. A., Quevillon, R. P., & Stricherz, M. (1990). Lessons from aftermath of Flight 232. Practical considerations for the mental health professions response to air disasters. *American Psychologist, 45*, 1329–1329.

Keane, T. M., Fairbank, J. A., Caddell, J. M., & Zimering, R. T. (1989). Implosive (flooding) therapy reduces symptoms of PTSD in Vietnam combat veterans. *Behavior Therapy, 20*(2), 245–260.

Kilpatrick, D. G., Veronen, L. J., & Resick, P. A. (1979). Assessment of the aftermath of rape: Changing patterns of fear. *Journal of Behavioral Assessment, 1*, 133–148.

Lindy, J. D. (1986). An outline for the psychoanalytic psychotherapy of post-traumatic stress disorder. In C. R. Figley (Eds.), *Trauma and its wake* (pp. 195–212). New York: Brunner/Mazel.

Lindy, J. D., Green, B. L., Grace, M., & Titchener, J. (1983). Psychotherapy with survivors of the Beverly Hills Supper Club fire. *American Journal of Psychotherapy, 37*(4), 593–610.

Marmar, C. R. (1991). Brief dynamic psychotherapy of post-traumatic stress disorder. *Psychiatric Annals, 21*(7), 405–414.

Marmar, C. R., Foy, D., Kagan, B., & Pynoos, R. S. (1993). An integrated approach for treating posttraumatic stress. In J. M. Oldham, M. B. Riba, & A. Tasman (Eds.), *Review of psychiatry* (pp. 239–272). Washington, DC: American Psychiatric Press.

McFarlane, A. C. (1986). Posttraumatic morbidity of a disaster: A study of cases presenting for psychiatric treatment. *Journal of Nervous and Mental Disease, 174*(1), 4–13.

McFarlane, A. C. (1992). Avoidance and intrusion in posttraumatic stress disorder. *Journal of Nervous and Mental Disease, 180*(7), 439–445.

McFarlane, A. C., Atchison, M., Rafalowicz, E., & Papay, P. (1994). Physical symptoms in posttraumatic stress disorder. *Journal of Psychosomatic Research, 38*, 715–726.

McFarlane, A. C., & Papay, P. (1992). Multiple diagnoses in posttraumatic stress disorder in the victims of a natural disaster. *Journal of Nervous and Mental Disease, 180*(8), 498–504.

McFarlane, A. C., & Raphael, B. (1984). Ash Wednesday: The effects of a fire. *Australian and New Zealand Journal of Psychiatry, 18*(6), 341–353.

Meichenbaum, D. (1985). *Stress inoculation training.* New York: Pergamon Press.

Mitchell, J. T., & Dyregrov, A. (1993). Traumatic stress in disaster workers and emergency personnel: Prevention and intervention. In J. P. Wilson & B. Raphael (Eds.), *International handbook of traumatic stress syndromes* (pp. 905–914). New York: Plenum Press.

Napier, M. (1991). The medical and legal trauma of disasters. *The Medical and Legal Traumas of Disasters, 59*(3), 157–181.

Pitman, R. K., Orr, S. P., Forgue, D. F., Altman, B., de Jong, J. B., & Herz, L. R. (1990). Psychophysiologic responses to combat imagery of Vietnam veterans with posttraumatic stress disorder versus other anxiety disorders. *Journal of Abnormal Psychology, 99*, 49–54.

Raphael, B. (1986). *When disaster strikes: A handbook for the caring professions.* London: Hutchinson.

Raphael, B., Linden, T., & Weisaeth, L. (1989). A research method for the study of psychological and psychiatric aspects of disaster. *Acta Psychiatrica Scandinavica* [Supplement] *353*, 8.

Regier, D. A., Myers, J. K., Kramer, M., Robins, L. N., Blazer, D. G., Hough, R. L., Eaton, W. W., & Locke, B. Z. (1984). The NIMH Epidemiological Catchment Area Program. *Archives of General Psychiatry, 41*, 934–941.

Resick, P. A., & Schnicke, M. K. (1992). Cognitive processing therapy for sexual assault victims. *Journal of Consulting and Clinical Psychology, 60*(5), 748–756.

Shalev, A., Bleich, A., & Ursano, R. (1990). Posttraumatic stress disorder: Somatic comorbidity and effort tolerance. *Psychosomatics, 31*, 197–203.

Smith, E. M., North, C. S., McCool, R. E., & Shea, J. M. (1990). Acute postdisaster psychiatric disorders: Identification of persons at risk. *American Journal of Psychiatry, 147*(2), 202–206.

Taylor, A.J.W. (1989). Victims of crime as victims of disaster. *Australian and New Zealand Journal of Psychiatry, 23*, 403–406.

Turner, S. W., Thompson, J., & Rosser, R. M. (1993). The Kings Cross fire: Early psychological reactions and implications for organizing a "phase-two" response. In J. P. Wilson & B. Raphael (Eds.), *International handbook of traumatic stress syndromes* (pp. 451–459). New York: Plenum Press.

van der Kolk, B. A. (1987). *Psychological trauma.* Washington, DC: American Psychiatric Press.

van der Kolk, B. A., Dreyfuss, D., Michaels, M., Shera, D., Berkowitz, R., Fisler, R., & Saxe, G. (1994). Fluoxetine in Posttraumatic Stress Disorder. *Journal of Clinical Psychiatry, 55,* 517–522.

Veronen, L. J., & Kilpatrick, D. G. (1983). Stress management for rape victims. In D. Meichenbaum & M. E. Jaremko (Eds.), *Stress reduction and prevention.* New York: Plenum Press.

Weisaeth, L. (1989). The stressors and the post-traumatic stress syndrome after an industrial disaster. Special issue: Traumatic stress: Empirical studies from Norway. *Acta Psychiatrica Scandinavica, 80,* 25–37.

Yehuda, R., Resnick, H., Kahana, B., & Giller, E. (1993). Long lasting hormonal alternations to extreme stress in humans: Normative or maladaptive. *Psychosomatic Medicine, 55,* 287–297.

Yehuda, R., Southwick, S. M., Mason, J. W., Ma, X., & Giller, E. L. (1992). Urinary catecholamine and severity of symptoms in PTSD. *Journal of Nervous and Mental Disease, 180,* 321–325.

13

Accidental Injury

Approaches to Assessment and Treatment

CONNIE L. BEST and DAVID P. RIBBE

INTRODUCTION

In an earlier chapter in this volume (Chapter 8), Scotti and colleagues offered a definition of accidental injury as those unintentional injuries caused by human error, technological disasters, or other unforeseen circumstances. Included in this definition are motor vehicle accidents, airplane crashes, train derailments, and other types of transportation accidents. Industrial accidents and construction failures are also frequently categorized as accidental injury. Falls, drownings, fires, and other home accidents often result in injuries that would be classified similarly. Citing figures from the Rice, MacKenzie, and associates' 1989 Report to Congress, Chapter 8 states that the total lifetime costs for accidental injuries are greater than all other leading causes of death (e.g., heart disease, cancer), when medical, disability, and lost work productivity costs are included. However, as Scotti and colleagues point out, those figures "do not specifically address the short and long term [sic] psychological sequelae of accidental injury." In their thoughtful and comprehensive chapter, Scotti and colleagues have addressed the psychological impact of accidental injury and the development of accident-related psychological trauma.

In this chapter we focus on the assessment and treatment of accident-related psychological trauma. The chapter begins with two case examples that we believe typify accidental injury victims and illustrate some of the specific concerns that these patient victims may have. Next, we provide a description of

CONNIE L. BEST · National Crime Victims Research and Treatment Center, Department of Psychiatry and Behavioral Sciences, Medical University of South Carolina, Charleston, South Carolina 29425.   **DAVID P. RIBBE** • National Center for Posttraumatic Stress Disorder, VA Medical and Regional Office Center, White River Junction, Vermont 05009.

Traumatic Stress: From Theory to Practice, edited by John R. Freedy and Stevan E. Hobfoll. Plenum Press, New York, 1995.

a variety of measures and interview schedules that have been found to be helpful when assessing psychological aspects of accident-related trauma. Although we attempt to present a comprehensive list of self-report measures, trauma history instruments, structured interviews, and psychophysiological methods, the assessment battery can easily be tailored for each accidental injury patient depending on the needs of the patient and the clinical picture. In this chapter we also attempt to outline an approach to treatment for accident-related trauma. Although we recognize that accident-related trauma can include a broad range of emotional responses and is not restricted to posttraumatic stress disorder (PTSD), the majority of the treatment interventions presented do address PTSD or PTSD-like symptoms, since these symptoms may be the most problematic for patients (APA, 1994). Embracing a tripartite model of anxiety that posits that a person may experience anxiety in the physical, cognitive, or behavioral channels, we utilize a cognitive–behavioral framework for treatment interventions. Specific interventions are offered to address symptoms that may be experienced in each of these channels. The chapter concludes with a discussion of special issues regarding assessment and treatment of this patient population. This chapter is primarily intended for use of clinicians who provide direct psychological services or for those professionals who provide consultation for multidisciplinary treatment teams that treat accidental injury patients.

The first author (CLB) of this chapter is a clinical psychologist who specializes in the assessment and treatment of psychological trauma. As the psychologist on the consultation/liaison service of a large tertiary hospital for 8 years, she has gained considerable experience providing clinical services to patients who have suffered from a variety of accidental injuries. She obtained one of the first federal research grants specifically designed to identify, assess, and treat seriously injured victims admitted to the surgical and trauma units of the hospital. Recognized for her expertise in the area of trauma, she is a frequent presenter at scientific meetings and conducts treatment workshops throughout the country. The second author (DPR) is a clinical psychologist whose clinical and research interests are in the areas of traumatic stress and disaster. As part of his professional background, he has worked with the victims of residential fires as well as with victims surviving a traumatic bus crash. He has also published and presented at professional conferences. Thus, the comments in the current chapter are informed by the rich professional background of both authors.

Case 1

Thomas was a 23-year-old male who had been in a serious motor vehicle accident with his family approximately 6 months prior to seeking treatment. While he was driving his mother-in-law's car, a tire blew, sending the car sliding onto the shoulder of the road. He tried to steer the car into a field, but skidded into a tractor trailer truck that was illegally parked on the shoulder of the road. His wife, 4-month old daughter, and mother-in-law, who were in the back seat were severely injured. All three passengers eventually died. Thomas and his wife's uncle, who were riding in the front seat, were only slightly injured. His

10-year-old nephew, who was sitting in the middle of the front seat, sustained serious head injuries. The nephew was expected to remain in a cognitive rehabilitation facility for the rest of his life.

Thomas lost consciousness for a few minutes in the ambulance but was fully alert in the emergency room where he could hear the medical personnel as they had frantically worked on his wife in the bed next to him. He could vividly describe the sounds and recount verbatim conversations occurring on the other side of the curtain that separated him from his wife. He presented for treatment with symptoms of PTSD and uncomplicated bereavement (APA, 1987, 1994). Surprisingly, his degree of grief was not at a level associated with full depressive syndrome: PTSD symptoms of psychological numbing and avoidance were the most prominent. He was also troubled by intrusive recollections of the sounds he had heard his wife make in the car immediately following the impact and those of the medical team as they assisted his wife in the emergency room.

Case 2

Robert was a man in his late 40s who initially was seen in the burn unit of a major medical university hospital with second- and third-degree burns covering 40% of his body. He had sustained the burns as the result of an unusual accident in which he and a friend were standing in his yard talking when a military jet from a nearby base developed engine trouble. As the plane flew overhead, Robert realized that the plane was in trouble only seconds before it crashed. He yelled to warn his friend and then jumped over a large barrel in which he had been collecting rainwater for his vegetable garden. As he jumped over the barrel for protection, the force from the crash caused the barrel to tip over, covering him with water at the moment that the flash of fire from the exploding jet fuel enveloped him. Robert certainly would have sustained even more severe burns over a greater extent of his body if it were not for being covered by the rainwater. His friend was not so fortunate. On his second day in the hospital, Robert was informed that his friend had died.

From the first day of admission to the hospital, Robert described symptoms of PTSD. He particularly was troubled by intrusive images and other intrusive sensory reexperiencing (i.e., smelling jet fuel, smelling burning flesh, and hearing the sounds of the engine sputtering). These symptoms persisted past the 1-month time frame required for a diagnosis of PTSD (APA, 1987, 1994). He also had some symptoms associated with depression but did not warrant a diagnosis of major depression.

ASSESSMENT

Overview

Until recently, comprehensive assessments of accident-related trauma were not found in the research literature. The studies that do appear in the literature have focused primarily on preexisting psychopathology in the accident victim (Malt, Myhrer, Bilkra, and Hoivik, 1987), pain associated with the accidental physical injury (Alcock, 1986), or examined only one type of accidental injury (Roca, Spence, & Munster, 1992). Much of what is known regarding a comprehensive posttrauma assessment comes from the combat or crime-related trauma literature. Published studies in those areas describe assessment of posttrauma symptoms and functioning that is multimethod, drawing from both self-report and collateral sources of information. Drawing on these literatures, we suggest that assessment measures range from taking trauma histories, to structured interviews, to standardized PTSD questionnaires, to standardized assessment of comorbid disorders such as depression or panic disorder, and, finally, to psychophysiological reactivity to trauma-related stimuli (in settings where this latter approach is feasible).

The assessment process and the number of instruments used may vary depending on the characteristics of each patient (e.g., the patient's reading level, the patient's ability to attend and concentrate, the patient's physical condition) and other constraints on therapy (e.g., patient will be moving from the area within a few weeks, lack of psychophysiological assessment equipment). However, whenever possible, the therapist should attempt to include a range of assessment procedures. The order of presentation is also important. The assessment process should flow from the more unstructured description of the accident (telling of the story), to an assessment of other traumatic events, followed by an assessment of PTSD and comorbid symptoms, and ending with psychophysiological assessment (if the latter is practical). Finally, the assessment process may be completed in one, lengthy session or accomplished in two or more shorter sessions depending on the needs of the patient and other practical considerations. The clinician may find the following instruments and measures helpful for the assessment of accident-related trauma.

Telling Their Story

A great deal of clinically useful information can be obtained by having the patient describe what happened just prior to, during, and immediately after the accident, how things are different for him or her since the trauma, and how he or she has been affected by it. Clinical experience indicates that greater fullness of detail and affective information are available when the patient first tells his or her story in an unstructured manner. Not only does the clinician receive content-specific information necessary for developing individualized treatment plans, but such patient narrative also gives an indication of the patient's particular style in attempting to cope with the trauma. For example, very detailed and precise accounts may indicate obsessive or intrusive symptomatology. Scattered and disorganized accounts may reflect impaired concentration caused by anxiety. If accounts provide only minimal details, it may suggest a tendency to use cognitive avoidance strategies as methods to reduce anxiety.

In addition to assisting in the diagnostic process, allowing the patient to tell his or her story can have tremendous therapeutic benefits. First, the process of telling the story may have a cathartic effect for the patient. Second, it also communicates to the patient that the therapist views him or her as an individual and wants to understand his or her unique experience. Third, in contrast to what may have been the reaction and the message received from other people, the process communicates to the patient that it is really "okay" to talk about what may have been a horrific event and the intense emotional response that resulted from the experience. Having the patient tell his or her story would best be accomplished during the first session and prior to completing the rest of the assessment process.

Potential Stressful Events Interview

This interview procedure was developed as part of the *Diagnostic and Statistical Manual*, Fourth Edition (DSM-IV) PTSD field trials (Kilpatrick, Resnick, & Freedy, 1991; Falsetti, Resnick, Kilpatrick, & Freedy, 1994). The Potential Stressful Events Interview (PSEI) assesses a comprehensive range of potentially stressful events (both traumatic and nontraumatic). The PSEI consists of five parts. Demographics, which are covered in the first part, are fairly straightforward. Part two assesses for low-magnitude stressors that may have occurred in the past year (i.e., job loss, marital difficulties, or serious illness). The third section assesses for lifetime incidence of high magnitude (traumatic) stressors, which are those stressors that are typically associated with increased risk for developing PTSD (APA, 1987, 1994). The last two sections assess both the objective and subjective characteristics of the first, worst, or most recent of the high-magnitude stressors. Objective characteristics would include injury and attributions about causal factors. The subjective characteristics are self-report factors that measure emotional (e.g., fearful or scared, emotionally numb, confused/disoriented) and physical (rapid heart rate, trembling or shaking, chest pain or discomfort) responses that are recalled from the time of the event. Because it may have a direct bearing on the therapeutic process, it is important before beginning therapy for a clinician to understand all types of potentially stressful events a patient may have experienced. The PSEI, therefore, may be an important instrument for the clinician. Because of the comprehensive nature of this instrument, it is especially well-suited for research purposes.

Trauma Assessment for Adults

The Trauma Assessment for Adults (TAA) was developed from the PSEI (see above) (Resnick, Best, Freedy, & Kilpatrick, 1993). The TAA is considerably shorter in length and may have more utility for most clinical practice settings. Like the PSEI, the TAA measures a broad range of traumatic events and the occurrence of multiple potential traumatic events across the life span. The need to obtain a trauma history for events other than the one for which the patient is seeking treatment was one that was recognized by the developers of the instrument based on their clinical experience. It was felt that a history of other stressful events might effect the complexity, length, or course of therapy. Therefore, if the clinician were aware of the other stressful or traumatic events, modifications or adjustments could be made earlier in the therapeutic process. Additionally, patients often report a resurgence of symptoms associated with previous stressful events after they experienced the stressor or accident for which they were seeking treatment. Obtaining a trauma history would allow the clinician to prepare the patient for this possibility. The authors of the TAA believe that this instrument or similar instruments are quite useful clinically and will see wide-spread use in a variety of clinical settings in the future.

NIMH Diagnostic Interview Schedule, Version III

The Diagnostic Interview Schedule (DIS) is a structured diagnostic interview designed as a psychiatric epidemiologic survey instrument intended to identify DSM-III-R psychiatric symptoms and make psychiatric diagnoses in adults (Robins, Helzer, Croughan, & Ratcliff, 1981; Robins, Helzer, Cottler, & Goldring, 1988; Resnick, Falsetti, Kilpatrick, & Freedy, in press). The DIS generates information about the intensity and duration, as well as the incidence, of psychiatric symptoms. The majority of the questions can be answered "yes" or "no," with "yes" indicating a positive symptom. Clinical assessment of accident victims may include the PTSD Module of the DIS. In this section, questions about the three types of clusters of PTSD symptoms are included: (1) intrusive reexperiencing phenomena (e.g., flashbacks, intrusive images); (2) avoidance behaviors or emotional numbing symptoms; and (3) symptoms of increased arousal. Additional questions assess whether the symptoms persisted for at least 1 month following the trauma. Symptoms of both lifetime and current PTSD are assessed.

Clinician Administered PTSD Scale

The CAPS-1 is a 30-item structured interview that bases its clinician ratings on specific behavioral descriptions of symptoms (Blake et al., 1990). It includes items that assess each of the PTSD symptoms defined by the DSM-III-R (APA, 1987). The CAPS-1 also includes eight items that assess associated features of PTSD in adults (e.g., survivor guilt, feelings of hopelessness, feelings of being overwhelmed, disillusionment with authority figures). A particular advantage of the CAPS-1 over other structured PTSD interviews such as the DIS, is the inclusion of separate frequency- and intensity-rating scales for each symptom. Frequency and intensity ratings are made on a 5-point continuum (where 0 would represent the lowest frequency and intensity, and 4 would represent the greatest frequency and intensity). Thus, the CAPS-1 can be used either as a dichotomous measure for making a DSM-III-R diagnosis of PTSD, or as a continuous measure for assessing lifetime or current (within the past month) severity of symptoms. Additional items assess the impact of PTSD symptoms on social and occupational functioning, global PTSD symptom severity, global changes in symptoms, the validity of the interviewee's responses. Excellent interrater reliability has been obtained on the frequency and intensity for each PTSD symptom group (criteria B, C, and D), with Pearson's correlation coefficients ranging from .92 to .99 for frequency ratings and greater than .98 for intensity ratings (Blake et al., 1990).

Impact of Event Scale

The Impact of Event Scale (IES) is a 15-item, self-report questionnaire designed to provide a cross-sectional picture of subjective psychological responses to a stressful life event (Horowitz, Wilner, & Alvarez, 1979; Zilberg, Weiss, & Horowitz, 1982). The IES measures the frequency of symptoms occurring within 7 days of administration. By asking the patient how true the items are for them, responses are indicated on a 4-point scale ranging from "not at all" (scored 0), "rarely" (scored 1), "sometimes" (scored 3), and "often" (scored 5). The IES yields three scores: an Intrusion subscale score (e.g., "I thought about it when I didn't mean to"; "Pictures about it popped into my mind"; "Other things kept making me think about it"); an Avoidance subscale score (e.g., "I tried not to talk about it"; "I stayed away from reminders of it"; "I tried not to think about it"); and a Total score. Due to the brevity of the test and the correlation of the subscales with symptoms of PTSD, the IES can be quite useful with accident victims for the initial assessment and also for monitoring PTSD symptoms throughout the course of treatment.

Symptoms Checklist-90-Revised

The Symptoms Checklist-90-Revised (SCL-90-R) is a 90-item, self-report inventory that assesses levels of psychological symptoms within 1 week of administration (Derogatis, 1977, 1983). Each item describes a psychological symptom. Items are rated on a 5-point scale ranging from "no discomfort" (scored 0) to "extreme discomfort" (scored 4) experienced within the past week. Nine primary factor scores can be determined: (1) somatization; (2) obsessive–compulsive; (3) interpersonal sensitivity; (4) depression; (5) anxiety; (6) hostility; (7) phobic anxiety; (8) paranoid ideation; and (9) psychoticism. Three additional measures of general psychological distress are: (1) global severity index; (2) positive symptom distress index; and (3) positive symptom total.

Based on the SCL-90-R, Saunders, Mandoki, and Kilpatrick (1990) developed a 28-item PTSD scale that successfully discriminated women who had PTSD resulting from crime-related violence from those who did not have PTSD. Findings from a second sample essentially replicated the utility of the 28-item PTSD scale in predicting the presence of PTSD in women who had previously experienced a violent crime (Arata, Saunders, & Kilpatrick, 1991). Although this scale appears to be a useful screening instrument for use with adult female crime victims, the utility of the scale has not been empirically examined with other populations (e.g., males, victims of other traumatic events). In clinical practice, it has been noted that elevated scores are typically reported by the victims of traumatic accidents. Higher scores on the SCL-PTSD scale and other SCL-90-R scales are indicative of more intense levels of psychological distress. It should be noted that, in every case, the SCL-PTSD scale should be administered only as part of the SCL-90-R given as a whole; it is not a stand-alone instrument. Also, this approach to assessment is a screening measure and should be supplemented with other questionnaires and interview-based information.

Beck Depression Inventory

The Beck Depression Inventory (BDI) is a 21-item, self-report instrument designed to assess the intensity of depressive symptoms and attitudes within the past week (Beck, Ward, Mendelson, Mock, & Erbaugh, 1961; Beck, Rush, Shaw, & Emery, 1979; Beck & Steer, 1984). The items can be rated from 0 to 3 in terms of intensity. Total scores between 0 and 10 are associated with no or minimal depression; between 11 and 17, mild to moderate depression; 18 to 24, moderate depression; and 30 to 63, severe depression. The coefficient alpha of the BDI is .87, and its test–retest reliability correlations are within the .80s. The BDI may be particularly useful with accident victims, as depressive symptomatology is often a clinical issue with them. Like other brief, self-report inventories, the BDI can be administered several times during the course of therapy to monitor the progress of symptoms over time.

Psychophysiological Assessment

One of the three symptom clusters of PTSD defined by the DSM-III-R and DSM IV is increased arousal (APA 1987, 1994). An effective means of assessing increased arousal among trauma victims is psychophysiological responsiveness to stimuli associated with the trauma. Combat veterans with PTSD have demonstrated robust physiological reactivity (e.g., increased heart rate and blood pressure, increased muscle tension, and changes in electrodermal activity) upon exposure to combat-related stimuli (Blanchard, Kolb, Gerardi, Ryan, & Pallmeyer, 1986; Malloy, Fairbank, & Keane, 1983; Pittman, et al., 1990).

Recently, psychophysiological reactivity has been studied among individuals who have PTSD secondary to motor vehicle accidents (MVAs) (Blanchard, Hickling, & Taylor, 1991; McCaffery & Fairbank, 1985; Ribbe & Jones, 1993). Although results are based on small samples, increased heart rate upon exposure to personalized scripts of the accident appears to be closely associated with PTSD among accident victims. High levels of physiological reactivity may persist from 6 months to 4 years after a traumatic accident (Ribbe & Jones, 1993).

Although psychophysiological assessment may provide valuable information for the treatment of accident victims that cannot be assessed by self-report measures, and its use is strongly encouraged, it does require sophisticated equipment and specialized training. Therefore, this type of assessment may not be practical for most clinical office settings, but it is well suited for research settings or some specialized clinical settings.

TREATMENT

Overview

The goals of this section of the chapter are three-fold: (1) to provide a theoretical overview for treatment, (2) to describe several therapeutic techniques for the treatment of accident-related trauma, and (3) to address several issues related to the treatment of accident victims.

Traumatic accidents may produce several psychological responses among individuals ranging from mild distress to extreme stress reactions, or anything along the continuum. If the accident was minor in nature and the level of distress determined by clinical interview and standardized assessment procedures such as those described above is low, the individual may not require any therapeutic intervention. In some cases, the simple provision of information, advice, and reassurance is sufficient. However, if the accident was more serious, or if the level of psychological distress is high, the victim may be in need of treatment. For treatment seekers, PTSD is probably the most common diagnosis (APA, 1987, 1994). Therefore, PTSD is the primary focus of the treatment section of this chapter.

It is helpful to think of many of the primary posttraumatic symptoms as predictable reactions to a fear-producing situation. Accident victims, like the victims of other traumatic events, may react to situations that remind them of the trauma with a fear response. The fear response will be manifested on three levels: physical, cognitive, and behavioral (Lang, 1968, 1979).

Physical reactions such as increases in heart rate, blood pressure, respiration rate, and muscle tension are automatic. Such reactions are considered an adaptive part of the "fight or flight" response when an individual perceives threat or danger. However, in the traumatized accident victim, these responses occur repeatedly when the victim is exposed to reminders of the threatening situation. The physical fear response may become maladaptive when it interferes with the individual's ability to function in day-to-day activities when no objective threat is present.

The fear response is also reflected in victims' cognitions. Thoughts about the accident may trigger other aspects of the fear response. Following a traumatic accident, victims may experience unwanted images or thoughts about the accident. These images or thoughts may persist despite the victim's efforts to stop them. The intrusive nature of these cognitions may cause concentration difficulties and lead victims to feel that they have little control in their lives. Sometimes, intrusive thoughts take the form of nightmares about the accident or night terrors, which leave the victim awake in a state of fear with no recall of the content of the dream.

After an accident, victims may respond to the physical and cognitive fear responses on a behavioral level, too. They attempt to control further exposure to situations that evoke fear-producing physical reactions and cognitions by avoiding situations that remind them of the accident. Victims may go to great lengths to avoid people, places, things, or situations that are associated with the trauma. It is important to note that trauma victims do not always recognize that they have developed patterns of avoidance because of the trauma. Often, the avoidance patterns become a routine part of life for victims. Thus, the clinician needs to assess when the avoidance behaviors began relative to the time of the accident. Avoidance that begins following an accident is probably a manifestation of adjustment to the accident.

Sometimes the physical, cognitive, and behavioral fear responses occur separately. Most frequently, however, the three levels of fear response occur simultaneously, or interact with one another. For example, having thoughts about the accident may trigger physical reactions, which, in turn, may lead to avoidance behaviors, which limit further exposure to fear-producing situations. However, avoidance behavior also prevents the individual from learning that feared people, places, or situations are objectively safe. Thus, physical, cognitive, and behavioral manifestations of anxiety may become self-sustaining.

Effective treatment focuses on each of the three levels of the fear response. A combination of relaxation procedures (e.g., Jacobsonian deep-muscle relaxation, controlled breathing), cognitive interventions (e.g., thought-stopping, activation–belief–consequences [ABC] training, rational emotive therapy [RET]), and behavioral techniques (role playing, exposure therapy, stress inoculation therapy) can be used to target the physical, cognitive, and behavioral aspects of the fear response.

In general, a cognitive–behavioral approach may be the treatment of choice for accident-related trauma. The following is a description of several of the cognitive–behavioral techniques that clinicians may find useful. The techniques are complimentary to Lang's tripartite model and are organized by the authors of this chapter to address each of the three channels of fear and anxiety.

Physical Treatment Techniques

Deep Muscle Relaxation

Some of the most effective techniques for reducing trauma-related anxiety in accident victims are those that train clients to engage in responses that are incompatible with fear responses. For instance, deep muscle relaxation techniques *can* produce a sense of calm and control that the client can employ when the accident victim begins to feel fearful or anxious. Jacobson (1938) deep muscle relaxation, which is described in clear and step-by-step fashion by Rimm and Masters (1979), involves tensing, holding, and releasing major muscle groups in a progressive manner, usually from head to toes. Patients are able to relax specific muscle groups that may be tense as a result of anxiety, and thereby causing pain or discomfort. Not only is this technique useful for individual muscle groups, but the resulting calm can become an automatic response after several practice sessions. The client can begin to experience relief of fear and anxiety relatively quickly after learning relaxation techniques. They then can become relaxed enough to think more clearly and to exercise control over their physical and emotional responses.

Deep muscle relaxation can be used in a systematic desensitization paradigm as well. This technique requires that the accident victim and the therapist construct a hierarchy of fear-producing stimuli (images, thoughts, sounds, situations) that progresses from those that are slightly distressing to those that are highly distressing. While in a state of relaxation induced through progressive muscle tensing and releasing, the accident victim is presented with stimuli at the least distressing end of the hierarchy. As the patient's anxiety reaches a level that is distressing, the patient then engages in his or her relaxation response until he or she feels calmer or more relaxed.

On a scale of 1 to 10 with higher scores representing extreme distress, the patient should continue to use the relaxation exercises until he or she is able to reduce his or her level of anxiety to a level equal to a 1 or 2. Once relaxed, the patient is then presented with the next scene in the hierarchy, and the process is repeated. Over several sessions, stimuli of increasing distress value are presented to the client. With time, the repeated pairing of a state of relaxation with distressing stimuli leads to a reduction in fear and anxiety in the presence of those stimuli. The patient eventually achieves a sense of mastery over the feared scenes. Thus, accident victims can learn to engage the relaxation response as a coping mechanism when confronted with stimuli or situations that arouse fear or anxiety (e.g., driving in a car, having a medical examination, flying in an airplane).

Cue-Controlled Breathing

Another useful technique for relaxation is cue-controlled breathing (Rimm & Masters, 1979). This technique involves having the patient take a deep breath, then exhale while saying aloud or silently to him- or herself words such as "calm," "relax," or "peaceful." This procedure generally serves to slow down the individual's rate of breathing, which typically becomes rapid and shallow during periods of stress. When taught and practiced repeatedly when the patient is already in a relaxed state (i.e., at the end of other relaxation exercises such as deep muscle relaxation), the patient can achieve significant levels of physical relaxation. Additional benefits of cue-controlled breathing are that it is easily mastered by patients, it is an abbreviated method of achieving relaxation compared to other more lengthy methods, and that it can be done discreetly virtually anywhere and at anytime the patient needs to reduce feelings of anxiety.

Pleasant Imagery

With pleasant imagery, as the name suggests, the patient tries to call to his or her mind's eye a pleasant scene. To ensure that the image is relaxing and free of associated stressful or unpleasant connotations, the patient (not the therapist), should choose the scene to be imagined. Richness in detail is best. Multiple sensory modalities (visual, auditory, kinesthetic, olfactory) should be included to maximize the relaxation response. Therefore, the therapist should have the patient provide as much detail as possible when describing the scene. For example, if the patient chooses a relaxing beach scene, the person should also be encouraged to describe how his or her skin feels with the warmth of the sun, the smell of the salt in the air, and the sounds of the waves and the seagulls. As with cue-controlled breathing, pairing the use of pleasant imagery with deep muscle relaxation may facilitate a relaxation response via classical conditioning principles.

Cognitive Treatment Techniques

Accident victims often develop distorted perceptions of the accident and of the consequences of the accident. They may develop complex belief systems about the conditions, real or imagined, that led to the accident, complicated it, or led to a less desirable outcome. Such cognitions may compound the distress that the accident victim experiences. In fact, when accident victims begin to act on misinterpretations and distorted beliefs, they may inadvertently be creating more difficulties in their physical and social environment, which further impair functioning. The goal of cognitive treatment techniques, then, is to limit and correct faulty thinking about the accidents, behaviors, and consequences of the accident.

Rational Emotive Therapy

First described by Ellis in the 1960s and refined during the 70s, RET is derived from a theory that assumes that emotional distress results from faulty or irrational patterns of thinking. An A–B–C paradigm is used to explain the theory, where A is the activation experience (real event), B stands for the person's belief system (thoughts) about the event, and C describes the emotional consequences (e.g., anxiety, depression, anger) related to the event. According to Ellis (1974), it is not the event itself that produces an emotional consequence, rather it is the person's belief system or thoughts that determine their emotions. Irrational thoughts are either empirically false or cannot be verified and have self-defeating consequences. The goal of RET is to help the patient to change or modify his or her belief systems, thereby modifying his or her feelings. In the case of Robert, some of the concurrent depression he suffered was related to his belief that his friend might have survived had he pulled him over the rain barrel. Helping Robert to challenge this belief, that there was actually a low probability that he would have been able to actually save his friend in light of the instantaneous circumstances of the accident, was an effective way to modify his beliefs and to reduce his feelings of self-blame and depression.

Cognitive Restructuring

Cognitive restructuring, a term popularized by Lazarus (1971), refers to a more general concept of cognitive therapy. Similar to RET, the goal of cogni-

tive restructuring is to discover the source of faulty beliefs or misinterpretations and to substitute those with other beliefs or ideas. In essence, it is a way to
think differently, and perhaps less negatively, about a situation. It is a way for
the patient to change his or her perceptions of the situation to more adaptive
ones. For example, in the case of Thomas, the patient initially had a great deal
of distress when he thought of the prospect of spending evenings alone. He
worried that he would begin thinking of his family and would be so consumed
with grief that he could not function. During therapy, a cognitive restructuring
approach was used to help him "reframe" his concept of "evening hours" from
one of dread to one of time to think about his tasks for the future (e.g.,
returning to school and purchasing his new business). Obviously, the horrific
circumstances of many traumatic events limit the degree to which cognitive
restructuring can occur, but every effort should be made to utilize this type of
therapy in order to mitigate the degree of the depression or anxiety experienced by the patient while at the same time demonstrate an appreciation for
the results of the accident.

Stress Inoculation Training

One other therapy which has been found to be quite effective in the
treatment of trauma is that of stress inoculation training (SIT). Developed
by Meichenbaum (1977), SIT is designed to help patients cope with anxiety
by enhancing their self-control skills. It consists of three stages. The first is
the Educational Stage in which the patient is provided with the conceptual
framework that maladaptive thoughts or beliefs produce aversive emotional
states and that self-statements play a critical role in such states. The second
stage is the Coping Skills stage in which patients are taught specific coping
skills. Stressful situations are conceptualized as having four sequential
phases: (1) preparing for a stressor, (2) confronting a stressor, (3) coping
with the fear of being overwhelmed by a stressor, and (4) the reinforcement
phase after dealing with a stressor. Patients are taught to modify their self-
statements or beliefs associated with each of these phases. During the third
stage (the Application Stage), homework assignments are given to patients to
practice in a covert or overt form the skills learned during the Coping Skills
Stage.

Veronen and Kilpatrick (1983) and Best, Amick, Veronen, and Kilpatrick
(1987) drawing on the specific model of Lang (1968), modified SIT for use with
sexual assault victims. By adding the notion that anxiety can be experienced
and manifested in three channels (physical, cognitive, or behavioral) to the SIT
paradigm, patients are taught specific techniques or skills to address symptoms
in each of these channels and given homework assignments to practice their
newly acquired skills. Foa and colleagues compared SIT with the in vivo component, with prolonged exposure therapy (PE) and supporting counseling (SC)
for recent rape victims (Foa, Olasov-Rothbaum, Riggs, & Murdock, 1991).
They found SIT to be the most effective therapy at the end of treatment, but
PE produced superior outcome on PTSD symptoms at 3-month follow-up. It
should be emphasized that SIT used by Foa was not the modified version as

used by Veronen and Kilpatrick or Best and colleagues, since it did not include the in vivo practice exposure component.

The first author has employed SIT with a variety of accident patients in inpatient and outpatient clinical settings and believes that the modified SIT can be generalized to this patient population. In the case of Thomas, a modified SIT package was developed to help him prepare for a civil trial stemming from the auto accident. Initially, he was unable to prepare for court because of his extreme level of PTSD symptoms. However, the SIT model broke the large, anxiety-provoking task (going to court) into smaller, more manageable parts (preparing for court, giving direct testimony, being cross-examined). By doing so, Thomas was then less anxious, able to design a plan of action to accomplish each of the smaller tasks, and accomplished each of the smaller tasks; thereby he accomplished the complete task.

Thought-Stopping

Thought-stopping is a technique used to interrupt ruminative thinking (Wolpe, 1958). When used with accident victims, the therapist instructs the patient to think about the accident for a brief period. When the patient signals with a raised finger that he or she has a clear image, the therapist shouts, "Stop!" The patient should then be queried to see if the thoughts are continuing. If so, the procedure is repeated until the thoughts stop. The patient can then be trained to stop his or her own intrusive, distressing, or ruminative thoughts in this way, first overtly (aloud), then covertly (silently). Although not all patients find thought-stopping to be beneficial, for some patients, this technique provides great relief from intrusive PTSD symptomatology. In the case of Thomas (auto accident victim), thought-stopping was successfully used to interrupt intrusive thoughts, images, and sounds of the hospital emergency room.

Behavioral Treatment Techniques

Role Playing

Following an accident, victims may have some difficulties interacting with other people. Previously acquired interpersonal skills may have temporarily fallen out of their repertoire of behavior as a result of the stress of the accident. Role playing can be useful to help the victim deal with stressful interpersonal situations and to help victims engage in behaviors that are more adaptive (Masters, Burisch, Hollon, & Rimm, 1987).

One criticism of role playing that has been heard by the first author of this chapter in the course of providing treatment workshops on accident-related trauma to mental health professionals is that this technique is patronizing to the patient. However, this technique assumes only that the level of stress in the patient may be so great that it affects his or her ability to cope with certain specific situations. It does not assume that the patient is generally socially unskilled, only that the patient is temporarily unable to generate a behavioral response because of extreme levels of anxiety. In Robert's case (the plane crash), role playing was quite beneficial. He was quite anxious at the thought of returning to his neighborhood, responding to questions about the accident, the loss of his friend, and the burns he received. Role playing helped him develop, in advance, responses for which he had previously felt ill-prepared or uncomfortable to make.

Role playing can uncover distorted cognitions or beliefs and reveal dysfunctional responses. A valuable variation of this technique is role reversal, where the therapist takes the role of the victims, and victim takes the role of other people in his or her sphere of functioning. Role reversal may help the victim discover his or her maladaptive beliefs about others' feelings and thoughts toward him or her.

Exposure Therapy

Exposure therapy is, perhaps, the most important element of successful treatment for patients with PTSD (Foa et al., 1991; Rothbaum & Foa, 1992, 1993). Consistent reexposure to reminders of the trauma allows the multifaceted fear response (physical arousal, intrusive cognitions, and behavioral avoidance) to extinguish in the absence of real danger. As the level of the fear response decreases, the victim can begin to feel, think, talk, and approach situations without feeling overwhelmed.

One type of exposure therapy is flooding (Lyons & Keane, 1989). Flooding can be produced imaginally without need for direct exposure to the actual traumatic situation. In therapy, exposure can be effected by encouraging the client to tell the story of the trauma. The therapist's task is to help the client to focus on many sensory details, thoughts, impressions, affective states, physical sensations at each part of the trauma. The therapist should have the client tell the story slowly, in minute detail, reporting every aspect of his or her experience including affective states and physical sensations. This part of therapy may be the most difficult for the therapist because the client's tendency is to try to escape or avoid confronting the traumatic memories. In order for extinction of the fear response to occur, the therapist must encourage the client to stay with the fear-producing memories to the point that he or she reaches a level of emotional arousal similar to that experienced during the traumatic accident. Attempts by the client to escape or avoid this level of distress must be prevented until he or she begins to show signs of calming down. Premature escape from fear-eliciting cues may unintentionally serve to reinforce the power of such cues to induce debilitating levels of fear. The most intense period of exposure may take several minutes. The entire exposure procedure (beginning, middle, and end) may take as long as 30 to 45 minutes.

Another type of exposure therapy is called gradual exposure (Masters, Burisch, Hollon, & Rimm, 1987). Unlike flooding where the process of therapy requires the patient to remain exposed (imaginal or in vivo), to the feared situation or thought until extinction can occur, gradual exposure is based on an anxiety-reduction model to address avoidance symptoms. A patient who is anxious and avoidant about returning to full-time employment at the same site of the industrial accident, would be encouraged to do so gradually. For example, the patient and therapist might develop a plan for the patient to initially begin work on a part-time basis, perhaps at a different part of the plant or on another shift, until he or she becomes more comfortable being in the feared environment. A slow but gradual return to preaccident functioning is the goal of therapy.

Integration of Treatment Procedures

As with any trauma, the length of treatment, order of treatment technique presentation, involvement of family members, and treatment format (i.e., individual vs. group format) will vary depending on the particular patient, the injuries received, and other practical constraints. Some patients may have the luxury of an unlimited number of sessions based on their insurance plan, whereas others are not so fortunate. For the former group, the therapist would want to teach treatment interventions for use in all three channels (physical, behavioral, and cognitive). For the latter group, however, the therapist must prioritized the treatment sessions to address those symptoms that are the most problematic for the patient. As will be discussed, those patients with very severe injuries and perceived life threat may require the most number of sessions. Therefore, length of therapy may vary from just a few sessions to weekly sessions lasting months. However, even with a limited number of sessions, the patient may benefit significantly from therapeutic interventions.

The order of therapy may also vary depending on the needs of the individual patient. However, the authors suggest that as a general rule of thumb therapeutic techniques should address symptoms in the physical channel first, followed by the cognitive channel, and then the behavioral channel. Therapists should begin with relaxation techniques that might provide some degree of immediate relief and increase the likelihood that the patient will continue with therapy. Exposure-based techniques designed for the behavioral channel may be more anxiety provoking and should be attempted later. Of course, the entire process should begin with an educational phase that includes goal setting and explanation of the therapy process, and it should conclude with an evaluation of therapeutic progress.

To our knowledge, no controlled treatment outcome studies exist comparing individual and group treatment for accident victims. This is clearly an area for future research. However, the clinician who treats accident victims may want to consider encouraging patients to join victim support groups as an adjunct to therapy. There are many national reputable groups (e.g., Mothers Against Drunk Driving, the Federation for the Blind, the Phoenix Society for burn victims) and local support groups (e.g., hospital-based burn victims groups, spinal cord injury groups, surviving family members groups) that may be beneficial to accident victims and their family members. Group membership may help the patient by normalizing his or her response to the trauma and by providing a feeling of affiliation at a time when he or she feels estranged from friends and families. Pragmatic advice on a range of postaccident concerns is also available through support groups. Most of the groups are free or at low cost to the patient.

For all types of trauma patients, certain factors may be associated with positive or negative outcomes. Although research in this area is also somewhat limited and often methodologically flawed, clinical experience would suggest the following. Factors associated with positive outcomes appear to be early intervention, a noncomplicated trauma history, a noncomplicated mental health and physical health history, less severe accident-related injury, good premorbid adjustment, and adequate social support. Factors associated with more negative outcomes may be late referral, complicated trauma history, complicated mental health and physical health history, severe accident-related injury, perceived life-threat, substance abuse, poor premorbid adjustment, and poor social support systems.

SPECIAL ISSUES

There are a few issues that appear to arise with sufficient frequency during the course of therapy with accident victims that the clinician may want to consider them early in the treatment process. These specific issues or factors are discussed below.

Perceived Life Threat

Perceived life threat has been shown to be a predictor of PTSD in rape victims (Kilpatrick et al., 1989) and in combat veterans (Foy, Resnick, Sipprell, & Carroll, 1987; Foy & Card, 1987; Grady, Woolfolk, & Budney, 1989; Jordan et al., 1991). It should be emphasized that perceived life threat may not necessarily include signs typically associated with increased danger, such as the use of a weapon during a rape, or the actual exposure to a toxic chemical during an explosion at a chemical factory, or the presence of high levels of radiation in a nuclear plant accident. Rather it is the victim's individual perception of danger that is important in determining posttrauma response. Clinically, the most efficacious way of determining perceived life threat is to ask the victim if he or she thought that they might be killed or seriously injured during the accident. There is no other accurate way to determine perceptions of life threat because it is a *subjective*, rather than an objective, assessment made by the *patient*, not by family members, therapists, employers, or witnesses to the accident. In the case of Thomas, although the auto accident was by all accounts very serious with several fatalities, at no time did he think that *he* was going to die. Robert, on the other hand, perceived a great deal of life threat when the plane crashed, killing his friend and severely burning him.

Assessing for perceived life threat is important for three reasons. First, for those victims who do report life threat, the clinician should be more alert to the possibility of the development of PTSD. Second, the victim may not recognize the relationship between life threat and intensity of symptoms in light of the apparent "minor nature" of some traumas or accidents (e.g., no physical injury, no death). Therefore, the victim and others may impute their high level of distress to "weak character" or malingering rather than to their subjective assessment of danger. Third, victims' family members, their employers, even third-party payers for therapy, may not understand the concept of perceived life threat as it relates to the development of PTSD and think that the victim is "overresponding" to the trauma. If others hold such beliefs, they may have unrealistic expectations of the victim and may be unwilling to offer necessary emotional, social, or financial support to the victim.

Physical Injury

Research has shown that physical injury can also be a predictor of PTSD (Kilpatrick et al., 1989). Although many accident-related traumas do not result in actual physical injury, a significant number do, and for those patients, the development of PTSD may be more likely. When physical injury is combined with other predictors, such as perceived life threat, the risk of PTSD may increase even more. Although physical injury can occur as a result of a trauma without perceived life threat, more often than not, the two coincide. Therefore, the patient may experience more symptoms of PTSD and/or have more intense symptoms of the disorder when both physical injury and a perception of threat to life have occurred.

For accident victims, several factors may account for the increase in the likelihood for developing PTSD when injury has occurred. First, physical injuries serve as constant visual and proprioceptive cues for the "reexperiencing" (intrusive) Category B cluster of PTSD (APA, 1987, 1994). The sight of a missing limb, the disfigurement of face from a serious burn, the need for a wheelchair because of a spinal cord injury, or even phantom limb pain, serve as hourly or daily reminders of the trauma because of the loss of function, pain, or other injury-related factors. The victim has a difficult time making what might be an adaptive cognitive avoidance response, even for a few minutes of the day. To put it into lay terms, it appears that "there is no rest for the weary" when it comes to intrusive symptomatology for some accident victims. In addition, physical injury, which is usually accompanied by significant levels of pain, may lower the patient's overall ability to handle stress. Although a discussion of psychoimmunology is beyond the scope of this chapter, it is generally recognized that a mind–body connection exists. Changes in hormonal functioning following an extreme stress may be associated with varying levels of PTSD (Yehuda, Resnick, Kahana, & Giller, 1993).

Physical injury resulting from a trauma has another deleterious effect on patients in addition to causing pain and suffering and increasing the likelihood of PTSD. Physical injury may limit the patient's ability to return to work. If the patient is capable of returning to work, it is often in a different position, for a reduced number of hours, or frequently interrupted for physical therapy or medical treatment appointments. Trauma patients who do return to work often report that they notice a decrease in their productivity. Combined with other possible productivity-reducing symptoms caused by PTSD, physical limitations of the job may result in the loss of employment. The loss of self-esteem that is often associated with loss of employment and the subsequent loss of financial resources may result in prolonged emotional strain and, in extreme instances, may result in a clinical depression. The connection between internal and external loss events and subsequent feeling of depression is consistent with the theoretical proposition that the loss of resources limits the individual capacity to adapt effectively (see Chapter 2, this volume; Hobfoll, 1989).

Physical injury may also markedly effect treatment interventions. For example, in the case example of Robert, who received burns as the result of the fire from the jet crash, many modifications were needed for teaching relaxation exercises. The tensing of muscles and the subsequent stretching of the affected overlying skin associated with deep muscle relaxation and deep breathing exercises would have been too harsh for the delicate condition of his skin. Therefore, these otherwise effective techniques had to be omitted. Helping Robert achieve a physiological relaxed state was achieved by the use of pleasant imagery.

Finally, the use of medications may be somewhat of a two-edged sword in treatment. It may offer the patient enough relief from physical pain or psychological symptoms so that he or she may be able to attend to, and process, the more cognitive components of therapy. On the other hand, heavy doses of some medicines may impair the patient's ability to comprehend and store verbally presented information. Use of medication may also make it more difficult to accurately assess trauma-related symptomatology and progress in therapy. The appropriate use of medication is an issue that should be carefully considered. The patient and relevant treatment professionals should collaborate in making appropriate decisions regarding medications. Kudler and Davidson (Chapter 4, this volume) provide informative comments regarding the integration of medication and psychosocial forms of treatment in treating trauma victims.

Immediate versus Long-Term Reactions

Clinicians may come into contact with accident victims immediately following the trauma (within a few days or weeks), or they may be asked to provide services to victims long after the accident (months or years later). Because victims may present quite differently depending on the acuteness or chronicity of the symptomatology, some discussion is in order.

Clinicians who work on a consultation/liaison service, an in-patient unit, or who are affiliated with emergency services (i.e., emergency medical services, law enforcement agencies, or trauma response teams), frequently see patients who are experiencing acute reactions. Although there may be wide variability in the clinical picture, these patients may be experiencing high levels of anxiety and fear, including symptoms associated with increased arousal (e.g., hypervigilance, exaggerated startle response, or sleep disturbances). They may describe vivid intrusive images, sounds, or smells related to the accident, or report feelings indicative of psychological numbing.

In other clinical settings, clinicians typically treat patients months to years after the accident. Patients with more long-term reactions may have developed both cognitive and behavioral avoidance patterns. Additionally, they may have distressing dreams or flashbacks of the accident. As growing awareness of the aftereffects of the trauma set in (possible loss of employment, loss of a body part due to injury, loss of a friend or co-worker who may have been killed during the accident), symptoms of depression may surface. Differences in symptom pictures dictate differences in the content, emphasis, and the course of treatment.

The Role of the Therapist as an Advocate

Patient advocacy is a topic typically not covered in professional school curricula or clinical practice. This is understandable in that most patients who access the mental health system are not in need of an advocate. However, trauma patients, especially accident victims, may be an exception. Why do accident victims need advocates? Accidents can be, and often are, physically and psychologically overwhelming. Consequently, the patients' usual effective coping mechanisms may be ineffective at the very time they need to function well to deal with increased demands. Accident victims may be required to interact with a multitude of agencies ranging from insurance companies, to employers, the medical community, mental health professionals, in addition to well-meaning, but possibly misguided family and friends. Because of all this, the patient may need assistance in dealing with others after the accident. For example, the patient may find it beneficial to have the clinician educate employers about PTSD symptomatology and the need to follow a gradual exposure model in order for the worker to return to the workplace or even to consider a temporary change in employment responsibilities. Or the clinician may need to speak on behalf of the patient to insurance carriers or employers explaining the rationale for, and the benefits of, a cognitive–behavioral framework for therapy. Otherwise, these groups may be hesitant to approve, or cooperate with, mental health therapies. Finally, for the victims who become involved in civil or criminal proceedings resulting from the accident, some advocacy may be extremely beneficial for providing information and assisting the patient throughout the process.

All of the above advocacy situations applied to Thomas (auto accident victim). He needed assistance in working with his employer who was initially somewhat nonsupportive, to temporarily change his job responsibilities because of his difficulties concentrating and his level of anxiety. The nature of his employment was quite important, since he worked for an agency involved in matters of national security. Thomas also needed accurate information regarding the workings of the legal system related to civil litigation.

SUMMARY

This chapter has attempted to make the reader aware of several clinical issues regarding the assessment and treatment of accident victims. It is suggested that a comprehensive assessment begin with an unstructured description of the accident, and be followed by a trauma history assessment, structured interviews, and possibly psychophysiological measures. A cognitive–behavioral, tripartite model for the treatment of accident-related PTSD was offered. Techniques to address the symptoms of anxiety manifested in the physical, cognitive, and behavioral channels were described, as were the course of therapy, length of therapy, and factors associated with positive outcomes. The chapter concluded with a section on special issues related to the treatment of accident-related trauma.

REFERENCES

Alcock, J. E., (1986). Chronic pain and the injured worker. *Canadian Psychology, 27*(2), 196–203.

American Psychiatric Association. (1987). *Diagnostic and statistical manual of mental disorders* (3rd ed.-rev.). Washington, DC: Author.

American Psychiatric Association. (1994). *Diagnostic and statistical manual of mental disorders* (4th ed.). Washington, DC: Author.

Arata, C. M., Saunders, B. E., & Kilpatrick, D. G. (1991). Concurrent validity of a crime-related Post-traumatic Stress Disorder scale for women within the Symptom Checklist-90-revised. *Violence and Victims, 6*(3), 191–199.

Beck, A. T., Rush, A. J., Shaw, B. F., & Emery, G. (1979). *Cognitive therapy of depression.* New York: Guilford Press.

Beck, A. T., & Steer, R. A. (1984). Internal consistencies of the original and revised Beck Depression Inventory. *Journal of Clinical Psychology, 40*, 1365–1367.

Beck, A. T., Ward, C. H., Mendelson, M., Mock, J., & Erbaugh, J. (1961). An inventory for measuring depression. *Archives of General Psychiatry, 4*, 561–571.

Best, C. L., Amick, A. E., Veronen, L. J., & Kilpatrick, D. G. (1987). *Manual for stress inoculation training treatment for rape victims.* Charleston, SC: Medical University Press.

Blake, D. D., Weathers, F. W., Nagy, L. M., Kaloupek, D. G., Klauminzer, G., Charney, D. S., & Keane, T. M. (1990). A clinician rating scale for assessing current and lifetime PTSD: The CAPS-1. *Behavior Therapist, 9*, 187–188.

Blanchard, E. B., Hickling, E. J., & Taylor, A. E. (1991). The psychophysiology of motor vehicle accident related posttraumatic stress disorder. *Biofeedback and Self-Regulation, 16*(4), 449–458.

Blanchard, E. B., Kolb, L. C., Gerardi, R. J., Ryan, P., & Pallmeyer, T. P. (1986). Cardiac response to relevant stimuli as an adjunctive tool for diagnosing post-traumatic stress disorder in Vietnam Veterans. *Behavior Therapy, 17*(5), 592–606.

Derogatis, L. R. (1977). *SCL-90: Administration, scoring & procedure manual—I for the DSM-R (revised) version.* Baltimore: Johns Hopkins University School of Medicine.

Derogatis, L. R. (1983). *SCL-90-R: Administration, scoring, and procedures manual—II* (2nd ed.). Baltimore: Clinical Psychometric Research.

Ellis, A. (1974). *Humanistic psychotherapy: The rational emotive approach.* New York: McGraw-Hill.

Falsetti, S. A., Resnick, H. S., Kilpatrick, D. G., & Freedy, J. R. (1994). A review of the "Potential Stressful Events Interview": A comprehensive assessment instrument of high and low magnitude stressors. *The Behavior Therapist, 17*(3), 66–67.

Foa, E. B., Olasov-Rothbaum, B., Riggs, D. S., & Murdock, T. B. (1991). Treatment of posttraumatic stress disorder in rape victims: A comparison between cognitive–behavioral procedures and counseling. *Journal of Consulting and Clinical Psychology, 59*(5), 715–723.

Foy, D. W., & Card, J. J. (1987). Combat-related post-traumatic stress disorder etiology: Replicated findings in a national sample of Vietnam-era men. *Journal of Clinical Psychology, 43*(1), 28–31.

Foy, D. W., Resnick, H. S., Sipprelle, R. C., & Carroll, E. M. (1987). Premilitary, military, and postmilitary factors in the development of combat-related post-traumatic stress disorder. *Behavior Therapist, 10*(1), 3–9.

Grady, D. A., Wollfolk, R. L., & Budney, A. J. (1989). Dimensions of war zone stress: An empirical analysis. *The Journal of Nervous and Mental Disease, 177*(6), 347–350.

Hobfoll, S. E. (1989). Conservation of resources: A new attempt at conceptualizing stress. *American Psychologist, 44*(3), 513–524.

Horowitz, M., Wilner, N., & Alvarez, W. (1979). Impact of Event Scale: Measure of subjective stress. *Psychosomatic Medicine, 41*(3), 209–218.

Jacobson, E. (1938). *Progressive relaxation.* Chicago: University of Chicago Press.

Jordan, B. K., Schlenger, W. E., Hough, R., Kulka, R. A., Weiss, D., Fairbank, J. A., & Marmar, C. R. (1991). Lifetime and current prevalence of specific psychiatric disorder among Vietnam veterans and controls. *Archives of General Psychiatry, 48,* 207–215.

Kilpatrick, D. G., Resnick, H. S., & Freedy, J. R. (1991). *Potential Stressful Events Interview.* Unpublished manual, Medical University of South Carolina, Crime Victims Research and Treatment Center, Charleston.

Kilpatrick, D. G., Saunders, B. E., Amick-McMullan, A. E., Best, C. L., Veronen, L. J., & Resnick, H. S. (1989). Victim and crime factors associated with the development of crime-related post-traumatic stress disorder. *Behavior Therapy, 20,* 199–214.

Lang, P. J. (1968). Fear reduction and fear behavior: Problems in treating a construct. *Research in Psychotherapy, 3,* 90–102.

Lang, P. J. (1979). A bio-informational theory of emotional imagery. *Psychobiology, 16*(6), 495–511.

Lazarus, A. A. (1971). *Behavior therapy and beyond.* New York: McGraw Hill.

Lyons, J. A., & Keane, T. M. (1989). Implosive therapy for the treatment of combat related PTSD. *Journal of Traumatic Stress, 2*(2), 137–152.

Malloy, P. F., Fairbank, J. A., & Keane, T. M. (1983). Validation of a multimethod assessment of posttraumatic stress disorders in Vietnam veterans. *Journal of Consulting and Clinical Psychology, 51,* 488–494.

Malt, U., Myhrer, T., Bilkra, G., & Hoivik, B. (1987). *Acta Psychiatrica Scandinavica, 76,* 261–271.

Masters, J. C., Burish, T. G., Hollon, S. D., & Rimm, D. C. (1987). *Behavior therapy: Techniques and empirical findings* (3rd ed.). New York: Harcourt Brace Jovanovich.

McCaffery, R. J., & Fairbank, J. A. (1985). Behavioral assessment and treatment of accident-related post-traumatic stress disorder: Two case studies. *Behavior Therapy, 16,* 406–416.

Meichenbaum, D. H. (1977). *Cognitive-behavior modification.* New York: Plenum.

Pittman, R. K., Orr, S. P., Forgue, D. F., Altman, D., DeJong, J. B., & Herz, L. R. (1990). Psychophysiological response to combat imagery of Vietnam veterans with posttraumatic stress disorder versus other anxiety disorders. *Journal of Abnormal Psychology, 99,* 49–54.

Resnick, H. S., Best, C. L., Freedy, J. R., & Kilpatrick, D. G. (1993). *Traumatic Events Assessment for Adults.* Unpublished manual, Medical University of South Carolina, Crime Victims Research and Treatment Center, Charleston.

Resnick, H. S., Falsetti, S. A., Kilpatrick, D. G., & Freedy, J. R. (in press). Assessment of rape and other civilian trauma-related post-traumatic stress disorder: Emphasis on assessment of potentially traumatic events. In T. W. Miller (Ed.), *Stressful life events* (2nd ed.). New York: International Universities Press.

Ribbe, D. P., & Jones, R. T. (1993). *Chronic psychological and psychophysiological sequelae among adolescents following a traumatic bus crash.* Presented at the annual meeting of the American Psychological Association, Toronto, Canada.

Rimm, D. C., & Masters, J. C. (1979). *Behavior therapy: Techniques and empirical findings.* New York: Academic Press.

Robins, L. Helzer, J., Cottler, L., & Goldring, E. (1988). *NIMH Diagnostic Interview Schedule Version III Revised (DIS-III-R).* St. Louis: Washington University.

Robins, L. N., Helzer, J. E., Croughan, J., & Ratcliff, K. S. (1981). National Institute of Mental Health Diagnostic Interview Schedule. Its history, characteristics, and validity. *Archives of General Psychiatry, 38,* 381–389.

Roca, R. P., Spence, R. J., & Munster, A. M. (1992). Posttraumatic stress disorder among adult burn survivors. *American Journal of Psychiatry, 149*(9), 1234–1238.

Rothbaum, B. O., & Foa, E. B. (1992). Exposure therapy for rape victims with posttraumatic stress disorder. *Behavior Therapist, 15*(10), 219–222.

Rothbaum, B. O., & Foa, E. B. (1993). Cognitive–behavioral treatment of post-traumatic stress disorder. In P. A. Saigh (Ed.), *Posttraumatic stress disorder: A behavioral approach to assessment and treatment* (pp. 85–110). New York: Pergamon Press.

Saunders, B. E., Mandoki, K. A., & Kilpatrick, D. G. (1990). Development of a crime-related post-traumatic stress disorder scale within the Symptom Checklist-90-revised. *Journal of Traumatic Stress, 3*(3), 439–448.

Veronen, L. J., & Kilpatrick, D. G. (1983). Stress management for rape victims. In D. Meichenbaum & M. E. Jaremko (Eds.), *Stress reduction and prevention.* New York: Plenum Press.

Wolpe, J. (1958). *Psychotherapy by reciprocal inhibition.* Stanford, CA: Stanford University Press.

Yehuda, R., Resnick, H. S., Kahana, B., & Giller, E. L., (1993). Long-lasting hormonal alterations to extreme stress in humans: Normative or maladaptive? *Psychosomatic Medicine, 55,* 287–297.

Zilberg, N. J., Weiss, D. S., & Horowitz, M. J. (1982). Impact of events scale: A cross-validation study and some empirical evidence supporting a conceptual model of stress response syndrome. *Journal of Consulting and Clinical Psychology, 50*(3), 407–414.

14

Treatment of Torture Survivors

Psychosocial and Somatic Aspects

PETER VESTI and MARIANNE KASTRUP

INTRODUCTION

In Chapter 9 (this volume) we reviewed the medical, psychological, and social sequelae of torture. The present chapter focuses on issues concerning assessment and treatment. Treatment requires the cooperation of medical, psychological, and social disciplines, but here we emphasize the psychotherapy of torture survivors. Our experience stems mainly from the group of tortured refugees living in Denmark. These individuals have been seen at the International Rehabilitation Research Center for Torture Victims (RCT) located in Copenhagen, Denmark. Although the content of this chapter is based largely on clinical practice at the RCT, when appropriate we refer to clinical work at other specialized treatment centers located throughout the world.

In Chapter 9 the short- and long-term physical and psychological consequences of torture were reviewed. This understanding of symptoms, however, is of fairly recent origin. Nevertheless, it has been recognized for hundreds of years that major traumatic events, including physical trauma and torture, can cause mental changes in the sufferers. Furthermore, it has been recognized that disturbances may persist across time. However, because of the strong influence of Freud's theories during the first half of this century, it was previously assumed that early psychopathology related to childhood trauma was largely responsible for emotional symptoms that occurred later in life. Thus, the potential role of adulthood trauma in determining adjustment was assumed to be minimal. This thesis was carried to an extreme after the Second World War

PETER VESTI and **MARIANNE KASTRUP** · Rehabilitation and Research Centre for Torture Victims, Borgergade 13, DK-1300 Copenhagen K, Denmark.

Traumatic Stress: From Theory to Practice, edited by John R. Freedy and Stevan E. Hobfoll. Plenum Press, New York, 1995.

when concentration camp victims, in order to obtain economic compensation from postwar West Germany, had to prove that they were not vulnerable or "neurotics" before they entered the camp (Krystal, 1976). Sufficient knowledge was gained only gradually to the effect that torture in itself causes long-term psychological dysfunction (Lederer, 1965). This understanding led to the development of treatment programs for torture survivors.

ASSESSMENT AND TREATMENT CONSIDERATIONS

All psychological treatment models for the treatment of torture survivors are based on the assumption that it is beneficial for the survivors to confront the trauma under controlled circumstances. However, the psychological symptoms and their treatment must be seen in a context of the treatment of the whole individual, and a model for treatment of torture sequelae thus includes the following aspects (Vesti, Somnier, & Kastrup, 1992): psychological treatment, social treatment, somatic treatment, legal advice, and spiritual guidance. No two torture survivors will have the same treatment needs, but the aspects mentioned should be considered, and a treatment plan tailored to particular needs and circumstances.

Cultural Aspects

Treatment will necessarily depend on local circumstances and should as far as possible take into account the cultural background of the individual survivor (Kinzie, 1989; Vesti & Kastrup, 1992). For example, in some societies (e.g., Middle Eastern) it is not in accordance with tradition and religion to address rape directly. Females from this background are often reluctant to talk about this part of their ordeal, whether at a treatment center in their country of origin or at a treatment center abroad. In such cases, it may be better to allow the emotions relating to sexual abuse to surface either symbolically in the form of art therapy or through massage or other forms of physiotherapy (Larsen & Pagaduan-Lopez, 1987). In this way emotions may be reexperienced and expressed without using language.

At this point it is relevant to consider the great divide between the traditions of the West, with its concepts of psychodynamics and cognitive restructuring, and those of the East, with a completely different religious tradition and even a different tradition in the viewing of the individual, not as a strictly independent individual, but as an integrated member of the extended family. Moslems may vehemently oppose our "Godless psychology," making reference to Freud's definition of religion as an illusion. Furthermore, the concepts of normality as understood in the West are also challenged:

> It is clear that the criteria which Western psychology upholds for the well-adjusted are not developed by empirical scientific research. They are rather derived mainly from a cultural concept of modern man as viewed by contemporary Western civilization. (Badri, 1979)

In contrast, western mental health practices contain a number of concepts, particularly cognitive restructuring, that can be accepted by Christians and Moslems alike (Badri, 1979).

Treatment Principles

Whereas the treatment itself is organized differently in different cultures, the following four basic principles have emerged as underlying all interventions (Jacobsen & Vesti, 1992). First, any procedure that may remind the survivors of their ordeal should be avoided if possible. This provision includes waiting time. Torture victims have often waited outside the torture chamber, hearing the screams and waiting for "their turn." To make a survivor wait at the hospital may provoke severe anxiety reactions, as might metallic sounds from the examination room. The same principle applies to the noisy handling of instruments, or shining sharp light directly into the eyes of the person being examined; these should be avoided because they often bring back memories of the torture chamber.

Second, treatment must be both physical and psychological and the two must run in parallel. Torture nearly always uses a combination of physical and psychological methods, producing damage in both areas. Because of this, an interwoven complex of somatic, psychological, and psychosomatic symptoms results. The survivors, particularly from non-Western parts of the world, may view their bodily symptoms as caused by some or other malfunctioning in the body and request treatment for this, tending to disregard any psychological cause. It is necessary to take all symptoms seriously so that no somatic complaint is disregarded. Two other factors also make parallel treatment important. First, the symptoms usually worsen when the trauma is approached in the therapy, and secondly, part of the torture is to convince victims that they have suffered irreparable harm ("Now we are going to destroy your brain so you will never be able to function normally again"). Only combined somatic and psychological treatment can resolve such fears.

Third, physical therapy is an important part of the treatment. As demonstrated in Chapter 9 (this volume), the survivors have a number of complaints from the various organ systems. However, the most frequent physical findings are from the musculoskeletal system. This is not surprising since common forms of torture include beatings all over the body, suspension, hyperextension of joints, fractures, and other direct trauma to the body. The physical therapy will address the sequels with physical methods. An example is the treatment of feet injured by repeated beating under the soles (falanga). As falanga can cause rupture of the balls of the feet, treatment will include strapping of the foot with tape, training the foot muscles, and help to provide the victim with shoes (occasionally after orthopedic measurement) that will alleviate the pain. The sequels of falanga in particular are interesting in as far as they appear pathognomonic for torture and thus will be of value in a court case. Physical therapy is also used to mobilize joints that have been held in a particular way as a result of the trauma. The muscles around the trauma frequently contract to protect the joint (Skylv, 1992). Physiotherapy (or other forms of physical treatment) is almost always necessary, not only to alleviate pain and mobilize joints, but also in conjunction with the psychotherapeutic sessions. Physiotherapy, before or after psychotherapy, influences the sessions and enhances the release of traumatic material. The reason appears to be the relaxation response to the physical methods, which lowers psychological defenses (Pagaduan-Lopez, 1987).

Fourth, treatment must include not only the torture survivor but also the whole family, offering assessment and treatment to spouse and children. The children of torture victims may suffer either from the disability of one or both parents or from the fact that the child has personally experienced traumatic episodes (Sack, Angell, Kinzie, & Rath, 1986; Figley, 1988; Kinzie, 1989). Also there frequently exists the phenomenon of "silence in the family." In clinical work at the RCT, the authors have frequently observed that the functioning of various family members becomes interdependent. For example, as the husband begins to improve in his level of functioning, his wife may become more symptomatic. At such a point in time, it is not unusual to learn that the wife had also been in prison, or that she had suffered greatly while the husband was in prison. Typically, she has repressed or minimized her symptoms for the sake of taking care of the family. Thus, it is important for mental health professionals to consider the welfare of family members as well as the identified torture survivor.

Our comments concerning basic treatment principles are consistent with our own clinical experience in working with torture victims and their family members. It should be understood that work at other treatment centers follows similar principles. As an example, treatment centers in the United States have been developed to address the mental health needs of Southeast Asian refugees (Kinzie, 1989; Mollica et al., 1990; Mollica, Wyshak, & Lavelle, 1987). Similar to the approach taken at the RCT, these centers take a broad approach toward clinical work. Individual treatment approaches (supportive psychotherapy and medication) are typically combined with other necessary intervention activities (case management, groups to encourage socialization and identification with other people). Thus, clinical work with torture victims must be multifaceted and characterized by flexible and creative thinking on the part of mental health professionals.

Indications and Contraindications

Not all torture survivors can benefit from the therapy outlined above. Some survivors cannot tolerate their own extreme levels of affect. In such cases (even with a gradual approach and the use of medication), it may be difficult for the individual to review his or her experiences and to gain insight into the causes of his symptoms. For other torture survivors, additional contraindications to insight-oriented therapy exist.

Supportive therapy is given for the former group (van der Veer, 1992). Even with clients who are able to use insight therapy, part of the session is allocated to practical problems (e.g., housing, financial concerns, family problems). It is clear that more time has to be given to these concerns than would be given to clients from our own cultural background, and it is estimated that 20% to 35% of the time in therapy is spent with these matters. If the clients are unable to obtain or use insight, the supportive element of the therapy is strengthened, and the sessions will concentrate on practical aspects (e.g., how to live with the symptoms that remain, and how the effects of recurrent nightmares may be lessened). The impact of nightmares may be lessened if the victim sleeps with a dim light on, and if some artifact relating to the new country is closed to the bed, for example the flag of the new country. The supportive therapy reinforces the survivor's self-confidence and helps that individual to believe that he or she can live a fulfilling life in spite of the torture and associated symptoms.

Insight therapy is contraindicated for some other clients. A full mental health history is taken when clients are evaluated for the first time. This includes both interview and psychological testing components (see Chapter 9, this volume). Particular attention is paid to the presence of any of the following conditions that might contraindicate insight therapy:

1. *Personality disorders.* The paranoid personality disorder and the antisocial personality disorder may cause concern and speak against insight therapy. The psychological handling of the traumatic material may cause acting out with consequences for the survivor and distress for the therapist.
2. *Weak ego boundaries,* as recognized by chronic anxiety and nervousness in interpersonal relationships. These persons may be overwhelmed by recollections of traumatic experiences and may experience reactive psychoses.
3. *Projection being used as the main defense mechanism.* These persons are usually unable to develop the necessary trust in the therapist and to be able to understand and use insight in their psychological functioning.
4. *Distorted normality,* as seen in individuals who have grown up in refugee camps who are constantly under threat of annihilation, witnessing atrocities, and often without parental support and schooling. These very unfortunate people need a long period of building up a new concept of normality and are better served by supportive therapy, including returning to school, help with the new language, and even support for the family (e.g., support groups, day-care centers).
5. *Severe substance abuse.* Insight-oriented therapy is not appropriate unless or until the substance abuse is under control. Often substance abuse may serve the function of producing a state of numbness or amnesia that serves the function of blocking painful memories or emotions. Generally, supportive approaches work better as an initial approach in these cases. More insight-oriented approaches may be attempted (cautiously) when or if substance abuse issues are under control.

THE CENTER CONCEPT

As a consequence of the understanding that trauma causes psychological sequelae, treatment programs have been developed. One of the first centers to open was the Rehabilitation and Treatment Center in Copenhagen, which developed from the work of the medical group of Amnesty International and was officially opened in 1984 (Marcussen, 1993). It is of interest to note that at the time of opening, many letters came from torture survivors, all expressing satisfaction that their symptoms had finally received some form of recognition. Many survivors expressed a sense of relief that their symptoms were not a sign of personal weakness or endogenous psychopathology. It was common to hear that survivors had suffered psychological and physical symptoms for years, but they had been unable to find any assistance for their suffering. Today more than 60 centers are in existence worldwide. A large proportion of these are organized under the umbrella of the International Rehabilitation Center for Torture survivors (IRCT), including centers in Argentina, the United States (Minneapolis), Zimbabwe, Turkey, Pakistan, and the Philippines (van Willigen, 1992).

In many countries, treatment of torture survivors is organized around centers devoted to the treatment of survivors. The main reason for centers is that few general hospitals or clinics will be able to provide treatment along the lines outlined above. Other advantages in establishing such a center include:

1. It is easy for the survivors to know where to seek help. They may have read about the center in the press, or their family physicians may know of its existence.
2. The staff at a center will be relatively permanent, allowing the victims to meet the same professionals at their visits in a small, secure environment.
3. Rehabilitation of torture survivors is relatively new. It involves several professions, and it is therefore of value for a number of trained professionals in this particular field to work together in one location. They will be able to communicate more easily, and their combined treatment will give better results than treatment given in various locations without communication across professions.
4. It is easier to obtain funding for a center with a clear purpose as to its function.
5. The large number of clients at a center specifically devoted to the rehabilitation of torture survivors results in expertise being gained faster than if a survivor is just one of many different categories of patients seen during the day.

There are several disadvantages inherent in running a center for torture survivors. These disadvantages include:

1. A center is an easy target for anyone wishing to destroy, threaten, or damage the idea of rehabilitating torture survivors (e.g., for political reasons). The idea behind rehabilitation is that the symptoms after torture constitute a psychological and medical problem. There may be many causes for the torture, but individual human beings are hurt, they have symptoms, and they present themselves as patients. But if therapists devote their professional lives to work at a rehabilitation center for

torture survivors, tortured by one political sector or structure in society, the therapists are easily seen as participating in a political struggle rather than as performing their duties as health professionals.

2. Therapists at the center may lose contact with the ordinary medical and psychological disciplines.

3. International funds may be available only for the first few years of operation, risking the loss of employees and experts as the center is cut down at the end of the first funding period.

4. A center cannot have all the facilities of modern medicine and will always need an external network of dedicated physicians and psychologists to help in the treatment of torture survivors. Because of this, treatment initiatives in some countries have been organized solely as a network of professionals referring to one another.

5. Because the need for treatment is larger than the capacity at the centers, the waiting time for rehabilitation is often more than 1 year.

Under all circumstances, treatment programs are narrowly defined as medical and social-psychological centers. In the vast majority of centers, it has been found advisable to follow this medical/psychological model rather than to venture into fact-finding or documentation and direct accusations of governments in power. This latter function is left to organizations such as Amnesty International and the American Society for the Advancement of Science, or similar organizations.

ASSESSMENT PROCEDURES

Methods have now been developed to measure symptoms as expressed before, during, and after therapy (Bøjholm et al., 1992). At the RCT, standardized questionnaires are used to evaluate exposure to trauma, psychosocial concerns, and somatic complaints. The Harvard Trauma Questionnaire is used to obtain information concerning previous trauma exposure and subsequent psychological symptoms (Mollica et al., 1992). The following standardized measures are also used to assess mental health symptoms: Hopkins Symptom Checklist (HSCL-25), Hamilton Rating Scale for Depression (HDS) and, the Hamilton Rating Scale for Anxiety (HAS) (Mollica, Wyshak, de Mameffe, Khuon, & Lavelle, 1987; Bech, Kastrup, & Rafaelsen, 1986). These scales, together with the clinical impressions, are recorded approximately every 3 months to allow an evaluation of treatment efficacy (Bøjholm et al., 1992). There is a great need to develop standardized measures for use in work with torture victims (Mollica & Caspi-Yavin, 1991). The current authors have outlined the instruments that have been used with success in the RCT in Copenhagen, Denmark. Other settings might use these or other instruments (including structured diagnostic interviews; e.g., Blake et al., 1990; Spitzer, Williams, Gibbons, & First, 1990) depending on local circumstances.

In addition to the use of measures to assess traumatic events and associated psychological and physical symptoms, the possibility of malingering and factitious disorder should be considered (Sparr & Pankratz, 1983). With respect to malingering, it seems rather unusual to find such persons in treatment settings, since there is little to be gained from pretending to be a torture victim. However, there is always the risk that informers, posing as victims, may approach the center in order to gather information about the clients there. Only a detailed history of the torture experience (i.e., exposure to traumatic events), combined with a careful history of psychosocial functioning, will reveal any inconsistencies in the presentation of the client.

Factitious disorders in this field have so far not been described. It is not unusual for paranoid schizophrenics to come to the center and complain about highly unusual experiences, (e.g., "The government has implanted a listening device in my brain"). When identified, these types of clients should be referred to more general mental health clinics.

TREATMENT PROCEDURES

Most torture survivors continue to live in their countries of origin. They seek whatever help is available, but when the regime responsible for the torture is still in power, they frequently do not mention the real cause of their symptoms. Some manage to flee and eventually present themselves as patients at clinics in the country of asylum.

In the following discussion on the psychotherapy of torture survivors, our theory and discussion is based primarily on the psychodynamic and humanistic approach to psychological dysfunction. The authors' experience is with tortured refugees living in the West who are treated at rehabilitation centers on an individual basis, particularly individuals primarily suffering from anxiety disorders, including posttraumatic stress disorder (PTSD) (APA, 1994).

This form of treatment rests on two basic assumptions: (1) that no increased level of psychopathology has been found in the torture survivors *prior to the torture;* and, (2) that confronting the trauma under controlled circumstances will be beneficial for the survivors.

Practical Aspects

Torture survivors live at home and come to the center for treatment once or twice a week. Sessions are run by psychologists or psychiatrists who have some years of experience in their various fields. The therapists undergo constant supervision, and time for this is allocated every week. The supervision is individual as well as in groups. In addition, RCT has found it advantageous to limit the time of direct client contact to a maximum of 50% of the therapist's work period. It has been found that spending hour after hour in therapy with torture survivors is indeed strenuous for the therapist, who risks vicarious traumatization and burnout. Time not used in direct client contact is spent in research, teaching, and supervision of other staff members. An interpreter is usually present during the sessions (see below) (Vesti et al., 1992).

The psychotherapeutic sessions last for 45 minutes, on average. The clients are treated individually, but their spouses and children can come to the facility for assessment and treatment, as needed. Great care must be taken to make sure that clients do not feel that they are psychiatric patients (i.e., stigmatized), and it is preferable to avoid an overly clinical atmosphere. It must also be kept in mind that a substantial number of torture survivors have been tortured with the help of health care professionals. Thus, presenting too formal a setting to clients (e.g., white lab coats, other uniforms, medical equipment, rooms without windows) may remind torture survivors of some aspect of their prior torture experiences. When this is the case, the effect is usually to exacerbate torture-engendered mental health symptoms. In some cases, this reaction can be so extreme that the torture victim has great difficulty in keeping subsequent treatment appointments.

The Phases of Psychotherapy

From a phenomenological point of view, the therapy of individuals may be divided into four phases. These are not rigid stages, but nevertheless, they are observed in most of the treatment conducted at the RCT in Copenhagen, Denmark. The order of these phases varies from case to case. Although the phases generally occur in the order presented (building trust, the cognitive phase, the emotional phase, and the reintegration phase), there can always be variability in individual cases. It is up to the therapist, in collaboration with the client, to ensure that each of these phases is incorporated into treatment.

Building Trust

During the initial phase of treatment, client, therapist, and (often) an interpreter meet for the first few times. It is the therapist's responsibility to establish confidence and trust with respect to the center itself and the absolute confidentiality of all information volunteered, and to the surroundings, the interpreter, and even the therapist himself or herself. Trust is gradually built up, but it may require several sessions.

It is to be expected and accepted that some survivors will ask personal questions; they should be answered with openness. The following are some examples from sessions with torture survivors:

- "Why do you work in a place like this, working with torture survivors?"
- "What is it that you want from me, what shall I tell you?"
- "Is it true that we are guinea pigs for the CIA, KGB (or its successor), Mossad, etc.?"
- "Even though you assure me of confidentiality, how can I trust you?"
- "What is preventing you from giving my secrets away?"
- "What do you know about torture, how can you understand what I am going through?"

It must be recognized that torture survivors have been subjected to ill-treatment by several authorities and professions, including the medical and even the psychological. Documentation for this is now widely available (Stover & Nightingale, 1985; Vesti, 1990). This means that the survivors, through psychological abuse, have lost trust in society, authority, professionalism, and even in fellow human beings. A survivor from the Second World War expressed how he changed as he was undergoing torture: "A crack went through the image of God."

The survivors have been abused and cheated in many ways, and even our professionalism may be questioned. Answers from the staff should be given openly, and, if confidentiality is a very sensitive area, it can usually be dealt with by arranging with the survivor that names are not necessary (or that fake names may be used in therapy to indicate fellow prisoners, torturers, etc.) and that detailed descriptions of the places of torture are not necessary.

At least one family has been punished because the victim went to the mass media in his country of asylum and "told the world what happened to me." We believe that the centers should not be engaged in direct accusations of governments and that clients who wish to bear testimony should be referred for this aspect to proper channels (e.g., Amnesty International or other large international human rights organizations that are aware of the risks involved). The question as to what we know about torture or how we could possibly understand its effects on the human mind cannot be answered as such, but only indirectly through the way we as professionals handle the interview and the way our questions reveal our knowledge of the torture situation and its effects on human beings. Furthermore, the therapist may need to put aside professional neutrality. In facing a torture victim, the professional is facing a person who has been through a direct onslaught on his survival and dignity. Thus, it may be of value to state our own attitude towards torture as an illegal criminal activity and assert that under no conditions do we condone it. Building trust is of prime importance for successful treatment, but it may take time. The first few sessions are vital for the therapy even to the extent that the obtaining of the trust has itself been seen as the treatment proper. It also takes professionalism to be exposed to this often massive distrust and yet handle the situation and turn it into one of confidence and trust.

The Cognitive Phase

The symptoms are reviewed when the former victim is confident about the situation at the center, and gradually the abusive acts that caused the symptoms will be discussed. Initially this will be in an emotionally detached way, and during this phase the torture survivors will talk about aspects of the arrest, detention, and torture. The survivor attaches a personal meaning to the events during the cognitive phase (e.g., "I know where I was taken because I realized in which area of town we drove and, even though hooded, I recognized where we were going;" or "Initially I thought they were criminals abducting me, only later did I realize that I was captured because they wanted to get my brother").

The Emotional Phase

As trust and confidence are established, the torture survivors become capable of confronting the trauma. This is initially on the cognitive level, but emotions will gradually be attached, and the individuals will experience the emergence of emotionally charged memories. Whereas in the cognitive phase they will be able to speak about dates and places, in the emotional phase they speak about what happened to others; remarks such as "I saw a man tortured this or that way" are frequent. As therapy unfolds, survivors talk about the torture itself and how it was carried out; they become anxious, depressed, or otherwise emotionally aroused as they speak about their ordeal. The memories will be painful, and pain will also be experienced again in the body. Viewed in psychodynamic terms, this will be understood as an abreaction or a catharsis (an abreaction is understood as an emotional release as the memories of the traumatic events are brought back to conscious awareness, and the emotions surface and become attached to them) (Somnier & Genefke, 1986). This abreaction often releases enormous amounts of tension and anxiety, as well as depressive symptoms. It is imperative during the therapy to observe constantly for signs of anxiety (e.g., unrest, the smoking of cigarettes, pacing up and down the floor) and sadness (e.g., wringing of hands, tears) and to allow these to run their course during the session. It is important to organize each session into a beginning, dealing with the happenings since the last session, the topic of the torture, and the emotional discharge, but always to leave time for the clients to abreact and reorient themselves back to the reality of the treatment center and the world outside. Until they have regained their composure, they should be allowed to stay in the center for a cup of coffee, a look at the newspapers, or otherwise calm themselves.

Extreme emotional abreactions, which may be so violent that they produce brief reactive psychoses, are infrequent, and we have only observed a limited number. One published study reported that reactive psychosis occurred, but rarely, among torture survivors (Kinzie & Boehnlein, 1989). We suspect, however, that the occurrence of psychotic symptoms is underestimated because there are frequent periods during the sessions when the clients become absorbed in their own world, going through some painful emotional crises which they talk about only later. We do not interrupt the clients during this period; we only observe them for signs of gross stress. There is no warning sign of the reactive psychosis, and it does not necessarily come at a particular point in the therapy. One patient was called to the doctor's office for a physical examination and when he was asked to remove his socks he immediately fell to the floor and had a flashback, believing himself back in the torture chamber and seeing the doctor as the torturer. He moaned on the floor and repeated his prayers over and over again. The doctor stayed with him and gradually helped him back to reality by pointing out objects in the room and mentioning names not related with the torture situation, as well as by bringing familiar sounds from the center to his notice. The patient's toe nails had been repeatedly torn off during torture.

This confrontation with the trauma will result in verbal expression of the emotions and some form of reenactment of the emotions from the torture chamber. Some therapists suggest having the patient's ordeal written down (Agger, 1989; Agger & Jensen, 1990). This method of treatment is referred to as the testimony method. The purpose of these written accounts is twofold. First, these accounts are viewed as a healing ritual for the torture survivor. Individuals are assisted in recording their experiences, expressing their emotions, and are supported and validated in this process. A written testimony can also be carried to later treatment providers, providing a source of valuable information regarding factors influencing personal adjustment. The second purpose of written testimony is judicial or political. These written accounts can be used to document terrible violation of human rights. It is typically recommended that the individual torture survivor be given the choice as to whether his or her personal testimony should be shared with human rights organizations or other collective entities. If a testimony is shared, it is important to disguise the description enough to protect the identity of the torture survivor.

It briefly needs to be mentioned that symptoms and their resolution during therapy may be viewed and conceptualized in different ways. We have stressed a more traditional psychodynamic understanding of the mind, talking in terms of defense mechanisms and abreaction of the traumatic material through therapy. It is evident, however, that this abreaction of repressed emotion may also be understood in cognitive–behavioral terms, for example as desensitization or habituation, meaning that repeated exposure to anxiety-provoking ideas will eventually lessen the anxiety reactions produced. More and more papers analyzing trauma-related symptoms in cognitive terms have become available, and the two directions frequently coexist within one institution (Keane, Albano, & Blake, 1992; Montgomery, 1992; Vesti & Kastrup, 1992).

The Reintegration Phase

Torture survivors gradually begin to understand their ordeal, what happened to them and why, and that they are healthy human beings who have been exposed to abnormal, exceptional, criminal circumstances. Survivors begin to understand that they have experienced physical and psychological sequelae that were predictable, and that the aim of the torturers was to change them as persons and make them function on a lesser level of fulfillment than before the torture. Memories, of course, will never be forgotten, but, as stated by a survivor after treatment:

> My memories of the torture are not overwhelming me the whole time any longer; I have put them in a drawer that I sometimes open to look at, but a drawer that I can close again. Yet I must admit that sometimes the drawer still springs open by itself.

In addition to the acceptance of cognitive and affective aspects of their experiences, the reintegration phase is marked by the establishment of more stable daily living routines (e.g., social relationships, work, recreation, finances).

Even though a number of residual concerns or functional compromises may exist, it is generally the case that the torture survivor is living a substantially more meaningful and productive life by the conclusion of mental health treatment efforts.

Treatment Techniques

Psychotherapy of torture survivors is generally based on the principles of psychodynamics and the relationship with the client, as in ordinary therapy. However, the therapist performs more direct interventions than in usual therapy for anxiety disorders (see below). The verbal psychodynamic psychotherapy used in most rehabilitation centers is concerned with the verbal interaction between client and therapist, with the possible aid of an interpreter. During therapy sessions, it is essential for the therapist to recognize the following issues:

1. As the psychotherapy unfolds, the clients will react emotionally, since emotions are attached to the memories of the trauma. When the traumatic material is confronted, signs of upheaval, uneasiness, irritability, and suspicion may be prominent, as may be depressive symptoms. Because of the emergence of the traumatic material, there is an initial worsening of somatic and psychological symptoms, even after the sessions. This phase passes, though it may last for weeks. To prevent dropout because of this phase, it is important to explain the reactions to the client before starting the therapy.

2. The clients will react to the emerging material with the use of defense mechanisms and coping strategies. Mechanisms that are often used by clients include projection, distortion, acting out, hypochondriasis, somatization, dissociation, intellectualization, and humor. It is useful for the therapists to recognize these and to explain them to the client to promote insight and successful adaptive strategies.

3. Transference phenomena mirror the reactions of the client toward the torturer and are frequently expressed in remarks such as: "You look like the torturer," or "You are my only friend." Naturally, transference phenomena as seen in ordinary psychotherapy are also encountered, but even though the psychodynamic framework is used, there should be no analysis of the transference phenomenon in the classical sense, except when it is directly related to the trauma (Krystal, 1978). The transference is not analyzed with respect to traumatic childhood factors, since we are dealing basically with people who were healthy and well-functioning before the torture.

4. Just as the clients react to the traumatic memories, so does the therapist, and he or she must be able to recognize his own reactions to the horror scenes of the described torture. The reactions span a range from guilt, regret, shame, identification, to privileged voyeurism.

5. The therapist must also be aware of his way of dealing with his reactions

to the traumatic material through defense mechanisms and/or coping strategies. The therapists' defense mechanisms and defense styles may span the entire spectrum, and the individual therapist's insight into these is important. In order to secure this insight, supervision is again vital in helping us to understand our own reactions and defense mechanisms in operation. In particular, identification, denial, and distancing are commonly observed.

6. Countertransference phenomena include overidentification and demonstration of solidarity, not to the survivor as a human being, but to the survivor's cause as such. It has even been suggested by some groups that we identify with the cause to the point of taking part in national holidays, demonstrations, and the like (Danieli, 1984). It is our experience that this does not promote the treatment, because the therapist will soon find his or her loyalties under stress when treating clients tortured by regimes of many different ideologies.

The therapy follows common psychotherapeutic guidelines, except in one area, that of direct interventions. Because of the extreme situation in the torture chamber, there is a specific psychology of the torture situation when the torturers play directly on the psychology of the victim to induce emotions that will destroy the victim's belief in him- or herself. It is therefore important for the therapist to have a very good working knowledge of the psychology of the torture chamber so as to be able to recognize the specific "psychological games" that have taken place. Furthermore, by demonstrating to the survivor awareness of these psychological reactions, the therapist will help the survivor to abreact the emotions involved and ensure trust. Several examples are presented to illustrate the type of feedback provided to clients:

1. "I broke when I signed the papers they wanted. I despise myself." Victims are frequently forced to sign papers either during the torture or before release. These papers may even testify that the torture survivor was well treated in prison. It is important for the therapist to understand that practically all human beings break under torture, that no guilt should come from this, and that breaking only testifies that the person is a human being.

2. "I broke, and he did not. I am a weak despicable person." One or two victims are sometimes allowed not to break, to make the other victims feel even more guilty: "They could take it. I could not because of my weakness."

3. "I feel so guilty: I gave the names of my friends." Many victims are put through "the impossible choice." They are forced to choose between giving names of their friends or having their family taken and perhaps even raped, tortured, or destroyed in front of them. The victims often do not realize at the time that there is no real choice and that whatever they say will not change the outcome in any way.

4. "Nobody believes me." Acts are carried out during torture that are so

extreme that the public often disbelieves the survivors, which is exactly what the torturers want. Several accounts of such unbelievably monstrous torture are available. A survivor stated, for example, that he and some other prisoners were taken to a cell, stripped naked, and suspended by an arm and a foot to chains in the ceiling. Some female prisoners were brought in, forced to undress, and to sit astride the suspended victims, causing excruciating pain in the limbs. The victim continued: "I know you probably do not believe me, but I still have the scar which I got when my head hit the wall," and the scar was demonstrated in the clinic. Obviously not all accounts should be believed, but it is our experience that the basis for such accounts as given above has been imposed deliberately to damage the credibility of the victim (i.e., acts perpetrated directly with his or her later testimony in view).

5. "My brain is damaged." The torturers tell the victims repeatedly that their bodies (e.g., brain, kidneys, etc.) or bodily functions (e.g., sexual capability, mental faculties) will be permanently injured. The goal is to misinform the victims, making them nihilistic in assessing their chances of returning to a normal life.

6. "What really broke me was when I realized that he was not my friend." The good man/bad guy psychological game is exploited to the extreme. A devastating feeling of loneliness and guilt can be induced in the victim through this principle of one torturer playing the bad guy and torturing the victim, whereas the other pretends to be the good guy trying to make the torturer stop (e.g., "Please tell me now, I am your friend, maybe I can make him stop"). The torture survivor is told that he was at fault for the lies and other actions of the torturers.

Key Factors in Successful Treatment

The treatment of torture victims is a relatively new field. Clinical work in this area has arisen largely out of practical necessity, rather than as a purely scientific endeavor. Therefore, no controlled studies concerning treatment efficacy with torture victims have appeared. Instead, a number of descriptive reports ranging from case examples to the description of multifaceted intervention programs have appeared (Agger & Jensen, 1990; Basoglu, 1992; Basoglu, Marks, & Sengun, 1992; Kinzie, 1989; Mollica et al., 1990). Most reports note the chronicity of mental health symptoms and related social problems suffered by torture victims and their families. Most of the reports argue for a combination of psychosocial (e.g., supportive therapy, case management) and medical (e.g., antidepressant medication) approaches. Most reports advocate the stabilization of presenting problems rather than a complete resolution of all difficulties. This modest goal is realistic given the many concerns that may be faced by torture victims and their family members.

Our work with torture victims at the RCT is similar to work conducted elsewhere. Successful treatment is predicated on several factors. To begin with, treatment should begin as early as possible to prevent the development of additional problems (e.g., secondary depression, family conflicts). Of course, the components of treatment should be tailored to the needs of the individual torture survivor (e.g., some will require physical therapy, some will not; some will require medications, some will not). It should be kept in mind, however, that torture victims are likely to have multiple needs. Therefore, psycho-therapy is generally only one component of an overall treatment regimen. Therapists and other treatment personnel should be knowledgeable concern-ing the nature of torture, including mental health effects. This understanding should be conveyed to torture victims early in treatment and repeatedly in order to facilitate trust and insight by the torture survivor. This often involves providing reassurances as to the purpose of the center and the integrity of the therapist (e.g., "the center is not an agent of the KGB," "I am here to help you"). Based upon the building of trust, psychotherapy and other treatment efforts have the most realistic chances of success.

A special problem may arise when an extorturer comes for treatment. We have occasionally experienced this at RCT. The torturers were initially in the service of a regime that later fell from power, and the torturers were then tortured by the new regime. Torture survivors should not be exposed to extor-turers. We have taken the stand that extorturers should be treated, but not on the same premises as the survivors. The few cases we have seen have been referred to professionals working outside RCT. In other countries (e.g., Argen-tina) another solution was found. Torturers were first to undergo whatever punishment society decided, after which treatment could begin (Kordon, Edel-man, Lagos, Nicoletti, & Bozzolo, 1988).

Interpreters

Work at RCT could not have started without interpreters. Whereas initially there was a distrust from therapists of the possibility for a therapeutic alliance when an interpreter was present, this fear has been alleviated over the last 10 years. It has increasingly been realized that interpreters work primarily bicul-turally, being capable of translating the small signs, nuances in language, and cultural expressions that would otherwise not be picked up (Marcos & Alpert, 1976; Egli, 1987). It is necessary, however, to select interpreters with care. At RCT we have tried to find interpreters with a high degree of personal maturity. They should be educated and have a stable background, if possible with a stable family situation. Working as an interpreter is strenuous because he or she will have to cope with the histories of torture and perhaps even put his or her own loyalty to a certain political system to the test. Interpreters are only accepted if they condemn torture unconditionally and under all circumstances. We dis-courage use of former torture survivors as interpreters and never use family members or relatives. It is furthermore imperative to ensure that it is the client who accepts the individual interpreter and that the client has the right to reject him or her. Finally, the interpreters also need supervision and ongoing training. The emotions aroused during therapy need to be worked through psychologically, and this is best done with the therapist in charge of the therapy immediately after the session. Sufficient time must therefore be interspersed between patients. This supervision may also be used better to understand the vocabulary of the torture situation, and has even led to a better understanding of the slang vocabulary of the torture situation in publications by the interpreters (Behbahani, 1992).

BEYOND INDIVIDUAL TREATMENT

The psychotherapy mentioned above is primarily used in the West, where organization, training, and trained personnel are available. Such treatment would be inaccessible in many countries, and other forms of psychotherapy have therefore been developed. One such form is counseling. It is a method in which nonprofessionals (e.g., volunteers, schoolteachers, religious leaders) acquire information, through courses and training, about trauma and its impact on the human mind. They then identify the torture survivors (often in a refugee setting) and offer to help them. Sympathetic listening, acceptance of the symptoms of the clients, and talking them through, perhaps with some emotional discharge, may alleviate the survivors' symptoms. A main issue is their understanding that torture survivors are not "mentally ill." The saying "a sorrow shared is a sorrow halved" plays a large part in this treatment, and of course the general support of fellow human beings is also of prime importance in psychotherapy proper (van der Veer, 1992).

Group and Mass Therapy

When a repressive regime falls from power, many torture survivors sometimes dare to seek treatment openly. In this situation group therapy has been offered: (1) because of its benefits per se; (2) because the people tortured often belong to one political movement in particular and often come from relatively similar socioeconomic backgrounds; and, (3) because the large number of survivors all too often outweigh the services available.

Group therapy has been developed particularly in Argentina (Kordon et al., 1988). It is used less frequently in Europe and the United States mainly because the survivors represent very divergent political views, even if they have been tortured in the same country by the same regime (e.g., it is not unusual for a regime to torture both its right- and its left-wing opponents). Also very few therapists speak the language of the survivors, making the running of a group almost impossible. However, Kinzie (1989) has described a "socialization group" for Southeast Asian refugees (victims of torture) that had relocated in the United States. This group was one facet of an overall treatment strategy. The purpose of the group was limited to providing a sense of belonging (in a strange culture) and to training participants in practical living skills (e.g., making purchases).

It is well known that repressive regimes cause many people to suffer. This suffering spans a range from outright torture to the fear of daily living in a dictatorship. When such regimes fall, a huge number of human beings surface who have been tortured, who for years have been subjected to other abuse of human rights, or who have lived under prolonged periods of fear and despair. One way to release the repressed feelings of a large number of people is through mass meetings organized to celebrate the downfall of the tyrants and the return to democracy. National hymns are sung during these meetings, and national symbols are displayed. The participants, who may be crying and expressing openly the formerly forbidden thoughts, may be sharing their bitter experiences with other human beings, perhaps for the first time. The effects of such arrangements are of great importance, and it must be realized both that the need for individual therapy always outweighs the availability and that other means to lessen symptoms stemming from all degrees of torture should be welcomed. After the decline of the Soviet empire, this mass expression of emotion, relief, and hope for the future was witnessed in the Baltic states (e.g., Estonia).

Auxiliary Services

As demonstrated in Chapter 9 (this volume), the sequels of torture affect several areas of human functioning. Psychotherapeutic intervention has been discussed above. The following is a review of the auxiliary services (somatic, social, legal, and spiritual) that are sometimes necessary in rehabilitation.

Somatic Treatment

Treatment of the sequelae of torture follows ordinary medical principles. Torture survivors may suffer from a large number of psychosomatic symptoms. Sometimes there is considerable discrepancy between symptoms and physical findings, except when they concern the musculoskeletal system (Juhler, 1993). It is nevertheless very important to take all somatic symptoms seriously and to recommend a thorough medical investigation whenever necessary. Because of the psychological reactions of the torture survivors, however, the individual specialists should have had training in the reactions that they may encounter (see also the case discussed above concerning brief reactive psychosis, this chapter). Such training can be organized from a central center, if there is one, which can approach the medical community and select and train those who are interested in this particular form of work (e.g., through workshops, case conferences, informal consultation with professional peers). A particular example of the above is general anesthesia for torture survivors. When drugs (e.g., pentobarbital) are given at the beginning of the anesthesia, it is not uncommon for torture survivors to become confused and highly agitated. These survivors may suffer enormous anxiety and even act as if they were back in the torture chamber. The same may occur when they regain consciousness, in both cases confusing or frightening health care personnel. It is not uncommon for such reactions to be labeled as histrionic or as otherwise indicative of personal psychopathology.

Social Treatment

In the industrial countries, social workers are of primary importance in the rehabilitation of torture survivors. Housing, jobs, education, and support for the family are vital. Many problems are met, and it has to be accepted that many torture survivors have to live on some kind of government assistance for extended periods. Torture survivors have the double burden of being severely traumatized and of being refugees (see Chapter 9) (Schlapobersky & Bamber, 1987). However, it should be recognized that many refugees are not familiar with social workers, and that a social worker in other parts of the world may be "someone who procures money for specific social causes." Even the introduction and use of social workers may be difficult with certain cultural groups. This is the case because in some cultures it is a strong ethic that the extended family should deal with all problems that are experienced by any family member, including any problems associated with torture. The goal for the social treatment of tortured refugees is modest. Although decent housing, a job, education, and further training are desirable, the goal often has to be reduced to more obtainable levels. Sometimes the goal with torture survivors is simply to ensure that the survivors are not worse off than other nontortured refugees.

Legal Problems

Legal problems may relate to posttorture issues (e.g., obtaining asylum, bringing the family to a new country, and other legal problems that all foreigners may run into in new countries). The legal aspects of obtaining asylum pose a particular burden on the health professions insofar as the UN 1984 Convention against Torture, Article 3, states that no person may be returned ("refouler") to another State where there are substantial grounds for believing that he would be in danger of being subjected to torture (Stæhr, Stæhr, Behbehani, & Bøjholm, 1993).

Relatively recently, survivors have started to take their torturers to court. Even when the survivors are living abroad, this is possible, either according to the national laws of the country of asylum, for example in the United States, or through the UN 1984 Convention against Torture, which allows the prosecution of perpetrators in any of the signing countries, regardless of where the crime took place. This topic is new to the law, but as health professionals we must be informed about the possibility and also be able to help our clients in this respect. It is often a problem in therapy that the survivors not only suffer the consequences of torture and have been forced into exile, but they also have to witness their torturers living in comfort, at no risk of being punished for their acts. Outgoing regimes regularly give amnesty to all personnel who have been in their service (i.e., freedom from all legal consequences), no matter what acts they have perpetrated during the years of repression. This places an extra burden on the survivors, as it increases their risk of meeting their former torturers.

Spiritual Assistance

The issue of spiritual aid will only be touched on, but many survivors understand the world and their torture in religious terms. Some may be concerned about having lost the protection of God or having had their world view changed dramatically, perhaps no longer seeing a just God; others see the torture as a trial or justified punishment from God. The moral dilemmas induced during the torture and imprisonment may for religious torture survivors indicate that religious advice should be approached. This is not a field that has been extensively researched, although papers on Islamic counseling of torture survivors have been circulated (Stæhr, et al., 1993) and may best be understood in western terms as similar to pastoral counseling.

That religion is of importance in extreme situations such as torture was also witnessed in the German concentration camps during the World War II.

> The religious interest of (concentration camp) prisoners, as far and as soon as it has developed, was the most sincere imaginable. The depth and vigor of religious belief often surprised and moved a new arrival. Most impressive in this connection were improvised prayers and services in the corner of a hut, or in the darkness of the locked cattle truck in which we were brought back from a distant work site, tired, hungry and frozen in our ragged clothing. (Frankl, 1964)

CASE HISTORIES

The following two case histories illustrate some of the above aspects of the psychotherapy of torture survivors.

Persistent Nightmares—Mr. P

Married, with two children, Mr. P was 37 years old when he was arrested. At the time of his arrest, he was to run for parliament. He comes from a major country in the Middle East and was politically active in an ordinary political party. As an electrical engineer, he had spent years in the rural areas trying to improve the living conditions of the peasants by introducing electricity in the villages. He was arrested in the first year of the revolution in the late 1980s and was kept for more than 6 months, severely tortured physically and psychologically. One form of the latter was mock execution. He was told that he was to be executed, was taken to a courtyard, and placed against a wall with a prisoner he knew on each side. The soldiers fired and he felt as if time had ceased to exist; when his hood was removed, he saw his two fellow prisoners lying dead by his side. He was taken to his cell and given another 24 hours before he was to be executed. The next morning he was taken to the same wall but this time he was placed not in the middle but to the side. He was thus fully convinced that he was about to be shot, but once more the two men next to him were killed, and he was spared. He was gradually proven innocent, was released, and escaped with his family to a Western country. He was suffering multiple symptoms, including severe recurrent nightmares about the mock executions, and he also felt that his whole world view had changed. He could not comprehend how the torture he had endured and seen perpetrated on other people could possibly happen.

In the first part of the therapy, great emphasis was placed on the restructuring of his cognition relating to "the ways of the world." He gradually began to understand that what had happened to him was a criminal, illegal activity carried out by a ruthless dictatorship, and that, although it could happen anywhere, it was not common in human society. Improvement occurred first in the physical symptoms. He had severe pain in the rectal area because a rod had been forced into his rectum, and he had a constant feeling that he was incontinent of feces. He was seen by a gastroenterologist and a rectoscopy was performed under full anesthesia. Internal hemorrhoids that were found were removed, after which the stools no longer caused problems. He had also been suspended and had severe back problems, with fixation of the lower part of the spine. Physical therapy lessened the spasms, and he regained full movement in his back, but he still has recurrent backache and has to have regular physical therapy. Mentally, he experienced an initial worsening of the symptoms, but as he knew that this was to be expected, he accepted it as part of the treatment. His ability to concentrate improved next, and he became able to follow classes and managed to learn the native language, to his own surprise since he believed that "my brain has been damaged." He attended the meetings of his political party and also enlisted in a similar party of his new country; he no longer had to avoid films from his own country when they were shown on the television. He continued to improve physically and psychologically, but he still had nightmares 5 to 7 nights a week. Mr. P never really woke up refreshed, and he had problems concentrating and learning the new language.

Several problems were superimposed on the therapeutic process. First, he took it upon himself to become a leader of his political party in his new country. This meant that people would call him in the middle of the night, complaining of their nightmares and worries, and he as a leader would have to comfort and counsel, never revealing his own problems. At times he felt desperate, wanted to kill himself, and wished that he had "died honorably" fighting the regime. Second, later in the process, he realized that a family member of his who belonged to the revolutionary party had been sent to assassinate him. He knew that many exiled colleagues had been killed, that he was in real danger, and that this danger was not fully appreciated by authorities in the new country.

During the last 2 years, he has attended RCT regularly. The nightmares have been reduced to about 3 to 4 nights a week, which is an improvement but is far from satisfactory. He still lives in constant fear of being killed, and there is little prospect of alleviating this short of change of the regime in his home country. He lives on social welfare, but he is able to be a father for the family and to bring up his son and daughter in the democratic ideas and spirit of

humanity for which he has always fought. The main achievement in the therapy appears to have been restructuring his cognitions to see the world once
more as a place that makes sense. He still, years after the therapy was initiated,
suffers nightmares once or twice a week despite prolonged therapy.

A Prolonged Court Case—Miss A

Miss A was in her 20s when she was picked up by the police. She was a
schoolteacher and was head of a small school when arrested, not because of her
own behavior, but because the police authorities wanted to arrest her brother,
who was accused of terrorism. She was taken to the local police station and kept
in isolation for 6 weeks. During this time she was regularly interrogated in a
small room by two or three police officers. She was kicked and beaten all over,
stripped naked, and abused verbally, all the while being blindfolded. Allegedly
she was not raped. On five occasions she was suspended in the "parrot's perch"
position, meaning that a stick was put between her flexed knees and elbows and
then lifted to rest on two chairs. By this, the feet are swung upwards, and in this
position she underwent falanga (i.e., beating on the soles of the feet). She was
burned repeatedly with cigarette butts and her head was pushed towards a wall,
to be jerked back just before impact. Her back was hyperextended, and she
reported excruciating pain. Her cell was next to the interrogation room, and
she had to listen to the screams and cries from the victims under torture.

Her brother was eventually arrested, and Miss A was transferred to a
prison, to the sick department. She was unable to walk because paralysis of both
legs had developed; she was plagued by repeated memories of the torture and
was frightened whenever a male orderly approached. Altogether she spent 4
years of detention under the provisions of an antiterrorist law. She was never
brought to trial.

After release from prison, she managed to come to Denmark and was
accepted for treatment. She was bedridden, with some atrophy of both legs, and
it became obvious that the initial trauma to the back had developed into a
functional paralysis. She still had scars from the cigarette butts and suffered
headaches and insomnia. She was also full of guilt because she had given some
names of innocent friends who had eventually been arrested, and she felt that
she had changed as a person and "that the world could never be the same again."

Rehabilitation was started with physiotherapy and training initially in a hot
bath and later at RCT itself. Because of the cultural and language differences,
psychotherapy was mostly supportive in the beginning. Only gradually did she
begin to understand her psychological reactions at the time of torture, that her
reactions were those of a normal person, and that at the time she had no
alternative to her actions. She began to realize that almost all victims break and
sign whatever papers or statements the torturers wish, as she had also heard
from her friends in prison. Her guilt gradually diminished, and she became less
frustrated by the nightmares. In one nightmare, she even managed to escape
from her assailants! Her physical condition improved considerably during the
next year, and she developed the ability to walk again. Her psychological symp-

toms also improved greatly. She finally understood her ordeal and her reactions and what had been done to her. She became angry and wanted to take her torturers to court. Proceedings started, and the court case has now continued for more than 10 years because of the defense's use (and misuse) of all the legal loopholes. Miss A's present level of functioning is close to her pretorture level. The case is still pending, but Miss A continues her fight to the bitter end.

The main achievements of the therapy have been to address the functional paralysis and to treat the physical and psychological symptoms in parallel, thereby starting a positive circle, with one aspect reinforcing another. The client, although angry with her torturers, was not motivated by private revenge; rather, she sought the civilized action of court proceedings.

SUMMARY

Torture sequelae affect all aspects of human life. As health professionals we are used to dealing with the physical, psychological, and social aspects of human existence, but the impact of torture involves other areas, such as the spiritual and world-view dimensions, and may also involve legal issues. Dealing primarily with the biological, psychological, and social aspects of treatment, this chapter has reviewed major areas of knowledge in the field, stressing the continuous monitoring and assessment not only of the clients but also of the treatment progress.

Treatment in different parts of the world differs not only in the approach to the torture survivors, but also according to local traditions and circumstances (e.g., the survivors may be treated on an individual basis or in group therapy). Many centers have been established for the treatment of torture survivors, and there are differing ways of organizing the treatment. But treatment, however organized, is based on the assumption that it is beneficial for the survivors to confront the trauma verbally or in other forms. Consequently, psychotherapy is of paramount importance, although it does not stand alone. The services of several health disciplines are needed, and it is vital that the involved staff and attached specialists all have a good working knowledge of what torture is, what it causes, and how to treat the victims without causing further traumatization. There is now sufficient understanding to allow us to treat torture survivors, and it is necessary for all decent human societies to provide this treatment for those of our fellow human beings who have been subjected to the devastating experience of torture.

REFERENCES

Agger, I. (1989). Sexual torture of political prisoners: An overview. *Journal of Traumatic Stress,* 2(3), 305–318.

Agger, I., & Jensen, S. B. (1990). Testimony as ritual and evidence in psychotherapy for political refugees. *Journal of Traumatic Stress, 3*(1), 115–130.

American Psychiatric Association. (1994). *Diagnostic and statistical manual of mental disorders* (4th ed.). Washington, DC: Author.

Badri, M. B. (1979). *The dilemma of Muslim psychologists.* London: MWH Publishers.

Basoglu, M. (Ed.). (1992). *Torture and its consequences: Current treatment approaches.* Cambridge: Cambridge University Press.

Basoglu, M., Marks, I. M., & Sengun, S. (1992). Amitriptyline for PTSD in a torture survivor: A case study. *Journal of Traumatic Stress, 5*(1), 77–83.

Bech, P., Kastrup, M., & Rafaelsen, O. J. (1986). Mini-compendium of rating scales of anxiety, depression, mania, and schizophrenia with corresponding DSM-III syndromes. *Acta Psychiatrica Scandinavia, 326*(73 suppl), 1–37.

Behbahani, M. (1992). *The argot of the victim.* Copenhagen: International Rehabilitation Council for Torture Victims.

Blake, D. D., Weathers, F. W., Nagy, L. M., Kaloupek, D. G., Klauminzer, G., Charney, D. S., & Keane, T. M. (1990). A clinician rating scale for assessing current and lifetime PTSD: The CAPS-1. *Behavior Therapist, 13,* 187–188.

Bøjholm, S., Foldspang, A., Juhler, M., Kastrup, M., Skylv, G., & Somnier, F. (1992). *Monitoring the health and rehabilitation of torture survivors: A management information system for a rehabilitation and research unit for torture victims.* Copenhagen: International Rehabilitation Council for Torture Victims.

Danieli, Y. (1984). Psychotherapist's participation in the conspiracy of silence about the Holocaust. *Psychoanalytic Psychology, 1,* 23–42.

Egli, E. (1987). *The role of bilingual workers without professional mental health training for refugee services in mental health.* Unpublished manuscript, University of Minnesota, Minneapolis.

Figley, C. R. (1988). A five phase treatment of post-traumatic stress disorder in families. *Journal of Traumatic Stress, 1,* 127–141.

Frankl, B. E. (1964). *Man's search for meaning.* London: Hodder and Stoughton.

Jacobsen, L., & Vesti, P. (1992). *Torture survivors—A new group of patients.* Copenhagen: International Rehabilitation Council for Torture Victims.

Juhler, M. (1993). Medical diagnosis and treatment of torture survivors. In J. P. Wilson & B. Raphael (Eds.), *The international handbook of traumatic stress disorders* (pp. 763–766). New York: Plenum Press.

Keane, T. M., Albano, A. M., & Blake, D. D. (1992). Current trends in the treatment of post-traumatic symptoms. In M. Basoglu (Ed.), *Torture and its consequences: Current treatment approaches* (pp. 363–401). Cambridge: Cambridge University Press.

Kinzie, J. D. (1989). Therapeutic approaches to traumatized Cambodian refugees. *Journal of Traumatic Stress, 2*(1), 75–91.

Kinzie, J. D., & Boehnlein, J. K. (1989). Post-traumatic psychosis among Cambodian refugees. *Journal of Traumatic Stress, 2,* 185–198.

Kordon, D. R., Edelman, L. I., Lagos, D. M., Nicoletti, E., & Bozzolo, R. C. (1988). *Psychological effects of repression.* Buenos Aires: Sudamerican/Planeta.

Krystal, H. (1976). *Massive psychic trauma.* New York: International Universities Press.

Krystal, H. (1978). Trauma and affects. *Psychoanalytic Study of the Child, 33,* 81–116.

Larsen, H., & Pagaduan-Lopez, J. (1987). Stress-tension reduction in the treatment of sexually tortured women: An exploratory study. *Journal of Sex and Marital Therapy, 13,* 210–218.

Lederer, W. (1965). Persecution and compensation: Theoretical and practical implications of the "persecution syndrome." *Archives of General Psychiatry, 12,* 464–474.

Marcos, L. R., & Alpert, M. (1976). Strategies and risks in psychotherapy with bilingual patients: The phenomenon of language independence. *American Journal of Psychiatry, 133,* 1275–1278.

Marcussen, H. (1993). *Annual Report 1992.* Copenhagen: Rehabilitation and Research Center for Torture Victims (RCT)/International Rehabilitation Council for Torture Victims (IRCT).

Mollica, R. F., & Caspi-Yavin, Y. (1991). Measuring torture and torture-related symptoms. *Psychological Assessment, 3*(4), 581–587.

Mollica, R. F., Caspi-Yavin, Y., Bollini, P., Truong, T., Tor, S., & Lavelle, J. (1992). The Harvard Trauma Questionnaire: Validating a cross-cultural instrument for measuring torture, trauma, and posttraumatic stress disorder in Indochinese refugees. *Journal of Nervous and Mental Disease, 180*(2), 111–116.

Mollica, R. F., Wyshak, G., de Marneffe, D., Khuon, F., & Lavelle, J. (1987). Indochinese versions of the Hopkins Symptom Checklist-25: A screening instrument for the psychiatric care of refugees. *American Journal of Psychiatry, 144*, 497–500.

Mollica, R. F., Wyshak, G., & Lavelle, J. (1987). The psychosocial impact of war trauma and torture on Southeast Asian refugees. *American Journal of Psychiatry, 144*(12), 1567–1572.

Mollica, R. F., Wyshak, G., Lavelle, J., Truong, T., Tor, S., & Yang, T. (1990). Assessing symptom change in Southeast Asian refugee survivors of mass violence and torture. *American Journal of Psychiatry, 147*(1), 83–88.

Montgomery, E. (1992). Co-creation of meaning: Therapy with torture survivors: A systemic constructionist view. *Human Systems: The Journal of Systemic Consultation and Management, 3*, 27–33.

Pagaduan-Lopez, J. (1987). *Torture survivors—What can we do for them?* Manila: Philippine Action Concerning Torture and Medical Action Group.

Sack, W. H., Angell, R. H., Kinzie, J. D., & Rath, B. (1986). The psychiatric effects of massive trauma on Cambodian children: II. The family, the home, and the school. *Journal of the American Academy of Child Psychiatry, 25*(3), 377–383.

Schlapobersky, J., & Bamber, H. (1987). Rehabilitation work with victims of torture. In D. Miserez (Ed.), *Refugees: The trauma of exile* (pp. 206–222). Dordrecht: Martinus Nijhoff.

Skylv, G. (1992). The physical sequelae of torture. In M. Basoglu (Ed.), *Torture and its consequences: Current treatment approaches* (pp. 38–55). Cambridge: Cambridge University Press.

Somnier, F. E., & Genefke, I. K. (1986). Psychotherapy for victims of torture. *British Journal of Psychiatry, 141*, 1628–1639.

Sparr, L., & Pankratz, L. D. (1983). Factitious posttraumatic stress disorder. *American Journal of Psychiatry, 140*, 1016–1019.

Spitzer, R. L., Williams, J. B., Gibbons, M., & First, M. B. (1990). *Structural Clinical Interview for DSM-III-R-Patient Edition* (SCID-P, Version 1.0). Washington, DC: American Psychiatric Press.

Stæhr, A., Stæhr, M., Behbehani, J., & Bøjholm, S. (1993). *Treatment of war victims in the Middle East.* Copenhagen: International Rehabilitation Council for Torture Victims.

Stover, E., & Nightingale, E. O. (1985). Introduction. In E. Stover & E. O. Nightingale (Eds.), *The breaking of bodies and minds: Torture, psychiatric abuse, and the health professions* (pp. 1–26). New York: W. H. Freeman.

United Nations. (1985). *United Nations convention against torture and other cruel, inhuman, or degrading treatment or punishment.* Geneva: Author.

Van der Veer, G. (1992). *Counselling and therapy with refugees.* Chistester: John Wiley & Sons.

van Willigen, L. H. M. (1992). Organization of care and rehabilitation services for victims of torture and other forms of organized violence: A review of current issues. In M. Basoglu (Ed.), *Torture and its consequences: Current treatment approaches* (pp. 277–298). Cambridge: Cambridge University Press.

Vesti, P. (1990). Extreme man made stress and anti-therapy: Doctors as collaborators in torture. *Danish Medical Bulletin, 37*, 466–468.

Vesti, P., & Kastrup, M. (1992). Psychotherapy for torture survivors. In M. Basoglu (Ed.), *Torture and its consequences: Current treatment approaches* (pp. 348–362). Cambridge: Cambridge University Press.

Vesti, P., Somnier, F., & Kastrup, M. (1992). *Psychotherapy with torture survivors: A report of practice from the Rehabilitation and Research Center for Torture Victims (RCT), Copenhagen, Denmark.* Copenhagen: International Rehabilitation Research Center for Torture Victims.

15

Traumatic Stress

A Blueprint for the Future

JOHN R. FREEDY and STEVAN E. HOBFOLL

OVERVIEW

This final chapter is an integrative summary of the major themes contained within this volume. As mentioned in the preface, the chapter authors are among the leading experts in the field of traumatic stress. State of the art research, clinical work, and teaching concerning trauma are their "daily bread." Therefore, the ideas and issues that have been raised provide an excellent sampling of where the field of traumatic stress is at today. We are also interested in where the field of traumatic stress will be, particularly in terms of clinical practice, in the future. With the future in mind, we summarize issues from the previous chapters with a special emphasis on clinical practice.

We have organized this chapter in six sections. Each section corresponds to a major theme addressed in one or more of the chapters. The content of the various sections represent our interpretations of work within this volume. We trust that our integrative statements do justice to the excellent work of the chapter authors. It is a challenging task to integrate such excellent and diverse ideas. In particular, the following major issues are addressed: (1) cultural and political factors impacting the field of traumatic stress; (2) evolving conceptual models concerning the linkage between traumatic events and subsequent adjustment; (3) the prevalence and nature (i.e., qualitative features) of traumatic events; (4) patterns of adjustment across time; (5) state of the art assessment

JOHN R. FREEDY · National Crime Victims Research and Treatment Center, Department of Psychiatry and Behavioral Sciences, Medical University of South Carolina, Charleston, South Carolina 29425   **STEVAN E. HOBFOLL** • Applied Psychology Center, Department of Psychology, Kent State University, Kent, Ohio 44242.

Traumatic Stress: From Theory to Practice, edited by John R. Freedy and Stevan E. Hobfoll. Plenum Press, New York, 1995.

techniques; (6) state of the art intervention models and practices; and, (7) case examples.

CULTURAL AND POLITICAL FACTORS

Throughout this book, cultural and political factors involved in the traumatic stress field are considered. Several chapters point out that it can be a struggle to examine the topic of trauma as a legitimate area of inquiry. For example, Weathers, Litz, and Keane (Chapter 5) trace the history of knowledge concerning war-related trauma. They highlight several points of discontinuity in the development of this knowledge base. It is suggested that political forces have played a major role in legitimizing attention toward the topic of war-related trauma (e.g., the unpopular nature of the Vietnam war). Similarly, Solomon and Shalev (Chapter 10) discuss acute and chronic aspects of war-related trauma. Elsewhere, Solomon (1993) has discussed the cultural pressures involved in minimizing documentation of potentially negative mental health outcomes of war. In a similar vein, several authors within the current volume argue that violence directed toward women is partially rooted in collective cultural attitudes that tolerate the mistreatment of women (Chapters 3 and 6). Efforts to change social attitudes or practices may be a legitimate focus for mental health professionals' organizations (e.g., advocacy for human rights, policy changes) as influencing some problems (e.g., wars, violence in urban areas) are beyond the power of individual control. It also seems critical that individual professionals face these issues so as to avoid perpetuating negative attitudes, beliefs, and practices toward trauma victims.

The two chapters by Vesti and Kastrup concerning torture victims (Chapters 9 and 14) also deal directly with political and cultural aspects of torture. At the political level, these authors argue that torture exists as a state sponsored or tolerated activity. An argument can be made that the problem of torture is worsened by nonrecognition or failure to sanction on the part of nonoffending countries. The Vesti and Kastrup chapters also address issues such as language barriers and differences in world view between treatment providers and sufferers from different cultural backgrounds. Through the use of interpreters and modification of westernized psychotherapeutic techniques (typically based on direct forms of verbal communication), they argue that it is possible to provide emotional support and healing to trauma victims from diverse backgrounds. There seems to be some universal healing power involved in meeting with a healer who provides information, advice, and emotional support.

McFarlane (Chapter 12) provides relevant commentary regarding the clinical implications of cultural attitudes toward trauma victims. On the one hand, he comments on the need to listen and to convey understanding and empathy toward trauma victims. Empathic listening, in the face of horrific suffering is not an easy task. On the other hand, McFarlane suggests that it is possible to either over- or underidentify with the needs of the trauma victim. Being overly sympathetic might lead to the failure to identify and aggressively treat the pathological manifestations of trauma-induced mental health problems. Several other authors in this volume make similar arguments for aggressive early-stage treatment efforts (Chapters 4 and 10). McFarlane (Chapter 12) also suggests that minimizing the role of trauma in creating current functional difficulties may lead to overly callous or judgmental attitudes toward trauma victims. Best and Ribbe (Chapter 13) recommend that clinical workers advocate for the legitimate needs of trauma victims (e.g., with employers, with insurance companies, with family members). Taking an active, nonjudgmental stance requires tempering traditional clinical attitudes toward issues such as malingering and secondary gain that may often amount to victim blaming in situations involving traumatic stress. Advocacy on behalf of trauma victims is viewed as an important contributor in facilitating a transition from a state of victimization (e.g., passiveness, hopelessness) to the state of a survivorship (e.g., activeness, confidence).

EVOLVING CONCEPTUAL MODELS

This volume highlights a number of conceptual models that have been suggested as potential explanations for the linkage between traumatic events and subsequent mental health problems. Overall, the trend within the traumatic stress field is toward etiological models that attempt to integrate biological, psychological, and social factors involved in the etiology and maintenance of trauma-induced mental health problems. Given the universal nature of traumatic experiences, it is somewhat surprising that current conceptual understanding is not at a more advanced stage. In part, this may result from cultural (and professional) discomfort in dealing openly with the frequent and devastating nature of traumatic events (see above). However, recent years have seen substantial advances in knowledge, due in part to the inclusion of posttraumatic stress disorder (PTSD) in the diagnostic nomenclature (APA, 1980, 1987, 1994; WHO, 1992). It is likely that the development of a common nomenclature has done a lot to encourage a growth in knowledge concerning trauma-based mental health problems (Saigh, 1993).

Several chapters review available models concerning the etiology and maintenance of PTSD. As a matter of fact, most of the chapters in this volume make at least some reference to an etiological model concerning the relationship between traumatic events and subsequent mental health adjustment. Two chapters will be singled out as they provide broad overviews concerning theoretical and etiologic issues. Readers interested in more detailed information concerning etiological models should consult individual chapters as needed (e.g., biological models are addressed in detail by Kudler & Davidson and Solomon & Shalev, Chapters 4 and 10).

The chapter by Freedy and Donkervoet (Chapter 1) provides a broad overview of psychological, biological, and integrative models concerning posttrauma adjustment. The psychological models are based upon either learning theory (classical and operant conditioning) or on cognition-based models (e.g., Horowitz, 1986; Foa, Steketee, and Olasov-Rothbaum, 1989; McCann & Pearlman, 1990; Resick, 1992). Basic biological models consider a range of possible etiological mechanisms (e.g., depletion of neurotransmitters due to inescapable situations; responsiveness to endogenous opiates; functional changes within the limbic system). Integrative models acknowledge the inadequacy of any single explanatory model and seek to combine the explanatory power of psychological and biological models. The current zeitgeist within the field of traumatic stress is to emphasize integrative conceptual models. A clinical implication of this trend is that practicing mental health professionals should integrate psychological and biological approaches in addressing the psychosocial needs of trauma victims.

A second chapter is particularly notable with regard to conceptual models. Hobfoll, Dunahoo, and Monnier (Chapter 2) suggest that trauma research is not adequately grounded in general knowledge concerning psychological stress. Therefore, they suggest a general model of stress and adaptation (i.e., the conservation of resources or COR stress model) as a template for understanding the profound impact of trauma upon individuals. From this viewpoint, it is suggested that the sudden and rapid loss of a broad range of resources (e.g., individual resources, family resources, organizational resources, and community resources) may have a profound and lasting impact upon the individual. To be consistent with COR theory, prevention and intervention efforts must seek to replace or limit the loss of resources that are vital to the biological and psychosocial survival of the individual. The dual emphasis upon the connection between individuals and their surrounding environment coupled with the emphasis upon the tangible nature of resource loss (e.g., work, family ties, possessions) are particularly appealing aspects of COR theory. In this volume, Hobfoll and his colleagues and Norris and Thompson (Chapter 3) address practical implications of COR theory for intervention and prevention efforts.

THE PREVALENCE AND NATURE OF TRAUMATIC EVENTS

Various chapters within this volume confirm the alarming frequency of the following types of traumatic events: war-related trauma (Chapters 5 and 10), violent crime (Chapters 6 and 11), natural and technological disasters (Chapters 7 and 12), accidental injury (Chapters 8 and 13), and torture (Chapters 9 and 14). Freedy and Donkervoet (Chapter 1) try to put perspective on the prevalence of traumatic events by citing a number of large general population surveys. Based on these surveys, it was estimated that between 40% and 70% of adults have experienced at least one traumatic event during their lives (Breslau, Davis, Andreski, & Peterson, 1991; Norris, 1992; Resnick, Kilpatrick, Dansky, Saunders, & Best, 1993; Kilpatrick, Saunders, Veronen, Best, & Von, 1987). One study indicated that as many as one fifth of adults in the general population may experience a traumatic event each year (Norris, 1992). It is also common clinical lore that trauma rates are higher in treatment-seeking, as opposed to nontreatment-seeking, samples. The obvious conclusion is that traumatic events are neither rare nor unusual. Until very recently the diagnostic nomenclature has underestimated the frequency of traumatic events (APA, 1987, 1994). Clearly traumatic events should be considered in trying to ascertain factors that may play an important role in determining individual adjustment.

A subtle, though crucial point follows from understanding the high prevalence of traumatic events in modern society. In particular, there is a bias in standard mental health practice toward the assessment and treatment of anxiety, depression, and other internalized psychological states. The emphasis is upon understanding and fixing things that are endogenous in nature. However, given the clear connection between trauma and mental health problems, it is very likely that a higher percentage of current mental health problems are *environmentally induced* than is currently recognized. If this assertion is correct, it implies that mental health professionals should focus more on preventing and managing the environmental causes of human suffering than is currently the case. Several chapters in the current volume make this same point (Chapters 2, 3, and 6).

The quality of traumatic events is also discussed within the current volume (e.g., Chapters 1, 2, 5–8, and 10–13). The basic idea is that event quality is a crucial factor in determining the degree to which a traumatic event may have a negative mental health impact. Some combination of either objective (e.g., physical injury, death, sexual penetration) or subjective (e.g., perception of threat to life, perception of loss of control) dimensions of the traumatic circumstances are believed to determine the risk for experiencing negative mental health outcomes. In particular, horrific experiences that involve extremely threatening experiences (to self or important other people) are believed to be responsible for determining negative mental health outcomes. A clinical implication of this knowledge concerning the importance of event quality lies in the assessment process. Clinical assessment should directly inquire both about a range of event types and about the particular qualities of any events that have been experienced (Chapters 11 and 13).

PATTERNS OF ADJUSTMENT ACROSS TIME

The current volume conceptualizes posttrauma adjustment as falling on a continuum ranging from little or no psychosocial damage through severe and lasting psychosocial impairment. The documentation of minor and severe mental health effects is largely referenced to existing systems of diagnostic nomenclature (APA, 1994; WHO, 1992). On the more mild end of the continuum, transient adjustment reactions are noted as the possible outcome of traumatic experiences (Chapter 1). On the more severe end of the continuum, PTSD is cited as perhaps the most common negative mental health outcome following traumatic events. Several chapters link PTSD symptoms to particular traumatic events and suggest that PTSD symptomatology can be chronic (e.g., Chapters 4, 5, and 7–13). In addition, many of these same chapters discuss the possibility of comorbid mental health problems (e.g., other anxiety disorders, depression, substance abuse, personality disorders).

Several chapters within this volume are particularly informative with regard to the issue of patterns of posttrauma adjustment across the course of time (e.g., Chapters 5, 7, 10, 12, and 13). Clearly, it is the case that many victims of trauma may experience acute adjustment difficulties following traumatic events. An example of the nature of severe, early posttrauma adjustment difficulties is provided in discussions of combat stress reaction (CSR) in the current volume (Chapters 5 and 10). A normal recovery curve may exist in the first several months posttrauma, such that mental health symptoms that are present by approximately 3 months posttrauma appear to be persistent across time (Falsetti & Resnick, Chapter 11). Thus, the presence of substantial PTSD symptoms as long as 3 months or more posttrauma should be treated with an active clinical orientation, as these symptoms are likely to become chronic and cascade into widening functional deficits. Delayed symptom onset is a possibility following traumatic experiences; however, the delayed onset of PTSD symptoms appears to be a relatively rare phenomenon (Chapters 1 and 10). As with other clinical conditions, the longevity of PTSD symptoms tends to increase the risk of comorbid symptomatology. Therefore, both early and aggressive clinical intervention may be a key to minimizing the development of complicated posttrauma mental health problems (Chapters 4 and 12).

Another important issue concerns the timing of traumatic events with regard to developmental level. It is generally assumed that the early onset of traumatic experiences and/or repeated exposure to traumatic events delays or distorts normal psychosocial development. Important capacities such as trust, self-esteem, optimism, or sustained motivation to achieve goals may be damaged as the result of traumatic experiences (Chapter 1). Although such processes are difficult to document with research data, the palpable quality of such developmental distortions is commonly noted in the course of clinical practice. Whether traumatic events overwhelm existing developmental capacities (e.g., sexual abuse of children) or interfere with the achievement of developmental milestones (e.g., difficulties with emotional intimacy among war veterans), the impact on personal and social adjustment can be substantial. A fuller understanding of the potential impact of traumatic experiences is achieved when the developmental range of the trauma victim is considered. One crucial focus of clinical work with trauma victims is to facilitate the further development of overwhelmed or damaged developmental capacities (e.g., trust, self-esteem, optimism).

STATE-OF-THE-ART ASSESSMENT TECHNIQUES

Several general issues emerged in this volume with regard to assessment techniques. One key issue concerns the importance of tailoring assessment procedures to the needs of the individual patient. Scotti et al. (Chapter 8) do a particularly excellent job in discussing the complexity and idiosyncratic nature of individual clinical cases. Using accidental injury cases as examples, Scotti et al. illustrate one way to tailor information-gathering strategies to the clinical situation. A second key issue concerns gathering and integrating an appropriate breadth of information. Kudler and Davidson (Chapter 4) do a particularly effective job in elaborating this latter point. These authors emphasize a standardized approach to assessment. Information is gathered from a variety of sources including: patient interviews, collateral interviews, record reviews, and testing material (psychological and biological tests). It is most helpful that Kudler and Davidson emphasize the integration of these diverse sources of information for the purposes of diagnosis and treatment planning. From this standpoint, it is apparent that the integration of psychosocial and biological treatment approaches flows from integrated conceptual models and assessment procedures.

Specific chapters within this volume outline the types of assessment procedures in use with particular types of trauma victims. Generally, a combination of interview and self-report techniques are recommended within these chapters (Chapters 10–14). Typically, the use of standardized procedures is recommended. In some cases, normative data specific to trauma populations are available. The brevity of some measures allows for the possibility of repeat assessments over time for the purpose of tracking treatment progress. Although the use of standardized assessment procedures that are specific to trauma populations has advantages (e.g., brevity, standardization), some caution is warranted. Assessment should not be considered a simple task. Expert clinical judgment should be used in selecting, administering, scoring, and interpreting assessment instruments. Attention should be paid to considering factors that might distort the accuracy of assessment findings (e.g., mental status, legal involvement). Assessment techniques are merely tools that, when used correctly, serve to inform the work of an expert clinician.

A final area of assessment practice involves insightful commentary that was offered by Falsetti and Resnick (Chapter 11). They suggest the importance of screening all treatment-seeking individuals for the presence of traumatic event exposure. This recommendation is justified based upon both the prevalence of traumatic events (particularly among treatment-seeking individuals) and the potential negative mental health impact of traumatic events. Falsetti and Resnick provide examples of assessment instruments that are designed to detect the presence of traumatic events. Additional chapters in this volume discuss how to approach treatment for a broad variety of trauma-induced mental health problems (Chapters 4, 10, 12–14).

INTERVENTION MODELS AND PRACTICES

Clinical practice with trauma victims should occur within the context of an overall intervention plan. In the current volume, Norris and Thompson (Chapter 3) provide an excellent model to guide the implementation of intervention efforts. Their model considers both the level (i.e., individual versus systems level) and the timing (i.e., prevention efforts that are primary, secondary, or tertiary in nature) of intervention efforts. Using the terminology from the Norris and Thompson chapter, corrective therapy is one of five approaches to intervening on behalf of trauma victims. Indeed, psychotherapy and medication interventions seem to be the bread and butter of most clinical work. Other intervention possibilities include: political action (e.g., legislation to control firearm availability), community development (e.g., helping community members to build their own strengths or resources), general education (e.g., crime prevention messages, safety belt messages, drinking and driving messages), and crisis counseling (e.g., rape crisis centers).

This volume also addresses the common points of effective interventions with trauma victims. For example, Freedy and Donkervoet (Chapter 1) describe the following general characteristics of trauma-based treatment: (1) an orientation toward prevention of traumatic events or limiting the impact of an event through early intervention; (2) remaining focused on trauma-based content; (3) building skills necessary to manage intense affect and troubling thought processes; (4) attempting to enhance internal (e.g., self-esteem) and external resources (e.g., social support); (5) facilitating the growth of delayed or distorted developmental capacities; and (6) integrating psychosocial and biological approaches. McFarlane (Chapter 12) makes a number of similar points in arguing that clinical work with trauma victims must be flexible and eclectic in nature.

Kudler and Davidson (Chapter 4) discuss general principles of biological intervention with trauma victims. This chapter provides an excellent model for the use of flexible and creative clinical management. The authors argue that psychosocial and medication approaches are complementary, and they present a step by step strategy for the utilization of medications in the management of the symptoms that may be presented by trauma victims. The chapter illustrates how selecting the correct type or dosage of medication is a collaborative process between the psychiatrist, patient, family, and other mental health treatment staff. Decisions regarding medication are based upon assisting the trauma victim in obtaining an optimal level of adjustment. In some cases, medication may be necessary to allow the trauma victim to tolerate the intense internal experiences that may be generated by focusing upon trauma-based material (see also McFarlane, Chapter 12).

A final factor concerning clinical intervention concerns the clinical management of chronic symptomatology. On the one hand, many of the chapters cite promising results for psychotherapeutic (typically cognitive and behavioral approaches) and medication-based approaches in addressing trauma-induced symptomatology. On the other hand, these same chapters clearly indicate limitations to available treatment approaches. Some people suffer from chronic symptomatology despite the best efforts of well-trained treatment professionals. In weaker moments, it may be tempting for treatment professionals to give up hope of making a positive difference. However, as treatment professionals, we are all called upon to do our best with the fullest range of treatment options that are currently available to us. It is also necessary that the field continues efforts to advance treatment knowledge. Kudler and Davidson (Chapter 4) offer four reasonable goals in addressing chronic trauma-induced symptoms: (1) reducing symptoms; (2) establishing a more satisfactory life style; (3) helping patients better understand their condition; and, (4) having patients develop a broader support system. These appear to be excellent and realistic goals for all trauma victims.

CASE EXAMPLES

A broad range of case examples are offered throughout the current volume. These examples provide excellent points of reference to inform the reader. A brief summary of the various case examples is offered here. Review of this summary of case examples provides an appreciation of the breadth of clinical material addressed within the current volume.

Kudler and Davidson (Chapter 4) provide two case examples. One case concerned an elderly combat veteran with PTSD. Their second case concerned a young female rape victim with PTSD. Medication, family consultation, an outpatient prisoner-of-war support group, and supportive follow-up sessions (mainly to manage medications) were used successfully with the elderly combat veteran. Medication, a rape support group, and supportive weekly psychotherapy were used with success with the young female rape victim.

Scotti et al. (Chapter 8) describe four case examples pertaining to the topic of accidental injuries. The first case example involved a young married couple involved in an auto accident. Both the husband and wife experienced a range of trauma-induced mental health symptoms (e.g., anxiety, intrusive memories). A second case example involved a young woman who had an auto accident in which she and her children experienced minor injuries. The mother experienced anxiety-based symptoms. The third case involved a young male soldier with severe PTSD secondary to driving a truck in an accident that killed two people. The fourth case example involved a mildly retarded young man who had experienced several traumatic experiences (auto accident, witnessing the beating death of his brother, and witnessing an industrial accident that killed a co-worker). He experienced both intrusive memories and anxious feelings. Scotti et al. use these case examples to illustrate their behavioral approach to clinical assessment. They emphasize the idiosyncratic nature of individual and environmental factors that may determine mental health adjustment following threatening accidents.

Solomon and Shalev (Chapter 10) do not provide case examples that pertain to individual soldiers in their chapter. They do, however, very carefully describe step-by-step procedures involved in crisis debriefing and other clinical-management strategies designed to address the needs of front-line mental health casualties. Suggested strategies include meeting physical needs, providing temporary relief from stressors, using human contact to legitimize fear while challenging self-depreciation, conveying the expectation of full recovery, promoting social support that allows a full return to military functioning, treating immediately, and removing from the unit as a last resort. Although Solomon and Shalev are dealing with combat soldiers, many of their lessons (e.g., providing for physical needs, providing temporary relief from stressors) may be usefully generalized to work with other trauma victims (e.g., violent crime victims, torture victims, disaster victims).

Falsetti and Resnick (Chapter 11) present a case example of a 35-year-old man with a history of physical assault among other traumatic events. His clinical presentation was complicated by the fact that he presented with PTSD symptoms and comorbid panic symptoms. One strength of this case example lies in the fact that the complicated presentation (i.e., complex trauma history, PTSD, and a comorbid disorder) is common in clinical practice. Therefore, the provided description of assessment procedures, the monitoring of symptoms over time, and the course of treatment provide a realistic model as to what many clinicians may face in conducting clinical work with trauma victims. Elsewhere, McFarlane (1989) has written about the complexity of trauma-induced mental health problems and has argued for the value of broad, flexible, and integrative approaches to clinical practice. Falsetti and Resnick (Chapter 11, this volume) describe the successful application of two cognitive behavioral treatment strategies (Mastery of Your Anxiety and Panic; Cognitive Processing Therapy) in this treatment case.

McFarlane (Chapter 12) briefly describes eight different case examples, illustrating a breadth of postdisaster clinical situations. One case example describes how a single mental health consultation reduced intrusive memories, illustrating that despite practical restraints a limited intervention effort may have substantial value. A second clinical example illustrates cognitive approaches to dealing with loss of control in life-threatening situations. A third case illustrates dealing with guilt issues when the trauma victim is resistant to receiving treatment. Support and pharmacotherapy were recommended as feasible options. A fourth example illustrates how family members (a husband and wife, both disaster victims) may support the avoidance of dealing with trauma-based symptoms. Joint consultation was recommended to clarify symptom patterns and to encourage the resolution of each person's symptoms. A fifth case example deals with the emergence of severe depression in the course of trauma-focused psychotherapy (not an uncommon phenomenon when death or loss of role function are at issue). An antidepressant was used with good effect in addition to the patient's psychotherapy. A sixth clinical example illustrates how the separation of parents from children may set the stage for later dysfunctional anxiety by either parents or the child. A seventh case example illustrates the utility of cognitive techniques in assisting an emergency service worker suffering from anxiety and guilt. The eighth case example illustrates how supportive psychotherapy coupled with antidepressant medication was appropriate with a trauma victim prone to dissociative episodes.

Best and Ribbe (Chapter 13) discuss two case examples. One case concerns a man involved in a serious auto accident in which three family members were killed (he was not seriously injured). At treatment presentation he suffered from PTSD and uncomplicated bereavement. The second case example involved a man who was severely burned while he and a friend unexpectedly witnessed a military plane crash. His friend was killed. This surviving victim manifested full PTSD symptoms with subclinical signs of depression. Best and Ribbe illustrate the application of cognitive–behavioral treatment techniques to address physical, cognitive, and behavioral manifestations of the fear experienced by the two victims from their case examples. These authors report that their clinical approach was largely successful in resolving trauma-induced mental health symptoms.

Vesti and Kastrup (Chapter 14) provide two case examples. One case example concerns a 37-year-old man who was held for political reasons and tortured by being subjected to mock execution where other prisoners were shot to death. Upon release, he managed to escape from his country and presented for treatment with PTSD symptoms. Approaches to his treatment included: insight oriented psychotherapy, medical treatment for torture-related injuries, and assistance with social benefits. Reflecting the complexity of his torture experiences and his current life circumstances (e.g., cultural displacement, economic difficulties, pressure to emotionally support fellow citizens worse off than he, threat of assassination), his anxiety-based symptoms were improved, but not entirely resolved. The fact that a partial resolution of mental health problems is a reasonable treatment goal calls to mind Kudler and Davidson's (Chapter 4, this volume) goals for evaluating treatment outcome (reducing symptoms, establishing a more satisfactory lifestyle, improving insight, and helping with the development of a broader support system). A second clinical case concerned a woman who had been arrested and tortured in various ways. She suffered from PTSD and depressive symptoms as well as a variety of torture-induced physical ailments. Her treatment consistent of: medical treatment for her injuries, physical therapy, insight-oriented psychotherapy, and support in pursuing legal actions against her torturers. Over the course of her integrated treatment, her anxiety and depression symptoms greatly improved, and her physical condition improved as well.

CLOSING REMARKS

The frequency of a broad range of traumatic experiences is an alarming fact that is clearly illustrated by chapters in this volume. The chapters further illustrate a clear connection between various traumatic events, event qualities, and negative mental health outcomes. A full range of adjustment possibilities ranging from mild to severe and short-lived to chronic may follow exposure to traumatic events. In the most tragic circumstances, PTSD and a variety of comorbid mental health conditions may follow trauma exposure. The occurrence of traumatic events and related mental health effects are a tragic reality in modern society.

Concerning the tragedy of trauma experiences and related mental health problems, this book offers hope to treatment professionals and trauma victims who require treatment. State of the art assessment and treatment techniques are carefully described in this volume, and the provision of multiple case example serves to illustrate suggested routes to implementation of assessment and treatment procedures. Prevention efforts and early intervention based upon the integration of psychosocial and biological approaches were emphasized, and clinicians were encouraged to consider these options through outreach and organizational efforts. Reading this volume is meant as a starting point. The editors hope that the volume provides the practical skills and insight to practicing mental health professionals interested in working effectively with the victims of traumatic events.

The editors appreciate the reader's attention. We trust that with our colleagues we have provided you with a useful and stimulating clinical guide. We wish you well in putting these important ideas into clinical practice. Most of all, we hope that your clients will suffer less because of your efforts, which may in part be influenced by the content of this volume. Perhaps together, as well-informed treatment professionals, we can make the world a safer and more humane place for all people.

REFERENCES

American Psychiatric Association. (1980). *Diagnostic and statistical manual of mental disorders*, (3rd ed.). Washington, DC: Author.

American Psychiatric Association. (1987). *Diagnostic and statistical manual of mental disorders* (3rd ed.-rev.). Washington, DC: Author.

American Psychiatric Association. (1994). *Diagnostic and statistical manual of mental disorders*, (4th ed.). Washington, DC: Author.

Breslau, N., Davis, G. C., Andreski, P., & Peterson, E. (1991). Traumatic events and post-traumatic stress disorder in an urban population of young adults. *Archives of General Psychiatry, 48,* 216–222.

Foa, E. B., Steketee, G., & Olasov-Rothbaum, B. (1989). Behavioral/cognitive conceptualizations of post-traumatic stress disorder. *Behavior Therapy, 20,* 155–176.

Horowitz, M. J. (1986). *Stress response syndromes* (2nd ed.). Northvale, NJ: Jason Aronson.

Kilpatrick, D. G., Resnick, H. S., Freedy, J. R., Pelcovitz, D., Resick, P. A., Roth, S., & van der Kolk, B. (in press). The posttraumatic stress disorder field trial: Emphasis on criterion A and overall PTSD diagnosis. In *DSM-IV source book.* Washington, DC: American Psychiatric Press.

Kilpatrick, D. G., Saunders, B. E., Veronen, L. J., Best, C. L., & Von, J. M. (1987). Criminal victimization: Lifetime prevalence, reporting to police, and psychological impact. *Crime and Delinquency, 33*(4), 479–489.

McCann, L., & Pearlman, L. A. (1990). *Psychological trauma and the adult survivor: Theory, therapy, & transformation.* New York: Brunner/Mazel.

McFarlane, A. C. (1989). The treatment of post-traumatic stress disorder. *British Journal of Medical Psychology, 62,* 81–90.

Norris, F. H. (1992). Epidemiology of trauma: Frequency and impact of different potentially traumatic events on different demographic groups. *Journal of Consulting and Clinical Psychology, 60*(3), 409–418.

Resick, P. A. (1992). Cognitive treatment of crime-related post-traumatic stress disorder. In R. J. McMahon and V. L. Quinsey (Eds.), *Aggression and violence throughout the life span* (pp. 171–191). Newbury Park, CA: Sage Publications.

Resnick, H. S., Kilpatrick, D. G., Dansky, B. S., Saunders, B. E., & Best, C. L. (1993). Prevalence of civilian trauma and posttraumatic stress disorder in a representative sample of women. *Journal of Consulting and Clinical Psychology, 61*(6), 984–991.

Saigh, P. A. (Ed.). (1993). *Posttraumatic stress disorder: A behavioral approach to assessment and treatment.* New York: Pergamon Press.

Solomon, Z. (1993). *Combat stress reaction: The enduring toll of war.* New York: Plenum Press.

World Health Organization. (1992). *The ICD-10 classification of mental and behavioural disorders.* Geneva: Author.

Index